EIGHTEENTH-CENTURY
BRITISH LOGIC AND RHETORIC

Eighteenth-Century
British Logic
and Rhetoric

WILBUR SAMUEL HOWELL

PRINCETON, NEW JERSEY

PRINCETON UNIVERSITY PRESS

1971

To Cecilia

PREFACE

In the long process of giving this book its present substance and form, I have received invaluable assistance of various kinds, and I should like now to acknowledge what the nature of that assistance has been, and what persons are to be identified as participants in it. Such acknowledgments might claim to have public interest, so far as they reveal that the advancement of learning is a truly cooperative enterprise, and that the individual scholar is indeed dependent for his success upon the good will of many other likeminded men and women. But in the present instance my acknowledgments are being set forth, not to paint a public moral, but to express my warm personal thanks to those who, in having confidence in me, have continuously renewed my confidence in the worth of what I have here tried to accomplish. Perhaps without their confidence I could have reached an acceptable goal on the present occasion, but I could not have exceeded my own initial estimates of the worth of this project, as I confess to believing that I have done here, nor could I have enjoyed as fully as I have the entire procedure that has led me at last to the writing of this prefatory postscript.

First of all, the John Simon Guggenheim Memorial Foundation awarded me a Fellowship for the academic year 1957-58 to enable me to begin the research that has led to this book, and in the same year and for the same purpose the Trustees of Princeton University granted me a leave of absence at half salary. My departmental chairman, Professor Carlos Baker, was instrumental in helping me to success in achieving both of these objectives. And in helping me to success in the first of them, I also owe thanks to Professor Gerald E. Bentley, Professor Donald C. Bryant, Professor Harry Caplan, Professor Louis A. Landa, Professor Whitney J. Oates, and the late Mr. Godfrey Davies.

Secondly, the Trustees of the Henry E. Huntington Library and Art Gallery bestowed a Fellowship upon me for the academic year 1962-63 in order that I might begin actually to write this book, and in support of that same endeavor the Trustees of

Princeton University once again granted me half salary and a leave of absence. In connection with my application for this Fellowship, Dr. John E. Pomfret, Director of the Huntington Library, gave me effective assistance, as did Professor Herbert A. Wichelns, Professor Julian P. Boyd, and several of those who had kindly supported my application for the Guggenheim award in 1957. In addition, my departmental chairman, Professor Willard Thorp, was instrumental in securing for me certain grants from the Annan Fund of the Department of English and from the University Committee on Research in the Humanities and Social Sciences to cover travel expenses and living costs associated with my scholarly work in that particular year.

Thirdly, the Council of the Humanities of Princeton conferred upon me one of their Senior Fellowships for the second term of the academic year 1965-66, and thus I was enabled to have a greatly reduced schedule of normal obligations for an uninterrupted period of five months, and to devote myself almost continuously in that period to the task of bringing this book nearer to completion. Professor Whitney J. Oates, chairman of the Council of the Humanities, was particularly helpful in arranging this appointment, as were my departmental chairman, the late Professor Alan S. Downer, and Professor J. Douglas Brown, Dean of the University Faculty.

Fourthly, the Trustees of Princeton University granted me a leave of absence at full salary for the second term of the academic year 1968-69, so that I might at last complete this book. My departmental chairman, the late Professor Alan S. Downer, was instrumental once again in bringing that arrangement about.

Finally, I wish to express my thanks for various other kinds of assistance. The University Committee on Research in the Humanities and Social Sciences helped me to defray the expenses involved in having the manuscript of this book typed and proofread. Professor Thomas Roche and Professor and Mrs. Louis A. Landa were so kind as to check some bibliographical points for me at the Bodleian Library and the British Museum on occasions when I could not conveniently have checked them myself. Mr. Benjamin F. Houston, Senior Staff Editor of Princeton University Press, expertly readied my manuscript for the printer, thus giving me good reason to express once more my gratitude to him. I owe to my wife a special word of thanks. She prepared the typed copy of my original handwritten manuscript and did so with an alertness and accuracy that made her work a model of excellence. Moreover, her interest in all aspects of the present undertaking has been a continuing source of encouragement and strength to me. This book is hers in important ways—a fact that is also emphasized by the entry which appears on the leaf preceding this Preface.

Beyond the acknowledgments just made, I should like to add a word or two of appreciation in a somewhat different sort of connection. As a direct result of the research done under the Guggenheim Fellowship which I mentioned above, I published in *The Quarterly Journal of Speech* for February 1959, an article entitled "Sources of the Elocutionary Movement in England: 1700-1748." Later, at a seminar meeting sponsored in 1963 by the Huntington Library, I read a paper called "The Plough and the Flail: The Ordeal of Eighteenth-Century Logic," and that paper was subsequently published in *The Huntington Library Quarterly* for November 1964. In December 1967, I published in *The Quarterly Journal of Speech* an essay, "John Locke and the New Rhetoric," and in *Speech Monographs* for November 1969, a longer essay, "Adam Smith's Lectures on Rhetoric: An Historical Assessment." *Action and Conviction in Early Modern Europe,* edited by Theodore K. Rabb and Jerrold E. Seigel (Princeton University Press, 1969) contains another long essay of mine, "John Locke and the New Logic." And most recently of all, I published in *University, A Princeton Quarterly* (Summer 1970), a short article, "Witherspoon on How to Speak and Write." This latter piece, and the others just enumerated, were originally written so as to stand alone, but they were also intended to figure in the present book at points where I would be discussing the subjects with which they deal. Thus it is that they appear in these pages after having been published in other formats. I should like at this time to thank their original publishers—the Speech Communication Association, the Huntington Library, and Princeton University Press—for their kindness in granting me permission to print these articles in whole or in part in the present book.

20 *Armour Road* WILBUR SAMUEL HOWELL
Princeton, New Jersey
April 22, 1971

CONTENTS

CHAPTER 1

Wee conclude therefore, that Rhetoricke *can bee no
more charged, with the colouring of the worse part,
than* Logicke *with* Sophistrie, *or* Moralitie *with Vice.
For wee knowe the Doctrines of Contraries are the
same, though the vse be opposite: It appeareth also,
that* Logicke *differeth from* Rhetoricke, *not onely as
the* fist, *from the* pawme, *the one close, the other at
large; but much more in this, that* Logicke *handleth
Reason exacte, and in truth; and* Rhetoricke *handleth
it, as it is planted in popular opinions and Manners:
And therefore* Aristotle *doth wisely place* Rhetoricke,
as betweene Logicke *on the one side, and* Morall *or*
Ciuile Knowledge *on the other, as participating of
both: for the Proofes and Demonstrations of* Logicke,
*are toward all men indifferent, and the same: But the
Proofes and perswasions of* Rhetoricke, *ought to differ
according to the Auditors,*

Orpheus in Siluis, inter Delphinas Arion.

Francis Bacon, *Of the proficience and aduance-
ment of Learning, diuine and humane*
(London, 1605), Bk. 2, pp. 67v-68r.

INTRODUCTION

This book undertakes to present an analysis of the major eighteenth-century British writings on logic and rhetoric and to place those writings in a chronological perspective, so that the reader may see them in relation to their antecedents in the seventeenth and their consequents in the nineteenth centuries and also in relation to their influences upon each other. Moreover, this book undertakes, as part of these two objectives, to introduce the reader to the authors of these writings and to make them and their works stand together as partners in an intellectual effort of appreciable size and duration. If history, as Carl Becker observed, is the memory of things said and done, then the present history is an attempt to tell our modern world what the chief British logicians and rhetoricians of the 1700's said when they wrote about their specialties, and what their works mean within the context of their particular time.

The main conclusion to be drawn from this history is that the changes which took place in logical and rhetorical doctrine between 1700 and 1800 are perhaps best interpreted as responses to the emergence of the new science.

The old science, as the disciples of Aristotle conceived of it at the end of the seventeenth century, had considered its function to be that of subjecting traditional truths to syllogistic examination, and of accepting as new truth only what could be proved to be consistent with the old. Under that kind of arrangement, traditional logic had taught the methods of deductive analysis, had perfected itself in the machinery of testing propositions for consistency, and had served at the same time as the instrument by which truths could be arranged so as to become intelligible and convincing to other learned men. In short, traditional logic prided itself upon being a theory of learned enquiry and of learned communication. Meanwhile, traditional rhetoric also prided itself upon having a share in these same two offices, its special purpose being to communicate truths through a process which, on the one hand, blended scientific conclusions with popular opinions and

5

manners, and, on the other hand, transmitted that blend to the general populace. For all practical purposes, the differences between logic and rhetoric, within the context of the old science, were derived from the differences between the learned and the popular audience. A good statement of the concepts which governed this view of the relations of these disciplines to each other is contained in the epigraph at the head of this chapter.

The new science, as envisioned by its founder, Francis Bacon, considered its function to be that of subjecting physical and human facts to observation and experiment, and of accepting as new truth only what could be shown to conform to the realities behind it. Bacon's vision became that of the Royal Society of London, and of similar organizations throughout Europe. The intoxicating novelty and enormous productivity of the new methods of investigation led young scientists and scholars to practice them with increasing sophistication; and logic, which had always claimed anyway to be the theory of enquiry, began to incorporate the new methods into its doctrines and ended by becoming so enamored of them that it allowed them to crowd out its waning interest in the methods of learned communication. Meanwhile, rhetoric began to see itself as the rightful claimant to the methods of learned communication and as the still unrivaled master of the arts of popular discourse; and by making these two activities its new concern, it came ultimately to think of itself as the art which governed all forms of verbal expression, whether popular or learned, persuasive or didactic, utilitarian or aesthetic. Thus in the context of eighteenth-century learning, rhetoric became the sole art of communication by means of language, and logic moved towards the realization that it was destined to become the science of scientific enquiry. A good statement of the concept which controlled these emerging relations of logic and rhetoric to each other was made by John Stuart Mill in the first half of the nineteenth century, and I have quoted it as the epigraph of Chapter 7, although in a real sense it also belongs to this Introduction.

The full story of these developments is arranged in the following pages as the materials themselves have dictated. Chapter 2 describes the old logic and Chapter 3 the old rhetoric of eighteenth-century Britain, some attention being given in each case to the posture of these two disciplines in the preceding era. Chapter 4 contains an account of a special eighteenth-century movement within the field of traditional rhetoric—a movement which this book explores completely for the first time. Chapter 5 and Chapter 6 deal respectively with the new British logic and rhetoric of the 1700's. Perhaps it should here be emphasized, moreover, that the initial sections of these two latter chapters ought to be regarded as parts of the present Introduction, and might well be turned to and read at this time, since they present introductory views of the chief happenings in their particular fields. As for Chapter 7, it is retrospective, but it also looks ahead.

The history of an intellectual revolution would not normally have a hero, but it is tempting in the present instance to pronounce this dictum inapplicable, and to confer the title of hero upon John Locke. Thanks to the inspiration which he drew from the writings of Bacon and Descartes, and from his association with the Royal Society of London, Locke produced in the 1690's two remarkable treatises, the *Essay concerning Human Understanding*, and an intended supplement to it, *Of the Conduct of the Understanding*. Together these works caused a great stir in Europe and exerted a powerful influence upon the intellectual life of the eighteenth century. So far as its dominant thrust may be said to be embodied in the works of one man, the movement under examination here is hardly anything more than the expression of Locke's influence in this or that of its many ramifications.

But various other eighteenth-century figures also played a large part in this movement, and when they are seen in the light which I am here endeavoring to shed upon them, they will, I hope, have new distinctions to add to those already associated with their names. For example, the ablest spokesmen for the new rhetoric of the 1700's are here identified as Adam Smith, founder of the science of economics; George Campbell, principal of Marischal College, Aberdeen; Hugh Blair, celebrated literary critic and scholar; Joseph Priestley, discoverer of oxygen; John Lawson, of Trinity College, Dublin; and John Witherspoon, the Scottish educator who became president of Princeton College in the American colonies and a signer of the Declaration of Independence. As for the movement which led in the eighteenth century towards the creation of a truly inductive logic, it was encouraged in various degrees by such men as Isaac Watts, well-known hymn writer; William Duncan, professor of natural philosophy in Marischal College; Thomas Reid, distinguished Scottish philosopher; Lord Kames, founder of philosophical criticism; and Dugald Stewart, the most brilliant academic personality in the Edinburgh of his time. All of these authors were Locke's disciples in direct or indirect ways, and not one of them would have treated rhetoric or logic as he did if Locke had not had an important hold upon him.

What of the old logic and rhetoric? Well, their spokesmen, too, are noticed here in detail, and some of them are also well known already for their accomplishments in other fields. There is John Sergeant, an articulate propagandist for Roman Catholicism in Great Britain; there is Henry Aldrich, Dean of Christ Church, Oxford; there is John Ward, fellow and vice president of the Royal Society; there is John Holmes, headmaster of Holt School, Norfolk; there are the popular actors Thomas Betterton, Thomas Sheridan, and John Walker; and there are writers and clergymen like John Henley, John Mason, and Gilbert Austin. If these names suggest that the old logic and rhetoric of eighteenth-century Britain were connected with substantial professions and men, my history itself as it unfolds will prove that this suggestion has ample evidence to back it up and that the logical and rhetorical doctrines of Aristotle and Cicero did not lack responsible advocates in the 1700's.

The antecedents of the movements and counter-movements described in the present history are set forth in detail in a book which I published in 1956. That book is called *Logic and Rhetoric in England, 1500–1700*. I should say, however, that, after I had finished it and had begun work upon the history of the same two disciplines in the eighteenth century, I saw that my earlier account needed to be extended, not by adding to its basic lines of emphasis, but by giving attention to some ramifications of its doctrines. In other words, I felt that Dean Aldrich's *Artis Logicae Compendium*, a late seventeenth-century Aristotelian logic which I had previously neglected, was so important in the eighteenth and early nineteenth centuries that it simply had to be discussed on the present occasion. Accordingly, I have made it one of my subjects in Chapter 2, and in dealing with it, I have not hesitated to repeat some of the things which my earlier book had to say about Bishop Sanderson's similar version of Aristotelian doctrine. Nor have I hesitated to comment in the same chapter upon four other seventeenth-century Aristotelian logics also omitted from my earlier history: Crakanthorp's *Logicae Libri Quinque*, Wallis's *Institutio Logicae*, and Sergeant's *Method to Science* and *Solid Philosophy Asserted*. Thus Chapter 2 must be identified as a supplement to *Logic and Rhetoric in England, 1500–1700*, but I hope that in its present context it will also be considered a proper introduction to eighteenth-century British Aristotelianism.

The present history stands alone in its field. Sketches of eighteenth-century British logic are available to the modern reader, as are sketches of eighteenth-century British rhetoric, and of course a great many of the individual logicians and rhetoricians whom I am presenting here have been the subject of previous books, articles, monographs, and the like.[1] But no author has hitherto attempted to bring together under a single view the two disciplines here examined. If the ensuing pages show that the histories of logic and of rhetoric shed significant light upon each other, at least so far as eighteenth-century Britain is concerned, this book will justify my having aspired to write it. But my larger hope is that the present history, in explaining the changes that occurred in logic and rhetoric at a climactic moment, will give these two disciplines an important new set of relations in modern scholarship and criticism. Modern rhetoric in particular suffers from many discordant and limited interpretations. Perhaps we can see it today in clearer perspective through this present examination of the posture which it had in the eyes of its eighteenth-century disciples and devotees. And perhaps its connection with logic during that time will enable us to understand what it needs to acquire if it is to gain as central a place in the learning of our time as it had in the learning of two hundred years ago.

[1] The most accessible account of British logic in the eighteenth century is that by Robert Blakey, *Historical Sketch of Logic, from the Earliest Times to the Present Day* (London and Edinburgh, 1851), pp. 342-372. See also William and Martha Kneale, *The Development of Logic* (Oxford, 1962), pp. 298-378. For a sketch of eighteenth-century British rhetoric, see William P. Sandford, *English Theories of Public Address, 1530-1828* (Columbus, Ohio, 1931), pp. 131-183, 198-200. See also Harold F. Harding, "English Rhetorical Theory, 1750-1800" (unpub. diss., Cornell University, 1937); Douglas Ehninger, "Dominant Trends in English Rhetorical Thought, 1750-1800," *Southern Speech Journal*, XVIII (September 1952), 3-12; P. W. K. Stone, *The Art of Poetry 1750-1820* (London, 1967), pp. 1-103; and W. Ross Winterowd, *Rhetoric, A Synthesis* (New York, 1968), pp. 45-75. As for specialized studies of authors and topics connected with my present history, they are cited below as the subjects to which they refer are severally examined.

CHAPTER 2

Inter Novae Logicae conditores Verulamium *quoque &*
Cartesium *numerat Gassendus; utriusque item Logicae Compendium exhibere profitetur. At* Cartesius
*de instauranda Logica ne per somnium quidem suum
cogitavit; quin videtur potius Philosophiam moliri
quae Arte Logica non utatur: eodem fortasse animo
quo scribendam censuit fine Demonstratione Geome-
triam. Longe alia* Verulamio *mens; cujus* Organon *cum
Aristotelico nihil habet commune praeter unum Nomen.*

*(Among the founders of the New Logic Gassendi num-
bers Verulam and Descartes, each of whom the* Logicae
Compendium *wishes also to notice. But yet, Descartes
did not plan upon the restoration of logic even in his
dreams; he rather seems to attempt a philosophy which
does not use the art of logic at all, perhaps in the same
spirit in which he considered that geometry ought to
be extended so far as to embrace all demonstration.
As for Verulam, he had quite another intention in a
distant sphere. His* Organon *has nothing in common
with that of Aristotle save the title alone.)*

Henry Aldrich, *Artis Logicae Compendium*
(Oxonii, MDCXCI), sig. G3v

THE ARISTOTELIAN INHERITANCE
IN LOGIC
(1615–1825)

1   Some Seventeenth-Century Peripatetics

At the very beginning of the eighteenth century, it looked as if English logicians had permanently turned their backs upon the possibility of reforming logical theory in the direction of the revolutionary teachings of Bacon and Descartes, and had instead decided to do all that they could to restore the logic of Aristotle to its former pre-eminence in education and learning. There were several writers who deserve credit for that state of affairs. The chief of them was Henry Aldrich, Dean of Christ Church, whose *Artis Logicae Compendium*, first published in 1691 at Oxford, was permeated with a spirit of dedication to the doctrines of the Peripatetics, and was destined to enjoy an astonishing popularity in England for the next hundred and seventy-five years. But Aldrich had impressive supporters. His distinguished colleague John Wallis, Savilian Professor of Geometry at Oxford, and a founder of the Royal Society of London, had published in 1687 a work called *Institutio Logicae, Ad Communes Usus Accommodata*; and in the Latin epistle dedicating it to the Lord President and other Fellows of the Royal Society, he had announced his hope of having his work serve in certain respects to recall to the Aristotelian or Peripatetic doctrine those logicians who, whether knowingly or unknowingly, had deviated from it. Not long before Wallis wrote those words, a treatise called *Manuductio ad Logicam, Sive Dialectica* had been given two successive editions at Oxford. That work, printed at Cologne in 1620 by a Belgian Jesuit, Philip Du Trieu, who survived until 1645, is thoroughly Aristotelian in its tone and content; moreover, its appearance at Oxford reflected the mild popularity that it had already

13

achieved on the Continent.[1] Then there had been Richard Crakanthorp's reconstruction of Porphyry's *Isagoge* and Aristotle's
Organon, entitled *Logicae Libri Quinque*, which came out first
in 1622 at London, and had three other editions within the next
sixty years. Before Crakanthorp were additional English Aristotelians, particularly Robert Sanderson, onetime fellow of
Lincoln College, Oxford, and Bishop of Lincoln between 1660
and 1663. Sanderson's *Logicae Artis Compendium*, published in
1615 at Oxford, was given a total of nine editions before the
seventeenth century ended, and it was to have four still later
ones, the last in the early 1840's, before its career in print was
over.[2] Its hold upon English education and learning is convincingly demonstrated not only by its having been one of Isaac Newton's important textbooks before and during his undergraduate
years at Trinity College, Cambridge, between 1661 and 1665, but
also by its having greatly influenced Jeremy Bentham exactly a
hundred years later when he was an undergraduate at Queen's
College, Oxford, and by its having entered in a significant way
into the distinguished scientific career and the logical doctrines
of George Bentham, Jeremy's nephew, during the early years of
the nineteenth century.[3] A textbook does not always have such
prolonged popularity or gain the attention of such formidable
talents as Sanderson's *Compendium* did. If we take account of the
many editions that it received, and add to them the many editions

---

[1] Donald Wing, in *A Short-Title Catalogue*, lists an edition of 1662 and
another of 1678, both at Oxford. A third English edition appeared at London
in 1826, and it was this work which figured in George Bentham's *Outline of
a New System of Logic* (London, 1827), pp. 108-109. Falconer Madan, *Oxford
Books* (Oxford, 1895-1931), III, 161-162, 359, describes each of the Oxford editions, and says that the work first appeared in 1615. The Bibliothèque Nationale holds copies of Continental editions dated 1620, 1628, and 1690. I have
examined the Oxford edition of 1662, a copy of which is in the Harvard University Library.

[2] See Madan, *Oxford Books*, III, 448, for a list of its seventeenth-century
editions. Later editions are dated 1705, 1707, 1741, and 1841.

[3] See David Brewster, *The Life of Sir Isaac Newton* (New York, 1831), p.
27; Louis T. More, *Isaac Newton, A Biography* (New York, 1934), pp. 31-32;
John Bowring, *The Works of Jeremy Bentham* (Edinburgh, 1838-1842), x, 37;
Thomas E. Holland, *The Encyclopaedia Britannica*, 11th edn., s.v. Bentham,
Jeremy; George Bentham, *Outline of a New System of Logic*, pp. 13, 22, 101,
107-110, 155; and Sir William Turner Thiselton-Dyer, *The Encyclopaedia
Britannica*, 11th edn., s.v. Bentham, George.

given to Aldrich's similar *Compendium* between 1691 and 1867,[4] we have no difficulty in concluding that these two treatises did more than any others to keep Aristotle's logical doctrines alive and influential in England for the entire period between Bacon's *Novum Organum* and John Stuart Mill's *A System of Logic*.

[4] For further details about editions of Aldrich's *Compendium*, see below, pp. 43, 58-60.

II Bishop Sanderson and the Attack on Ramus

When Sanderson's *Compendium* first appeared in print, the prevailing logical system in England was not that of the traditional Aristotelians, but that of the articulate and argumentative disciples of Peter Ramus.[5] Ramus, a Frenchman, had come upon the European scene during the middle years of the sixteenth century, when the Reformation was reaching its climax, and when bitter controversy was taking place everywhere in Europe, now as the prologue and again as the epilogue to military struggles between Catholicism and Protestantism. Ramus's logic perfectly fitted its times. It was a logic conceived, organized, and taught less as a master guide to philosophical enquiry than as a master guide to controversy, in times when two great hostile forces confronted each other in Europe, and each was committed to winning converts by words or by force at the expense of the other.

In this historical situation Ramus proceeded to define logic as the art of disputing well and to organize logical theory into two operations. One operation consisted in the invention of arguments. The theory of this operation showed the disputant how to visit the ten topics or places and to find in them the lines of argument to be followed and the ideas to be used in proving his case against an opponent. The other operation surveyed the entire field of organizing an argumentative discourse, and Ramus made this operation consist of teachings related to the logical proposition, the syllogism, and method. In a very real sense he thought that the ability to combine words into logical propositions, the ability to combine those propositions into valid syllogisms of one of the three available Aristotelian figures, and the ability to combine syllogisms into whole discourses, were the three arts that the successful disputant had to master, after he had taught himself to find the wherewithal for his argument within the ten places.[6]

Method was to Ramus a point of great emphasis in logical theory, and even Sanderson, a firm opponent of his teachings,

[5] See Wilbur S. Howell, *Logic and Rhetoric in England, 1500-1700* (Princeton, 1956), pp. 299-309.

[6] *Ibid.*, pp. 146-165. Ramus's ten places of invention prescribed that a disputant argue from causes, effects, subjects, adjuncts, opposites, comparatives, names, divisions, definitions, witnesses. See below, nn. 27, 28, 45, 68.

went so far as to commend him for his industry in goading men of genius into a more careful consideration of this part of logic.[7] In line with his overwhelming interest in disputation, Ramus thought of method as the theory of organizing learned and popular discourses. The system of organizing a learned discourse he termed the method of nature or science, that is to say, the method by which philosophers would naturally arrange their subject matter when they addressed each other and sought to win a philosophic assent to disputed points of theology, metaphysics, or ethics. Ramus designated the system of organizing popular discourse as the method of prudence, and he obviously intended it for use in popular debate and oratory upon occasions when speakers and preachers, needing to win the assent of the multitude, would find it disadvantageous to proceed by strict definition, by exhaustive dichotomous divisions, and by following throughout the order of descending generality, but would resort instead to more familiar and less taxing procedures of expression.

Sanderson's *Compendium* noted that the recent opponents of Ramism had sought to take a middle ground between Ramus and Aristotle, but had tended to make their compromises less Aristotelian than Ramistic.[8] He himself was interested, not in repudiating the compromise, but in altering the emphasis within it. He accordingly described logical theory so as to point out that "logic, which under the figure of synecdoche can also mean dialectic, is an instrumental art directing our minds in the knowing of all things knowable."[9] This definition, it can be seen, contains no reference to what Ramus had insisted upon above all when he began his famous treatise by terming dialectic or logic the art of disputing well.[10] Sanderson attempted instead to suggest that logic must ultimately be conceived in terms wide enough to include the entire *Organon* (or "Instrument") of Aristotle, and not simply Aristotle's *Topics* and the two treatises on analytics, which the Ramistic system tended to stress rather exclusively.

The *Compendium* proceeded next to indicate what the parts

[7] Robert Sanderson, *Logicae Artis Compendium* (Oxford, 1618), p. 122.

[8] *Ibid.*, pp. 122-123.

[9] *Ibid.*, p. 1. Sanderson's Latin text, which I have translated here and below, reads as follows: "*Logica*, quae & Synecdochicè Dialectica, *est ars instrumentalis, dirigens mentem nostram in cognitionem omnium intelligibilium.*"

[10] Peter Ramus, *Dialectique* (Paris, 1555), p. 1.

of logic are, and at this point Sanderson was careful to show how these parts relate severally to the great classics of the Aristotelian tradition. Again we may see that he did not follow Ramus, who, it will be remembered, had supported the view that the parts of logic are invention and judgment or arrangement.[11] Sanderson said:

> Its parts are three, by virtue of the number of mental operations directed out of it. The first part gives direction to the first operation of the mind, namely, simple perceiving; and this part deals with simple terms. To it pertain Porphyry's *Introduction* and the Book of Aristotle's *Categories.*

> Its second part gives direction to the second operation of the mind, namely, unifying and dividing; and it deals with propositions. To it relates Aristotle's Book *On Interpretation.*

> Its third part gives direction to the third and last operation of the mind, namely, discoursing; and it deals with argumentation and method. To it relate the Two Books of the *Prior Analytics,* the same number of Books of the *Posterior Analytics,* the Eight Books of the *Topics,* and finally the Two Books of the *Sophistical Elenchi.*[12]

The four criticisms that Sanderson went on to direct against the Ramists were that they had altered logical terms and idioms current for a very long time in the schools, that they had mutilated logic by depriving it of some of its parts, that they had used passages from exoteric writers like poets and orators to illustrate the esoteric precepts of logic, and that they had reduced the theory of method to the meagre and painful routine of definition and division by dichotomies.[13] Sanderson's own *Compendium* can really be described as a determined attempt to correct these faults. Thus he restored to logical theory such terms as those belonging to the five predicables and the ten predicaments, which Ramus had abandoned in favor of the ten places of invention. Thus also, as we have just seen, he divided logic into three parts, not two, and in treating of the third part, he spoke of fallacies, which Ramus had omitted from his scheme. Thus also he avoided illustrating logical precepts by quoting from oratory and poetry. And finally he expanded the theory of method and made it some-

---

[11] *Ibid.,* p. 4.   [12] *Compendium,* pp. 2-3.   [13] *Ibid.,* p. 122.

thing that reflected the new scientific interests of the seventeenth century, as Ramistic method had reflected the sixteenth-century interest in disputation and propaganda.

The point just mentioned deserves a word of comment. Sanderson's theory of method embraced two opposite procedures, one of which he called the method of invention, and the other, the method of doctrine. The former method, he explained, is used in discovering new truth, the latter, in teaching what has been discovered. Sanderson described these two aspects of method as follows:

> Each proceeds from that which is more known by us to that which by us is less known; but one and the other in a different manner, nevertheless. For we discover precepts by ascending, that is, by progressing from the concrete and the particular, which to us are more directly known, towards the intelligible and universal, which are more known by nature. But we transmit precepts by descending, that is, by progressing from the universal and intelligible, which are more known by nature, and more clearly known by us also, to that which is less universal, and closer to the senses, and as it were less known.[14]

The very fact that Sanderson's theory of method involves a consideration of the method of invention as well as the method of doctrine or communication, whereas Ramus's theory had emphasized only the latter point, should be remembered as we turn later to the discussion of the logics of the eighteenth century. So far as eighteenth-century logicians discussed method at all, they followed Sanderson and not Ramus. That is to say, they emphasized method as investigative as well as presentational, not as presentational alone. Indeed, Sanderson's description of the method of invention or investigation was to be echoed more than once during the eighteenth century by English writers seeking to supplement the Aristotelian doctrines of Aldrich as Sanderson in his day had sought to supplement and correct Ramism. Sanderson's description of the four steps to be followed in the method of invention is perhaps one reason why his *Compendium* appealed in later days to scientists and philosophers who wanted logic to serve as an instrument for the advancement of learning:

[14] *Ibid.*, p. 226. See Howell, *Logic and Rhetoric in England*, p. 306.

19

The method of invention has four means, and as it were four stages through which we ascend. First is perception, by the help of which we assemble some notion of individual things. Second is observation or seeing accurately, in the course of which we collect and arrange what we have assimilated at different times by perception. Third is the proof by experiment, wherein we subject the multitude of assembled observations to fixed tests. Fourth and last is induction, in which we summon the multitude of collected and tested proofs so as to make up a universal conclusion.[15]

Sanderson's account of the other method, that of doctrine, begins by recognizing that, in presenting knowledge to others, either of two procedures may be used, one of which concerns the theoretical sciences, the other, the practical wisdoms. The former of these Sanderson called the unitive or compositive or synthetic method. It is governed by two laws, one of which, the *lex unitas*, is that the unity of a science depends upon unity of subject, while the other, the *lex generalitatis*, echoed Ramus's injunction that the more universal should precede the less universal. The three major concerns of this method are the subject itself, its elements, and its general relations. Sanderson envisaged this method as working thus:

Accordingly for theoretical sciences the doctrine of method is as follows: First in few words there should be a treatment of the concept of the subject, so far as it can in some way be understood in advance. Secondly, there should be a treatment of its elements, then of its general relations, then of its species. The line of descent should be from the simpler to the more complex, until the bottom is reached. Aristotle used this method accurately in treating the subject of physics.[16]

The system of transmitting the practical wisdoms to students or others was called by Sanderson the divisive or resolutive or analytic method. Its three major concerns are the end, the subject, and the means. Like its companion procedure, it is governed by two laws respectively prescribing that the unity of a practical wisdom depends upon unity of aim, and that in organizing a dis-

---

[15] Sanderson, *Compendium*, pp. 226-227. See also Howell, p. 307.
[16] *Compendium*, p. 231.

course the more universal precedes the less universal. The method is put into operation as follows:

> Hence among the practical wisdoms the theory of method is, first, that the discipline should be treated in relation to the idea of end, as a matter of foreknowledge, then in relation to subject, wherein the end is realized, then in relation to the elements of the means, and then in relation to the means themselves, first in general, then in species, and finally in the individual case. As in practical ethics, first is treated happiness as end; then are treated intellect, will, human passions, as the subjects of happiness; and then are treated choice, avoidance, custom, etc., which are the elements of virtues; and finally are treated the virtues themselves, as the means to happiness in general and in its species.[17]

[17] *Ibid.*, p. 232.

In thus correcting and supplementing Ramus's theory of method and in restoring to logic certain traditional Aristotelian elements that the Ramists had omitted from their logical system, Sanderson merely did what several of his contemporaries were also doing. One of these, Richard Crakanthorp, deserves some mention, not as a serious rival of Sanderson in the front rank of seventeenth-century Peripatetics, but as a logician whose moderate vogue endured for several generations and who was mentioned as an effective and true Aristotelian along with Sanderson and Wallis by Dr. Samuel Johnson in the preface which he contributed to Robert Dodsley's *The Preceptor* in 1748.[18]

Crakanthorp's *Logicae Libri Quinque*, which first appeared seven years after Sanderson's *Compendium* was published, abandoned the theory of method altogether as a part of logic, and dwelt exclusively upon the doctrines relating to the predicables, the predicaments, the theory of logical terms, the classes of propositions, the demonstrative and the dialectical syllogisms, the places or topics of argument, and sophisms or fallacies. Thus Crakanthorp proved to be a better Aristotelian than Sanderson, who in treating method had bowed to a Ramistic rather than a Peripatetic convention, even if his actual theory of method had gone considerably beyond what Ramus dictatorially ordered.

In the Latin Introduction to his logic, Crakanthorp took the trouble to declare his allegiance to Aristotle and to specify that his doctrine was based upon Aristotle's treatises *On Interpretation*, the *Prior Analytics*, the *Posterior Analytics*, the *Topics*, and the *Categories*.[19] He also mentioned Porphyry's *Isagoge* with respect, and claimed it as authority for his own treatment of the predicables, Aristotle having discussed the latter subject so indirectly as to give Porphyry an excuse for his own more elaborate exposition of it. Crakanthorp, a zealous Puritan as well as a learned man, added that Porphyry's little book and Porphyry

[18] See Robert Dodsley, *The Preceptor* (London, 1748), I, xxv-xxvi. See also below, Ch. 5, pp. 307, 342.

[19] Richard Crakanthorp, *Logicae Libri Quinque* (London, 1641), sig. A6r-v. My discussion of Crakanthorp is based upon this edition, which is the second. The first edition appeared at London in 1622; the third at London in 1670; and the fourth at Oxford in 1677. The excerpts which I quote are in my translation.

himself were detestable, at least so far as Augustine had been right in testifying to Porphyry's bitter hostility to Christianity. But Crakanthorp then softened this verdict by noting that Jerome had told of Porphyry's later change of heart towards the Christians after he had been exiled by Constantine the Great as a punishment for his hatred of them.

It should not for a moment be supposed that Crakanthorp chose to follow Aristotle without thoroughly knowing of the reformed logic of Ramus. What he rather did was to attempt to counteract the reforms that Ramus had emphasized, and to take occasion now and then to attack Ramus by name. At least one such attack deserves our notice. It occurs soon after Crakanthorp had mentioned the three laws that Aristotle had established for testing the scientific acceptability of propositions. Those laws were that the predicate of a proper scientific proposition must apply to all cases of the subject, must be in harmony with itself, and must not extend beyond the limits of the nearest general class to which the subject can belong.[20] Without deigning to take notice of the way in which these three laws had been applied to logic by Ramus, Crakanthorp turned next to the discussion of axioms and theses, and at that point he criticized Ramus with some asperity. He said:

> An axiom in any discipline is an undemonstrable proposition or principle of such clear and conspicuous truth that he who would learn that discipline could hardly ignore it. Here are some axioms in metaphysics: it can truly be said of anything that it exists or does not exist; or that it is so-and-so or not so-and-so; or that it is impossible for it at one and the same time to be the same and not the same. Here is one in mathematics: any whole is greater than its part. And in physics: God and nature make nothing in vain. And in ethics: all who strive aim for the good. And so on.
>
> Surely these shine in their own light, and therefore they are deservedly called by the all-inclusive and truly elevated term axiom, that is, something thought most worthy and greatest;

[20] *Ibid.*, p. 297. Crakanthorp calls them by their traditional Latin terms: "Primus vocatur *de Omni*, Secundus *Per se*, Tertius *Quatenus ipsum*." These three laws were important elements in scholastic and Ramistic logic. See Howell, *Logic and Rhetoric in England*, pp. 41-43, 149-153, 181-182, 295-296.

because on account of their very great self-evidence, in which you may put the greatest trust, they are most worthy. For certainly it always stirs my bile and distaste because that "new" man, the late Peter Ramus, who turns everything both up and down, dares to call all propositions axioms, and dares to teach his disciples to call them so. Among the disciples you read or hear of nothing more frequently than of contingent axioms, of probable axioms, even of false axioms, and indeed of absurd and impossible axioms. But away with such idiocies! Let us send Ramus to the Peripatetic schools, so that he may often be flogged, and never be flogged enough. Let us call a fig a fig, a spade a spade, and a proposition a proposition. And let us leave this truly noble term axiom to those things which are in truth thought greatest and most worthy of honor.[21]

If Crakanthorp had had his way, he would also have wanted Ramus to be flogged for his attempt to alter the traditional connections between logic and rhetoric. What Ramus had done in that respect was fateful. As we have noticed,[22] he defined logic as the art of disputing well, and he limited it strictly to invention and arrangement, which had been the parts of dialectic in Aristotle's *Topics* and in Cicero's similiar work. When Ramus came to the subject of rhetoric, he had to make a decision of some consequence. If he chose to regard rhetoric in its Aristotelian and Ciceronian formulations, he would have had to recognize that it too treated invention and arrangement, as well as style, memory, and delivery, these five operations having been regarded in the fully developed Peripatetic rhetoric of Cicero as the fundamental procedures in the composing and the pronouncing of a speech. But Ramus felt that redundancy would be involved if he allowed rhetoric to treat invention and arrangement after he had assigned invention and arrangement to logic. He could in large measure have avoided the redundancy, of course, by regarding rhetoric

---

[21] Crakanthorp, *Logicae Libri Quinque*, pp. 302-303. Crakanthorp notes in the margin that he is referring to Ramus's *Dialecticae Libri Duo*, Bk. 2, Ch. 3. Crakanthorp's concept of axiom is derived etymologically from the Greek word ἀξίωμα, which means "that of which one is thought worthy, an honor, that which is thought fit." Thus in science an axiom is "that which is assumed as the basis of demonstration, a self-evident principle."

[22] See above, pp. 16-17. For other details, see my *Logic and Rhetoric in England*, pp. 146-172.

as the art of dealing with the popular audience, "the audience of untrained thinkers," as Aristotle had said,[23] while keeping to the ancient notion that dialectic, as an arm of demonstrative logic, was the art of dealing with discourse addressed to men of learning. Thus under the subject of rhetoric he could have treated invention and arrangement as they would need to be conducted in developing a popular discourse, and under the subject of dialectic, as they would need to be conducted for a discourse before an audience of philosophers. Ramus's contemporary, Thomas Wilson, in writing his *Rule of Reason* and his *Arte of Rhetorique* in the 1550's, had followed that very plan. The former work, the first treatise in English on learned controversy, divided dialectic or logic into two parts, invention and judgment or arrangement; and the latter, as a treatise on popular discourse, followed the Peripatetic and Ciceronian scheme of dividing rhetoric into invention, arrangement, style, memory, and delivery. Ramus, however, did not accept that kind of solution. He argued, instead, that logic should treat invention and disposition in such a basic way as to reveal everything that any dialectician or any orator would need to know in finding or arranging ideas for any possible discourse, learned or popular. He also argued that rhetoric should thus be left only with its traditional procedures of style and delivery, and should confine itself to the lore of the tropes and the figures and to the practical manipulation of the voice and the body. In regard to memory as a part of rhetoric, Ramus argued that it was a common factor in many arts, and that it did not belong in particular to the speaker, whose proper training for any kind of dispute could be confined to what he may say, in what order he may say it, and by what means.[24] Thus Ramus's final

---

[23] *Rhetoric*, 1357a 10-15.

[24] Ramus's words on this point, as quoted from his *Scholae Rhetoricae*, Lib. 3, by John Holmes, *The Art of Rhetoric made Easy* (London, 1755), Bk. 1, p. 4, are as follows: "*Dicis Oratori tria esse videnda*, quid dicat, quo quidque loco, & quomodo; *primo Membro* Inventionem, *secundo* Collocationem, *tertio* Elocutionem & Actionem *comprehendis*: Memoriam *igitur in hac trium Membrorum Partitione praetermittis*. Communis est *ais* multarum Artium, *propterea omittitur*." Ramus could of course use Cicero as authority for alleging that memory is not a part of rhetoric, and could cite *Orator*, 17.54, where Cicero says that it is not necessary to discuss memory in connection with oratory, since it is common to many arts. It should be remembered, however, that Cicero elsewhere insisted upon including memory among the standard

decision was that rhetoric and dialectic differed from each other as the process of discovering and arranging arguments differs from the process of expressing arguments in unusual patterns of language and pronouncing them with suitable intonation and gesture. The assumption behind this thinking is, of course, that matter and form can be profitably divorced from style and delivery, and that the problems of subject matter and organization in literature are not solved by the same art that considers the problems of verbal and oral expression.

To Crakanthorp, trained as he was in an older tradition, this Ramistic solution did not appeal at all. He conceived of logic as the study of argumentation both in general and in respect to its two species. The general aspects of argumentation are covered by Crakanthorp's first three books, where he dealt successively with predicables, categories, terms, propositions, and syllogisms. At the beginning of Book IV, he took up the two species of argumentation with these significant words:

> We have thus far treated argumentation in general, without respect either to the matter in which it consists, whether necessary or probable, or to the end on account of which it exists, whether for teaching, or for disputing, or for persuading. Now follow the species of argumentation, which are going to be treated in respect to the matter in which they consist and the end which they exist to serve. There are two species of arguments: the argumentative or demonstrative syllogism, which is called Demonstration; and the probable syllogism, which, if it is used for the discovery of truth, is called the dialectical syllogism, and, if it is used for persuading, is called the rhetorical syllogism.[25]

These links between logic, dialectic, and rhetoric are of course thoroughly Aristotelian, and Crakanthorp could have found a dozen passages in Aristotle's logical and rhetorical writings to support them, including the famous statement at the beginning of his treatise on rhetorical theory that "rhetoric is the counterpart of dialectic." But Crakanthorp did not consider it necessary to treat the relations among these three arts as if they were open to question. Instead, he assumed them as already established, and

---

parts of rhetorical theory. See his *De Inventione*, 1.7.9; also *De Oratore*, 1.31.142, 1.42.187, 2.19.79; also *De Partitione Oratoria*, 1.3.

[25] *Logicae Libri Quinque*, p. 294.

he went on to devote his fourth book to the demonstrative syllogism, that is to say, to the form of proof that employs necessary materials, that argues from cause or effect, that reaches the highest degree of certainty in its conclusiveness, and that can be used both as an instrument of discovery and a method of teaching. And in his fifth and last book, he discussed dialectic, which he defined in itself and in its relation to rhetoric in the following way:

> Dialectic is the species or part of general logic which teaches how to argue probably to the end that the truth may be uncovered through disputation.

> Rhetoric is the part of general logic which teaches how to argue probably to the end that it persuades or dissuades in respect to the doing of something.[26]

Crakanthorp's view of disputation is that the successful disputant visits the places of argument and finds in them the argumentative materials needed for the conduct of a debate upon the question under examination. There are thirteen such places listed and analyzed in his fifth book. The first four were famous as heads of enquiry in metaphysical disputes, and they consisted in discussing any abstract phenomenon in terms of its efficient cause, its final cause, its material cause, and its formal cause. The fifth place referred to the phenomenon in terms of its effects. Then came the consideration of its subordinates, its collateral circumstances, its contraries, its matchings with equals, its matchings with disparates, its division, its sign, and its witnesses or testimonies.[27] Crakanthorp differs from Sanderson and Ramus in respect to the names and the total number of places only in ways that would be considered unimportant today.[28] What is important

---

[26] *Ibid.*, p. 340; see also pp. 118-129, for Crakanthorp's earlier discussion of dialectic and rhetoric, and of science, grammar, poetry, and history as parts of logic.

[27] The Latin terms for these "loci" in Crakanthorp's scheme serve as thirteen of his chapter headings in Book v as follows: "à Causa efficiente; à Causa Finali; à Causa materiali; à Causa formali; ab Effectu; à Subjecto; ab Adjuncto seu Accidente; à Dissentaneis; à Comparatis paribus; à Comparatis imparibus; à Distributione; à Signo; à Testimonio seu Authoritate." See above, n. 6; below, nn. 28, 45, 68.

[28] Sanderson's *Logicae Artis Compendium* (Oxford, 1618) treats of the places under the following heads and on the following pages: De Locis Topicis (p. 183); De Locis à Causâ & Effectu (p. 185); De Locis à Subiecto & Accidente (p. 189); De Locis à Dissentaneis & Comparatis (p. 192); De Locis à Coniu-

about this part of logical theory in the Renaissance is that it derived ultimately from Aristotle's *Topics* and from Cicero's similar work, and it provided the dialectician with a machinery which not only yielded him a store of argumentative materials when he was engaged in debate but also made him similar to the rhetorician who under the Aristotelian and Ciceronian theory of rhetoric had a prearranged network of places to examine when he was in search of materials for his popular orations.[29] The rhetorician sought his materials, of course, in order that he could persuade a popular audience through the medium of a continuous discourse, while the dialectician sought his in order that he might establish truth through the medium of disputation.

Crakanthorp's Epilogue adds to the value of his work by mentioning a few of the laws that ought to be observed in a formal academic dispute by the opponent who challenges the thesis under examination and by the respondent who answers the challenge.[30] Thus to the end he kept in mind that logic was the instrument for establishing and communicating both the certainties of science and the tested probabilities of practical knowledge, and that in respect to the communication of tested probabilities it had a close partnership with rhetoric. Ramus would have protested that Crakanthorp's logic covered more than it needed to cover when it analyzed the predicables and predicaments, and less than it needed to cover when it omitted method; and he would have insisted that rhetoric functioned in a proper theory of the arts only to guarantee ornament as a relief from plainness of style in the finished oration and only to assure propriety in movements of the voice and body as the speaker pronounced his words in public. But Ramus's views were obsolete by the time of Crakanthorp, and thus it became possible not only to undo many of his reforms but to establish in their place the very dogmas that he doubtless credited himself with having eliminated forever.

---

gatis & Notatione (p. 199); Loci à Toto & Parte (p. 202); De Locis à Genere & Specie (p. 204); De Locis à definitione & divisione (p. 207); De Loco à Testimonio (p. 208).

Ramus's reform of this part of logic resulted in his allowing only ten places. See above, nn. 6, 27; below, nn. 45, 68.

[29] For a discussion of the places or topics of rhetoric in eighteenth-century rhetorical theory, see below, Ch. 3, pp. 91-94, 97-101.

[30] *Logicae Libri Quinque*, pp. 473-474.

iv John Wallis's *Institutio Logicae*

In 1638, three years before the date of the second edition of Crakanthorp's *Logicae Libri Quinque*, a Cambridge student named John Wallis, who had recently become bachelor of arts from Emmanuel College and was currently proceeding towards a master's degree, acted as respondent in an academic disputation by defending the thesis that a singular proposition in the context of a syllogism always has the force of a universal. The same young scholar in the following year argued again in a formal disputation in support of the thesis that on the plane of actuality the extension of a term is equivalent to its object extended in the same amount. And a few years later in a more mature spirit he composed a formal argument to prove that hypothetical syllogisms and all other composite arguments ought to be considered as Aristotelian forms of the categorical syllogism. These three essays on the theory of logic did not reflect a merely transitory interest on the part of Wallis. Indeed, he preserved them and published them in 1687 as an appendix to his *Institutio Logicae*, a textbook which was to have four eighteenth-century editions and was to achieve the honor not only of being repeatedly singled out for respectful contradiction by Dugald Stewart between 1785 and 1809 in his distinguished lectures at Edinburgh on the philosophy of the human mind, but also of being mentioned with approval by Richard Whately in his *Elements of Logic* in 1826.[31]

Wallis's fame as a logician, however, was overshadowed by his other accomplishments. After having been awarded the degree of master of arts at Cambridge in 1640, he gained reputation as a cryptographer, a mathematician, a member of the parliamentary party in the Civil War, and an enthusiastic supporter of the scientific reforms that Francis Bacon had called into being, and that Wallis's friend Robert Boyle was carrying forward in a way

[31] For Wallis's three theses, see *Institutio Logicae* (Oxford, 1687), pp. 219-262. My entire discussion of Wallis's logic is based upon this edition, the first, the translations being mine. Other editions appeared at Oxford on the following dates: 1699, 1702, 1715, 1729, 1763. See Dugald Stewart, *Elements of the Philosophy of the Human Mind*, Vol. II (New York, 1814), pp. 125, 155, 236, 240, 333-335, 338, for references to Wallis; also see Richard Whately, *Elements of Logic* (London, 1831), pp. 125, 142, 224.

later regarded as decisive.[32] In fact, the Royal Society of London grew out of the meetings that Wallis, Boyle, and other believers in experimental science arranged and attended between 1645 and 1660. Wallis was appointed by Cromwell in 1649 to be Savilian Professor of Geometry at Oxford, and he succeeded in holding that post after the Restoration until his death in 1703. His *Arithmetica Infinitorum*, published at Oxford in 1655, is his most important work. Louis Trenchard More says of it that it "displays and greatly extends the methods of analysis introduced by Descartes and Cavalieri." More adds: "It became the standard work on the subject and is constantly referred to by Fermat, Barrow, Newton, and Leibniz. His solution for finding the areas of curves by the use of infinite series was so close to the discovery of the calculus that Newton and Leibniz had principally to clarify and advance his method into a formal system."[33]

"It hath been my lot," wrote Wallis in 1697, "to live in a time wherein have been many and great changes and alterations. It hath been my endeavour all along to act by moderate principles, between the extremities on either hand, in a moderate compliance with the powers in being. Hereby I have been able to live easy and useful, though not great."[34] The crucial changes and alterations to which Wallis referred in these refreshingly modest words proceeded of course from the publication in 1620 of Francis Bacon's *Novum Organum*, from the publication in 1637 of René Descartes' *Discours de la Méthode*, from the announcement by Boyle in 1662 of the law of the inversely proportional relation between volume and pressure in a compressed gas, and from the fateful publications of Newton's *Principia* in midsummer of 1687 and of Locke's *An Essay concerning Human Understanding* in 1690. These are the documents which made the span of John Wallis's life the most decisive era between the end of Christ's ministry and the beginning of the twentieth century. These are the documents which revealed new horizons in scientific thinking and threw into sharp relief the differences between those new horizons and the old landscape of mankind's past journeyings. It

[32] My biographical account relies upon that by Agnes Mary Clerke in *The Dictionary of National Biography*.

[33] *Isaac Newton, A Biography*, p. 36, n. 21.

[34] Quoted from Miss Clerke's article on Wallis in *The Dictionary of National Biography*.

was Wallis's lot, as he perceptively recognized, to avoid penetrating to the edge of the new horizons and yet to resist the comforting impulse to take refuge in the oldest districts of the country behind. No work of his better illustrates this moderation than does the *Institutio Logicae*.

The Latin epistle which dedicates this work to the Lord President and other Fellows of the Royal Society has been mentioned in the first section of this chapter as announcing Wallis's hope that his treatise would recall logic in some respects to the teachings of Aristotle. Wallis took pains in the epistle to specify what those respects were. He felt compelled, he said, to depart from the common path of traditional logicians by recalling singular propositions to the class of universals, and by enclosing hypothetical syllogisms and other composite arguments within the rules governing categorical syllogisms. He added that these two points merely restore to Aristotle what was rightfully his anyway, and that he had included suitable dissertations upon them at the end of his present work. Thus he associated his *Institutio Logicae* with one of the academic exercises that he had performed some fifty years earlier at Cambridge, and with another exercise that he had written not too long after he took his master's degree.[35] When he went on to conclude his dedicatory epistle by remarking that the entire *Institutio Logicae* had been composed some years ago and had been adapted then to the uses of the Royal Society and even dedicated to them at that time, he makes it almost certain that the work was probably one of the first things he wrote after he began in 1645 to attend the meetings of the group constituting the Royal Society in its earliest form.

The *Institutio Logicae* begins in the approved manner by defining its subject. Its first words are as follows: "Logic is *the art* (or practical knowledge) of *reasoning* (or of skilfully using the

[35] Preceding the three theses in the first edition of the *Institutio Logicae* is a short preface (p. 218) headed "Monitum ad Lectorem," which ends as follows: "And indeed the first and the third of these dissertations I really wrote some time ago as theses (as they are called); and I defended them A.D. 1638 and 1639 in Emmanuel College, Cambridge, in public disputation (I was then a youth); and they were published in 1643. The other was written somewhat more seriously (but many years ago), and is here published for the first time." The Bodleian Library holds a copy of the two previously published dissertations under the title, *De Propositione Singulari, et De Quantitate* (Londini, 1643).

rational faculty); it directs the mind (or intellect) in the due and neat conducting of thought. This conducting is called *ratiocina-tion* or *discourse*; it is also called *logic* (λογική) ἀπὸ τοῦ λόγου, which word signifies both *thinking* and *speaking*. The *objects* of logic (around about which it turns) are all things (whether real or imaginary); all things, indeed, whatever they be, which we dis-course about, or think about, or make use of in reasoning."[36] This description, it will be noticed, suggests an emphasis upon the mental operations as they take place without necessarily resulting in speech, and as they take place in order that speaking may occur. In other words, Wallis wanted his readers to understand that reasoning is both a silent discourse with oneself in thought and an open discourse with others in spoken words. After explain-ing this distinction in Greek and Latin concepts, he remarked: "In like manner in our English language we say *Discourse* at one time in relation to the inward *reckoning* of the mind, and at an-other time concerning external *colloquy*."[37]

This distinction permitted Wallis to treat of two sorts of dis-course, the inward and the outward. In connection with the first sort he discussed the familiar terms emphasized in Porphyry's *Isagoge* and in the six treatises making up Aristotle's *Organon*. The second sort permitted him to discuss method, upon which the Ramists had laid great stress as far as it concerned the tasks of presentation. Thus like Sanderson before him Wallis produced a logic that was a compromise between Aristotelianism and Ram-ism. Accordingly, he did not come fully to grips with that revolu-tionary doctrine which derived its authority from Bacon and Des-cartes and was to be called in the eighteenth century the new or the inductive logic.

Whether discourse is outward or inward, the mental operations involved are basically the same. Thus Wallis divided his logic into three Parts, each of which dealt with one of the three fundamen-tal operations of the mind. Part One, consisting of twenty-three chapters, analyzed the first intellectual operation, simple appre-hension, and it spoke of terms, predicables, predicaments, and so on. Part Two, with eleven chapters, analyzed judgment, the sec-ond intellectual operation, which consists in putting terms to-

---

[36] *Institutio Logicae*, p. 1. In this and the following quotation my italics parallel Wallis's.
[37] *Ibid.*, p. 1.

gether into propositions, and in taking cognizance of such aspects of the latter as their parts, their quality, their quantity, their opposition, their equivalence, their conversion, and their modality. Part Three, having twenty-four chapters, analyzed discourse, the third operation of the mind, in which propositions are combined into syllogisms of the three standard figures and of that controversial fourth figure which Wallis called the Galenian, "from Galen's having introduced it originally, it appears."[38] Not only the four figures, but their modes, occupied Wallis's attention in this section of his treatise. He devoted some time to the errors that Ramus and his followers, notably Downham, had made in discussing the syllogistic moods, and he had a special chapter on the expository syllogism as it had been treated by the Ramists.[39] He then discussed such other forms of argument as enthymeme, sorites, induction, example, hypothetical syllogisms, disjunctive syllogisms, dilemmas, fallacies, demonstrative syllogisms, and topical syllogisms. These kinds of argument are all presented by him as examples of inward discourse or private thinking. When logicians wish to combine them into larger units for outward discourse, they need to have the theory of method added to the considerations that guide the third intellectual operation, and thus it is by treating method that Wallis brings his treatise on logic to a conclusion.

It is customary to suppose that induction was not an element in Aristotelian logic, and that Bacon and his followers are to be given credit for introducing it into logical theory. But such is not the case. Induction was recognized by Aristotle as one of the two foundations of belief and of proof, the other foundation being syllogism. At one point in the *Prior Analytics* he said: "For all our beliefs are formed either by means of syllogism or from induction."[40] And in the *Rhetoric* he echoed this same thought, remarking, "And since every one who proves anything at all is bound to

[38] *Ibid.*, p. 127; also pp. 152-156 (for Wallis's treatment of the fourth figure). For a discussion of the unreliability of the tradition that Galen added the fourth figure to Aristotle's syllogistic theory, see William and Martha Kneale, *The Development of Logic*, pp. 183-184.

[39] *Institutio Logicae*, pp. 158-160.

[40] 68b 14. Trans. Hugh Tredennick. See *Aristotle: The Organon, I*, in the Loeb Classical Library (Cambridge, Mass. and London, 1938), p. 513. For other references to induction in that same work, see pp. 327, 329, 503, 515, 517.

use either syllogisms or inductions (and this is clear to us from the *Analytics*), it must follow that enthymemes are syllogisms and examples are inductions."[41] But the induction that Aristotle envisaged was interpreted generally by him and his followers to be a variant form of the syllogism, and to require analysis as a distinct type of argument only because it seemed to be different from the syllogism in the eyes of the untrained reasoner. Wallis is certainly a solid Aristotelian in his treatment of induction as an argumentative form, as can be seen in the following passage, which begins his chapter entitled, "De Inductione & Exemplo":

> Two customary forms of argumentation still remain to be examined here: induction and example. These, indeed, like a great many other forms, yield uncertain and doubtful proof, although it may be probable enough. In any case, they cannot be reputed perfect syllogisms (except when the induction is complete) because they are not perfect argumentative forms. To whatever extent they are argumentative, however, just so far are they syllogistical. And in proportion as they are imperfect argumentations, so far are they (and in the same degree) imperfect syllogisms. So that, on this account, it should not be necessary to deduce that this kind of argumentation is in a different class from the syllogistical kind.

> Induction is a form of argumentation or syllogism by which a statement concerning a general matter under any circumstances is proved to be the truth by showing what the truth is concerning all the particulars beneath that general, or at least by counting up so many of the particulars as may make it credible to suppose that what is true of them is likewise true of the remaining ones.

> And indeed if the enumeration be complete, it has the force of a perfect syllogism. That is, if anyone should argue the proposition that all planets with the exception of the sun borrow light from the sun, it has to be proved by showing that it is separately true of Saturn, Jupiter, Mars, Venus, Mercury, and the moon. In truth, this is a syllogism in "Darapti," in this form:

[41] 1356b 7-10. Trans. W. Rhys Roberts in *The Works of Aristotle*, ed. W. D. Ross (Oxford, 1924), Vol. XI.

Da-   Saturn, Jupiter, Mars, Venus, Mercury, and the moon
       separately borrow light from the sun; but

rap-   These are all of the planets with the exception of the sun;
       therefore

ti-   All planets, with the exception of the sun, separately bor-
       row light from the sun.[42]

Wallis proceeded at once to answer the technical objection that
this argument is not a legitimate syllogism in "Darapti," inasmuch
as it has a universal conclusion instead of the required particular.
His answer, which points out that the minor term, "all planets except the sun," is a collective universal, and thus a singular, seems
to insist upon formal considerations at the expense of meaning
and reality; but the important thing to notice about his whole

---

[42] *Institutio Logicae*, pp. 167-168. "Darapti" is one of the Latin terms invented to help young scholars remember the various figures and moods of the
syllogism. It designates a syllogism in the first mood of the third figure. Such
a syllogism would contain two universal affirmative premises ("a" being the
symbol of the universal affirmative), and a particular affirmative would be
produced as a conclusion ("i" being its symbol). The complete mnemonic
pattern is given as follows by Wallis, pp. 130, 152:

   Figure i: Barbara, Celarent, Darii, Ferio,—
   Figure ii: Cesare, Camestres, Festino, Baroco,—
   Figure iii: Darapti, Felapton, Disamis, Datisi, Bocardo, Ferison,—
   Figure iv: Cadere, Fedibo, Digami, Fegano, Balani.

The four figures of the syllogism are determined by the position of the
middle term in the two premises. When the middle term is subject of the first
premise and predicate of the second, the syllogism is in the first figure. When
the middle term is predicate of both premises, the syllogism is in the second
figure. When the middle term is subject of both premises, the syllogism is in
the third figure. And when the middle term is predicate of the first premise
and subject of the second, the syllogism is in the fourth figure.

Since each premise may theoretically be a universal affirmative, a universal
negative, a particular affirmative, or a particular negative, and since each conclusion in a syllogism may theoretically fall into one of these same four categories, it follows that in theory there are sixty-four possible syllogisms (4 possible first premises × 4 possible second premises × 4 possible conclusions).
But of these sixty-four possibilities, only nineteen are valid syllogisms under
the rules, and these nineteen are represented by the nineteen words in Wallis's
mnemonic pattern. The letter "a" represents a universal affirmative; "e" a
universal negative; "i" a particular affirmative; "o" a particular negative. For
a variant mnemonic pattern, see below, p. 47.

approach to induction is that he did not associate it with observation, experiment, and the discovery of causation, but merely made it the process of noting a common characteristic among physical objects of a predetermined class. Dugald Stewart was to argue some hundred years later that induction as envisaged by Aristotle and his followers was incapable of advancing mankind a single step in the acquisition of new knowledge, and he was to use Wallis's very syllogism in "Darapti" to demonstrate his point.[43]

It should be noted, however, that Wallis was not unaware of the importance of induction in human affairs. Having discussed the example as a form of imperfect induction in which a general statement is proved, not by enumerating all the particulars concerned, but by pointing to a few or even to a single one, he offered the following comment upon the role of that form of argument and of induction itself in experimental philosophy, the social sciences, ethics, mechanics, history, and law:

> Either of these two arguments (however uncertain because of the uncertainty of their matter) has yet a great and frequent use.
>
> Either is a principal instrument of investigation whenever by examining and observing particulars we come to the knowledge of a universal, which we gather up by those means. And in that direction tends (what is called) the experimental philosophy. For although in the order of nature the progression is from causes to effects, yet in the order of knowing the progression is from observed effects to the investigation of causes. And indeed in the magnetic effects which I have already noted, unless it shall have been observed before (and that originally in a concrete case, I believe), that a magnet attracts iron and points to the north, no one would know or indeed suspect such a thing from the nature of the magnet. And so equally in many other things.
>
> In carrying on our practical affairs (whether in politics, or economics, or ethics, or even in mechanical matters) good sense derived from the examples of those things which were analogous in the past (however much you may not from them predict with

[43] See Dugald Stewart, *Elements of the Philosophy of the Human Mind*, II (1814), 333.

assurance what will be in the future)—good sense, I repeat, is the principal guide in directing our actions. For where a variety of chances and accidents which cannot certainly be foreseen induces a great uncertainty in predicting, it is necessary that we be held in check by that probability which the nature of the case allows. Indeed, probability borders rather upon what ought reasonably to be expected as more likely to come about than upon what is certain. And it is necessary to guide our actions by that standard.

Likewise among historians and among judges in legal cases themselves (where the enquiry is directed towards a matter of fact), a strong presumption and a great probability as to the happening (in the absence of infallible proof) suffice for settling a very great many questions; and, in doubtful matters, the major probability should prevail over the minor.[44]

Despite this recognition that arguments by imperfect induction and example exert a major influence upon the advancement of knowledge, Wallis did not alter his position that they were subordinate forms of the syllogism and had to be explained in those terms if they were to have any place at all in logic. He was equally on the side of the Peripatetics in his attitude towards the topics or places. Chapter 23 of Part Three of his treatise is entitled "De Syllogismo Topico," and it treats of the process of deriving inspiration for arguments from the consideration of causes and effects, of subjects and accidents, of contraries and comparisons, of conjugates, etymologies, and derivations, of whole and parts, of genus and species, of definition and division, and of testimony.[45] These places are more numerous than those allowed by Ramus, but they exemplify the same basic point of view towards the sources of ideas in disputation and towards the usefulness of disputation itself as a form of enquiry. They would serve, indeed, as excellent heads of analysis to anyone who wanted to

---

[44] *Institutio Logicae*, p. 172.

[45] Wallis clusters his places into pairs or triads, except for the last one, and numbers each group. Thus he has eight groups, as follows: i. De Causa & Effectu; ii. De Subjecto & Accidente; iii. De Dissentaneis & Comparatis; iv. De Conjugatis, Notatione, & Derivatione; v. De Toto & Partibus; vi. De Genere & Specie; vii. De Definitione & Divisione; viii. De Testimonio. See above, nn. 6, 27, 28; see below n. 68.

study the argumentative structure of the three theses that Wallis attached to his *Institutio Logicae,* or the argumentative structure of theological and philosophical controversy during the entire period of the Reformation.

Chapter 24 of Part Three of the *Institutio Logicae* is entitled "De Methodo," and it discusses method as the guide to the third intellectual operation at the moment when discourse ceases to be inward thinking and becomes external colloquy. Early in this chapter Wallis spoke as follows:

> For as logic teaches us to dispute in such a way that our argument may be well knit and conclusive, so does it teach us to divide or arrange our argument by method in order, to the end that it may conform more aptly to the nature of things themselves or at least to the purpose of disputing.
>
> Since in truth there may be great diversity now in the goal which the debates set for themselves and again in the capacity, the inherent quality, and the prejudices of those with whom the debate is held, it is difficult to prescribe for method any firm rules which may give satisfaction to everybody.[46]

In line with these relaxed words, Wallis did not attempt to be rigid in his theory of method. What he said was intended to have reference not only to disputants but to all classes of writers and authors—to historians, poets, orators, practical philosophers, speculative philosophers, mathematicians, enquirers, and teachers. In fact, he openly made each of these groups a separate subject of discussion, and he considered for each one the characteristic methods that seemed best for the presentation of its particular kind of subject matter or for the conduct of enquiry, where the latter aspect of method seemed to apply with special point in a given situation. Thus his comments amount to a practical demonstration of the role of seventeenth-century logical method in the whole theory of communication and scientific enquiry.

Many of his observations on method were so widely accepted as to be useful only to the inexperienced author. For example, the veteran historian would not have needed Wallis's doctrine that he should follow a chronological order in presenting his subject matter, whether he dealt with events in the fashion of the chroni-

[46] *Institutio Logicae,* p. 212.

cler or with events distributed under such heads as civil and ecclesiastical, or under such national groupings as the English, the French, and the Spanish. Nor would the experienced writer of comedy, tragedy, or romance have been especially enlightened by Wallis's remark that he would give his audience a feeling of elegance and pleasure by inverting the order of time and by beginning in the middle of things so as to create suspense and curiosity about earlier happenings. Nor would the seasoned orator have thought himself benefited by Wallis's observation that oratorical arrangements are dictated by calculating what will have weight with the audience and whether this or that should be said or not said to them, oratory being the art of concealment as well as the art of statement.[47] But even if advice of this kind is fully useful only to beginners, it is nevertheless sound and helpful, and it has a place in the theory of discourse and in the preparation of young men and women for the tasks of authorship.

What Wallis said on method in the speculative sciences is also intended primarily for young natural philosophers; yet it has a special interest for us now, not only because of Wallis's having dedicated the work in which it appears to the officers and fellows of the Royal Society, but also because of its relation to the concepts of method in the logics of Ramus and Sanderson. Let us hear Wallis speak at some length on this matter.

If we consider philosophy, the methods therein are likewise diverse.

In practical affairs and the prudential sciences, the method is customarily to begin with the end or the proposed goal (as in ethics with blessedness) and to consider what it is or in what it consists; and then to speak concerning the means by which it is achieved.

In the speculative sciences, the method is to begin with the cause (or what is first in regard to the way of operating) and from there to proceed to the effect; or alternatively to begin with the subject (the name, nature, and species of which are first investigated) and thence to proceed to accidents, adjuncts, properties, and relations, along with the principles and causes of these last; and finally to come to concomitants, or consequences, or contraries.

[47] *Ibid.*, pp. 212-213.

39

But also in the speculative sciences there is one method to be used for investigation, and another for teaching or education.

The method of investigation proceeds from particulars to universals. For instance, by observing what concerns Thomas, Richard, John, Socrates, Plato, and so on, we assemble from this source what may be a common possession of human kind, and what may be the property of this or that person, or the peculiarity of this or that race. Thereafter, by observing what concerns men, quadrupeds, fishes, birds, and so on, we gather together from that source what may be common to animals, and what may be the property of what species. Afterwards, by observing what concerns animals, plants, metals, minerals, and so on, we collect from that source what may be peculiar to each of these genera, and what is common to them all. Next we proceed to investigate the nature of Body in general or of Substance, and finally, the common relations of Being.

But whereas in investigating we aspire to the knowledge of these things, the method of transmission or of education and teaching is plainly the contrary. Indeed, in this field (since it should be necessary that the learner have confidence in what is being said), the generals are taught first, and thence we descend to particulars. As for example, we speak first of what that may be which is Being; then of what Substance may be, and Accident; and what each of these may have in common, and what may be proper to each. Then we come down to the species of Substance—what Body is, and what Spirit—and from there to subordinate genera, to species, and at last to individuals. Thus things are taught at once and together which have a great many aspects in common, in order that it may not be necessary to repeat each same thing in connection with each separate individual.[48]

Wallis went on to lay down seven rules for the method of teaching—the rule of brevity, harmony, homogeneity, proper sequence, clear division, perspicuity, and decorum or uniformity. These need not be explained here, for what Wallis meant by them is sufficiently indicated by the terms which he used to name them. After he stated them, he brought that chapter to an end by dis-

[48] *Ibid.*, pp. 213-214.

cussing method in mathematics, where one proceeds by laying down definitions, citing axioms and postulates, and proving propositions. This aspect of method was to receive stress in eighteenth-century logic, although of course it would be discussed there as an aspect of the broader method of synthesis, which always moves from generals to particulars. Hence we shall have occasion to revert to it later.[49]

[49] See below, Ch. 5, pp. 323-326, 355-359.

v Dean Aldrich's Famous *Artis Logicae Compendium*

Wallis's *Institutio Logicae* was only four years off the press, and its second edition was still eight years in the future, when Henry Aldrich published at Oxford his *Artis Logicae Compendium*. This work demands the attention of the historian of British logic because it took the place of Sanderson's similar treatise in the study of logical theory at Oxford and elsewhere, and because it not only carried the outlines of Aristotelian doctrine across the years between 1691 and 1825 in England, but it also provided the inspiration for the tremendous increase in the popularity of Peripatetic logic among English logicians of the first three decades of the nineteenth century. Thus it has an importance that contradicts the expectations created by its small size, its condensed style, and its status as a textbook for college undergraduates.

The author of this unusual work was a churchman, scholar, composer, and architect at Oxford in the latter half of the seventeenth century. Born in Westminster in 1648, and prepared for college at Westminster School, he enrolled as a student at Christ Church, and went on to take the degree of bachelor of arts in 1666 and of master of arts in 1669. Several years later he was made canon of Christ Church and doctor of divinity. In 1689 he became dean of Christ Church and held the office until his death in 1710. He served as vice chancellor of Oxford in 1692. Not only did he publish the *Artis Logicae Compendium* and a few other books, but he interested himself deeply in musical activities, in engraving, and in architecture. It was as an architect, indeed, that he achieved a lasting reputation. He was responsible for the whole or the partial design of the construction or repair of such distinguished Oxford buildings as St. Mary's Church, the Old Ashmolean, Trinity College Chapel, the Library, Hall, and Chapel of Queen's College, the Library and beautiful Peckwater Quadrangle of Christ Church, and All Saints Church in the High Street. Those who have seen All Saints will agree with the recent verdict that "it is a church of which Wren would have been proud."[50]

[50] W. G. Hiscock, *Henry Aldrich of Christ Church 1648-1710* (Oxford, 1960), p. 29. Hiscock's discussion of Aldrich's work in music, engraving, and

The *Artis Logicae Compendium* as it appeared at Oxford in 1691 has two distinct forms in two separate publications, although both publications are in the same apparent format and bear the same title and imprint. One publication contains 107 pages made up of a *Praefatio* of 8 unnumbered pages devoted to the history of ancient logic, of a First Book of six chapters covering 34 pages, of a Second Book of six chapters covering 65 pages, and of a brief *Conclusio* at the bottom of the last page of the text.[51] The other publication contains 67 pages made up of the same *Praefatio*, a First Book of four chapters and 29 pages, a Second Book of two chapters and 18 pages, an Appendix of 1 page on method, an Appendix of 2 pages on the uses of logic as given by Sanderson, and a *Conclusio* of 9 pages on the history of recent logical doctrine.[52]

In round terms, the long *Compendium* contains two things which the short *Compendium* omits altogether—a chapter of 22 pages on the ten categories or predicaments of Aristotle, and a chapter of 10 pages on the boundary of logical questions. On the other hand, the short *Compendium* has a valuable feature that the long *Compendium* lacks—the *Conclusio* of 9 pages on recent logic and logicians. There are other differences between these two publications, but they are slight and do not have value for our present discussion. What needs emphasis is that these two versions of the *Compendium* had a total of fourteen editions before they began in the early nineteenth century to enjoy their really astonishing popularity. Taken together in their entirety, they reinforce the Aristotelianism of Sanderson, Crakanthorp, and Wallis, and they provide an insight into the way in which the Peripatetics were setting themselves to oppose reform in logic.

Aldrich's definition of logic and his division of the discipline

---

architecture is detailed and conclusive, but he barely mentions the *Compendium*. My sketch of Aldrich's life depends upon Hiscock's recent work and upon the older account by Sir Leslie Stephen in *The Dictionary of National Biography*.

[51] There is a copy of this full *Compendium* in the Bodleian Library and in the British Museum. Its title page reads: "Artis Logicae Compendium. Oxonii, E Theatro Sheldoniano, *An. Dom.* MDCXCI." Later editions were issued at Oxford in 1692, 1704, 1771, 1793, 1804, and 1810.

[52] The only copy of a 1691 edition of the abridged *Compendium* that I have been able to find is in the British Museum. Its title page reads: "Artis Logicae Compendium. Oxonii, E Theatro Sheldoniano, *An. Dom.* MDCXCI." Later editions appeared at Oxford in 1692, 1696, 1704, 1723, 1771, and 1793.

into its parts are directly borrowed from Sanderson's *Compendium*. After saying that the three operations of the mind are simple apprehension, judgment, and discourse, and that these operations are subject respectively to the defects of indistinctness, falsehood, and incorrect reasoning, Aldrich remarked that the system formulated to protect the mind against being paralyzed by these defects is called logic or the art of reasoning. He added at once: "Logic is therefore an instrumental art directing the mind in the knowledge of things. Its parts are three in relation to the mental operations which it directs: 1) That part which concerns simple apprehension; 2) that which concerns judging; and 3) that which concerns discoursing."[53] These three operations, Aldrich went on, find expression in three respective equivalents— terms, propositions, and syllogisms. "And hence in the same proportion," he remarked, "it is commonly said that the first part of logic deals with simple terms, that is, with simple words expressing simple perceptions; the second part, with propositions, or with words combined to express a judgment; and the third part, of course, with syllogisms or with the doubly combined words by which argument or discourse is made up."[54]

The doctrines connected with these parts provided the entire contents of the *Compendium*, except for the historical *Praefatio* and the historical *Conclusio*. Thus as major topics in the first main part of his work, Aldrich discussed the five predicables—"*Genus, Species, Differentia, Proprium, Accidens*,"[55] and the important logical problems of division and definition.[56] The second main part was devoted to propositions, although, after mentioning that these were either categorical or hypothetical, so far as their sub-

[53] *Artis Logicae Compendium* (Oxford, 1696), p. 2. Translation mine. Aldrich's Latin text reads: "Est igitur *Logica* Ars instrumentalis dirigens mentem in cognitione rerum: ejusque partes tres sunt, pro operationibus mentis quas dirigit. 1. *De Simplici Apprehensione*. 2. *De Judicio*. 3. *De Discursu*." (The punctuation followed here is that of Aldrich's text.) Copies of the 1696 text are in the family of the short *Compendium*. For Sanderson's similar definition of logic, see above, n. 9.

[54] *Ibid.*, p. 3. Aldrich's Latin reads: "Atque hinc adeo vulgo dicitur Pars prima Logicae versari circa *terminos simplices*, i.e. voces simplices Apprehensionem simplicem exprimentes: secunda circa *Propositionem*, sive Vocem complexam quae Judicium exprimit: tertia vero circa *Syllogismum* sive Vocem decomplexam qua Argumentatio sive Discursus exprimitur."

[55] *Ibid.*, pp. 6-8. [56] *Ibid.*, pp. 9-10.

stance was concerned, he limited himself at first to the former kind, and spoke of them as affirmations or negations, as universals or particulars, and as objects of study in relation to opposition and conversion.[57] The syllogism as the very center of Aristotelian logic received the major share of attention in the third main part. And in view of the attacks which were made against this aspect of logical theory in the closing years of the eighteenth century, Aldrich's treatment of it deserves special comment here.

Aldrich approached the syllogism by using the accepted language of the Peripatetic tradition. "The third part of logic," he said, "concerns proof or syllogism, which is the outward sign of the third operation of the mind, and which is beyond question discourse, or the expression of reasoning by means of propositions."[58] Since discourse, he went on, is a progress of the mind from one judgment to another, it clearly requires something from which it sets out, something at which it arrives, and something to weigh by turns in such a manner that one thing becomes known from another and by the force of the other; indeed, to know a following thing as the result of a previous thing is often to that extent to judge them. The things from which the discourse sets out are the antecedents; the point at which it arrives is the consequent. And the process of progression is of two kinds, material and formal. Aldrich explained this important distinction as follows:

> *Material* progression takes place when a consequent is inferred from an antecedent solely by the import of the terms, this import being the *material of the argument*. As for example, *man is an animal,* therefore *he is a living creature.*

> *Formal* progression takes place when a consequent is inferred from an antecedent on account of the very manner of bringing them together, the manner being the *form of the argument.* As for example, *B is A, C is B,* therefore *C is A.*[59]

As a result of these distinctions, Aldrich went on at once to define the syllogism as "an utterance in which, certain things having

[57] *Ibid.,* pp. 10-17.

[58] *Ibid.,* p. 17. The text reads: "Tertia pars Logicae agit de *Argumento* sive *Syllogismo* quod est signum tertiae operationis intellectus: nempe *Discursus* vel *Ratiocinium* Propositionibus expressum."

[59] *Ibid.,* p. 17. My italics parallel those in Aldrich's text.

been laid down and granted, there necessarily emerges another thing beyond and on account of the things that were granted and laid down."[60]

Having explained that he was going to limit himself at first to the categorical syllogism, which has two antecedent propositions called premises, and a consequent called the conclusion, Aldrich pointed out that the conclusion always contains two terms, a subject and a predicate, and that the relation between them is established by establishing the relation of each to a third term. The latter process, Aldrich went on, is conducted according to the following canons, upon which the force of every syllogistical argument is founded:

1. Two terms which meet together in one and the same third term, meet together in each other.

2. When one term meets in a third, and a second term does not meet in that third, the first and second do not meet in each other.

3. When two terms both fail to meet together in one and the same third term, they fail to meet in each other.

4. If neither one of two terms has anything included in it that is not included in the other, the two terms do not differ from each other.

5. If either of two terms cannot be proved to meet together in one and the same third term, they cannot be proved to meet together in each other. In fact, it must remain doubtful whether a third term in which the two others might meet can be found, and that very doubt is not yet removed.

6. If one term has not been proved to meet in a third, and if a second term has been proved not to meet in that third, the first and second term cannot be proved not to meet in each other. In fact, it must remain doubtful whether a third term of that sort could be found, that is, whether one of the two agrees in what the other differs from, and that very doubt is not yet destroyed.[61]

[60] *Ibid.*, pp. 17-18. The text reads: "Hisce intellectis, opinor satis constare quo sensu definiatur *Syllogismus, Oratio in qua positis quibusdam atque concessis necesse est aliud evenire praeter & propter ea quae posita sunt atque concessa.*"

[61] *Ibid.*, p. 18.

We need not follow Aldrich through his statement of the twelve rules that can be applied to the syllogism as a consequence of the six canons just stated. Nor do we need to enter into his analysis of the four figures and the total number of syllogisms that can be created in each. What he said is summed up in the mnemonic verses which he would have students memorize in order to keep the mysteries of the syllogism in mind. Since his verses differ from those proposed by earlier logicians, and since his were to have a later popularity in the nineteenth century, I shall give them for their value to this present history:

> *Barbara, Celarent, Darii, Ferioque*, prioris:
> *Cesare, Camestres, Festino, Baroko*, secundae:
> Tertia *Darapti, Disamis, Datisi, Felapton,*
> *Bokardo, Ferison,* habet: Quarta insuper addit
> *Bramantip, Camenes, Dimaris, Fesapo, Fresison:*
> Quinque *Subalterni* totidem *Generalibus* orti
> Nomen habent nullum, nec si bene colligis usum.[62]

It is necessary at this point to take account of Aldrich's statement of the basic principle of Aristotelian logic, the dictum concerning all or nothing. This dictum became a great point of attack in the criticisms that were directed at the syllogism in the late eighteenth century, and it afterwards provided a rallying cry for the nineteenth-century defenders of Peripatetic logic. Sanderson and Wallis had both dealt with this dictum in the same standard way that Aldrich followed,[63] but we shall confine ourselves

[62] *Ibid.*, p. 26. See above, n. 42.

[63] See Robert Sanderson, *Logicae Artis Compendium* (Oxford, 1618), p. 126. Sanderson's text reads: "Dictum de Omni est hujusmodi: *Quicquid affirmatur vniversaliter de aliquo subiecto, affirmari necesse est de ijs quae sub eo continentur.* Dictum de Nullo hujusmodi: *Quicquid negatur vniversaliter de aliquo subiecto, negari necesse est de ijs quae sub eo continentur.*" Italics are Sanderson's. See also John Wallis, *Institutio Logicae* (Oxford, 1687), p. 135. His definition reads: "Fundamentum quo nititur *Modorum* omniun jam memoratorum, (unde probetur *Conclusivos* esse;) est *Postulatum* illud quod dici solet *Dictum de Omni & de Nullo*: quod tam per se evidens praesumitur ut probatione non indigeat. Nimirum, *Quicquid de Subjecto quopiam vniversaliter Affirmatur aut Negatur, id similiter vel Affirmatur vel Negatur de omni eo de quo hoc subjectum dicitur.*" Wallis added, p. 137: "Nonnulli autem Logici (nostri seculi, aut superioris) posthabita veterum probatione per *Dictum de Omni & de Nullo*; aliud substituunt illius loco Postulatum, nimirum *quae conveniunt in eodem tertio, conveniunt inter se.*"

here to Aldrich's formulation of it. Having explained in his own terms the principle behind syllogistic reasoning, Aldrich said:

> Aristotle demonstrated this same thing otherwise and better, according to this manner: he first established the theorem which the Schoolmen call the *dictum de omni & nullo*; to wit, "What is predicated universally concerning a term (that is, a distributed term), whether affirmatively or negatively, is similarly predicated of all things contained in it."[64]

We shall have occasion later to show in what precise manner this dictum was criticized by logicians seeking to end the reign of syllogistic theory or at least to establish induction as an equal of deduction in logical doctrine.[65] It is sufficient now merely to call attention to the dictum, and to say that it had traditionally been regarded as the principle which was not only so far self-evident as to require no proof but was also of such fundamental importance that all valid knowledge rested ultimately upon it.

Aldrich did not neglect the other important features of Peripatetic logic. After he had treated the full categorical syllogism, he mentioned such imperfect forms of it as enthymeme, induction, example, and sorites. Borrowing from Wallis, he said of induction that "in it is proposed whatever may be needful concerning particulars, and thence the thing proposed is claimed concerning universals, as *this, and that, and the other magnet attract iron,* and therefore, *all magnets do*"; but unlike Wallis, to whom the induction is a syllogism in "Darapti," Aldrich called it a certain kind of enthymeme, and added that his own example of it was "beyond question a syllogism in 'Barbara,' whose minor premise is silent."[66] Later, he devoted a chapter to hypothetical (as distinguished from categorical) propositions and syllogisms.[67] He also treated the probable arguments of dialectic, and in connection with them he discussed the seven places in which the dialectician seeks for his artistic proofs and the single place in which

[64] *Compendium*, p. 27. Aldrich's text reads: "Idem aliter & melius demonstrat Aristoteles ad hunc modum. Statuit primo Theorema quod Scholastici vocant *Dictum de Omni & Nullo*; scil. 'Quod praedicatur Universaliter de alio (i.e. de termino distributo) sive affirmative, sive negative, praedicatur similiter de omnibus sub eo contentis.'"

[65] See below, Ch. 5, pp. 388-389, 395-396, 418-421; also Ch. 7, p. 705.

[66] *Compendium*, p. 31. See above, pp. 34-36.

[67] *Compendium*, pp. 34-39.

nonartistic proofs are found.[68] In the long *Compendium*, as I noted earlier, he explained the doctrine connected with the ten categories of Aristotle.[69] And of course in both the long and short *Compendium* he gave some attention to the subject of fallacies and of method.[70] His teachings upon all of these points were not original, and in fact his analysis of method closely followed that of Sanderson, although in the spirit of Wallis he added some special comments upon method in mathematics.[71] The point is, however, that he covered these broad subjects in narrow compass, and his condensation was such that he touched upon every one of them without creating a work of discouraging bulk or offensive pretension.

In one respect, his *Compendium* in its shorter form has a feature of such great value to the historian of British logic that it deserves further consideration here. I refer to the *Conclusio*, which traced the history of logic from the time of Ramon Lull in the early thirteenth century to Aldrich's own day. Some of that history had been covered in Sanderson's *Compendium*, and Aldrich did not hesitate to quote Sanderson directly on Lull, Ramus, and the Systematics.[72] But between 1615, when Sanderson's *Compendium* first appeared, and 1691, when Aldrich brought out his similar work, Bacon's *Novum Organum*, Descartes' *Discours de la Méthode*, and Locke's *Essay concerning Human Understanding* had all been published, and the ideas of Bacon and Descartes had already had time to produce changes that were revolutionizing scientific practice and, so far as Descartes was concerned, had already to some extent influenced log-

---

[68] *Ibid.*, pp. 47-49. Aldrich's seven sources of artistic arguments are designated as follows: 1. Causa & Causatum. 2. Subjectum & Accidens. 3. Dissentanea & Comparata. 4. Conjugata, i.e. Dictiones cognatae vocis & significationis; & Notatio. 5. Totum & Pars. 6. Genus & Species. 7. Definitio & Divisio. The single place in which nonartistic arguments are found is that of testimony—divine testimony and the testimony of experience in one's own occupation. See above, nn. 6, 27, 28, 45.

[69] *Artis Logicae Compendium* (Oxford, 1691), pp. 35-36.

[70] *Ibid.*, pp. 33-34, 69-80. See also *Artis Logicae Compendium* (Oxford, 1696), pp. 51-62, 62-64.

[71] Compare Aldrich's *Compendium* (Oxford, 1696), pp. 62-64, with Sanderson's *Compendium* (Oxford, 1618), pp. 225-232, and with Wallis's *Institutio Logicae* (Oxford, 1687), pp. 212-217.

[72] *Compendium* (Oxford, 1696), sig. F4v and F5r-v. See Howell, *Logic and Rhetoric in England*, pp. 302-303.

49

ical theory. Aldrich's *Conclusio* shows what sort of impact this new logic was having upon the convinced Peripatetics just seventy-one years after the date of Bacon's *Novum Organum*.

Aldrich thought (the year, I repeat, was 1691) that Descartes had not even dreamed of reconstructing logic and had envisaged geometry instead as the real science of proof, whereas Bacon's *Novum Organum* had been so remote from the concerns of logic as to have nothing in common with the *Organon* of Aristotle except the title. The epigraph with which my present chapter opens is taken from Aldrich's *Compendium* and to it the reader may refer for Aldrich's very words upon this matter.[73] But Aldrich had something further to say about Bacon, and we should now listen to it:

> That distinguished man denies that there is need for the syllogism in the enterprise which he has in mind, namely, the enterprise of setting up experiments. He does not in fact disapprove of Aristotle's logic, but he often praises it in that celebrated work, the *Advancement of Learning*. Nevertheless, as he generally wishes for something in the rest of the sciences, he principally wants two things in logic, the first of which goes farther than Aristotle did: 1) he wants an art of inventing and surveying the sciences as a whole; and 2) he wants to know what proofs ought to be applied to what materials or subjects (a question which Aristotle is said to have noticed but not to have treated anywhere). Nobody should require the orator to achieve certainty in proof or propose that the geometer argue only to the point of probability. But it is so far enough if logic shall have kept this last problem in mind. In fact, such a matter as that involved in the last problem cannot be taught directly, unless the whole encyclopedia is being taught. In the future the duty of logic will not be to invent sciences, especially the ones which Bacon terms the mechanical sciences, but to aid the person who wishes either to teach or to learn the inventions which they call the liberal arts. Logic acknowledges this one aim, and logic performs it amply.[74]

[73] In the 1696 edition of the *Compendium*, these words appear at sig. F6r.
[74] *Ibid.*, sig. F6r. For Bacon's treatment of the two points mentioned by Aldrich, see the *Advancement of Learning*, Book II, in James Spedding, Robert L. Ellis, and Douglas D. Heath, eds., *The Works of Francis Bacon* (London, 1857-1874), III, 384, 397.

In reading these words, which so carefully separate the new experimental philosophy of the *Novum Organum* from the domain of logic, and which even question the propriety of making logic responsible for correcting the two deficiencies attributed to it in the *Advancement of Learning*, we might at first be disposed to think that Aldrich is merely behind the times, and that Bacon's ideas were making greater progress towards a reform in logical doctrine than the dean of Christ Church had the capacity to recognize in 1691. To be sure, reform was in the air. Locke's *Essay concerning Human Understanding* had been published a year earlier, and it had made some severe criticisms of the theory of syllogistic reasoning; moreover, it would not be long until Locke's essay *Of the Conduct of the Understanding* would appear, and that little work was destined to enter into competition with textbooks in Aristotelian logic during the eighteenth century, and to give English logicians a new set of perspectives.[75] But Aldrich's attitude towards Bacon's *Novum Organum* was by no means an outmoded opinion when he expressed it. It did not represent the temporary reversal of a trend towards the acceptance of Bacon's work by British followers of Aristotle. Indeed, one hundred and fifty-five years after Aldrich had said what he did, Sir William Hamilton, the professor of logic and metaphysics at Edinburgh, and an ardent Aristotelian, said much the same thing. In his edition of the complete works of one of his own masters, Thomas Reid, an edition, by the way, that appeared in an unfinished form in 1846, and was later completed by Henry L. Mansel in 1863, Sir William faced the unpleasant necessity of editing Reid's treatise, "A Brief Account of Aristotle's Logic, with Remarks," which is a destructive analysis of the theory of the syllogism; and he performed that particular task by attaching to Reid's text a set of remarkably quarrelsome footnotes, one of which contradicts in the following words Reid's claim that Bacon's *Novum Organum* offers a more effectual method of attaining truth than did Aristotle's *Organon*:

> The Organon of Aristotle and the Organum of Bacon stand in relation, but the relation of contrariety: the one considers the laws under which *the subject* thinks; the other the laws under which *the object* is to be known. To compare them together is

[75] These two works are considered below, Ch. 5, pp. 266-279.

therefore, in reality, to compare together quantities of different species. Each proposes a different end; both, in different ways, are useful; and both ought to be assiduously studied.[76]

But let us return to Aldrich. After he had finished his comments upon Bacon and Descartes, he next took up the other members of the new school of logicians, mentioning two in particular. The first one was Gassendi, the French philosopher, who had died in 1655; and the other is identified only as the author of the *Ars Cogitandi*. Aldrich confessed that he did not know the name of this latter logician, but that he suspected him of being a Jansenist concealing his true identity in order that his work on logic might serve as a rehearsal for the war which the Jansenists later declared against the Protestants.[77] To these two logicians Aldrich devoted the closing six pages of his *Conclusio*, and in view of the many and distinguished things that, as he said, were being reported in connection with the *Ars Cogitandi*,[78] he gave it the lion's share of space.

As a guide to his comments upon Gassendi, Aldrich adopted a theme from Cicero's *De Finibus*, where Cicero compared Epicurus and Democritus as natural philosophers. "The words which Cicero spoke concerning the relations of Epicurus to his master," remarked Aldrich, "apply on the present occasion to Gassendi in

[76] *The Works of Thomas Reid, D.D.*, ed. Sir William Hamilton, 6th edn. (Edinburgh, 1863), II, 712. Sir William Hamilton's philosophy owes much to Aristotle and to Reid, as well as to Kant. But his indebtedness to Reid did not go so far as to interfere with his devotion to Aristotle's logic, despite the persuasive brilliance of Reid's attack on the syllogism. Nor did his devotion to the cause of the Peripatetics go so far as to permit him to accept Aldrich's *Compendium* at its true and obvious value, even if he and Aldrich had an equal enthusiasm for Aristotle and a common inclination to deny Bacon's *Novum Organum* a place in logical theory. In fact, Sir William is unexpectedly and unconvincingly contemptuous of Aldrich's *Compendium*, and says of it that "absolutely considered, it has little or no value." See Sir William Hamilton, *Discussions on Philosophy and Literature, Education and University Reform*, 3rd edn. (Edinburgh and London, 1866), p. 124.

[77] *Compendium* (Oxford, 1696), sig. F6v. Aldrich's text reads: "De Autore *Artis Cogitandi* nihil habeo dicere, praeter ea quae Interpretationi Latinae sunt praefixa; Conversum scilicet Librum è Gallico tertium recognito, quem scripsisset Jansenista aliquis, qui nomen suum premebat, ut praeluderet bello contra Protestantes ab iis postea indicto."

[78] *Ibid.*, sig. F6r.

such a way that what Epicurus did to Democritus, Gassendi in turn does to Aristotle—he adds by changing a very few things, and the changes which he makes in the hope of improving his original succeed only in making things worse."[79] This verdict does not lack in wit what it may lack in justice, at least so far as it concerns Gassendi. But Aldrich did not state his criticism only in a sparkling turn of phrase. Instead, he went on specifically to examine certain points in Gassendi's handling of the syllogism in order to show that his attempts to improve Aristotle had not been a contribution of value to logic.

The *Ars Cogitandi,* which Aldrich discussed next at some length, happens to be the most famous and the most original of the popular logics written in the seventeenth century. As we have seen, Aldrich did not know who its author was, but he was right in thinking that the work was somehow associated with Jansenism. The Jansenists were a group of religious mystics and educational reformers who congregated at Port-Royal near Paris in the middle years of the 1600's and who dedicated themselves to the austere moral code of their founder, Cornelius Jansen, and to an educational philosophy that was in general opposed to the traditionalism of the Jesuits and the universities. The most celebrated member of the group was Pascal, and the most distinguished contribution by the group to educational reform was the work which Aldrich called the *Ars Cogitandi,* and which he specifically described as a Latin version of the third edition of a French treatise.[80] In actual fact, the French treatise, which had first been published anonymously at Paris in 1662, was entitled *La Logique, ou L'Art de Penser*. Ultimately it came to be known in France as the *Logique de Port-Royal* and in England as *The Port-Royal Logic*. It also came ultimately to be known as a work of composite authorship, its chief author being Antoine Arnauld, who had composed a first draft of it for circulation in manuscript, while his colleague, Pierre Nicole, had helped prepare it for publication, and had expanded the text somewhat for later editions. At the time when Aldrich's *Compendium* first appeared, *The Port-Royal Logic* had already achieved a phenomenal popularity in France, and had been published in England not only in a Latin version

[79] *Ibid.,* sig. F6v. See Cicero, *De Finibus Bonorum et Malorum,* 1.6.17.
[80] See above, n. 77.

then in its fourth printing, but also in a French text and in an English translation.[81] Its importance in the history of logical theory lies in its having been one of the first logical treatises to have reflected the teachings of Descartes and to have become widely influential as an expression of what Aldrich called the *Nova Logica.*[82]

Aldrich began his discussion of *The Port-Royal Logic* by paraphrasing three points made by Arnauld in the first and second dissertations prefacing the text of his work. Arnauld had claimed that his major concern was to assemble those precepts which were most conducive to forming the human judgment; that he had preserved all of the useful teachings in the hallowed traditions of the subject, and some teachings which were of little use but had to be included because students would expect them; and that he had ventured to introduce into logic many new things from other fields—rhetorical doctrines which would not be found in the usual textbooks in rhetoric, ethical, physical, and metaphysical doctrines which students ought generally to know, and as many doctrines from other subjects as a teacher would want his students to remember and to use. Having quoted these claims as if they were more consecutive and discrete in his source than in fact

---

[81] The Huntington Library holds a copy of the third Latin edition to be published in England. Its title page reads: "Logica, sive Ars Cogitandi: In qua praeter Vulgares Regulas plura nova habentur ad Rationem dirigendam utilia. *E tertia apud Gallos Editione recognita & aucta in Latinum versa.* Londini: Impensis *R. Littlebury, R. Scot, G. Wells,* Bibliopolarum *Londinensium,* & *R. Green Cantabrigiensis.* MDCLXXXII." Other editions of this work appeared at London in 1674, 1677, and 1687.

A French edition was published at London in 1664 under the title, *Logique, ou l'Art de Penser.* There is a copy in Dr. William's Library, London.

The first English version of this work appeared at London in 1685 under the title *Logic; Or, The Art of Thinking.* Later editions of this particular version appeared at the same place in 1693, 1696, and 1702. A second English version was done by John Ozell and published at London in 1717; a third English version by Thomas Spencer Baynes appeared at Edinburgh in 1850 and went through several editions; James Dickoff and Patricia James are authors of a fourth English version published at Indianapolis in 1964.

For details concerning its authorship, see [G. Du Pac de Bellegarde and J. Hautefage], *Oeuvres de Messire Antoine Arnauld* (Paris, 1775-1781), XLI, iv-v, 101-104. Cited below as *Oeuvres d'Arnauld.*

[82] For a discussion of Descartes's influence upon *The Port-Royal Logic,* see Howell, *Logic and Rhetoric in England,* pp. 342-363.

they are, Aldrich proceeded to criticize *The Port-Royal Logic* and its author in the light of them.[83] Here is a partial expression of his critical approach:

> What remains, then, you ask? Nothing but this: that having cast away all other books, we should swallow only his. In truth, I won't hinder anyone from doing so. But I am compelled to confess that scarcely anything more irksome could befall me than the task of reading his work through to the end. For it abounds in declamations, a great many of them superfluous, and all of them arrogant. Thus the author disparages other writers, especially Descartes and Pascal, whose bookshelves he has pillaged; and he hardly names any person without abusing him. Everything which he puts forth on his own behalf, he pronounces haughtily, as if ex cathedra. What he borrows from scholastic logic he so obscures in his presentation that a person who already knows in advance everything that he says may nevertheless have great difficulty in understanding what he wishes to say. And then he approaches with so much labor those most familiar points of scholastic doctrine and those things which are obscure to no one, as for example, the rules of conversion and of the syllogism; and he perspires in explaining them as if he were giving assistance to a collapsing world. Yet meanwhile he thinks it suitable to his work that he remain in ignorance of what directly concerns the *Argumentum Syllogismo*.[84]

There are other comments of the same sort throughout the remaining pages of Aldrich's historical *Conclusio*. Thus he remarked that Arnauld's attack on the Protestants contains nothing but logical fallacies. Thus he accused Arnauld of talking about Euclid in miserable ignorance of the principles of geometry. Thus he castigated Arnauld for pretending to contribute so much of his own to logic in the very work in which he condescendingly ad-

---

[83] The 18-line passage quoted by Aldrich in the *Compendium* (1696), sig. G1v, lines 11-28, is a patchwork of five passages from scattered parts of the first and second dissertations prefixed to Arnauld's *Logica, sive Ars Cogitandi* (London, 1674), p. viii, lines 7-12; p. ix, lines 6-14; p. xviii, lines 27-30; p. xii, lines 3-5; and p. xx, lines 4-8. In the edition of the *Ars Cogitandi* at London in 1682, these passages are found at the following points: p. vii, lines 28-33; p. viii, lines 21-28; p. xvii, lines 21-22; p. xi, lines 13-15; p. xviii, lines 30-34.

[84] *Compendium* (1696), sig. G1v-G2r.

mits that he himself starts out from Aristotle and that Aristotle's *Analytics* contain all that is known of logic as a science. And thus he ridiculed Arnauld for claiming the basic principle of syllogistic reasoning to be that one premise of a good syllogism contains the conclusion, and the other premise shows that it does so, when as a matter of fact this principle is merely a disguised version of what the scholastics had always called the *dictum de omni et nullo*.[85] The final words of Aldrich's *Conclusio* indicate the warmth of his devotion to Aristotle and the intensity of his disapproval of *The Port-Royal Logic*:

> Daylight would fail me if I should even reckon up by enumeration all the rest of the things which I cannot endorse in that *Ars Cogitandi*. But in truth I do not therefore ask that anyone else should not read and approve it. I ask only one thing which I would to heaven I were able to get: that if I am wrong, I be allowed to enjoy my error in silence. For nothing is more irksome indeed to me than to disapprove of a stranger's work which, if I could be deceitful, I would prefer to praise. But as I have to bring my work to some conclusion or other, I would commend to you, Carolus, and to all like you, the words of the Apostle: "Prove all things; hold fast that which is good." Perhaps there will be some of you who may feel with me that, by as much as you shall have understood all the others better, by that much do you make Aristotle of greater value.[86]

The fundamental issue concealed beneath Aldrich's hostility to *The Port-Royal Logic* did not become clear until the eighteenth century was well advanced, and other spokesmen had appeared on the scene to represent the claims of the Peripatetics and the counterclaims of the new logic. Even when the issue emerged distinctly, it was not at first resolved with any great statesmanship, although there were brilliant presentations on both sides, as we

[85] For Arnauld's statement of the basic principle of syllogistic reasoning, see *Logica, sive Ars Cogitandi* (London, 1682), p. 162. Arnauld's words are: "*Debet praemissarum altera continere conclusionem, idque ab alterâ ostendi.*" Italics are those of the original text. Aldrich, *Compendium* (1696), sig. G2v, quoted it thus: "*Boni Syllogismi praemissa altera continet Conclusionem, idque reliqua ostendit.*"

[86] "Carolus," that is, Charles Boyle, Aldrich's favorite pupil, for whom he wrote the *Compendium*. See *Compendium* (1696), sig. a1r. The Biblical reference is of course to I Thessalonians 5.21.

shall see later. What really was involved, however, was the question whether logic should ally itself with the experimental sciences and seek to describe in philosophical terms the processes by which new scientific truth is discovered, or whether logic should continue as in the past to be allied with the humanistic disciplines, with language and literature, and with the processes by which ethical truth could be worked out by disputation and communicated by logical method. Descartes had called attention to this issue in his *Discours de la Méthode*. Looking around him in an effort to formulate a method for the investigation of nature, he had turned first to the logicians. He said of their subject:

> But, on examination, I found that, as for Logic, its syllogisms and the majority of its other precepts are of avail rather in the communication of what we already know, or even as the Art of Lully, in speaking without judgment of things of which we are ignorant, than in the investigation of the unknown; and although this Science contains indeed a number of correct and very excellent precepts, there are, nevertheless, so many others, and these either injurious or superfluous, mingled with the former, that it is almost quite as difficult to effect a severance of the true from the false as it is to extract a Diana or a Minerva from a rough block of marble.[87]

It was in the endeavor to give logic a concern for the method of investigating the unknown that *The Port-Royal Logic* was written, and that it contained so many things which formerly had been carefully insulated from the rules of the syllogism and carefully allocated among the disciplines of physics, metaphysics, ethics, and geometry. And it was to protest against what *The Port-Royal Logic* had done that Aldrich composed his criticisms of that work. Aldrich wanted logic to remain as it had traditionally been—the guide to the learner and the teacher in the field of the liberal arts. He foresaw no future for logic in the experimental sciences that Bacon had set in motion. And his views had powerful support for well over a century after his *Compendium* was published. But there was to be powerful opposition to those views, too, and the opposition was ultimately to change

[87] *Discours de la Méthode*, trans. John Veitch in *The Method, Meditations, and Selections from the Principles of Descartes* (Edinburgh and London, 1887), p. 18. See also Howell, *Logic and Rhetoric in England*, pp. 342-350.

logic into a discipline built upon that proposed by the Port-Royal-ists and their followers rather than upon that so zealously admired by the Peripatetics.

In concluding this account of Aldrich's *Compendium*, I feel that I cannot do better than present some of the most interesting of the facts connected with its later history. It was translated in three or four hours on March 24, 1750, in a little cottage at Traeth Mawr in Wales by John Wesley, the founder of Methodism, as he waited for the tide to ebb and permit him to continue his journey to Trefollwyn; and Wesley's translation was published several times in the next eighty-six years.[88] The nineteenth century was only in its second decade when the short *Compendium* acquired a new title and an amazing new popularity. At Oxford in 1817 it appeared as the *Artis Logicae Rudimenta*, having dropped the historical *Praefatio*, the practice of arranging the text into a First and a Second Book, the discussion of the uses of logic as set forth by Sanderson, and the *Conclusio* that dealt so revealingly with the history of logic in the seventeenth century. Later editions of this particular form of the *Rudimenta* were issued at Oxford in 1820, 1841, 1848, and 1867. Several other forms of it rolled meanwhile from the presses. Before 1821 it appeared in a Latin text with each chapter given an English commentary by John Hill of St. Edmund Hall, Oxford, who had taken his master's degree in 1812.[89] It was published in an anonymous translation at Oxford in 1817,[90] in a translation of the first three chapters by John Hill

---

[88] Wesley's translation was first published anonymously. The title page of its first edition reads: "A Compendium of Logick. Bristol: Printed by Felix Farley, MDCCL." A second edition appeared at London in 1756; a third at London in 1790; a fourth at London in 1811; and another at London in 1836. See Richard Green, *The Works of John and Charles Wesley. A Bibliography* (London, 1896), pp. 68-69. See also *British Museum Catalogue of Printed Books*, s.v. Compendium, and also s.v. Wesley, John. See also *The Journal of the Rev. John Wesley, A.M.*, ed. Nehemiah Curnock (London, 1938), III, 459.

[89] I have been unable to locate copies of the first or the fifth edition of this work. The title page of the second edition reads: "Artis Logicae Rudimenta. With Illustrative Observations on Each Section. Second Edition. Oxford: Printed by W. Baxter, for J. Parker; and F. C. and J. Rivington, St. Paul's Church Yard, London 1821." A third edition appeared at Oxford in 1823; a fourth at Oxford in 1828; and a sixth at Oxford in 1850, with John Hill's name given on the title page.

[90] The title page of this translation reads as follows: "A Compendium of Logic, by H. Aldrich, D.D. Abridged and Translated. To which are added,

at Oxford before 1823,[91] and in another translation of the same three chapters by John Huyshe at Oxford in 1827.[92] It was adapted to the uses of younger students by John Woolley in 1840.[93] Several sets of questions on Aldrich's logic appeared at Oxford between 1824 and 1836 to aid students in reviewing for their examinations in that subject.[94] Henry L. Mansel, the prominent Oxford metaphysician and follower of Sir William Hamilton's philosophy, edited the *Rudimenta* with notes and marginal references in a bulky volume of 300 pages in the middle years of the nineteenth century.[95] But of all the interpreters of the *Compendium*, Richard Whately was the one who brought its doctrines

---

Explanatory Notes, and a Complete Analysis. Oxford, Printed and Sold by N. Bliss. 1817." The Preface expresses the translator's diffidence and promises to correct in a second edition the errors that may be pointed out in this one.

[91] The title page of the earliest edition that I have been able to locate reads: "The Rudiments of the Art of Logic; with Explanatory Notes. To which are added, Questions for Examinations. A New Edition. Oxford: Printed for J. Vincent, near Brasennose College; and G. and W. B. Whittaker, Ave Marie Lane, London, 1823." The copy of this work in the Bodleian Library contains the words, "By John Hill," written in pencil on the inside of the original pamphlet cover. Later editions appeared at Oxford in 1827, 1832, and 1843.

[92] The title page reads: "A Treatise on Logic, on the Basis of Aldrich. By John Huyshe. Oxford, 1827." This translation is based upon the Latin text of Aldrich's *Rudimenta* as published first in 1817. It translates Aldrich while citing Whately's *Elements of Logic* as a friendly recent authority on Aristotelian doctrine; and it devotes much attention to answering the objections which George Bentham's *Outline of a New System of Logic* had raised against Whately. Huyshe's translation appeared in a second edition at Oxford in 1833 with all the objections to Bentham removed.

[93] See John Woolley, *An Introduction to Logic, Designed for the Use of Younger Students* (Oxford, 1840).

[94] See, for example, the anonymous little book of 65 pages entitled *Questions on Aldrich's Logic, with References to the Most Popular Treatises* (Oxford, Published by J. Vincent, 1829). References in this work indicate that "the Most Popular Treatises" are Hill's *Logic*, Huyshe's *Treatise*, Whately's *Elements*, and Samuel Hinds's *Introduction to Logic*. Hinds was vice principal of St. Alban Hall, Oxford (1827-1831), and Whately its principal (1825-1831). Hinds's *Introduction to Logic* (Oxford, 1827) was based upon Whately's *Elements*. Other editions of the *Questions* appeared at Oxford in 1824 and 1836.

[95] *Artis Logicae Rudimenta . . . With notes and marginal references* by the Rev. H. L. Mansel . . . Second edition, corrected and enlarged. Oxford: William Graham, 1852. There was a third edition at Oxford in 1856, and a fourth at the same place in 1862. I have not identified the date of the first edition.

into the greatest prominence by founding upon them his remarkably successful *Elements of Logic* in 1825. That work will receive
special consideration later. Without Aldrich's logic, however, it
might never have come into being at all, and the impressive burst
of enthusiasm for Aristotelian logic at Oxford in the early nineteenth century might never have occurred.

VI Syllogisms and Science: John Sergeant's View

One other clash between the Peripatetics and the new logicians remains to be mentioned in the period between the date of publication of Aldrich's *Compendium* and the beginning of the eighteenth century. On this occasion the spokesman for the Peripatetics identified himself merely as J. S., but we now know him to have been John Sergeant. Sergeant graduated from Cambridge in 1643, after having prepared for his degree at St. John's College. Somewhat later he became a convert to Roman Catholicism and studied for the priesthood at the English College in Lisbon. He returned to England in 1652 and was for the most part occupied from that time until the very hour of his death in 1707 as a propagandist for the cause of the Roman church in England, although he studied in France for a time during the middle 1670's. He deserves a small place in my present history because he published at London in 1696 a book entitled *The Method to Science* and one year later a supplementary work called *Solid Philosophy Asserted, Against the Fancies of the Ideists: or, The Method to Science Further Illustrated, with Reflexions on Mr. Locke's Essay Concerning Human Understanding.*[96] Both of these works are devoted to a criticism of the new logic and to an assertion of the superiority of the old, and although they never went beyond their first edition, they have some originality, and they reinforce in English the position that Aldrich's *Compendium* was maintaining in the same time and place in Latin.

In a lengthy Preface dedicating the first of these works "to the Learned Students of Both Our Universities," Sergeant confessed that he was adding one more treatise on logic to those already available, and that he might on that account be thought presumptuous or disrespectful. But he insisted that his regard for

---

[96] These works indicate their authorship by the initials "J. S." The imprint of the first reads as follows: "London, Printed by *W. Redmayne* for the Author, and are to be Sold by *Thomas Metcalf*, Bookseller, over against *Earl's Court* in *Drury-lane*, 1696." The imprint of the other reads: "London, Printed for *Roger Clavil* at the *Peacock*, *Abel Roper* at the *Black Boy*, both in *Fleet-street*, and *Thomas Metcalf*, over against *Earl's-Court* in *Drury-Lane*, 1697."

My sketch of Sergeant follows that by Thompson Cooper in *The Dictionary of National Biography.*

truth was so compelling as to force him to declare current logics to be defective in containing dry, unproved rules, dubious definitions, unnecessary divisions, a needless elaboration of the predicaments, and many superfluous doctrines concerning the syllogism. Four of the five works which he mentioned as having these faults in various degrees were Continental in origin, as we would expect from his having studied in Portugal and France during his earlier career. First on his list was *The Port-Royal Logic*, which he considered to be excellent in divers ways and to make "many good steps towards *True Logick*," although "in the main," he said, "it amounts to no more but *The Schools Reform'd* into Method and Elegancy."[97] The only logic by an Englishman on Sergeant's list was Thomas Lushington's *Logica Analytica de Principiis, regulis, et Usu Rationis Rectae*, which had been published at London in 1650, and never reprinted, although its author, who took his bachelor's degree from Lincoln College, Oxford, in 1616, had the distinction of having been one of Sir Thomas Browne's teachers when Browne was at Broadgates Hall between 1623 and 1626.

The Method to Science may be described not only as a statement of what Sergeant believed to be the true way of achieving scientific knowledge, but also as a refutation of the claim that the ways proposed by Bacon and Descartes were legitimate alternatives to his own. The true way he found of course in Aristotelian logic, and he devoted the body of his work to an analysis of that discipline in terms with which we are already in the main familiar. Thus in the three Books that make up his treatise he spoke respectively of notions, judgments, and discourse, as the three operations of the understanding, and of words, propositions, and syllogisms, as their respective logical equivalents. Within these boundaries lay what he considered to be the proper scientific

---

[97] *The Method to Science*, sig. [b1]r. I reverse the style of Sergeant's Preface in respect to the use of roman and italic type. In addition to *The Port-Royal Logic*, which he called the *Ars Cogitandi*, Sergeant mentioned the following Continental works: 1) "Mr. *Le Grand's Method*," that is, Antoine Le Grand, *Institutio philosophiae, secundum principia R. Descartes. Nova methodo adornata et explicata* (published at London in 1672 and on various later dates); 2) "*Burgersdicius*," that is, Franco Burgersdijck, *Institutionum Logicarum Libri Duo* (published at Leiden in 1626 and 1634); 3) "Mr. *Clark*," that is, John Clerke or Joannus Clericus or Jean Le Clerc, *Logica, sive Ars Ratiocinandi* (published at Amsterdam and London in 1692 and at various other places and times, including Cambridge in 1704 and Leipzig in 1710).

method as distinguished on the one hand from the method laid down by the speculative philosophers, who recognized Descartes as their leader and who proceeded through reason and principle, and on the other hand from the method of the experimental philosophers or Baconians who proceeded through induction.[98]

It must be understood that to Sergeant the superiority of his method lay in its being essentially mathematical in its basic procedures. The disagreements which prevail among most classes of reasonable men, he remarked, do not extend to mathematicians. Has the same coherent way been taken in the other parts of philosophy as in the latter science? Manifestly not. Mathematicians use self-evident propositions and lucid definitions as axioms, and their conclusions force everyone to agree with them, whereas other sorts of philosophers have not followed the same clear method. "Whence we have good reason to suspect," argued Sergeant, "that the want of observing this Method, or something Equivalent to it, has been the sole occasion of all those Deviations from Truth and Disagreements among Philosophers in their Conclusions and Tenets, which we find in the World."[99]

Something equivalent to the method of mathematics could be formulated, thought Sergeant, if the following line of enquiry were applied. Nature gives us our notions, on which all science is grounded. We must make these notions clear and distinct by taking three steps. The first is that of distributing the notions under common heads, dividing those heads by intrinsical differences, and coming at last to the notion that we are to discourse of, having defined it along the way and having arrived by the entire process at a distinct and clear conception of it. The next step is that of judging how the notion under consideration may truthfully be joined into a proposition involving another notion. And the third step is that of connecting the terms of the proposition with yet another notion, a third term, in order to prove it true, if its truth is not self-evident. These three steps make up the method of science, and Sergeant summed it up in the following way:

For, our Notions being clear'd, First Principles establish'd, the true Form of a Syllogism manifested, Proper Middle Terms found, and the Necessity of the Consequence evidenced; all

[98] *The Method to Science*, sig. [b6]r - [b7]r, [d5]r-v.
[99] *Ibid.*, sig. [a4]r.

those Conclusions may be Deduced with *Demonstrative Evidence*, which ly within our Ken, or which we can have occasion to enquire after; that is, all that we have *Notions* of: provided those Notions be not meerly *Accidental*, or very *Remote* from one another, and therefore Incapable of being Connected.[100]

In the final analysis, Sergeant believed that each one of the particular sciences was founded upon its own special set of axioms or self-evident propositions, and that it was the business of scientific enquiry to take the self-evident propositions in a given science and make use of them in such a way as to perceive in them other self-evident propositions through the process of immediate inference or to wrest from them new and less evident propositions through the process of syllogistic reasoning. If Sergeant had been asked to explain where each science got its allotment of self-evident propositions at the outset, he would have replied that they were furnished by the science of metaphysics. He said just that, indeed, when he concluded one part of his discussion of first principles by remarking, "Hence is seen how Metaphysicks give the Principles to all *Inferiour* Sciences that treat of *particular Subjects*; and how they establish both the Truth, Certainty and Evidence of those respective Principles."[101] Although one science differs from another in having its own special subject to investigate, the basic self-evidence belonging to the first principles of all the sciences is found by Sergeant in the concept of the identical proposition. "The *Self-Evidence* belonging to First Principles consists in this," he declared, "that the two Terms must be *Formally Identical*."[102] What he meant by this is explained a few pages later when he remarked that "all the Force of Inference, nay, all possibility of Concluding or proving any thing is entirely grounded on this Self-evident proposition, *Idem est Idem sibi ipsi*, or, *A Thing is the same with it self*."[103] This concept is closely akin to what Aldrich called the *dictum de omni et nullo*, and to what the Port-Royalists had made the principle of every proper syllogism.[104] Its true import is to assert the principle of consistency as the underlying principle of all science. According to it, scientific truth is achieved in any given subject when the principles of

[100] *Ibid.*, sig. [a6]v - [a7]r.
[101] *Ibid.*, p. 157. The italics follow those in Sergeant's text.
[102] *Ibid.*, p. 131.   [103] *Ibid.*, p. 158.   [104] See above, pp. 48, 56.

that subject are consistent with each other and with the basic self-evident propositions from which they are derived. A false proposition is of course one which can be shown not to agree with other demonstrated or self-evident principles in its system. It is in these terms that the syllogism can be called the great instrument of science. Its function is to establish consistency between the self-evident principles allotted to a particular science and the conclusions that remain to be derived from those principles by the process of finding middle terms through which the two terms of one of the principles involved can be examined in an effort to exhaust the entire range of its implications. The following quotation shows how Sergeant thought of applying the concept of identical propositions or the principle of consistency to actual scientific discourses:

> Hence, *Homo est Homo, Quantitas est Quantitas, &c.* being Self-evident, are the *First Principles* to all Discourses treating about the Nature of *Man* or *Quantity*; that is, they are the *last* and most *Clear* propositions in that Matter or Subject, into which all that can be said of *Man* or *Quantity* is finally resolv'd; and, moreover, the *Test* of the Truth or Falshood of all that can be said of them. So that if any part of those Discourses do hap to violate those Principles, that is, if it deviates from those Natures, or does, by consequence, make Man *not to be* Man, or Quantity *not to be* Quantity, 'tis most evidently convicted of *Falsity*: As, on the other side, if those Discourses do proceed *Agreeably* to these Principles, it must most certainly and evidently be *True*.[105]

Involved in Sergeant's theory of method is the postulate that a scientific truth differs from what he called conclusions founded on opinion and conclusions founded on faith. A scientific truth is one which is either self-evident or the result of syllogistic proof. Once the two terms in the thesis to be proved are placed correctly in relation to each other and to a suitable middle term, nothing more can be required to make the thesis acceptable as science. Sergeant argued as follows in support of this point:

> For, this done, the Conclusion so necessarily follows, that it is as Impossible it should not be True as it is that an Identical

---

[105] *The Method to Science*, pp. 136-137.

Proposition should be False; or (which is the same) that a Contradiction should be True, which are the highest Impossibilities. Wherefore, since to have *Science* of any thing, is to know evidently the thing *is so* and *cannot but be so*, and this is known by the means now mentioned; it follows that no thing more can be requir'd to gain Science of any Proposition whatever.[106]

Opinion and faith are terms given to conclusions which cannot be conclusively demonstrated from self-evident principles or from conclusions correctly proved by syllogisms. A conclusion rests upon faith when it emerges from a syllogistic argument which depends upon our willingness to accept testimony as true. Sergeant illustrated this sort of knowledge by stating as a conclusion that it is true that there is such a city as Rome, and by resting that conclusion upon our tendency to believe that what many witnesses say under normal circumstances can be accepted as true, and that the existence of Rome has been attested by many witnesses speaking under normal circumstances. A conclusion rests upon opinion when it emerges from a syllogistic argument which depends upon our willingness to accept what commonly happens as if it properly or inevitably happens. Thus, said Sergeant, I may conclude that my debtor will pay me tomorrow, and I may rest my conclusion upon the argument that promises are usually kept, and that my debtor in saying that he will pay me tomorrow has made me a promise. Neither opinion nor faith can be accepted as science, Sergeant declared, for each rests upon the presence of an extrinsic or a common middle term within its syllogistic structure, whereas only an intrinsic middle term in a syllogism can produce scientific certainty.[107]

Sergeant's attack upon the method which Descartes had proposed as a proper means of achieving scientific truth did not consist in alleging that that method would produce mere opinion or faith, but that that method did not observe true logic in laying down its principles and thus could not produce true science. We need not enter here into the details of Sergeant's examination of Descartes.[108] What he did, in effect, was to show that the famous first principle of Descartes' philosophy, *Cogito, ergo sum*, violated

---

[106] *Ibid.*, p. 249.   [107] *Ibid.*, pp. 322-323.

[108] For the outline of Sergeant's attack upon the Cartesians, see *The Method to Science*, sig. [b7]r - [d5]r.

the requirement that a first principle must be self-evident and must always be treated as needing no proof. At one point he gave his criticism of Descartes a nationalistic turn:

> Farther, I must declare, for the Honour of our English *Genius,* that, tho' we do not match the French in the Finery, Gayity, and Neatness of their delivering their Conceptions (a Talent in which they are very Excellent) any more than we do in our Outward *Garb*, and *Dress*; yet, that there are more Solid Productions, well-built Truths, and more Judicious and Ingenious Thoughts of his own in our Learned Countryman Mr. *Locke's* Treatise, Entitled, *An Essay concerning Human Understanding,* than (as far as I have observ'd) is found in great Multitudes of such slight Discoursers put together.[109]

When he turned to the experimental philosophers, and analyzed their alleged method to science, the method, that is, of experiment and induction, Sergeant dismissed it as capable of producing not science but opinion, not demonstrative certainty but probability. He spoke on this point in his Preface and in the text of his work.[110] What he said in his Preface well represents the tenor of his objections to the inductive method, and I shall quote it in part:

> We are come now to consider the Other pretended *Method to Science,* which is the Way of *Experiments* or *Induction.* Concerning which, (not to repeat what I have occasionally, by way of *Reason,* alledg'd against it in my following Book) I need say no more, but that *Matter of Fact* shows evidently, that this Method, *alone,* and Unassisted by *Principles,* is Utterly Incompetent or Unable to beget *Science.* For, what one Universal Conclusion in Natural Philosophy, (in knowing which Kind of Truths *Science* consists) has been Demonstrated by *Experiments,* since the time that Great man, Sir *Francis Bacon,* writ his *Natural History*? The very Title of which laborious Work shows, that himself did not think *Science* was attainable by that Method. For, if we reflect well on what manner such pieces are writ, we shall find that it is, (as he calls it) meerly *Historical,*

[109] *Ibid.,* sig. [d5]r. I reverse the style of Sergeant's Preface in respect to the use of roman and italic type.

[110] *Ibid.,* sig. [d5]r - [d6]v; also pp. 173-174, 246, 283.

67

and Narrative of *Particular* Observations; from which to deduce *Universal* Conclusions is against plain Logick, and Common Sense. To aim at *Science* by such a *Method,* may be resembled to the Study of finding out the Philosopher's Stone. The
Chymist lights on many Useful and Promising things by the
way which feed him with *false hopes, and decoy* him *farther*;
but he still falls short of his *End.* What man of any *past,* or of
our *present* Curious Age, did ever so excell *in those* Industrious
and Ingenious Researches, as that Honour of our Nation, the
Incomparable Mr. *Boyle?* Yet after he had ransack'd all the
hidden Recesses of Nature, as far as that Way could carry him,
he was still a *Sceptick* in his *Principles* of Natural Philosophy;
nor could, with the utmost Inquisitiveness, practic'd by so great
a Wit, arrive at any Certain Knowledge whether there was a
Vacuum or no: And certainly, we can expect no Science from
such a Method that can give us no Certain Knowledge, whether
in such a Space there be *Something,* or *Nothing*: which, of all
others, should be the most easily *Distinguishable* and *Knowable.* Lastly, we may observe, that when an *Experiment,* or
(which is the same) a *Matter of Fact* in Nature is discover'd, we
are never the nearer knowing what is the *Proper Cause* of such
an *Effect,* into which we may certainly *refund* it, which, and
onely which, is the Work of *Science.*[111]

Although Sergeant's *The Method to Science,* as we have noticed, mentioned with approval Locke's *Essay concerning Human
Understanding,* Sergeant had not read that work with any attention when he complimented Locke upon his well-built truths and
solid and ingenious thoughts. This fact became obvious in 1697
when Sergeant published his *Solid Philosophy Asserted.* Although
he dedicated the new treatise to the Right Honourable Robert,
Lord Viscount Dunbar, not to the students and dons of Oxford
and Cambridge, he nevertheless addressed to the latter a special
Preface, which he opened as follows:

Gentlemen:

After I had Publish'd my *Method to Science,* which I Dedicated to your selves, I came to receive certain Information that
very many *Students* in both the Universities, and not a few of
those also who were to *instruct others,* did apply themselves to

[111] *Ibid.,* sig. [d5]r - [d6]r.

the *Way* of *Ideas,* in hopes to arrive by that means at Philosophical Knowledge. My best Judgment, grounded on very Evident Reasons, assur'd me, that that Method was far from *Solid,*
and utterly Unable to give you the True Knowledge of *any
thing* in Nature; being it self altogether *Groundless,* and meerly
Superficial.[112]

As the Preface proceeds, it clearly appears that the way of ideas
as an avenue to philosophical knowledge is the way recommended by Locke's *Essay concerning Human Understanding.* It
is interesting to have Sergeant's testimony that in 1697 Locke's
famous work was being eagerly read at Oxford and Cambridge.
And it is also interesting to be told that a year earlier, when his
Method to Science was published, Sergeant had reached the point
of having given Locke's *Essay* a superficial reading and of having
formed an imperfect judgment of it, whereas now in the light of
a more careful scrutiny he wanted to examine its doctrines in detail and expose their weaknesses. After lamenting that a great wit
like Mr. Locke should be half lost to the commonwealth of learning by having lighted unfortunately upon "such an Unaccountable
Method,"[113] Sergeant expressed himself vigorously thus:

This wrought up my Thoughts higher, and made me conceive
a greater Indignation against this New Way of Philosophizing;
and that, very particularly, for *his* sake; tho' I saw the *Cartesians* as much wanted Rectifying in their Grounds, as he, or
rather more.[114]

The *Solid Philosophy Asserted* is not a revised version of *The
Method to Science.* It is rather an examination of Locke's doctrine
of ideas in the light of the method that Sergeant had explained in
his earlier work. We need not pause here to examine the *Solid*

[112] *Solid Philosophy Asserted,* sig. a1r. I reverse Sergeant's style in respect to
the use of roman and italic type.

[113] *Ibid.,* sig. a2r.

[114] *Ibid.,* sig. a2v. By "Cartesians" Sergeant meant among others Antoine
Le Grand, a French priest of the Franciscan order, who was stationed at Oxford during a large part of the seventeenth century. Le Grand wrote a work
which Sergeant had mentioned disparagingly in *The Method to Science* (see
above, n. 97). Subsequently Sergeant devoted to Le Grand a work which he
called *Ideae Cartesianae* (London, 1698), and which replied to Le Grand's
criticism of *The Method to Science* and the *Solid Philosophy.*

Philosophy. But we should note that Locke himself read and heeded it. "I have Locke's copy of Sergeant's *Solid Philosophy Asserted,* 1697, 8vo," said James Crossley, "the margins of which are filled with answers in Locke's autograph to the animadversions contained in that book. It is somewhat strange that neither these nor his manuscript notes on the pamphlets of Dr. Thomas Burnett of the Charter-house, written against the *Essay,* which are also in my possession, have ever been published or noticed by his biographers."[115] And we should perhaps also note that a good statement of Sergeant's criticism of Locke is contained in the Preface to the *Solid Philosophy Asserted,* where Sergeant took Locke and Descartes to task in the following words:

> What our several Methods are, the Title of my Book tells my Reader in short, *viz.* that, (as I have hinted in my Dedicatory) *Theirs* is to ground all their Discourses on *Ideas*; that is, (as themselves express it, and as the Word [*Idea*] *declares,*) on *Similitudes,* or *Resemblances*: which *Similitudes,* (as is abundantly demonstrated in my three first Preliminaries,) are meer *Fancies*: Mine is to build them solely and entirely on the *Things* themselves, in which, as the Footsteps or Effects of his Essential Verity, the Creative Wisdom of the *God of Truth,* has planted and imprinted all Created Truths whatever.[116]

The point to be emphasized about Sergeant's *Solid Philosophy Asserted* and about *The Method to Science* as well is that both of these works call attention primarily to the investigative function of Peripatetic logic without thereby undermining or calling into question its important and equally basic communicative function. All logics of the sixteenth and seventeenth centuries had had these two functions in mind but had tended for the most part to overemphasize the uses of logic for communication while underemphasizing its uses for investigation and enquiry. There can be no doubt whatever that Ramus had exemplified these very tendencies. His great success in convincing the learned world that

[115] See James Crossley, ed., *The Diary and Correspondence of Dr. John Worthington,* in Remains Historical & Literary Connected with the Palatine Counties of Lancaster and Chester, Published by the Chetham Society, Vol. xxxvi (1855), p. 193, n. Quoted in the sketch of Sergeant in *The Dictionary of National Biography.*

[116] *Solid Philosophy Asserted,* sig. a4v.

logic is the art of disputing well had acted to diminish the concept that logic is also interested in the processes of discovering truth. Dissatisfied in particular with a logic that was interested only in the communication of what we already know, Descartes had called for a new logic that would be concerned with the investigation of the unknown. But even the Port-Royalists, who had caught something of Descartes' vision, had remained so far traditional as to emphasize both of these functions when they defined logic to be "the art of using the reason well in acquiring a knowledge of things, as much for oneself as for the instructing of others."[117] Now Sergeant, who was a much more determined traditionalist than the Port-Royalists had been, chose to place stress upon enquiry rather than instruction. To be sure, the passage just quoted from the *Solid Philosophy Asserted* makes discourse one of the points of attention in logic, and discourse in its major role is the means by which knowledge is transmitted from person to person and from age to age. But Sergeant has another point of attention, and it turns out to be the main preoccupation of his two works. It comes into being because discourse has to be grounded upon something, inasmuch as the words of human speech have to have referents in human experience. Therefore the process of grounding discourse either upon things or upon the ideas of things becomes a potential concern of logic. Sergeant's personal view was that discourse must be grounded rather on things than on ideas, and that things are not only the real objects upon which God's truth has been imprinted but also the final sources of all human wisdom through the methods of syllogistic derivation. The new logicians of the eighteenth century would question whether man was to approach real objects with preconceived ideas as to the meaning which God had imprinted upon them or was rather to approach them in an effort to discover what God's meaning might originally have been. This important issue must be reserved for later consideration. Meanwhile, we can thank Sergeant for his help in allowing us to see how Peripatetic logic could be considered a method to science, and what its exact procedures were as an instrument for research and investigation.

[117] See [Antoine Arnauld and Pierre Nicole], *Logica, sive Ars Cogitandi* (London, 1682), p. 1. Translation mine. The Latin text reads: "Logica est *Ars bené utendi ratione in rerum cognitione acquirenda, tam ad sui ipsius, quam aliorum institutionem.*"

CHAPTER 3

For logic contents itself with such principles of reasoning, which arising from the nature of things, and their relations to each other, may suffice to discover truth from falsehood, and satisfy thinking and considerate persons. Nor does it propose any thing more than assent, upon a just view of things fairly represented to the mind. But rhetoric not only directs to those arguments, which are proper to convince the mind; but also considers the various passions and interests of mankind, with the bias they receive from temper, education, converse, and other circumstances of life; and teaches how to fetch such reasons from each of these, as are of the greatest force in persuasion. It is plain therefore that rhetoric not only supplies us with more heads of invention *than logic, but that they very much differ from each other in the use and design of them; the one imploying them only as principles of knowledge, but the other cheifly as motives to action.*

John Ward, *A System of Oratory, Delivered in a Course of Lectures Publicly read at Gresham College, London* (London, 1759), I, 31-32.

THE EIGHTEENTH-CENTURY
CICERONIANS
(1700–1759)

1 Rhetoric as the Counterpart of Logic

The subject matter of rhetorical theory in the opening years of the eighteenth century was the product of the same movements and countermovements that I have just outlined in tracing the development of Henry Aldrich's logic. Aldrich clearly recognized that he was committing himself in 1691 to the logical system of Aristotle in a serious attempt on the one hand to restore to logic certain concepts and terms denied it by the Ramists and on the other hand to reinterpret ancient doctrine and offer it as a valid response to the challenge of modernism. Early eighteenth-century rhetoricians were likewise under the influence of a venerated classical tradition that had been drastically curtailed by Ramus, and were aware that Ramism and the classical tradition itself were being challenged by new conditions. But one difference between the orientation of logic and rhetoric in that era must be carefully remembered. When eighteenth-century logicians referred to ancient logic, they thought only of Aristotle, whereas their rhetorical colleagues in conceiving of ancient rhetoric were completely unable to think of anyone but Cicero. All studious men of that age had learned from Cicero and Quintilian, of course, that Ciceronian rhetoric had derived its basic teachings and its halo of authority from the rhetorical writings of Aristotle, and thus they would have been essentially correct if they had chosen Aristotle rather than Cicero as the spokesman for the rhetorical doctrine which represented ancient civilization. But Cicero had three advantages over the Stagirite when the eighteenth century came to select someone to symbolize traditional rhetoric: he had treated rhetorical theory much more voluminously and much more exoterically than Aristotle had done; his rhetorical writings had entered so completely into European culture of the Middle Ages as to have established the only terms within which the rhetoric of successive later centuries could normally be understood by teachers, learners, critics, scholars, and poets; and he was counted the greatest writer on rhetoric ever to have achieved first rank both as orator and man of letters. Thus it would have been unthinkable in the year 1700 to have overlooked Cicero in naming the ancient rhetorical system that was being put forward in company with Peripatetic logic as the best doctrine for that particular era. But to us it is important to see Ciceronianism in rhetoric as the counterpart of Aristotelianism in logic. The two systems are so intertwined that the problems of the one are in fact variations upon the problems of the other, and a firm grasp of the history of both is essential to the understanding of the fate of either one.

Ciceronian rhetoric meant so very much more to Cicero and his many followers than rhetoric means popularly today that a real effort has to be made to keep his definition in mind if his theory of rhetoric is to have the exact contours for us that he intended it to have. Cicero did not think of rhetoric as if it were exclusively the art of writing well in prose in contrast to the art of writing well in verse. He did not employ the glib modern distinction between the practical and the aesthetic in order to separate rhetoric from poetry while stigmatizing rhetoric in the same breath. He did not understand rhetorical expression to be elegant and stylish and grand as distinguished from a more mundane kind of expression in which everything was plain and homely and unadorned. Nor did he think of rhetoric in any of its pejorative senses: as artificial elegance of language, or as studied pomposity of style, or as declamation unaccompanied by sincere conviction and earnest feeling, or as persuasion by emotional means against the weight of reason and conscience, or as discourse that is slanted, devious, and deceitful rather than sober and honest. He knew speakers and writers who represented all of the abuses that rhetoric is heir to, and he knew others who thought contemptuously of rhetoric because it seemed to be taught in some quarters as if those abuses were its only concern. But he saw far deeper realities beneath such externals. He recognized, as all of us must, that the exchange of ideas between one person and another, or between one generation and another, is at the very center of man's social, political, moral, economic, and cultural life, and that any art which improves man's capacity to exchange ideas is at the very center of all the other arts. To Cicero, grammar, rhetoric, and logic were the studies upon which all linguistic exchanges of ideas were based. Grammar sought to establish an accurate and orderly language in which discourses could be phrased for comprehension by all who possessed that language in common. Logic sought to make discourses consistent both in themselves and in their relation to the basic assumptions of their time. Rhetoric sought to make discourses effective with people who must act wisely in concert if civilization is to endure, and who are given to emotionalism, prejudice, ignorance, and stupidity unless they are constantly reminded that these impulses must not be allowed to nullify reason and good sense. Cicero did not use these exact terms in expressing his ideas upon communication in general, or upon the relation of grammar, logic, and rhetoric to each other. But he had these ideas in mind as the self-evident truths upon which the arts of discourse were founded. Moreover, in his view, rhetoric was certainly the chief art of discourse, and it consisted of all the principles and precepts which regulated all speaking and all writing addressed to popular audiences on occasions when some doctrine had to be taught, some thesis proved, some great achievement or great man celebrated for public enlightenment, or some course of action proposed as the best response to the facts of the case and to the human interests and feelings concerned.

Beneath these assumptions Cicero constructed a rhetorical theory which made rhetoric consist of five major procedures, each being considered as an integral part of a single whole, and that whole being regarded as covering the entire problem of authorship in the field of popular oral and written exposition and persuasion. These five procedures will be fully discussed when I deal later with the eighteenth-century works concerned with them. Here I need only say that they were mentioned in the previous chapter during my discussion of Crakanthorp, Ramus, and Thomas Wilson,[1] and that Cicero's own terms for them are *inventio, dispositio, elocutio, memoria,* and *pronuntiatio.*[2] In the most general way, the first of these terms involved the machinery by which the subject matter of a discourse was arrived at, whereas the others respectively involved the theory of arrangement or

---

[1] See above, Ch. 2, pp. 24-26.   [2] Cicero, *De Inventione,* 1.7.9.

form, of style or wording, of retaining the discourse in mind, and of pronouncing it in public. So full of import did Cicero consider every one of these procedures to be that he called each in its own right a great art; and with his eye on rhetoric as a whole, he declared, "One may guess therefore what power is inherent in an art made up of five great arts, and what difficulty it presents."[3]

Although these five great arts formed the basis of Thomas Wilson's important English work, *The Arte of Rhetorique*, first published at London in 1553, and although they were everywhere accepted in Elizabethan England as the constituents of ancient rhetorical theory, they tended to duplicate the subject matter of logic, which at that time, as I indicated earlier, was engaged in providing a machinery for the invention and arrangement of arguments in learned controversy. This duplication occasioned the reforms collectively known as Ramism. Genuinely disturbed by the untidiness involved in having logic and rhetoric cover the same ground, Ramus decided that the most efficient way to correct the untidiness would be to have logic assume complete responsibility for the whole theory of subject matter and arrangement in discourse, while rhetoric would be allotted the theory of style and delivery.[4] This solution did not interfere with the traditional associations between content and form as elements in the philosophical conception of discourse, but it effectively excluded rhetoric at the very threshold of the modern era from any concern with those elements, and it made logic the only art which speculated upon them. In effect, while Ramus damaged logic by underemphasizing its interest in the method of discovering new truth, he at least left it with important things to think about; but what he did to rhetoric threatened it with catastrophe. Limited to delivery and to the mere externals of style, rhetoric no longer had anything of real importance to say or do. It had to content itself with enumerating in pedantic detail the names, derivations, and literary applications of the tropes and the figures, on the one hand, and with issuing the commands of a drill master about the use of voice and gesture in delivering a speech, on the other. These matters, which have some significance when they are not

[3] *Brutus*, 6.25. Translation by G. L. Hendrickson in The Loeb Classical Library (Cambridge, Mass. and London, 1939), p. 37.

[4] See above, Ch. 2, pp. 25-26. For additional details, see Howell, *Logic and Rhetoric in England*, pp. 146-172.

detached from considerations of content and form, appeal only to a limited and dogmatic mind when they are made into separate arts or are ordered to become the sole constituents of a single art. Ramus put rhetoric precisely where architecture would be if the traditional concern of the latter art for materials and design were completely transferred to the science of engineering, and architecture were accordingly left stranded with nothing of importance to claim as its own, and with the prospect of having to disappear altogether from the scene or of trying to console itself with such residual tasks as those of the house painter and the paper hanger.

In actual fact, rhetoric did not disappear from the scene in England as a result of the reforms of Ramus. But during the seventeenth and eighteenth centuries, it lent its ancient and well-understood name to each of three distinct enterprises, and thus the term rhetoric began to acquire the ambiguity that afflicts it throughout modern criticism. One of these enterprises, which will be the subject of my present chapter, involved rhetoric in the attempt to recover in the name of Cicero what Ramus had taken from it in the name of reform. This segment of the history of rhetoric follows the same impulses that the English Peripatetics exhibited in their efforts to restore Aristotelianism to logic in the era between 1615 and 1825. The second of these enterprises involved rhetoric in an oppressively narrow concern with the flowers of style and the graces of delivery, until at length in the eighteenth century rhetoric carried Ramism to its farthest extremity and convinced itself that voice and gesture alone were its proper and sole responsibility. This latter segment of the history of rhetoric is known as the elocutionary movement, and it will be the subject of my next chapter. The last of the three enterprises was devoted to the attempt to create a new rhetoric, which would on the one hand be as comprehensive as that of Cicero, and on the other would recognize that the Ciceronian machineries for the invention of subject matter, for the organization of ideas, and for the development of style, were unsuited to a democratic and scientific age. This new rhetoric, which corresponds in spirit to the new inductive logic of the eighteenth century, grew up as the theory of topics and commonplaces for the invention of rhetorical subject matter was challenged repeatedly between 1662 and 1750, and as the demand became more and more insistent for the use of simple rhetorical forms and a plain style in an era of popular government and tremendous scientific achievement.[5] My sixth chapter will be devoted to the new rhetoric of the era between 1646 and 1800.

In turning to the eighteenth-century Ciceronians and their efforts to restore to rhetoric its ancient concern for a place in the theory of subject matter and form, we should remember that these rhetoricians had had important English predecessors in the age preceding theirs. This is not the place to discuss what those predecessors did,[6] but a few of them should be mentioned to show that they were men of as much substance and learning as their contemporaries were whom I named in the previous chapter in connection with the revival of Aristotelian logic in the seventeenth century. The chief English Ciceronian of that same century would unanimously be identified as Thomas Farnaby, distinguished as a classical scholar, schoolmaster, and friend of Ben Jonson. His *Index Rhetoricus*, published at London in 1625, treated four of the five constituent parts of Ciceronian rhetoric, the theory of memory being omitted, as indeed Cicero himself had occasionally done.[7] Not only did that work achieve a thirteenth edition by 1713, but its discussion of rhetorical style, as the third part of rhetoric, was published separately at London in 1648 under the title, *Troposchematologia*, and that little book enjoyed great popularity thereafter, reaching its fifteenth edition by 1767.[8] Along with Farnaby in the ranks of seventeenth-century Ciceroni-

[5] For an account of the beginnings of the new rhetoric, see Howell, *Logic and Rhetoric in England*, pp. 364-397.

[6] Readers interested in them might want to consult pp. 318-326 of the work cited in the preceding note.

[7] See *Orator*, 17.54; see also above, Ch. 2, n. 24.

[8] For dates of editions of the *Index Rhetoricus*, see Howell, *Logic and Rhetoric in England*, p. 321, n. 10.

A copy of the first edition of the *Troposchematologia* (London: Apud Ri: Royston, 1648) is held at the British Museum. Its Preface is signed "T. S.," that is, Thomas Stephens. The seventh edition (London, 1683), also held at the British Museum, was edited by "E. L." The fifteenth edition (London, 1767) was edited by John Williams, Vicar of Catherington, who added some miscellaneous adages to the work.

Attention should also be called to a book entitled *Farnaby illustrated: or, the Latin text of Farnaby's Rhetoric exemplified by various passages from the sacred Scriptures, the Roman classics, and the most distinguished British Authors* (York, 1768). There is a copy at the Bodleian Library.

ans we should place William Pemble, lecturer in divinity at Magdalen Hall in Oxford, whose *Enchiridion Oratorium*, published at Oxford in 1633, also recognized invention, arrangement, style, and delivery as the constituent parts of rhetoric, although it treated only with invention and arrangement.[9] Thomas Vicars, clergyman and scholar, rebuilt rhetoric in terms of the five constituent parts authorized by Cicero in a work called Χειραγωγια, *Manuductio ad Artem Rhetoricam*, published at London in 1621, and thus he belongs with the Ciceronians of his time.[10] And so does Obadiah Walker, who became master of University College, Oxford, in 1676, and whose work called *Some Instructions conerning the Art of Oratory*, published at London in 1659, and given a second edition at Oxford in 1682, dealt with invention, arrangement, style, and delivery.[11] Incidentally, Walker and Henry Aldrich were contemporaries at Oxford, and Walker as a Roman Catholic published in 1688 a work which answered Aldrich's previously printed attack as an Anglican upon two pro-Catholic discourses by Abraham Woodhead, Walker's protégé.[12]

Walker and the other English Ciceronians just mentioned had support from the Continent in their efforts to restore the full rhetorical tradition as an aftermath of Ramism. Of the several Continental rhetoricians who might be named in this connection, I shall here identify only two as being of particular interest to the English Ciceronians of the eighteenth century. The first of these is Cypriano Soarez, Spanish Jesuit, whose *De Arte Rhetorica Libri Tres ex Aristotele, Cicerone et Quinctiliano Deprompti*, published first at Coimbra around 1560, had a great number of European editions throughout the sixteenth and seventeenth centuries, and was issued at Venice in 1589, and at various other Continental cities on later occasions, in an abridgment edited by Ludovico Carbone under the title, *Tabulae Rhetorices*.[13] The

[9] Howell, *Logic and Rhetoric in England*, pp. 323-324.

[10] *Ibid.*, pp. 320-321.   [11] *Ibid.*, pp. 324-325.

[12] See *The Dictionary of National Biography*, s.v. Walker, Obadiah; also W. G. Hiscock, *Henry Aldrich of Christ Church 1648-1710*, pp. 42-45.

[13] A brief biographical sketch of Soarez may be found in Nicolas Antonio, *Bibliotheca Hispana Nova* (Matriti, 1788), I, 261. A briefer sketch of his life and a much fuller bibliographical account of his writings are given by Augustin and Aloys De Backer, *Bibliothèque de la Compagnie de Jésus*, new edn. by Carlos Sommervogel, S.J. (Brussels and Paris, 1890-1909), VII, 1331-1338. Soarez was born at Ocaña in Spain in 1524 and died at Plasencia in the same

other Continental rhetorician to have influenced the English Ciceronians was Gerardus Johannes Vossius, Dutch classical scholar, Protestant theologian, friend of Hugo Grotius, and author not only of the *Oratoriarum Institutionum Libri Sex*, but also of the *Rhetorices Contractae, sive Partitionum Oratoriarum Libri Quinque*, and of the *Elementa Rhetorica, Oratoriis ejusdem Partitionibus Accommodata*, the latter two of which had editions at Oxford, London, and Cambridge during the seventeenth and eighteenth centuries.[14] Indeed, the *Elementa Rhetorica* as published at London in 1724 was accompanied by a little treatise entitled *De Ratione Interpungendi*, which dealt with the problem of punctuation, and was written by John Ward, Professor of Rhetoric in Gresham College, London, and the leading English Ciceronian rhetorician of the eighteenth century, whose *A System of Oratory* will be discussed immediately.[15]

---

country in 1593. After having joined the Jesuit order in 1549, he taught rhetoric and the humanities for seven years, and the Holy Scriptures for twenty. He also served as governor of the colleges of Braga and Évora in Portugal.

[14] The *Rhetorices Contractae* appeared at Oxford in 1631, 1651, 1655, 1664, and 1672; the *Elementa Rhetorica* had an edition at Cambridge in 1663 and editions at London in 1663, 1707, 1724, and 1739.

[15] For further details concerning Ward's contributions to Vossius's *Elementa Rhetorica*, see *British Museum General Catalogue of Printed Books*, s.v. Vossius, Gerardus, and Ward, John.

When John Ward was appointed professor of rhetoric at Gresham College on September 1, 1720, he became one of the seven faculty members of an institution that could trace its own beginnings to the days of Henry VIII and Queen Elizabeth. It was actually founded in 1596 upon a bequest from the estate of Sir Thomas Gresham to the City of London and the Mercers' Company. Sir Thomas was a financial genius who served in various important and honorable public capacities under Henry VIII, Edward VI, Mary Tudor, and Elizabeth, and who built up a great fortune from the gifts of those monarchs and from his own personal success as a merchant. At the time of his death in 1579, his princely income included a substantial annual return upon his initiative in having founded the Royal Exchange. His will directed that at the death of his widow his impressive residence in Bishopgate Street and his income from the Royal Exchange be used by the City of London and the Mercers' Company to establish a college that would offer academic courses of high quality for the public benefit. Some nineteen years after its founding, a contemporary historian, Sir George Buck, described Gresham College as follows:

> This is a little Uniuersitie or Accademies Epitome as *Rome* when it flourished was, *Orbis Epitome* in the conceit of *Athenaeus* and others, for in this colledge are by this worthy Founder ordained seauen seuerall lectures of seauen seuerall Arts and faculties, to be read publikely, to wit, a lecture of Diuinitie, a lecture of Ciuill law, a lecture of Physicke, a lecture of Rhetorike, a lecture of Astronomy, a lecture of Geometrie, and a lecture of Musicke, by seauen seuerall renowned professors of these Arts and learnings.[16]

[16] Sir George Buck, "The Third Vniversitie of England," in *The Annales, or Generall Chronicle of England*, by John Stow and Edmond Howes (London, 1615), p. 980. An edition of *The Annales* in 1605 had contained an appendix entitled, "Of the Vniuersities in England" (pp. 1438-1447), which gave an account only of Cambridge and Oxford. That same account appeared again in the edition of 1615, but this time it was accompanied by Sir George Buck's sketch of the third university, the two surveys being now collectively entitled, "An Appendix or Corollary of the Fovndations and Discriptions of the Three Most Famovs Vniversities of Englande, viz. Cambridge, Oxford, and Lon-

Sir George added that each professor received a stipend of £ 50 per year under Sir Thomas's bequest "and a fayre lodging within this his pallace-like house, now their colledge which this magnificent Knight built. . . ."

Much of the early history of Gresham College comes down to us from the same John Ward whose appointment as professor of rhetoric was just now mentioned. In the year 1740 Ward published at London a work called *The Lives of the Professors of Gresham College*. The only thing we learn about Ward himself from this volume is the date of his appointment as professor. But we learn many other interesting things. We learn that the City of London and the Mercers' Company, in putting Sir Thomas Gresham's will into practical effect, appointed in 1597 to the first faculty of Gresham College three Oxford graduates and three Cambridge graduates, and that the seventh professor, appointed by Queen Elizabeth, held degrees from both of those universities.[17] We also learn that the City and the Mercers' Company proceeded to arrange a weekly schedule of lectures so that each professor had a certain day assigned to him, and would deliver his lecture twice on that day, once in the morning between eight and nine in Latin, and once in the afternoon between two and three in English. The beginning arrangement, according to Ward, was this: the lecture on physic (it would now be called hygiene or medicine) was scheduled for Mondays; on law, for Tuesdays; on divinity, for Wednesdays; on geometry, for Thursdays; on astronomy, for Fridays; and on rhetoric, for Saturdays. Music had a special schedule of its own. Its first lecture, ordinarily comprising a half-hour of exposition of theory in Latin, and a half-hour of practice by voice or instrument, fell on Thursday afternoons between three and four; and its second lecture, comprising a half-hour of exposition of theory in English, and another half-hour of practice, fell between three and four on Saturday afternoons.[18]

---

don. . . ." By London University Sir George meant all of the schools of higher learning in the city, including King's College in Chelsea, the Inns of Court, and the various establishments for the study of medicine and theology. One of the constituent parts of this third university was Gresham College, and Sir George devoted his thirtieth chapter (pp. 980-981) to it.

[17] Ward, *Lives of the Professors*, p. 38.

[18] *Ibid.*, pp. v-viii. Each of the two lectures on law was to consist of three quarters of an hour of explaining the subject in Latin, and one quarter of

The requirement that each professor deliver one lecture in Latin was flexible; Ward noted that the first professor of music could speak no Latin and was permitted to deliver both his lectures in English. We also learn from Ward that it was agreed to divide the academic year into the four terms of court sittings under the English common law, and that the first lectures at Gresham College were delivered in Michaelmas Term of 1598.[19] Ward gives us many other illuminating details concerning the history of the institution during its first century, the chief of which is that various members of its faculty belonged actively to the group of experimental philosophers who later grew into the Royal Society of London, and that, through the circumstance of the Society's having a special meeting room assigned to it in Gresham College, it could claim Sir Thomas's palace-like house as the nursery in which it had spent its earliest childhood.[20]

Ward's account of the Gresham College faculty covers the first one hundred and twenty-four years of the history of that institution. He gave separate biographical sketches of each of the successive professors of divinity, astronomy, geometry, music, law, physic, and rhetoric. One of the longest and most laudatory of his sketches is devoted to Sir Christopher Wren, who was a scientist before he gained fame as an architect, and who served between 1657 and 1661 as professor of astronomy at Gresham College and as member of the group later recognized as the Royal Society.[21] There were twelve professors of rhetoric at Gresham College before Ward, four of whom were connected with the Royal Society, and four of whom had some few publications to their credit.[22]

---

an hour of summarizing the exposition in English. Ward noted, p. x, that the schedule of lectures had been changed somewhat by 1633, the lecture on rhetoric having been moved to Friday, for one thing.

[19] *Ibid.*, pp. iv-v, ix.

[20] *Ibid.*, pp. x-xii, xviii. Ward remarked that the Royal Society ceased its connection with Gresham College in 1710, and at that time began to hold its meetings in its own newly acquired house. Thus, as he said, the two bodies enjoyed a close association lasting for fifty years.

[21] *Ibid.*, pp. 95-111.

[22] The Gresham professors of rhetoric, as listed by Ward, are enumerated below, their dates at Gresham College being given first, then their names, and finally their educational pedigrees:

1596-1598. Caleb Willis.   Christ Church, Oxford.
                              B.A. 1589, M.A. 1592.

But the disheartening fact for the historian of English rhetoric is
that the organizers of Gresham College drew up no mandate for
the professors of rhetoric to follow, although they gave other professors specific advice about their duties; and it is also disheartening that the twelve professors of rhetoric between 1598 and 1720
lectured on their subject without ever having published anything
in that field or without having left behind for Ward's records any
trace of the doctrine which they presumably considered to have
been included in the necessary topics of their lectures. Thus
Ward's sketches of them in not mentioning what their lectures

1598-1613.	Richard Ball.	Magdalen College, Oxford.
		B.A. 1590-1, M.A. 1594, B.D. 1602.
1613-1619.	Charles Croke.	Christ Church, Oxford.
		B.A. 1608, M.A. 1611, B.D. & D.D.
		1625.
1619-1627.	Henry Croke.	Christ Church, Oxford.
		B.A. 1613-4, M.A. 1616, B.D. 1635.
1627-1638.	Edward Wilkinson.	Magdalen Hall, Oxford.
		B.A. 1622, M.A. 1625.
1638-1654.	John Goodridge.	Balliol College, Oxford.
		B.A. 1601-2, M.A. 1606, B. Med.
		1618-9.
1654-1659.	Richard Hunt.	King's College, Cambridge.
		B.A. 1649, M.A. 1653.
1659-1670.	William Croone	Emmanuel College, Cambridge.
	(or Croune).	B.A. 1650-1, M.A. 1654, M.D. 1663.
1670-1676.	Henry Jenkes.	King's College, Aberdeen.
		M.A. 1646. Fellow of Caius College,
		Cambridge, 1653-97.
1676-1686.	John King.	Caius College, Cambridge.
		M.B. 1670.
1686-1696.	Charles Gresham.	Trinity College, Oxford.
		B.A. 1680-1, M.A. 1683.
1696-1720.	Edward Martyn.	King's College, Cambridge.
		B.A. 1692-3, M.A. 1696.

The professors in this list to have had connections with the Royal Society
are William Croone, Henry Jenkes, John King, and Charles Gresham. Croone
is counted one of the Society's founders.

The four who were authors of published works are Charles Croke, Richard
Hunt, William Croone, and Henry Jenkes.

Caleb Willis, Richard Ball, Henry Croke, Edward Wilkinson, John Good-
ridge, Richard Hunt, John King, Charles Gresham, and Edward Martyn do
not appear in *The Dictionary of National Biography*, but the other professors
of rhetoric in Ward's roster do.

were about give us no way to understand how they faced the issues of an age in which Ramistic rhetoric was on the wane in England, and neo-Ciceronian rhetoric was on the rise, and new critics of rhetoric like Robert Boyle and Thomas Sprat from the precincts of the Royal Society itself were voicing eloquent objections to the idea that the ancient lore of the tropes and the figures was the very heart of the theory of rhetorical style.[23]

Ward's own position in the history of the eighteenth century has been so imperfectly understood that the most accessible biographical sketch of him begins by calling him the biographer of the Gresham professors.[24] He himself would have wanted to be identified above all as professor of rhetoric at Gresham College, and he would have wanted that aspect of his career to be emphasized in any account of his life. He must at times have felt it strange that he was appointed to such a position in the first place. The appointment occurred when he was forty-one years of age. Before that time he had successively been a clerk in the navy office and the proprietor of a school in Tenter Alley, Moorfields. Whereas each of his predecessors in the chair of rhetoric at Gresham College had had affiliations with Oxford or Cambridge, he himself had had no connection whatever with any university, his advanced education having been secured under the tutelage of John Ker at Bethnal Green Academy, a favorably known nonconformist school in London, the place of Ward's birth. He had reached the age of seventy-two before he acquired an academic degree, and that came to him from the University of Edinburgh, which named him an honorary doctor of laws on April 15, 1751.[25] Each of the previous professors of rhetoric at Gresham College

[23] Ward, *Lives of the Professors*, pp. 301-334. Boyle's thesis that Greek rhetorical standards were not to be accepted as the sole criteria for judging masterpieces of other cultures is contained in his famous book, *Some Considerations Touching the Style Of the H. Scriptures* (London, 1661), an account of which is given below, Ch. 6, pp. 464-481. For an account of Sprat's criticism of the rhetoric of tropes and figures, see Howell, *Logic and Rhetoric in England*, pp. 388-390; see also below, Ch. 6, pp. 485-486.

[24] I refer to the account of him by Thompson Cooper in *The Dictionary of National Biography*.

[25] See *A Catalogue of the Graduates in the Faculties of Arts, Divinity, and Law, of the University of Edinburgh, since its Foundation* (Edinburgh, 1858), p. 256. The date of the degree as given by John Nichols, *Literary Anecdotes of the Eighteenth Century* (London, 1812), v, 522, is not correct.

served there for an average of ten years, and most of them had then resigned and gone on to other activities. But Ward held his professorship for thirty-eight years, and he was still holding it at the time of his death, which occurred on October 17, 1758, in his chambers above what Vertue numbers as the sixteenth entry of the handsome building once occupied by Sir Thomas Gresham.[26] During most of his life at Gresham College, Ward was a fellow of the Royal Society, having been elected to that body on November 30, 1723, when Sir Isaac Newton was its president. Ward was himself appointed one of its vice presidents in 1752. He also was a fellow, a director, and a vice president of the Society of Antiquaries, and a trustee of the British Museum.[27] And unlike any of the previous Gresham professors of rhetoric, he left a full record of his lectureship behind him when he died, having carefully transcribed the fifty-four English lectures that he delivered over the years, and the Latin oration that he delivered publicly in 1720 at the beginning of the Michaelmas Term when he first entered upon his collegiate duties. These lectures were all published in the year after his death in two volumes at London under the title, *A System of Oratory, Delivered in a Course of Lectures Publicly read at Gresham College, London: To which is prefixed An Inaugural Oration, Spoken in Latin, before the Commencement of the Lectures, according to the usual Custom.*[28] As we shall see

[26] In Ward's *Lives of the Professors*, facing p. 33, is an attached folded sheet containing George Vertue's attractive engraving of Gresham College, dated 1739. My numbering of the entry to the lodgings of the rhetoric professor is based upon that in the engraving. A different numbering is used by John W. Burgon, *The Life and Times of Sir Thomas Gresham, Knt.* (London, 1839), II, facing p. 437, where Vertue's plate is reproduced, and number 10 is assigned to the rhetoric professor's lodgings, the entry to them not being separately indicated.

[27] My account of Ward is based mostly upon that in *The Dictionary of National Biography*. For a useful recent study of him and his works, see Douglas Ehninger, "John Ward and His Rhetoric," *Speech Monographs*, XVIII (March 1951), 1-16.

[28] It would seem that by 1720 the practice of delivering lectures both in Latin and in English at Gresham College had been abandoned, and that it had become the custom for each professor to present only his inaugural lecture in Latin. At any rate I find no indication that a Latin version of Ward's lectures on rhetoric exists among the papers that he bequeathed to the British Museum, although these papers include the manuscript of his English lectures.

later, the eighteenth century was to produce many courses of lectures on rhetoric and rhetorical subjects—Adam Smith's and Hugh Blair's at Edinburgh, John Lawson's at Dublin, Joseph Priestley's at Warrington, Thomas Sheridan's and John Walker's at Oxford, and George Campbell's at Aberdeen. But it must be remembered that those lectures were all delivered long after John Ward began his professorship of rhetoric at Gresham College, and that, had Ward not set as conscientious and as learned an example as he did, there might have been no thought of lecturing upon that same subject, and little public interest in rhetoric to appeal to, when those later lecturers found themselves before the audiences of their own time and place.

Ward's *System of Oratory* contains an anonymous notice saying that the reputation of its author for learning would long ago have recommended his lectures for publication, had it not been that he was constantly using them in his professorship. The notice adds that Ward had told several friends of his desire to have the lectures published after his death, and that his manuscript, which was at that time on deposit at the bookseller's, testified to that same desire. Indeed, concludes the notice, it was with the publication of his lectures in mind that Ward "caused a fair copy of them to be transcribed, after he had from time to time revised them with his usual accuracy, during the space of thirty eight years, in which he most punctually discharged the duties of his Professorship at Gresham College, having been elected into it on the 1st of September 1720, and dying on the 17th of October 1758."

The Latin inaugural address, entitled "Oratio, Quam in Collegio Greshamensi, cum rhetorices praelegendae provinciam illic suscept [*sic*], publice habuit Iohannes Wardvs, v. Kal. Nov. MDCCXX," was designed, according to its subtitle, to speak "De

---

See *Index to the Additional Manuscripts, with those of the Egerton Collection, Preserved in the British Museum, and Acquired in the Years 1783-1835* (London, 1849), pp. 475-476. According to Burgon, *Life of Gresham*, ii, 518, all professors of music were excused from lecturing in Latin after the first lecturer in that subject was given permission to speak in English. But Burgon implies that the rule requiring each professor to deliver one of his lectures in Latin was still among the college regulations in the nineteenth century, although he does not indicate how strictly it was enforced.

Usu et Praestantia Artis Dicendi."[29] Since the fifty-four lectures that follow it are not unconnected with the same general theme, I need not bother to summarize the Latin oration here. But one thing might be noted about it, as we approach the other lectures: the authorities which it quotes include Aristotle's *Rhetoric*, Cicero's *De Oratore* and *De Partitione Oratoria*, Horace's *De Arte Poetica*, Plutarch's *Cicero*, and Quintilian's *Institutio Oratoria*. No possible list of other ancient works could compare with this in indicating the basic sources of Ward's rhetorical theory or in preparing his listeners for the kind of doctrine that the subsequent lectures contain.

Ward's fifty-four lectures cover 863 printed pages, and are organized so as to give proper emphasis to each one of the five great arts which Cicero had named as the necessary constituents of rhetoric. After three preliminary lectures respectively dealing in 42 pages with the history, the nature, and the divisions of the orator's discipline, Ward spoke of invention in eight lectures embracing 132 pages, of disposition or arrangement in eight lectures covering 127 pages, and of style, his major topic, in twenty-seven lectures sprawling over 123 pages at the end of the first printed volume and 312 pages at the beginning of the second volume. Then he dealt with pronunciation or delivery in four lectures taking up 65 pages, and with memory in one lecture of 15 pages. Following this conscientious exposition of ancient rhetoric, Ward devoted a final three lectures occupying 47 pages to such related matters as listening, reading, writing, and imitating the masters. Nothing that Cicero considered essential is missing from

[29] For its text, see *A System of Oratory* (London, 1759), I, i-xvi. The title and subtitle would be translated as follows: "The Oration Concerning the Use and Eminence of the Art of Speaking, which John Ward delivered in public at Gresham College five days before the kalends of November, 1720, when he entered there into the duty of lecturing upon rhetoric." In *The Lives of the Professors*, p. x, Ward noted that the day assigned to the lecture on rhetoric was changed to Friday in the early sixteen hundreds, and that the new arrangement was kept thenceforth. Five days before the kalends of November in the Roman reckoning is October 28, the kalends themselves being counted as the first day in such a backward-going series. Thus October 28, 1720, is the date of Ward's first lecture. In that year, October 28 fell on a Friday, as an English calendar for 1720 will testify. It appears that Ward did not change the day assigned to the lecturer on rhetoric. It also appears that Gresham College must have opened that year on Monday, October 24.

Ward's program, and everything that Ward considered essential is expressed or implied in Cicero's rhetorical writings and in the elaborate synthesis that Quintilian formulated from the works of his Ciceronian and Aristotelian predecessors. Nor did Ward ignore the influential rhetorics of the period just before his own, as we shall have occasion to notice later.

In terms of its value as an exposition of ancient rhetorical theory, Ward's *System of Oratory* invites comparison with the best works of its kind in English. Only Thomas Wilson's *Arte of Rhetorique*, published just two hundred and six years before Ward's lectures were put into a printed book, can be said to surpass the *System of Oratory* as a latter-day interpretation of classical Roman doctrine, and the advantage is on Wilson's side, not because he adhered more fully to Ciceronian teachings than Ward did, not because his learning in the whole field of classical rhetoric was broader or deeper than Ward's, but because his imagination was alert, his style attractive, and his spirit triumphant; and in these latter traits Ward was not outstanding. Indeed, Wilson put ancient Latin rhetoric into English with the enthusiasm of an apostle making available to his countrymen the accepted doctrine behind the mighty eloquence of Greece and Rome, whereas Ward carefully reinterpreted Aristotle, Cicero, and Quintilian with the defensive patience of an antiquarian. It is not inaccurate to suggest that Wilson wrote out of the exuberant readiness of Renaissance humanists to claim victory, and Ward, out of the stubborn unwillingness of the eighteenth-century Ciceronians to accept defeat.

In justifying this latter observation, the historian of rhetoric could truly say that Ward was attempting to revive the five great arts of Cicero in the spirit of one who, knowing the criticisms directed in his own times against a major part of the Ciceronian system, lacked the insight himself to reconstruct ancient rhetoric by creatively responding to those criticisms. Ward had read Bernard Lamy's *De l'Art de Parler* in the English translation entitled *The Art of Speaking*, published at London in 1676 and reprinted there in 1696 and 1708;[30] and in that work, which had

---

[30] In *A System of Oratory*, II, 126, Ward quoted from Lamy's *The Art of Speaking*, p. 4, c. 24, and that particular reference, construed in fact as designating Part 4, page 24, makes use of the peculiar system of pagination found in the first London edition of Lamy's work, which Ward probably owned.

been attributed erroneously to the Port-Royalists, but which is properly to be linked with the reforms proposed in *The Port-Royal Logic*, Ward would certainly have come in contact with the abrasive attack made by Lamy upon the use of the topics as a means of arriving at the subject matter of a discourse. Lamy had said:

> Those who reject these Topicks, do not deny their Fecundity; they grant that they supply us with infinite numbers of things; but they alledg that that Fecundity is inconvenient; That the things are trivial, and by consequent the Art of *Topicks* furnishes nothing that is fit for us to say. If an Orator (say they) understands the subject of which he treats; if he be full of incontestable Maxims that may inable him to resolve all Difficulties arising upon that subject; If it be a question in Divinity, and he be well read in the Fathers, Councils, Scriptures, &c. He will quickly perceive whether the question propos'd be Orthodox, or otherwise. It is not necessary that he runs to his Topicks, or passes from one common place to another, which are unable to supply him with necessary knowledg for decision of his Question. If on the other side an Orator be ignorant, and understands not the bottom of what he Treats, he can speak but superficially, he cannot come to the point; and after he has talk'd and argued a long time, his Adversary will have reason to admonish him to leave his tedious talk that signifies nothing; to interrupt him in this manner, Speak to the purpose; oppose Reason against my Reason, and coming to the Point, do what you can to subvert the Foundations upon which I sustain my self.[31]

After this kind of attack, any discussion of the topics of rhetorical invention in ancient rhetoric would need special alertness and perhaps would even have to recognize that that part of the Ciceronian system was not fully applicable any longer to an age predominantly interested in the empirical approach to knowledge. But Ward, as we shall see, gave the topics conventional treatment in his lectures, after making a somewhat embarrassed apology for

[31] *The Art of Speaking* (London, 1676), Pt. v, pp. 104-105. For a discussion of the relation between Lamy's attack on the topics, and a similar attack in *The Port-Royal Logic*, see Howell, *Logic and Rhetoric in England*, pp. 355-357, 380-381.

them as being useful to those without the genius or the opportunity to find stronger arguments by more direct investigation.[32]

Lest it be argued in defense of Ward that he could hardly have been expected to be so far ahead of his time as to have stated between 1720 and 1758 what was later to become the modern view of the topics of rhetorical invention, the point should be firmly made that the modern view had already been stated before Ward assumed his professorship at Gresham, and that Ward knew what that statement entailed. His own words at the end of his first English lecture prove this point beyond question. Having reviewed in that lecture the rise and progress of oratory, and having mentioned the chief authorities on rhetoric in the classical period, Ward ended on this note:

> And a very good judge has not long since given it as his opinion; that the method of forming the best system of oratory, is to collect it from the finest precepts of Aristotle, Cicero, Quintilian, Longinus, and other celebrated authors; with proper examples taken from the choicest parts of purest antiquity. This method, therefore, I shall endeavour to pursue in my following discourses.[33]

Now, the very good judge to whom Ward referred in this passage is the distinguished French author and churchman, Fénelon, the Archbishop of Cambrai, as Ward indicated in a marginal note to one side of the quotation. Thus Fénelon takes his place in Ward's list of authorities as the originator of the very idea that Ward's own *System of Oratory* is to carry out. Fénelon had voiced this idea in outlining in 1714 a "Projet de Rhétorique" in his famous "Lettre à M. Dacier, Secrétaire Perpétuel de l'Académie Française, sur les Occupations de l'Académie"; and he had said then that a rhetoric founded upon the choicest parts of purest antiquity would be a work that was short, exquisite, and delightful.[34]

---

[32] See below, pp. 97-101.   [33] *System of Oratory*, I, 15.

[34] Fénelon said in the passage paraphrased by Ward: "Une excellente Rhétorique seroit bien audessus d'une grammaire et de tous les travaux bornés à perfectionner une langue. Celui qui entreprendroit cet ouvrage y rassembleroit tous les plus beaux préceptes d'Aristote, de Cicéron, de Quintilien, de Lucien, de Longin, et des autres célèbres auteurs: leurs textes, qu'il citeroit, seroient les ornemens du sien. En ne prenant que la fleur de la plus pure antiquité, il feroit un ouvrage court, exquis et délicieux." See *Oeuvres Complètes de Fénelon* (Paris, 1850), VI, 618.

Ward knew this letter, as the page reference in his marginal note proves, from the English translation given it by William Stevenson in a volume published at London in 1722 under the title, *Dialogues Concerning Eloquence In General; And particularly, that Kind which is fit for the Pulpit: By the late Archbishop of Cambray. With His Letter to the French Academy, Concerning Rhetoric, Poetry, History, and A Comparison betwixt the Antients and Moderns.*[35] And Ward had read not only the first edition of Stevenson's translation of Fénelon's "Lettre" but also the translation of the *Dialogues on Eloquence* accompanying it; for on two occasions in his course of lectures he referred to the latter work, and each of his references is given page numbers that correspond with those on which the same passage occurs in that earliest edition of Stevenson's translation.[36] Ward's second reference to the *Dialogues* was especially complimentary to Fénelon—it spoke of him as "a very great man" and "this excellent writer." It is hard to understand why Ward, admiring Fénelon in terms as eulogistic as these, and having Fénelon's *Dialogues on Eloquence* fully in mind, would not have seen that Fénelon himself had carried out in his own *Dialogues* the very mandate laid down in the "Lettre." In other words, Fénelon's *Dialogues* meet his own prescription for rhetoric—they are short, exquisite, and delightful, and they preserve only the choicest and the most timeless parts of ancient rhetorical doctrine. Thus they omit all the precepts regarding the topics of invention; and they include what has become the modern view of the origin of rhetorical subject matter and the modern view of the doctrine of disposition, style, and delivery.[37] Had Ward followed Fénelon's example more understandingly, he would have created a rhetoric that might have outlasted the eighteenth century. And this can be said without belittling his accomplishments as a careful and dedicated interpreter of a system that was not in its entirety to survive beyond his time except as a monument of an ancient habit of thought.

[35] Ward's note placed the passage by saying, "A.B. of Cambr. *Lett. p.* 213." Thus we know that he is referring to the first edition of Stevenson's translation, for the passage paraphrased by him may be found on page 213 of that publication.

[36] See *System of Oratory*, II, 112-113, 321. See below, n. 95.

[37] For a discussion of Fénelon's *Dialogues* as the first modern rhetoric, see my *Fénelon's Dialogues on Eloquence, A Translation with an Introduction and Notes* (Princeton, 1951), pp. 44-46. See also below, Ch. 6, pp. 504-519.

Before we turn to Ward's treatment of the five great arts, we should mention that his second and third lectures contain a Ciceronian definition of rhetoric, and some necessary comments upon the relations among rhetoric, grammar, and logic as arts of discourse. After having asserted that rhetoric and oratory are interchangeable terms, the only difference between them being that the first is of Greek and the second of Latin origin, Ward defined the subject of his course of lectures by saying that "Oratory is the art of speaking well upon any subject, in order to persuade."[38] On the other hand, grammar "is the art of speaking *correctly*."[39] It includes making the proper choice of words, using them in the usual senses, and joining them properly in relation to the form and idiom of the language involved. Ward immediately stressed that both grammar and rhetoric concern themselves equally with speaking and writing, each from its own point of view. It might be good grammar, but it would be bad oratory, he remarked, to use flowery language with an ordinary subject, or to treat a lofty subject in lowly language. If grammar and rhetoric have these points of similarity and difference, and if each pursues its own aim in relation to all of the possible subjects of discourse, what then of logic? "Indeed," said Ward, with the relations between rhetoric and logic primarily in mind, "the subject of *logic* is equally extensive; but the difference both in its short and concise way of reasoning from the fluency and copiousness of oratory; and the end it proposes, which is only the knowledge of truth, while the other carries us to action, render it intirely a distinct art."[40]

With the reforms of Ramus in the back of his mind, Ward later said that some would assign invention and disposition wholly to logic, and exclude them from rhetoric, but that he himself saw no reason why rhetoric and logic could not be conversant about these two procedures without interfering with each other. "Thus both logic and rhetoric," he observed, "teach us to reason from the same principles, as from the cause, effects, circumstances, and many others, whence arguments are usually taken."[41] But rhetoric goes on from there to other considerations, and seeks materials which, being designed to conciliate and arouse passion, are not of any concern to logic. At this point Ward made the statement

[38] *System of Oratory*, I, 19.
[39] *Ibid.*, I, 22.   [40] *Ibid.*, I, 25.   [41] *Ibid.*, I, 31.

that appears as the epigraph to the present chapter, and the reader who would consider further his views on the relations of logic and rhetoric might want to consult it.

As for the interest of logic and rhetoric in disposition or arrangement, here again, said Ward, the two arts differ as they differ in respect to invention. The logician arranges the propositions of a syllogism by a certain prescribed method so that the relation between the terms of the argument may be evident, and the conclusion proceed from the premises. But the orator is not tied down to mood and figure. He seldom uses perfect syllogisms. He begins sometimes with his conclusion, sometimes with either one of his premises; he proves each point before he goes on to another; by using diversity in his method, he pleases and entertains as well as instructs. In the light of such considerations as these, Ward concluded, the theory of disposition in oratory is quite different from that in logic.[42] Although he proceeded later to devote eight chapters to Cicero's theory of rhetorical disposition, he did not discuss further the subject of disposition in logic, and thus he missed the opportunity to show how traditional rhetoric might in this part of its doctrine have been improved by merging its interest in method with the interest that logic had been showing in that subject during the sixteenth and seventeenth centuries. Once more, it seems, he proved himself to be more of an antiquarian preserving the exact contours of ancient rhetoric than a creative scholar bent upon adapting the timeless parts of ancient rhetoric to the challenges confronting modern man.

The parts of invention, remarked Ward at the beginning of his tenth lecture, are considered to be three: the first respects the subject of the discourse, the second, the speaker, and the third, the hearers.[43] In devoting eight lectures to the theory of rhetorical invention, Ward spoke successively of each of these three heads, which are of course to be understood, not as if the doctrine of any one of them excluded all consideration of the other two, but as if the interest of rhetoric in the theory of subject matter involved three different approaches to the basic ideas that an author on a given occasion would want to convey. In other words, a speaker or writer in arriving at the content of his discourse would always need to consider his words in relation to what they would announce about the subject under discussion, what they would re-

[42] *Ibid.*, I, 32-33.   [43] *Ibid.*, I, 140.

96

veal about the author doing the talking or writing, and how they would affect the audience of listeners or readers. There could be little objection to these three heads as valid and exhaustive categories for the discussion of subject matter in discourse. Objection could only come to the doctrines and concepts enunciated under these categories, as questions of scientific accuracy, morality, and human psychology began to operate upon what was being said about a given subject by a given speaker before a given audience.

Ward treated the first of these heads by considering arguments or proof. If one statement is to be proved by another, a relation must be established between them by means of a third statement. Ward elaborated this idea as follows:

> Now this third thing logicians call the *Medium* or *middle Term*, because it does as it were connect two extremes, that is, both parts of a proposition. But rhetoricians call it an *Argument*, because it is so applied to what was before proposed, as to become the instrument of procuring our assent to it.[44]

Arguments come by nature to the quick and the ingenious, said Ward, and by art to those who wish systematically to supplement what nature may provide. In this latter connection, he declared, "the greatest help to invention is, for a person to consider well before hand the subject, upon which he is to speak, and not to venture to affirm any thing concerning it, which he has not first a clear notion of himself."[45] "The better any one understands a thing himself," he added, "the better is he able to explain it to others. . . . And the more thoroughly he is himself persuaded of the truth of what he sais, he will be qualified to impress it with greater strength and clearness upon the minds of those, to whom he speaks."[46]

The matter might well have been allowed to rest upon these truths, which are the basic theme of the doctrine of invention in Fénelon's *Dialogues*.[47] But what would happen then to the system of topics? It would disappear, of course, from rhetorical theory, and somehow Ward did not want that to happen. Accordingly, he saved the system by offering it to speakers as a way of getting around the handicaps of scanty knowledge and lack of time for

[44] *Ibid.*, 1, 48.   [45] *Ibid.*, 1, 50.   [46] *Ibid.*, 1, 50, 51.
[47] See Howell, *Fénelon's Dialogues on Eloquence*, pp. 82-87. See also below, Ch. 6, pp. 512-513.

study. To those who have these handicaps, he said, "art has pre-scribed a method to lessen in some measure these difficulties, and help every one to a supply of arguments upon any subject. And this is done by the contrivance of *common places,* which Cicero calls the *seats* or *heads of arguments,* and by a Greek name *topics.*"[48]

Topics, said Ward with Cicero still in mind, are internal or external. The internal topics arise in connection with the subject itself, and there are sixteen of them: Definition, Enumeration, Notation, Genus, Species, Antecedents, Consequents, Adjuncts, Conjugates, Cause, Effect, Contraries, Opposites, Similitude, Dissimilitude, and Comparison. Ward devoted the last part of his fourth lecture to explaining these terms, to illustrating their use in Cicero's speech in defense of Milo, and to remarking that the topics not only help the man of few intellectual resources but also him who knows his subject and yet does not know what to say about it. The external topics, which Ward introduced by calling them inartificial,[49] and by noting that Aristotle had called them by that name to distinguish them from the internal or artificial topics, embrace all the arguments arising from what may be characterized as testimonies: the oracles and auguries of the ancients; the divinely inspired scriptures of the Christians; all human statements in the form of written laws, wills, charters, written or oral testimony, private contracts, and public treaties between nations. These inartificial proofs were severally discussed by Ward in his fifth lecture.

The distinction between internal and external topics had been authorized by Aristotle, as Ward correctly observed; and it had had great currency in Latin rhetoric throughout classical and postclassical times.[50] It must now be understood, however, not as

[48] *System of Oratory,* I, 51. Ward's reference, as he indicated in the margin beside this passage, is to Cicero's *Topics,* 6-8.

[49] *System of Oratory,* I, 61.

[50] See Aristotle, *Rhetoric,* 1355b 35-39. Quintilian, *Institutio Oratoria,* 5.1.1, spoke as follows of this distinction: "To begin with it may be noted that the division laid down by Aristotle has met with almost universal approval. It is to the effect that there are some proofs adopted by the orator which lie outside the art of speaking, and others which he himself deduces or, if I may use the term, begets out of his case. The former therefore have been styled ἄτεχνοι or *inartificial* proofs, the latter ἔντεχνοι or *artificial.*" (Translation by H. E. Butler in The Loeb Classical Library, London and New York, 1921-

a narrow technical distinction between two sorts of proof, but as the very crux of the difference between the ancient and the modern approach to rhetoric. According to the distinction, as Aristotle articulated it, the foundations of external or nonartistic proofs were there at the outset of a case, and such proofs themselves consisted of arguments derived from actual physical evidence. We could illustrate these proofs by saying that, if an eyewitness swore to having seen the accused commit the murder in question, his testimony would be counted as the basis of nonartistic proof, in the sense that the art of rhetoric could claim no part in supplying to a speaker such materials of discourse. Conclusions derived from these materials, said Aristotle, have merely to be used. Internal or artistic proofs, on the other hand, were directly devised by the art of rhetoric itself. An example of them would be afforded if the accused, being positively identified as having committed a previous murder when he had had little to fear from his victim, were now said to have committed the present murder because the present victim was known to have been a man whom the accused greatly feared. This particular argument, by the way, could be said to have originated in the topic of comparison—if X actually did Y under minor pressure, then X would surely do Y under major pressure.

It is one of the astonishing vagaries of history that these so-called artistic arguments should ever have been taken as having anything but subsidiary probative value in a court of law or should ever have been made into a major goal of an artistic system of rhetorical invention. But they were taken as decisive proofs in cases before Greek courts in the latter fifth and the entire fourth centuries B.C., and they were given a prominent place in inventional theory in classical Greek and Roman rhetoric. The earliest Greek rhetoric had apparently been founded upon the theory of the priority of nonartistic proofs. What explains the amazing shift from that state of affairs to one in which a studied machinery is devised to produce mere probabilities? The best answer that I have seen to this question is given in George Ken-

1936. The italics are Butler's.) Quintilian added that in his opinion those rhetoricians who wanted to eliminate from the rules of oratory all discussion of inartificial proof deserve the strongest condemnation. He himself gave full attention to both kinds.

nedy's *The Art of Persuasion in Greece*.[51] Kennedy shows that the application of the democratic process to judicial procedures during the fifth and fourth centuries B.C. resulted in cases being tried, not before the trained Areopagus or single magistrates of earlier times, but before large popular juries called *dikastéria* consisting of more than two hundred jurors who were required to determine questions of fact.[52] This development was accompanied by a widening of the political base of the government in the fifth century to include more and more people with less and less background.[53] And during the whole of that time there was a growing realization that direct evidence could be fabricated, that witnesses could be bought and documents forged. Says Kennedy:

> According to Isocrates fifteen people once swore in court to the death of a slave who was subsequently produced from hiding alive and well. Probabilities, however, as Aristotle says, do not deceive for bribes. In the *Laws* Plato forbids oaths to be taken by parties to a suit in his state "for it is somehow dreadful, when there are so many lawsuits in a city, to know well that almost half of the people are perjurers who meet each other readily at meals and other assemblies and private meetings."[54]

Factors such as these could explain why probabilities, which Aristotle advised the legal orator to justify as incapable of being convicted of perjury,[55] came into prominence in theories of rhetorical invention, and even tended to crowd out the consideration of nonartistic proofs. Besides, probabilities do have a value when decisions must be made and tangible evidence is completely lacking. Other factors could explain why probabilities and the rhetorical machinery for producing them through the use of topics were painstakingly maintained in dialectical and rhetorical theory throughout the Middle Ages. After all, the central truths of those times were theological, and were laid down in divinely inspired scriptural writings, and thus rested firmly upon divine

[51] Published at Princeton, New Jersey, by Princeton University Press, 1963.
[52] *The Art of Persuasion in Greece*, pp. 27-28.
[53] *Ibid.*, p. 28.
[54] *Ibid.*, pp. 89-90. Kennedy documents the references in this passage as follows: Isocrates, *Against Callimachus*, 53f.; Aristotle, *Rhetoric*, 1376a 19ff.; Plato, *Laws*, 948d 6.
[55] *Rhetoric*, 1376a 20.

testimony, the strongest possible foundation of argument, and itself an example of nonartistic proof. All the speaker or controversialist had to do was to create probable arguments to supplement and explain the certainties of scriptural testimony, and the ancient topics of rhetorical and dialectical proof were admirably suited to that enterprise.

The difficulties that began later to afflict the theory of topics in rhetoric and logic came in part from the Baconian and Cartesian emphasis in the seventeenth century upon the value of acquiring empirical knowledge. In one sense, this emphasis amounted to a recognition that human beings in attempting to make up their minds upon any issue must abandon probable arguments and seek arguments based upon the facts of the case in dispute. But the new interest in the empirical as distinguished from the a priori approach to knowledge was only one of the factors that encouraged criticism of the theory of topics. Another factor was the Reformation, which challenged the accepted authority of past centuries, and sought new alignments and new beliefs by testing the facts of contemporary Christian behavior against the tenets of Christian faith. Still other factors were the rise of Anglo-Saxon law and the development of Anglo-Saxon political institutions, both of which encouraged the empirical attitude, the desire to base legal and political decisions upon testimony, precedents, contracts, treaties, and statistics. All of these factors had acted to reinforce the destructive criticism that Bernard Lamy leveled at the art of topics when he wrote *De l'Art de Parler*, and they had also acted to make John Ward approach the topics apologetically in his fourth lecture on rhetoric at Gresham College. It is regrettable, however, that these factors operated upon Ward merely to produce an apologetic attitude towards the topics rather than a creative revision of them.

We must not attempt to follow Ward throughout the remaining portion of his discussion of rhetorical invention, lest the treatment of him here become tedious and disproportioned. What he did after discussing the topics was to complete his analysis of the first part of invention by devoting a full lecture to the theory of the states of controversies, and other lectures to the problem of devising arguments for demonstrative, deliberative, and forensic discourses. The theory of the states of controversies had been designed in ancient rhetoric to help speakers locate the issue in a particular case.[56] It taught that an issue arises whenever an affirmation and a denial clash; that issues fall into classes; that some issues concern the question whether the accused or someone else committed the crime; that some concern the question whether the crime is to be called by one name or another; and that some concern the question whether the crime was justified or not. Ward illustrated these issues by showing how they could be found in various ones of Cicero's orations, and thus to his auditors, who probably had been taught to regard those orations merely as performances in grammar, he must have imparted some truly rhetorical principles. The second part of invention, which concerns the speaker's character, was treated by Ward in one lecture after he had finally finished his lengthy analysis of everything that pertains to the speaker's subject. One striking feature of his discussion of the speaker's character is that, after requiring wisdom, integrity, benevolence, and modesty to be shown in the words of an oration, Ward talked about the various types of human character in respect to emotions, moral qualities, ages, and fortunes, and in discussing these four things, he gave a good digest of Aristotle's remarkable profiles of youth, old age, and the prime of life.[57] In the last of his eight lectures on invention, Ward treated the hearers as the third main consideration in devising the subject matter of discourse, and this consideration led him to analyze the passions, not as an improper object of oratory, but as the only means of getting men to act according to reason. His procedure was to assign to each type of discourse its appropriate emotions, and to discuss each emotion by following what Aristotle had said about it in his *Rhetoric*.[58] Demonstrative oratory Ward found to

[56] Ward relied for this theory upon Cicero's *De Inventione* and *De Oratore* and upon Quintilian's *Institutio Oratoria*. For an exposition of the theory, see my *The Rhetoric of Alcuin and Charlemagne, A Translation, with an Introduction, the Latin Text, and Notes* (Princeton, 1941), pp. 34-59.

[57] See *Rhetoric*, 2.12-14. See Ward, *System of Oratory*, Lecture 10.

[58] Early in his lecture on the third part of invention, Ward said that Aristotle in his *Rhetoric*, Bk. 2, Ch. 1, had defined the passions as "*Commotions of the mind, under the influence of which men think differently concerning the same things.*" See *System of Oratory*, I, 158-159. See also Aristotle, *Rhetoric*, 1377b 31, 1378a 19. Ward made four other specific references to Aristotle's *Rhetoric* in the course of his discussion of the passions, and his dependence

require appeals to joy and sorrow, love and hatred, emulation and contempt; deliberative oratory, appeals to fear, hope, and shame; and forensic oratory, appeals to anger, lenity, pity, and indignation. These Ward felt to be the principal passions, so far as oratory was concerned, and he closed his lecture upon them by saying that the orator must feel them himself as a prerequisite to exciting them in others.[59]

Ward's treatment of disposition, the second of the great arts making up Ciceronian rhetoric, has already been said to have followed the standard Latin theory and to have shown no inclination whatever to adjust that theory to the doctrine of logical method, despite the relevancy of the latter to the problem of organizing oratorical discourse. One further criticism of Ward's eight lectures on disposition should receive notice. In adopting the idea that an oration falls into six parts, the introduction, narration, proposition, confirmation, refutation, and conclusion, Ward deliberately chose one of the most elaborate of the ancient accounts of oratorical form after citing and rejecting one of the simplest of the ancient accounts, which had required a speech to have at the very least a proposition and confirmation, and at most two additional parts, an introduction and conclusion. In other words, Ward elected to follow Cicero's *De Inventione*, which he quoted throughout his lectures on disposition, rather than Aristotle's *Rhetoric*, which he also quoted in respect to its theory of rhetorical form.[60] The significance of this choice is that Ward was once again falling into the role of antiquarian rather than that of creative scholar. The Ciceronian formula was a hallowed convention. It had appealed mightily to the taste for ceremony and

---

upon Aristotle can be further established by comparing what he said about each emotion to what Aristotle said.

[59] A truism in Latin literary theory. Ward quoted it from Horace, *De Arte Poetica*, 102-103. But see also Cicero, *De Oratore*, 2.45.189-190, and Quintilian, *Institutio Oratoria*, 6.2.26 and 11.3.61-64.

[60] For the Ciceronian sources of Ward's lectures on disposition, see *De Inventione*, 1.14.19-109. Ward also made passing references to *De Partitione Oratoria* and *De Oratore* as well as to Quintilian's *Institutio Oratoria* during these particular lectures, and among the moderns to Vossius's *Rhetorices Contractae, sive Partitionum Oratoriarum Libri Quinque* and *Oratoriarum Institutionum Libri Sex*. For the Aristotelian theory which Ward referred to, see *Rhetoric*, 3.13-19.

ornateness in successive ages of empire, monarchy, aristocracy, and ecclesiastical usurpation of political authority. But when Ward was lecturing at Gresham College, the taste had changed, and a simpler formula for rhetorical disposition was coming into use. Fénelon had already outlined this simpler formula in his *Dialogues on Eloquence*.[61] It was to consist basically of the Aristotelian requirement that a speaker should state his case and prove it, and perhaps use an introduction and conclusion if circumstances demanded them, without feeling obliged to perform six major operations, each with subdivisions and elaborations, in composing a persuasive discourse. One of the great rhetorical works of Ward's own century, the American Declaration of Independence, is an example of the simpler formula that was becoming popular, but the Declaration owed its structure to the theory of method in eighteenth-century logic rather than to the doctrine of disposition in rhetoric.[62] Needless to say, the simpler rhetorical formula was being produced by new times, new philosophies, new conceptions of political life, and new attitudes towards knowledge. But Ward thought more carefully upon preserving the ancient doctrine than upon making it serve modern needs.

It should be emphasized that confirmation and refutation as two of the most important parts of the theory of rhetorical disposition involve the use of logical theory within the confines of rhetoric, even as rhetorical invention involves logic whenever arguments are sought as proof of the orator's case. In other words, logic and rhetoric overlap in the field of proof, whether the speaker is seeking arguments or trying to arrange them. Accordingly, Ward devoted his fifteenth lecture to proof by means

[61] See Howell, *Fénelon's Dialogues on Eloquence*, pp. 111-114. Fénelon attributed his theory of rhetorical arrangement to Cicero, not to Aristotle; but he was thinking of the mature Cicero who wrote *De Oratore*, not of the youthful Cicero who wrote *De Inventione*. Had Ward elected to reduce everything Cicero said on disposition to its essentials, he too would have been less pedagogical and more philosophical about it, and would probably not have chosen to follow *De Inventione* as closely as he did.

[62] See my article, "The Declaration of Independence and Eighteenth-Century Logic," *The William and Mary Quarterly*, Third Series, XVIII (October 1961), 463-484. Jefferson owned a copy of Ward's *System of Oratory*, however. See E. Millicent Sowerby, *Catalogue of the Library of Thomas Jefferson* (Washington, 1952-1959), V, 17.

of the syllogism and enthymeme, and his sixteenth lecture to proof by means of induction and example. What he said upon these matters was borrowed from standard Aristotelian logic, and to summarize his doctrine would be merely to repeat things already said in the previous chapter. But by way of showing that Ciceronian rhetoric had a fully serious logical dimension, we might comment upon one aspect of Ward's treatment of proof. This aspect was that Ward as rhetorician followed Aristotelian logicians in thinking of the syllogism as the fundamental form of reasoning. At the end of his discussion of the enthymeme, he remarked that this kind of argument was in appearance closer to natural logic than to the syllogism. "However syllogistical reasoning," he added, "is very useful, tho not in popular discourses: for every argument may be reduced to a syllogism, and if it will not hold in that form, there is certainly some flaw in it, which by that means will most easily be discovered."[63] Even the induction, which consists in inferring one thing from several others, and the example, which infers one thing from another, are basically syllogistical. Said Ward: "For in every induction and example, the thing or things, from a comparison with which we infer our conclusion, carries in it the force of a medium or argument, and the whole induction or example has the nature of an *Enthymem* or imperfect syllogism."[64]

The third of the great arts of the orator under the Ciceronian system is elocution or style, and Ward discussed it in full detail, after having concluded his treatment of disposition by devoting a whole lecture to the structural niceties of digression, transition, and amplification as defined respectively by Quintilian, Vossius, and Cicero. Elocution, it will be remembered, had been made the first of the two parts of rhetoric under Ramus's reform, and accordingly it had had many Ramistic treatises devoted to it in the two centuries preceding Ward's professorship at Gresham College.[65] But it had also been often treated before and after the time of Ramus as something that could be detached from the other parts of Ciceronian rhetoric and given an independent consideration of its own under circumstances emphasizing that in this guise it had not lost its traditional affiliation with invention, disposition,

[63] *System of Oratory*, I, 237.
[64] *Ibid.*, I, 249-250.
[65] See Howell, *Logic and Rhetoric in England*, pp. 247-281.

delivery, and memory.[66] Of all of the parts of rhetoric except delivery, elocution was the greatest favorite in classrooms of European grammar schools of the sixteenth and seventeenth centuries,
and in the literary studies that the precollege student of those
days was required to undertake. The reason behind this state of
affairs is not hard to explain. It was more obviously within the
capacities of lower school children to be able to identify the
tropes and the figures of style in the poems of Horace or Virgil
and in the orations of Cicero than it would have been for them to
comment upon the state of the controversy in one of Cicero's
forensic speeches or to show how Cicero had derived one of his
arguments from such a topic as adjuncts or contraries. The tropes
and the figures, in the Latin and Greek terminology that was assigned to them in textbooks on rhetorical style, must have appealed mightily to the mentality of the pedagogue. Here were
long lists of definitions that students could be made to memorize
in Greek and Latin and to illustrate from the classics as passages
were translated aloud and facts of style and grammar noted. Here
also was material to serve as a point of reference for student writers. They could be instructed, for example, to develop their Latin
theme on one day in terms of such figures as repetitions and contraries, and on another day in terms of such tropes as irony or
allegory. Considered only as a means of cultivating the student's
verbal aptitude and dexterity in the Latin language, at a time
when he could use that language only in the world of learning but
never in the world of everyday life, the tropes and the figures had
great value, and it would be impossible to overrate their importance as a factor in determining Latin literary style and taste in
western Europe during the Middle Ages and the Renaissance.
Vernacular style and taste were also of course the outgrowth of
training in the Latin grammar schools, and thus all modern European literatures owe a profound and frequently acknowledged
debt to the third part of Ciceronian rhetoric.

Ward opened his discussion of elocution by insisting, as the
ancients had done, that this art should never be separated from
the art of providing subject matter and guaranteeing form in discourse. It is precisely this insistence that differentiates him from
Ramism and from various debased modern concepts of rhetoric.
Cicero, said Ward, required the orator to consider what he should

[66] *Ibid.*, pp. 116-137, 326-335.

say, what order he should follow, and what manner of expression he should adopt; and in the light of these three requirements he himself, having disposed of the theory governing the first two, would now discuss that governing the third.[67] "This has always been esteemed so necessary and essential to an orator," he went on, "that some have placed the whole art of oratory only in *Elocution*."[68] But Cicero, he emphasized, had taken a broader view, and Quintilian, while stressing that a mastery of words was of great importance in oratory, had pointed out that as an absolute necessity a concern for subject matter must accompany it.[69]

Ward divided the doctrine of elocution into two main parts, speaking first of the general characteristics that all verbal expression has throughout the entire range of its applications, and then of its particular configurations when it is respectively applied to lowly, intermediate, or elevated subjects and to such literary types as the epistle, the dialogue, the historical work, and the oration. These two divisions were doubtless suggested to him by the *Rhetorica ad Herennium*, which he himself had attributed to Cornificius in his first lecture, but which he nevertheless rightly regarded as an organic part of the Ciceronian rhetorical tradition.[70] He did not follow this source, however, in respect to the

[67] *System of Oratory*, Lecture 20. See Cicero, *Orator*, 19.43.

[68] *System of Oratory*, I, 303.

[69] Ward documented this statement by referring to Quintilian, *Institutio Oratoria*, 8.Pr. Ward doubtless had the following statements of Quintilian in mind: "For I am compelled to offer the most prompt and determined resistance to those who would at the very portals of this enquiry lay hold of the admissions I have just made and, disregarding the subject matter which, after all, is the backbone of any speech, devote themselves to the futile and crippling study of words in a vain desire to acquire the gift of elegance, a gift which I myself regard as the fairest of all the glories of oratory, but only when it is natural and unaffected" (8.Pr.18). "Therefore I would have the orator, while careful in his choice of words, be even more concerned about his subject matter. For, as a rule, the best words are essentially suggested by the subject matter and are discovered by their own intrinsic light" (8.Pr.20-21). H. E. Butler's translation.

[70] Modern scholarship holds that the *Rhetorica ad Herennium* could not have been composed by Cornificius, and that there is no evidence to show who might have written it. For an authoritative review of this problem, see [*Cicero*] *Ad C. Herennium de Ratione Dicendi* (*Rhetorica ad Herennium*), trans. Harry Caplan, in The Loeb Classical Library (Cambridge, Massachusetts, and London, 1954), pp. vii-xiv. For the source of Ward's division of the subject of elocution, see *Rhetorica ad Herennium*, 4.7.10-18.

order in which he discussed the two divisions, and he did not hesitate to supplement it by drawing upon many other sources both ancient and modern. Thus he frequently referred to such classical works as Aristotle's *Rhetoric,* Cicero's *De Oratore* and *Orator,* Quintilian's *Institutio Oratoria,* and Longinus's *On the Sublime,* and among more recent writers to Chaucer, Lord Bacon, Milton, Dryden, Bernard Lamy, Locke, Joseph Addison, Vossius, Fénelon, and Anthony Blackwall.

Having remarked that the general characteristics of all verbal expression could be identified as elegance, composition, and dignity,[71] Ward proceeded to discuss elegance first, and he made this aspect of style fall under two heads, which he called purity and perspicuity.[72] Since purity consisted in choosing words and phrases that agreed with the forms and meanings of the language being used, and in avoiding solecisms and barbarisms, it was in truth a grammatical matter, and its discussion in rhetoric was necessary only because an art which studies persuasiveness in language cannot avoid considering that ungrammatical forms are usually unpersuasive. In proposing the following analogy between cultivated speech and proper dress, Ward indicated some of the social dynamics that lead people of the middle class to seek to improve their conversational manners, and that lead people of the upper classes to make that improvement difficult:

> For polite and elegant speakers distinguish themselves by their discourse, as persons of figure do by their garb; one being the dress of the mind, as the other is of the body. And hence it comes to pass, that both have their different fashions, which are often changed; and as the vulgar affect to imitate those above them in both, this frequently occasions an alteration, when either becomes too trite and common.[73]

Perspicuity, the second aspect of elegance, was made the subject of an entire lecture by Ward, and in it he advised that each in-

[71] Ward's three terms are taken from the following passage in the *Rhetorica ad Herennium,* 4.12.17; "Quae maxime admodum oratori adcommodata est tres res in se debet habere: elegantiam, conpositionem, dignitatem." Professor Harry Caplan translates them as Taste, Artistic Composition, and Distinction.

[72] That is, "Latinitas" and "explanatio" in the *Rhetorica ad Herennium.* Professor Caplan translates them as Correct Latinity and Clarity.

[73] *System of Oratory,* I, 309-310.

dividual word in a discourse must be used in its acknowledged sense and must be combined with other words so as to make a plain natural order. These two requirements would guarantee that a speaker or writer did not become unintentionally obscure. The possibility that obscurity might be deliberately sought for one reason or another received some of Ward's attention, and in this connection he recalled Quintilian's story of the rhetorician *"Who used to order his scholars to cloud their discourses. And his highest applause was: Bravely said, I did not understand it myself."*[74]

There is not much that we need now notice in Ward's discussion of composition, the second of the general characteristics of style, except that it concerned the structuring of the periodic sentence, the ordering of words, phrases, and clauses, the joining of letters and syllables into agreeable combinations of sound, and the arranging of words with regard to quantity or number. Ward considered all of these matters important in oratory or writing for their bearing upon the music, cadence, and harmony of discourse. We should perhaps observe that at this point in his lectures, Ward balanced his veneration of the ancients against his recognition that modern English cannot effectively adhere to classical patterns of composition, and thus here at least he did not recommend to his generation a mere obedience but rather a creative accommodation to ancient doctrine. In respect to word order, for example, he recognized the order of nature and the order of art, and he pointed out that the English could not accommodate themselves to the latter as effectively as the Latins did. His illustration was pertinent. The Latins, he noted, have three ways of saying that Aristotle taught rhetoric—they can put the subject first, or second, or third, in the sentence, and arrange the verb and object accordingly.[75] But the English would have to say, "Aristotle taught rhetoric," since it would amount to an absurdity to declare that rhetoric taught Aristotle, and it would make the

[74] *Ibid.*, I, 334. Italics are Ward's. See Quintilian, *Institutio Oratoria*, 8.2.18. Quintilian said that he had got the story from Livy.

[75] Ward put this sentence in three forms in his twenty-third lecture: "Aristoteles docuit rhetoricam. Rhetoricam docuit Aristoteles. Docuit Aristoteles rhetoricam." It would of course be clear from the case ending that "Aristoteles" is subject and "rhetoricam" is object, and thus word order would not be a necessary clue to grammatical function.

thought quite incomplete to say, "taught Aristotle rhetoric." Ward concluded his lecture on word order by striking an impartial note in his observations upon Latin and English:

> Upon the whole, therefore; in English the nearer we keep to the natural or grammatical order, it is generally best; but in Latin we are to follow the use of the best writers; a joint regard being always had to the judgement of the ear, and perspicuity of the sense, in both languages.[76]

The third general characteristic of elocution is what Ward called dignity, and this quality rested upon a distinction between the patterns of ordinary speech and the patterns of literary expression. "Dignitas," the Latin term for this quality, involves the basic notion that something is suited to something else, "dignus," its Latin root, being the word that denotes the suitability or fitness of one thing for another. Thus a feeling of mutual respect by two men for each other would be a "dignity," in the sense that the feeling is suited to their recognition of each other's humanity. It would by opposition be an indignity if one man had a feeling of contempt for a fellow man, since such a sentiment would not be suited to that sense of common humanity which all men share. A rhetorician could say that literary style would have dignity when the language of a thought was suited to the thought itself— a plain style for a plain thought, a figured style for an elevated thought, and so on. Indeed, dignity in literary style often meant no more than that, and perhaps that is what it always should mean. But in Latin rhetoric of the Republic, the Empire, and the European Middle Ages, the term dignity inevitably acquired some natural and influential sociological overtones. There was, for example, the speech of the people, ordinary speech, vulgar speech, on the one side, and learned speech, diplomatic speech, aristocratic speech, royal speech, on the other. This meant that literary style, the offspring of learning and politeness, would be deemed suitable, would be deemed to have dignity, when it was fitted to the patterns of educated speech of the court and university, and stood opposed to the patterns of ordinary, vulgar speech.

[76] *System of Oratory*, I, 366.

In this connection it is significant that the tropes and the figures, which were the main instruments for giving dignity to rhetorical style, were regarded as departures from something usual and common in speech, and were considered the embodiment of something unusual and uncommon.[77] What Ward did in his lectures on these instruments was to reflect this established state of affairs. He defined a trope as a word used outside of its common orbit of meaning. "A *Trope*, then," he observed, "as it has been usually defined, is, *the change of a word from its proper signification to some other with advantage*," and he indicated that he borrowed this definition from Quintilian.[78] Thus if one said that Hannibal defeated the Romans, one would be using the word "Hannibal," not in its accepted reference to one man, the distinguished Carthaginian general, but in a changed reference in which it meant "Hannibal and his army defeated the Romans," and this changed reference is called by the term synecdoche, in which the name of a part is used to stand for an entire thing.[79] The departure from ordinary usage in the case of a trope is of course at times a matter of plain necessity, as when a language does not yet have a vocabulary of literal terms to express all of the ideas and things that men want to discuss, and recourse must be had to metaphorical expression. And at other times such departures are a matter of emphasis, as when a given literal word will not impart to the expression of an idea the strength that could be imparted to it by a metaphor or metonymy. But beyond necessity and emphasis as motivations for the use of tropes there is the desire for beauty, and it is this latter desire that leads writers and speak-

[77] The trait which the tropes and the figures have in common, said Quintilian, is that "both involve a departure from the simple and straightforward method of expression coupled with a certain rhetorical excellence." See *Institutio Oratoria*, 9.1.3. (H. E. Butler's translation.)

[78] *System of Oratory*, I, 384. Italics are Ward's. He took this definition, he said, from Quintilian's *Institutio Oratoria*, 8.5, but the definition is actually found in 8.6.1. The *Rhetorica ad Herennium*, 4.31.42, uses the term "exornationes verborum" rather than the term "tropi," but otherwise it anticipates Quintilian's definition. It says: "They indeed [i.e., the *exornationes verborum*] all have this in common, that the language departs from the ordinary meaning of the words and is, with a certain grace, applied in another sense." (Harry Caplan's translation.)

[79] *System of Oratory*, I, 385.

ers to depart from the ordinary ways of speech and by doing so to achieve what the rhetoricians call dignity of style.[80] As for the figures, they involve even more strikingly the notion of a departure from the language of everyday life. There is a sense in which any particular form of language is a figure of thought, the form of language being as it were the figure that the thought cuts when it becomes visible or audible; "but rhetoricians," said Ward, "have restrained the sense of the word to such forms of speech, as differ from the more common and ordinary ways of expression; as the theatrical habits of actors, and their deportment on the stage, are different from their usual garb and behavior at other times." And he at once defined a figure in these words: "A *Figure* therefore, in the sense [in which] it is used by rhetoricians, is: *A mode of speaking different from, and more beautiful and emphatical, than the ordinary and usual way of expressing the same sense.*"[81]

The notion that dignity of style is achieved when a pattern of verbal expression repudiates the patterns of ordinary speech and suits itself to the patterns of learning and politeness was fully worked out by Ciceronian rhetoricians of the sixteenth and seventeenth centuries in their elaborate and endless analysis of each one of several hundred tropes and figures. Ward was more selective than many of his predecessors and contemporaries were, and accordingly his discussion of these departures from popular speech made a reasonably successful attempt to handle only the more basic and distinctive of them.

The tropes that he emphasized were metaphor, metonymy, synecdoche, and irony, and this list could hardly be curtailed by anyone seeking to handle the subject adequately. But in his lecture on the secondary tropes, he talked briefly of eight others, one of which was allegory, and there he indicated how numerous the tropes threatened to become whenever a desire to cover them in all their nuances got the better of good judgment. Ward acknowledged his indebtedness to Vossius when he defined metaphor as "*A trope, which changes words from their proper signification to*

[80] *Ibid.,* I, 388-390. Ward acknowledged that he followed Quintilian in setting forth these three reasons to explain why tropes were used in discourse. For Quintilian's discussion of this matter, see *Institutio Oratoria,* 8.6.6: "Id facimus, aut quia necesse est aut quia significantius est aut (ut dixi) quia decentius."

[81] *System of Oratory,* II, 33-34.

another different from it, by reason of some similitude between them."[82] And he partly envisaged the modern practice of analyzing metaphors into tenor and vehicle when he commented that this kind of trope involved three components, a thing, another thing to which the first is compared, and a likeness between them. We of course would think of the first thing as the tenor, the second as the vehicle, and the likeness between them as the meaning.[83] When Ward turned later to synecdoche and spoke of it as the trope produced by putting the whole for a part, or the part for a whole, he talked briefly of universal wholes, essential wholes, and integral wholes, and he took the occasion to illustrate the third of these by restating the favorite thesis of the Ciceronian rhetoricians that "rhetoric is an integral whole in respect to the four parts that comprise it, namely, invention, disposition, elocution, and pronunciation."[84]

Not long after this remark was made, Ward brought the last of his five lectures on the tropes to an end, and entered upon the first of five lectures on the figures. Perhaps the best way to indicate the shift in his own interest as he went from the one to the other subject is to say that he had remarked earlier in differentiating them that *"Tropes* are chiefly designed to represent our thoughts, but *Figures* our passions."[85] This same idea he repeated in his first lecture on the figures,[86] and he gave it heavy emphasis as he went on. His method, like that of the *Rhetorica ad Herennium* and Quintilian before him, was to divide this part of elocution into two classes, verbal figures and figures of sentences,[87] each of which he discussed with more frugality than his contemporaries usually showed. "The difference between these classes consists in this," he said, "that in the former, if you alter the words, or sometimes only the situation of them, you destroy the *Figure*; but in the latter the *Figure* remains, whatever words are made use of;

[82] *Ibid.,* I, 399. Ward's note refers to Vossius, *Oratoriarum Institutionum Libri Sex*, 4.6.1. The italics are Ward's.

[83] For an influential analysis of metaphor, see I. A. Richards, *The Philosophy of Rhetoric* (New York, 1936), Lecture V.

[84] *System of Oratory*, II, 3.

[85] *Ibid.,* I, 384. Italics are Ward's.

[86] *Ibid.,* II, 37.

[87] See *Rhetorica ad Herennium*, 4.13.18, and Quintilian's *Institutio Oratoria*, 9.1.17.

or in what manner soever the order of them is changed."[88] Ward made this distinction clear by remarking that epistrophe, as one of the verbal figures, consists in ending two or more successive clauses or sentences with the same word, whereas apostrophe, as one of the other kind, comes into being when the orator changes the direction of his speech and suddenly addresses himself not to the audience as a whole but to some special group within it or to some absent person.

We need not follow Ward through his discussion of these two classes of figures, although the dryness of his method can be suggested by remarking that he mentioned and discussed eighteen verbal figures in one lecture and nineteen figures of sentences in three lectures. A feature of his treatment of the latter subject was that six of these figures were considered to be especially suited to proof, and the remaining thirteen to moving the passions.[89] One of these thirteen, aporia or doubt, was described by Ward as a debate between the mind and itself, characterized by hesitation, by the stating of several lines of thought, and by the failing to come to a fixed resolution. Thus modern criticism could say with accuracy that the rising of Shakespeare's *Hamlet* to the final crisis is an example of the figure of aporia, and that the whole play, as a movement from certainty into doubt and from doubt into certainty, is a complex application of the figure of aporia working within the wider figure of antimetabole.

One structural disproportion in the Ciceronian doctrine of elocution must be noted as we approach Ward's next five lectures, in which he began to deal with the second main part of elocution, and took up first the concept of the plain, middle, and grand styles. Although widely recognized throughout Latin rhetoric, this concept derived its chief sanctions from the *Rhetorica ad Herennium*, from the *Orator*, and *De Oratore* of Cicero, and from

[88] *System of Oratory*, ii, 46-47.

[89] The six figures suited to proof are prolepsis or anticipation, hypobole or subjection, anacoinosis or communication, epitrope or concession, parabole or similitude, and antithesis or opposition. The last of these included oxymoron (see Lecture 32). The thirteen figures suited to moving the passions are epanorthosis or correction, paralepsis or omission, parrhesia or reprehension, aparithmesis or enumeration, exergasia or exposition, hypotyposis or imagery, aporia or doubt, aposiopesis or concealment, erotesis or interrogation, ecphonesis or exclamation, epiphonema or acclamation, apostrophe or address, and prosopopeia or fiction of a person (see Lectures 33 and 34).

the *Institutio Oratoria* of Quintilian.[90] These treatises intended the distinction to mean that different subjects require different treatments, and that true excellence in oratory consists not in cultivating the grand style at the expense of the plain but in being always able to command the three styles as the subjects demand. In the classical view, great oratory was as much at home in one of these styles as in another, and, since each style had its own particular function to perform, it would be the essence of bad oratory to use any style for a purpose that was unsuited to it. When Cicero said that the plain style is best for proving, the middle style best for pleasing, and the grand style best for persuading,[91] he certainly was counting on the possibility that a plain logical statement could achieve the distinction of being considered great oratory. But the attention which Latin rhetoric could not restrain itself from giving to the tropes and the figures somehow seemed to belie the theory that oratory in the plain style had a real place in rhetorical literature. In other words, what Latin rhetoric implied by the very abundance of its emphasis upon the tropes and figures as instruments of beauty in discourse was much more weighty than what it said when it allowed plainness in style to be on occasion the criterion of true excellence in oratory. Nowadays, proper oratory is carelessly considered to have genuine associations only with grandiloquent expression. An oration in the plain style is almost a contradiction in terms. In fact, some critics have to go so far as to say that the Gettysburg Address is not an oration at all, but a work of literature, and if they were pressed to justify this opinion, they would contend that only the figures and ornate style should be called oratory, while the simple style should be dignified by a fairer term. It is obvious that this present attitude has descended from that part of Latin rhetoric which gave the tropes and figures such an interminable emphasis as to discredit by implication the rhetorical function of plainness.

Ward did nothing to anticipate and prevent this modern confusion when he gave the three styles his specific attention. In fact,

[90] See *Rhetorica ad Herennium*, 4.8.11-16; *Orator*, 5.20-32, 21.69-112; *De Oratore*, 3.45.177, 3.52.199, 3.55.212; Quintilian, *Institutio Oratoria*, 12.10.58-68. For an invaluable documentation of the concept of the three styles in Greek and Latin rhetoric, see Professor Harry Caplan's translation of the *Rhetorica ad Herennium*, pp. 252-253.

[91] *Orator*, 21.69.

it did not apparently occur to him that his ten previous lectures on the tropes and the figures shouted down what he said in his single lecture on the plain style. But aside from this shortsightedness, which he had inherited from the ancients themselves, his treatment of the three styles is faithful and accurate. He devoted one preliminary lecture to the different characters of style as they are determined by differences between one man and another in respect not only to their personal habits of thought, imagination, and memory, but also to the impersonal influences of geography, nationality, historical situation, and language. "But the cheif distinction of stile," he said as he brought that lecture to a close, "arises from the different subjects, or matter of discourse."[92] It is in considering the adaptation of style to subject matter, he explained, that rhetoricians have evolved the concept of the three styles; and he enumerated these styles as "the *low* or *plain* stile, the *middle* or *temperate*, and the *lofty* or *sublime*," these precise terms being borrowed, as he acknowledged, from Bernard Lamy's *Art of Speaking*.[93] He found an instance of the plain style in the *Spectator*; and in outlining what the plain style required in the way of purity, perspicuity, composition, and dignity, he emphasized among other things that care should be taken in it to use the tropes and the figures cautiously. But he did not intimate that the plain style might in fact be the characteristic rhetorical style of the modern world, although he thought it well fitted to epistles, dialogues, philosophical dissertations, and other discourses not addressed to the passions. The middle style has fine thoughts as its distinguishing mark, he said in his lecture on that subject; and he paused to contrast it to the plain style, which reflects plain thoughts, and to the lofty style, which expresses the elevated and the sublime. Longinus became one of his chief authorities when the sublime style occupied him for his next two lectures. "Noble and lofty thoughts," remarked Ward, "are principally those, which either relate to divine objects; or such things as among men are generally esteemed the greatest and most illustrious."[94] Among the latter Ward mentioned power, wisdom, courage, and beneficence. He added the profound remark that the true sublime is consistent with the greatest plainness and simplicity of expression; but, as if this were not an admission that

[92] *System of Oratory*, II, 126.   [93] *Ibid.*, II, 126. See above, n. 30.
[94] *Ibid.*, II, 169.

sublimity and the plain style should be treated as one, he turned in his next lecture to the kind of language that the lofty style requires, and here he reviewed once more the characteristics of elegance, composition, and dignity, stressing under the latter head that a proper use of the tropes and the figures was a most necessary part of grandeur in style. In view of his having cited Fénelon's *Dialogues on Eloquence* at the beginning of his first lecture on the concept of the three styles, and in view of his having there approved not only of Fénelon's distaste for the pompous and luxuriant elocution of the youthful Cicero but also of his preference for the more correct and nervous style of Cicero's maturity,[95] it is difficult to understand why Ward should not have considered the *Dialogues on Eloquence* to be a better and a more modern approach to the problem of sublimity in oratory and literature than he could have found in Longinus or Quintilian, and why he should not therefore have altered correspondingly his whole treatment of the styles, the tropes, and the figures.

Two points should be briefly mentioned in taking note of the lecture which Ward delivered on wit and humor immediately after his lectures on sublimity. The first is that he considered Cicero to have provided the incentive for rhetoricians to be interested in this topic, and to have furnished the two main heads under which it should be properly discussed. In other words, he linked his lecture to Cicero's *De Oratore*, and like Cicero he divided wit into *cavillatio*, that is, continued wit or humor, and *dicacitas*, concise wit or jesting.[96] But it should be emphasized as a second point that he cited examples of wit from such modern sources as the *Guardian* no less than from the classics, and at the beginning of this lecture he quoted Locke as having described wit justly and accurately in the following words:

It lies most in the assemblage of ideas, and puting those together with quickness and variety, wherein can be found any resemblance or congruity, thereby to make up pleasant pictures and agreable visions in the fancy. Which therefore is so agreable to all people, because its beauty appears at first, and there is required no labor of thought to examine what truth or reason

---

[95] *Ibid.*, II, 113. Ward's marginal note at this point refers to "*Dial. of Eloq.* p. 70." The reference is to p. 70 of Stevenson's translation. See above, pp. 93-94.
[96] *System of Oratory*, II, 199. See *De Oratore*, 2.54.218.

there is in it. The mind, without looking any farther, rests satisfied with the agreableness of the picture, and the gaiety of the fancy.[97]

Ward concluded his lengthy discussion of elocution by giving six lectures on the style to be used in epistles, dialogues, history writing, and oratory. What he did in effect was to show which of the three styles was suited to each of these types of literature. He repeated his earlier statement that epistles and dialogues were best adapted to the plain style, since each is close to conversation. As for historical writing, it may not properly be part of an orator's province, he said, but "it has so near a relation to it, that in the opinion of Cicero, an orator is best qualified to write a good history."[98] Ward observed later that "Cicero has given us the whole art of composing history, in a very short and comprehensive manner." And he quoted to his audience at Gresham College a long passage in English from Cicero's *De Oratore*, in which Cicero reduces the writing of history to two laws, the first being that the historian must not dare to tell anything but the truth, and the second, that he must dare to let the whole truth be told.[99] It is of course in carrying out these laws in terms of subject matter, arrangement, and style that history needs the assistance of the art of rhetoric, and Ward devoted attention to each of these three rhetorical considerations, and to such other requisites of history as the narration of facts, the reflection upon them by way of interpretation, the reporting of speeches, and the management of digression. In connection with his discussion of the style of historical writing, he declared that "in general, an historical stile is said to be of a middle nature, between that of a poet and an orator, differing from both not only in ornamental parts, but likewise in the common idioms and forms of expression."[100] What

[97] *System of Oratory*, ii, 195-196. See Locke, *An Essay concerning Human Understanding*, Book 2, Ch. 11, §2. Ward gave this quotation in italics; he omitted a passage in which Locke contrasted wit and judgment; and he altered Locke's text in three or four minor respects. Except for the italics, I have given the quotation in Ward's punctuation, language, and spelling.

[98] *System of Oratory*, ii, 230-231. See *De Oratore*, 2.9.36.

[99] *System of Oratory*, ii, 235-236. Ward quoted in English the whole passage from *De Oratore*, 2.15.62-64, beginning "Nam quis nescit, primam esse historiae legem," and ending "et sine sententiarum forensium aculeis persequendum est."

[100] *System of Oratory*, ii, 289.

makes the historian differ from the orator, he later observed, is that the orator must be master, not of the middle style alone but of the three styles, and thus his art is the one truly comprehensive art in the whole field of nonpoetic discourse. After defining the orator's task as that of proving what he asserts, that of representing his assertions in an agreeable light, and that of presenting them so as to move the passions, Ward said:

> Now each of these parts of an orator's province require [sic] a different stile. The low stile is most proper for proof and information. Because he has no other view here, but to represent things to the mind in the plainest light, as they really are in themselves, without coloring or ornament. The middle stile is most suited for pleasure and entertainment, because it consists of smooth and well turned periods, harmonious numbers, with florid and bright figures. But the sublime is necessary in order to sway and influence the passions.[101]

Soon after uttering these words, Ward brought his lectures on elocution to an end, and he turned next to pronunciation, another of the great arts of the Ciceronian system. This art required four lectures, one on oral delivery in general, and three on the particular aspects of voice and gesture. Inasmuch as a group of rhetoricians during the eighteenth century severed this art from the body of Ciceronian rhetoric, and made it into an independent pursuit, as if the part could by mere dictate assume the functions of the whole, it will need special attention in my history, and I propose to devote my next chapter to it, as I indicated earlier. Thus a discussion of what Ward had to say about it would merely anticipate the things that are to be considered later. In omitting to review this part of his program, however, I feel it necessary to mention that he rested his doctrine not only upon ancient sources but also upon certain modern works which like his own lectures were devoted to a careful reconstruction of the full classical view of the art of oral delivery. Thus while he borrowed many precepts about this part of rhetoric from Cicero's *De Oratore* and Quintilian's *Institutio Oratoria*, and occasionally referred to the *Rhetorica ad Herennium*, he counted also for assistance upon Fénelon's *Dialogues on Eloquence*, upon Vossius's *Oratoriarum*

[101] *Ibid.*, II, 300. These words echo Cicero's *Orator*, of course. See above, n. 91.

Institutionum Libri Sex, upon Louis de Cressolles's *Vacationes Autumnales, sive de Perfecta Actione et Pronunciatione Libri III,* and upon the third edition of an anonymous English pamphlet entitled *Some Rules for Speaking and Action,* which in turn had borrowed heavily and without acknowledgment from Michel Le Faucheur's *Traitté de l'action de l'orateur, ou de la Prononciation et du geste,* as translated into English around 1702 under the title, *An Essay Upon The Action of an Orator.*[102] Cressolles and Le Faucheur are the primary modern sources of much of what eighteenth-century Englishmen were to declare and endlessly repeat on the subject of voice and gesture in speaking and acting, as my next chapter will demonstrate in detail. Thus Ward was quite abreast of his times in respect to his learning upon this subject. But he was opposed to his times in refusing to make voice and gesture the sole ingredients of rhetorical theory, and that refusal provides an important instance in which he may have followed the ancients not because they were venerable but because they were right.

Ward's only remaining lecture to interest us here is that on memory, although the three later lectures, which brought the series to an end by discussing how to listen, to read, to write, and to imitate, must be acknowledged to have an auxiliary connection

---

[102] Ward referred to Cressolles's *Vacationes Autumnales* four times in the course of his four lectures on pronunciation. See *System of Oratory,* II, 315, 325, 327, 358. On two occasions he quoted from *Some Rules for Speaking and Action. . . . In a Letter to a Friend,* each time with full acknowledgments. See *System of Oratory,* II, 333, 375. The third edition of *Some Rules* (London, 1716) conforms to the pagination indicated in Ward's references. The earlier editions (London, 1715, 1716) do not. Copies of the second and third editions are held at the Huntington Library. I have not been able to locate a copy of the first edition, but it may safely be assigned to 1715, inasmuch as the "Letter" as printed in the third edition is dated Feb. 4, 1715-16 (p. 32), and inasmuch as the Preface of that edition says (p. 5) that the work was first written and printed "about Six Months ago." I have not examined copies of the fourth edition (London, 1732), nor of the edition at Dublin around 1750. For further details, see below, Ch. 4, pp. 190-192.

A comparison of *Some Rules* with the English translation of Le Faucheur's *Traitté* will immediately establish the fact that the former borrows heavily and without acknowledgment from the latter.

For a discussion of the problem of dating the first edition of the English translation of Le Faucheur's *Traitté,* see my article, "Sources of the Elocutionary Movement in England: 1700-1748." *The Quarterly Journal of Speech,* XLV (February 1959), 6-8. See also below, Ch. 4, pp. 165-168.

with eighteenth-century rhetoric. Memory, as one of the five great arts of the Ciceronian tradition, is not considered by Ward to belong to rhetoric in any organic way. In fact, in his third lecture, he did not include it among the parts of rhetoric, and he did not mention it when he mentioned the parts that rhetoric has as an integral whole.[103] But his veneration for the ancients was so strong, and his desire to recapture the full outline of classical rhetoric so absorbing, that he decided to say something at last about memory, even though some of the best modern writers and Aristotle himself would have supported him in not doing so, on the theory that memory is of concern to all arts, not to oratory alone. Its value to oratory, said Ward, is that, since every "discourse pronounced in public, must either be spoken by memory, or read,"[104] and since reading allows little room for warmth and vehemence, the orator must speak *memoriter* in order to give proper tone and modulation to his voice and to accompany his words with proper gestures. But some good judges, he observed, have recommended that orators should not memorize every word of their speeches, but should get each subject well in mind, and prepare a plan for its presentation, and even design certain chief figures and expressions for its delivery, while leaving room "to add what may occasionally be suggested from present circumstances, when they come to speak."[105] As for cultivating the memory, Ward gave some prudential advice about the need for understanding what is being memorized, and for committing to memory one part of a discourse at a time. At length he came to the question whether the natural memory could be improved by using a contrived memory system, and he answered it by referring to classical rhetoric. Remarking that some "antient writers speak of an artificial memory, and lay down rules for attaining it,"[106] he invoked the authority of the *Rhetorica ad Herennium* and Cicero's *De Oratore* on this point, and he proceeded to explain the ancient practice of contriving a system of places in the mind, and storing each place with an image, and fixing upon the image some idea to be remembered, so that by mentally visiting the places, the speaker would recall first the image and then the

[103] *System of Oratory*, I, 29; II, 3.

[104] *Ibid.*, II, 381.

[105] *Ibid.*, II, 383. Ward may have Fénelon in mind as one of these good judges. See Howell, *Fénelon's Dialogues on Eloquence*, pp. 105-110.

[106] *System of Oratory*, II, 389.

idea concerned.[107] This memory system is ingenious, but the question would always arise whether it would not be more difficult to memorize its details than it would be to memorize directly what one needed to recall on a given occasion. Ward saw this difficulty plainly enough, and he conceded at the end of his lecture that perhaps the best way to gain a good memory was by constant exercise in direct memorization.

In taking leave of Ward, we should mention that three honors were paid his *System of Oratory* within fifty years after its publication. One honor consisted in its being quoted at great length on the whole subject of rhetorical invention by John Walker in the third and later editions of his popular work, *A Rhetorical Grammar, or Course of Lessons in Elocution.*[108] Another honor involved its being cited as a leading authority on such subjects as Oratory, Elocution, Figure, Gesture, and Voice in Oratory in Ephraim Chambers's *Cyclopaedia: or, an Universal Dictionary of Arts and Sciences,* as that work was constituted in the five-volume edition appearing at London in 1788-1789. Indeed, the article on Oratory in that edition is admiringly credited to "the learned Dr. Ward," and is acknowledged to be based upon his first English lecture in the series at Gresham College.[109] A third

[101] See *Rhetorica ad Herennium,* 3.16.28-40, *De Oratore,* 2.85.350-360. See also Quintilian, *Institutio Oratoria,* 11.2.1-51. For a discussion of various explanations of the ancient memory system by English rhetoricians before the time of Ward, see my *Logic and Rhetoric in England,* pp. 85-87, 88-89, 96-98, 103-104, 143, 207, 317, 341.

[108] The third edition appeared at London in 1801. The following notice appeared in the Second American Edition (Boston, 1822), pp. 302-303: "As rules for invention, or, as Dr. Priestly more properly calls it, *recollection,* are established by such good reasons, and on so respectable authority, I shall present the student with a large extract from the System of Oratory of the learned Dr. Ward, professor of Gresham College. And as this book has long been out of print, and is scarcely to be got, I flatter myself I shall make my reader no unacceptable present, by giving him the learned professor's lectures on *Invention,* or that part of rhetoric which treats on the method of finding out arguments for the proof of what is proposed." This edition proceeded to devote its final eighty pages to the extract from Ward's *System of Oratory.*

The first edition of *A Rhetorical Grammar* appeared at London in 1785; the second at London in 1787. Neither of these editions contains the extract from Ward.

[109] In respect to its treatment of the subjects of Rhetoric and Oratory, the sixth edition of Chambers's *Cyclopaedia* (London, 1750) offers an interesting

honor paid to the *System of Oratory* came from its being reduced to a summary in eighteen double-columned folio pages and given currency not only as a pamphlet entitled *Treatise on Oratory* but also as the article on Oratory in the third volume of the second and third editions of William Henry Hall's *The New Encyclopaedia*.[110] A note affixed to the end of that article reads as follows:

> Upon a review of the respective authors on this subject, we have made choice of Dr. Ward's Treatise, conceiving it best adapted to the purposes and oeconomy of this work. We have omitted all the superfluous definitions and examples, and made such occasional remarks and additions as we conceived would best tend to elucidate this treatise.[111]

---

contrast to the expanded edition published in 1788-1789 under the supervision of Abraham Rees. In 1750, Oratory is briefly defined as the art of speaking well, and is said to be the synonym of Rhetoric, the only difference between the terms being that the first is of Latin, the second of Greek origin. Rhetoric is given a somewhat more substantial treatment in that edition, however, and is discussed not only with reference to definitions by Lord Bacon and Vossius but also with reference to the notion that Rhetoric and Oratory differ from each other as theory differs from practice, "the *rhetorician* being he who describes the rules of eloquence; and the orator he who uses them to advantage and speaks elegantly." In 1788-1789, the *Cyclopaedia*, as enlarged by Rees, gives Rhetoric very brief treatment, without reference to Bacon or Vossius, and deals at length with Oratory, citing Ward as the primary authority, and using here the same definitions from Bacon and Vossius that had appeared in 1750 in the entry on Rhetoric. Plainly Ward's *System of Oratory* is responsible for this shift in emphasis.

[110] The title page reads: "The New Encyclopaedia; or, Modern Universal Dictionary of Arts and Sciences, On a New and Improved Plan. In which all the . . . sciences are arranged into complete systems, the arts digested into distinct treatises, and philosophical subjects introduced in separate dissertations. . . . Including all the material information that is contained in Chambers's Cyclopaedia, the Encyclopaedia Britannica, and the French Encyclopedie. . . . By William Henry Hall. . . . The Third Edition. . . . London, Printed for C. Cooke [1797?]." This work was originally published around 1788 under the title, *The New Royal Encyclopaedia*.

The Princeton University Library holds a pamphlet entitled *Treatise on Oratory; Or, The Art of Speaking well upon any Subject, in order to persuade*. This pamphlet is a bound gathering of the pages of the article on Oratory in Hall's *The New Encyclopaedia*, Vol. III.

[111] I do not know the identity of the author of this note. The second and third editions of Hall's *Encyclopaedia* are said on their title pages to have been "Revised, corrected, and enlarged, with considerable Additions, Improve-

It is certain, of course, that Ward's lectures on oratory at Gresham College exerted a continuing influence through the abridgment that this anonymous scholar made of them for the pages of Hall's *New Encyclopaedia*, and it is equally certain that Ward's reputation as a learned interpreter of classical rhetoric suffered no impairment by the attention given him in Walker's *Rhetorical Grammar* and in Chambers's famous *Cyclopaedia*. But, even so, the *System of Oratory* as a full separate work was not enough in demand during the latter half of the eighteenth century to warrant its being given a second edition. Indeed, when it first appeared in 1759, it already belonged not to its time or to the immediate future but to the past. The new rhetoric then in the making was not in the mood to be satisfied with the vanishing tradition which had cast its venerable spell upon Ward.

---

ments, and modern Discoveries, by Thomas Augustus Lloyd, Assisted by Gentlemen of Scientific Knowledge."

After the preceding detailed account of Ward's handling of the five great arts of Ciceronian rhetoric, I do not need to explain further how these arts were treated by other Ciceronian rhetoricians of the eighteenth century. But at least it must be emphasized that Ward was not alone in seeking to keep alive that hallowed and remarkable tradition, and that his colleagues in the enterprise ranged all the way from those who had Cicero's entire system in mind to those who were interested only in certain parts of it. A few comments upon these colleagues will serve to bring this chapter to an end.

A close second to Ward in the ranks of energetic and scholarly British Ciceronian rhetoricians of the eighteenth century was John Holmes, master of the public grammar school in Holt, Norfolk. Holmes shared with Ward a zealous enthusiasm for the educational value of all the essential arts of Ciceronian rhetoric, and he also had reason to participate with Ward in respecting the name of Gresham. The grammar school in Holt, where Holmes taught for many years in the central period of the seventeen-hundreds, had been founded by Sir John Gresham, uncle of the founder of Gresham College.[112] It was Sir John, indeed, who had taught Sir Thomas some of the intricacies of a merchant's occupation in sixteenth-century England, and who may therefore be considered a kind of foster parent of Sir Thomas's own great riches and subsequent benefactions. An eighteenth-century advertisement described in the following words the school which Sir John had founded some two hundred years before:

> At *Holt* in *Norfolk*, in a large commodious House, pleasantly situated, Young Gentlemen are Boarded, and completely qualified for all manner of Business, in LATIN, GREEK, FRENCH, ARITHMETIC in all its Parts, *Book keeping* by Double Entry, called MERCHANTS ACCOUNTS, the USE of the GLOBES, and WRITING in all the Hands used in *Great-Britain*.[113]

[112] See *The Dictionary of National Biography*, s.v. Gresham, Sir John; Gresham, Sir Richard; Gresham, Sir Thomas.

[113] This advertisement appears on the page following the Index in Holmes's own *The Art of Rhetoric Made Easy* (London, 1755). My quotation follows the punctuation of the original. At the end of the advertisement is a statement that the school is kept by Holmes *"and proper Assistance."*

Holmes himself was not only the headmaster of Holt but an author as well. The advertisement just quoted falls at the end of a list of nine books which his publishers, C. Hitch and L. Hawes, had brought out for him, and which were declared to be on sale at their establishment, the Red Lion, in Paternoster Row, London.[114] Of these his *New Grammar of the Latin Tongue* and his *Greek Grammar* were popular with schoolmasters everywhere. He himself offered testimony to this general effect when on one occasion he thanked the Visitors of Holt School for their kind recommendation and encouragement of the use of his books, and when he indicated that the Visitors had aided him within a few years in selling "about *Six Thousand* Latin Grammars, and near *Four Thousand* Greek Grammars."[115] He added that *The Art of Rhetoric Made Easy* had a proportionate popularity, but he gave no figures to show us how widely it had sold.

The latter work, however, has more concern for us than any of Holmes's other textbooks. It appeared in a first edition at London in 1739, and in a second edition at the same place in 1755, just four years before the date of publication of Ward's lectures at Gresham College. The second edition, to which my present discussion will mainly refer, has a title page that not only describes the book in general outline but also offers to modern readers a glimpse into the mind of an earnest and devoted teacher of two hundred years ago. It reads as follows:

The Art of Rhetoric Made Easy: or, The Elements of Oratory Briefly stated, and fitted for the Practice of The Studious Youth of *Great-Britain* and *Ireland*: In Two Books.

The First comprehending the Principles of that excellent Art, conformable to, and supported by the Authority of the most accurate Orators and Rhetoricians, both Ancient and Modern, *viz.*

---

[114] The list, exclusive of *The Art of Rhetoric Made Easy*, contains the following titles: 1) *A New Grammar of the Latin Tongue*; 2) *The Greek Grammar*; 3) *The History of England*; 4) *Rhetorick Epitomiz'd; or, The Principles of that whole Art briefly exemplified on a Copper-Plate, engrav'd by Mr. Pine*; 5) *The Key; or, Questions to the Latin and Greek Grammars*; 6) *The Grammarian's Arithmetic; or, A Compendious Treatise of the Art of Cyphering*; 7) *The French Grammar*; 8) *The Grammarian's Geography and Astronomy, Ancient and Modern*.

[115] *The Art of Rhetoric Made Easy* (London, 1755), sig. a4v.

Isocrates,	Farnaby,
Aristotle,	Butler,
Cicero,	Smith,
Dionysius *Halicarnass.*	Walker,
Quintilian,	Burton,
Vossius,	Blackwall,
Petrus Ramus,	Lowe,
Cyp. Soarius,	Rollin,
Aud. Talaeus,	A.B. of Cambray,
Dugard,	Mess. de Port-Royal, *&c.*

The Whole being distinguished into what is necessary to be *repeated*, and what may be made only Matter of *Observation*.

The Second containing the Substance of Longinus's celebrated Treatise on the Sublime.

In Both which all *Technical Terms* are fully explained, with their *Derivations*, and proper *Examples* applied to demonstrate and illustrate all the Tropes, Figures, and Fine Turns, that are to be met with, or imitated, either in the Scriptures, Classics, or other polite Writings as well *Oratorical* as *Poetical*.

The Second Impression Corrected and Improved.

By John Holmes, *Master of the Publick* Grammar-School, *in* Holt, Norfolk.

London: Printed for and sold by C. Hitch, and L. Hawes, in *Pater-noster Row,* and the Booksellers in *Cambridge, Norwich* and *Dublin.*

MDCCLV.

This elaborate description will be dismissed as pretentious and overcareful only by those who expect the past to conform to the present. In actual fact, title pages of learned works in the seventeenth and eighteenth centuries were prevailingly detailed and explicit. Holmes used his in the present instance to acquaint teachers with the contents of his work, and anybody who takes the pains to read his rhetorical doctrine will see that his title did not mislead or exaggerate.

In his Preface he admitted the existence of many rhetorics like his own, but he felt that not one of them was adapted to the capacity or fitted to the use of students in grammar schools, "especially in this Day, when School-Boys are expected to be led, sooth'd, and entic'd to their Studies by the Easiness and Pleasure of the Practice, rather than by Force or harsh Discipline drove, as in Days of Yore."[116] He then said that he proposed to remedy these defects by adhering to the following plan:

First, That we might always keep in View the glorious and extensive Plan of the *Ancients,* strict Care has been taken to follow their Method entirely, and (by leaving out the copious Parts of their Works, which were principally design'd as Models for *Men* and *Proficients,* tho' jumbled together by modern *Rhetoricians* among their Precepts for the Use of *Boys*) to extract from them all the *Terms* we make use [*sic*] in our Divisions and Subdivisions of the Art. . . .

Secondly, That Nothing might be wanting that's necessary for the young Scholar to be here inform'd of, or what perchance he cannot obtain elsewhere without abundance [*sic*] more Trouble, I have not only inserted those *Tropes, Figures,* and *Repetitions,* which the learned and judicious Mr. *Blackwall* with his Followers call the *Chief* and *Principal,* but likewise all others, great and little, the less useful as well as the more useful; however with this Caution, that they're *distributed* according to their several Degrees of Merit and Distinction. So that, *Young Gentlemen,* you'll meet with here about 250 *Figures,* &c. That is all, and indeed many more than all that are treated of in any other One Book, as may readily be perceived by the *Index.* . . .

Thirdly, As to *Method,* That a proper Distinction may be made between Things of ordinary Use and such as are rare and extraordinary, I propose Nothing *to be got by Heart* but the *Principal Matters* which are printed in the largest Character, the Lines set at greater Distance, and mark'd with *A, B, C,* &c. All which should be brought into Practice and explained by the *Examples annex'd,* as the Learner goes on. . . .

Thus much concerning *Book I.* which when I had finished, there still seemed to be something wanting towards perfecting *a Compleat Compendium of Rhetoric,* and that was, To point out to the young Student *The Height and Excellency of good Writings.* To perform which, I humbly conceive Nothing could be more properly introduced than the Substance of the Cele-

[116] *Ibid.,* sig. a2r. Here and below I reverse the style of Holmes's Preface in respect to the use of roman and italic type.

brated *Longinus on the Sublime*. This therefore I have proposed for *Book II*. and to be, as it were, a Crown to the Whole.[117]

In carrying out this plan, Holmes defined rhetoric as "the Art of *Speaking* or *Writing well and ornamentally* on any Subject," and he then proceeded not only to give it the function of instructing, persuading, and pleasing in any field whatever, whether moral, philosophical, or divine, but also to make it consist of invention, disposition, elocution, and pronunciation.[118] As he discussed each of these divisions, he designated every important idea by placing in the margin to the left of it a capital letter of the alphabet, and thus in all he used every letter except J and V. The result was that he reduced the whole doctrine of Ciceronian rhetoric to twenty-four principles, four of which concerned its definition, its divisions, and its first part, invention, whereas three concerned disposition, thirteen concerned elocution, three concerned pronunciation, and the final one lumped pronunciation and elocution together in a mercifully short doggerel verse summarizing the whole. These twenty-four principles were presumably to be memorized by the students. If Holmes and other teachers were successful in enforcing this requirement, the students at Holt and elsewhere would have learned by heart that arguments for instruction, persuasion, and pleasure on any subject whatever are grounded in reason, morals, and affections, that orations should be arranged into the exordium, narration, proposition, confirmation, refutation, and peroration, that written themes should be arranged into proposition, reason, confirmation, simile, example, testimony, and conclusion, that elocution consists in achieving grammatical propriety, elegance, and dignity, the last of which involves the use of tropes, figures, and beautiful turns, and finally that pronunciation requires the proper control of the voice and the body in delivering a discourse to an audience.

Holmes's text was supplemented throughout by footnotes in fine print and double columns, and in these he cited at one time or another each of the twenty authorities whom he had listed on his title page. These references, many of them actual quotations, lent depth and extension to the twenty-four principles. Aristotle's

[117] *Ibid.*, sig. a2v-a4v. Holmes begins line 19 with a lower-case "t."
[118] *Ibid.*, pp. 1-2. Italics are Holmes's.

Rhetoric was quoted in Greek and English on the definition of rhetoric, on the three kinds of oratorical topics, on the affections of the mind, and on the distinction between simile and metaphor.[119] Cicero was cited over and over again on similar points of doctrine, as was Quintilian.[120] Moreover, two works by Isocrates, *Nicocles or the Cyprian* and *Against the Sophists*, received quotation in Greek and English, as did *On Literary Composition* and *On the Ancient Orators* by Dionysius of Halicarnassus.[121] Among more recent authorities, Holmes emphasized particularly his use of Ramus, Talaeus, Soarez, Vossius, Fénelon, Charles Butler, William Dugard, John Smith, Obadiah Walker, William Walker, Anthony Blackwall, and Nicholas Burton.[122]

[119] *Ibid.*, pp. 2-3, 7-8, 13, 27. See also p. 29, where Aristotle is referred to but not quoted. The *De Rhetorica ad Alexandrum*, ascribed to Aristotle by Holmes, is also quoted in Greek and English, pp. 16-17, on the parts of the classical oration.

[120] Holmes attributed the *Rhetorica ad Herennium* to Cicero, and he borrowed from that treatise as follows: in a reference to the outline of a whole legal case, p. 10; in an enumeration of the parts of the classical oration, p. 18; in an enumeration of the three parts of elocution, p. 25; in a reference to *collocatio*, pp. 25-26; in a reference to the parts of *pronuntiatio*, p. 76; and in a reference to the countenance in delivery, p. 78.

Cicero's *De Oratore* is cited by Holmes as follows: on the nature of the orator's power, pp. 2, 3; on the need for the orator to be a good man, p. 12; on the need for the orator to feel the emotions that he would arouse, p. 14; on the analogy between garments and metaphorical expression, p. 27; on faults of tropes, p. 29; on the several abilities required in an orator, p. 74; on the proper variation of the voice, p. 76; and on the pre-eminence of action in delivery, p. 77.

Cicero's other works to be silently or openly used by Holmes are *De Inventione*, *Orator*, *De Partitione Oratoria*, and *Topica*. See Holmes, pp. 4, 7, 11.

As for Quintilian's *Institutio Oratoria*, Holmes silently paraphrased it in the opening words of his dedicatory epistle, as can be seen by comparing his "Quoniam Naturâ tenacissimi sumus omnes eorum . . ." with the *Institutio Oratoria*, 1.1.5; and he referred openly to it for confirmation or elaboration of points of doctrine as follows: pp. 3, 4, 7, 8-9, 9-10, 18-20, 21-23, 25, 26, 27, 28, 29, 30, 74-75, 76, 78.

[121] See Holmes, pp. 2, 25-27.

[122] See Holmes as follows: for Ramus, pp. 3, 4, 6; for Talaeus, pp. 28, 78; for Soarez, pp. 2, 7, 29-31, 75; for Vossius, pp. 14, 78; for Fénelon, pp. 12, 14, 48, 74, 79; for Butler, pp. 76, 77, 78; for Dugard, pp. 76, 77; for Smith, p. 67; and for Obadiah Walker, pp. 6-7. Holmes's use of William Walker is men-

The second book of Holmes's treatise presents a digest of Longinus's *On the Sublime* in a series of nine letters from Holmes himself to an unidentified correspondent, addressed only as "Sir." From the first letter it appears that Holmes had previously borrowed his correspondent's copy of Gabriel de Petra's Greek text and Latin translation of Longinus, and was then engaged in comparing it with the second edition of the more recent Greek text and Latin translation by Zachary Pearce, an English scholar and ecclesiastic, who had also published an edition of Cicero's *De Oratore*.[123] The implication is that Holmes's digest is the result of his comparative study of the versions by de Petra and Pearce, although there were already in existence four English translations of Longinus, and he may also have drawn upon one or more of them.[124] Holmes proceeded to present a brief summary of each of the forty-four chapters of Longinus's treatise and to illustrate the various points by quoting Greek, Latin, and English verses.

---

tioned below, n. 139. For a discussion of his use of Blackwall and Burton, see below, pp. 138-141.

[123] Since the second Book of Holmes's *The Art of Rhetoric Made Easy* in the edition of 1755 has a separate title page and separate pagination, it will be necessary in referring to it to use roman numeral II before its page numbers. For Holmes's reference to Pearce and de Petra, see II, 5 6.

In a note at this point, Holmes listed various editions of Longinus's *On the Sublime*, indicating not only that de Petra, professor of Greek at Lausanne, had published along with the Greek text the first Latin translation of that work at Geneva in 1612, but also that Pearce's Greek text and Latin translation, published at London in 1724 and in a second edition in 1732, was "the most accurate and beautiful Edition of *Longinus*, as well in respect to the *Greek* Text as the *Latin* Version and Notes, the World will perhaps ever see." Certainly Pearce's edition had great popularity in the eighteenth century. The British Museum holds copies of it dated as follows: Londini, 1724, 1732, 1752, 1773; Glasguae, 1751, 1763; Oxonii, 1778, 1806; Amstelaedami, 1733; and Lipsiae, 1769.

For a good study of the Longinian tradition in England, see Samuel H. Monk, *The Sublime: A Study of Critical Theories in XVIII-Century England* (New York, 1935), pp. 10-28.

[124] Monk, *The Sublime*, pp. 10, 21-22, 244-245. William Smith's translation, published first in 1739, would not have helped Holmes, who had completed his digest by June 8, 1738, according to the date affixed to his dedicatory epistle. But he could have used the translation by John Hall (London, 1662), or John Pulteney's English version of Boileau's French version (London, 1680), or the anonymous translation published at Oxford in 1698, or the translation by Welsted (London, 1712).

The English work which he used almost exclusively to exemplify aspects of the sublime is James Thomson's "The Seasons," which in 1738, when Holmes brought *The Art of Rhetoric Made Easy* to publication, had been in circulation for only eight years.[125] In the main, the notes provided by Holmes in this second book are designed to explain how many editions of Longinus's *On the Sublime* there had been, what specific authors are mentioned in it, how many other works Longinus wrote, and what his text means in respect to its historical references, its doctrine, and its seeming hiatuses. It is obvious that Holmes intended these notes to be interesting and helpful to his schoolboy readers, and that his intention would have succeeded.

But there is one note which fulfills an additional and quite unintended function. It consists in a quotation from Fénelon's *Dialogues on Eloquence*, which Holmes had repeatedly cited in his first book. As I said earlier, Fénelon's *Dialogues* are concerned with the same subject that Longinus's *On the Sublime* had analyzed from the point of view of ancient rhetoric—the subject of genuine eloquence in oratory and literature.[126] But unhappily Longinus had been unwilling to confine himself to those effects which lofty conceptions and vehement passions have upon style. Instead, after discussing these two sources of the sublime as innate or natural constituents, he had proceeded in the spirit of ancient stylistic theory to discuss such acquired or artistic constituents as the proper management of figures of thought and speech, the proper choice of words and metaphors, and the striving for lofty and magnificent composition.[127] It may be said of

---

[125] Holmes said (II, 39-40): "I dare say, Sir, you'll excuse me, if for the future, instead of Longinus's Instances out of the *Ancients*, I should produce Examples from a *Modern Author* equally *Sublime*. For, indeed, such to me appear the Passages that I shall transcribe from Mr. James Thomson on the *Seasons*, viz. *Spring, Summer, Autumn, Winter*; late Pieces of Poetry, which, according to Longinus's *Criterion of Sublimity*, have upon a repeated Perusal irresistably [*sic*] forced my Attention and lasting Admiration. [N.B. *They are taken from his first Edition.*]" Italics are Holmes's.

In line with this tribute, Holmes repeatedly quoted full stanzas from "Seasons" to illustrate such figures as Apostrophe (II, 40-44), Erotesis or Interrogation (II, 44-47), Asyndeton (II, 47-48), Congeries of Anaphora, Diatyposis, and Asyndeton (II, 48-49), Collective Singular (II, 51), Historical Present (II, 51-53), Parabole (II, 58-60), and Loftiness and Magnificence in Composition (II, 63-71).

[126] See above, p. 117.

[127] See Holmes, *The Art of Rhetoric Made Easy*, II, 21-22, for a statement of

Fénelon that his conception of genuine eloquence rested upon the first two of Longinus's five principles, and that he avoided the other three, not because they are unimportant in the retrospective analysis of style, but because, as terms addressed to a prospective speaker or writer, they seem to make eloquence consist of outward and visible signs rather than of inward and spiritual graces. In these respects Fénelon speaks on the subject of eloquence with a modern voice, and Longinus with the voice of the irretrievable past. Holmes's note on this subject caught the essential meaning of Fénelon's theory of eloquence without recognizing also that, if Fénelon was right, the theory of Longinus would have to be curtailed to the point of losing the three constituents which it drew from art and learning. Said Holmes:

> The A.B. of *Cambray* in his Dialogues of Eloquence gives much the same Characteristic of *True Oratory*, as *Longinus* does of *Sublimity*. His words are—'*Plato* says an oration is so far eloquent as it affects the Hearer's Mind. By this Rule you may judge certainly of any Discourse you hear. If an Harangue leave you cold and languid, and only amuses your Mind, instead of enlightening it; if it does not move your Heart and Passions, however florid and pompous it may be, it is not truly Eloquent. *Tully* approves of *Plato's* Sentiments on this Point; and tells us . . . that the whole Drift and Force of a Discourse should tend to move those secret Springs of Action that Nature has placed in the Hearts of Men. Would you then consult your own Mind to know whether those you hear be truly Eloquent? If they make a lively Impression upon you, and gain your Attention and Assent to what they say; if they move and animate your Passions, so as to raise you above yourself, you may be assured they are *True Orators*. But if instead of affecting you thus, they only please or divert you, and make you admire the Brightness of their Thoughts, or the Beauty and Propriety of their Language, you may freely pronounce them to be meer *Declaimers*.'[128]

---

these five constituents of sublimity. For Longinus's own statement of them, see the text and translation of *"Longinus" On the Sublime* by W. Hamilton Fyfe in The Loeb Classical Library (London and New York, 1927), pp. 140-141.

[128] *The Art of Rhetoric Made Easy*, II, 20. Italics are Holmes's. Holmes credited the reference to Tully to *"Lib.* I. §. 5. and *Lib.* II. §. 82," that is, to

This discussion of *The Art of Rhetoric Made Easy* has been silent on the subject of memory as a constituent part of Ciceronian rhetoric for the reason that Holmes did not include it in his essential program. But he did devote a footnote to it, and that deserves brief mention. In connection with his division of rhetoric into invention, disposition, elocution, and pronunciation, he remarked that memory is properly speaking no part of rhetoric, even if it is a part of the orator's business.[129] And he justified this statement by invoking the authority of Cicero and Ramus.[130] Cicero in one place had failed to include memory among the parts of rhetoric, although, as Holmes confessed, he had in other places taken an opposite stand. And Ramus had excluded memory from rhetoric by invoking the former rather than the latter Ciceronian indicant, and by remarking that memory was a common faculty in many arts. At this point, Holmes did three things: he recalled that "most of the ancient Orators, to help the *Memory*, recommend and give some obscure Hints of an *Artificial* or *Local Memory*, from what they call *Locis & Imaginibus*"; he mentioned that two memory systems of his own day, Richard Grey's *Memoria Technica* and Solomon Lowe's *Mnemonics*, were singular improvements upon the ancient system; and to guide students in committing things to memory he laid down six practical rules that are ultimately derived from those which Quintilian outlined, after he had explained the formal system requiring the use of places and images and had then promised some simple precepts of his own. Holmes's rules advise that a longer oration should be memorized part by part after the whole thing has been read and understood; that it be memorized from the same sheets on which it had in the first place been written; that it be memorized in the morning, but reviewed several times the preceding night before sleep comes; that more difficult passages should be associated with some note or sign to prompt the mind to remember them;

Cicero's *De Oratore*, 1.5.17; 2.82.337. The passage from Fénelon he credited to "Stevenson's Cambray's *Dial.* p. 64," that is, to page 64 of the work mentioned above, p. 94. Stevenson's translation of this passage is not fortunate in its use of the expression, "however florid and pompous it may be." For details, see below, Ch. 6, n. 156.

[129] *The Art of Rhetoric Made Easy*, p. 4.

[130] See above, Ch. 2, n. 24.

that it is preferable to learn not by declaiming hurriedly but by declaiming steadily and with gestures; and that the greatest aid in respect to building and preserving one's memory is frequent exercise.[131] With these rules, all of which were given in Latin, Holmes brought his brief discussion of memory to a close.

The two modern memory systems mentioned by him were well known in the seventeen-hundreds. Grey's *Memoria Technica*, the more influential of the two, was first published at London in 1730, and after receiving eight other editions in the next seventy years, it was combined with Lowe's *Mnemonics*, a much briefer treatise dating from 1737, and the joint edition had a large vogue in the next century.[132] Grey's work presented an ingenious system for remembering dates and other useful figures. Suppose, for example, that a student wanted to remember the dates when Cyrus, Alexander, and Julius Caesar founded their respective empires, and that he understood those dates to be 536 B.C., 331 B.C., and 46 B.C. All he had to do was to master the use of an arbitrary scheme in which each of the numbers from naught to nine stood

[131] These rules are based ultimately upon the following paragraphs in Quintilian's *Institutio Oratoria*: 11.2.27, 32, 43, 28, 33, 40.

[132] My discussion of Grey's treatise is based upon the copy of the third edition in the Huntington Library. Its title page reads: "Memoria Technica: or, A New Method of Artificial Memory, Applied to, and exemplified in Chronology, History, Geography, Astronomy. Also Jewish, Grecian, and Roman Coins, Weights, and Measures, &c. With Tables proper to the respective Sciences, and Memorial Lines adapted to each Table. By Richard Grey, D.D. Rector of *Hinton* in *Northamptonshire*. . . . The Third Edition, Corrected and Improved. London, Printed for John Stagg in *Westminster Hall*; and sold by A. Bettesworth and C. Hitch in *Pater Noster Row*, F. Clay, and D. Brown without *Temple Bar*, 1737."

Grey was fully aware of the principles of the memory system of ancient rhetoric, and he briefly explained them in his Introduction, pp. xi-xiii.

I have not seen a copy of Solomon Lowe's *Mnemonics delineated, in a small Compass and easy Method* (London, 1737). The *British Museum General Catalogue of Printed Books*, s.v. Lowe, Solomon, and s.v. Grey, Richard, says that it was intended as a supplement to Grey's *Memoria Technica*. Nevertheless, it was first published separately, and it was not given a second edition until 1806, when apparently for the first time is was combined with Grey's work, and the two came out together thereafter in 1812, 1819, 1824, 1836, 1861, and 1865. Grey's work as a separate publication was also given at least seven nineteenth-century editions.

for a particular vowel or diphthong on an upper scale, and for a particular consonant on a lower scale. Thus the vowel a and the consonant b would represent the number 1; e and d, 2; i and t, 3; o and f, 4; u and l, 5; au and s, 6; oi and p, 7; ei and k, 8; ou and n, 9; y and z, 0.[133] Now, applying this scheme to 536, the date when Cyrus founded his empire, the student would be able to convert the numerals into the syllable, "uts"; and then, to complete the job, he would deprive the word Cyrus of its final letters and replace them with the syllable that stood for the date in question, so as to create the artificial word "Cyruts." In like manner he would convert the word Alexander into the artificial word "Aléxita," and Julius Caesar into "Julios." He would now be in a position where (if he could remember the artificial word in its precise form and the numbers represented by each letter of the word's final syllable) he would be able to recall when Cyrus, or Alexander, or Caesar founded their respective empires.

The reason why this memory system sold well in the eighteenth century is perhaps easier to discover than one would think as he contemplated the intricacies of the method proposed. Grey's work contains historical dates, tables of coins, weights and measures, and scientific statistics, all of which would be useful to have at hand, if one could remember where he had put the book that contained them. From the historical dates one could learn that Creation had occurred in 4004 B.C., the universal deluge in 2348 B.C., the call of Abraham in 1921 B.C., the exodus from Egypt in 1491 B.C., and the founding of Solomon's temple in 1012 B.C. Grey proposed, by the way, that these dates could be remembered in relation to the founding of Cyrus's empire by keeping in mind the following line: "C*rothf* Del*etok* Ab*aneb* Ex*afna* Tem*bybe* Cyr*uts*."[134] He added that "Cr denotes the Creation, *othf* 4004, Del the Deluge, Ab the Calling of Abraham, Ex Exodus, Tem the Temple, and Cyr Cyrus," and he repeated that the "Technical Endings of each represent the respective Year according to the Rules already laid down." By similar devices one could also recall that the building of Rome had taken place in 753 B.C. (Rom*put*), the mariner's compass had been invented in 1302 (Comp*atze*),

---

[133] Grey, *Memoria Technica* (London, 1737), pp. vi-vii, 2.

[134] *Ibid.*, pp. 6-7. On p. 5, Grey explained that "th" may be used to signify "thousand" in order to avoid having to say "zyzy." Hence the form "Crothf," rather than "Crozyzyf," as the date of Creation.

gunpowder had been invented in Germany by a monk in 1344 (Gun*patfo*), printing had been invented in 1449 (Pin*afon*), and Columbus had discovered Cuba and Hispaniola in 1493 (Colum*bont*).[135]

Holmes's *The Art of Rhetoric Made Easy* maintained a degree of popularity for well over a hundred years after its publication. The two editions already noticed were followed at London in 1766 by a third, which retained the form of its predecessors. Then in 1786 it was combined with John Stirling's *A System of Rhetoric,* and in this new guise, stripped of its learned footnotes, reduced in bulk by the omission of its digest of Longinus, and rearranged so as to set forth its doctrine in a sequence of questions and answers, it survived for the rest of the eighteenth century.[136] In the nineteenth century it received at least two other editions more or less in the format just described. Stirling's *System of Rhetoric,* first published at London in 1733, was a treatise on *elocutio,* the third part of Ciceronian rhetoric, and it was made up of two entities, the second of which was an abridged version of Farnaby's Latin treatise on the tropes and figures, and the first, Stirling's English version of Farnaby.[137] Stirling's originality consisted in

---

[135] *Ibid.,* pp. 9, 13.

[136] The Huntington Library holds a copy of the combined treatises of Stirling and Holmes, the latter of which is directed no longer merely to the studious youth of Great Britain and Ireland but to the youth of a land divorced not long before from the British Empire. Its title page reads: "A System of Rhetorick, In a Method entirely New. Containing All the Tropes and Figures necessary to illustrate the *Classicks,* both Poetical and Historical. For the Use of Schools. By John Sterling, M.A. . . . To which is added, The Art of Rhetorick Made Easy: or, The Elements of Oratory, Briefly stated, and fitted for the Practice of The Studious Youth of Great-Britain, Ireland, and the United States of America. Illustrated with proper Examples to each Figure, and a Collection of Speeches from the best English Authors. By John Holmes. Dublin, Printed: New-York: Re-printed by Hugh Gaine, at the Bible, in Hanover-Square. M, DCC, LXXXVIII."

By 1795, Stirling's *System of Rhetoric,* which I have seen only in this Huntington copy, had reached its twelfth edition as an independent publication, and it continued to be reprinted in that form during the early nineteenth century.

The combined treatises of Holmes and Stirling were printed as follows: Dublin, 1786; Dublin and New York, 1788; Dublin, 1806; Dublin, 1864. There must have been other editions, too, but I have not tried to locate them.

[137] See John Stirling, *A System of Rhetorick* (Dublin and New York, 1788), p. iii. Stirling here said that he would only mention the laws followed in com-

his attempt to enliven his English definitions by putting them into rhymed couplets, but it is unhappily true that his couplets would hardly have advanced the cause of poetry in the eyes of the schoolboys of the time.[138] The editor who made the combined edition of Holmes and Stirling can be said to have presented through Holmes a digest of the four great arts of Ciceronian rhetoric, and through Stirling a digest of one of those same four arts. This combination, of course, has the effect of giving elocution an exorbitant amount of emphasis, and of making invention, arrangement, and pronunciation seem unimportant by comparison. It also has the effect of illuminating the source of the ambiguity that since the Renaissance has surrounded rhetorical doctrine itself, inasmuch as the treatises of Holmes and Stirling in close proximity to each other afford an example of the use of the term rhetoric to name a discipline on the one hand as Cicero conceived of it and on the other as it was interpreted by those who limited it to the ornaments of style.

The chief authority behind this latter kind of rhetoric during the eighteenth century was not Stirling or such older writers as Thomas Farnaby or William Walker,[139] but Anthony Blackwall,

---

posing his work, "so far as it is my own, the *Latin* Definitions being mostly *Farnaby's*."

[138] *Ibid.*, pp. iii, 1. Here are two examples of Stirling's couplets:

A *Metaphor*, in place of proper Words,
Resemblance puts; and Dress to Speech affords.

A *Metonymy* does new Names impose,
And Things for Things by near Relation shews.

[139] As I indicated above, p. 80, Farnaby was author of a Ciceronian rhetoric, the *Index Rhetoricus*, a part of which was made into a separate treatise on style, the *Troposchematologia*, and was given repeated printings during the eighteenth century.

William Walker, not to be confused with his namesakes Obadiah and John, was a seventeenth-century rhetorician who wrote a work on the tropes and figures called *Troposchematologiae Rhetoricae Libri Duo* (London, 1668), which Holmes cited in *The Art of Rhetoric Made Easy*, pp. 27, 28, 75. This Walker also wrote on invention as one of the principal arts of discourse, and his work in that field has the following title page: "De Argumentorum Inventione Libri Duo, Quorum prior agit de Inventione Logica, alter de Inventione Rhetorica, In Studiosae Juventutis tam Scholasticae quàm Academicae Usum conscripti. Authore *Guilielmo Walker* Scholae *Granthamiensis* in Agro *Lin-*

whom Holmes mentioned on the title page that I quoted earlier. Blackwall's *An Introduction to the Classics* contained an essay "on the nature and use of those emphatical and beautiful figures which give strength and ornament to writing."[140] It is unnecessary here to discuss that essay, inasmuch as an attempt to do so would merely involve a repetition of observations already made in our discussion of Ward. But we should keep in mind, nevertheless, that the book in which it appeared, first published in 1718, not only influenced Ward and Holmes, but went through six editions on its own by 1746, and in 1748 it became the treatise selected to represent the subject of rhetoric and poetry in Robert Dodsley's famous *The Preceptor*, enjoying in that form a total of eight editions before the century ended, and being given a separate publication as an extract from Dodsley in 1796 for the use of students at Harvard.[141]

---

colniensi Magistro. . . . Londini, Typis *J. Macock*, impensis *Josephi Clark*, sub signo Stellae in vico vulgò vocato Little-Britain. 1672."

This latter work placed the inventional system of dialectic or logic alongside that of rhetoric, and showed clearly wherein the two systems overlap and wherein they differ. Thus it represents one more illustration of the extent to which the influence of Ramus had waned in England by 1672. Ramus, of course, believed that one inventional system could serve both rhetoric and logic, and that logic was properly entitled to formulate it.

[140] This quotation is borrowed from the title page of the first edition (London, 1718).

[141] For Homes's references to Blackwall, see *The Art of Rhetoric Made Easy*, pp. 30, 41, 44, 48.

In Dodsley's *The Preceptor*, I, 319-364, Blackwall's work appeared as the treatise that would introduce youth to the first principles of rhetoric and poetry. "I found this Subject so concisely and sensibly handled by Mr. *Blackwel*, in the second Part of his Introduction to the Classicks," said Dodsley in a footnote, p. 321, "that, despairing to get any thing better, or more to my Purpose, I prevail'd with the Proprietor of the Book, to give me leave to make such Use of it as should be thought proper. Some small Alterations therefore have been made, and many Examples from the Poets to explain and illustrate the Rules, exchang'd or added; in which last Particular alone this Treatise seem'd defective."

The editions of *The Preceptor*, all from the presses of R. Dodsley, R. & J. Dodsley, or J. Dodsley, in London, are dated as follows: 1748, 1754, 1758, 1763, 1769, 1775, 1783, 1793.

Blackwall's *Introduction to the Classics*, as published for Harvard students, has the following title page: "Rhetoric and Poetry. Extracted from the Preceptor. For the Use of the University in Cambridge. Printed at *Boston*: By I.

The only other eighteenth-century stylistic rhetoric that I shall mention here is Nicholas Burton's *Figurae Grammaticae & Rhetoricae Latino Carmino Donatae*, published at London in 1702 as a textbook to be used in the school at Durham.[142] This work played an important part in Holmes's *The Art of Rhetoric Made Easy*. After recognizing that the number, the names, and the definitions of the tropes, figures, and turns will always be an uncertain matter, Holmes spoke thus of a part of his general plan in treating them, referring to himself in the third person:

> The FIGURAE METRICAE following, which he has rank'd in the same *Method* with his own, were compos'd by Mr. N. BURTON for the Use of *Durham School*, and are the *briefest, smoothest, most correct*, and most *expressive* of any extant. These, as the Author could not mend 'em, he here proposes to his own *Scholars*, as containing, like the *Iliad in a Nutshell*, a noble Fund of *Troposchematological* Knowledge; promising to each *Sixpence*, whoever he is, that will learn 'em by Heart, and *repeat* 'em to him with Understanding.[143]

The record does not tell us how many students made use of this opportunity to reap a profit for doing what they probably would not have done otherwise, or what consequences in literature or

---

Thomas and E. T. Andrews, Faust's Statue, No. 45, Newbury Street. 1796." There is a copy in the Princeton University Library.

[142] The following treatises having to do with ornaments of style were also current in the eighteenth century, but I have not examined them in composing the present work: 1) Edward Bysshe, *The Art of English Poetry: containing, I. Rules for making Verses. II. A Dictionary of Rhymes. III. A Collection of the most Natural, Agreeable, and Noble Thoughts . . . that are to be found in the best English Poets* (London, 1702) (There were later editions at London in 1705, 1714, 1724, 1725, 1737, 1762); 2) John Brightland, *A Grammar of the English Tongue, with Notes, giving the Grounds and Reason of Grammar in General. To which are now added, the Arts of Poetry, Rhetoric, Logic . . .* (London, 1712; this work reached its eighth edition at London in 1759); 3) Henry Felton, *A Dissertation on Reading the Classics, and Forming a Just Style* (London, 1713; there were later editions at London in 1715, 1718, 1730, 1753); 4) Daniel Turner, *An Abstract of English Grammar and Rhetoric* (London, 1739); 5) Daniel Turner, *An Introduction to Rhetoric; containing all the Tropes and Figures in English Verse* (Abingdon, 1771); 6) Thomas Gibbons, *Rhetoric; or, A View of its Principal Tropes and Figures . . . with Rules to . . . attain Propriety and Elegance in Composition* (London, 1767).

[143] *The Art of Rhetoric Made Easy*, pp. 31-32.

life followed from Holmes's schoolmasterly offer. But the terms of the offer seem clearly to indicate that Holmes himself was the teacher of rhetoric at Holt. As for the verses which he borrowed from Burton, they are rhythmical and informative. Here is what the student would have understood in the formulations of his own mother tongue if he had memorized Burton's Latin verses on metonymy and had repeated them to Holmes in an effort to earn sixpence for some private indulgence:

METONYMY changes one name to the name of a kinsman.
The doing and done switch positions, one first or the other;
The inventor denotes the invention, the author the work;
Its material stands for the object, the tools for the labor;
The end takes the place of the means, and the means of the end;
An adjunct is put for its subject, the subject for adjunct;
Seals are what is sealed, and a place becomes what it contains;
And a country will point out its people, and all they have done.[144]

[144] *Ibid.*, p. 32. Translation mine. Burton's Latin verses are quoted by Holmes as follows:

> Cognato mutat METONYMIA Nomine Nomen:
>   *Effecti Efficiens* vice fungitur, hujus & illud;
>   Inventor notat Inventum, notat Autor Opusque;
>   Materies Rem Signat, & Instrumenta Laborem;
>   Finis pro Medio, Medium pro Fine locatur;
>   Ponitur *Adjunctum* pro *Subjecto*, & vice versâ;
>   Sunt Signatorum vice Signa, Locata Locorum;
>   Et Locus Indigenas, & quae sunt gesta notabit.

IV Separative Tensions in Rhetoric: A Retrospect

This discussion of Ciceronian rhetoric in eighteenth-century England has shown not only the main outlines of what Holmes affectionately called "the glorious and extensive Plan of the *Ancients*," but also the structural and doctrinal weaknesses in the ancient plan itself. The Ciceronians thought of rhetoric as an integral whole made up of parts, each of which was vital in the operation of the total organism of communication, but not one of which by itself could presume to do what all could do together. Yet at the same time the Ciceronians were unable to resist the impulse to stress elocution rather more than invention, disposition, and pronunciation. Indeed, some of them, beguiled into an apparent literal interpretation of the figure of synecdoche, came to think of elocution as if the part were in reality the whole, and as if the tropes and the figures of style were in fact the whole of rhetoric. In this connection it should not be forgotten that Stirling in good faith called his treatise on the tropes and figures *A System of Rhetoric*, even as Holmes called his work on the entire plan of the ancients *The Art of Rhetoric Made Easy*. Here is an instance where the same word is used in two distinct senses, and each sense suggests that it is the proper one, while in fact one sense is a greatly reduced version of the other. This double meaning was of course acquired by the word rhetoric when in the sixteenth century Ramus had confronted the Ciceronians of his day, and had in the name of Cicero stripped rhetoric of two of her parts and given them to logic. From that day onward, rhetoric carried a narrow and a broad signification, and it is always difficult to know which signification is intended when the word is used in the idiom of a given time. Some modern scholars are sure, for example, that the narrow signification is the precise and proper one to use in analyzing rhetorical values in the writings of the sixteenth, seventeenth, or eighteenth centuries. But there is evidence in each of those periods that the broad signification also flourished. In the eighteenth century the narrow signification took a new direction, as rhetoric began to be associated with pronunciation and to lose its ancient affiliation with style, disposition, and invention. This new direction is the subject of the next chapter.

CHAPTER 4

Here it may be observed, that there is no argument urged to enforce the study of eloquence for the use of the pulpit, which is not equally cogent in regard to the senate-house, and the bar.

Indeed the necessity of it to all three is so very manifest to any one, who reflects ever so little upon the point, that it might be judged a waste of time to have dwelt so long upon this topick, did not the total neglect of it, and a general deficiency, consequential from that, warrant an opinion, that it has either not been considered sufficiently by those whose business it is, or that it has not appeared to them to be of so important a nature as is here pretended.

But it may be asked, supposing the great use, importance, and necessity of this art were established in their utmost extent, beyond all possibility of doubt or cavil, it may be asked, I say, how is it to be acquired? The Romans have pointed out the way, and their example is a sufficient light to guide us. Cicero when he gives a definition of this art, in the same sentence points out the means to attain it.‡ 'Elocution is a graceful management of the voice, countenance, and gesture.' It is to be acquired as all other arts are, by precept, by example, by practice. 'Till these means were tryed, we find that oratory was at a very low ebb in Rome.

‡ *Pronunciatio est vocis, & vultus, & gestus moderatio cum venustate. Haec omnia tribus modis assenqui* [sic] *poterimus: arte imitatione exercitatione.*

Thomas Sheridan, *British Education*
(London, 1756), pp. 157-158. [The Latin is
transcribed as Sheridan's text gives it.]

THE BRITISH ELOCUTIONARY
MOVEMENT
(1702–1806)

1 Rhetorical Delivery Adopts a New Name

The title of this chapter would suggest that, if elocution is being
used here to mean what it meant in the rhetorical treatises of
Ward and Holmes, a further consideration of the third part of
rhetoric in the Ciceronian scheme is about to be undertaken, and
another discussion of the tropes and the figures is now to unfold.
But such is happily not the case. Although Ward and Holmes
were always careful to equate the English term elocution with the
contents of the Latin doctrine of *elocutio,* as the literal analogy
between the two languages would dictate, a quite different arrangement began to prevail in the early eighteenth century, and
the elocutionary movement was responsible for giving it wide
currency and increasing public acceptance. This new arrangement involved the use of elocution as the equivalent of the Latin
pronuntiatio or *actio,* which in Cicero's program not only designated the fifth rather than the third part of rhetoric, but also
stood, as we have mentioned, for precepts related to voice and
gesture. In confining their attention to this part of the total rhetorical program, the elocutionists continued to think of themselves
as rhetoricians and to refer formally to their subject as rhetoric,
even as John Stirling had done in regard to his teaching of the
tropes and the figures. But the practices which the elocutionists
encouraged inevitably led to declamation without sincere conviction and earnest feeling, as students recited discourses devised
and organized by somebody else. And when these practices came
to stand in the public mind for the whole of rhetorical doctrine,
rhetoric came to mean empty and insincere speaking, even as the
practices of Stirling and to some extent Holmes and Ward in
overemphasizing the tropes and figures made rhetoric the term,
not for the whole art of speaking, but for artificial elegance of

style. Much as the historian of rhetoric may question the wisdom and doubt the literary insight of those who reduce the rhetorical discipline to this or that fragment of itself in the name of the ancients, he has to reckon with them, for they are a part of the record which he must interpret. So far as the English elocutionists are concerned, they acquired a place in the record shortly before the date when Ward began his professorship at Gresham College, and they maintained it for an astonishingly long time. They seem now to have endorsed a futureless idea that was destined against logic and common sense to have a two-hundred year future in England and America. Their strange movement is our present concern.

Why was it that the fifth part of rhetoric should have been called elocution in some quarters of the eighteenth century in Britain, when it had been consistently termed *pronuntiatio* or *actio* by the great Roman authorities, and pronunciation by the Englishmen who wrote vernacular treatises on Ciceronian rhetoric during the sixteenth, seventeenth, and eighteenth centuries?[1] There is no easy answer to this question, but the happening occurred anyway, and the following observations are intended to indicate that it was not wholly a matter of caprice.

First of all, while pronunciation had been established since the early sixteenth century as the technical English term for the oral delivery of discourse, it had even earlier been used to designate the process of sounding an individual word in relation to its correct accent. Thus it had an ambiguity connected with it, as do many words that have both a technical and an ordinary meaning. The ambiguity in this case did not become really bothersome, however, until the science of phonetics began to emerge, and pronunciation began to be used to denominate the activity to which

---

[1] For the use of *pronuntiatio* or *actio* as the technical name of the fifth part of rhetoric, see *Rhetorica ad Herennium*, 1.2.3 ("Pronuntiatio est vocis, vultus, gestus moderatio cum venustate"); Cicero, *De Inventione*, 1.7.9 ("Pronuntiatio est ex rerum et verborum dignitate vocis et corporis moderatio"); Quintilian, *Institutio Oratoria*, 11.3.1 ("Pronuntiatio a plerisque actio dicitur, sed prius nomen a voce, sequens a gestu videtur accipere"); Cicero, *De Oratore*, 1.31.142 ("Cumque esset omnis oratoris vis ac facultas in quinque partes distributa; ut deberet reperire primum, quid diceret; deinde inventa non solum ordine, sed etiam momento quodam atque iudicio dispensare atque componere; tum ea denique vestire atque ornare oratione; post memoria saepire; ad extremum agere cum dignitate ac venustate"); *Ibid.*, 3.59.222 ("Est enim actio quasi sermo corporis, quo magis menti congruens esse debet"); Cicero, *Orator*, 17.55 ("Quo modo autem dicatur id est in duobus: in agendo et in eloquendo. Est enim actio quasi corporis quaedam eloquentio, cum constet e voce atque motu"); Cicero, *De Partitione Oratoria*, 7.25 ("C. F. Actio igitur sequitur, ut opinor. C. P. Est ita: quae quidem oratori et cum rerum et cum verborum momentis commutanda maxime est. Facit enim et dilucidam orationem et illustrem et probabilem et suavem non verbis sed varietate vocum, motu corporis, vultu, quae plurimum valebunt si cum orationis genere consentient eiusque vim ac varietatem subsequentur").

For various instances where *pronuntiatio* has been rendered into English as "pronunciation," see Howell, *Logic and Rhetoric in England*, pp. 81-82, 89, 104, 112, 255, 256, 325. Ward and Holmes are eighteenth-century instances, of course.

this science addresses itself. At that point the term acquired a new technical sense without having lost either of its previous applications.

In 1617 Robert Robinson published at London a work called *The Art of Pronuntiation*. In reality, this was a treatise on phonetics, or on the science of determining the sounds of speech and of indicating them by an arbitrary system of diacritical marks. Robinson left absolutely no doubt about his own intention in writing the work. He wanted, he said, to describe the art by which "the true pronuntiation of languages might be learned."[2] He set forth this art under two headings, "*Vox Audienda*, Or The Elements of Mans *Voice*," and "*Vox Videnda*, Which is writing, or the Characters of Mans *Voice*." In the first part, he was going to apply himself "to set foorth the elements and parts of the voice," he declared; in the second, he was going to appoint "for euery simple sound in mans voice sundry letters and characters, that the voice being thereunto once committed may by any (who shall know the vse of them) without any other expositor or instructor be aptly and truly pronounced vpon view of the writing, how strange soeuer the language be."[3] Needless to say, Robinson carried out his plan exactly, and his treatise has accordingly taken its place in the history of the science of phonetics in England.[4]

But because in Robinson's time the art of pronunciation as an English concept would technically have referred to the art of delivering a speech, and would technically have fitted a work on voice and gesture, an unfortunate tendency has persisted to think of his treatise as if it dealt with these latter subjects. A mere reading of it would have dispelled this illusion, but for some reason its contents have not always been consulted by those who have sought to characterize what it contains. William Phillips Sandford said of it, for example, that it was "probably the first book written in English devoted exclusively to the subject of delivery,"[5] and there can be no doubt that Sandford used "de-

[2] Robert Robinson, *The Art of Pronuntiation* (London, 1617), f.A6. Robinson's work is reproduced in *The Phonetic Writings of Robert Robinson*, ed. E. J. Dobson, Early English Text Society, No. 238 (London, 1957), pp. 1-28, my quotation being taken from p. 6.

[3] Dobson's edition, p. 7.

[4] See E. J. Dobson, *English Pronunciation 1500-1700* (Oxford, 1957), I, 200-214.

[5] *English Theories of Public Address, 1530-1828*, pp. 113, 170, 195, 209. My quotation is from p. 113.

livery" to mean the fifth part of the art of rhetoric. His words have been echoed by others, and his mistake will doubtless continue to be made.[6] Careless and unimportant as it is, it illustrates the dangers involved in having two different technical meanings assigned to the same word. The elocutionists are perhaps to be thanked at least for attempting to withdraw the term pronunciation from its setting in rhetoric and to free it for an unambiguous technical meaning in lexicography and phonetics.

Nevertheless, it is not easy to understand why these rhetoricians happened to choose elocution as the new English term for the fifth part of rhetoric. After all, was not elocution already recognized in England as the term for the lore of the tropes and figures and for the doctrine of the three kinds of style? If so, how was a new ambiguity to be avoided when the term was made also to mean oral delivery? This very difficulty occurred to Ephraim Chambers in the early eighteenth century. In the second edition of his famous *Cyclopaedia*, published at London in 1738, he printed an article on Pronunciation, and in it he recognized not only that this word had a meaning in phonetics as well as in rhetoric, but also that an unfortunate tendency was afoot to give it a new and undesirable synonym within rhetoric itself. Said he:

Pronunciation is also used for the fifth and last part of rhetoric, which consists in regulating and varying the voice and gesture agreeably to the matter and words; so as more effectually to persuade, and touch the hearers. See RHETORIC.

The *pronunciation* is of such importance, that Demosthenes called it the first, the second, and the third part of eloquence.[7] See ACTION.

Quintilian defines the *pronunciation, vocis, & vultus, & corporis moderatio cum venustate*; a decent, agreeable manner of managing the voice, gesture, and action of the whole body.[8]

[6] See Warren Guthrie, "The Development of Rhetorical Theory in America, 1635-1850: V, The Elocution Movement—England," *Speech Monographs*, XVIII (March 1951), 18. See also Lester Thonssen and A. Craig Baird, *Speech Criticism* (New York, 1948), p. 127.

[7] For the attribution of this famous saying to Demosthenes, see Cicero, *De Oratore*, 3.56.213, and Quintilian, *Institutio Oratoria*, 11.3.6.

[8] This definition seems to be based upon that in the *Rhetorica ad Herennium*, 1.2.3. See above, n. 1. I do not find this exact language in Quintilian.

Cicero somewhere calls it *quaedam corporis eloquentia,* a certain eloquence of the body; and in another place, *sermo corporis,* the language or speech of the body.[9]

Pronunciation is the same with what we otherwise call *action.* See ACTION.

Some writers, particularly Mr. Henley, confound it with *elocution,* which is a very different thing. That author, when he styles himself *restorer of the ancient elocution,* means of the ancient *pronunciation.*[10] See ELOCUTION.

The elocutionists could have avoided this sort of confusion, of course, by calling the fifth and last part of rhetoric by the alternate term action, as classical authorities would have authorized, or by the new term delivery, as the twentieth century was going to do. But they ignored both of these possibilities, and there was some reason why they might have done so. Delivery was after all a term that did not have roots in the Latin rhetorical tradition, as the elocutionists may have realized, although not many of them can be said to have mastered that tradition with competence. As for the term action, it was associated in English with the notion of physical movement and gesture rather than with oral utterance, and thus it must have seemed too narrow to cover both of these activities.

It may be that the elocutionists considered their new word to have two distinct advantages as the technical name for the fifth part of rhetoric. First, it was descended from the same root that had produced the word eloquence, itself a term for excellence in oratory and for the art which would bring oratorical excellence into being; and thus it would have the effect of designating a part in such a way as to suggest that the part was the whole. Thomas Sheridan, one of the most influential of the English elocutionists, really believed, as we can see from the epigraph at the head of this chapter, that the ancient term *pronuntiatio* was not only best rendered into English by the word elocution, but that elocution in this sense was what the ancients had meant by the art of rhetoric or of oratory in the large. Secondly, there was a seventeenth-

---

[9] See *Orator,* 17.55; *De Oratore,* 3.59.222. See above, n. 1. See also Quintilian, *Institutio Oratoria,* 11.3.1.

[10] For a discussion of Henley as one of the early elocutionists, see below, pp. 193-203.

century English precedent for calling oral presentation in rhetoric by this new name.[11] So far as writings on rhetoric are concerned, that precedent was at least as old as John Wilkins's *Ecclesiastes, or, A Discourse concerning the Gift of Preaching.* Originally published at London in 1646, and given six later editions before 1700, this treatise divided its doctrine into three headings, that is, Method, Matter, and Expression; and when it came to speak of Expression, it first discussed "Phrase," and secondly, "Eloquution."[12] There can be no doubt that "Phrase" designated for Wilkins what the ancient rhetoricians had called *elocutio*, and that "Eloquution" designated for him what the ancients had called *pronuntiatio* or *actio.* "The *phrase*," he said, "should be plain, full, wholesome, affectionate,"[13] and these four terms provided the framework for his discussion of the problem of style in sermon-making. As for the problem of oral presentation, Wilkins briefly developed the single thesis that "In the elocution there are two extremities to be avoided: too much Boldnesse, Fear,"[14] and these two qualities as Wilkins explained them refer to the speaker's attitude as it is reflected in his voice and bearing. Wilkins concluded his discussion of these qualities by saying, "In brief, the most proper manner of eloquution is with modesty and gravity, which will best sute our calling and businesse."[15]

[11] At this point my wording is largely that of an article which I published some years ago on the English elocutionists, entitled, "Sources of the Elocutionary Movement in England: 1700-1748," *The Quarterly Journal of Speech,* XLV (February 1959), 1-18. That article supplies the wording of portions of the first eight sections of this chapter.

[12] See *Ecclesiastes, or, A Discourse concerning the Gift of Preaching As it fals under the Rules of Art,* 3rd edn. (London, 1651), pp. 5, 128-133. *A New English Dictionary,* s.v. Elocution, gives Robert Cawdrey's *A Table Alphabeticall, containing and teaching the true writing and vnderstanding of hard vsuall English Words,* 3rd edn. (London, 1613), as the earliest English work to define elocution as delivery. The next instance listed in the *NED* is dated 1678, and the third, 1739.

[13] *Ecclesiastes,* p. 128.

[14] *Ibid.,* p. 132.

[15] *Ibid.,* p. 133. For other details concerning the shift of the term elocution from the context of the tropes and figures to that of voice and gesture, see Frederick W. Haberman, "The Elocutionary Movement in England, 1750-1850," unpublished doctoral dissertation, Cornell University, 1947, Ch. III.

III Why Delivery Aroused Urgent Interest

The question whether one technical term or another is to be used to designate a given activity is rarely of vital interest to the public at large. A much more important question is whether the activity itself has value, and whether its value is greater at one time than at another. There can be no doubt that the activity of pronouncing a speech to an audience is an important part of speechmaking, and that, whether it is called pronunciation, or action, or elocution, or delivery, it deserves a place in the theory of rhetoric. Aristotle recognized that delivery "is, essentially, a matter of the right management of the voice to express the various emotions— of speaking loudly, softly, or between the two; of high, low, or intermediate pitch; of the various rhythms that suit various subjects." But he said that "no systematic treatise upon the rules of delivery has yet been composed," and he added, "Besides, delivery is—very properly—not regarded as an elevated subject of inquiry."[16] There he let the matter rest. The great Latin rhetoricians went further than he by writing systematically on delivery as one of the five arts to be mastered by speakers; but while they regarded this art as important, and treated it with respect, they were never tired of keeping it tied to the other parts of rhetoric and of devoting less space to it than they devoted to invention, disposition, and style. Why was it, then, that in eighteenth-century Britain the subject of delivery should have become so important in some minds as to crowd out all other aspects of rhetoric and to stand as the only rhetorical discipline worth cultivating intensively? A few observations may help to show what has to be considered in arriving at an answer to this question.

First of all, as the preceding chapter has suggested, every part of Ciceronian rhetoric except delivery had been under attack or revision during the seventeenth century, and the eighteenth century was left with the task either of keeping the old rhetoric alive in some sort of relation to the changes proposed, or of creating a new rhetoric for a new time. Rhetorical invention had been transferred to logic by Ramus, and in being restored to rhetoric in the reaction against his reforms, it had come under attack by the Port-Royalists and Lamy for its reliance upon the use of topics and of merely probable arguments, and for its seeming indiffer-

[16] *Rhetoric*, 1403b 26-38. Trans. by W. Rhys Roberts.

ence to factual proofs and empirical knowledge. Rhetorical disposition had also been transferred by Ramus to logic, and logic liked it so well that she did not surrender it when she sought to recover what Ramus had taken from her. The seventeenth-century English logicians, as we saw in Chapter 2, did much useful and sophisticated work on disposition as they addressed themselves to the subject of method, and their work contained as much of the essence of the theory of rhetorical form as could be found in the more elaborate rhetorical accounts of the six parts of the classical oration. Rhetorical elocution, as that aspect of rhetoric which concerned style, had been required by Ramus to deal only with the tropes and the figures, and those ornaments had been attacked as disgusting superficialities by Thomas Sprat of the Royal Society at the very time when they were being endlessly refined and elaborated in connection with the effort to restore to rhetoric the other functions that Ramus had taken from it. Memory had been declared by Ramus to have affiliations with all the arts, and thus to require no special rhetorical treatment, and this judgment had not been seriously challenged in the seventeenth century or by Holmes and Ward at a later date; nor had there been any serious effort to keep an art of memory alive within the boundaries of the theory of rhetoric. Only rhetorical pronunciation had remained free of attack during the period which Ramus had started by making delivery the second division of his bifurcated rhetoric and his opponents had ended by returning delivery to its former place in the scheme which included invention, arrangement, and style. The elocutionists in seeking to elevate the fifth part of rhetoric into a new prominence at least could have claimed that they were responding to the criticisms against the traditional system in such a way as to preserve only what that system itself had saved from successful assault. In other words, the basic justification of their school could have been that the previous immunity of *pronuntiatio* to attack entitled it to be regarded as having a continuing validity. Meanwhile, Ward had sought without conspicuous success to meet the attacks on traditional rhetoric by a patient elaboration of its ancient doctrine, and later in the eighteenth century Adam Smith, Campbell, and Blair would attempt to meet those same attacks in a more resourceful way, as indeed Fénelon had already done. Perhaps the elocutionists could have been criticised for a lack of boldness in their efforts to keep the old system alive by surrendering all of it except delivery, and by implying that delivery was all that ever mattered anyway; but when even so they are seen in the framework of the struggle between the old and the new, their movement begins to have more relevance and purpose than it might otherwise appear to possess.

In the second place, the religious services of the Church of England consisted so much more basically of readings from the *Book of Common Prayer* than of original preachings and exhortations in the form of evangelical sermons that when the combative mood of the Reformation had finally subsided, the theory of *pronuntiatio* in ancient rhetoric began to seem especially pertinent to the early training of English pulpit orators, whereas the partly controverted ancient doctrines of invention, arrangement, and style appeared less fruitful by comparison; and the eighteenth-century elocutionists seized upon this point with some emphasis. On Saturday, August 18, 1711, Richard Steele devoted an issue of *The Spectator* to showing that the reading of the liturgy in a strong and effective way was an important but neglected accomplishment; and forty-five years later his words were quoted, and their theme almost endlessly elaborated, by Thomas Sheridan, in his book called *British Education*, which was the opening tract in his campaign to revive ancient *pronuntiatio* conceived as the entire art of ancient rhetoric.[17] Taking as his text the Latin proposition, "Pronuntiatio est Vocis & Vultus & Gestus moderatio cum venustate," and crediting it to Tully although it actually comes from the *Rhetorica ad Herennium*, Steele had said:

Mr. Spectator,

The well Reading of the Common Prayer is of so great Importance, and so much neglected, that I take the Liberty to offer to your Consideration some Particulars on that Subject: And what more worthy your Observation than this? A thing so Publick, and of so high Consequence. It is indeed wonderful, that the frequent Exercise of it should not make the Performers of that Duty more expert in it. This Inability, as I conceive, proceeds from the little Care that is taken of their Reading, while Boys and at School, where when they are got into *Latin*, they

[17] See *The Spectator*, No. 147, and *British Education* (London, 1756), pp. 96-100.

are look'd upon as above *English*, the reading of which is wholly neglected, or at least read to very little purpose, without any due Observations made to them of the proper Accent and manner of Reading; by this means they have acquir'd such ill Habits as won't easily be remov'd. The only way that I know of to remedy this, is to propose some Person of great Ability that way as a Pattern for them; Example being most effectual to convince the Learned, as well as instruct the Ignorant.[18]

By Sheridan's time, as we shall see, many efforts had been made to cope with the problem that so concerned Steele, and an art of oratory defined exclusively in terms of the ancient doctrine of delivery had been in existence for a half-century. Sheridan needed only to help it advance, not to revive it. But he thought of himself as bringing it back into existence after it had been in oblivion for centuries, and its chief value, as he saw it, was that it would make religion a force capable of remedying the widespread and potentially fatal evils of immorality, ignorance, and false taste in British society. Speaking of oratory conceived as the art of delivery, he said:

> The study, or neglect of this art, can not possibly be a matter of indifference to us. It must be productive of the best, or attended with the worst consequences. It must either effectually support religion against all opposition, or be the principal means of it's destruction. The church service, according as it is either well or ill administered, must excite great emotions, or set people to sleep; it must give delight, or occasion disgust; it must carry conviction of truth with it, or appear fictitious. And

[18] Steele went on to propose that a certain reader of the Service in St. James's Garlic Hill Church, whom he had recently heard with great attention and profit, be named annual reader at the assembly of the Clergy of Sion College, and thus be put in a position where he could show the clergy how reading should be done. Indifference to the meaning of the words being read was attributed by Steele to the desire to avoid an imputation of cant. "Cant," he remarked, "is, by some People, derived from one *Andrew Cant* who, they say, was a Presbyterian Minister in some Illiterate part of Scotland, who by Exercise and Use had obtained the Faculty, *alias* Gift, of Talking in the Pulpit in such a Dialect, that it's said he was understood by none but his own Congregation, and not by all of them." Steele continued by saying that cant had recently come to mean anything unusual in delivering a passage, and that proper emphasis and accent should not be confused with it.

indeed nothing can contribute more strongly to make the latter opinion prevail, than hearing it's doctrines delivered in tones and accents quite foreign from nature and truth. In this, as in life, the general maxim will hold good, that before you can persuade a man into any opinion, he must first be convinced that you believe it yourself. This he can never be, unless the tones of voice in which you speak come from the heart, accompanied by corresponding looks, and gestures, which naturally result from a man who speaks in earnest.[19]

In addition to the need for improvement in the reading of the liturgy, and the desire to keep ancient rhetoric alive in its least controversial aspect, there was a cultural problem involved in the activities of the English elocutionists, and it was perhaps the most interesting of the incentives behind their movement. During the eighteenth century the British became aware that the many forms which their language had in various districts of England, and the many differences which existed between London English, on the one hand, and Scottish or Irish or American English, on the other, were no longer to be regarded merely as attractive and desirable variations from locality to locality, but as positive hindrances to the cultural, political, commercial, and occupational welfare of a growing and dynamic world empire. What was a young Irishman to do, for example, if he took his university training at Trinity College, Dublin, and came later to desire a career as actor on the London as well as the Dublin stage? What was a young Scot to do if, having prepared for the legal profession in Edinburgh, and having been enrolled as a Scottish advocate, he at length decided that the English bar offered him larger opportunities than he could have in his native land, and that he should accordingly seek his fame and fortune as a lawyer in London? These two questions are not hypothetical. They apply to actual historical incidents of the eighteenth century.

The first incident concerns Thomas Sheridan, the future elocutionist, who went on the Dublin stage soon after his graduation from Trinity College in 1739, and who was actively associated with the theatres of Dublin and London between 1743 and 1759. His own experience as an Irish lad at Westminster School must

[19] *British Education*, pp. 91-92. The next to the last sentence in this quotation is accompanied by a two-line Latin footnote quoting Cicero, *De Oratore*, 1.19.87; the last sentence, by a four-line Latin footnote quoting the same work, 3.57.216.

first have taught him that his career, and the careers of all ambitious and able young Irishmen, would be greatly assisted by the standardizing of English pronunciation, and by the eliminating of all provincialisms from the speech of the Irish, the Scots, the Americans, and even the English. At any rate, he conceived of the revival of the ancient theory of oratorical delivery as the chief means to this end, and he devoted to it the last thirty years of his life. As a first step he published in 1756 a treatise on British education. Thereafter he delivered lectures on elocution throughout Great Britain, he published those lectures in 1762, and he brought out in 1780 his *General Dictionary of the English Language,* "one main object of which," its title page declared, "is to establish a plain and permanent standard of pronunciation."[20]

The second incident involves Alexander Wedderburn. Wedderburn was born in Scotland in 1733 and was educated at the University of Edinburgh, where in his student days he associated with such eminent men as David Hume, Adam Smith, William Robertson, Lord Monboddo, and Lord Kames.[21] Even at that time he dreamed of achieving success at the English bar and of becoming the first Scotsman ever to be named Lord Chancellor of England; "but he was conscious," says Lord Campbell, his biographer, "that as yet he could not speak the language of the country where he meditated such achievements, and that beyond the *res angusta domi* there might be obstacles in his way which were wholly insurmountable."[22] Indeed, after visiting London in 1753 and seeing at first hand that he appeared to be qualified on almost all counts for the practice of law in England, he continued to be concerned, his biographer records, about the disadvantages that would attend "his defective knowledge and vicious pronunciation of the vernacular tongue."[23] Campbell revealingly adds: "Although he could write English, as well as Latin, with tolerable purity, in common conversation he was often reduced to great embarrassment from not being sure that he knew how to express

---

[20] See below, pp. 214-243, for a more specific discussion of these matters.

[21] This account of Wedderburn depends upon that by A. H. Millar in *The Dictionary of National Biography* and upon the Life by John, Lord Campbell, in *The Lives of The Lord Chancellors and Keepers of the Great Seal of England* (London, 1845-49), VI, 1-366, cited here as Campbell, *Life of Lord Loughborough.*

[22] Campbell, *Life of Lord Loughborough,* pp. 8-10; the quotation is from p. 10.

[23] *Ibid.,* p. 12.

himself properly about the most trifling matters; and he could easily perceive that, notwithstanding the politeness of the Englishmen he met, they had great difficulty in commanding their gravity when he spoke in the native accent of the Canongate, and still more when he rashly attempted to imitate them, and came out with the jargon called 'High English.' " This linguistic deficiency Webberburn felt he would have to remove before he could join the legal profession in London.

Upon his return to Scotland, he pursued his legal studies further and was duly called to the Scottish bar on June 29, 1754. For the next three years he practiced law in Edinburgh; but his chief case in that period was not in the Court of Session, but in the General Assembly of the Church of Scotland, where, as a Ruling Elder, he defended David Hume against an attempt by some members of the Assembly to enquire into the question of Hume's being subversive in matters of religion. Meanwhile, as member of the Select Society, to which Hume, William Robertson, Hugh Blair, Adam Smith, and Lord Kames also belonged, Wedderburn practiced himself in public speaking, "a department of education which had hitherto been almost entirely neglected in Scotland."[24] After one of the debates in a meeting of the Society, Charles Townshend jestingly asked the members "why they did not learn to speak as well as to write the English language," and he proposed that an interpreter be appointed to describe what their debates were about.[25] At this very moment Thomas Sheridan was lecturing on elocution in Edinburgh, and, as Lord Campbell somewhat sarcastically puts it, he was endeavoring in his strong Irish brogue "to teach all the delicacies of English intonation."[26] Sheridan's lectures had the effect of causing the Select Society to pass the following unanimous resolution:

> That it would be of great advantage to this country, if a proper number of persons from England, duly qualified to instruct gentlemen in the knowledge of the English tongue, the manner of pronouncing it with purity, and the art of public speaking, were settled in Edinburgh; and if at the same time a proper number of masters from the same country, duly qualified for teaching children the reading of English, should open schools in Edinburgh for that purpose.[27]

[24] *Ibid.*, p. 31.   [25] *Ibid.*, p. 35.   [26] *Ibid.*, p. 36.
[27] *Ibid.*, p. 37.

And the unanimous resolution was accompanied by a decision to found an organization to be called "The Society for promoting the reading and speaking of the English Language in Scotland," the members of which would not only contribute money for the realization of the Society's objectives, but also, in the irreverent words of Wedderburn's biographer, "would all begin to speak English, according to the rules of grammar, and Sheridan's scale of progression—'tĭ-tùm or tùm-tĭ-tum-tĭ.' "[28] To this organization, of course, Wedderburn and all members of the Select Society belonged.

In late July or early August, 1757, Wedderburn left Edinburgh for London, at the end of a dramatic episode in which, refusing to apologize for his invectives against a fellow attorney, Lockhart, in a case in the Inner House, he stripped off his gown and said that he would never wear it again.[29] We do not know exactly what progress he had made by that time in purifying his speech of its Scottish provincialisms; but we are told that, upon his arrival in London, it was still his passionate desire to correct his accent, and that Sheridan, who happened to be in London at that time to negotiate an appearance on the stage and to supervise the publication of his *Course of Lectures on Elocution*, was pleased to come each day to Wedderburn's quarters in the Inner Temple and give him long lessons in talking, reading, reciting, and declaiming.[30] Wedderburn's later success at the English bar and in English politics included his being made Lord Chancellor in 1793, as his boyish dream had anticipated; and thus in the end he proved that his provincialisms in speech had either disappeared or had at least not been a serious handicap in his career. There can be no doubt that many young men in Ireland, Scotland, and the remoter parts of England were aware during Wedderburn's lifetime of having the very disability which had caused him such concern, and that they recognized the necessity of removing it if they were to gain glory and riches in the cultural center of Great Britain. For them some teacher of elocution in their own school or community must often have performed services like those which Thomas Sheridan performed for Alexander Wedderburn.

[28] *Ibid.*, p. 37.   [29] *Ibid.*, pp. 47-48.   [30] *Ibid.*, p. 51.

IV Continental Backgrounds of British Elocution

The English elocutionary movement thus received its motivations
from actual forces at work in British society in the eighteenth century, and it derived its distinctive English name from native
sources, but it borrowed its first doctrines from a French Jesuit
and a Protestant clergyman of Swiss extraction, each of whom
exercised a measurable influence upon the forerunners and the successors of Thomas Sheridan.

The first of these in point of time, but the second in influence
among English elocutionists, was Louis de Cressolles. As we have
seen, Cressolles was regarded by Ward as a respected authority
on *pronuntiatio*,[31] and thus he would deserve mention in any history of English rhetoric. But he deserves special mention for his
contribution to the early and the later history of the elocutionary
movement in the eighteenth century. Born in a small village in
Brittany in 1568, he entered the Society of Jesus at the age of
twenty, and for the rest of his life he devoted himself to study,
pedagogy, and ecclesiastical administration, serving as professor
of humanities, rhetoric, philosophy, and theology in his earlier
career, and as secretary to the General of the Society for the fifteen years that preceded his death in Rome in 1634.[32] It would
seem at first glance that the work which he published in 1620
under the title *Vacationes Autumnales* was primarily interested
either in describing what its author had done in his various
autumn holidays or in presenting an anthology of classical de-
scriptions of such periods of freedom. Yet the *Vacationes Autumnales* has neither of these objectives in mind. As the following
transcript of its title page reveals almost at once, it is a treatise on
the two aspects of the ancient theory of oratorical delivery:

> Vacationes Avtvmnales sive De Perfecta Oratoris Actione et
> Pronvnciatione Libri III. *In quibus è scriptorum elegantium
> monumentis, gestuum & vocum rationes non indocta copia &
> varietate explicantur, & vitia in agendo notantur.* Opus omni-
> bus eloquentiae studiosis, & qui vel sacro, vel profano in loco

[31] See above, Ch. 3, n. 102.
[32] De Backer, *Bibliothèque de la Compagnie de Jésus*, II, 1654-1655; also
Nouvelle Biographie Générale, s.v. Crésol, Louis.

publicè dicunt, vtilissimum. *Auctore* Lvdovico Cresollio *Armorico, è Societate* Iesv. Lvtetiae Parisiorvm. . . . M.DC.XX. . . .[33]

The *Vacationes Autumnales* in its seven hundred and six pages of actual text presents no doubt the largest extant collection of observations by classical authors on the subject of voice and gesture in oratory. Its First Book, the shortest of the three parts into which it is divided, contains ninety-nine pages serving as a general introduction to the whole work. Indeed, the subject of oratorical action is taken up only in the last two of its twelve chapters. Book II devotes three hundred and fifty-three pages to the subject introduced in those two chapters, discussing not only the oratorical actions to be cultivated but those which should be avoided as faults. It deals fully with gestures and expressions of the head, countenance, forehead, eyes, eyebrows, ears, nostrils, mouth, trunk, hands, fingers, forearm, shoulders, and feet. Book III contains two hundred and fifty-four pages dealing with the whole problem of managing the voice. Not only does it discuss in detail such matters as the natural and the cultivated voice, and the voice to be used in proof and in repulsing a verbal attack, but it also concerns itself with such properties of the voice as virility, effeminacy, abundance, greatness, distinctness, indistinctness, thinness, harmoniousness, moderateness, prodigality, smoothness, pleasantness, brightness, harshness, hoarseness, hardness, dissonance, variety, and monotony. Certainly these topics and many later ones relating to correct pronunciation, distinct pronunciation, grave pronunciation, swelling pronunciation, rough pronunciation, and the like, make Book III a great storehouse of precepts on the voice in oratory, as Book II is a similar storehouse of precepts on the actions of the body during the presentation of a public discourse.

[33] The title page would read as follows in English: "Autumn Recesses, or Three Books concerning the Finished Action and Pronunciation of the Orator. In which the doctrines of gesture and voice are set forth with not unlearned copiousness and variety from the works of choice writers, and the faults in action are noted. A work most useful to all students of eloquence and to all who speak publicly on sacred or secular occasions. By the author Louis Cressolles of Brittany, of the Society of Jesus. Paris . . . 1620. . . ." This work appears never to have had a second edition. A copy of the edition just cited is in the New York Public Library and in the Library of the University of Illinois.

The second authority behind the doctrines of the English elocutionists, and the more important by far, is to be identified as
Michel Le Faucheur.[34] Le Faucheur was born in Geneva in the
late fifteen-hundreds and died at Paris on April 1, 1657. His chief
occupation was that of Protestant clergyman at Montpellier, at
Charenton, and at Paris. At one point his career as churchman
was threatened, however, by a rule forbidding foreigners to
preach in France, and it was then that he considered but did not
finally accept an offer to be the professor of theology at Lausanne.
He is said to have been distinguished for his learning and his oratorical ability, and to have earned the respect of French Catholics
for his honesty of speech and conduct. At the end of his life he
had published several religious tracts and sermons, and had written various other treatises destined for later publication. The
most famous of these unpublished writings turned out to be a
work called *Traitté de l'action de l'orateur, ou de la Prononciation
et du geste*, which was seen through the press shortly after his
death by his friend and coreligionist Valentin Conrart, noted as
the father of the French Academy.[35] At the end of the seventeenth

[34] My account of his life depends upon that in the *Biographie Universelle*
and that in the *Nouvelle Biographie Générale*. To Le Faucheur and Cres
solles as foreign authorities behind English elocutionary doctrine should be
added Jean Lucas, whose *Actio Oratoris, seu de Gestu et Voce, Libri Duo*,
was published at Paris in 1675, and reprinted at Paris in 1761 in the second
edition of Joseph Antoine Toussaint Dinouart's *L'Éloquence du corps, ou
l'Action du prédicateur*. Lucas's *Actio Oratoris*, a slight book of 58 pages, is
mentioned by Hugh Blair, *Lectures on Rhetoric and Belles Lettres* (Dublin,
1783), II, 439. Lucas (1638-1716), a member of the Society of Jesus, taught
rhetoric at Paris between 1671 and 1677. See De Backer, *Bibliothèque de la
Compagnie de Jésus*, v, 147-150. For reference to Lucas's influence upon
Gilbert Austin, see below, p. 255.

[35] The title page of the first edition does not mention the name of the author. It reads as follows, if all bracketed explanations usually included in it by
bibliographers are omitted: "Traitté de l'action de l'orateur, ou de la Prononciation et du Geste. Paris, Augustin Courbé, 1657." A later edition of the
Traitté attributed the work to Conrart. Its title page reads: "Traite de l'Action
de l'Orateur, *Ou de la* Prononciation et du Geste. Tres-nécessaire à tous
ceux qui ont à parler en public. Par Mr. Conrart, *Secrétaire du Roy, Maison &
Couronne de France. Jouxte la Copie* A Paris, Chez Sebastien Mabre-Cramoisy,
Imprimeur du Roy, ruë St. Jaques [*sic*], aux Cicognes. MDCLXXXVI." This edition was done from a Paris copy by P. vander Aa at Leyden.

The *Traitté* has thus been said on occasion to be Conrart's work. Robert
Watt, *Bibliotheca Britannica*, listed it under Conrart's name, saying: "He pub-

century this book had received at least seven editions in its own tongue, and at Helmstadt in 1690 it had been made available to the learning of Europe in a Latin translation by Melchior Schmidt.[36] In the eighteenth century it was to have a great influence upon the early English elocutionists, as we shall see in the following section of this chapter.

---

lished, A Treatise on Oratorical Action. Paris, 1657, 12 mo. Reprinted under the name of Michel Le Faucheur. 1686." The *British Museum General Catalogue of Printed Books* lists the first and two later editions of the work under Conrart's name without any cross reference to Le Faucheur, and it lists later editions of the work under the name of Le Faucheur without any cross reference to Conrart.

Philbert in his article on Le Faucheur in *Biographie Universelle* complains that the *Traitté* had originally been attributed to Conrart because of his having published the first edition of it, and that the same error had occurred on the title page of the Latin translation which Melchior Schmidt gave the work at Helmstadt in 1690. See below, n. 36.

[36] The French editions that I have been able to find in accounts of Le Faucheur's life and in listings in library catalogues occurred as follows: Paris, 1657; Paris, 1667; Paris, 1676; Lyon 1676; Paris, 1686; Leyden, 1686; Amsterdam, 1697.

The title page of the Latin translation reads as follows: "De Actione oratoria, sive de Pronunciatione et gestu liber utilissimus, gallico idiomate sine auctoris nomine premium aliquoties, deinde Parisiis et in Belgio sub Conrarti, Secr. Reg., nomine editus, nunc, ut pluribus usui esse possit, latinitate donatus . . . Helmstadii, typis et sumptibus G. W. Hammii, 1690." I have not seen this work. My wording is taken from the *Catalogue Général des Livres Imprimés de la Bibliothèque Nationale*, s.v. Le Faucheur, Michel, and s.v. Conrart, Valentin.

v Le Faucheur's *Traitté* in England

A few years after the publication of Schmidt's Latin version of Le Faucheur's *Traitté*, the French work was brought out at London in an anonymous English translation, and its title page described it as "An Essay upon the Action of an Orator; As to his *Pronunciation & Gesture*. Useful both for *Divines* and *Lawyers*, and necessary for all *Young Gentlemen*, that study how to *Speak* well in *Publick*."[37] In 1727 this same translation was given another printing at London, its title page having been altered to read "The Art of Speaking in Publick: or an Essay on the Action of an Orator; As to his Pronunciation and Gesture. Useful in the Senate or Theatre, the Court, the Camp, as well as the Bar and Pulpit. The Second Edition Corrected. With an Introduction relating to the Famous Mr. Henly's present Oratory."[38] Twenty-three years later, in 1750, this translation was given a third edition, and its title page now read, "An Essay upon Pronunciation and Gesture, Founded upon the Best Rules and Authorities of the Ancients, Ecclesiastical and Civil, and Adorned with the finest Rules of Elocution."[39] Small wonder that these three different titles would lead to the supposition that three different works are designated by them. Small wonder, also, that the absence of Le Faucheur's name from the title pages would make it difficult to identify him as connected with these works in any way. Yet the fact of the matter is that these works differ from each other only as later editions differ from their prototype, and that the prototype in this case is of course an English translation of Le Faucheur's French *Traitté*.

[37] The title page continues: "Done out of *French. Aliud est eloquentiam callere; aliud, eloqui.* London: Printed for *Nich. Cox* at the *Golden Bible* without *Temple-Barr.*" No date is given. In the work there is no mention that Le Faucheur is the author. The italics are those of the original text. See above, n. 11, for a comment upon my wording at this point in the present chapter.

[38] The title page continues: *"Aliud est Eloquentiam callere. Aliud est Eloqui.* London: Printed for N. Cox in *Story's Passage, Westminster*, and sold by him and the Booksellers in *London, Oxford*, and *Cambridge*. 1727."

[39] The title page continues: "London: Printed for C. Hitch, in *Pater-noster-row*. MDCCL." Francis Orton, an English clergyman, erroneously attributed Le Faucheur's *Traitté* to Simon Foucher and published in 1848 at Altrincham a metrical version of the translation under examination here. Orton called his work *An Essay, upon the Action of an Orator, or, his Pronunciation and Gesture.*

The date of the first publication of this translation is to be regarded as the moment when the English elocutionary movement formally began, and the name of the translator is to be accepted as that of the English founder of the movement. It is exasperating, therefore, to be forced to confess that the translator does not identify himself and that the first edition does not proclaim its date of publication. To be sure, John Henley is credited with being the author of the edition published in 1727,[40] no doubt because his name is mentioned on its title page, as we have seen; but a mere glance at "The Editor's Introduction and Apology for this Edition" within the work itself promptly dispels any thought that Henley had anything to do with it, except as the unwilling victim of the editor's hostility. So far as I know, there is at present no firm clue to the identity of the editors of the second and third editions, or of the translator responsible for putting Le Faucheur's work into English in the first place. But there is a way to be sure that the first edition was published early in the eighteenth century, probably in the year 1702, although this statement contradicts the accepted belief that it appeared around 1680.[41] The evidence in support of an early eighteenth-century date appears to be conclusive, even if the exact year is something of a question. At any rate, here is the evidence that we have.

The first and most important piece of evidence is that the second edition, which, I repeat, was published in 1727, spoke of the first edition as "having been buried upwards of twenty Years in the most profound *Silence* and *Oblivion*."[42] This statement conclusively points to the first decade of the eighteenth century as that in which the translation was originally published, and it leaves us only with the problem of deciding whether some one year in that decade has any special claim above another as the date when the work appeared.

The second piece of evidence consists in taking note that the

---

[40] See *The Dictionary of National Biography*, s.v. Henley, John, where *The Art of Speaking in Public* (1727), is listed as if it were one of Henley's own works. In reality what is there attributed to him is the second edition of the anonymous English translation of Le Faucheur's *Traitté*.

[41] See Donald Wing, *Short-Title Catalogue*, s.v. Le Faucher [*sic*], Michel. Wing follows the dating given for the work in the *British Museum General Catalogue of Printed Books*, s.v. Traité; also s.v. Le Faucheur, Michel.

[42] *The Art of Speaking in Publick* (London, 1727), p. xi. Italics are those of the original text.

first edition was dedicated "*To the Honoured* Christopher Rawlinson, *Esquire*," and that the dedicatory letter complimented him on the honorable part which he had played in the commonwealth of learning.[43] It seems obvious that this compliment is a reference to Rawlinson's only literary endeavor, his edition of King Alfred's Old English version of Boethius's *Consolationis Philosophiae Libri V*, which was published at Oxford in 1698; and if it is such a reference, then the dedicatory letter itself could not have been written before that same date.

The third piece of evidence is somewhat speculative. The Translator's Preface to the Reader, as it appears in the first edition, confessed "that this *English Translation* of that *Tract*, is wholly owing to the extraordinary Character which the Incomparable Sir *Roger L'Estrange* and the Reverend Dr. *Wake* have been pleased to give it;"[44] but "The Editor's Introduction and Apology" for the second edition changes this particular passage to read that the work had been made English because of the character and recommendations given it "by two very *eminent* Persons of their Time, the incomparable Sir *Roger L'Estrange*, and *his Grace the present Arch-bishop of Canterbury*, when Preacher to the *Honourable Society of Gray's Inn*."[45] The phraseology of the first of these passages is such as to indicate that Sir Roger L'Estrange was still giving his sponsorship to the translation at the time when the passage was being written; but the wording of the second passage naturally puts his sponsorship into an appreciably distant past. Since Sir Roger died in 1704, we may assume that the first edition of the translation was published before that year. Thus its probable date would seem to lie between 1698 and 1704.

The fourth piece of evidence is also speculative. But it tempts us by the wording of the reference to the Reverend Dr. Wake in the first of the passages just cited to guess that 1702 is the probable year in which the English translation of Le Faucheur's *Traitté* first appeared. William Wake, the object of this reference, had studied at Christ Church, Oxford, and had been granted the

[43] *An Essay upon the Action of an Orator*, sig. A2r-A5v.

[44] *Ibid.*, sig. A6v-A7r. In quoting from this Preface here and below, I reverse the style of the original in respect to the use of roman and italic type.

[45] *The Art of Speaking in Publick*, p. xii. Italics are those of the original text.

degree of bachelor of arts in 1676, of master of arts in 1679, and of bachelor and doctor of divinity ten years later. Between 1682 and 1685 he had served in Paris as chaplain to Richard Graham, Viscount Preston, ambassador to the court of Louis XIV, and had come to know French literature and scholarship at first hand. Upon his return to England he filled the office of preacher of Gray's Inn between 1688 and 1695, and of canon of Christ Church, Oxford, between 1689 and 1702. In 1703 he became dean of Exeter, holding that office until 1705. And thereafter he was successively Bishop of Lincoln and Archbishop of Canterbury.[46] The printed reference to him as "the Reverend Dr. *Wake*" in the first edition of the translation of Le Faucheur's *Traitté* would have been made only at that time in his career when he did not have other special titles that a public mention of him would in propriety have included; and in his particular life such a time would in all likelihood have been late in the year 1702, when the sole office that he held was the rectorate of St. James's in Westminster.[47]

No doubt as a young preacher of Gray's Inn between 1688 and 1695 Dr. Wake recommended Le Faucheur's *Traitté* to one of his young friends, not only as a treatise which he had heard praised during his stay in Paris, but also as something which Englishmen would profit by reading. No doubt Sir Roger L'Estrange, who was always interested himself in making French works available in English, conveyed the same recommendation to the same

[46] *The Dictionary of National Biography*, s.v. Wake, William (1657-1737).

[47] Authors were careful in the eighteenth century (and of course in other centuries as well) to refer to prominent living persons by the present titles which those persons held. A very good example can be cited in relation to Dr. Wake himself. In the year 1708 a pamphlet appeared at London with two quotations on its title page, one of which was identified as being from Juvenal's *Satires*, and the other, as being from "Dr. *Wake*, Bishop of *Lincoln*, his Appeal to the True Members of the Church, *p*. 120." Dr. Wake's current title in 1708 was that of Bishop of Lincoln; he did not become Archbishop of Canterbury until 1716.

The pamphlet just mentioned is by Matthew Tindal, and it has the following title and imprint: *A Second Defence of the Rights of the Christian Church. Being a Vindication of the Passages taken out of that Book, and inserted in two Indictments in the Queen's Bench against a Bookseller and his Servant . . . . In a Letter from a Gentleman in* London *to a Clergyman in the Country.* . . . London, Printed in the Year 1708. There is a copy in the Huntington Library.

young man at the same time. No doubt that young man in the course of the next few years did the translation and published it, mentioning the famous Sir Roger in a prefatory compliment that would do no injury to the aspirations of a rising young scholar, and naming his other sponsor, Dr. Wake, by the only title that he could possibly have applied to him at that point, although Wake himself was later to become a celebrated church dignitary.

While 1702 is thus a most probable date for the first publication of the English version of Le Faucheur, the rival date, 1680, is impossible for two reasons, either of which by itself should be conclusive. William Wake could not have been given the title of doctor in the year 1680 or in any other year before 1689. Moreover, the Christopher Rawlinson to whom the first edition of the translation is dedicated, and who is mentioned as a mature scholar at the time when the dedication was being penned, would have been only three years of age in 1680, and thus as that moment hardly eligible for active membership in the commonwealth of learning, even under the passport of flattery.[48]

Le Faucheur's *Traitté* is one of the most respectable works of scholarship in the whole history of the elocutionary movement and one of the leading treatises on delivery in the history of rhetorical theory. With some reservations the same comments apply to the English version, which should now receive a brief consideration.

Immediately after the letter which dedicates the first edition of the English version to Christopher Rawlinson is "The Translator's Preface to the Reader," and in it we learn something of the attitude of English learning towards rhetoric conceived as the art of voice and gesture. Having mentioned the many successful French editions of the work, and the sponsorship of the present translation by Sir Roger L'Estrange and Dr. Wake, the translator indicated that a question had arisen in France "whether *Action* or *No Action* ought to be used in Publick,"[49] and the controversy which ensued between the party of fanaticism and that of foppery had made necessary the discussion of this issue in an introductory chapter of this book. He justified the book itself as follows:

[48] *The Dictionary of National Biography*, s.v. Rawlinson, Christopher (1677-1733).

[49] *An Essay upon the Action of an Orator*, sig. A7r.

But the *Subject* is wholly *New*, and the *Novelty* is worth any *Young Gentlemans* Money in the Kingdom; especially if he lays under any Temptation of the *Air, Gallantry* and *Grace* of a good *Pronunciation* and *Gesture*, either for the *Church*, the *Court*, or the *Camp*. The *Divine*, the *Lawyer* and the *Soldier* are the Men of the World, who have most occasion to *speak well in Publick*: And if our *English Youth* were train'd up more in the *Art of Oratory* and better instructed in the Rules of *Action*, why might they not become as *Great Men* and as *Good Speakers*, as ever *Greece* or *Rome* yet produc'd.[50]

It became an obsession with the later elocutionists, as we shall see, that the art of oratory consisted wholly in acquiring the air, gallantry, and grace of a good pronunciation and gesture, and that proper training in these accomplishments was not only the secret of the mighty eloquence of ancient Greece and Rome, but the sure promise, as well, of greatness of character and eloquence of speech in eighteenth-century England. Thomas Sheridan, who might be called the second founder of the elocutionary movement, thought that this idea originated with himself. But it is stated plainly enough in the passage just quoted from the translator of Le Faucheur. These words from the same source also anticipate other aspects of Sheridan's approach to elocution:

In fine, This *Book* is no Enemy to *Good Breeding*, and it intrenches upon no Mans *Education* or *Profession*. The *Dancing-School* indeed teaches *Gesture* or *Motion* wonderfully well, and the *Ballance of the Body* to Perfection; but it can never do the whole Business of an *Orator* nor accomplish him with all necessary *Action* either for the *Pulpit* or the *Barr*, till the *Feet* can speak *Figures* and the *Hands* plead *Causes*. 'Tis certain however, that *Eloquence* does not lay in the *Heels*, nor *Rhetorick* in *Frisking* and *Gesticulation*.[51]

There is ambiguity in the words just quoted—a tendency both to assert and to deny the thesis that delivery is all that matters in oratory. But the assertion rather than the denial seems to predominate in the following two justifications which the translator saw for his efforts in making Le Faucheur available to the English public:

[50] *Ibid.*, sig. A7v-A8r.   [51] *Ibid.*, sig. A8r-A8v.

First then, the thing is *New, Learned* and *Ingenious* in General. It treats of *Pronunciation* and *Gesture* in particular; which are the very Life and Soul of *Rhetorick*. It is founded upon the best *Authorities* of the Ancients, Ecclesiastical, Secular and Civil; and yet plausibly adapted to *Modern Practice* and the *Genius* of the *present Age*. It is adorned with the finest *Figures* and *Beauties* of *Elocution*, and illustrated with the most *Glorious Examples*. Insomuch that I might by an easy *Metaphor* call it an *Universal Constellation* of *Eloquence*. But as for *Gesture,* there never was any thing done like it *before*; the *Rules* are so very *Nice*, and *New*, even to a *first Discovery*. A Genteel regular *Movement of the Body*, without doubt, goes a great way in the Character of a *Publick Orator*; for there is nothing so taking or so much admir'd now-a-days as that which is *Acted* to the Life; strikes the *Senses* and captivates the *Mind*. So that *Gesture*, in fine, is not improperly called the *Eloquence of the Body* and the last *Accomplishment* of *Speech*.

In the next Place: Besides the *Intrinsick Worth* of this *Treatise*, I may with good Reason also recommend the *usefulness* of it to the *Grammar-Schools*, the *Universities* and the *Inns of Court*; And I hope I shall not be charged either with *Impertinence* or *Praesumption* for my Pains, after a fair Perusal. However I shall take upon me to say, that it will make as excellent a *School-Book* for *Boyes* as any extant; to reform the *vitious Habits* of their *Pronunciation*; to refine the affected Rudeness of their *Behaviour*; to polish the natural *Clownishness* of their *Gesture*, and to give them a true *Light* at last into the main end and design of *Rhetorick,* which is to express themselves *distinctly* and *handsomely* in their *Exercises* upon all Occasions. I am confident over and above, that it will not be thought unworthy of any *Young Gentlemans* Pocket or *Study*, who has any value for the Graces of *Action*, and the Charms of *Eloquence*. But I will be so bold at last as to assert, that if this little *Tract* were rightly made use of, with a just *Application,* by *Students* either of *Divinity* or the *Law*; they would have no occasion to run so often to the *Play-Houses*, nor fall in *Love* somuch with *comical Fopperies* and *extravagant Postures*. Farewel.[52]

[52] *Ibid.*, sig. A9r-A11r.

We shall have occasion later to remark that the English translator of Le Faucheur's *Traitté* had not yet settled upon the term
elocution as the proper name for the fifth part of ancient rhetoric.
In the passage just quoted, for example, it is noticeable that he
preferred the older terminology in which delivery was called pronunciation and gesture, and that he used the word elocution to
designate the tropes and the figures of style. But this matter was
strictly an issue between the English translator and his English
public. It was not an issue between Le Faucheur and his French
readers. We see how Le Faucheur conceived of his work and of
the public reaction to it in "The Author's Preface to the Reader,"
which in this edition of the translation follows immediately after
"The Translator's Preface." Le Faucheur thought that his work
needed defense against those who "will say that I am *overlarge*
and more *nice* then I need be upon the *variation of the Voyce*,"
and those who "may think that my *Rules of Rhetorick* are over-
stockt with *Examples*, and needed not all that Train of Illustration."[53] He answered these criticisms as follows:

> *First*, As to *those* on the one hand, that think I am too *long* and
> *exact* upon the Business of *Pronunciation*, and have said *too
> much* of the *Variation of the Voice*; They cannot in Justice
> blame me for being so *particular* upon the two *main Points* of
> *Oratory*. . . .
>
> *Secondly*, As for *those*, on the other hand, that find fault with
> me for stuffing my Discourse with too *many Examples*, and for
> gathering up such a *Cloud of Testimonies* to make good the
> *Rules* here propounded; I have *this* to say for't. *First*, That
> these Authorities, quoted out of the best *Writers* and *Orators*,
> so famous all over the World for their Learning and Eloquence,
> do add a certain Beauty and Lustre to the *Rules of this Art*.
> Besides, they give my *Praecepts* a Reputation and Credit as
> well as an agreeable *Light, Air* and *Grace*. . . . But, *secondly*,
> I have *this* also to urge further, that *these Examples* do not only
> adorn my *Praecepts*, which are not so very pleasing perhaps or
> agreeable *of themselves*; but illustrate them too, and make
> them more easy and intelligible.[54]

[53] *Ibid.*, sig. a1v. The italics are those of the original text here and below.
[54] *Ibid.*, sig. a1v-a3r.

Early in the first chapter of the English translation of the *Traitté* the statement is made that "the *Great Masters* of *Rhetorick* have set up *Invention, Disposition*, and *Elocution* for the *three first parts* of *Oratory*," and that later, in recognition of the influence of the passions in human affairs, they added "a *Fourth Part*. That is, *Action*; which consists of *Speaking* and *Gesture*," and which Demosthenes rated as the first, the second, and the third among the accomplishments of an orator, as did Cicero too.[55] It is important to notice in this declaration not only that oral delivery is considered to be of special importance in arousing the passions of a hearer but also that it is being treated by Le Faucheur as the fourth rather than the only part of the classical rhetorical program. Le Faucheur's translator was not always careful to preserve the notion that, while delivery has an important place in the hierarchy of oratorical arts, it must never be allowed to become the sole member of the hierarchy. In fact, we have seen in his own preface that he slides constantly towards the acceptance of distinct and handsome delivery as the main end and design of rhetoric, despite his awareness that Le Faucheur's own text gave rhetoric more than that one responsibility. The translator's attitude seems to be a native English contribution to the classical theory of *pronuntiatio*; but, as an English contribution, it is confined to the elocutionists, not to the learned traditionalists like Ward and Holmes. In fact, as we shall see later, the objectionable feature in Thomas Sheridan's elocutionary program was that he saw nothing in classical rhetoric except delivery, even when he was quoting from Cicero and Quintilian the very passages that denied so limited a thesis. Le Faucheur would not have authorized the concept behind Sheridan's program. Le Faucheur's English translator, however, was beginning to suggest that that concept was really what Le Faucheur's treatise had been about in the first place.

The latter part of the first chapter of the *Traitté* is devoted to the considerations which led Le Faucheur originally to write on delivery. Excellence in this part of rhetoric, said he, can make up for deficiencies in invention, arrangement, and style, whereas excellence in those parts can go for nothing if the faculty of pronunciation and gesture is poorly developed. "So Powerfull an

[55] *Ibid.*, p. 2; see also p. 78.

Influence has this Faculty over the *Senses*," he picturesquely re-marked, "That the Impression and *Farewell* it leaves upon us, is the *Orator's* Fate."[56] It is therefore to be wished, he observed, that the ancients had established delivery "in as ample a manner as they have established the other three parts of *Rhetorick*." But they did not. Aristotle gave no precepts for it, believing it a gift of nature; Cicero did not supply it with laws; Cornificius treated it, to be sure, but in an imperfect way; and Quintilian, who sur-passed all the rest, did not meet modern requirements—"His instructions also are only for the *Barr*, and Rules of *Action* are still wanting as well for the *Pulpit*."[57] This book, at the urging of friends, said Le Faucheur, was written to supply this latter need, and to eliminate from Quintilian's treatment of legal speaking cer-tain fopperies that are no longer customary or desirable.

But is a studied delivery becoming to a divine or a lawyer? Should preachers of the word of God have a care for voice and gesture? Is it not unworthy of their ministry for them to consider "how to *frame their Voyce* and *move their Body*"?[58] If congrega-tions are won by grace and elegance in speaking, has not preach-ing become a craft more suited to actors in playhouses than to ministers in the pulpit? Did the Apostles study and practice "*this Art of Action*" in making the remarkable conversions that are characteristic of their role in history?[59] And as for lawyers, did God appoint men to administer justice by fine words and fair speeches? Is it not the task of speakers at the bar of justice before learned judges "to tell them the *naked truth* of things, to shew 'em the bare *matter of Fact* they are to *Try*, in the plainest character and Stile. . . ?"[60] These questions are raised and answered in Le Faucheur's second chapter.

Le Faucheur did not approach these questions solely in the spirit of a philosopher determined to decide whether the study of rhetorical means is to be avoided under all circumstances or is to be undertaken only when rhetorical means are subordinated to religious or legal ends. He approached them instead with the attitude of a thoughtful pragmatist. Thus he argued that he did not intend his book for those who had already acquired the art

[56] *Ibid.*, pp. 3-4.
[57] *Ibid.*, pp. 8-9. Many scholars of Le Faucheur's time attributed to Cornifi-cius the *Rhetorica ad Herennium*; Le Faucheur's reference is to that work.
[58] *Ibid.*, p. 14.   [59] *Ibid.*, p. 15.   [60] *Ibid.*, p. 25.

of speaking. Rather, he intended "only to instruct *Youth* and assist those that are bred up to *Divinity* or the *Law*."[61] Moreover, he went on, he did not want to suggest by his book that graceful action was the whole of a minister's concern. Graceful action, he said, is an external thing, and if preachers became more preoccupied with it than with proclaiming the glory of God or seeking the salvation of man, they would indeed profane their ministry "and turn the *Pulpit* of *Jesus Christ* into a *Theatre* of their own *Pomp* and *Vanity*."[62] My design, he insisted, is only to show preachers how to edify their congregations "not only with their discourse and Style, but in some measure also by the decency of their *Speaking* and the Fineness of their *Action*."[63] Although the Apostles may not have observed these niceties, St. James and St. John were nevertheless called by Christ *"the Sons of Thunder,"* and these two never exhorted people except in the voice of terror and vehemence; besides, the Apostles had the immediate inspiration of heaven and the power to work miracles, and if modern preachers had similar resources, the study of action would be as irrelevant for them as it was for the original evangelists.[64] As for the court of law, the study of a graceful delivery by speakers who practice there is essential for three reasons. First of all, judges are not perfectly learned, and they need more than a bare recital of the merits of a case to make them give a fair hearing to a legal speech. "Now," declared Le Faucheur, "there is nothing like a fine way of *Speaking* and *Gesture* to make them take notice of a *Plea*. . . . The *best Cause* in the world may soon be lost for want of *Action*."[65] Secondly, good speaking and fine action help to convince judges that the orator is sincere. As one authority for this statement Le Faucheur quoted Cicero himself. It appears that Marcus Calidius had charged in court that Quintus Gallius had attempted to poison him. Appearing in defense of Gallius, Cicero argued that the charge of Calidius must be false or Calidius would not have presented it with such detachment and indifference. To clinch his point, Cicero turned to Calidius and demanded, *"Where was your Grief and your Grievance, your Fury*

[61] *Ibid.*, p. 16. [62] *Ibid.*, p. 17. [63] *Ibid.*, p. 18.

[64] *Ibid.*, pp. 20-22. For the reference to St. James and St. John, see St. Mark 3.17.

[65] *Ibid.*, p. 28.

and your Fire?"[66] In the third place, declared Le Faucheur, "if honest Men should deny themselves *these Arts* of persuasion in a *Good Case*, others yet would make use of them in a *Bad One*"; and his long quotation from St. Augustine on this theme concludes by issuing the following challenge to those who hesitate on moral grounds to master the art of rhetoric: *"why should not* Good Men *study it to maintain the Cause of* Truth, *when* Ill Men *put it in practice to defend* Injustice, *to support* Error, *and to compass their own* Wicked Ends?"[67]

After having devoted his third chapter to advising young men that they should begin early to study action before an "ungenteel *habit*" has been allowed to develop, and that they should learn "to fly the *Bad* and follow the *Good*" in selecting their elders for imitation, Le Faucheur turned to the first division of his subject, voice or speaking, and for the next eight chapters he successively analyzed the problems of being heard without difficulty or trouble, of being heard with delight, and of being able to get variety into the voice not only in respect to loudness or lowness, vehemence or softness, and swiftness or slowness, but also in respect to differences among rhetorical subjects, among passions, among the formal parts of the oration, among the figures of rhetoric, and among words and sentences. An indirect effect of Le Faucheur's manner of treating this first aspect of the fifth part of ancient rhetoric was that he made his reader aware of many of the traditional terms belonging to the other parts, as when he enumerated the figures of rhetoric, the six parts of the formal oratorical discourse, the kinds of rhetorical subjects, and the passions to which appeals must be made by speakers. Thus a distinct but faint outline of classical rhetoric emerges from Le Faucheur's discussion of voice in oratory. The flavor of this section of his *Traitté* comes out everywhere in the chapters just mentioned, but it is especially evident in the last words of Chapter VIII. Said Le Faucheur at that point:

[66] *Ibid.*, p. 30. For the episode to which Le Faucheur here refers, see Cicero, *Brutus*, 80.277-278. To Le Faucheur's reference I have added essential names and details about the episode.

[67] *Ibid.*, pp. 32-34. For the quotation, see St. Augustine, *De Doctrina Christiana*, 4.2.3.

I must add this; That the only way to acquire the Faculty of *varying* the *voyce* upon all kinds of *Subjects* as well as *Passions,* is to be often *reading* of *Comedies, Tragedies,* and *Dialogues* a loud [*sic*], or some other Discourses of *Authors,* whose Stile comes nearest up to the *Dramatick*: For nothing can be more serviceable to the Emprovement of *Action* and *Elocution*.[68]

Chapters xii and xiii of the *Traitté* deal with the subject of oratorical gesture, at first in general, and then as it involves the whole body and its individual parts—the head, face, eyes, eyebrows, mouth, lips, shoulders, trunk, and hands. It is plain, however, that in Le Faucheur's opinion the most important movements for the orator consist in those which he makes with his hands and eyes.

On the latter subject he said among other things that ancient actors in trying to acquire the faculty of shedding tears upon the stage would keep their imagination at work, not upon the troubles of the characters whom they were portraying, but upon personal afflictions of their own, and thus they were able to make their eyes reflect the grief that their role demanded. One of his examples was based upon an episode in the life of Cicero. When Cicero was in exile, his friend Claudius Aesopus, the actor, performing in the role of the exiled Telamon in a play by Accius, spoke his lines with his mind fixed not on his own part but on Cicero, and so transported the people, and so released their tears, that they took to heart what he meant, and saw the true injustice that Cicero was undergoing. The effect which Aesopus had upon them, said Le Faucheur, went a long way towards bringing Cicero home again.[69] "*Passions,*" he later observed, "are wonderfully convey'd from *one person's Eyes* to *another's*; the *Tears* of the *one* melting the *Heart* of the *other,* and making a *visible sympathy* between their *Imaginations* and *Aspects.*"[70] Le Faucheur then recalled that one of the most famous preachers of a recent age, speaking to a great congregation about the vices of his parish, and about the miseries that God would send upon them in retaliation, suddenly exclaimed, "*And, in fine, God will forsake us.*" And with these words the preacher broke into tears, and ad-

[68] *Ibid.,* pp. 117-118.

[69] *Ibid.,* pp. 187-188. As Le Faucheur indicated, Cicero told this story himself in his *Oratio Pro P. Sextio,* 56-58.

[70] *Ibid.,* pp. 189-190.

dressing himself to God, he imploringly asked, *"And if thou for-sake us*, Good God! *what will become of Us?"* His passionate rap-ture, said Le Faucheur, reduced to Christian tenderness and tears the entire congregation.[71]

In discussing gestures of the hands, "the chief Instruments of *Action,"* Le Faucheur enumerated seventeen specific rules, many of which he presented not as matters of option but as outright prescriptions.[72] Thus the orator is commanded never to clap his hands or thump the pulpit or beat his breast—"for that smells of the *Juggler* and the *Mountebank*, and 'tis good for nothing."[73] The orator is also told to make gestures only with his right hand and to use the left in company with the right solely in such a way as to keep the right above the left. "But to use an *Action* with the *left Hand* alone," Le Faucheur advised, "is a thing you must avoid for its indecency."[74] There were, however, some exceptions to this particular rule: if the speaker needs to indicate where the unjust would be placed on judgment day, he could use his left hand alone, as he also could in illustrating Christ's command to the faithful servant to cut off his right hand if it offend him. The speaker is later advised to put his right hand on his breast in speaking of himself; to make his gestures pass from left to right and end at the right; to begin gesturing only after the speech has begun, and to end gesturing as the speech ends; to accommodate the nature of the gesture to the nature of the thing mentioned, as by beckoning a welcome when uttering a welcome; to allow ges-tures of the hand to rise no higher than the level of the eyes; to keep the hands always in view in any gesturing that takes place; to make no attempt to use action everywhere, and to keep from falling into what the ancients called the vice of *"the babbling of the Hands"*;[75] to imitate no base, filthy, or dishonest action; to be decent and well mannered and modest in all gestures; and to be sure, in a prosopopoeia, that, when the speaker has to represent a person speaking, he gives him gestures proper to that person, or when he represents a person acting, he does nothing discord-ant. It would be discordant, said Le Faucheur, if the preacher, in repeating Christ's agonized cry upon the cross, "My God, my God, why hast thou forsaken me," gestured by clapping his hands together or by lifting them up towards heaven.[76] These rules, Le

[71] *Ibid.*, p. 190. [72] *Ibid.*, pp. 194-205. [73] *Ibid.*, p. 196.
[74] *Ibid.*, p. 197. [75] *Ibid.*, p. 202. [76] *Ibid.*, pp. 203-204.

Faucheur concluded, are not the only ones that could be laid down; "but I think I have taken notice," he remarked, "of the most *principal, useful and necessary Actions*."[77]

The fourteenth and final chapter of Le Faucheur's *Traitté* is devoted to instructions for putting all the precepts for voice and gesture into practice. He acknowledged that in being presented to students the rules "seem *flat, low* and of *little importance*; but being well and exactly *observed*, they give a wonderful *Lustre* and *Grace* to a Discourse."[78] In short, they are not to be despised, not to be dismissed, as light and childish. Nor are they to be objects of conscious attention to the lawyer pleading his cause or to the divine preaching his sermon. For the speaker in the act of speaking, said Le Faucheur, "ought to think of nothing at that time but the matter in hand; and he must not be studying any other *Motions* or *Passions* then, but use *those only* which arise naturally from the *Subject* of his *Discourse*, from the *Place* where he speaks and the *Presence* of the *Person*, to whom he addresses himself: For the very thought of *Rules* and the *care* of *observing* them would mightily distract and amuse him upon *that Conjuncture*."[79] Le Faucheur also made it plain that the actions which were used in the course of an actual speech need not be studied or rehearsed beforehand. Even if time were available to the speaker for such rehearsals, "it would be but ill spent upon the Study of so *trivial* a Business as *Action* is in comparison; instead of giving themselves up entirely to meditate upon the *grave things* they have to say and the *important Affairs* they have to manage."[80] Audiences in the theatre may be wholly taken up with the elegancy and grace of pronunciation and gesture. "But when they hear an *Orator*, they attend chiefly to *serious things*, and to the *important points* of his *Discourse*; and as for his *Action* they are well enough satisfied, if it be but *reasonable* and *agreeable*, and do not offend either their *Ears* or their *Eyes*."[81] In sum, said Le Faucheur, all that I would have a man do is to understand the precepts of action before he speaks—to try them out and practice them in private and endeavor to acquire in that way a good habit of speaking in public. The young speaker should memorize some fine passages and rehearse them until he can pronounce them according to the rules governing delivery. He should observe these

[77] *Ibid.*, p. 206. [78] *Ibid.*, p. 208. [79] *Ibid.*, p. 209.
[80] *Ibid.*, p. 210. [81] *Ibid.*, p. 211.

rules in his own conversation, submitting to a master if he is unable to follow them by himself. He should notice how far famous contemporary advocates and preachers adhere to these rules in their actual discourses. In his first year of applying these rules to his own public delivery, he should solicit criticisms from his intimates and should eliminate any fault that they call to his attention. Above all, said Le Faucheur in his final sentence, the speaker should "neglect nothing that may render him more *accomplisht* and *agreeable* to his *Auditors*."[82]

The French title of Le Faucheur's work—*Traitté de l'action de l'orateur, ou de la Prononciation et du Geste*—was rendered into English by an exactly equivalent English title—*An Essay upon the Action of an Orator; As to his Pronunciation and Gesture*; and the same relationship of literal equivalence prevails for the most part between Le Faucheur's French text as a whole and its English translation. In general, the translator used the English term action to translate Le Faucheur's French term *action*, as we see not only in the title but also in one of the passages cited above.[83] And Le Faucheur in turn used that term to translate the Latin word *actio* or *pronuntiatio*. In general, the translator thought of action as having two aspects, pronunciation or vocal utterance, and gesture or bodily utterance, as his English title proclaimed, and as Le Faucheur and Latin rhetoric had authorized in their own parallel vocabularies. Moreover, the translator, as we have also seen, tended to use the English word elocution to translate what Le Faucheur called *élocution* and Latin rhetoric called *elocutio*.[84] But every now and then, as if to offer evidence that the English word elocution, as used in the context of rhetorical theory, was gradually being transferred from the third to the fifth of the five great arts of Ciceronian rhetoric, Le Faucheur's translator introduced it as the term for vocal utterance or voice. The best illustration of this usage occurs in a passage where Le Faucheur's text contains the word *prononciation* and the English text renders that word as elocution. Le Faucheur was speaking of the unequal importance of human actions and of human events, so far as atrocious and extraordinary crimes are of greater consequence than ordinary vices, so far as the interest of honor and life is of

[82] *Ibid.*, p. 217.   [83] See above, p. 172.

[84] See above, p. 172. See for another example *An Essay upon the Action of an Orator*, p. 78.

deeper concern than the pecuniary interest, and so far as the heroic deeds of a conqueror and the safety or ruin of a nation are of more profound significance than ordinary human actions or the welfare of an individual person. All of these matters, great or small, said Le Faucheur, demand that the orator speak of each in the voice best suited to it—"ils demandent aussi une Prononciation beaucoup plus émeuë et plus véhemente les uns que les autres."[85] The English translation rendered this sentence as follows: "They also require a quite *different Elocution* according to the diversity of the *Subject*; some of them a far more *vehement Accent* and *Passionate Pronunciation* than others."[86]

As if to emphasize his delight in using elocution as a resonant and brave new term for vocal utterance, the translator of Le Faucheur introduced the word on three occasions when the French text did not authorize him to do so, and when he simply embroidered his source by throwing that word in. One good illustration of this exuberance appears in the passage which closes Le Faucheur's eighth chapter, and which I quoted above.[87] The last sentence in that quotation—"For nothing can be more serviceable to the Emprovement of *Action* and *Elocution*"—not only used the word elocution to refer to vocal utterance in speaking but also generously contributed the sentence itself to the text without having any authority in Le Faucheur for doing so.[88] Another illustration of the same sort occurs when the translator, having rendered into English Le Faucheur's analysis of the unpleasant fault of uttering words from a mouth held well open, added on his own inspiration, but without authority in his source, the rhetorical question, "And where's the Elocution of unintelligible *Gibberidge*?"[89] Still another illustration of the same sort occurs when the translator rendered into English Le Faucheur's advice that the speaker must understand the importance of variety in general terms, but "he must have *Particular Rules* also for all the *changes* and *variations* of the *Voyce* that are necessary to set-off his Discourse with a *taking Air* of Elocution, according to the quality of

[85] *Traicté de L'Action de L'Orateur* (Paris, 1676), p. 110. (This edition does not spell the title word in the same way as the first French edition did.)
[86] *An Essay upon the Action of an Orator*, p. 96.
[87] See above, p. 176.
[88] Compare the *Essay*, p. 118, with the *Traicté*, p. 132.
[89] Compare the *Essay*, p. 63, with the *Traicté*, p. 74.

the *Subjects* he treats of, the nature of the *Passions* he would shew in *himself* or raise in *others,* the several parts of his *Discourse,* the different *Figures* he makes use of, and the *variety* of his *words* and his *Phrase.*"[90] The "taking Air of Elocution" in this passage is not authorized in Le Faucheur's French text, and the appearance of the phrase in the translation is to be regarded as one more indication of the strange fascination that the word elocution was coming to have in 1702 in England as a term for vocal utterance. Ultimately the term was to dominate all other competitors in that particular usage, and was even to become the term for the entire art of rhetoric.

[90] Compare the *Essay,* pp. 92-93, with the *Traicté,* p. 106.

Le Faucheur had intended his *Traitté* to be useful primarily to the pulpit and the bar, and this fact was stressed on the title page of its first edition in English. But in its second English edition, the title page enlarged the sphere of its usefulness to include the senate, the theatre, the court, and the camp as well. Lest these new-found beneficiaries be regarded merely as the brain children of promoters bent upon improving the sale of their product, I should like to say that, long before the date of its second edition, the English version of the *Traitté* had been adapted to the uses of the theatre. In fact, it had been utilized to support a discussion of the art of acting, and its influence upon that discussion had been so far concealed as to be difficult for the casual reader to detect or even to suspect.

The work in which this development took place was published at London in 1710, and its title I shall quote in full, precisely because the first part of it seems to indicate that the book itself is a biography of a distinguished actor rather than an attempt to apply the rules of oratorical delivery to the conduct of an actor upon the stage. The title page reads thus:

The Life of Mr. *Thomas Betterton*, The late Eminent Tragedian. Wherein The Action and Utterance of the *Stage, Bar*, and *Pulpit,* are distinctly consider'd. With The Judgment of the late Ingenious *Monsieur de St. Evremond*, upon the *Italian* and *French* Music and Opera's; in a Letter to the Duke of *Buckingham*. To which is added, The Amorous Widow, or the *Wanton Wife*. A Comedy. Written by Mr. Betterton. Now first printed from the Original Copy. . . . London: Printed for Robert Gosling, at the *Mitre*, near the *Inner-Temple Gate* in *Fleetstreet*. 1710.

Despite the failure of this title page to designate the author of the work, Charles Gildon can be positively assigned to that role, owing to the fact that, in some (but not all) copies of its first and only edition, his name is affixed to the letter which dedicates the work to Richard Steele, the famous essayist and politician.[91] Gil-

[91] The Huntington Library holds two copies of the first edition, one containing Gildon's name at the end of the dedicatory letter, and the other, no name at all.

don was a distinctly minor figure in the literary world of London during the eighteenth century. Indeed, Leslie Stephen in his sketch of him in *The Dictionary of National Biography* calls him a hack author and indicates that his entire literary output shows little genius. As we shall see, the part which he played in the work now under discussion does not afford us reason to doubt that verdict.

In addition to the dedicatory epistle, *The Life of Betterton* contains not only a preface and some verses penned by Nicholas Rowe and spoken by Mrs. Barry at a performance on April 7, 1709, for the benefit of Betterton, but also a collection of documents loosely associated with that great actor's career. This collection is made up of the following items: 1) a 4-page introduction promising a biography of Betterton and an account of his precepts on acting;[92] 2) a 6-page sketch of Betterton's life;[93] 3) a 131-page work devoted to the precepts for action and utterance of the stage, the bar, and the pulpit;[94] 4) a 32-page treatise which is a continuation of the preceding item and which devotes itself to critical observations on dancing, music, and opera;[95] 5) a 3-page list of plays in which Betterton had acted;[96] and 6) a separately-paged text of Betterton's play, *The Amorous Widow*. It might be difficult to find a title that would on the one hand be as short as the first six words of Gildon's present one and on the other hand would be comprehensive enough to describe with reasonable accuracy such a miscellany of items as his work actually holds; but it would be equally difficult to find a title that advertises the contents of the book more inaccurately than those six words have managed to do.

The third and fourth sections of the book are in the form of a dialogue faintly reminiscent of Cicero's *De Oratore*. The dialogue is represented to have taken place the year before Betterton's death, and to have been held at his country house in Reading, its characters being Betterton himself and two friends who have called upon him.[97] The conversation begins as the three men re-

[92] Charles Gildon, *The Life of Mr. Thomas Betterton* (London, 1710), pp. 1-4.

[93] *Ibid.*, pp. 5-11.　　[94] *Ibid.*, pp. 11-142.　　[95] *Ibid.*, pp. 142-174.

[96] *Ibid.*, pp. 174-176.

[97] *Ibid.*, p. 11. Betterton's death occurred in 1710. Hence the dialogue is figured to have taken place in 1709.

tire to the garden after having dined together. They naturally fall into a discussion of famous actors and actresses and of the graces of action and speaking. As they proceed, Betterton is urged to deliver his sentiments upon this latter subject, so that from what he says his friends will be able to form "a System of *Acting*, which might be a Rule to future Players, and teach them to excel not only themselves, but those who have gone before them."[98] Betterton professes himself unable to construct such a system because of his ignorance of the learned tongues; "yet not to disappoint you entirely," he observes, "I shall fetch you a Manuscript on this Head, written by a Friend of mine, to which I confess I contributed all, that I was able."[99] It turns out that this manuscript, which one of his guests casually notes to be in Betterton's own handwriting,[100] concerns itself with action and utterance in oratory and in acting, and that it contains two shorter papers. The first shorter paper discusses the meaning of various natural gestures, and is said by Betterton to have come to him by way of another friend "from a learned Jesuit who wrote on this Subject."[101] The second shorter paper treats of the several natural defects, vices, and virtues of the voice, and Betterton indicates that it came through still another friend from Julius Pollux's *Onomasticum Graece & Latine*, Book ii, Ch. 26.[102] After both of these short papers have been read aloud by Betterton, and the presentation of the manuscript surrounding them has been completed, the conversation turns away from acting and takes up dancing, singing, and opera. At this point Betterton reads still another manuscript from still another friend upon these latter topics, and he plainly indicates that this paper in its later portions is based upon a letter addressed by the French critic Saint-Évremond to the Duke of Buckingham.[103] When this paper has been read, the dialogue comes to an end, and Betterton's two guests take their leave and set out on their return to London.

Gildon's readers would be aware, as this account of the third and fourth sections of his book has indicated, that Betterton is relying upon outside sources for stipulated parts of his discourse on action and utterance. It would be simple indeed for those

[98] *Ibid.*, p. 17. [99] *Ibid.*, pp. 17-18. [100] *Ibid.*, p. 18.
[101] *Ibid.*, pp. 43-48. [102] *Ibid.*, pp. 89-93.
[103] *Ibid.*, pp. 147-174. This letter represents the singing of France as superior to that of Italy, and the regular stage as superior to opera (pp. 160-166).

readers to identify one of these sources as the Julius Pollux who flourished in the capacity of a Greek rhetorician and grammarian of the second century of the Christian era. Nor would it be particularly laborious for them to consult that author's *Onomasticum* and to see for themselves that this treatise, which is acknowledged to be the source of the second of the two shorter papers presented by Betterton, actually contains the ideas which Betterton reads aloud to his guests as a part of his discussion of the voice.[104] As for the "learned Jesuit" who is openly acknowledged to have furnished the substance of the first of the two short papers, the reader who knew something about seventeenth-century treatises on oratorical delivery would have no difficulty in identifying him as Louis de Cressolles and in proceeding to satisfy himself that the passages attributed to him by Betterton in an indirect way are in fact passages from the *Vacationes Autumnales*, to which I have earlier had occasion to refer.[105] Thus

[104] In strict terms, Gildon borrowed from Book II, Ch. 4, Section 26, of the *Onomasticum*. See *Julii Pollucis Onomasticum Graece & Latine* (Amstelae-dami, 1706), pp. 210-215. Section 26 is headed, "*De voce, aut his quae a voce derivantur.*" Paragraphs 116-117 of this Section contain the words upon which Gildon's account of the virtues, defects, and vices of the voice is based. Under the heading Voice, Pollux was interested in listing all of the principal words which describe the thing named by that term. Thus he said in these two paragraphs: "In truth you will refer to the voice as elevated, lofty, clear, broad, heavy, impressive, clean, sweet, seductive, exquisite, persuasive, deceitful, pliant, rapid, soft, hissing, plain, perspicuous; black, that is, obscure, hoarse, unpleasant, meagre, contracted, annoying, dusky, confused, discordant, in-elegant, feeble, unpersuasive, rigid, harsh, disconnected, sullen, hollow-sounding, brassy, piercing." (Translation mine.) Compare with Gildon, pp. 89-93. See also below, p. 255.

[105] See above, Ch. 3, p. 120; Ch. 4, pp. 160-161. That Betterton's "learned Jesuit" is Cressolles can be seen by comparing Gildon's work with the *Vacationes Autumnales*, as follows:
For Gildon, p. 43, lines 17-23, see Cressolles, p. 134, lines 3-7.
For Gildon, p. 43, lines 24-29, see Cressolles, p. 109, lines 11-18.
For Gildon, p. 43, lines 30-32, see Cressolles, p. 105, lines 19-22.
For Gildon, p. 44, lines 4-9, see Cressolles, p. 162, lines 12-15, 17-22.
For Gildon, p. 45, lines 30-32, see Cressolles, p. 367, lines 19-23.
For Gildon, p. 46, lines 1-3, see Cressolles, p. 374, lines 6-10.
For Gildon, p. 46, lines 18-31, see Cressolles, p. 317, lines 15-21.
For Gildon, p. 47, lines 1-2, see Cressolles, p. 317, lines 15-21.
This table does not offer an exhaustive account of Gildon's borrowings from Cressolles's vast work. It is designed rather to offer concrete proof that Better-

up to a point Gildon has been careful to emphasize that the dialogue which he composed and attributed to Betterton and his two guests is based upon certain properly identified sources.

Even beyond that point it must in fairness to Gildon be noticed that he has shown a tendency to warn us against supposing the other parts of Betterton's discourse to have been offered as that actor's own advice upon action and utterance on the stage. Thus he said that his only excuse for writing a preface to his book was "to prevent an Objection, which may be made, and that is, that I have been a *Plagiary*, and deliver'd Rules for my own, which are taken out of other Authors." He even added the following admission at once:

I first allow, that I have borrow'd many of them from the *French*, but then the *French* drew most of them from *Quintilian* and other Authors. Yet the *Frenchman* has improv'd the Ancients in this Particular, by supplying what was lost by the Alteration of Custom, with Observations more peculiar to the present Age.[106]

If Gildon's candor, however, had been as complete as the actual situation demanded, he would have had to say more than he did about this French source. He would have had to declare that the source was in fact Le Faucheur's *Traitté*. And he would have had to say in addition that Betterton's discourse was not based directly upon Le Faucheur's French text, but upon the text of the English translation that we have been examining. A comparison of the following pairs of quotations will show the nature of Gildon's reliance upon this unacknowledged English source:

Gildon, p. 32:

Pericles, tho 'tis said he had the Goddess Persuasion on his Lips, and that he thundred and lightned in an Assembly, and made all *Greece* tremble when he spoke, yet would never publish any of his Orations, because their Excellency lay in the ACTION.

---

ton's "learned Jesuit" and Cressolles are one and the same person. More work is needed on the problem of referring Gildon's other borrowings from the "learned Jesuit" to their source in the *Vacationes Autumnales*.

[106] Gildon, pp. ix-x; see also pp. 28, 31, for guarded references suggesting his dependence on a translation. My quotations reverse Gildon's style in respect to the use of roman and italic type.

Le Faucheur's Translator, p. 6:
> *Pericles*, for all the *Poets* said that the *Goddess of Persuasion* sat upon his Lipps; that he *thunder'd* and *lighten'd* in an *Assembly*, and made all *Greece* tremble again when he *Spake*; never made any of his *Orations* Publick: For why, *says one*, their Excellency lay in the *Action*. . . .

Gildon, p. 72:
> The *Mouth* must never be writh'd, nor the *Lips* bit or lick'd, which are all ungenteel and unmannerly Actions, and yet what some are frequently guilty of. . . .

Le Faucheur's Translator, pp. 192-193:
> As for the *Mouth*, you must never *wry* it at all; for that's very *disagreeable*. . . . As for your *Lips*, you must take care not to *bite* 'em, nor to *lick* 'em with your *Tongue*; as I have seen some People do sometimes: Which is very *Ungenteel* and *Unmannerly* in an *Orator*.

Gildon, p. 101:
> There are, in short, two things to make the Speaker heard and understood without Difficulty; first, a very distinct and articulate Voice, and next a very strong and vigorous Pronunciation. The first is the most important; for an indifferent Voice, with a distinct Pronunciation, shall be far more easily understood, than one, that is stronger and more audible, but which does not articulate the Words so well.

Le Faucheur's Translator, pp. 64-65:
> *First*, there are two things requisite to qualify a Man for this Work: That is, a very *Distinct* and *Articulate Voyce*, and a very *Strong* and *Vigorous Pronunciation*; but the *former* is the more important and necessary of the *Two*. For a Man that has only an *indifferent Voyce*, if his *Pronunciation* be but Distinct, he shall be understood with far more ease than another that has a stronger and more Audible Faculty of *Speaking*, but does not *articulate* his words so well.[107]

[107] Gildon's borrowings from the English version of Le Faucheur are sometimes close to verbatim quotations, as in the passages shown here; sometimes, however, Gildon's text consists in verbal echoes of his source, or in the adaptation of Le Faucheur's oratorical doctrine to the special uses of the actor. For

As we reflect upon the whole dialogue between Betterton and his friends, it is proper to observe that in certain respects Gildon has succeeded despite the woodenness of his method in making Betterton as attractive a character in this work as he was in fact. Thus Gildon shows Betterton to be modest and unassuming, and to feel that even his eminence as an actor does not entitle him to speak in his own person upon a subject so fully considered by ancient Greek and Latin authors as the technique of oratorical delivery was. Thus also Gildon shows Betterton to have the unmistakable right to contribute to the art of delivery something from his own impressive experience on the stage. In this latter connection, we may perhaps assume that Betterton's repeated and admiring references to Hamlet's famous words on utterance and gesture in the theatre are consciously contrived by Gildon to indicate what Betterton himself would want his own experience to mean in terms of a modern enrichment of ancient theory, and what Hamlet's words must have meant to Betterton in his many celebrated appearances in the role of the prince of Denmark as he was advising the strolling players on the pronunciation of the lines that they were to utter in the attempt to trap the conscience of Claudius.[108]

One final word about Gildon's *Life of Betterton*. Some of what it says on stage history, and much of what it says on stage gesture, appeared almost verbatim later in the eighteenth century in a work called *The History of the English Stage* (London, 1741), attributed on its title page to Betterton, but more properly to be regarded as a miscellany compiled by Edmund Curll. This work runs to 167 pages, 66 of which can be positively identified with pages that Gildon had written himself or had borrowed from the

---

illustrations of each of these two latter kinds of borrowings, compare Gildon's text with that of the English version of Le Faucheur, as follows:

p. 26 with p. 172	pp. 33-34 with pp. 173-177
p. 26 with pp. 39-55	p. 51 with pp. 171-172
pp. 26-27 with pp. 39, 54-55	p. 57 with p. 178
p. 27 with pp. 58, 175	p. 78 with p. 202
p. 28 with pp. 115-116	

[108] For Betterton's references to *Hamlet*, see Gildon, pp. 23-24, 38, 70-71, 81-84, 87-88.

English version of Le Faucheur.[109] With his eye fixed upon the possibility of exploiting human weaknesses for his own profit, Curll distributed these 66 pages in such fashion that sections of doctrine on stage action preceded and followed sections devoted to accounts of the lives and loves of famous actors and actresses and to episodes in the history of the theatre. Curll omitted almost everything that Gildon had said on utterance or voice; and this latter topic, it should be emphasized, had been made much less important by Gildon than it had been by Le Faucheur. But Curll gave most of Gildon's precepts on gesture, and thus it is possible for us to say that the elocutionary movement during its first fifty years in England was as closely concerned with the art of acting as it was with oratorical delivery in speeches made in the pulpit, at the bar, or in the parliament.

[109] The following sections of Curll's *History* and Gildon's *Life of Betterton* may be consulted and compared by those interested in seeing how far the later work is based upon the earlier:

Ch. I (pp. 5-12) of Curll is drawn from Gildon, pp. 2, 5-10.

Ch. II (pp. 13-31) of Curll is partly drawn from Gildon, pp. 13-17.

Ch. IV (pp. 36-54) of Curll is drawn from Gildon, pp. 23-40.

Ch. V (pp. 55-78) of Curll is partly drawn from Gildon, pp. 41-55.

Ch. VI (pp. 79-110) of Curll is partly drawn from Gildon, pp. 57-68, 71-84.

The fact that Curll's *History*, p. 36, attributes its fourth chapter to "Mr. Betterton's Papers" has led to the conclusion that Curll's treatment of stage gesture is taken directly from the notes of the famous actor himself. This conclusion is apparently endorsed by *The Cambridge Bibliography of English Literature*, II, 403. But such an opinion appears to have nothing to support it except Curll's words as just quoted, and Curll, of course, is merely echoing Gildon's assertion in the *Life of Betterton* that the manuscript read by Betterton was in his own hand. Once we recognize that Curll was borrowing Gildon's text, and that Gildon in turn was attributing to Betterton what Le Faucheur had actually said, we cannot take seriously the assumption that Curll was giving us Betterton's own views.

Alan S. Downer, "Nature to Advantage Dressed: Eighteenth-Century Acting," *PMLA*, LVIII (1943), 1007, 1031-1032, was I believe the first to note that Curll's *History* borrows much of its material from Gildon's *Life of Betterton*. The connection between Gildon and Le Faucheur appears not to have been recognized until it was pointed out in the article to which I referred above, n. 11.

The next episode, and a crucial one, in the early history of this movement in England concerns an anonymous pamphlet entitled *Some Rules for Speaking and Action; To be observed At the Bar, in the Pulpit, and the Senate, and by every one that Speaks in Publick. In a Letter to a Friend.* This little treatise was first published at London in August or September of 1715, and it had an immediate run of popularity, with the result that it reached a third edition by the following February, and had two later editions by 1750.[110] My present discussion of it is based upon a copy of the third edition at the Huntington Library. That copy contains 32 pages, and is made up of a short Preface, a division called "The Portraiture of a Compleat Orator," a quotation "Out of Bishop Sprat's Charge to his Clergy," another quotation "Out of Bishop Burnet's Pastoral Care," and an unsigned Letter dated Feb. 4, 1715/16, and headed "Some Rules for Speaking and Action." The Preface is brief enough to be quoted in full:

> This Letter was writ and printed about Six Months ago at the Request of a *Friend*; and the *Bookseller* being now about Publishing another Edition, and desiring me to give him what farther *Collections* I have made; I have prefix'd to it, *The Portraiture of a Compleat Orator*, which is agreeable enough to the Letter, as taken from *Quintilian*, and an *Epitome* of what the Bishop *Sprat* and *Burnet*, the one the *English Cicero*, the other one of the greatest Orators of the Age, have written upon this Subject. What other *Observations* I have since made, are inserted in the Letter; and indeed I should have digested what is prefix'd into the same Method, but only I thought there was no Occasion to be nicely Methodical in such a short Discourse, and which consists wholly of Hints and Sketches. I *submit* it to the World as it is, and shall be glad to see it mended.[111]

As these words indicate, the author of the pamphlet considered that his own contribution to his subject was contained in his Let-

---

[110] See above, Ch. 3, n. 102. See also *British Museum General Catalogue of Printed Books*, s.v. Rules (col. 128).

[111] I reverse the style of the original text in regard to the use of roman and italic type.

ter on speaking and action. When we turn to it, we find that it begins on a note of apology for the author's unfitness, and that it declares its intention of relying only upon what others have said.[112] The author later added that "this *Letter* is an *Epitome* of Volumes."[113] Despite this amiable pretension, however, he depended completely upon the first edition of the English version of Le Faucheur's *Traitté*, as a reading of the two works will reveal to anyone interested.

Perhaps the most significant aspect of *Some Rules for Speaking and Action*, apart from its connection with Le Faucheur's influence upon the early history of the elocutionary movement in England, is that it was cited not only in John Ward's lectures on rhetoric at Gresham College, as we have noticed,[114] but also in John Mason's little work, *An Essay on Elocution, or, Pronunciation*, first published at London in 1748. Mason openly acknowledged his reliance upon it for the dictum that words of quality and distinction must be pronounced with strong emphasis.[115] But despite his attempt to show that he had predecessors, it has been carelessly assumed in our time that he was the originator of the elocutionary movement in England, and that his *Essay* stands at the head of the list of great English works on elocution.[116] In actual fact, Mason occupies a modest position in the movement, as we shall see when we come to consider him later in this chapter. Meanwhile, those who wish to examine his use of *Some Rules* as one of his acknowledged sources should also be aware of his occasional unacknowledged reliance upon the first or the second edition of the English version of Le Faucheur's *Traitté*. For example, his observations upon the problem of varying the voice according to the tenor of the passions and according to the differing moods of the different parts of the classical oration have a much

---

[112] *Some Rules for Speaking and Action* (London, 1716), p. 20.

[113] *Ibid.*, p. 30.

[114] See above, Ch. 3, n. 102.

[115] See his *Essay on Elocution, or, Pronunciation* (London, 1748), p. 27.

[116] The latter view is expressed by Warren Guthrie, "The Development of Rhetorical Theory in America, 1635-1850: V, The Elocution Movement—England," *Speech Monographs*, XVIII (March 1951), 21, 23; the former, by W. M. Parrish, "Elocution—A Definition and a Challenge," *The Quarterly Journal of Speech*, XLIII (1957), 2.

clearer source in Le Faucheur and his English translator than in
Some Rules for Speaking and Action.[117]

[117] In *An Essay on Elocution, or, Pronunciation*, p. 26, Mason in a very
summary fashion characterized the kind of voice that should be used to express love, anger, joy, sorrow, fear, courage, and perplexity. In *An Essay Upon
the Action of an Orator*, pp. 99-100, Le Faucheur's translator in an equally
summary fashion characterized the kind of voice to be used to express love,
hatred, joy, grief, fear, confidence, anger. There can be no doubt that Mason's
account of these passions follows that of Le Faucheur's translator.

Also on p. 26, Mason briefly designated the kind of voice that ought to be
used for exordiums, narrations, reasoning, and persuasion. His advice on these
points is a severely reduced version of that in Le Faucheur's translator, pp. 119,
125, 126, 127.

The author of *Some Rules for Speaking and Action* handled the emotions
merely by saying, p. 24: "Joy and Sorrow, Fear and Boldness, Resentment and
Compassion, Esteem and Contempt, demand *Different Looks* and *Actions.*"
As for the parts of the oration, he remarked, p. 25: "An Orator, Sir, should
Begin with a low and modest Voice, *Raise* it by Degrees as the Subject re-
quires, and *Conclude* with Joy, and Triumph, and Satisfaction."

Merry-Andrew

The next episode of my present story concerns John Henley, who attracted more attention to the elocutionary movement than did anyone else of his time. As early as 1738 his title as the *"restorer of the ancient elocution"* had become sufficiently well known to be recognized by Ephraim Chambers in the second edition of his popular *Cyclopaedia*, and sufficiently inappropriate to invite Chambers to remark with a touch of contempt that if Mr. Henley wanted an accurate description of what he was actually engaged in doing, he should call himself the restorer of the ancient pronunciation.[118] Henley was only forty-six years of age when Chambers thus memorialized and corrected his way of characterizing himself. It is no small accomplishment for a man in middle life to be mentioned in this special way in an important reference work, even with a rebuke implied in the notoriety.

This prominent early elocutionist is also known to fame as Orator Henley.[119] Son of the vicar of Melton Mowbray and grandson of the vicar of the same parish on his mother's side, Henley was born in 1692 and educated at St. John's College, Cambridge. He became a schoolmaster in his native village, where, says his biographer, Mr. Welstede, he established the "Practice of improving Elocution by the publick Speaking of Passages in the Classicks, Morning and Afternoon, as well as Orations, &c."[120] During this time he began an extensive work on universal grammar, wrote an historical poem called *Esther*, refused an invitation to apply for a fellowship at his college in Cambridge, was ordained deacon by Dr. Wake (the sponsor of Le Faucheur's English translator), and, after receiving his M.A. in 1716, was admitted into the clergy of the Anglican church.

Successful at once as a preacher, and ambitious to succeed in this new career, he went to London equipped with thirty letters

[118] See above, p. 150.

[119] See *The Dictionary of National Biography*, s.v. Henley, John.

[120] John Henley, *Oratory Transactions, No. I* (London, 1728), p. 5. This quotation occurs in connection with a biographical sketch of Henley attributed to "Mr. *Welstede*" and included in this volume of *Oratory Transactions*. According to T. F. Henderson's brief life of Henley in *The Dictionary of National Biography*, Welstede is probably to be identified as Henley himself.

of recommendation, "and preach'd more Charity-Sermons about Town, was more numerously followed, and raised more for the poor children at those Sermons than any other Preacher, however dignify'd, or distinguish'd."[121] In delivering these sermons, Henley placed open stress upon proper utterance and gesture, influenced no doubt by the popularity of such treatises as the English translation of Le Faucheur, Gildon's misnamed *Life of Mr. Thomas Betterton*, and the anonymous pamphlet, *Some Rules for Speaking and Action*. At this same era of his life, Henley did a considerable amount of literary work. He published translations of Pliny the Younger's *Epistles* and *Panegyric*, of various works of René Vertot, of Montfaucon's *Diarium Italicum*, of Jean-Pierre de Crousaz's *Logique*, and of Addison's Latin poems. He also edited *The Works of Sir Philip Sidney* (London, 1724-25).[122]

But his obvious concern for success, his flamboyance in advertising elocutionary techniques through his sermons, and his studied program of attracting attention to himself, began soon to tell against him. Mr. Welstede says that Henley's "Popularity, with his enterprizing Spirit, and introducing regular Action into the Pulpit, were the true Causes, why some obstructed his rising in Town, from Envy, Jealousy, and a Disrelish of those who are not qualify'd to be compleat Spaniels."[123] There is also a possibility, not mentioned by Welstede, that Henley's career in the Anglican establishment was impaired by rumors of his having been forced to leave Melton Mowbray because of a scandal linking him to a married woman, Mrs. Tolson, who was subsequently alleged to have followed him to London and to have passed as his wife.[124] At any rate, about the year 1724 Henley was relieved of his ecclesiastical duties in London and tossed "into a country-Benefice by the Way of the Sea, as far as *Galilee* of the *Gentiles*."[125] Not in the mood to endure this exile from town, Henley gave up his country benefice and his career in the established church; and he returned to London to open on July 3, 1726, in quarters above the market

[121] *Oratory Transactions, No. I*, p. 12.

[122] See *Books Written, and Publish'd, By the Reverend John Henley, M. A.* (London, 1724), pp. 5-15. See also *Oratory Transactions, No. I*, p. 12.

[123] *Oratory Transactions, No. I*, p. 12.

[124] See William Whiston, *Mr. Henley's Letters and Advertisements, Which concern Mr. Whiston* (London, 1727), pp. 14-16.

[125] *Oratory Transactions, No. I*, p. 13.

house in Newport Market, an institution which he called The Oratory.

The Oratory had two aspects, one religious and the other secular.[126] On the former side its practices rested upon the legal right of private judgment in religion, and upon the liturgy of the primitive Christian church. As a secular institution, it was declared to be an academy of the sciences and languages to supply the want of a university in London.[127] Thus Henley preached sermons on Sundays; and on week days he conducted public conferences, or had others conduct them, on a variety of subjects.[128] He widely advertised himself as a preacher who applied the proper rules of voice and gesture to the presentation of his sermons; and in describing the educational aims of The Oratory in the first sermon that he preached there, he said, "Above all, what shall most strongly engage our attention, shall be the beautiful, and long neglected science of rhetoric and elocution."[129] The Oratory, it would appear, is the true forerunner of the elocutionary academy that Thomas Sheridan was to dream of founding later in the eighteenth century, and of the schools of oratory, elocution, and speech that were to be established in America during the nineteenth and twentieth centuries.

Henley attracted so much attention with his concern for elocu-

---

[126] For an account of the plan of The Oratory, the principles governing its conferences, the procedures followed in its system of instruction, the text of the first sermon preached there, the text of its liturgy, and so on, see John Henley, *The Appeal of the Oratory to the First Ages of Christianity* (London, 1727).

[127] The University of London was not incorporated until 1836. But the Oratory was hardly correct in pretending in 1726 that higher instruction was not then available in London. See above, Ch. 3, pp. 83-86.

[128] See John Henley, *Oratory Transactions, No. II* (London, n.d.), which contains a list of sermons, theological lectures, and academic lectures delivered at The Oratory from July 3, 1726, to August 31, 1728.

[129] For the text of this sermon, see *The Appeal of the Oratory to the First Ages of Christianity*, where the sermon is paged with "Four Discourses," pp. 25-41. My quotation is from p. 38. In restoring the science of elocution, Henley delivered a series of lectures on July 6, 13, 20, and 27, 1726, on the following topics: "The general Principles of Speaking"; "The general Principles of Action"; "The Antient History of Action"; "Remarks on some Rules of *Quintilian*." On August 31 of that year, he delivered a lecture on "The Action of the Eye and Features." See *Oratory Transactions, No. II*, under "The Academical . . . Subjects of the Oratory."

tion that by 1727 the publisher of the first edition of the English version of Le Faucheur's *Traitté* decided that a second edition would be a profitable enterprise. Accordingly he commissioned an editor whose identity is now unknown to see it through the press and to supply, as its title page declared "an Introduction relating to the Famous Mr. *Henley's* present Oratory." Thanks to that editor's work, we are given a revealing account of Henley's efforts to restore the ancient elocution. The editor began his introduction with these words:

> The Town having been of late very much alarm'd at the *Reverend* and *ingenious* Mr. *Henly's* extraordinary Performances and Attempts, to revive the antient Manner of Speaking in Public, upon all Occasions; several Pamphlets have appear'd in the World, and particularly one, written by Mr. *Wood*, which mightily condemns Mr. *Henly's* Gestures, comparing them to the absurd and indecent Gesticulations of a *Merry-Andrew* or *Harlequin*. Mr. *Wood* lashing the *Newport Market* Orator's Gestures so satyrically, and at the same time referring his Readers to the following Sheets, whereby they might judge how different Mr. *Henly's* Gestures were from the Rules laid down in them; Great Demands were made for them, which is the real and true Occasion for their appearing abroad once more in public Print. . . .[130]

Having thus justified the republication of the English version of Le Faucheur, the editor went on to speak of the circumstances under which that work had been first published in England and

---

[130] *The Art of Speaking in Publick*, pp. x-xi. The Wood here mentioned called himself elsewhere William Wood of Christ Church, Oxford. He had offered himself in 1726 as a lecturer in The Oratory, and had been commissioned by Henley to collect for delivery at a conference an hour's worth of passages from Cicero on the subject of voice and gesture. But it seems that at this same time Wood was preparing to publish an attack upon Henley. When the latter discovered Wood's duplicity, he accused him of making improper advances to one of the boys in a school where Wood had been employed as teacher, and he later offered to meet Wood in a duel. The details of this earthy episode are set forth in William Wood's pamphlet, *The Dueling Orator delineated* (London, 1726).

It could well be that this William Wood is the anonymous editor of *The Art of Speaking in Publick*, and that he took revenge upon Henley by writing unfavorably of him in the introduction of that work.

composed in France. Then he offered some comments of his own on speaking and action in oratory, and at length returned to the subject of Henley:

> To Conclude. Notwithstanding the great Pains and Industry, of the *Reverend Mr. Henley,* and his under Strapers to collect Passages from Authors upon *Elocution;* Yet it is very much feared he will have but little longer Success, because his own Gestures are thought by many experienc'd *Orators* not conformable to the Precepts he lays down, and if they were, as they really in Fact are not; yet his Auditors cou'd never attain it, without a diligent and constant Practice.[131]

As for Henley's own actual contributions to the doctrine of the elocutionary movement, we shall confine ourselves here to his chief effort in that field. It is contained in one of his sermons, and it circulated widely in its time. But we should bear in mind that among the voluminous Henley manuscripts in the British Museum and the Guildhall Library in London, there are other writings of his on this subject, and that these might possibly yield something to give Henley a higher standing among rhetoricians than that which his printed works or his promotional activities can possibly justify.[132]

On Sunday, November 15, 1724, when he was still in charge of his country benefice, and had not yet broken with the Anglican establishment, Henley preached in the Church of St. George the Martyr, in London, a sermon containing his theory of elocution. The sermon was published the following year at the request of many in the audience under the title *The History And Advantages of divine Revelation, with the Honour, that is due to the Word of God; especially in regard to the most Perfect Manner Of delivering it, form'd on the antient Laws of Speaking and Action: Being an Essay to restore them.*[133] This work was given a second

---

[131] *The Art of Speaking in Publick,* pp. xxiii-xxiv.

[132] I have not examined the Henley manuscripts in the Guildhall Library, but I have looked at some of those in the British Museum, and I have read the following ones, which, although only of minor interest and scant value, do bear upon speaking and action in oratory: "Eloquence of the Pulpit"; "The Action of the Eye, and Aspect"; "Action of the Hands." See Additional Mss. 19, 925.

[133] The imprint reads: "*London*: Printed for *T. Longman,* at the *Ship* and *Black-swan* in *Pater-noster-row*; *J. Mac-Euen,* in the *Strand*; and sold at his

edition in 1727, appearing as one of the units in Henley's *The Appeal of the Oratory to the First Ages of Christianity*, and upon that edition my present discussion is based. That same second edition was included in one of Henley's later publications, *Oratory Transactions, No. II*.

The sermon is on the text of I Samuel 3.1: "And the word of the Lord was precious in those days; there was no open vision." Henley followed three lines of thought in developing this text. He first offered comment upon the several methods that God had used to reveal his will to mankind in the period between the Creation and the writing of the Gospels. Secondly, he endeavored to show what honor and happiness had come to human beings as a result of those revelations. Thirdly, he considered what respect should be paid to God's word in general, and how respect should be shown in particular in preaching upon it. Under this third heading he developed his theory of elocution. Thus he spoke, as indeed he explicitly emphasized, "of sacred eloquence, or the oratory of the pulpit; with regard to the publick exercise of it."[134] I presuppose, he said, that the preacher is qualified for his task by nature and training, and that he has "a well weigh'd composition, or, a discourse in the mind, and a ready mastery of it in speaking."[135] What, then, should be the preacher's chief concern in utterance and gesture?

Henley's answer to this question sounds familiar indeed to anyone who has followed Le Faucheur's ideas into their first English edition and into their subsequent abridgment by Gildon and by the anonymous compiler of *Some Rules for Speaking and Action*. In fact, in the second edition of the sermon now under consideration, Henley inserted a note which refers to what Bishops Ken, Burnet, Sprat, and Gibson had said in recommending greater attention to delivery on the part of clergymen,[136] and, as anyone can verify, Henley could have found in the third edition of *Some Rules for Speaking and Action* the very passages in question, so far as Bishops Burnet and Sprat are concerned. But let us give

---

shop in *Edenburgh*; and *G. Dommer*, 1725." There is a copy at the Bodleian Library.

[134] *The Appeal of the Oratory to the First Ages of Christianity*, p. 15.
[135] *Ibid.*, p. 15.
[136] *Ibid.*, p. 19. A different note appears at this point in the first edition.

Henley a full opportunity to state his own theory of elocution as he would have it applied by preachers in the pulpit. He said:

> That manner of delivery, which is the most just, forcible, and compleat, on this important head, is that, which takes in all the powers of the whole man. . . .

> Since then, the compleat, which must be the only just delivery, includes all the faculties together; it demands a right management of the utterance, and of the behaviour, as parts of those faculties, otherwise it must be imperfect and deficient, and therefore not just, or proper.

> This right management of the utterance and behaviour implies a freedom from all the faults which may attend either of them; all levity, excess, affectation, indecency, and in general any impropriety: it implies also a concurrence of those due qualities, that should adorn them, to be natural, easy, lively, graceful, harmonious, and solemn.[137]

These words were uttered some nineteen months before the date when Henley founded The Oratory and started to give practical instruction in sacred elocution. But even so he was already thinking of the opportunity to be more explicit on this subject than the limitations of a sermon would allow. Thus he told his congregation in the church of St. George the Martyr that the practical teachings which he could not give in that place "shall sometime, by the blessing of God in another form, be offer'd to the publick."[138] And the following words indicate that his future teachings would parallel those in Le Faucheur's *Traitté*. He said:

> In proper speaking and gesture, the nature of the thing spoken, strongly imprinted on the mind, and present feeling of the orator, is the only guidance; and as things are, in their own nature, various, they necessarily require a variation of the voice, and of the deportment, that is conformable to each of them: and the precise fitness of one certain sound and movement of the whole person, even to a line of the countenance, to one certain thing, most properly and perfectly express'd, and the consequent unfitness of any other, to it, are as demonstrable, as any proposition in the Mathematics.[139]

[137] *Ibid.*, p. 16.   [138] *Ibid.*, p. 16.   [139] *Ibid.*, p. 17.

Henley's congregation was not aware that, as he uttered the words which I have just quoted, he was thinking of utterance and action in aesthetic terms. But the readers of his sermon can see that he had that very concept in mind. For he affixed a note to the printed text of this passage, and in it he observed that "the true masters of speaking and action" are the masters of music and painting, inasmuch as the principles of both are "taken from philosophy, that is, a just, clear, distinct sense of the nature of things in general; and in particular, from the mathematicks." Thus, he went on to emphasize, the pathetic close of a discourse ought to be spoken with the greatest force, and not "as the method is, by lowering the voice to the end of it." Thus the passions require a language and address differing among themselves. All things vary: good and bad qualities, prosperous and unhappy events, the several ways of addressing God. Le Faucheur's influence seems particularly striking in Henley's next observation: "These, and all other subjects, claim a diversity of pronunciation, and of the conduct, agreeable to the distinct and true nature and merits of them. And this should be carefully study'd, in reading the offices of those churches, where prayers are to be read, as well as in the discourses."[140]

Prompted by an enthusiasm that distorted the facts of history, Henley saw the study of oral delivery as an object of reverent dedication among the ancients, and as the very cause of their superiority throughout aftertime in the world of literature, whereas the literary inferiority of the modern era could be traced directly to the modern neglect of that study. Here are two passages from the concluding movement of Henley's sermon to illustrate this diagnosis:

> The antient greeks and romans, who have furnish'd the most conspicuous lights, the most lasting names of distinction, in the letter'd world, study'd the art of publick speaking and gesture, as it really is, as a distinct science. . . . Demosthenes has made the manner of delivery only to be the very essence of a public speaker. Quintilian has left us the most minute directions imaginable for each note and motion; and Tully was remarkable for his unweary'd application to the skill of it. The most venerable characters of the good old days of christianity, the Basils, the Chrysostomes, the Augustines, and a train of others, excell'd in

[140] *Ibid.*, p. 18.

it. To see St. Paul preaching with a vehemence, an energy, like the blaze from heaven at his conversion, was a famous wish of one of the first doctors of the faith; and sure it is, when he open'd himself to the court of the Areopagus, ye men of Athens; his gesture, as well as his voice, was the most forcible that can be conceived. . . .

The principal causes of our defect in this noble talent, are the disadvantages of our public education, which is so calculated, as not to train us up to it: the inconvenience of the place, to which we are confin'd; the method of entire reading what we speak, which is commonly injurious to the graces of eloquence; join'd with some ill grounded prejudices. The countenance of the knowing, the polite part of the world might conduce to remedy this failure; all good men should think it a duty: all judicious men should account it a delight to encourage the contrary.[141]

Soon after these words were uttered, Henley brought his sermon to a close, expressing the hope as he did so that what he had been saying "may suffice, with regard to the nature of sacred elocution, the rules, the advantages, and history of it, the causes of our defects in it, the proper remedies, and the right treatment of objections to it." The themes enumerated in these words were to constitute a main part of his educational program when he founded The Oratory in 1726,[142] and the substance that he himself contributed to them in the sermon just discussed and in his other

[141] *Ibid.*, pp. 19-20. It was St. Augustine whose dearest wish was that he could have seen St. Paul preaching. On the title page of the first edition of the sermon now under discussion, there is a circular engraving of a preacher standing in a classical setting with his arms raised in gesture. Around the circumference is a band containing the Latin words, "Paulum Videre Praedicantem Votum Augustini." The engraving is signed "J. Pine Sculp."

[142] In *Oratory Transactions, No. I,* pp. 4-5, Mr. Welstede (who was no doubt Henley himself, as I indicated above, n. 120) spoke thus of Henley's educational program in founding The Oratory: "He likewise found it a great Defect that tho' he was brought up for a Clergyman, he was not instructed to preach, or pray, or read Prayers, or speak, or catechise, or confer, or resolve a Case of Conscience, or understand the Scriptures, or form any natural and clear Idea of the Christian Religion: He determin'd there sometime to lay a Foundation for removing such a Complaint, that Men may be educated for their proper Business, and not be under the greatest Disadvantages in that Station, where they ought to be the most Excellent. This he now professes to do in his present Institution."

teachings was to offer to later generations a true measure of his quality as a rhetorical philosopher. What, then, is the verdict that his theory of rhetoric should receive as we look back upon it and seek to assess its value?

The verdict has to be that his theory of rhetoric does not deserve to be taken seriously, although it beguiled him and many of his contemporaries and successors so extensively that the historian of rhetoric must give it serious consideration.

The fundamental count against Henley as a rhetorician is that, in deliberately presupposing the preacher to have a well-weighed composition in mind as he approached the problem of rhetoric, and in construing the task of oral utterance as the very essence of the rhetorical enterprise, Henley was emphasizing that rhetoric should waive all interest in the quality and persuasiveness of a preacher's thought, organization, and style, and should concentrate all its energies upon the physical acts of speaking and gesture, as if these physical acts could be profitably studied apart from the intellectual and spiritual acts which they reflected.

Henley invoked the authority of Cicero, Quintilian, and St. Augustine in support of his view of rhetoric. But he did so without bothering to understand what they had really intended to say. Thus he made them witnesses against themselves. When he declared that they "study'd the art of publick speaking and gesture, as it really is, as a distinct science," he was completely at odds with the facts. What Cicero and Quintilian actually did was to make the study of voice and gesture one of the five arts that the speaker had to master, and they always insisted that this one art must never be studied as a distinct science but must always be construed in a context which included each of the other four arts. In fact, their rhetorical writings, and Aristotle's as well, have this insistence as their clearest and most fundamental thesis. He who invokes their authority on details of their system does so mistakenly if he ever makes them say anything that calls this thesis into serious question.

Henley certainly never read any of these ancient rhetoricians in their entirety. As the editor of *The Art of Speaking in Publick* made plain in 1727, and as we gather from other sources, Henley hired university graduates to collect passages on delivery from classical authors, and he caused those passages to be read as lectures at The Oratory.[143] The inevitable result of such a method of scholarship was that ancient rhetoric under Henley's auspices shrank to a mere fraction of itself, and that fraction, as Ephraim Chambers pointed out in 1738, received a name not hitherto fixed finally upon it in British usage.

In these respects, a comparison between Henley and Ward is instructive. In the very era when The Oratory was founded, Ward was lecturing in nearby Gresham College, and, as we have seen, he was presenting a scholarly interpretation of the entire classical system of rhetoric, the only limitation of his lectures being that they did not show any genius in adapting that system to the needs of his own time. And what of Henley as scholar and lecturer? Judged in relation to Ward, his scholarship in rhetoric is a thing of shreds and patches.

Another comparison is equally instructive. Two years before Henley preached his sermon on sacred elocution, Fénelon's *Dialogues on Eloquence* were published at London in an English translation. Henley could have read them in connection with his interest in pulpit oratory. Fénelon handled the topic of pulpit oratory in relation to the problems of subject matter, organization, style, and delivery, and he achieved the enviable distinction of writing eloquently on eloquence. He applied to modern preaching the best of ancient doctrine, and he ignored in ancient doctrine what no longer made sense for the modern preacher. Measured against his robust and vital rhetoric, Henley's theory seems thin and perverse. Indeed, Henley's reduction of the theory of preaching to the domain of voice and gesture against the whole tenor of Fénelon's teachings is the hardest thing of all to reconcile with the favorable verdict which generosity and indulgence might normally want us to pronounce upon Henley as a rhetorician.

[143] See above, p. 197; also n. 130.

John Mason's *An Essay on Elocution, or, Pronunciation*, which
has already been mentioned in my discussion of *Some Rules for
Speaking and Action*, needs separate consideration in the present
history only because certain other writers have given it a higher
standing in the elocutionary movement than it actually deserves.[144] First published at London in 1748, and given a second
edition at the same place later that year, it continued to be popular for the next four decades, reaching its fifth edition in 1787. But
its chief value is that it reasserts and reinforces the themes to
which the translator of Le Faucheur and his imitators like Gildon
and Henley had already given repetitious and well-publicized
attention. In its own right it is not even remotely original in its
approach to the fifth part of ancient rhetoric. Indeed, it appears
initially to strip that part of one of its dimensions.

As we know, the fifth part of ancient rhetoric was called *pronuntiatio* or *actio*, and it was made to consist of the act of voicing
words and accompanying them with proper gesture. Both of
these two divisions of the ancient concept seem at first glance to
have been associated in Mason's mind with the meaning that he
intended to affix to the newly emerging term elocution. For example, he chose as title a phrase in which elocution and pronunciation were made synonymous; in naming and characterizing the
five divisions into which Cicero and Quintilian had divided rhetoric, he specified that by elocution those two authors "always
meant, what we call, *Diction*; which consists in suiting our Words
to our Ideas, and the Stile to the Subject"; he went on to stress
that by pronunciation the ancients always meant "the Art of
managing the Voice, and Gesture in speaking";[145] and then he
deliberately explained that he was going to alter this system of
terminology, and that the alteration which he proposed was intended merely to make elocution mean what pronunciation had
meant to the Roman rhetoricians. Thus after he had said by way
of definition that "Elocution is a Branch of Oratory, the Power
and Importance of which is greater than is generally thought;

[144] See above, p. 191n.
[145] *An Essay on Elocution, or, Pronunciation*, The Second Edition (London, 1748), p. 4.

insomuch that Eloquence takes it's Name from it," he added the following as a footnote:

Eloquentia ab *eloqui*. I use the word *Elocution* here in it's common and vulgar Sense, to signify *Utterance, Delivery,* or *Pronunciation*, in which Sense we frequently use it in the English Language, and which its Latin Etymology very well justifies; tho' I know some good Writers apply to it a different Idea, in conformity to the Sense in which the Latin Orators used the word *Elocutio*. But it's no uncommon Thing for derivative Words in one Language to be taken in a different Sense from that, in which the Words they are derived from are taken in another.[146]

But after these explanations, it is surprising to find Mason introducing a refinement of his own into the elocutionary terminology that he appears to have been following up to this point, and it is perplexing to note that his refinement consists in making elocution refer, not to ancient *pronuntiatio* as a whole, but only to one of its parts, the voicing or uttering of words. He said:

So that by *Pronunciation*, the Antients understood both *Elocution* and *Action*; and comprehended in it the right Management of the Voice, Looks, and Gesture. To the former of these the present Essay is chiefly confined; *viz.* the right Management of the Voice in reading or speaking; which is indifferently called by us, *Elocution* and *Pronunciation*.[147]

Having made elocution and pronunciation seem at first to refer only to the voicing of words, Mason said that the "great Design and End of a good Pronunciation is, to make the Ideas seem to come from the Heart; and then they will not fail to excite the Attention and Affections of them that hear us: From which the Great Benefit and Usefulness of this too much neglected Art may be seen." He added at once:

The Design of this Essay is to shew
I.   What a bad Pronunciation is, and how to avoid it.
II. What a good Pronunciation is, and how to attain it.[148]

[146] *Ibid.*, pp. 3-4. Only the three Latin words at the beginning make up this note in the first edition of Mason's essay.
[147] *Ibid.*, p. 5.   [148] *Ibid.*, p. 6.

A bad pronunciation, according to Mason's subsequent discussion, consists in speaking too loudly, in speaking too softly, in speaking in a thick, hasty, or cluttering voice, in speaking too quickly, or too slowly, in speaking with too much irregularity, in speaking with too much monotony or uniformity, and in speaking in some unpleasant prevailing tone—a womanish tone, a singing tone, a theatrical tone, a pretentiously awesome tone, a uniform tone, or an odd, whimsical, whining tone. The cure for each of these defects, as stated by Mason, is so much a matter of common sense that we need not dwell upon them. His advice on how to avoid disagreeable tones indicates his general approach to faulty pronunciation as a whole:

> In reading then attend to your Subject, and deliver it just in such a Manner as you would do if you were talking of it. This is the great, general and most important Rule of all; which, if carefully observed, will correct not only this but almost all the other Faults of a bad Pronunciation; and give you an easy, decent, graceful Delivery, agreeable to all the Rules of a right Elocution.[149]

Mason began the discussion of his second topic by observing that "A good Pronunciation *in reading*, is the Art of managing and governing the Voice so as to express the full Sense and Spirit of your Author in that just, decent, and graceful Manner, which will not only instruct but affect the Hearers; and will not only raise in them the same Ideas he intended to convey, but the same Passions he really felt."[150] With this definition as his controlling idea, Mason urged readers to do the seven following things for achieving a just pronunciation: 1) to have a particular regard to their pauses, emphasis, and cadence; 2) to take in the full sense and enter into the spirit of their author; 3) to study nature—"the nearer our Pronunciation in Publick comes to the Freedom and Ease of that we use in common Discourse (provided we keep up the Dignity of the Subject, and preserve a Propriety of Expression) the more just and natural and agreeable it will generally be";[151] 4) to endeavor to keep their mind collected and composed; 5) to be sure to keep life, spirit, and energy in the expression, and let the voice vary naturally according to the variation

[149] *Ibid.*, pp. 20-21.   [150] *Ibid.*, p. 22.   [151] *Ibid.*, p. 34.

of style and subject; 6) to hear as often as possible those who excel in the art of pronunciation—it "is better learnt by Imitation than Rule";[152] and 7) to exercise themselves frequently in reading aloud.

As he concluded this part of his discussion, Mason said that he had originally planned to bring his essay to an end at this point. "But as under the Word [Pronunciation] the Antients comprehended *Action* as well as *Elocution*; and as a few general Rules concerning that may be of Use to such as speak in Publick, I thought it might not be improper," he said, "here briefly to subjoin them."[153] And subjoin them he did, speaking of proper actions of the head, the countenance, the eyes, the hands, and the body. His reliance upon Le Faucheur is obvious in this division of his subject, as it also is in his two previous headings. We can see a plain example of this by comparing what Mason and the translator of Le Faucheur's *Traitté* say in part when they speak of gestures of the head:

Mason, p. 39:

It should always be on the same Side with the Action of the Hands and Body, except when we express an Abhorrence, or a Refusal of any thing, which is done by rejecting it with the Right-hand, and turning away the Head to the Left; as in that Sentence—*Dii talem terris avertete pestem*—where such an Action is very proper in pronouncing the Word *avertete*.[154]

Le Faucheur's Translator, p. 181:

To this I must add that the *Head* ought always to be turn'd on the same side with the other *Actions* of the Body, save only when they are exerted upon *things* we *refuse*: As for instance, when the *Poet* says;

I think my self not worthy of such Praise.

Or, upon *things* we *detest* and *abhorr*; as when he says again;

Good Gods! divert from Us so great a Plague.

For *these* things we must reject with an *Action* of the *right Hand* and turn the *Head* away at the same time to the *left*.

[152] *Ibid.*, p. 37.

[153] *Ibid.*, p. 38. The bracketed word in this quotation is a bracketed word in Mason's text.

[154] The Latin quotation is from Virgil, *Aeneid*, III, 620.

Despite Mason's recognition that *elocutio* in classical rhetoric meant style, and that the elocutionists had deliberately chosen to convert that term into the English word for pronunciation or the voicing of discourse, he did not succeed any better than Henley had done in keeping his own distinctions in mind. Thus he allowed his central concept to become cloudy and confused. A conspicuous illustration of his looseness and imprecision in regard to that concept occurred even as he was in the act of acknowledging that to him elocution meant delivery rather than style. Delivery, he said, "was much cultivated by *Quintilian*, and before him by *Cicero*, and before him by *M. Antonius*; but before his Time, it was too much neglected by the *Roman* Orators: Which made him say, *He had seen many Men famous for Eloquence, but not one of them that understood Elocution.*"[155] In this quotation, Mason made Antonius into an elocutionist upholding the thesis that the understanding of delivery was the great historical dividing line between the instinctive natural eloquence of early Rome and the superior cultivated eloquence of its maturity. Mason even cited Quintilian's *Institutio Oratoria*, 8.Pr.13, as the authority for this thesis. But Quintilian had borrowed the thesis of Antonius from Cicero's *De Oratore*, 1.21.94, where Cicero had made Antonius declare that the difference between the merely accomplished speaker and the true man of eloquence was not so much the possession of skill in delivery on the part of the latter as it was his possession of an admirable and splendid style in treating any of his chosen subjects, and his command of all the resources concerned in oratory. In other words, Mason was forcing the classical writers to support a narrow view of rhetoric, and was quoting them to this effect in a passage which plainly stated a broad and comprehensive view. It is something of a mystery that men trained in the classics as were Mason and Henley could have permitted themselves such inexcusable laxities in interpreting for their time the ancient rhetorical tradition. The fact that they did so makes it difficult to respect their theories highly.

[155] *An Essay on Elocution, or, Pronunciation*, p. 4.

A pamphlet entitled *An Essay on the Action Proper for the Pulpit,* printed at London for R. and J. Dodsley in 1753, has sometimes been credited to John Mason.[156] It does not appear, however, to have been written by a clergyman, and on that score alone Mason can be effectively disqualified as its author.[157] Moreover, it does not use the term elocution to describe its subject, as Mason would most certainly have done; it speaks instead of "Just *Action*" or "Right *Manner*," and it divides that procedure into voice and gesture.[158] But its ideas are similar to those advanced by Mason, and thus it belongs without question among the documents of the English elocutionary movement.

This work opens by recounting a very recent episode in which the author had heard two contrasting preachers. One had a weighty subject, a fine taste and learning, a great ability in language, a masterly skill in composition, a proper arrangement of his sermon, and a series of bold, noble, natural figures and images; but he had no proportionable effect upon his hearers because he "pronounced his Discourse without the least Justness, Grace, or Pathos."[159] The other preacher was a plain, ordinary man, with little literature, no refinement, an everyday subject, an indifferent method, a mediocre style; but his delivery was so strong, significant, and agreeable that he made his auditors profoundly attentive and sensibly moved.

A fabricated episode of this sort might well have led the author to seek to correct the public taste that could go so far astray as to permit itself to be deceived by sound rather than sense. After all,

---

[156] It is listed among Mason's works in the card catalogue of the Huntington Library, which in this matter follows the authority of the Library of Congress.

[157] The last eight pages of the pamphlet are presented as an address by the author to young ministers urging them to pay greater attention to the delivery of their sermons. This address is not that of an older clergyman to the younger men in his calling, but rather that of a layman or member of the congregation to the clergy itself. At one point in the address (p. 81), the author says: "Degenerate as the most of us Hearers are, be assured we secretly respect and admire the Image of *Virtue* wherever we behold it; but above all we respect and admire it in a *Clergyman*." This is merely one of many passages in which the pamphlet identifies its author as a layman.

[158] *An Essay on the Action Proper for the Pulpit* (London, 1753), pp. 3, 60.
[159] *Ibid.,* p. 2.

the two audiences on display here can be accused of mistaking the outward show for the inner reality, and for responding to the former rather than the latter, as the ancient Pharisees did when they observed the external appearance of religion but lacked its very heart. In other words, this episode calls for the development of the kind of education in which audiences are made into thinking adults, and for the kind of rhetoric which those audiences would require. But our author neglected this aspect of the episode and began instead to reflect "on the vast importance of Just *Action* or a Right *Manner* in the Pulpit."[160] A superficial treatise on delivery rather than a profound discourse on rhetoric was the result.

The first part of the treatise consists in a set of arguments to show that pulpit orators should cultivate the art of voice and gesture. The arguments are not advanced in a systematic and critical way, but if they were reduced to a system, they would resolve themselves into the following propositions: 1) that attention to proper voice and gesture in a sermon would make the preacher's message appeal to the eyes and ears as well as the understanding of the audience and thus would increase the influence of the preacher; 2) that every accent, every look, every gesture stands naturally for a corresponding sentiment and passion, and that when they are joined with fit words, "the Impressions produced by their United Force must be strong and lively,"[161] as the impressions must be weak when fit words are delivered without proper utterance and action; 3) that the bar, the bench, parliament, and the stage have spirited speakers in abundance—"the Pulpit alone [seems then to be] an Enemy to Beauty of Address, Truth of Expression, and Harmony of Sound";[162] 4) that while sense and truth in a homely dress will affect a perceptive mind, they will not affect the careless, inattentive hearer, who needs the added benefits of a graceful and lively delivery, which indeed even the perceptive profit by having; 5) that advocates of religion are engaged to plead its cause before judges prejudiced against it, and that it is their duty to remove those prejudices by practicing "all the honest Wiles that a just Rhetoric teaches for catch-

---

[160] *Ibid.*, p. 3.   [161] *Ibid.*, p. 5
[162] *Ibid.*, pp. 6-7. I express as a statement what the pamphlet presents as a rhetorical question.

ing the Attention, and stealing upon the Heart";[163] 6) that history affords numberless instances to show how far people are moved by Eloquence and by that part in particular "which in the largest Sense of the Word may be called Action";[164] 7) that nothing being said here is to be construed as recommending "*Action* as separate from *Truth* and *Reason*, the only natural Sources of Persuasion";[165] 8) that in reality, action is only just when it "is a Genuine Exhibition of *Nature*, which represents her Feelings and Perceptions, and gives to these a Voice and Body";[166] and 9) that religious passions, like any others, have certain peculiar features, tones, and gestures adapted to them by nature—Raphael's picture of St. Paul preaching at Athens shows bold, majestic action, the action which perfectly expresses nature, although Raphael by some connoisseurs is said to have shown the apostle's arms raised up too high.[167]

The anonymous author of this treatise turns next to the practical suggestions which the young preacher should follow in perfecting his pulpit voice. He should be modest, he should listen to criticism, and when he finds a friend who will criticize him, he should "*grapple him to his Soul with Hooks of Steel.*"[168] He should imitate a good model; he should have an exalted conception of his art; he should cultivate a deliberate pronunciation, with frequent pauses; he should avoid the careless tone of one reading a newspaper; he should avoid an insipid, unvaried, monotonous tone of voice; he should allow each of the passions to express itself in the voice naturally suited to it; he should avoid falling into a tune; he should please the soul as well as the ear of the hearer—as Mr. Pope says, "The Sound must seem an *Echo* to the Sense";[169] and he should allow his voice to react to the different moods of the different parts of his sermon.

At this point in the pamphlet, the author made a suggestion which Henley had already tried to carry out in a feeble and eccentric way, and which Thomas Sheridan would make a cardinal point in his program. It was that students of the ministry should be provided with schools like those in which the ancients taught youth to be speakers. These ancient schools became part

[163] *Ibid.*, p. 12. [164] *Ibid.*, p. 15. [165] *Ibid.*, p. 18.
[166] *Ibid.*, p. 19. [167] *Ibid.*, p. 27. [168] *Ibid.*, pp. 32-33.
[169] *Ibid.*, p. 49. For the quotation from Pope, see his *An Essay on Criticism*, Part II, line 165.

of the legend that the elocutionists fabricated about classical Greece and Rome. They never discussed these schools in concrete terms. They never listed the subjects in their curriculum, or related those subjects to the theory of ancient rhetoric as a whole. They simply assumed that the ancients had institutions devoted exclusively to teaching the routines of voice and gesture, and that from those schools were produced the generations that made Greek and Roman eloquence and literature pre-eminent in the history of man. Our pamphlet observes that those ancient schools esteemed pronunciation and action the most essential part of civil eloquence, and that young men learned in those schools the decorum and various powers of delivery. It also mentions that Cicero after having gained a reputation at the bar spent two years abroad in the intensive study of pronunciation, and that the lack of eminent speakers in England was caused by the lack of schools like those which the ancients had.[170] But into a factual account of the ancient schools, the pamphlet does not go.

After giving a few more practical hints upon the cultivation of a proper voice, and after recommending that young preachers speak the speech trippingly, on the tongue, as Hamlet had recommended, the author brought his discussion of this part of his subject into its final stages by writing as follows:

> Their studying to *melt* their Sounds into a fine *Liquidity*, or to *swell* them into an ample *Majesty*, is of peculiar importance to the Grace and Efficacy of their Public Performances. Next to *following Nature*, which is the general and all-controuling Law in the Art I talk of, This is perhaps the highest thing in the whole Magic of Pronunciation.[171]

This pamphlet turns quite practical as it takes up for its final topic "that part of *Action*, which relates to *Gesture*. . . ."[172] It echoes Hamlet's advice that a speaker should suit the action to the word, the word to the action, and should beget a temperance to give all smoothness.[173] And it also echoes Le Faucheur repeatedly, as indeed it had done already in directing the speaker to allow his voice to react differently to each of the different passions and to each of the different parts of his speech. Thus it says,

---

[170] *Ibid.*, pp. 53-55.
[171] *Ibid.*, p. 58.   [172] *Ibid.*, p. 60.   [173] *Ibid.*, pp. 62, 65.

as had Le Faucheur, that the hands should never be raised higher than the eyes, nor brought lower than the edge of the pulpit; that the left hand should never be employed to express anything by itself, nor ever be used except with the right; and that both hands should everywhere be kept within the speaker's view.[174] But when in that same place it declares "The *Connoisseurs* in this Art" to be of opinion "that the Speaker should move always from the *right* to the *left*, but neither much nor quick," it gives a rule that does not appear to be authorized by Le Faucheur, and that would seem anyway to be impossible to apply in any actual situation.

[174] *Ibid.*, pp. 68-69. For Le Faucheur's teachings on these points, see *An Essay Upon The Action of an Orator* (London, 1702?), pp. 196-197, 198, 200.

Although the British elocutionary movement was about fifty years of age when the pamphlet that I have just discussed was published, and although that movement was to enjoy immense popularity in Great Britain and America from that time until the end of the nineteenth century, I shall nevertheless close my account of it by discussing in detail only one more of its many adherents, Thomas Sheridan. Sheridan has already been mentioned several times in this chapter, and on one occasion he was called the second founder of the elocutionary movement. There is no reason to modify the latter title in any respect. In fact, Sheridan was so much luckier than Le Faucheur's translator or Gildon or Henley in getting himself remembered by posterity that to this day the diminishing band of elocutionists still consider him the most important figure among their predecessors, and many of them would go so far as to call him not only the originator but the greatest apostle of this school of rhetoric.

Thomas Sheridan's son, Richard Brinsley Sheridan, became a brilliant parliamentary orator and the author of such famous plays as *The Rivals* and *The School for Scandal*. Thomas's father, also called Thomas, was an outstanding schoolmaster in Dublin and throughout much of his life a warm friend of the distinguished satirist and churchman Jonathan Swift. As if nature intended him to establish the theatrical and oratorical talents of such a son and to reflect the pedagogical interests of such a father, Thomas had two careers, one as actor on the Dublin and London stages, and the other as an educator bent upon giving the art of oratory a central place in the educational system of Great Britain. He was born in Ireland in 1719 and educated at first at Westminster School in England and later at Trinity College, Dublin, where he took his degree as bachelor of arts in 1739, and was later given his master's degree.[175] His biographer, William Fraser Rae, says that his father wished Thomas "to become a schoolmaster, but the young man preferred to go on the stage, for which, while an undergraduate, he had written a farce called

[175] George Dames Burtchaell and Thomas Ulick Sadleir, *Alumni Dublinenses* (London, 1924), s.v. Sheridan, Thomas; W. B. S. Taylor, *History of the University of Dublin* (London, 1845), p. 404.

Captain O'Blunder, or the Brave Irishman."[176] As we shall see in a moment, this account of Thomas's choice of a career is in need of considerable revision. But nevertheless Thomas did go on the stage after his graduation from college, and between 1743 and 1759 he was connected except for a two-year interval with the Theatre Royal in Smock Alley, Dublin, at first as actor and later as actor-manager. This phase of his career ended when he was forty years of age, and a new phase began, in which he devoted himself to the cause of educational reform. His reforms extended to the advocacy of improvements in the elementary schools of Ireland and to the publicizing of a proposal for an academy of elocution to prepare university graduates for careers in the pulpit, in parliament, or at the bar. These matters occupied him for the rest of his life, and at the time of his death in 1788 he had become so completely identified with the elocutionary movement that his earlier career in the theatre seemed almost to have been the work of another man.

But the Sheridan who became a successful actor-manager and the other Sheridan who preached educational reform and advocated the founding of an elocutionary academy are not antagonistic to each other. Rather, the first of the two pursued what he considered to be the practical side of the same fundamental calling that the other followed on the side of its doctrinal and pedagogical implications. Indeed, we have Sheridan's own word for this exact connection between his two careers, and there is no reason to doubt it. But since his word has been neglected in the account of him in *The Dictionary of National Biography*, and thus is not likely to figure in the average student's estimate of his career,[177] it can profitably be quoted here. Besides, it gives Jonathan Swift a role in Sheridan's plan to become an elocutionist, and it introduces us to the very language of Sheridan's thought about his two lines of endeavor. On December 6, 1757, when his career

[176] *The Dictionary of National Biography*, s.v. Sheridan, Thomas (1719-1788).

[177] The sketch of Sheridan in Alexander Chalmers, *The General Biographical Dictionary* (London, 1816), XXVII, 458-466, contains a much better evaluation of him than does that in *The Dictionary of National Biography*. For a good recent evaluation of him, see Wallace A. Bacon, "The Elocutionary Career of Thomas Sheridan (1719-1788)," *Speech Monographs*, XXXI (1964), 1-53.

on the stage was drawing to an end and his career as educational reformer had just been launched, he delivered an oration in the Music Hall in Fishamble Street, Dublin, and became so far autobiographical in the course of it as to reveal the following facts about himself:

It is not yet forgotten that my Father's Employment was the Education of Youth; nor was he amongst the least eminent in his Profession. As I ever esteemed that to be one of the most useful and honourable Stations in Life, I resolved to make Choice of it for mine. It was therefore the chief Point I had in View in my Course of Reading.

As I had passed the two most important Years, in finishing my School Studies at *Westminster*, I was not the worse qualified for the Undertaking; and as I had my Father's Reputation to build upon, and some very advantageous Proposals made to me upon that Head, I had the most flattering Prospect of Success, and should certainly have entered upon the Office, immediately after taking my Degree of Master of Arts, but for one Objection. Upon the maturest Deliberation, I thought I saw a great Deficiency in our early Part of Education; and that too in some of the most essential Points. 'Till I should be able to remedy this, I determined not to enter upon the Employment; and, not liking the beaten Way, resolved to pass some Time in search of a new Path.

That which chiefly gave my Mind this Turn, was a Conversation which I once had with Dr. *Swift*, soon after my Entrance into the College: He asked me what they taught there? When I told him the Course of Reading I was put into, he asked me, Do they teach you English? No. Do they teach you how to speak? No. Then, said he, they teach you *Nothing*. As I was instructed from my boyish Days to reverence him as one of a superior Class of Beings, his Sayings always passed with me for Oracles, and this particularly sunk deep into my Mind.

In my Progress thro' the College, I had often Occasion to apply it, and long before I had finished my Course, was fully convinced that all our other Studies turn to little Advantage, to the Inhabitants of *Great Britain*, and *Ireland*, thro' a Neglect of these. I then set to work to make myself Master, if possible, of those two necessary Branches; but was a long time puzzled and perplexed in the Intricacies of a Labyrinth thro' which I could find no Clue.

After much Time spent in this Way, at length I found, that there never could be any Settlement of the *English* Language, nor could it possibly be reduced to Rule, unless the Art of Speaking were first revived. The Grounds of this my Opinion, being already given to the Publick need not here be repeated; and as the Arguments there used, have never yet been confuted, but, on the contrary, have received Sanction from the Approbation of many judicious Persons, I have reason to believe that they were not ill founded. The revival of the long lost Art of Oratory, became, therefore, the first necessary Step towards my Design. A Task of so arduous a Nature, so surrounded with Difficulties, as would have deterred any one from the Attempt, who was less zealous in the Pursuit of his Point.

In my first Motions towards it, I was only groping my Way in the Dark, and my Journey ended in a Chaos, where there could not be said to be Light, but, as *Milton* expresses it, rather Darkness visible.

At length I found that *Theory* alone would never bring me far on my Way; and that continual *Practice* must be added to furnish me with Lights to conduct me to my Journey's End. To obtain this, there was but one Way open, which was the Stage.[178]

Sheridan then went on to say that his career on the stage at first allowed him no opportunity to master the oratorical technicalities which he deemed necessary to have mastered before he could proceed with his educational aims. But in the course of time, he said, he was called upon to assist and instruct young actors in his

[178] Thomas Sheridan, *An Oration, Pronounced before a Numerous Body of the Nobility and Gentry, Assembled at the Musick-Hall in Fishamble-street, On Tuesday the 6th of this instant December, And now first Published at their unanimous Desire*, The Third Edition (Dublin, 1757), pp. 19-21. Cited below as *An Oration*. In quoting this passage, I have made certain paragraph divisions where the original does not do so. Otherwise I have followed the style of Sheridan's text.

The reference in the fifth paragraph of this quotation to the recent publication of "The Grounds of this my Opinion" is a reference to Sheridan's book, *British Education* (London, 1756), which was the opening step in his educational campaign. A discussion of it will follow.

company so that they would become proficient performers; and, as many others have discovered, Sheridan became aware that one gets hold of the fundamental principles of an art when he tries to teach it. Those principles once known, he remarked, "it was not difficult thro' Time and Application to trace the whole System." And he added at once: "So that it is now some Years, since I could have undertaken to shew, that the Art of Oratory, might have been taught in these Kingdoms, upon as certain Principles, and with as good a Prospect of Success, as it ever was by the Rhetoricians of *Greece* or *Rome*; or as the Arts of Musick, Painting, &c. are now taught by their several Professors."[179]

Having mastered the long lost art of oratory through his efforts to instruct young actors in the art of acting, Sheridan felt that he could then turn to the task of educational reform, and to the problem of finding the proper place for oratorical instruction within the whole scheme of Irish education. He came soon to the conclusion that elementary education in Ireland was in no way comparable in quality to that offered in the renowned English public schools like Eton and Westminster, and that the first of his measures of reform would therefore be to seek to provide better masters and a more demanding curriculum in the Irish lower schools. This reform, he urged, would arrest the tendency on the part of the Irish gentry to send their sons to England for an education and thus to alienate them from their native land.[180] He also came to the conclusion "that the present Course of Education in the College of *Dublin*, is in itself superior to that of any in *Europe* of the same Kind," and that certainly no reform would need to be undertaken there.[181] But even so there was a defect in Irish higher education and indeed "a Defect under which the *English* labour as much as we"—"*the Want of proper Places to finish the Education of a Gentleman.*"[182] The founding of such a school became the object of Sheridan's ambition as an educational reformer. And, as he saw it, the most likely method for making that reform prosper would be to speak to men of influence and position and to get them not only to favor "*a Society established for the Improvement of Education,*" but also to contribute money to the Society and to accept Sheridan's own program as its ultimate

---

[179] *An Oration*, p. 22.
[180] *Ibid.*, pp. 6, 8, 9, 10, 11, 13, 14.
[181] *Ibid.*, p. 13.
[182] *Ibid.*, pp. 13-14. Italics are Sheridan's.

aim.[183] Speaking of the plan that he would lay before such a Society, Sheridan said:

> The Ends proposed by it, amongst many others, are these; 1st. to qualify every young Gentleman to make a figure proportionable to his Talents, in whatever Profession or sphere of Life he shall make his Choice, or into which his Lot shall have cast him. Whether it be the Pulpit, the Senate-house, or the Bar; whether he seeks for Glory in the Field, or prefers the Quiet of a rural Life. 2dly. to qualify him in all the Accomplishments of a Gentleman to make a Figure in polite Life, and to assist him in acquiring a just Taste in the liberal Arts, founded upon Skill.[184]

As for the actual academy that he dreamed of having the Society create, Sheridan visualized it as an annex of the theatre to which he had devoted the early phase of his career. He declared:

> For I considered that such Theatre might supply no inconsiderable Helps to an Academy. The same Man who led the Band there, might be the Instructor in Musick: The same who presided over the Scene-painting, might be the Preceptor in Drawing; and the same who gave most Pleasure by his Performance on the Stage, might be the properest master in dancing. The double Encouragement which in this Case they would receive, might at all Times secure to us some of the best Masters in *Europe*, in those several Arts. Besides, as I had intended to erect a small Academy purposely for the regular Instruction of young Persons, who were possessed of Genius and Talents for the Stage, and who should have all proper helps towards fitting them for that Profession, it might be hoped in time, that the Theatre would become an admirable Assistant to the School of Oratory, by furnishing to the young Students constant good Models and Examples in all the different species of Eloquence.[185]

Earlier in this chapter I mentioned that the elocutionary movement as a concentrated study of the correct speaking of English derived some of its strongest incentives not only from the lack of a standardized English pronunciation throughout the world empire which Englishmen had been creating during the seventeenth and eighteenth centuries, but also from the handicaps

---

[183] *Ibid.*, pp. 18, 25. Italics are Sheridan's.
[184] *Ibid.*, p. 25.   [185] *Ibid.*, pp. 23-24.

which the Irish, the Scots, and the Americans felt themselves to suffer when their inability to speak standard English stood in the way of their occupational success in the British capital. During my discussion of those incentives, I mentioned Thomas Sheridan and Alexander Wedderburn to show that men actually handicapped by provincialism in speech deliberately set out during the eighteenth century to teach themselves to speak English as the British court spoke it. It is now appropriate to mention Sheridan again in this same connection. He envisioned his school of oratory as an Irish center for the study of correct English speech, and he thought that students would flock to it from Scotland, from Wales, from America, from the other British Colonies abroad, from Europe, and even from England, where that particular branch of education was as defective as it was everywhere else.[186] He even specified that his school would remedy the political disadvantages of provincialism in speech throughout the English-speaking world. He remarked:

> Would it not then evidently be the Interest of the Gentlemen of *Scotland* and *Wales*, I mean such as would otherwise send their Sons to *England* for Education, to give this Country the Preference, where English and the Art of Speaking would be systematically taught, without which Experience shews it is impossible they can ever get the better of their first vitiated Pronunciation? How many Gentlemen of those Countries now lament the Want of such an Opportunity in their early Days, when they find themselves disabled, on Account of that Defect, from making such a Figure in publick Assemblies, as their Talents, Knowledge, and Literature would otherwise intitle them to? . . .

> Is it not reasonable to believe, considering our Situation, that we should be supplied with Numbers from *America*, and the *British* Colonies Abroad? especially when we reflect that the Form of the *British* Constitution is established in most of them; and that a Knowledge of the *English* Language, and Oratory, are equally necessary to them, to make a Figure in their several Assemblies. . . .[187]

[186] *Ibid.*, p. 15.
[187] *Ibid.*, pp. 14-15. My indication of a new paragraph is not authorized by Sheridan's text.

Sheridan evidently dreamed these dreams during the period when, as actor-manager of the Theatre Royal in Smock Alley, he was enjoying financial success and was beginning to hope that his own resources would soon be great enough to allow him to found a school of oratory near his playhouse. But on March 2, 1754, his hopes were rudely shattered. A riot occurred at the Theatre Royal during a performance of James Miller's adaptation of Voltaire's *Mahomet* when the audience took offense at Sheridan because of his assumed refusal to allow one of his players to give an encore and repeat some lines which condemned wicked ministers of state. Those lines had possible reference to the Irish scene, and the applause for them had plain political overtones. The riot caused expensive damage, and it raised such hostility to Sheridan that he decided to withdraw for a time from his theatrical career and to lease his theatre to the deputy-manager, Benjamin Victor.[188] In the oration which we have here been quoting at length, Sheridan called the riot an earthquake, and remarked that it reduced his plans for a school of oratory to a heap of ruins. "Thus at once," he added, "were all my Hopes blasted. The only Fruits I reaped from a Nine Years incessant toil both of Body and Mind, were the loss of a considerable Sum of Money, by the whole of my Undertaking and a broken Constitution."[189] But in reality he reaped other fruits that he did not mention in the speech. He made a break of two years from his Dublin theatre and went to England, where he wrote and published *British Education*, and where he also began his active career as lecturer on elocution. After that two-year interval, he returned to Smock Alley for a time, but on April 20, 1759, he ordered his theatrical company dissolved,[190] and from that time on he devoted himself to his attempt to establish a standard of English pronunciation and to awaken public sentiment in support of his plan for a school that would teach oratory in accordance with his own personally established conception of its fundamental principles. "I should be sorry," he declared in 1757, "that an Art which cost me so much Pains to acquire, the Propagation of which appears to me to be fraught with the highest Benefits to the Publick, should perish

[188] For an account of this episode, see Benjamin Victor, *The History of the Theatres of London and Dublin, From the Year 1730 to the present Time* (London, 1761), I, 159-174. Cited below as Victor.

[189] *An Oration*, p. 24.   [190] Victor, I, 267.

with me."[191] Through Sheridan's own efforts from 1759 to 1788, when he died, his idea of that art did not perish. Instead, it was widely diffused throughout the English-speaking world.

Sheridan's *British Education*, published at London in 1756 and again at that same place in 1769, is of immense value to students of the elocutionary movement because it enables them to grasp in an early form the educational program that Sheridan was later to explain in his speech of 1757 before the nobles and gentry of Ireland; and it also permits those students to inspect in detail the sources to which Sheridan went when he started to recover what he repeatedly called the long lost art of oratory. Few writers on Sheridan have paid much attention to *British Education*. Without it, however, his later lectures on elocution are deprived of the only context in which their meaning can be understood and their value appraised.

Prefixed to the first edition of *British Education* is a letter addressed to Lord Chesterfield, who had served as lord-lieutenant of Ireland for a period of eight months between the summer of 1745 and the spring of 1746, and who during that time had lent assistance to one of Sheridan's undertakings in such a way as to cause Sheridan to acknowledge himself Chesterfield's debtor.[192] Sheridan made it plain in the letter that he was not in any formal sense dedicating *British Education* to his lordship; he was rather, he said, speaking in the name of the people of Great Britain and asking Chesterfield "to patronize and encourage a scheme, peculiarly calculated to promote their honour and interest."[193] And what was that scheme? In Sheridan's own words, as he himself put emphasis upon them, it was this: *"A design to revive the long lost art of oratory, and to correct, ascertain, and fix the English language."*[194] Sheridan went on to mention Chesterfield's unique fitness for the office of patron of such a design, and he quoted part of the proposal which Jonathan Swift in 1712 had addressed to the Lord High Treasurer of Great Britain on the subject of correcting, improving, and ascertaining the English tongue.[195] Of

[191] *An Oration*, p. 24.

[192] For Sheridan's acknowledgement of his indebtedness to Chesterfield in this matter, see *British Education* (London, 1756), pp. xxiii-xxiv.

[193] *Ibid.*, p. v.   [194] *Ibid.*, p. vi.

[195] *Ibid.*, pp. vii-viii. See "A Proposal for *Correcting, Improving* and *Ascertaining* The English Tongue; in a Letter To the Most Honourable Robert

particular interest is Sheridan's indication that Chesterfield as lord-lieutenant of Ireland had had many plans for the betterment of that country, one of the most promising of which was his "proposal publickly made to the provost and fellows of the university, for the endowment of proper lectures and exercises in the art of reading and speaking English." "I own, my Lord," added Sheridan, "that this proposal, and the unexpected honour you did me, in mentioning my name, as one who might be useful on such an occasion, first made me think a scheme practicable, which had long before taken possession of me in idea."[196] There can be no doubt from this statement that Chesterfield had had a part in Sheridan's decision in 1756 to turn away from the stage and devote himself to the cause of the elocutionists. Nor can there be any doubt from Sheridan's whole address to Chesterfield that he actively hoped for a renewal of Chesterfield's interest in him as he presented himself to the public with a settled statement of the importance of his educational design in rectifying what he deemed to be the great evils of British cultural, moral, political, and religious life.

The first of the three Books into which Sheridan divided *British Education* argues that the British Constitution survives only as the spirit of dedication to the Christian religion exists among the British citizenry, and that the art of oratory is the only effective means of inducing citizens to maintain their dedication to that religion. In making Christianity the basis of the British Constitution and the pillar of the British state, Sheridan cited from Montesquieu's *De l'Esprit des Lois* the doctrine that each of the three possible forms of human government, the monarchical, the despotic, and the republican, had its own principle, monarchies being supported by the cultivation of the love of honor, despotisms, by the cultivation of fear, and republics, by the cultivation of the love of virtue.[197] Then Sheridan went on to argue that the

---

Earl of Oxford *and* Mortimer, *Lord High Treasurer* of Great Britain. London: Printed for Benj. Tooke, at the *Middle-Temple-Gate, Fleetstreet.* 1712"; in *The Works of Jonathan Swift,* ed. Sir Walter Scott, Second Edition (London, 1883), IX, 133-155.

[196] *British Education,* p. xiv.

[197] *Ibid.,* p. 37. A translation of Montesquieu's great work was made by Thomas Nugent and published at London in 1750 under the title *The Spirit of Laws.* That translation enjoyed an immense popularity in Great Britain

British government, as a combination of these three forms, needed a principle of its own to regulate it, and that its principle consisted in its being supported by the cultivation of the Christian religion,[198] inasmuch as that religion taught the people to regard eternal punishment as the greatest object of fear, to seek eternal happiness as the greatest honor, and to lead the virtuous life as the best means of avoiding eternal damnation and gaining eternal salvation. Oratory, Sheridan went on, had been the great instrument used in the republics of Greece and Rome to promote and encourage virtue. Having been originally established to guarantee liberty, these republics owed to the love of virtue their very existence; and they proceeded on the assumption that the best means of encouraging virtuous conduct was through the diffusion of wisdom. "To do this," said Sheridan, "it was necessary that their thoughts and words should be ranged in due order, and the whole delivered with proper tones and gestures. Or, in other words, the art of oratory was essential to those who spoke in publick." Sheridan added: "Accordingly we find, that in the education of their youth, after having taken care to instil strongly the principle of virtue, their chief attention was to instruct them in the most accurate knowledge of their own language, and to train them from their childhood in the practice of oratory, as the sure means to preferment in the state."[199] The study of oratory, Sheridan then declared, was even more necessary in Britain than it had been in Greece and Rome, inasmuch as the Christian religion, as the foundation of British society, was aided in all of its observances by skill in speaking. In connection with this argument Sheridan uttered the words which I quoted earlier in this chapter.[200] "Indeed," he subsequently said, "it is so evident that the proper arms for the use of the members of the church militant here on earth, for the soldiers in Christ, can be drawn from no stores but those of oratory, that it is astonishing how it could be so entirely neglected."[201]

The second Book of *British Education* develops the thesis that only by taking care to cultivate its language to the greatest possi-

---

throughout the rest of the eighteenth century. Thus Sheridan was referring to a work already well known to his countrymen.

[198] *Ibid.*, pp. 40-42.   [199] *Ibid.*, pp. 47, 48.   [200] See above, pp. 154-156.
[201] *British Education*, p. 146.

ble extent can a civilization triumph over time and oblivion, and that only by cultivating the art of oratory to the greatest possible extent can a language be perfected.[202] The proof offered by Sheridan in support of this thesis consisted largely in the argument by analogy. Thus he maintained that the Greek and Latin languages, which have defied oblivion and time, were rich, flexible, accurate, excellent; that their development towards perfection was chiefly owing to the study and practice of oratory; and that, if English is to achieve among competing modern languages the status of a great classical tongue, England must follow the illustrious example of the ancients.[203]

In the third Book of *British Education*, Sheridan argued the following propositions: "That the liberal arts never flourished, or arrived at perfection in any country, where the study and practice of oratory was neglected. That in those countries, where the liberal arts arrived at their highest pitch of glory, there were no traces of them, previous to the study of oratory. That the liberal arts always followed oratory in their progress towards perfection; arrived at their summit soon after that did; declined as that declined; and, when that was banished, wholly disappeared."[204] He even devoted a chapter to the thesis that "it is much more probable that oratory raised and supported the liberal arts, than that the liberal arts raised and supported oratory."[205] From these arguments he concluded that if poetry, music, and painting are to arrive at perfection in England, they must have the support which only the cultivation of oratory can give. The great masters of the art of creating beautiful representations of human nature derived the highest advantage from having lived in those periods and countries when oratory was at its height. Poetry, which uses language as the means of representing human nature, can only achieve perfection when oratory has perfected the language in which the poet expresses himself.[206] Music, which studies the various sounds and tones annexed by nature to the various passions, goes to oratory for its inspiration; for is it not the orator's necessary task "to express all the different passions in their nat-

---

[202] *Ibid.*, pp. 175-192.   [203] *Ibid.*, pp. 217-379.

[204] *Ibid.*, pp. 387-388.

[205] *Ibid.*, pp. 398-403. The quotation appears as the italicized chapter heading for Bk. III, Ch. v.

[206] *Ibid.*, pp. 413-415.

ural and suitable tones and sounds?"[207] As for painting, the same general truth prevails. Said Sheridan:

> Here it must at once occur, that as the business of the history-painter is to represent human nature in a manner which shall be at once graceful and expressive, when animated by all it's variety of passions and affections; and that, in order to do this, he must be able to give all the various configurations of the muscles of the face, together with the whole deportment of the body, and action of the limbs, which are the natural concomitant signs of those passions; and all these must be in the most exact degree of due proportion; he could no where meet with such perfect subjects as amongst the orators. . . . Nor is it possible to conceive any look, attitude, or gesture, which the painter might have occasion for in all the several styles, whether of the grand, the terrible, the graceful, the tender, the passionate, the joyous; whether expressive of the more furious and violent passions, as anger, hatred, &c. or of the more calm and pleasing, as of pity, joy, &c. which he might not have frequent opportunities of catching warm from the life in the endless variety of subjects treated of by an impassioned orator.[208]

In fairness to Sheridan, we should not expect that his work on British education has about it anything but a borrowed originality. In the Preface to the first edition, he asserted that he hoped for the reader's indulgence in regard to errors and inaccuracies in his treatise, and that he had no intention of interfering with the existing educational establishment in Great Britain. He supported this latter assertion by saying that a recent revolution in the two great schools of England had given him the notion for his own scheme of education; and he went on not only to apply to Dr. William Markham, the headmaster of Westminster since 1753, the words which Quintilian had used to describe the ideal teacher, but also to single out Dr. Edward Barnard for special compliment as the headmaster of Eton. "It is with great pleasure," said Sheridan with himself in mind, "that the author can assure the publick, that amongst many other good customs introduced into both those schools, pronunciation and the art of speaking are now made essential points."[209] As for his request that the reader

---

[207] *Ibid.*, p. 416.   [208] *Ibid.*, pp. 428-429.
[209] *Ibid.*, p. xxxi. Sheridan's text is in italics.

pardon any shortcomings to be found in his work, Sheridan is even more disarming, even franker, about disclaiming special authority in the field of education. The present treatise, he explicitly said, "was begun and finished during a few months recess in the last summer," when he was ill and unable at best to devote more than three or four hours to it in any one day; and speaking still in the third person, he added the following statement about his own lack of serious preparation for the task of educational reform:

> It is now more than ten years since he has been an alien to all learned studies, and a stranger to books in general, except such only as were necessary to the discharge of a troublesome and laborious employment. This is his first attempt as a writer, without any previous steps taken, without any pains to qualify him for so difficult an office. Thus circumstanced, how vain were all hopes of praise! Happy indeed shall he think himself, if he can escape censure![210]

But unfortunately we have to recognize that Sheridan expressed in his preface a modesty which he promptly forgot. The authorities upon whom he relied for most of his quotations about the long lost art of oratory, so far as *British Education* is concerned, are Cicero and Quintilian. On many occasions and at some length he cited these great rhetoricians, now in Latin footnotes, and now in English translation in his text.[211] His favorite source was Cicero's *De Oratore*, the masterpiece of the Latin rhetorical tradition; but Quintilian's *Institutio Oratoria*, the most learned and most complete of the ancient commentaries on classical rhetoric, is often quoted in his text or notes, and he occasionally cited Cicero's *Brutus* and *De Optimo Genere Oratorum*, and the anonymous *Rhetorica ad Herennium*, which he regarded as one of Cicero's works. Certainly these sources would have revealed to anyone that ancient rhetoric, as a central discipline in ancient education, was much more than the study of voice and gesture; yet Sheridan saw only this one part of the total picture,

[210] *Ibid.*, p. xxvi. Sheridan's text is in italics.

[211] The heaviest concentrations of references to Cicero and Quintilian in *British Education* occur as follows: in Bk. I, Chs. 10, 15, 16; and in Bk. II, Chs. 3, 10.

and became certain that what he saw was all there was to see.[212] No trace of self-doubt betrays itself in his rambling, repetitious, dogmatic argument. He really felt that he alone had discovered the lost art of oratory, and that without him the art would die forever.

It is not easy to explain why Sheridan quoted so much from the ancient system and understood it so imperfectly. But some speculations upon this matter are at least permissible. First of all, an actor-rhetorician, having always had to interpret lines written for him by someone else, is inevitably more concerned with the problem of delivery than with the problems of invention, arrangement, and style, and thus he might carelessly tend to think that, because delivery is his only concern, it is the only concern of rhetoric in general. At any rate, that is what Sheridan as actor-rhetorician actually thought. Secondly, an actor-rhetorician would naturally turn to others of the same breed for guidance in matters connected with oratorical and theatrical delivery. Hence it is entirely plausible to assume that Sheridan turned to Betterton's theory of acting as it had been presented in Gildon's *Life of Mr. Thomas Betterton* and in Curll's *The History of the English Stage*, and that he found in those works, known most certainly by him at first hand, a rhetorical doctrine which in the course of time he made his own as he discovered in patches its classical origin. Besides, Betterton was a theatrical legend in the world of Sheridan's youth, and a theory that Betterton sponsored would have had special appeal to Sheridan when he began to teach the art of acting to his younger colleagues. Thirdly, when *British Education* was first published, John Ward's *System of Oratory* had not yet appeared in print, and it would be three years before it made available to the British public a careful scholarly account of the full art of ancient rhetoric. Thus Sheridan lacked a contemporary source above the level of schoolboy rhetorics like that of Holmes to give him direction in his search for the ancient scheme; and

[212] The epigraph at the head of the present chapter affords a capital instance of the way in which Sheridan's *British Education* used the authority of the ancients to promote the definition of *pronuntiatio* into a definition of elocution, and then allowed the latter definition to stand for the whole art of ancient rhetoric. Sheridan's *Lectures on Elocution*, however, offer final proof that to him the long lost art of oratory is merely what the ancients regarded as oratorical delivery.

after his long absence from studious pursuits during his active connection with the Theatre Royal, he would suffer from lack of direction if anyone ever did. Finally, Sheridan might well have assumed that, in making pronunciation and gesture the whole of rhetoric, he had the support of George Berkeley, the distinguished eighteenth-century Irish philosopher and churchman. Berkeley was an important influence upon Sheridan's *British Education*.[213] In *The Querist,* which was first published at Dublin in three parts in the middle seventeen-thirties, Berkeley had posed a series of rhetorical questions concerning economic, financial, political, sociological, and moral subjects, and had plainly intended the questions not only to provoke enquiry and debate by their acuteness and brevity but also on occasion to call satirical attention to human foolishness and perversity. As published in final form at Dublin and London in 1752 in a work devoted to certain ones of Berkeley's miscellaneous writings, *The Querist* wanted at one point to know "Whether *Homer's* Compendium of Education, Μύθων μὲν ῥητῆρ ἔμεναι, πρηκτῆρά τε ἔργων, would not be a good Rule for modern Educators of Youth? And whether half the Learning and Study of these Kingdoms is not useless, for want of a proper Delivery and Pronunciation being taught in our Schools and Colleges?"[214] The second of these questions seemed to Sheridan to call attention to the very thesis that he was advocating in *British Education,* and it doubtless seemed also to put Berkeley on the side of the elocutionists. At any rate, Sheridan quoted it twice, and each time the implication was that this conception of the nature and value of rhetoric had the sanction of the

[213] For Sheridan's major references to Berkeley, see *British Education,* pp. 9-10, 83, 201, 225-226, 486, 520-523, 524, 531-533.

[214] This query, numbered 203, appears in George Berkeley's *A Miscellany, containing Several Tracts on Various Subjects* (London: Printed for J. and R. Tonson and S. Draper in the Strand, MDCCLII), p. 141.

As given in the recent standard text by T. E. Jessop in *The Works of George Berkeley, Bishop of Cloyne,* ed. A. A. Luce and T. E. Jessop (London . . . and New York, 1948-1957), VI, 122, this query contains a misprint which consists in the substitution of "punctuation" for "pronunciation." For a discussion of this error, see Wilbur Samuel Howell, "A Misprint in Berkeley," *Times Literary Supplement* (October 13, 1961), p. 683.

The verse by Homer is from the *Iliad,* IX, line 443. Jessop translates it "To be skilled in both words and deeds."

brilliant Bishop of Cloyne.[215] Indeed, as he quoted it on the second occasion, Sheridan was speaking of ancient Athens and Rome as having had two successive systems of education, one of which marked the golden age of those states and consisted in the union of oratory and philosophy, whereas the other marked the period of their degeneracy and saw oratory neglected and philosophy elevated into the only subject of study. Britain, Sheridan asserted, had chosen the latter of these two systems.[216] "To give a sanction to the sentiments which I have delivered upon this head," he declared, "I shall subjoin a few queries of the bishop of Cloyne, extracted from a pamphlet called the Querist."[217] He proceeded at once to quote eight of Berkeley's questions, and the last one which he quotes is given in his text in the following way:

> Whether Homer's compendium of education, Μυθων τε ρητηρ εμεναι πρηκτηρα τε εργων, would not be a good rule for modern educators of youth? and whether half the learning and study of these kingdoms is not useless, for want of a proper delivery and pronunciation being taught in our schools, and colleges?[218]

In thus starting from the ancient union of rhetoric and philosophy, as described so perceptively in Cicero's *De Oratore*, and in going onward to the plain implication that Cicero meant only to emphasize the union of philosophy and oratorical delivery, and that Berkeley himself endorsed this latter view of rhetoric and thought its revival the salvation of British education—in doing these things, Sheridan illustrates how distorted and incomplete was his view of the place of rhetoric in ancient civilization, and how clear was his conviction that Berkeley had authorized him to preach delivery and pronunciation as the means of putting British learning on the road to glory.

Three years after the date of the first edition of *British Education*, and two years after the delivery of his oration before the nobility and gentry of Ireland, Sheridan published his next con-

[215] See *British Education*, pp. 201, 532-533.
[216] *Ibid.*, pp. 529-530.   [217] *Ibid.*, p. 531.
[218] Sheridan's footnote on the line that he quotes from Homer reads as follows: "This is a line from a speech of Phoenix to Achilles, in the 9th book of the Iliad; and may be thus translated: Alike to practice eloquence and valour."

siderable work on elocution. It was called *A Discourse Delivered in The Theatre at Oxford, in The Senate-House at Cambridge, and at Spring-Garden in London*.[219] "To The Two Learned Universities of Oxford and Cambridge," read its dedicatory statement, "The following Discourse (As a small token of gratitude For the candour with which they received, And the generosity with which they encouraged, His attempt Towards improving Elocution, And promoting the study of the English Language) Is, With all humility, And the most profound respect, Inscribed, By their very faithful and devoted servant, Thomas Sheridan." The treatise belonging to this complimentary dedication contains a restatement of the ideas which we have already suggested in speaking of Sheridan's previous works. In fact, it includes many passages surrounded by quotation marks but not identified with any specific source; and these passages turn out to be quotations from *British Education*.[220] Sheridan told his audiences in Oxford, Cambridge, and London that many bad consequences attended the neglect of the study of English and the art of speaking; that any practical plan for removing this neglect deserved the attention of

---

[219] Following the title as just given, the title page reads as follows: "By Thomas Sheridan, M.A. Being Introductory to His Course of Lectures on Elocution and the English Language. Ut enim hominis decus ingenium, sic ingenii ipsius lumen est eloquentia. Cic. de Orat. London: Printed for A. Millar, in The Strand; J. Rivington and J. Fletcher, in Pater-noster-Row; J. Dodsley, in Pall-Mall; and sold by J. Wilkie, in St. Paul's Church-yard. M.DCC.LIX."

The student of Sheridan's sources soon learns to accept carelessness and inaccuracy as the hallmark of Sheridan's scholarship. The quotation attributed to Cicero's *De Oratore* on this title page is actually from Cicero's *Brutus*, 15.59.

[220] For example, the quotation in *A Discourse*, p. 6, is taken from a footnote in *British Education*, p. 52; the quotation on pp. 6-7 of *A Discourse* is taken from *British Education*, p. 53; the quotation on p. 17 of *A Discourse* is paraphrased from *British Education*, p. 85; the quotation on pp. 17-18 of *A Discourse* is partly taken from *British Education*, pp. 85-86; and the quotation on p. 48 of *A Discourse* is taken from a quotation from John Locke in *British Education*, pp. 200-201. Incidentally, in introducing this last quotation into *A Discourse*, Sheridan made it appear that the passage referred specifically to "elocution." But the longer quotation from Locke in *British Education* specifies that Locke had in mind the necessity of teaching English students to speak and write English. Thus Locke was not thinking of elocution as Sheridan used the term. But the latter made no attempt to avoid the erroneous implication that Locke was a supporter of the elocutionists.

the best and wisest men; that the English were the only civilized people of ancient or modern times "who neglected to cultivate their language, or to methodize it in such a way, as that the knowledge of it might be regularly acquired";[221] that the English were the only people who never studied the art of elocution or founded any institutions in which those professionally required to speak in public "might be instructed to acquit themselves properly on such occasions, and be enabled to deliver their sentiments with propriety and grace";[222] that this neglect of the study of elocution was the more astonishing because the support of the English ecclesiastical and civil establishment depended "upon the powers of elocution in public debates, or other oratorical performances, displayed in the pulpit, the senate-house, or at the bar";[223] that the study of oratory was as necessary to the English as it had been to the ancient Greeks and Romans; that the difference between "ourselves" and the ancients was that we have pursued most of the studies which they pursued, "but some we have wholly omitted";[224] that the "chief points in which they differed from us, were the study of their native language, and oratory";[225] that the true source of our neglect of these studies was founded upon a wrong linguistic bias which caused us to neglect the spoken language and favor the written; that the spoken language works by the whole force of natural and artificial means, whereas the written language works only by artificial means; that a nation which bestows all its care upon cultivating the artificial and neglecting the natural language is taking a wrong course;[226] that the effects which a beautiful composition is capable of producing depend upon the art of speaking; that the current English system of education reflected the preoccupation of the Renaissance with the mastery of Latin as a vehicle of written communication throughout Europe; that the English had left the pronunciation of their native language wholly to chance, and accordingly "those who taught English, were amongst the most ignorant of mankind";[227] that the way towards reform was that of tracing the principles of elocution, of reducing the art of oratory to a system, and of drawing up rules by which a knowledge of English might be methodically obtained; that the purpose of Sheridan's course

---

[221] *A Discourse*, p. 3.
[222] *Ibid.*, p. 4. [223] *Ibid.*, p. 4. [224] *Ibid.*, p. 10.
[225] *Ibid.*, p. 11. [226] *Ibid.*, p. 20. [227] *Ibid.*, p. 33.

of lectures was "to lay open the principles of elocution, and the peculiar constitution of the English language, with regard to the powers of sound and numbers, in a method, which should it prove to be as rational as it is new, will, I hope, give the author of these lectures no cause to repent of the time and pains which his researches into these abstruse subjects have cost him";[228] that the introduction of these studies will have a beneficial effect upon two new institutions recently created at Oxford, the Vinerean endowment for the study of law, and Lord Clarendon's benefaction for the introduction of physical exercises;[229] that should eloquence establish her throne in England, English students would gladly pay her homage; and that the study of elocution might reasonably be supposed to produce beneficial results.

I fear, said Sheridan as he began to conclude his discourse, that I have exhausted your patience, and I shall close "with the same exhortation to the revival of the art of elocution, which Quintilian used to the Romans, to engage them in the support of it, when in its declining state."[230] And he thereupon ended his lecture with a 31-line Latin quotation from the last chapter of the last book of Quintilian's *Institutio Oratoria*, where Quintilian mentioned the inducements which ought to lead the student to carry out the difficult task of becoming excellent in all the departments of the rhetorical discipline.[231] Quintilian spoke as he did after he had exhaustively discussed invention, arrangement, style, memory, and delivery. Sheridan used Quintilian's words as if Quintilian were suggesting that only delivery presented difficulties to the student of eloquence, and that true excellence in oratory lay solely in mastering that one art.

Sheridan's lectures on elocution, as we are told on the title page of the work just discussed, were delivered at Oxford, Cambridge, and London. But they were also delivered at Edinburgh, Bath, and Belfast. As we have already mentioned, Wedderburn heard them in the Scottish capital before he left that city for London in 1757, and he was led by them not only to seek Sheridan's aid in improving his pronunciation, but also to join with other Scots in

---

228 *Ibid.*, p. 50.   229 *Ibid.*, pp. 54-55.   230 *Ibid.*, p. 58.

231 Sheridan's quotation from Quintilian is presented as a continuous passage, but it is in fact made up of several passages in its source; see *Institutio Oratoria*, 12.11.25, 26, 29-30. This same Latin passage appeared at somewhat greater length as a footnote in *British Education*, pp. 376-377.

founding "The Society for promoting the reading and speaking of the English Language in Scotland."[232] We have James Boswell's word that Sheridan repeated his lectures at Edinburgh at a later date. "In the summer of 1761," said he in his *Life of Johnson*, "Mr. Thomas Sheridan was at Edinburgh, and delivered lectures upon the English Language and Publick Speaking to large and respectable audiences." "I was often in his company," Boswell added, "and heard him frequently expatiate upon Johnson's extraordinary knowledge, talents, and virtues, repeat his pointed sayings, describe his peculiarities, and boast of his being his guest sometimes till two or three in the morning."[233] Of Sheridan's lectures at Bath, Dr. Samuel Johnson himself is quoted by Boswell as having predicted that "Sheridan will not succeed at Bath with his oratory." "Ridicule," explained Johnson, "has gone down before him, and, I doubt, Derrick is his enemy."[234] Some of the ridicule which Johnson thus recorded as having been aroused against Sheridan by his lectures was possibly the outcome of the growing conviction of men of learning that Sheridan was solemnly claiming to have made a significant new discovery when in reality what he had found was considerably less than a discovery, considerably less than new, and considerably less than significant. The publication of John Ward's *System of Oratory* in 1759 would have taught the learned world to suspect that Sheridan was really confused about the true nature of ancient rhetoric, and that he was unable to recognize how inadequate his conception of it was. And the publication at London in 1762 of the actual lectures that he had been giving here and there since 1756 would have offered the hard testimony of print in support of the widespread belief that the long lost art of oratory was lost more completely after Sheridan's efforts to recover it than it would have been if he had done nothing whatever in that direction.

The first edition of Sheridan's *Course of Lectures on Elocution*

[232] See above, pp. 157-159.

[233] *Boswell's Life of Johnson*, ed. G. B. Hill, rev. F. F. Powell (Oxford, 1934-1950), I, 385. Boswell mentioned in the same work that he himself had been at some pains to improve his pronunciation, and had received help in that direction from "old Mr. Sheridan." *Ibid.*, II, 159.

[234] *Ibid.*, I, 394. The Derrick mentioned by Johnson is Samuel Derrick (1724-1769), who served as master of the ceremonies at Bath from 1761 to the time of his death. See *The Dictionary of National Biography*, s.v. Derrick, Samuel.

features eight discourses, one of which serves as the introduction to the others.[235] Between this introduction, which is dated July 10, 1762, and the seven following lectures, which are undated, is a ten-page list of subscribers to the edition, and the list contains 643 names, some of whom are recorded as having signed for more than one copy. A note at the top of the first of these ten pages indicates that "many of the Names in this List were hastily taken down at the door of the several places where the Lectures were delivered." Since the names were not ordinarily written by the subscribers themselves, the note goes on, it is feared that the list will be found to contain many errors in the spelling of names and the recording of titles and proper distinctions for each. Moreover, it adds, the names of more than a third of those who attended the lectures have been lost. In the list itself are such names as that of James Boswell, Mr. Burgh, Mr. Blair, Mr. Bentham, Lord Kames, and Mr. Walter Scott. Sheridan himself estimated that 1700 persons had heard him deliver this present course of lectures on elocution and a former course of the same nature.[236] Following the eight lectures on elocution are two dissertations on the state of language in different nations, and a document setting forth the "Heads of a Plan for the Improvement of Elocution." To these papers are added a dissertation on the difficulties of learning English, and the first edition of Edward Young's poem, *Resignation*, the latter of which appears with its own title, imprint, and pagination. The present discussion will deal only with Sheridan's eight lectures on the fifth part of rhetoric, since the other ingredients of the volume in which they appeared either will have been covered already in this account of Sheridan or do not relate to the rhetorical aspects of the elocutionary movement.

The introductory lecture that is printed in this volume contains one element which seems intended by Sheridan to make his theory of rhetoric into a natural complement of Locke's *Essay concerning Human Understanding*. "Is it not amazing to reflect,"

---

[235] The title page of the first edition reads thus: "A Course of Lectures on Elocution: Together with Two Dissertations on Language; and Some other Tracts relative to those Subjects. By Thomas Sheridan, A. M. London: Printed by W. Strahan, For A. Millar, R. and J. Dodsley, T. Davies, C. Henderson, J. Wilkie, and E. Dilly. MDCCLXII." My discussion is based upon this edition, which I cite as *Lectures on Elocution*.

[236] *Lectures on Elocution*, p. xv.

said Sheridan, "that from the creation of the world, there was no part of the human mind clearly delineated, till within the last sixty years? when Mr. Locke arose, to give us a just view, of one part of our internal frame, 'the understanding,' upon principles of philosophy founded on reason and experience."[237] And it was Locke, declared Sheridan, who discovered the chief cause of the erroneous views of human nature before his time. In explanation of this point, Sheridan spoke thus:

> His discovery was, that as we can not think upon any abstract subject, without the use of abstract terms; and as in general we substitute the terms themselves, in thinking, as well as speaking, in the room of the complex ideas for which they stand; it is impossible we can think with precision, till we first examine whether we have precise ideas annexed to such terms: and it is equally impossible to communicate our thoughts to others with exactness, unless we are first agreed in the exact meaning of our words.[238]

But although Locke was careful, remarked Sheridan, to examine all of his own terms and to give them clear definitions "for the benefit of others, in communicating to them his thoughts,"[239] his successors tended exclusively and avidly to emphasize the acquisition of knowledge, as indeed Locke himself did, and they also tended to ignore the process by which knowledge is made useful to society. In fact, Locke himself did not make any contribution to the latter process except to insist that men should carefully examine the meaning of their terms and use each term steadily in the same sense. What Locke did not do, Sheridan went on, was to trace disordered thinking to its source, and to see "that the study of our own language, has never been made part of the education of our youth."[240] Sheridan then admitted that Locke's *Some Thoughts concerning Education* had complained of the neglect of the study of English and had attributed that neglect to the indifference of teachers and tutors in English schools and universities towards the mother tongue. The fault rather lay, said Sheridan, with the failure to make the mother tongue a distinct branch of education and to train masters to teach it as their sole employment, not as their casual employment in intervals between

[237] *Ibid.*, p. v.   [238] *Ibid.*, p. vi.   [239] *Ibid.*, p. vi.
[240] *Ibid.*, p. vii.

their efforts to teach Greek and Latin. This failure explained why Locke's *Essay concerning Human Understanding* had proved of so little benefit to the world. Men do not think or reason more clearly now, declared Sheridan, than they did before the publication of Locke's *Essay*. He added: "Upon the closest examination, indeed, it would appear, that little or no benefit in point of practice, has resulted from a display in theory, of the only part of the human mind, which has hitherto been laid open with accuracy, upon principles of true philosophy."[241]

Thus Sheridan conceived his own task to be that of emphasizing the study of the English language as a way of contributing to the art of communicating knowledge and as a way of supplementing Locke's demand for carefully defined ideas described by carefully defined words. As Sheridan saw it, the prime necessity was that two languages be recognized, the spoken and the written, the former the gift of God, the latter the invention of man. "It will be allowed by all persons of reflection," said Sheridan, "that there is no speculative point more ardently to be wished for, than to have it in our power to contemplate those parts of the human mind, which are still concealed from us, or falsely viewed thro' the mists of errour, with the same clear satisfaction that we find in examining Mr. Locke's view of the understanding."[242] Those parts of the human mind which Sheridan wanted specifically to investigate were the passions and the imagination, and they were in need of investigation precisely because all previous studies of them had been based upon the assumption that they could be described objectively in written language when as a matter of fact they could never be objectively described at all but had to be treated demonstratively in terms of the accents and gestures of spoken language. It must never be forgotten, said Sheridan, "that the passions and the fancy have a language of their own, utterly independent of words, by which only their exertions can be manifested and communicated."[243] This language Sheridan proposed for study, even as he proposed the mother tongue. We must, he urged, regulate the marks of the spoken language, settle their use precisely, and thus create a language in which the passions and taste can be treated, even as Locke had created a language for treating the understanding. Previous attempts to reform the pas-

[241] *Ibid.*, p. ix.　　　[242] *Ibid.*, p. xi.　　　[243] *Ibid.*, p. x.

sions and imagination as Locke reformed the understanding failed because "some of our greatest men have been trying to do that with the pen, which can only be performed by the tongue; to produce effects by the dead letter, which can never be produced but by the living voice, with its accompaniments."[244]

> This [added Sheridan] is no longer a mere assertion; it is no longer problematical. It has been demonstrated to the entire satisfaction of some of the wisest heads in these realms: And readers of but moderate discernment, will find it fully proved in the sixth and seventh lectures, on Tones and Gesture; and in the two following Dissertations on Language.[245]

Sheridan turned to the contemporary scene for an illustration of the power of the spoken over the written language, and he chose William Pitt, first earl of Chatham, as the embodiment of the power of speech. It was Pitt "who by the mere force of cultivating the language bestowed by the Deity on humankind, as far as he could carry it by his own pains, raised himself to the sole direction of affairs in this country: and not only so, but the powers of his living voice shook distant thrones, and made the extremities of the earth to tremble."[246] These words, to be sure, are applied by Sheridan to a man identified only as "a late minister"; but the true identity of that minister is not really in doubt.

That minister's skill in using the language of nature, Sheridan went on, emphasized how great its power continued to be, even when the study of it was neglected. Restore it to the position which it held among the Greeks and the Romans, and England would add their distinction in the arts to her own distinction in the sciences, and thus create the perfect society. Sheridan added:

> Now they had no arts whatsoever, in which they excelled us, that did not take their rise, either immediately, or consequentially, from the pains bestowed upon the culture of the language of nature, the living speech. What is there wanting then amongst us, but to apply ourselves with industry to the same means, in order to attain the same ends?[247]

The lectures which followed the introductory discourse defined elocution as "the just and graceful management of the voice,

[244] *Ibid.*, p. xii.   [245] *Ibid.*, pp. xii-xiii.   [246] *Ibid.*, p. xiii.
[247] *Ibid.*, p. xiv.

countenance, and gesture in speaking,"[248] and divided it into the headings of voice and gesture, only one lecture, the seventh, being devoted to the latter subject. We do not need to be reminded that this definition of elocution, and this division of it into two parts, went back in Sheridan's thinking to the pages of *British Education* and to *A Discourse Delivered in The Theatre at Oxford*; nor do we need to be told again that Sheridan borrowed his definition from the *Rhetorica ad Herennium,* where it stands as the classical outline of the doctrine relating to the fifth part of rhetoric.[249] But it needs emphasizing that Sheridan made rhetoric impotent when he reduced the rhetorical doctrine of Aristotle and Cicero to his own little measure. Did he not leave rhetoric with the duty of accounting for the eloquence of Chatham by confining its remarks to Chatham's voice and gesture? And did he not give rhetoric the task of producing future Chathams by taking England's young men into Sheridan's academy and teaching them there the mysteries of vocal and physical expression as the true secrets of effectiveness in oratory? The Burkes, the Lincolns, and the Churchills of the future would not owe their full endowment of eloquence to Sheridan's stunted formula, although they would find oratorical delivery important among their other rhetorical accomplishments. It was Sheridan's tragedy as a rhetorician that he glimpsed a peninsula through the fog of his own folly and thought his discovery a continent.

In speaking of voice as the first part of elocution, Sheridan discussed articulation, pronunciation, accent, emphasis, pauses, pitch, and tones. The whole of his discussion need not be summarized here, but there are a few points that should receive attention, and I shall mention them briefly.

"A good articulation, consists," he said, "in giving every letter in a syllable, its due proportion of sound, according to the most approved custom of pronouncing it; and in making such a distinction, between the syllables, of which the words are composed, that the ear shall without difficulty acknowledge their number; and perceive at once, to which syllable each letter belongs."[250] This ability, he went on, is to the ear what good handwriting is to

[248] *Ibid.,* p. 19.
[249] See *British Education,* pp. 119, 158-159; *A Discourse,* p. 49; *Rhetorica ad Herennium,* 1.2.3.
[250] *Lectures on Elocution,* pp. 19-20.

the eye; but whereas it is not thought necessary for a gentleman to have a good handwriting, this accomplishment being required only of a clerk, it should be considered a disgrace for a gentleman to omit syllables in pronouncing words, or to huddle his words together, so as to be unintelligible.

When Sheridan took up his second topic, pronunciation, he acknowledged that, among the ancients, this word took in "the whole compass of delivery, with its concomitants of look and gesture." But with us, he added, the term "refers only to the manner of sounding our words."[251] Thus he pointed up the difficulty of continuing to use pronunciation as an English term for delivery when it had come to have a settled meaning in phonetics. In discussing pronunciation in this latter sense, he spoke of the differences shown by the Scots, the Irish, and the Welsh in sounding English words, and of the differences in London English between cockney dialect and court speech. The latter, he observed, represents fashionable pronunciation; all other dialects "are sure marks, either of a provincial, rustic, pedantic, or mechanic education; and therefore have some degree of disgrace annexed to them." What he at once added affords us an insight into the elocutionary movement as having its chief value, not in its recovery of the lost art of oratory, not in its enlargement of the ancient art of oratorical delivery, but in its function as a means by which the newly affluent English middle class could acquire court speech in a series of lessons like those given Wedderburn by Sheridan himself, and could thereafter enjoy the feeling of superior status involved in having divested themselves of provincialisms:

> And as the court pronunciation [explained Sheridan] is no where methodically taught, and can be acquired only by conversing with people in polite life, it is a sort of proof that a person has kept good company, and on that account is sought after by all, who wish to be considered as fashionable people, or members of the beau monde. This is the true reason that the article of pronunciation has been the chief, or rather only object of attention, in the whole affair of delivery. Yet tho' this is a point, the attainment of which is ardently desired by an infinite number of individuals, there are few who succeed in

[251] *Ibid.*, p. 29.

the attempt, thro' want of method, rules, and assistance of masters; without which old habits can not easily be removed.[252]

In connection with his discussion of emphasis, which, as he said, "discharges in sentences, the same kind of office, that accent does in words,"[253] Sheridan took the question, "Shall you ride to town to-morrow," and demonstrated how, by emphasizing successively each one of the words in it, a speaker could produce a succession of different meanings. Sheridan's debt to the earlier English elocutionists is not often a matter of his having borrowed details from them. But in regard to his use of this particular question, which he called "a trite instance," he was in fact borrowing directly from Mason's *Essay on Elocution*.[254]

Sheridan's sixth lecture not only dealt with tones but also concluded his treatment of voice as the first grand division of elocution; and his seventh, which brought the series to an end, discussed gesture. Upon the use of these two instruments, he said, "all that is pleasurable, or affecting in elocution, chiefly depend."[255] Thus it would not be out of place to note that these concluding lectures contain what Sheridan regarded as his own contribution to the doctrine of oratorical delivery.

Most people, he observed, regard language as if it were composed only of words, but such a concept is in reality too narrow. "For language, in its full extent," said he, "means, any way or method whatsoever, by which all that passes in the mind of one man, may be manifested to another."[256] If nothing passed through the mind but ideas, he remarked, and if men were merely directed by reason, like Swift's Houyhnhnms, a language composed only of words would sufficiently answer the needs of communication. Then he added:

But as there are other things which pass in the mind of man, beside ideas; as he is not wholly made up of intellect, but on the contrary, the passions, and the fancy, compose great part of his complicated frame; as the operations of these are attended with an infinite variety of emotions in the mind, both in kind and degree; it is clear, that unless there be some means found, of

[252] *Ibid.*, p. 30.   [253] *Ibid.*, p. 57.
[254] *Ibid.*, p. 58. Compare with John Mason, *An Essay on Elocution* (London, 1748), pp. 21-27.
[255] *Lectures on Elocution*, p. 93.   [256] *Ibid.*, p. 94.

manifesting those emotions, all that passes in the mind of one man can not be communicated to another. Now, as in order to know what another knows, and in the same manner that he knows it, an exact transcript of the ideas which pass in the mind of one man, must be made by sensible marks, in the mind of another; so in order to feel what another feels, the emotions which are in the mind of one man, must also be communicated to that of another, by sensible marks.[257]

The sensible marks which transfer feelings from one person to another, said Sheridan, are "tones, looks, and gestures."[258] As every passion has its peculiar tone, he explained somewhat later, so does it have its peculiar gesture, its own exact look.[259] And tones and gestures are related in such fashion that "The one, may be justly called the speech, the other, the hand-writing of nature."[260]

Sheridan took the trouble to deny that a system of rules could be devised to demonstrate what particular tones and gestures are best adapted to express the several emotions of the mind. Just as people cannot be taught to sing and dance by precept, he argued, but have to be taught by masters and by patterns of imitation, in a course of actual practice, so people cannot be taught tones and gestures by a system of rules.

> Were there masters to teach this, in the same manner as other arts are taught, such a system of rules, [he said] would not only be useful but necessary. And indeed, without such a system of rules, to qualify persons for the office of instructing pupils methodically in the art, we can never hope to see proper masters arise amongst us.[261]

Till such masters arise, added Sheridan, the best I can do is to advise each person that his proper course is to try on his own to avoid artificiality and to keep to his own natural manner of delivery.

It was of course the masters who were to cause trouble later on. They did not value Sheridan's notion that perfection could be achieved without teachers if a person followed his own manner and like Betterton sought only to be in earnest.[262] They valued

[257] *Ibid.*, p. 99. [258] *Ibid.*, p. 100. [259] *Ibid.*, p. 114.
[260] *Ibid.*, p. 113. [261] *Ibid.*, p. 123. [262] *Ibid.*, p. 127.

instead his idea that rules could be devised to enable ordained teachers to instruct other teachers in the art of arousing passions by a system of fixed tones and gestures. And it became their passionate conviction that these other teachers were alone qualified to indoctrinate pupils in the mysteries of oratory, and that the title of orator must be denied to anyone who did not earn it in the school of elocution. Systems of fixed tones and gestures became the bane of the elocutionary movement, and, as they were often accompanied by mysticism and quackery, they increasingly attracted the poseurs and the charlatans into the ranks of the teachers of oratorical delivery. Such teachers brought rhetoric into the deepest disrepute that it had ever known.

Sheridan was not himself responsible for all the abuses that his elocutionary theory fostered. Indeed, so far as his attempts to fix a standard for English pronunciation are concerned, he performed a praiseworthy service for his generation. But he cannot be excused for advocating in one breath that the only way in which English pronunciation could be standardized was through the revival of the ancient art of oratory, and for claiming in the next breath, against the very tenor of his own quotations from Cicero and Quintilian, that the ancient art of oratory was a matter of voice and gesture alone. The true rhetorical system of Aristotle, Cicero, and Quintilian, creatively adjusted to the conditions in eighteenth-century Britain, would have had great value not only in helping to fix a standard for English pronunciation but also in helping to strengthen the whole enterprise of civilized living so far as that enterprise is in need of a wide diffusion of competence in speaking and writing and of disciplines to foster that competence. But the rhetorical system sponsored by Sheridan in the name of the ancients was not only blighted by its having been a misreading of the rhetoric of ancient Greece and Rome, but it was foredoomed to become a leading influence in reducing rhetoric to a lowly estate in the English and American academic communities of the twentieth century, and to a condition in which it began in the modern vocabulary to mean merely declamatory rather than fully persuasive utterance.

XII Burgh, Herries, Walker, Austin

The history of the elocutionary movement in Britain during the last thirty-eight years of the eighteenth century will not concern us here in any detail. Indeed, the movement did not significantly change its basic philosophy throughout its entire lifetime, and thus its later features would largely be a repetition of those which I have already delineated. Moreover, the story of its acceptance in late eighteenth-century England has been well told by Frederick W. Haberman, and to him the reader who wishes full information on that subject may profitably turn.[263] What I shall do in closing this chapter is to mention the more important of the other eighteenth-century British teachers of elocution and to comment briefly upon their work, in order that their names and their achievements may not be wholly ignored in connection with the present account of Sheridan and his predecessors.

One of the earliest textbooks on elocution by a Briton was published at London six years after the appearance of Sheridan's *British Education*. It was called *The Art of Speaking*, and its author was James Burgh, headmaster of an academy which he himself had founded at Stoke Newington in 1747.[264] In the year in which he founded his academy, Burgh published a little treatise on education, the strangest characteristic of which is that it contained nothing to indicate any interest on Burgh's part in the subject of elocution as an element in his own educational thinking. What he actually did in that work was to stress the need to base a curriculum for boys upon such subjects as they would use in passing decently and comfortably through their life on this earth, and upon such subjects as they would require to prepare them for "the *ever-lasting duration* after this life is at an end."[265]

[263] See in particular his essay, "English Sources of American Elocution," *History of Speech Education in America Background Studies*, ed. Karl R. Wallace (New York, [1954]), pp. 105-126. Cited below as Haberman.

[264] See *The Dictionary of National Biography*, s.v. Burgh, James (1714-1775). For an analysis of Burgh's work on elocution, see Donald E. Hargis, "James Burgh and *The Art of Speaking*," *Speech Monographs*, XXIV (November 1957), 275-284.

[265] James Burgh, *Thoughts on Education, Tending Chiefly To recommend to the Attention of the Public, some Particulars relating to that Subject; which are not generally considered with the Regard their Importance deserves* (Bos-

A thorough education in the Christian religion was the method which Burgh recommended for the latter of these two aims; and the former aim could in his view be accomplished by the acquisition of such subjects as grammar, Latin, Greek, French, penmanship, drawing, music, mathematics, bookkeeping, geography, astronomy, anatomy, history, biography, and political principles of the rational sort. Grammar, he thought, was particularly useful "for leading people into a method of speaking or writing their thoughts correctly and intelligibly, and of rightly apprehending those of others."[266] But beyond this one brief reference to the art of speaking he did not go in 1747, when he was founding his academy and thinking of the ideal program of education for boys preparing themselves for the university or for a life in business. Fifteen years later, his *Art of Speaking* was published in the earliest of its many editions,[267] and it stands as proof by itself that Burgh had now added elocution to the list of subjects which he deemed important for the first of the two aims assigned by him to the educational system. No doubt the appearance in 1756 of Sheridan's *British Education* had called his attention to elocution as a deserving subject of study; no doubt as a professional schoolmaster he saw elocution as much better suited to the grammar school than to the university, despite Sheridan's own repeated insistence that the art of speaking deserved to become the postgraduate phase of the education of young men for the pulpit, the bar, the parliament, or the theatre; no doubt he desired to give his school prestige by establishing in its curriculum the same kind of elocutionary study that Sheridan had praised headmaster William Markham for introducing at Westminster School and headmaster Edward Barnard for introducing at Eton;[268] and no doubt his own early addiction to the Scottish accent of his native Perthshire, and his later occupation as teacher of boys who spoke in the

---

ton: Reprinted and Sold by Rogers and Fowle in Queen Street, 1749), p. 11. The original edition was published at London in 1747.

[266] *Ibid.*, p. 12.

[267] Burgh's *The Art of Speaking* was first published at London in 1762, and it had at least six other editions in Great Britain before the century ended. It also had a great vogue in America. Charles Evans's *American Bibliography* (Chicago, Ill. and Worcester, Mass., 1903-1959, XIV, 59) shows American editions in 1775, 1780, 1782, 1785, 1786, 1790, 1793, 1795, and 1800.

[268] See above, p. 226.

South British accent of Stoke Newington in metropolitan London had shown him the practical necessity of giving more attention in the schools to the problem of establishing a uniform standard of English pronunciation throughout the United Kingdom, and of emphasizing frequent practice in oratorical delivery as a possible means to that end. At any rate, his *Art of Speaking* gave elocutionary doctrine a real place in education and made it continuously available to the elementary schools of Great Britain from the early seventeen-sixties to the end of the eighteenth century; and it deserves recognition for those reasons, but not necessarily for its intrinsic worth. It is to Burgh's credit, however, that he amended Sheridan's program by addressing elocution to the needs of grammar school students rather than to the needs of the advanced scholar.

An author not usually counted among British elocutionists of the eighteenth century must receive brief mention here. He is a shadowy figure named John Herries, and he is chiefly remarkable for attempting as Sheridan had done to make elocution popular among adult citizens and university students. His chief work was entitled *The Elements of Speech*, and it invited scholars to become its readers when it was published at London in 1773. "To the Honourable and Learned Members of the Universities of Great Britain and Ireland," said its dedicatory address, "the following essay on the human voice, is most respectfully inscribed, by their most devoted, and most humble servant, John Herries." The first of the two parts into which this work is divided dealt with the formation of voice and language, and it devoted separate chapters to the organs of speech, the elements of speech and vocal music, the alphabet, the cultivation of the voice in children, the impediments in speech, the teaching of speech to the deaf and dumb, and the origin of simple sounds. The second part discussed the qualities and the control of speech. Its elocutionary content is indicated in its chapters on the exercise of the breath, the strength of the voice, graceful pronunciation, gradation and extent of tone, medium and management of voice, and harmony, emphasis, and pathos of speech. In a panegyrical introduction Herries echoed Sheridan by observing that, "Upon a review of the state of eloquence in these kingdoms, we shall find that the chief cause of its decline, is the neglect of cultivating the VOICE in our younger years." "Almost the whole effect of publick speaking," he added with a typical elocutionary disregard for the facts, "results from the skilful use of this one faculty."[269] Perhaps the most interesting feature of the work as a whole is that it relied upon William Holder's *Elements of Speech* (London, 1669) for parts of its discussion of the art of teaching the deaf to converse.[270] As for its elocutionary bent, Herries developed the thesis that "the true criterion of just speaking is, when each of the articulate sounds is uttered forcibly and distinctly,"[271] and he outlined a plan that should be followed in dealing with the articulate sounds of English speech.[272]

The efforts of Herries to spread the elocutionary gospel were not confined only to the work just discussed. He also lectured on the theory and practice of speaking, his discourses being presented at Essex House in London, at the Music Hall in Dublin, at the New Assembly Room in Glasgow, at the Concert Room in Edinburgh, and at the Mitre in Oxford. There is in the Bodleian Library a pamphlet devoted not only to an outline of the seven lectures that Herries delivered on these occasions, but also to an announcement of the appointed days, hours, and admission costs of the seven lectures as they were to be presented in the Great Room of the Mitre.[273] Herries intended each of the lectures to

[269] John Herries, *The Elements of Speech* (London, 1773), p. 4. I have been unable to establish Herries's dates or to find out much of anything about him.

[270] *Ibid.*, pp. 64-80. Herries mentions Holder (p. 70) among former writers on the art of teaching the deaf to speak. He is directly but silently indebted to Holder for his statement about the cause of deafness, and for his illustration of the tendency of loud noises to relieve deafness while they last. Compare Herries, pp. 67-68, with William Holder, *Elements of Speech* (London, 1669), pp. 113, 167.

[271] *The Elements of Speech*, p. 152.

[272] Herries's plan is printed on a folio leaf bound between pp. 24 and 25 of his book. This leaf is reduced to the size of the regular pages by being folded into eight rectangular divisions. It is headed "The Elements of Speech and Vocal Music, on a New Plan."

[273] The title page of the pamphlet reads as follows: "Analysis of a Course of Lectures on the Theory and Practice of Speaking, As they were delivered at Essex House, London; the Musick Hall, Dublin; the New Assembly Room, Glasgow; and the Concert Room, Edinburgh. By John Herries, A. M. To be delivered (by Permission) at the Great-Room, at the Mitre, Oxford. To begin on Tuesday next, at Seven o'Clock in the Evening, and to be continued on the Wednesday, Thursday, and Friday, of that Week; and the Tuesday, Wednes-

emphasize some one aspect of the art of delivery in its theoretical ramifications, and to demonstrate those ramifications by showing how they applied to the most striking passages of eloquence and poetry in the English language. For abstruse philosophical and anatomical doctrine not likely to be of interest to those attending the lectures, he referred his hearers to his own published work, *The Elements of Speech*.[274]

John Walker is the foremost English elocutionist of the generation following that of Sheridan.[275] Walker was born in Middlesex, and thus he never had to face the handicap of speaking to the English community in a Scottish or an Irish accent. But he did have to carry on his profession for a few years in Ireland, and at that time his English accent would certainly have called his attention to the problem presented by differing customs of English pronunciation and to the need of establishing standards for English speech. He had almost no formal education in language or any other academic subject. In fact, he was apprenticed to a trade early in his life, and it was not until after his mother's death that he decided to change his occupation and embark upon a theatrical career. He became in due time a successful actor. His first connections were with provincial companies; later he performed under Garrick at Drury Lane and under Barry in Dublin. His career in the latter city began in 1758, when he joined Barry's company at the Crow Street Theatre and so became a member of the theatrical enterprise organized to rival Thomas Sheridan's company at the Theatre Royal in nearby Smock Alley. On Barry's side the rivalry was successful enough to help Sheridan decide in 1759 to end his theatrical career and become a lecturer on elocution. Perhaps Sheridan's success in this new venture gave Walker an example that he could apply to himself. At any rate, he quit his theatrical career in 1768 and became a lecturer on elocution

---

day, and Thursday, of the Week Following. Tickets for the whole Course, at Half a Guinea each, to be had of Mr. Prince, Mr. Fletcher, and Mr. Bliss, Booksellers. —Where likewise may be had an Analysis giving a full Account of each Lecture. Admittance to nonsubscribers 2s. 6d. [n. p., c. 1775]." Cited below as *Analysis*.

[274] *Analysis*, p. 2.

[275] My account of Walker (1732-1807) is based in part upon that written by Thompson Cooper for *The Dictionary of National Biography*.

about 1771. In the latter capacity he was well received by audiences in Ireland, Scotland, and England. He himself testified that he gave "public lectures on English Pronunciation at the university of Oxford" and that some time afterwards he was "invited by several of the Heads of Houses to give private lectures on the Art of Reading, in their respective colleges."[276] Out of these invitations emerged a determination on Walker's part to throw his instruction into a system, and out of that determination emerged his most important elocutionary work, *Elements of Elocution. Being the Substance of a Course of Lectures on the Art of Reading; Delivered at several Colleges in the University of Oxford.*

The nature of this work, and one of the influences behind it, are indicated in the Preface that Walker attached to its first edition, and some of what he said on that occasion deserves quotation here.

> While I was engaged in the present undertaking [he remarked], I met with a work called *Prosodia Rationalis*. This ingenious treatise undertakes to reduce speaking sounds to such rules as shall enable a person to imitate the notes of a speaker or reader, as closely as he can follow him in singing. For this purpose, a notation is invented, which brings every word to some part of the musical scale, and marks its force, extent, and duration. . . . Mine was an humbler attempt; I could only flatter myself with being able to convey such turns and inflexions of voice as accompanied the pauses and emphasis of a good speaker; and this, had that great actor and excellent citizen Mr. Garrick lived, I should have exemplified in some of his favourite speeches; but death, which deprived the stage of its greatest ornament, bereft me of a most valuable friend and patron. . . . Unassisted, therefore, and unpatronized, the work is at length completed: without any breach of modesty, it may be asserted, that the general idea is new, curious, and important: and, without any false humility, I am ready to allow, that the manner of treating it has a thousand faults and imperfections. It wants that strength and correctness of the college, united with the ease and elegance of a court, which is found in several of the present productions; and it partakes of that haste, that interruption, and want of finishing, which must necessarily

[276] John Walker, *Elements of Elocution* (London, 1781), I, vii.

249

accompany a life of labour and uncertainty; for though nothing but long practice, in actual tuition, could have enabled me to construct such a system, it required the leisure and liberty of affluence to produce it to the best advantage.[277]

Walker's reference in the passage just cited to "actual tuition" probably suggests that he himself taught elocution when for two years he conducted a school in partnership with James Usher immediately after he quit the stage. At any rate, his interest in being a teacher of that subject had been shown before he printed his Oxford lectures, and the chief evidence of that interest is his work called *Exercises for Improvement in Elocution*, published at London in 1777. Another evidence of the same sort is his *Rhetorical Grammar, or Course of Lessons in Elocution*. The first two editions of the latter work were strictly occupied with delivery, the fifth part of Ciceronian rhetoric. But, as I pointed out earlier, the third edition, published at London in 1801, contained a lengthy account of invention, the first part of Ciceronian rhetoric, and that account was an acknowledged extract from John Ward's *System of Oratory*.[278] Thus Walker's *Rhetorical Grammar* is something of a milestone in the history of the elocutionary movement, inasmuch as it represented in its third edition a temporary break in the custom of making delivery stand as the whole of

[277] *Ibid.*, I, xi-xiv. The *Prosodia Rationalis; or, An Essay Towards Establishing the Melody and Measure of Speech to be Expressed and Perpetuated by Peculiar Symbols*, was written by Joshua Steele, and published at London in 1775. For further illustration of the influence of this work on Walker, see the latter's essay entitled *The Melody of Speaking Delineated; or, Elocution taught like Music, by Visible Signs* (London, 1787). Steele's contribution to the elocutionary movement is discussed by John B. Newman, "The Role of Joshua Steele in the Development of Speech Education in America," *Speech Monographs*, XX (March 1953), 65-73. Newman's evaluation of Steele needs to be corrected, however, in respect to his assertion that "Of all those who made use of Steele's formulations in the development of elocution in both England and America, John Walker was probably the only one who did not in some way acknowledge Joshua Steele." Certainly Newman's statement is contradicted by the passage that I have just quoted from the Preface to Walker's *Elements of Elocution*. Newman's statement that Steele devised the formula for the mechanical method of elocution needs correction also. The formula came from Jean Baptiste Du Bos's *Réflexions Critiques sur la Poësie et sur la Peinture*, Pt. III, secs. IV, IX. What Steele did was to work out an application of Du Bos's idea.

[278] See above, Ch. 3, p. 122 and n. 108.

rhetoric. But it earned that distinction by borrowing from Ward, not by attempting to do anything original with invention on its own.

Although Gilbert Austin's *Chironomia; or a Treatise on Rhetorical Delivery* belongs to the nineteenth century by virtue of its having been published in 1806, I should like to mention it as a way of summarizing my entire account of eighteenth-century elocution and as a means of softening some of the criticism that the elocutionists invite by reason of their chronic ignorance of ancient rhetoric and their exaggerated enthusiasm for rhetorical delivery as a completely independent art. Austin may safely be called the earliest Briton to bring a real grasp of classical learning to bear upon the problem of composing a treatise limited to the fifth part of ancient rhetoric. John Ward and John Holmes were learned in the entire subject matter of Ciceronian rhetorical theory, as we have seen; Sheridan was not really well informed on any part of that theory, despite his pretended knowledge of the ancient art of speaking; Austin at least took the pains to examine what the best ancients and the best moderns had said on oratorical delivery, and to keep his readers constantly aware of the actual writings upon which the theory of delivery rested. Like Sheridan, Austin was born in Ireland and brought up in a community habituated to an Irish accent. Like Sheridan he held the degree of bachelor of arts and master of arts from Trinity College, Dublin.[279] But unlike Sheridan he was a clergyman rather than an actor, and a scholar rather than a novice in learning. Thus his theory of elocution was superior to Sheridan's in richness of background, although like Sheridan's it was narrow and sterile in its willingness to lend monumental support to the thesis that the fifth part of rhetoric could be isolated from its natural context and studied profitably by itself.

Austin recognized full well that ancient rhetoric consisted of invention, disposition, style, and memory, as well as pronunciation or action, and he also knew that the fifth of these aspects was always presented by the classical authorities in company with the

[279] Born in County Louth, Austin was admitted to Trinity College on February 1, 1770, at the age of 17. He was named scholar in 1772, bachelor of arts in 1774, and master of arts in 1780. See Burtchaell and Sadleir, *Alumni Dublinenses*, s.v. Austin, Gilbert.

other four. His apparent excuse for making pronunciation an independent subject of investigation was that it concerned the exterior or outward manifestations of speechmaking, whereas the rest of the orator's task had to do with internal matters—with processes that were hidden from the eye and ear of the audience. "The management of the voice, the expression of the countenance, and the gesture of the head, the body, and the limbs," he said at the very beginning of his vast work, "constitute the external part of oratory; and relate to the personal talents and efforts of the public speaker, in like manner as the other divisions of rhetoric, invention, disposition, choice of words, and memory, relate to those of his understanding."[280] Presumably Austin did not question the propriety of treating these externals of the orator's total procedure as if they could be separated from the internal operations of the orator's mind. At any rate, he treated the externals by themselves, and he thus convicted himself at the outset of the charge that he like the other elocutionists had no concern for the human reason as a factor in determining how man expressed himself.

Austin did not elect, however, to follow Sheridan and Walker in using elocution as the proper word for the fifth part of rhetoric. "The term elocution," he said, "is, by this acceptation, diverted from its original signification as established by the ancient rhetoricians."[281] Correctly observing that the ancients had used this term to apply to the choosing and arranging of words in a discourse, Austin declared that "To express what the Roman writers understood by *pronunciatio* and *actio*, we shall use the word Delivery, which is already established, in this sense, in our language."[282] Here, at least, is accuracy of outlook and understanding, although it is strange that anyone who comprehended

---

[280] *Chironomia* (London, 1806), p. 1. The notion that oratorical delivery was the external part of rhetoric could have come to Austin from a continental treatise on elocution entitled *Petri Francii Specimen Eloquentiae Exterioris ad Orationem M. T. Ciceronis pro A. Licin. Archia accommodatum* (Amstelaedami, 1697). Francius, also known as Pierre Fransz (1645-1703), was a professor of eloquence, history, and Greek at Amsterdam, and his interest in teaching oratorical delivery did much to foster the elocutionary movement in Europe. Austin indicated (*Chironomia*, p. iii) that he knew the *Specimen Eloquentiae Exterioris* only by title.

[281] *Chironomia*, p. 2. [282] *Ibid.*, p. 3.

this much of the Roman program would have proceeded to vitiate that program by treating delivery by itself.

The classical authorities whom Austin cited most frequently are Quintilian and Cicero. Indeed, he had so many Latin quotations from these two authors, and he so often gave lengthy English translations of passages from their rhetorical writings, that his work is a treasury of their ideas on the subject of voice, countenance, and gesture. His main title, *Chironomia*, comes from Quintilian, who said that the law of gesture had in heroic times been signified by that technical word.[283] It is to be noted that Austin cited the *Rhetorica ad Herennium* in full awareness of its not being a work by Cicero,[284] and it should also be noted that he referred in easy and familiar terms to Aristotle's *Rhetoric*, quoting it in Greek and English on the subject of the three means of persuasion, on the proverb that modesty dwells in the eyes, on the doctrine of pity and the conditions which prompt that emotion, and on the debatable propriety of devoting space to delivery and style in a treatise on rhetorical theory.[285]

But in the last analysis the best way to describe Austin's *Chironomia* is to say that it is an English replica of Louis de Cressolles's *Vacationes Autumnales*. The *Vacationes Autumnales* has already been briefly described in this chapter,[286] and its connection with Ward's *System of Oratory* and Gildon's *Life of Betterton* has been indicated so far as to demonstrate its importance to the English Ciceronian rhetoricians and to the English elocutionists of the early eighteenth century.[287] A vast compilation of passages from Greek and Roman rhetoric, biography, and history on the subject of voice, countenance, and gesture, and on the exercises in pronunciation and declamation by Greek and Roman school children, actors, orators, poets, and even emperors, the *Vacationes Autumnales* encouraged the historically naive belief that the ancients did almost nothing but strive to improve their

---

[283] Austin quoted on his title page the passage in which Quintilian made this observation. The passage is found in the *Institutio Oratoria*, 1.11.17. See *Chironomia*, p. 2, for Austin's comment on his use of Quintilian as the authority for his title.

[284] *Chironomia*, pp. 172-173.

[285] *Ibid.*, pp. 22, 107, 110-111, 170-172.

[286] See above, pp. 160-161.

[287] See above, Ch. 3, p. 120; Ch. 4, pp. 185-186.

oratorical delivery, and that their educational program had no purpose except that of concentrating upon the fifth part of rhetoric. An uncritical corollary of this belief was that the truly impressive eloquence in ancient literature came from training in voice and action, and that eloquence would come again to Europe if such an educational program were restored. Austin's *Chironomia* is dedicated to the task of fostering these beliefs in English as Cressolles had fostered them in Latin. Austin depended upon Cressolles by quoting several long passages from the *Vacationes Autumnales* in English translation, and in footnotes he gave the Latin text on which his translations were based. Throughout his work he referred to Cressolles over and over and over again.[288] In fact, he depended upon that writer more fully than upon any postclassical authority. Small wonder, then, that he like Cressolles seems to confine the interests of rhetoric and of classical civilization itself to the narrow confines of speech and gesture.

A special word should be said about the connection between the *Chironomia* and Le Faucheur's *Traitté de l'action de l'orateur, ou de la Prononciation et du geste*. If Austin had been asked whether he knew of the *Traitté*, he would have replied that, although he had not read it, he had heard of it by title, and that, according to his best information, it was the work not of Le Faucheur but of Conrart. In this connection we remember that Le Faucheur's *Traitté* had at first been published anonymously under the supervision of his friend, Valentin Conrart, and had been printed under Conrart's name in one of its later editions, before it finally began to appear as the work of its true author.[289] Austin's authority for believing the *Traitté* to be by Conrart was Johann Matthias Gesner's *Primae Lineae Isagoges in Eruditionem Universalem*. In that guide to knowledge, Gesner listed Conrart's *Traitté* as an essay on delivery, and Austin, in mentioning Gesner's reference, said that he had not been able to get hold of Conrart's book.[290] In actual fact, however, Austin had seen it, not in one of its French editions, not in its Latin edition, but in its English version as published at London in the first years of the

---

[288] For Austin's references to Cressolles, see *Chironomia*, pp. 9-11, 23, 24, 26, 75, 77-78, 96, 103, 104, 109, 113-115, 121-122, 126-127, 139, 175, 248, 303, 324, 325, 326-327, 332-333, 334, 336, 339, 340, 341, 350-352, 399, 401, 402, 403, 426, 434-435, 455, 459, 555-557.

[289] See above, p. 162 and n. 35.   [290] *Chironomia*, pp. iii-iv.

eighteenth century and as plagiarized soon after by Charles Gildon in his *Life of Betterton*. Without knowing that he was really objecting to Le Faucheur, Austin disagreed with a passage that he quoted from Gildon's *Life*.[291] Thus Le Faucheur's important *Traitté*, so instrumental in bringing the elocutionary movement to England in the early seventeen-hundreds, and so much a part of that movement between 1700 and 1750, must also be recognized for its momentary presence in Austin's elaborate summary of elocutionary doctrine at the beginning of the nineteenth century.

That elaborate summary can hardly be dismissed without some notice of its reliance upon many other sources than those already mentioned. Like Betterton, Austin quoted the list of qualities of the voice as that list had appeared in Julius Pollux's *Onomasticum*.[292] Like Hugh Blair, Austin knew Jean Lucas's *Actio Oratoris, seu de Gestu et Voce, Libri Duo*, and he devoted fifteen pages of the Appendix of the *Chironomia* to a lengthy quotation from that Latin poem on gesture and articulation.[293] Like John Walker, Austin was familiar with Joshua Steele's *Prosodia Rationalis*, and he thought it ingenious and perfect in its plan for recording inflections and modulations of the voice.[294] Austin himself regarded Nicolas Caussin's *De Eloquentia Sacra et Humana, Libri XVI*, as one of his major authorities, and he quoted repeatedly from it.[295] He knew François Pithou's *Antiqui Rhetores Latini*, and he quoted excerpts from it on various aspects of rhetorical theory, specifically using passages written by Curius Fortunatianus, Cassiodorus, Isidore, and Alcuin.[296] He also cited ancient rhetorical doctrine in the interpretations given it by Vossius and Henisch.[297] He even made two references to Omer Talon.[298] He cited his elocutionary predecessors, Sheridan and

---

[291] *Ibid.*, p. 441.

[292] *Ibid.*, pp. 553-554. See also above, pp. 184-185 and n. 104.

[293] See pp. 563-577. See also above, n. 34.

[294] *Chironomia*, pp. 276, 290, 367. See above, pp. 249-250.

[295] *Chironomia*, pp. 32, 74, 88, 175-177, 285, 325, 483.

[296] *Ibid.*, pp. 2 (for Cassiodorus); 2 (for Isidore); 13, 175 (for Alcuin); 175, 558-559 (for Fortunatianus). Austin, pp. 263, 265, also quoted Cassiodorus and Isidore in other connections than those provided by Pithou.

[297] *Chironomia*, pp. 2, 40, 175, 322, 457, 578-583.

[298] *Ibid.*, pp. 175, 177-178.

Walker.[299] He quoted from Fénelon, Dubroca, Marmontel, Rollin, Du Bos, Buffon.[300] He cited Hugh Blair, Kames's *Elements of Criticism*, and Burke's *Philosophical Enquiry into the Origin of our Ideas of the Sublime and Beautiful*.[301] He made very extensive use of Johann Jakob Engel's *Ideen zu einer Mimik* in its French translation, *Idées sur le geste et l'action théatrale*.[302] And beyond all these he quoted and used many other works.

Thus Austin brought great learning for the first time to the elocutionary movement in England, and although his *Chironomia* never had a second edition, it contributed influentially to the teachings of the elocutionists in England and America throughout the nineteenth century, and it was rightfully called by A. M. Hartley "incomparably the ablest treatise on delivery in general, that has yet appeared in our language."[303] Even so, however, it is a work so seriously limited in perspective as to have had no beneficial effect upon the fortunes of rhetoric in the modern world. The very fact that it was a work of real learning, indeed, tended to encourage the belief among the later elocutionists that they were being truly learned themselves and truly conversant with the ancients in restricting rhetoric to the study of voice and gesture.

[299] *Ibid.*, pp. 7, 17, 51, 63-65, 73-74, 81, 82, 175, 235, 482, 485 (for Sheridan); 51, 56, 60, 71, 78-79, 175, 482 (for Walker).

[300] *Ibid.*, pp. 80, 101, 175, 441, 442-443 (for Fénelon); 94-95, 201, 271, 287, 380, 414, 486 (for Dubroca); 101, 175, 225, 234, 240-241, 262, 277, 280, 281, 380, 381, 442, 496 (for Marmontel); 175, 178-179, 375, 380, 426-427, 487-488 (for Rollin); 252, 253, 257-258, 265, 266, 274, 275, 475-478 (for Du Bos); 99, 117, 122, 485-486 (for Buffon).

[301] *Ibid.*, pp. 175, 179-180 (for Blair); 54, 97, 468, 469-473, 474 (for Kames); 175, 181-183, 294 (for Burke).

[302] *Ibid.*, pp. 106, 252, 272, 277, 282-283, 294, 375, 386, 423, 424, 455, 461-462, 478-483, 490-494, 499-500.

[303] Quoted by Haberman, p. 118.

CHAPTER 5

The art of syllogism produced numberless disputes, and numberless sects, who fought against each other with much animosity, without gaining or losing ground; but did nothing considerable for the benefit of human life. The art of induction, first delineated by Lord Bacon, produced numberless laboratories and observatories, in which Nature has been put to the question by thousands of experiments, and forced to confess many of her secrets, which before were hid from mortals. And by these, arts have been improved, and human knowledge wonderfully increased.

Thomas Reid, "A Brief Account of Aristotle's Logic. With Remarks," in Lord Kames's *Sketches of the History of Man* (Edinburgh, 1774), II, 236.

THE NEW LOGIC

(1690–1814)

I   Seven Points of Friction

As we have seen in Chapter 2, the logic adopted in seventeenth-century Britain was intended to replace Ramism not only by restoring the tradition which Ramus had curtailed and rearranged, but also by continuing to emphasize certain features especially prominent in Ramus's program itself. As formulated by Sanderson, Crakanthorp, Wallis, Aldrich, and Sergeant, this logic may in retrospect be said to possess seven dominant traits. The first of these was that it stressed the investigative as well as the presentational offices of logical doctrine, thus reasserting the traditional belief that logic is an instrument of philosophical enquiry, without repudiating Ramus's insistence upon the equally traditional notion that logic also contributes important elements to the theory of presentation. Its second trait was that it defined its investigative mission to be the subjecting of axioms and other self-evident verbal propositions to deductive analysis in an effort to wring from them conclusions whose validity could not be questioned if the analysis had been conducted according to rule. Its third trait was that it regarded the syllogism as the pre-eminent instrument of enquiry and proof, induction being thought an imperfect form of that instrument. Its fourth trait was that it considered the *dictum de omni et nullo* to be the one self-evident principle from which the entire art of logic and all the figures and rules of the syllogism could be deduced. As its fifth trait, it believed disputation to be the outstanding philosophical activity in the fields of enquiry and communication, inasmuch as truths could by debate be tested and simultaneously transmitted throughout the world of learning. Its sixth trait was that it deemed the places or topics of invention to be especially useful as a machinery for subjecting questions to systematic investigation, on the one hand, and for presenting the results of that investigation on the other. Ramus, it will be recalled, had reduced the ancient lore of invention to ten places, and his successors, however opposed to him they may have been, endorsed the traditional view of the utility of this branch of logic, although of course they did not follow Ramus in limiting these places to his precise formulations. The final trait of seventeenth-century British logic was bound up with its underlying but usually unstated assumption that truth and consistency are completely equivalent concepts. That is to say, it thought of truth as the quality which a proposition has by virtue of its being exactly consistent with a proposition already known to be true. In this connection we should remind ourselves that the syllogism is the most efficient instrument ever perfected for testing the consistency of verbal propositions—a fact which helps to explain the enduring popularity of deductive logic. Bacon and Descartes had not questioned the efficacy of this function of the syllogism. But they had doubted the truth of many of the standard propositions usually cited to illustrate syllogistic major premises, and they had questioned whether those propositions were entitled to guarantee the truth of any conclusion drawn from them in conformity to rule. Earlier ages had sought to cope with such doubts by postulating metaphysics and revelation as the proper authorities behind all fundamental truths, and by confidently using such truths to authenticate the derivative truths making up theology, politics, and ethics. In general it may be said that seventeenth-century British logic, as it was taught in the universities and understood in learned circles, followed the past in accepting truths based upon the authority of metaphysics and revelation; and that it also followed the past in thinking the test of consistency to be the proper means of establishing subordinate truths throughout the realm of science.[1]

The logic just described continued to be popular during the eighteenth century in Great Britain, as I pointed out in Chapter 2. In fact, it was still current in 1825, when Richard Whately's

---

[1] See above, Ch. 2, pp. 61-71, for a discussion of John Sergeant's advocacy of this view of scientific inquiry.

A preliminary statement of the essential differences between the old logic and the new in Great Britain during the seventeen-hundreds was attempted in the present author's essay, "The Plough and the Flail: The Ordeal of Eighteenth-Century Logic," *The Huntington Library Quarterly*, xxviii (1964-1965), 63-78.

Elements of Logic gave a large part of it a new interpretation and a further lease on life. It may be said of Ramus that his logical system had been largely forgotten in England and in Europe by 1700. But it may also be said that the system which replaced his during the sixteen-hundreds survived until the middle of the nineteenth century.

The new logic, as I mean to call the doctrine which offered an increasingly effective competition in eighteenth-century Britain to the Aristotelianism of Aldrich and his school, moved in the direction of emancipating itself from its rival, and the nature of that emancipation is best understood by discussing it in terms of the dominant traits that we have found the rival to possess. In short, the new logic contrasts with the old in seven ways. As you read it, you become increasingly aware that logic is heading towards a final break with the theory of communication, and is readying itself for an exclusive affiliation with scientific enquiry. Moreover, you are constantly reminded that the kind of scientific enquiry in which logic is most interested consists no longer in the verbal examination of propositions but in the empirical examination of the realities of nature. Again, you are not allowed to forget that the syllogism is losing its pre-eminence as an instrument of enquiry, and that induction is being recognized as the equal of syllogism in some systems of thought, or in other systems as the more basic of the two forms of reasoning. Then too you begin to find the *dictum de omni et nullo* treated with decreasing respect, and you come to predict that it will ultimately be replaced by canons derived from the experimental sciences. You also notice that disputation is losing its hold, not as an academic exercise intended to sharpen wits and develop verbal skill, but as a means of testing and establishing truth; and that controlled experiments and the observation of facts beneath the magnifying glass or beyond the telescope are replacing disputation as the recognized means of determining the validity of scholarly hypotheses. Still again, you repeatedly read arguments against the use of the topics in investigating problems or in discovering arguments for discourse, and it becomes obvious that, even if disputation were going to be able to retain any part of its traditional investigative function, the factual approach to the invention of arguments is on the way towards being accepted in place of the old method of sitting in your armchair and thinking up proofs drawn from such topics as adjuncts, contraries, or similitudes. And finally you see the emphasis shifting in eighteenth-century British logic from an acceptance of consistency as the criterion of truth to an acceptance of the idea that a statement is valid when it accords with the facts under examination. This shift tended unfortunately to make it look as if mankind had to choose between these two conceptions of truth—as if he had to reject the one if he accepted the other. In actuality, however, no such choice is ever required. Neither of these two conceptions has to be rejected if the other is made a principle of scholarship or morality. Nevertheless, the principle of consistency is of maximum use in an age which believes that its major truths have all been discovered, and that its great problem is to establish a consistency between those truths and the rules of conduct. On the other hand, the principle which equates truth with factual accuracy is naturally of first importance in an age of scientific revolution, when old truths are being struck down and new truths established. To a certain extent, every age in human history falls into both of these categories. But the eighteenth century gradually became more conscious of itself as an age of scientific revolution than as an age of ideological stability, and thus the new logicians of that era were eventually more prone to overvalue the means that satisfied the demand for accuracy of statement than to value properly the means required to make statements consistent with each other. Nor can we say with any assurance that the same disproportions have been avoided by scholars and philosophers of the nineteenth and twentieth centuries.

Before we turn to the actual authors of the new logic of eighteenth-century Britain, we should understand that their work was a gradual rather than a sudden growth. Locke's vision of the new logic as he formulated it in the closing years of the sixteenhundreds was of cardinal importance, and his thinking was to have great consequences later on. But during the first half of the eighteenth century, the new logic was not greatly different from the Aristotelianism of Aldrich, although it was beckoning to change as Aldrich never did. Not until 1774 did the rate of change become accelerated, and it did so at that time because Thomas Reid published then his important little essay, "A Brief Account of Aristotle's Logic. With Remarks." Something of the revolutionary flavor of that essay can be savored in the extract selected from it to serve as the epigraph of this present chapter. Reid's work inspired George Campbell in 1776 to subject syllogistic logic to a devastating attack in his famous book, *The Philosophy of Rhetoric,* and within the next ten years Dugald Stewart was delivering at Edinburgh the lectures which can now be seen as the most brilliant statement of the principles of inductive logic before the time of John Stuart Mill. Thus the new logic did not reach maturity until the eighteenth century was nearly over. But it was in being as that century began, and its origins belong to the preceding century, as Reid so accurately noted.[2] Its unfolding in the period between the first publication of Locke's *Essay concerning Human Understanding* and the eventual printing of Stewart's lectures on logic at Edinburgh is the subject of the present chapter.

[2] For a discussion of the seventeenth-century antecedents of this new logic, see Howell, *Logic and Rhetoric in England,* pp. 342-363.

II   John Locke and the New Logic

John Locke was born at Wrington in Somerset on August 29, 1632, and he died at Oates, the country estate of Sir Francis Masham, in Essex, on October 28, 1704.[3] He attended Westminster School between 1647 and 1652, his residence there being marked by his appointment as a King's Scholar through his having demonstrated special ability in Latin, in grammar, and in literary composition. One of his schoolmates at Westminster was John Dryden, later to be famous as poet and dramatist. Locke's career at Oxford began in 1652 with his admission to Christ Church, and it ended some thirty-two years later, in 1684, when his suspected activity against the government of Charles II led to his being expelled from a senior studentship, that is, a fellowship, which he had continuously held at Christ Church for the preceding twenty-six years. He was awarded the degree of bachelor of arts on February 14, 1656, his college courses having included grammar, rhetoric, logic, moral philosophy, mathematics, and Greek, and his college exercises having involved him in public disputations.[4] His studies in logic had brought him into contact with the apostles and opponents of Ramus, and with the logical theory expounded by such Aristotelians as Sanderson and Crakanthorp. Dr. John Wallis, the Savilian professor of geometry at Oxford between 1649 and 1703, was Locke's teacher in various branches of mathematics. Later, of course, Wallis was to publish his influential treatise on Aristotelian logic, the *Institutio Logicae*, and to include in it two of his own disputations from his student days at Cambridge. It was during Locke's pursuit of the

[3] For this brief account of Locke, I rely mainly upon H. R. Fox Bourne's *The Life of John Locke in Two Volumes* (London, 1876) and Maurice Cranston's *John Locke, a biography* (London, 1957). I have also consulted Jean Le Clerc's memoir of Locke as it appears in the seventh edition of *The Works of John Locke, in Four Volumes* (London, 1768), I, vii-xxii; also the short life by Leslie Stephen in *The Dictionary of National Biography*; and the little pamphlet by Maurice Cranston entitled *Locke*, cited below, Ch. 6, p. 502.

My present discussion of Locke's contribution to logic is a somewhat extended version of the article which appeared in *Action and Conviction in Early Modern Europe*, ed. Theodore K. Rabb and Jerrold E. Seigel (Princeton, New Jersey: Princeton University Press, 1969), pp. 423-452.

[4] See Bourne's *Life of John Locke*, I, 41-52, for additional details concerning Locke's studies as an undergraduate at Oxford.

degree of master of arts, which was conferred upon him June 29, 1658, that he began to read Descartes and to become absorbed in the new philosophy.[5] Soon after he took his master's degree, he was named by Christ Church to the senior studentship which I mentioned above, and within the next few years he held various positions in his college—that of lecturer in Greek in 1661 and 1662, that of lecturer in rhetoric in 1663, and that of censor of moral philosophy in 1664.[6] Meanwhile, he belonged to an Oxford scientific group which at an earlier time had started to hold regular meetings in London, and which in the late sixteen-fifties numbered among its members the great scientist Robert Boyle, the geometer and logician John Wallis, the future bishop of Chester John Wilkins, and young Christopher Wren, then serving as professor of astronomy at Gresham College. Thanks especially to the efforts of Wilkins, this group was chartered in 1662 as the Royal Society of London, and Locke was elected fellow of that new organization on November 23, 1668. Six years later, he took the degree of bachelor of medicine at Oxford, having embarked upon medical studies sometime before 1666.

But while these events were in progress, Locke had begun a second career, which was to lead towards public service and towards undying fame as a philosopher. In the autumn of 1665 he was appointed secretary to the British ambassador to Brandenburg, and he spent a few months late in that year and early in the next in the capital city of that little country. Then in July, 1666, he met Lord Ashley, afterwards the notable first Earl of Shaftesbury, and was persuaded to attach himself to the family of that nobleman as physician and friend. Between 1667 and 1683, Locke resided for many long periods of time at Exeter House or at Thanet House, Shaftesbury's London homes, or at Shaftesbury's

[5] *Ibid.*, I, 61-62.

[6] Cranston, *John Locke, a biography*, p. 73, says of Locke's lectureship in rhetoric, "The duty of the Praelector Rhetoricus was not to give orations but to teach philosophy." The final phrase in this statement is surely open to question. It would be more accurate to say that Locke's own mature proficiency in speaking and writing Latin came in part at least from his undergraduate course in rhetoric, where he would have studied Latin oratory, poetry, and epistles, and would have practiced himself in these types of compositions. Thus as Praelector Rhetoricus in 1663, he would have encouraged similar occupations among his students, and would have taught them meanwhile his own austere rhetorical theories. See below, Ch. 6, pp. 489-502.

country estate in Dorsetshire. Locke himself always had a frail physical constitution, and he spent four years in France between 1675 and 1679 in search of a climate that would help him maintain his health. He was again on the Continent between 1683 and 1688, this time in Holland, an exile during the troubles that had arisen in England in connection with Shaftesbury's attempt to prevent James II from ascending the English throne; and this sojourn was the occasion of his friendship with Jean Le Clerc, whose journal, the *Bibliothèque Universelle et Historique*, printed in French an epitome of the *Essay concerning Human Understanding* two years before the English text was first brought out in London. By the way, Le Clerc's *Logica; sive, Ars Ratiocinandi; Ontologia, sive de Ente in Genera; Pneumatologia seu de Spiritibus*, published together in a single volume at London and Amsterdam in 1692, were the first works to reveal traces of the influence that Locke's *Essay* came to exert upon logic, ontology, and pneumatology; and William Molyneux, a scientist and philosopher who resided in Dublin and carried on a scholarly correspondence with Locke, was the earliest Briton to point out this fact.[7] Locke's exile in Holland ended when the revolution of 1688 brought William and Mary to power in England, and Locke himself played a part in that historic transaction. The closing years of his life, except for some public activity between 1693 and 1700, were spent in retirement at Oates in the household of his devoted admirers and warm friends, Sir Francis and Lady Masham. Lady Masham, who was twenty-six years younger than Locke, and who had first met him when he was forty-nine and she was twenty-two, held him in the greatest esteem, and bestowed upon him a devotion of heart and a responsiveness of mind that earned his lasting affection and that must have made the ill health of his final days more endurable than it could possibly otherwise have been.

The lasting significance of Locke's greatest work, *An Essay con-*

[7] In a letter dated from Dublin, December 22, 1692, Molyneux told Locke that he had recently seen Le Clerc's three treatises, "in all which," Molyneux adds, "he has little extraordinary but what he borrows from you; and in the alteration he gives them, he robs them of their native beauties; which can only be preserved to them by the same incomparable art that first framed them." See *Some Familiar Letters between Mr. Locke, and Several of his Friends* (London, 1708), pp. 16-17. Cited below as *Some Familiar Letters*. For a discussion of Le Clerc's *Logica*, see below, pp. 299-304.

cerning Human Understanding, consists in its having outlined more influentially than any previous work the modern method by which knowledge is to be sought, validated, and understood. It did not set forth a system of beliefs that people should accept in regard to the substance of the sciences and the scholarly disciplines; rather it defined the program to be followed in order that enquiries in those fields would yield dependable results. What should a man do when he sets out to obtain valid knowledge about himself and his world? This was the question which Locke's *Essay* raised, and his reply turned out to be the right answer at the right time. The tradition which he demolished had said that man obtained valid knowledge about himself and his world by examining propositions previously established in connection with all of the subjects of human concern, and by treating those propositions as alone capable of yielding complete certainty in all sciences. This tradition meant on the simplest level that if a man wanted knowledge about the realities of his environment, he examined the opinions and beliefs which he had been taught to regard as the proper interpretation of those realities, and by examining them he derived fresh truths to guide his beliefs and actions. But doesn't this tradition involve the risk of seeing reality, not as it might appear if one looked at it directly, but as it appears when seen through the errors of the past? Aren't we always in danger of having false ideas about things unless we endeavor in the first place to form our ideas as accurately as we can from a careful observation of the things, and unless we continuously attempt thereafter to study the things afresh in an effort to keep our ideas of them constantly responsive to any changes that better means of observation might lead us to see in them? Locke believed profoundly that the method of the past confined men not only to past truths transmitted in a spirit of indifference, but also to past errors that could not be put to death. He saw with utter clarity that past truths could be appreciated as living present truths only if the present undertook to examine them afresh in the light of the realities behind them and to recognize again how accurately they interpreted those realities. He saw with equal clarity that errors could be detected as errors and avoided as dangers only if the present undertook to eliminate them after taking another look at the facts behind them and after seeing that the facts did not support them. There is nothing in this program ever to become obsolete. And yet, so fond are men of their preconceptions, their prejudices, their inherited or previously formed convictions, that they will resist to the end of time the labor involved in testing their beliefs against the facts and the anguish produced by seeing some beloved idea proved false. Thus they will always stand in need of Locke's program, as his age stood in need of it. And they will always benefit when they apply it rigorously and in the love of truth, if the accurate correspondence between our ideas and the realities behind them is our only safe guide to understanding and conduct. The chief difference between the twentieth century and the seventeenth century, in regard to the benefits to be derived from reading Locke's *Essay*, is that we today are taught the lesson of Locke in every one of the sciences and the arts to have been influenced by him, and thus we know him even when we have not read him at first hand, whereas the seventeenth century was taught only to respect the tradition that Locke was to demolish, and had little inclination to doubt that tradition, although Bacon and Descartes had flung the heaviest of challenges against it, in what turned out to be the prelude to Locke's success in transforming it at last into a minority voice in modern culture. Thus the seventeenth century was shocked by Locke's *Essay* into realizing that it had been blindly groping along the trails of the past and listening only to the past, at a moment when the new science was following Bacon in making many of the beliefs of that past obsolete. If Locke's *Essay* is seen today largely through eyes which have been already taught its essential lesson, it may appear to the unwary to have lost its uniqueness as a shaper of the modern mind. He who turns to it today, however, will be benefited as by a lesson which teaches new things in being reviewed again.

The actual content of the *Essay concerning Human Understanding* can best be indicated by reminding ourselves that it is divided into four books, and that those books deal respectively with innate notions, with ideas, with words, and with knowledge and opinion. Book I contains the famous denial of the existence of innate notions in the mind. Book II establishes experience as the source of all of our ideas, sensation and reflection being the forms of experience, and ideas being accepted as having various degrees of simplicity and complexity. Book III presents the classical analysis of words considered as the signs of ideas and of the things that ideas represent. And Book IV concerns itself with the identification of our knowledge of things with our ideas of things, and with the degrees, the extent, the reality, the validity, and the means to improvement of knowledge. A summary of Locke's arguments under each of these heads would be out of place at this time. Moreover, any summary would do violence to a work which does not easily lend itself to the arts of condensation and epitome. But those who have not the time for a reading of the *Essay* and yet have a wish to understand its major teachings would be well satisfied, I believe, to turn to Richard I. Aaron's book, *John Locke*, the second part of which gives the *Essay* an illuminating analysis.[8]

If a work can be called classic when it is accepted into the universities as part of the undergraduate program, Locke's *Essay* became a classic almost at once. It was first published at London in 1690, and it was incorporated into the curriculum of Trinity College, Dublin, before December 22, 1692. Earlier in that year, the new provost, Dr. St. George Ashe, ordered the undergraduates of Trinity to make the *Essay* one of their required books, and he stipulated that they would be strictly examined during their progress through it. The authority for this statement is William Molyneux, who has been mentioned earlier as having called Locke's attention to Le Clerc's indebtedness to the *Essay*. In the same letter in which he referred to Le Clerc, Molyneux said that he was the first to have recommended and lent the *Essay* to Dr. Ashe, and that Dr. Ashe was so wonderfully pleased and satisfied with it that he took steps to have his students make it part of their formal program.[9] Molyneux said one other highly significant thing in that letter—Locke's next work, he observed, "should be of a model wholly new, and that is by way of logick; something accommodated to the usual forms, together with the consideration of extension, solidity, mobility, thinking, existence, duration, number, &c. and of the mind of man, and its powers, as may make up a complete body of what the schools call logicks and metaphysicks."[10] A large discourse upon these matters, added Moly-

---

[8] My reference is to the second edition of Mr. Aaron's book (Oxford, 1955).

[9] *Some Familiar Letters*, p. 17. Dr. Ashe is said to have given the *Essay* an abridgment for the use of students; but no copy of it appears to have been found. See H. O. Christophersen, *A Bibliographical Introduction to the Study of John Locke* (Oslo, 1930), p. 28. Cited below as Christophersen.

[10] *Some Familiar Letters*, p. 16.

neux, would be attractive in all universities, "wherein youths do not satisfie themselves to have the breeding or business of the place, unless they are ingaged in something that bears the name and form of logick." This recommendation did not mean, however, that Molyneux had no regard for the *Essay* itself as an important contribution to logical theory. In a letter dated eight months later than the one just quoted, he chided Locke gently for having failed in *Some Thoughts concerning Education* to name specific authors whom he would advise gentlemen to read in the various parts of learning. "Had you done this," said Molyneux, "I know no *logick* that deserves to be named, but the *Essay of Humane Understanding*. So that I fear you would rather have left that head open, than recommended your own work."[11]

Not long after Dr. Ashe's pioneering step at Dublin, Oxford began to show interest in Locke's *Essay* as a treatise on logic. In a letter to his Dublin admirer on April 26, 1695, Locke wrote that Molyneux, in view of his expressed wish to have Locke compose a work on logical theory, might be pleased to hear of an abridgment of the *Essay* then being prepared by an Oxford don, who had already written two letters to Locke in connection with his undertaking, and who seemed in Locke's judgment to be an ingenious man and to write sensibly about what he was doing.[12] The abridgment, said Locke, was being planned to take the place "of an ordinary system of logick" in the education of young scholars at Oxford. "From the acquaintance I had of the temper of that place," Locke tartly commented, as he no doubt thought of the reception of his *Essay* in the Oxford of Dean Aldrich, "I did not expect to have it get much footing there." Molyneux, who had become a veteran admirer of the *Essay*, and had confessed on December 23, 1693, to having already given it a third reading,[13] rejoiced in the prospect of an abridgment of it "from a judicious hand in *Oxford*," and added, " 'tis what I always thought might be of good use in the universities, where we yet want another sort of language, than what has hitherto prevail'd there, to the great hindrance of science."[14] On July 2, 1695, Locke wrote again to Molyneux as follows:

> The abridgment of my *Essay* is quite finish'd. It is done by a very ingenious man of *Oxford*, a master of arts, very considera-

[11] *Ibid.*, p. 54. This letter is dated August 12, 1693.
[12] *Ibid.*, pp. 109-110.   [13] *Ibid.*, p. 66.   [14] *Ibid.*, p. 112.

ble for his learning and virtue, who has a great many pupils. It is done with the same design you had in view, when you mention'd it. He has generally (as far as I could remember) made use of my words; he very civilly sent it me when it was done, and, upon looking it over, I guess you will approve of it, and think it well done.[15]

"I am mightily pleased that your *Essay* is abridg'd," replied Molyneux on August 24 of that year, "tho', for my own reading, I would not part with a syllable of it." " 'Tis to me," he went on, "no small argument of the curious genius of the english [sic] nation, that a work, so abstract as yours, should now suffer three impressions in so short a time."[16]

In fact, however, the abridgment of the *Essay* did not finally appear in print until the following spring. Its compiler was John Wynne, of Jesus College, who dedicated the work "To the Much Esteemed *Mr. John Locke,*" and who remarked in the dedicatory epistle that, while his epitome could not take the place of the complete *Essay,* it would nevertheless serve "to make the way to Knowledge somewhat more plain and easie; and afford such Helps for the improvement of Reason, as are perhaps in vain sought after in those Books, which profess to Teach the *Art of Reasoning.*"[17] These words squarely aim the abridgment at the target which Molyneux had wanted it to hit.

But when Molyneux received a copy of the abridgment from its London publisher at the request of Locke himself,[18] he was no longer mightily pleased, nor did he think it well done. He wrote as follows to Locke on June 6, 1696:

> I have read over Mr. *Wynne's* abridgment of your *Essay.* But I must confess to you, I was never more satisfy'd with the length of your *Essay,* than since I have seen this abridgment; which, tho' done justly enough, yet falls so short of that spirit which every where shews it self in the original, that nothing can be more different. To one already vers'd in the *Essay,* the

[15] *Ibid.,* p. 116.   [16] *Ibid.,* p. 123.

[17] [John Wynne], *An Abridgment of Mr. Locke's Essay concerning Humane Understanding* (London, Printed for *A.* and *J. Churchill* at the *Black Swan* in *Pater-noster-Row,* and *Edw. Castle* next *Scotland-Yard Gate,* near *Whitehall* [sic], 1696, sig. A3v. I reverse the style of the original quotation in respect to the use of roman and italic type.

[18] *Some Familiar Letters,* p. 145.

abridgment serves as a good remembrancer; but, I believe, let
a man wholly unacquainted with the former, begin to read the
latter, and he will not so well relish it. So that how desirous soever I might have formerly been of seeing your *Essay* put into
the form of a logick for the schools, I am now fully satisfy'd I
was in an error; and must freely confess to you, that I wish Mr.
Wynne's abridgment had been yet undone. That strength of
thought and expression, that every where reigns throughout
your works, makes me sometimes wish them twice as long.[19]

When he answered these complimentary words in a letter to
Molyneux on July 2, 1696, Locke did not enter into a dispute with
his friend on the merits of Wynne's abridgment. In fact, he could
with justice have felt that Molyneux's opinion of it was not open
to serious question. What interested him, however, was that the
undergraduates at Cambridge seemed suddenly to be reading the
Essay, as they had not previously done, and that Wynne's abridgment might have played a part in that development. He wrote to
Molyneux as follows:

'Tis your pre-occupation, in favour of me, that makes you say
what you do of Mr. *Wynne's* abridgment; I know not whether
it be that, or any thing else, that has occasion'd it; but I was
told, some time since, that my *Essay* began to get some credit
in *Cambridge*, where, I think for some years after it was published, it was scarce so much as looked into. But now, I have
some reason to think it is a little more favourably received
there, by these two questions held there this last commencement; *viz. Probabile est animam non semper cogitare*: And,
Idea dei non est innata.[20]

Locke did not live to see the abridgment succeed in giving the
Essay an audience of undergraduates in Scottish universities, nor
did he have an early admirer in Scotland to recommend the full
Essay to Aberdeen, or Edinburgh, or Glasgow, or St. Andrews,
as Molyneux had recommended it to Dublin. But the abridgment
and its original were certainly influential in the schools of Scotland from the late seventeen-twenties to the end of the century.
One of the graduation theses at Aberdeen in 1730 proposed that

[19] *Ibid.*, p. 149.   [20] *Ibid.*, pp. 156-157.

"omnis idea, aut oritur a sensibus aut a reflectione,"[21] and thus was Locke's doctrine of the origin of ideas made evident in Scottish educational circles some twenty-six years after his death. At the University of Edinburgh, the story of his early influence is connected with John Stevenson, who was appointed to the chair of logic and metaphysics on February 25, 1730, as successor of Colin Drummond. In *The Scots Magazine* for August, 1741, in an article entitled "A Short Account of the University of Edinburgh, the present Professors in it, and the several parts of Learning taught by them," we read that Stevenson was discharging his duties in respect to logic by lecturing "upon *Heineccii Elementa Philosophiae Rationalis,* and the abridgment of Mr. Locke's *Essay on Human Understanding.*" Sir Alexander Grant, classical scholar and historian, observed that Stevenson substituted Heinecke and Locke for Aristotle and Ramus with such success as to cause a principal of Edinburgh to remark in 1826 upon the extreme scarcity of lectures at that institution on Aristotle's logic after the year 1730.[22] In the same connection it might be noticed that during the eighteenth century there were ten editions of Wynne's abridgment, and that two of these appeared at Edinburgh, the earlier in 1767 and the other in 1770, both obviously printed to meet the needs of undergraduates in their course in logic.[23] No doubt to perform a similar service for students at the University of Glasgow, Wynne's abridgment was published in that city in 1752 by Robert and Andrew Foulis, university printers. Similar evidence that it was used at St. Andrews seems not to exist, although Henry Rymer, professor of logic, rhetoric, and metaphysics at that uni-

---

[21] See William L. Davidson, "The University's Contribution to Philosophy," in *Studies in the History and Development of the University of Aberdeen,* ed. Peter J. Anderson (Aberdeen, 1906), p. 75.

[22] Sir Alexander Grant, *The Story of the University of Edinburgh* (London, 1884), II, 328-329. For a full account of Stevenson's career as professor of logic at Edinburgh, see Alexander Bower, *The History of the University of Edinburgh* (Edinburgh, 1817-1830), II, 269-281. See also James McCosh, *The Scottish Philosophy, Biographical, Expository, Critical, From Hutcheson to Hamilton* (New York, 1875), pp. 107-108.

[23] As I indicated above, the first edition appeared at London in 1696. There was a second edition at London in 1700; a fourth at London in 1731; a fifth at London in 1737; a seventh at Glasgow in 1752; a new edition at Edinburgh in 1767, at Edinburgh in 1770, and at Boston in 1794. I have been unable to locate copies of the third or the sixth editions.

versity between 1747 and 1756, is said to have replaced the old system of Aristotle and Ramus with the new logic of Bacon and Locke, and his example was clearly followed by his immediate successor, Robert Watson, between 1756 and 1778, and by Watson's successor, William Barron, between 1778 and 1803.[24]

Perhaps Molyneux's warm admiration of Locke's *Essay* as a new and effective logic for the mature philosopher, and his desire to have Locke write something himself on that subject for university students, were instrumental in shaping events, once Wynne's abridgment had not satisfied Molyneux's expectations. At any rate, Locke embarked upon a new project just as Wynne's abridgment was celebrating its first anniversary as a printed book, and the project can certainly be construed as having reference to what Molyneux had proposed almost five years before. As if indeed to suggest Molyneux's part in it, Locke announced the new project to Molyneux himself in a letter dated April 10, 1697. He wrote thus:

> I have lately got a little leisure to think of some additions to my book, against the next edition, and within these few days have fallen upon a subject that I know not how far it will lead me. I have written several pages on it, but the matter, the farther I go, opens the more upon me, and I cannot yet get sight of any end of it. The title of the chapter will be *Of the Conduct of the Understanding*, which, if I shall pursue, as far as I imagine it will reach, and as it deserves, will, I conclude, make the largest chapter of my *Essay*. 'Tis well for you you are not near me, I should be always pestering you with my notions, and papers, and reveries. It would be a great happiness to have a man of thought to lay them before, and a friend that would deal candidly and freely.[25]

Molyneux died a year and a half after he had received this letter from his friend, and Locke's new project had not yet been published. But Molyneux might have seen some part of it in manu-

---

[24] See Blakey, *Historical Sketch of Logic*, pp. 436-438. Barron's logical theory, which was completely in the spirit of the new logic of Bacon, Descartes, and Locke, has been preserved in his *Lectures on Belles Lettres and Logic* (London, 1806), II, 357-597. See below, p. 296. Barron gave fourteen lectures on the second of his two main topics.

[25] *Some Familiar Letters*, p. 194.

script during his visit to England in the summer of 1698 when he met Locke for the first and only time of his life. Progress upon the rest of it might have been slow. At any rate, it was not incorporated in the fourth edition of the *Essay*, printed "with large Additions" in 1700; nor did it ever appear within that work in subsequent editions. Its first printing, in fact, occurred in 1706, two years after Locke's death, when it was included in a collection of his hitherto unpublished writings bearing the general title, *Posthumous Works of Mr. John Locke*.[26] At that time, and not until that time, did it become a matter of public knowledge that Locke had made another contribution to logic, as Molyneux had wanted him to do all along.

This contribution, the title of which may for convenience be shortened to *The Conduct of the Understanding*,[27] established itself in its introductory paragraphs as a timely substitute for the logical theory then being studied in universities. It spoke as follows in this connection:

> The Logick now in use has so long possessed the Chair, as the only Art taught in the Schools for the Direction of the Mind in the Study of the Arts and Sciences, that it would perhaps be thought an affectation of Novelty to suspect, that Rules that have served the learned World these two or three thousand Years, and which without any complaint of Defects the Learned have rested in, are not sufficient to guide the Understanding. And I should not doubt but this Attempt would be censured as Vanity or Presumption, did not the great Lord *Verulam's* Authority justifie it; who not servilely thinking Learning could not be advanced beyond what it was, because for many Ages it had not been, did not rest in the lazy Approbation and Applause of what was, because it was; but enlarged his Mind to what might be.[28]

[26] Its imprint reads: "London, Printed by *W. B.* for *A.* and *J. Churchill* at the *Black Swan* in *Pater-Noster-Row.* 1706."

[27] It has repeatedly been published not only under the title originally assigned to it by Locke, but also under the slightly shorter title which I am using. Moreover, it has appeared as *Some Thoughts on the Conduct of the Understanding in the Search of Truth* and as *A Treatise on the Conduct of the Understanding.*

[28] *Posthumous Works of Mr. John Locke* (London, 1706), p. 4.

Locke supported his reference to Bacon's authority by quoting next a Latin passage from the *Novum Organum* and by translating it at once into English. The translation ascribes the following sentiments to Bacon:

> *They*, says he, *who attributed so much to Logick, perceived very well and truly, that it was not safe to trust the Under standing to it self, without the Guard of any Rules. But the Remedy reach'd not the Evil, but became a part of it: For the Logick which took place, though it might do well enough in civil Affairs, and the Arts which consisted in Talk and Opinion, yet comes very far short of Subtilty in the real Performances of Nature, and catching at what it cannot reach, has served to confirm and establish Errors, rather than to open a way to Truth.* And therefore a little after he says, *That it is absolutely necessary that a better and perfecter use and employment of the Mind and Understanding should be introduced.*[29]

In line with these opening words, *The Conduct of the Understanding* devotes itself to procedures calculated to guide the enquirer seeking an accurate understanding of the performances of nature. It is not a closely organized work. It does not follow Molyneux's original suggestion that it be accommodated to the usual forms of logic. But it has an adequate degree of order, and it may perhaps best be described as a logic for the guidance of the mental states which the enquirer should achieve if he is ever to succeed in establishing truth of any sort.

Thus it deals first with the "three Miscarriages that Men are guilty of in reference to their Reason, whereby this Faculty is hindred in them from that Service it might do and was design'd for."[30] One of these miscarriages occurs to those who do not use their reason at all but merely follow the thinking of their parents, their neighbors, or their spiritual advisers. Another miscarriage occurs to those who put passion in the place of reason and who hearken to their own or other people's thinking only so far as it

---

[29] *Ibid.*, p. 5. My quotation follows the original in respect to the use of italics. The passage quoted by Locke is from Bacon's preface to the *Novum Organum*. For Bacon's Latin text and James Spedding's translation of it, see James Spedding, Robert L. Ellis, and Douglas D. Heath, eds., *The Works of Francis Bacon* (Boston, 1860-1865), I, 204-205, 206; VIII, 31-32, 33. Cited below as *Works of Bacon*.

[30] *Ibid.*, p. 7.

suits their humor, interest, or party to do so. The third miscarriage, to which Locke devoted a considerable amount of space, occurs to those who readily and honestly follow reason, "but for want of having that which one may call *large, sound, round about Sense,* have not a full view of all that relates to the question, and may be of moment to decide it."[31] In his subsequent discussion of this part of his subject, Locke pointed to a human faculty which, if properly used, will make the rules of formal logic unnecessary. He said: "Every Man carries about him a Touchstone, if he will make use of it to distinguish substantial Gold from superficial Glitterings, Truth from Appearances. And indeed the Use and Benefit of this Touchstone, which is natural Reason, is spoil'd and lost only by assumed Prejudices, overweening Presumption, and narrowing our Minds."[32]

The next and only other major topic of this work concerns "several Weaknesses and Defects in the Understanding, either from the natural Temper of the Mind, or ill Habits taken up, which hinder it in its progress to Knowledge."[33] The tendency to be too forward or too slow in making observations on the particular facts which constitute the foundations of our civil and natural knowledge, the tendency to cram the mind with particular facts without digesting them, the tendency to draw general conclusions and raise axioms from every particular fact which one encounters, the tendency to resist "the proper business of the Understanding," which is "To think of every thing just as it is in it self," and instead, in open defiance of common sense, to do the exact contrary,[34] the tendency to hunt arguments "to make good one side of a Question, and wholly to neglect and refuse those which favour the other side,"[35]—these are a few of the imposing number of just weaknesses and defects which Locke wanted the searcher of truth to be aware of and to correct in the process of making himself capable of basing his knowledge upon accurate ideas of things as they are.

The Conduct of the Understanding and its parent work, *An Essay concerning Human Understanding*, were without question the most popular, the most widely read, the most frequently reprinted, and the most influential, of all English books of the eighteenth century. Between 1700 and 1800 Wynne's abridgment was

[31] *Ibid.*, p. 8.   [32] *Ibid.*, p. 12.   [33] *Ibid.*, p. 47.
[34] *Ibid.*, p. 50.   [35] *Ibid.*, p. 51.

given a total of nine editions, and these, as we have seen, greatly contributed to the influence of the *Essay* in academic circles, where the leaders of eighteenth-century thought were being educated. Thanks to the assistance which it received from the popularity of the abridgment, and thanks above all to its own capacity to attract readers and admirers, the *Essay* flourished in the eighteenth century as no other English work did. If Molyneux found it a mark of the curious genius of the English nation that a work as abstract as the *Essay* could have received three editions between 1690 and 1695, the admirers of Locke in the year 1805 would have been even more complimentary towards the genius of Great Britain and Europe, for in that year the *Essay* was given its twenty-first edition at London, while it could take added pride in having been included in each one of the ten editions which Locke's complete works had been given by that date, and it could claim to have had not only four editions in a Latin translation made by an Irish friend of Molyneux's, Richard Burridge, for circulation in the learned world, but also to have made eight appearances in the French translation by Pierre Coste, and at least three appearances in German translations.[36] As for *The Conduct of the Understanding*, it had made twenty appearances in print by the year 1805. These included its first printing in 1706 among hitherto unpublished writings of Locke, its later presence, of course, in each of the first ten editions of Locke's complete works, its appearance on seven occasions as a separate volume, and its publication once in company with the full *Essay*, and once in company with an abstract of the *Essay* made by Sir Geoffrey Gilbert.[37] Blakey says that *The Conduct of the Understanding*

---

[36] See Christophersen, pp. 26-28, 92-99. See also Bourne, *Life of John Locke*, II, 440-441. The British Museum holds three different copies of eighteenth-century German translations of Locke's *Essay*, one published at Altenburg in 1757, one at Mannheim in 1795, and one at Jena and Leipzig in 1795-97. Bourne (II, 441) states that the first German translation of the *Essay* appeared at Königsberg in 1755, but no copy of it seems to have survived. See Christophersen, p. 97.

[37] See Christophersen, pp. 71-73. *The Conduct of the Understanding*, Christophersen notes, also had eighteenth-century German and French translations. Christophersen's list of appearances of this work fails to include the edition published in the year 1741, supposed to have been printed by R. Foulis at Glasgow, a copy of which is in the Princeton University Library. This copy represents the first separate edition of the work. See below, n. 40. Christopher-

was often used in British universities as a textbook on logic.[38] Doubtless his remark applies especially to the work in its separate editions, which, so far as the period between 1700 and 1805 is concerned, appeared at Glasgow in 1741, 1754, and 1763, at London in 1762, 1800, and 1802, and at Dublin in 1782. Such printings all have the character of the textbook about them, and in the hundred years that followed 1805, the work was given many other editions of similar character, including eleven in company with Bacon's *Essays Moral, Economical, and Political.* But these latter publications are part of the story of the long duration of Locke's influence. Our present concern is to emphasize that the eighteenth century is the century of his special greatness, and that his famous *Essay*, and its supplement, *The Conduct of the Understanding,* contributed more than his other works did towards making his influence dominant.

Now that the *Essay* and *The Conduct of the Understanding* have been delineated as contributions to logical theory in the eyes of Locke's contemporaries, and have been established as offering an increasingly influential alternative to conventional logic in British universities and throughout the community of European learning during the eighteenth century, we need next to comment upon the precise nature of the revolution wrought by these two works in supplying the schools with a new logic containing what Molyneux called "another sort of language, than what has hitherto prevail'd there, to the great hindrance of science."[39] We need next, in short, to describe Locke's contribution to the kind of new logic which was fully to emerge in the late eighteenth century. Perhaps the best way to describe that contribution is to say bluntly that Locke founded the new logic in respect to each of the seven traits which we have described it as possessing in its fully developed form. No one would want to deny, of course, that Bacon and Descartes had prepared the way towards the new logic, and that without them Locke's achievement might have been substantially diminished in importance, or might have been prevented altogether. But it must always be remembered that Locke's *Essay* was getting its first readers at the very moment in

---

sen also fails to mention the edition published at Dublin by W. Wilson, the printer, in 1782, a copy of which is listed in *Bibliotheca Lindesiana.*

[38] *Historical Sketch of Logic,* p. 281.   [39] See above, p. 270.

history when Henry Aldrich in his Aristotelian treatise, *Artis Logicae Compendium*, was denying to Bacon and Descartes the right to be considered as true logicians, and that under Aldrich's guidance the old logic seemed to have withstood successfully the assaults of its two most formidable early seventeenth-century adversaries, and to be no longer in danger from them for the indefinite future. Thus without the appearance of Locke's *Essay*, Bacon and Descartes might have had to wait another century or two for full recognition in the field of logical theory, whereas with its appearance an improved form of their views began at once to get a fresh scrutiny. That is to say, the *Essay* gave their views a fully modern treatment, and stripped from them the backward-looking vocabulary in which Bacon and Descartes had expressed them. Such achievements would entitle any work to a place in the history of logic. But the *Essay* possesses one other excellence to give it special influence in its own time—an excellence at once curious, puzzling, inexplicable, wonderful. For in addition to being a good, helpful, timely, and useful book, it had the luck to be also a masterpiece. In that capacity it gave the new logic of the eighteenth century an auspicious beginning indeed.

In their ultimate influence upon logical doctrine, *The Conduct of the Understanding* and the *Essay* may be said to give the new logic the first of its important characteristics—that of emphasizing its connection with the theory of scientific enquiry and of dissociating itself from the theory of learned communication. These two works, in short, tie logic to the inductive sciences and free it from its traditional association with the humanistic enterprise of transmitting ideas. When *The Conduct of the Understanding* was first given a separate identity of its own through being published by itself, it received a new title made up of thirteen words, only five of which had been part of Locke's own original title; and the thirteen words identified the work as containing some thoughts on the conduct of the understanding in the search of truth.[40] The

---

[40] As I indicated above, in n. 37, there is a copy of this first edition in the Princeton University Library. Its title page reads in part as follows: "Some Thoughts On the Conduct of the Understanding In the Search of Truth. . . . By John Locke Esq; *Quid tam temerarium . . . defendere?* Cic. de Natura Deorum, lib. I. Printed in the Year M DCC XLI." Written by hand above the last clause in this title are the following words: "Glasgovv Printed by R. Foulis." I do not find this work listed in the "Catalogue of Books Printed

accuracy of the final phrase in this title is obvious to all who examine what the work discusses. And the same phrase could equally well be used to designate Locke's paramount interest in writing the *Essay*, as that work reveals throughout its full extent, and in particular in the winning terms of its "Epistle to the Reader," where Locke spoke as follows:

> I shall always have the satisfaction to have aimed sincerely at Truth and Usefulness, though in one of the meanest ways. The Commonwealth of Learning, is not at this time without Master-Builders, whose mighty Designs, in advancing the Sciences, will leave lasting Monuments to the Admiration of Posterity; But every one must not hope to be a *Boyle*, or a *Sydenham*; and in an Age that produces such Masters, as the Great—*Huygenius,* and the incomparable Mr. *Newton*, with some other of that Strain; 'tis Ambition enough to be employed as an Under-Labourer in clearing Ground a little, and removing some of the Rubbish, that lies in the way to Knowledge; which certainly had been very much more advanced in the World, if the Endeavours of ingenious and industrious Men had not been much cumbred with the learned but frivolous use of uncouth, affected, or unintelligible Terms, introduced into the Sciences, and there made an Art of, to that Degree, that Philosophy, which is nothing but the true Knowledge of Things, was thought unfit, or uncapable to be brought into well-bred Company, and polite Conversation.[41]

It must be emphasized that Locke's *Essay*, in associating itself with the method of enquiring into the true knowledge of things,

---

by Robert and Andrew Foulis," in *Notices and Documents Illustrative of the Literary History of Glasgow, During the Greater Part of Last Century* (Glasgow, 1831), pp. 49-78. Nor for that matter is it listed among the works published by the other prominent eighteenth-century Glasgow printer, Robert Urie. See *Records of the Glasgow Bibliographical Society* (Glasgow, 1915), III, 98-108. It is quite probable, however, that the Princeton bibliographer is correct in saying that Foulis printed it. The fact that its imprint omits the name of its publisher would explain why it was not listed among works known to have been put out by Foulis.

[41] *An Essay concerning Humane Understanding, In Four Books,* The Fourth Edition, with large Additions (London, 1700), sig. b3v-b4r. In this particular quotation I reverse the style of the original in respect to the use of roman and italic type.

did not disparage the enterprise associated with the communication of truth to others. Locke felt, however, that the method of acquiring knowledge and the method of communicating it should not be allowed to dictate one to another in such a way as to impair the functioning of either one. The method of communicating knowledge from specialist to specialist or from specialist to student, for example, had not only been a part of Ramistic logic and of early post-Ramistic Aristotelianism, but had also tended to create in the old logic as a whole a false sense of values in respect to scientific enquiry. Thus the citing of maxims at the beginning of a learned discourse, and the subsequent reference to them in order to demonstrate the truth of a relevant but less familiar statement, were standard parts of the procedures recommended by the old logic for teaching truths to others; but at the same time these very procedures tended to make truth appear to issue from maxims rather than from the facts of experience, with the result that maxims were regarded as being the highest of the objects of study, while the facts of experience were deemed lower objects, and were often dismissed contemptuously for producing merely probable knowledge as distinguished from the certainty to be derived from maxims syllogistically examined. Locke had in mind this unfortunate impact of learned communication upon learned enquiry when he condemned the use of maxims as follows.

They are not of use to help Men forwards in the Advancement of Sciences, or new Discoveries of yet unknown Truths. Mr. *Newton*, in his never enough to be admired Book, has demonstrated several Propositions, which are so many new Truths, before unknown to the World, and are farther Advances in Mathematical Knowledge: But for the Discovery of these, it was not the general *Maxims, What is, is;* or, *The whole is bigger than a part,* or the like, that help'd him. These were not the Clues that lead him into the Discovery of the Truth and Certainty of those Propositions. Nor was it by them that he got the Knowledge of those Demonstrations; but by finding out intermediate *Ideas,* that shew'd the Agreement or Disagreement of the *Ideas,* as expressed in the Propositions he demonstrated. This is the great Exercise and Improvement of Humane Understanding in the enlarging of Knowledge, and advancing the Sciences; wherein they are far enough from receiving any Help from the Contemplation of these, or the like magnified *Maxims*. Would those who have this Traditional Admiration of these Propositions, that they think no Step can be made in Knowledge without the support of an *Axiom*, no Stone laid in the building of the Sciences without a general *Maxim*, but distinguish between the Method of acquiring Knowledge, and of communicating it; between the Method of raising any Science, and that of teaching it to others as far as it is advanced, they would see that those general *Maxims* were not the Foundations on which the first Discoverers raised their admirable Structures, nor the Keys that unlocked and opened those Secrets of Knowledge. Though afterwards, when Schools were erected, and Sciences had their Professors to teach what others had found out, they often made use of *Maxims, i.e.* laid down certain Propositions which were self-evident, or to be received for true, which being setled in the Minds of their Scholars as unquestionable Verities, they on occasion made use of, to convince them of Truths in particular Instances, that were not so familiar to their Minds as those general *Axioms* which had before been inculcated to them and carefully setled in their Minds. Though these particular Instances, when well reflected on, are no less self-evident to the Understanding than the general *Maxims* brought to confirm them: And it was in those particular Instances, that the first Discoverer found the Truth, without the help of the general *Maxims*: And so may any one else do, who with Attention considers them.[42]

As in this passage, so in the *Essay* in general, Locke kept clearly in mind the distinction between the method of learned enquiry and the method of learned communication, and it was towards the former method, I repeat, that he directed his thought. If he had been asked to speculate upon the future of the latter method in a world in which logic no longer administered it, he might, I believe, have expressed the hope that it would identify itself with the concerns of the emerging new rhetoric, and that the new rhetoric would accordingly provide the theory and doctrine for learned communication as it had historically provided the theory and doctrine for popular communication between the orator and the public. This is not the place, however, for an analysis of

[42] *Ibid.*, pp. 359-360.

Locke's view of rhetoric. I shall deal with that subject in my next chapter, where I am going to point out that the *Essay* contains not only Locke's memorable attack upon the accepted stylistic rhetoric of his time, but also his prophetic indication of the direction in which a reconstructed rhetoric might develop out of the necessity to recognize that language is abused or deficient when it fails to convey with ease and quickness a true knowledge of things between one man and another. It was in part Locke's idea of the new rhetoric that Adam Smith and George Campbell fulfilled in the middle years of the eighteenth century, and thus Locke helped found the new rhetoric as well as the new logic. But of that anon.

The long passage last quoted points to another characteristic of the new logic, and this was the belief that the discoverers of the truths of science found those truths in particular instances, not in general maxims. "For in particulars," said Locke in another passage, "our Knowledge begins, and so spreads its self, by degrees, to generals."[43] At still another place, Locke devoted himself to a criticism of the syllogism, the central implement of the old logic, and in the course of that criticism, after citing the rule "That no Syllogistical Reasoning can be right and conclusive, but what has, at least, one general Proposition in it," he remarked with some firmness, "As if we could not *reason*, and have knowledge *about Particulars*. Whereas, in truth, the Matter rightly considered, the immediate Object of all our Reasoning and Knowledge, is nothing but Particulars."[44] Statements like this turned the old theory of scientific enquiry upside down. For had not the old theory, as understood, for example, by John Sergeant, insisted that true science addressed itself to general principles supplied by metaphysics, and that it considered its true task to be one of extracting from those principles the whole range of particular truths which could be shown to be consistent with them? It was Locke's attack upon this assumption that not only led Sergeant to write *Solid Philosophy Asserted*, but also led the new logic of the eighteenth century to place particular things above traditional generalizations in its theory regarding the proper objects of scientific enquiry.

Locke did not address himself to the problem of constructing

[43] *Ibid.*, p. 362.
[44] *Ibid.*, p. 412. Italics are those of the original passage.

an inductive logic, as Dugald Stewart and John Stuart Mill were later to do with great authority and perceptiveness. But his *Essay* had certain things to say against the syllogism, in addition to the criticism noted just above; and the sum of his objections to this great instrument of the old logic gave the new school of logicians of the eighteenth century still another of its dominant characteristics. His objections were set forth in the famous seventeenth chapter of Book IV, and at that point the *Essay* is closer to the history of logical theory than it could claim to be in any other of its parts. In the first edition of the *Essay*, this chapter did not contain seven subsections which were to appear in later editions as supplements in Section IV. And the second edition of Wynne's abridgment gave this part of the *Essay* more space than the first edition had done. Thus there can be no doubt that Locke's unfavorable attitude towards syllogistic logic grew stronger during his own lifetime, and that the abridgment gave the unfavorable attitude an increasing amount of attention. Small wonder, then, that the new logicians became increasingly disposed to think of the syllogism with disfavor and disrespect.

The seventeenth chapter of Book IV is entitled "Of Reason." This word has various different meanings in English, but as he would use the term, said Locke, it would stand "for a Faculty in Man, That Faculty, whereby Man is supposed to be distinguished from Beasts, and wherein it is evident he much surpasses them."[45] There are four degrees in reason, he declared: "the first and highest, is the discovering, and finding out of Proofs; the second, the regular and methodical Disposition of them, and laying them in a clear and fit Order, to make their Connexion and Force be plainly and easily perceived; the third is the perceiving their Connexion; and the fourth, the making a right conclusion."[46] It is with such a vision of the full scope of reason and its several aspects that Locke proceeded to consider whether the syllogism is or is not the proper instrument and the most useful exercise of this faculty. Four considerations led him to conclude that it was not.

"*First,*" he argued, "Because Syllogism serves our Reason, but in one only of the forementioned parts of it; and that is, to shew the connexion of the Proofs in any one instance, and no more: but in this, it is of no great use, since the Mind can perceive such Con-

[45] *Ibid.*, p. 404.   [46] *Ibid.*, p. 405.

nexion where it really is, as easily, nay, perhaps, better without it."[47] When Locke made this statement, he wanted it to indicate that the syllogism applied solely to the third of the four degrees of reason, and that it applied there, not as the primary means of establishing a connection among the truths under inspection, but as a device for confirming the connection seen in a previous flash of insight. He also wanted this statement to make very clear the lack of value of the syllogism even in that one capacity. His elaboration of these lines of argument contains many trenchant and memorable observations, some of which are of special significance in cutting the syllogism down to a new unimportance. If we will observe the way in which our own minds behave, he remarked, we shall find ourselves reasoning best and most clearly, when we pay attention, not to the rule of the syllogism, but to the actual connection of the proof. "If Syllogisms must be taken for the only proper instrument of reason and means of Knowledge," he remarked, "it will follow, that before *Aristotle* there was not one Man that did or could know any thing by Reason; and that since the invention of Syllogisms, there is not one of Ten Thousand that doth."[48] But God had been more bountiful to man, Locke continued, than to give him two legs while leaving it to Aristotle to make him rational. In other words, God had given men a mind that can reason "without being instructed in Methods of Syllogizing: The Understanding is not taught to reason by these Rules; it has a native Faculty to perceive the Coherence, or Incoherence of its *Ideas*, and can range them right, without any such perplexing Repetitions."[49] "For the natural order of the connecting *Ideas*," Locke added somewhat later, "must direct the order of the *Syllogisms*, and a Man must see the connexion of each intermediate *Idea* with those that it connects, before he can with Reason make use of it in a *Syllogism*. And when all those Syllogisms are made, neither those that are, nor those that are not Logicians will see the force of the Argumentation. *i.e.* the connexion of the Extremes one jot the better."[50] Indeed, said Locke with mounting sarcasm, as he concluded this first phase of his objections to formal syllogistic logic, the chief use of syllogisms in or out of the schools is to allow men "without shame to deny the connexion of

[47] *Ibid.*, p. 405. [48] *Ibid.*, p. 406. [49] *Ibid.*, p. 406.
[50] *Ibid.*, p. 408.

Ideas, which even to themselves is visible."[51] By contrast, he observed, the ingenuous enquirers, having no aim but to find truth, "must see the connexion, that is between the intermediate *Idea,* and the two other *Ideas* it is set between, and applied to, to shew their Agreement, and when they see that, they see whether the inference be good or no, and so *Syllogism* comes too late to settle it."[52] And if the lovers of truth allow themselves to think syllogisms useful in detecting the fallacies that are hidden in florid, witty, involved, or rhetorical discourses, they would be better advised, said Locke, "to lay the naked *Ideas* on which the force of the Argumentation depends, in their due order, in which Position the Mind taking a view of them, sees what connexion they have, and so is able to judge of the Inference, without any need of a Syllogism at all."[53]

"Secondly," Locke declared, "Another reason that makes me doubt whether Syllogism be the only proper Instrument of Reason in the discovery of Truth, is, that of whatever use *Mode* and *Figure* is pretended to be in the laying open of Fallacy (which has been above consider'd) those scholastique Forms of Discourse, are not less liable to Fallacies, than the plainer ways of Argumentation: And for this I appeal to common observation, which has always found these artificial Methods of reasoning more adapted to catch and intangle the Mind, than to instruct and inform the Understanding."[54] In supporting this argument, Locke pointed to the fact that men might be silenced by a chain of formal syllogisms and might even admire the virtuosity of the one who used them, but that they would nevertheless not be truly convinced by such a means. "And therefore," said Locke, "Syllogism has been thought more proper for the attaining Victory in dispute, than for the Discovery or Confirmation of Truth, in fair Enquiries."[55] To those, however, who might feel the syllogism genuinely useful in their own quest for knowledge, Locke had a word of comfort. They ought, of course, to continue to employ whatever they found really helpful, and syllogisms were no exception to this rule. "All that I aim at," said Locke, "is, that they should not ascribe more to these Forms than belongs to them; And think that Men have no use, or not so full a use of their rea-

[51] *Ibid.,* p. 408. [52] *Ibid.,* p. 408. [53] *Ibid.,* p. 409.
[54] *Ibid.,* p. 410. [55] *Ibid.,* p. 410.

soning Faculty without them."[56] And with these mollifying sentiments he turned to his third argument against the syllogism.

This argument consisted in the brief observation that, however
lacking in utility the syllogism might be in respect to the processes by which true knowledge is established, it is of even less use
in dealing with probabilities. The mind, he argued, judges
whether a proposition is probable or not by weighing all the
proofs and all the circumstances on both sides, and by deciding
where the preponderance of weight lies. Such a process requires
that the mind have freedom to move wherever it feels it needs to
move, whereas the syllogistic process dictates that it examine one
assumed probability so exhaustively as to lose sight of the real
question at issue. Locke's imagery at this point strongly reinforces
his philosophical opinion. Thus he spoke of the mind as being
held "fast," "intangled perhaps, and as it were, manacled in the
Chain of Syllogisms," instead of being at liberty to show "on
which side, all Things considered, is the greater Probability."[57]
Since in traditional rhetorical doctrine probabilities were regarded as the chief materials of rhetorical proof, the force of this
argument tells ultimately against the theory that rhetorical syllogisms or enthymemes are indispensable instruments for deciding which argument is the more probable or the more weighty for
deliberative speeches, debates, and popular controversies. Thus
Locke's disparagement of the syllogistic process implies a necessary reappraisal of the value of the enthymeme in rhetoric.

Locke's fourth and final objection to the syllogism was that it
has no value whatever in directing the reason towards the making
of new discoveries in science and scholarship. Since these discoveries are the object of the reason in its hardest task, as Locke himself had indicated, this objection tells not only against the syllogism but also against continuing the affiliations between scholastic logic and scientific enquiry. Locke's words upon these matters
have lasting significance, and they should be quoted at some
length:

> The Rules of *Syllogism* serve not to furnish the Mind with those
> intermediate *Ideas*, that may shew the connexion of remote
> ones. This way of reasoning discovers no new Proofs, but is the
> Art of marshalling, and ranging the old ones we have already.

[56] *Ibid.*, p. 410.   [57] *Ibid.*, p. 411.

The 47th. Proposition of the First Book of *Euclid* is very true; but the discovery of it, I think, not owing to any Rules of common Logick. A Man knows first, and then he is able to prove syllogistically. So that *Syllogism* comes after Knowledge, and then a Man has little or no need of it. But 'tis chiefly by the finding out those *Ideas* that shew the connexion of distant ones, that our stock of Knowledge is increased, and that useful Arts and Sciences are advanced. *Syllogism*, at best, is but the Art of fencing with the little Knowledge we have, without making any Addition to it. And if a Man should employ his Reason all this way, he will not do much otherwise, than he, who having got some Iron out of the Bowels of the Earth, should have it beaten up all into Swords, and put it into his Servants Hands to fence with, and bang one another. Had the King of *Spain* imployed the Hands of his People, and his *Spanish* Iron so, he had brought to Light but little of that Treasure, that lay so long hid in the dark Entrails of *America*.[58]

Somewhat before Locke uttered the words just quoted, he had described in terms of two practical illustrations what he considered to be the natural way of arriving at knowledge. This natural way consisted in the process which the human reason would follow by itself in forming ideas that were in agreement with the realities which the human being has to interpret. Locke called this process inference. "To infer," he declared, "is nothing but by virtue of one Proposition laid down as true, to draw in another as true, *i.e.* to see or suppose such a connexion of the two *Ideas*, of the inferr'd Proposition."[59] Locke's first illustration of this process indicates that he considered it an instantaneous action of the rational faculty in its environment of sensation and reflection. "Tell a Country Gentlewoman," he said, "that the Wind is South-West, and the Weather louring, and like to rain, and she will easily understand, 'tis not safe for her to go abroad thin clad, in such a day, after a Fever: she clearly sees the probable Connexion of all these, *viz.* South-West Wind, and Clouds, Rain, wetting, taking Cold, Relapse, and danger of Death, without tying them together in those artificial and cumbersome Fetters of several Syllogisms, that clog and hinder the Mind, which proceeds from one part to another quicker and clearer without them:

[58] *Ibid.*, p. 411.   [59] *Ibid.*, p. 407.

and the Probability which she easily perceives in Things thus in their native State, would be quite lost, if this Argument were managed learnedly, and proposed in Mode and Figure."[60] Locke's other illustration of the natural process of inference applies not primarily to the conclusions of everyday life but to the world of philosophical argument.[61] And yet it too is close to familiar experience. He said:

> Let this be the Proposition laid down, *Men shall be punished in another World*, and from thence be inferred this other, *then Men can determine themselves*. The Question now is to know, whether the Mind has made this Inference right or no; if it has made it by finding out the intermediate *Ideas*, and taking a view of the connexion of them, placed in a due order, it has proceeded rationally, and made a right Inference.

After a precise denial that the mind would in the first instance resort to syllogisms in determining whether there was a rational connection between the idea of men's punishment in another world and the idea of men's freedom and self-determination, Locke went on:

> In the instance above mentioned, what is it shews the force of the Inference, and consequently the reasonableness of it, but a view of the connexion of all the intermediate *Ideas* that draw in the Conclusion, or Proposition inferr'd. *v.g. Men shall be punished,—God the punisher,—just Punishment,—the Punished guilty—could have done otherwise—Freedom—self-determination*, by which Chain of *Ideas* thus visibly link'd together in train, *i.e.* each intermediate *Idea* agreeing on each side with those two it is immediately placed between, the *Ideas* of Men and self-determination appear to be connected. *i.e.* this Proposition, *Men can determine themselves* is drawn in, or inferr'd from this *that they shall be punished in the other World.*

Those who deny the belief in freedom of the will might be disposed to quarrel with the content of the passage just quoted, but they should not allow such a doctrinal consideration to cloud their awareness that Locke's two illustrations present a revolu-

[60] *Ibid.*, p. 406.   [61] *Ibid.*, p. 407.

tionary picture of the human mind at work upon the facts of its environment. Locke saw the mind engaged with such concrete realities as the southwest wind, the clouds, the likelihood of rain, the thought of getting wet and catching cold, the recollection of a recent fever, and the sense of danger in a relapse and death. He saw the mind proceed from its own conviction that it would face punishment in the other world to its sense of God and justice and guilt and innocence and freedom. To Locke, these were the sequences which began with things and ended in knowledge. These were the sequences which the old logic called an imperfect form of the syllogism, but which were in reality the perfect form of inference. Moreover, these were the sequences which would give learned discourse a new pattern of organization and a new theory of method, in contrast to the scholastic theory of arranging ideas in a strict descending order of generality or in a syllogistic or enthymematic formulation. The new rhetoric, so far as it would seek to describe the method of communication to be used in the world of scholarship and science, could be expected to recommend the natural movement of discourse from a factual statement to its successive logical consequents and to find completely unusable the methods that had been dictated by Ramus, Sanderson, and Aldrich. It could be expected to do so, that is to say, wherever it had the courage to follow Locke into the modern world.

In his evaluation of the syllogism, Locke did not discuss the *dictum de omni et nullo,* even though traditional logicians had considered it to be the principle from which the whole impressive structure of syllogistic logic had been deduced. Nevertheless, when the new logicians of the eighteenth century began to disparage the *dictum,* they were reflecting an attitude that can be traced to implications in Locke's *Essay,* and thus Locke may also be supposed to have supplied the new logic with this particular characteristic. In a very real sense, of course, Locke's whole theory of the origin of human knowledge tells against what the *dictum* took for granted—that the foundation of our understanding of the individual case rests upon our previous understanding of the whole class to which the individual case belongs. This assumption, indeed, was not only at odds with the concepts which Locke evolved to explain the actions of the human mind in the quest for truth; it was also contrary to his view of the generating forces behind the development of any given science. "There is, I know," said he, "a great deal of Talk, propagated from Scholastick Men, of Sciences and the *Maxims* on which they are built: But it has been my ill luck, never to meet with any such Sciences; much less any one built upon these two *Maxims, What is, is*; and *It is impossible for the same thing to be and not to be.*" "And I would be glad to be shewn," he continued, "where any such Science erected upon these, or any other general *Axioms* is to be found: and should be obliged to any one who would lay before me the Frame and System of any Science so built on these, or any such like *Maxims*, that could not be shewn to stand as firm without any Consideration of them."[62] If these words cannot be construed to suggest that Locke would have no regard for the *dictum* considered as the main source of the principles of logic, then the new logicians of the eighteenth century may be assumed to have acquired their own disrespect for the *dictum* from some other source than the *Essay*. But the chances in favor of this latter eventuality are not numerous or convincing.

The chances are excellent, however, that Locke's distaste for the disputation as an effective instrument in the establishment and propagation of truth was a direct influence in providing the new logic with the same attitude and thus with another of its major characteristics. From the quotations which I have used to clarify Locke's adverse opinion of the syllogism, it can be seen that he regarded disputation more as an exercise in entangling the mind of an opponent in fallacies, or in achieving a victory over him in debate, or in fencing against him with what little knowledge one may have than as an instrument for discovering or confirming truth in fair enquiries. This selfsame unfavorable attitude towards disputation appears in other parts of the *Essay*.

For example, in Chapter x of Book iii, in speaking of the deliberate resort to obscure words as one of the abuses of language, Locke said:

> To this abuse, and the mischiefs of confounding the Signification of Words, Logick and the liberal Sciences, as they have been handled in the Schools, have given Reputation; and the admired Art of Disputing, hath added much to the natural imperfection of Languages, Whilst it has been made use of, and

[62] *Ibid.*, p. 359.

fitted, to perplex the signification of Words, more than to discover the Knowledge and Truth of Things: And he that will look into that sort of learned Writings, will find the Words there much more obscure, uncertain, and undetermined in their Meaning, than they are in ordinary Conversation.[63]

Another disparagement of disputation occurs when Locke, in his chapter on maxims, speculated upon the possibility that these were used in debate, not as the true originals and sources of knowledge, but as conventions which, on being invoked by a disputant, would require his opponent as a matter of ritual to admit the force of the argument to which they were tied, and thus to concede defeat. And why were such rituals acceptable? Because, said Locke, the schools, "having made Disputation the Touchstone of Mens Abilities, and the *Criterion* of Knowledge, adjudg'd Victory to him that kept the Field: and he that had the last Word was concluded to have the better of the Argument, if not of the Cause."[64] Certainly these opinions show little of the respect lavished by the old logic upon maxims, and much of the disrespect which Locke cherished towards the philosophical disputes of his own day.[65] But of course it must be remembered that his disapproval was directed less against the dispute as a preparatory academic exercise than against its presumption in claiming for itself a crucial role in the search for the true knowledge of things.

I noted earlier that the new logic of eighteenth-century Britain was to question the propriety of allowing the topics to be considered as possible sources of scientific proofs for propositions under investigation, and that ultimately the topics would disappear as subjects of attention in logical theory. Locke encouraged this development, and thus he may be said to be connected with still another characteristic of the new school of logicians. But so far as his logical writings are concerned, he did not condemn the topics in any detail, no doubt because their use was directly contrary to his whole theory that true understanding originates in the study of things rather than in the manipulation of words, and be-

[63] *Ibid.,* p. 291. [64] *Ibid.,* p. 360.

[65] For further confirmation of Locke's disapproval of disputation, see his *Some Thoughts concerning Education,* in *The Works of John Locke in Four Volumes,* 7th Edn. (London, 1768), IV, 116-117.

cause the topics had been so severely questioned by *The Port-Royal Logic* and by Bernard Lamy's *The Art of Speaking* that little remained to be said against them.[66] Nevertheless, Locke did speak directly upon this subject, and I shall indicate his attitude by pointing to a few remarks concerning it in *The Conduct of the Understanding.*

The first set of these remarks is made in connection with his discussion of the need to apply patterns of mathematical reasoning to all arguments which seek to establish certainties on the one hand or probabilities, on the other. A conclusion can sometimes be established as a certainty, he asserted, by tracing in a single sequence the exact connection between it and the ideas upon which it rests; but in establishing a conclusion as the best of the probabilities that are available in a given case, the reasoner must trace several sequences of connection between opposing conclusions and the ideas which support them, and then must balance one sequence against another, in order for the understanding to determine what the most probable conclusion is. Locke added:

> This is a way of reasoning the Understanding should be accustomed to, which is so different from what the illiterate are used to, that even learned Men oftentimes seem to have very little or no notion of it. Nor is it to be wondered, since the way of disputing in the Schools leads them quite away from it, by insisting on one topical Argument, by the success of which the truth or falshood of the Question is to be determined, and victory adjudg'd to the Opponent or Defendant; which is all one as if one should balance an account by one Summ charged and discharged, when there are an hundred others to be taken into consideration.[67]

Since the theory of topics in traditional logic was always applied in the first instance to the investigation of probabilities, the words just quoted may be said to represent an attack upon that theory at its vital center, and to indicate that mathematics offered a better pattern for arriving at probable truth. Thus did Locke lend heavy weight to the belief that the topics were of little or no value in argument.

[66] See Howell, *Logic and Rhetoric in England*, pp. 355-357, 380-381.
[67] *Posthumous Works of Mr. John Locke*, p. 31.

The second set of remarks against the topics occurs as Locke considered the problems arising when the understanding out of laziness or haste contents itself with improper ways of searching for the truth. Sometimes, he observed, the understanding is satisfied with testimony in cases where testimony does not suffice. Sometimes, when the situation calls for a balancing of one probability against others, the understanding contents itself with a single argument, as if that would be enough. "In some Cases," he went on, "the Mind is determin'd by probable Topicks in Enquiries where Demonstration may be had."[68] "All these," he added, "and several others, which Laziness, Impatience, Custom, and want of Use and Attention lead Men into, are misapplications of the Understanding in the search of Truth."

Locke's third set of remarks against the topics falls in the final pages of *The Conduct of the Understanding* where he emphasized once more that in any question under scrutiny, the most important thing was "to examine and find out upon what it bottoms."[69] Here he delivered a broader and more devastating condemnation of topical argument than he had previously done.

> Most of the Difficulties [he said] that come in our way, when well consider'd and trac'd, lead us to some Proposition, which known to be true, clears the Doubt, and gives an easie Solution of the Question, whilst Topical and Superficial Arguments, of which there is store to be found on both sides, filling the Head with variety of Thoughts, and the Mouth with copious Discourse, serve only to amuse the Understanding, and entertain Company without coming to the bottom of the Question, the only place of Rest and Stability for an inquisitive Mind, whose tendency is only to Truth and Knowledge.

Locke did not concede that the topics might be useful in teaching youngsters to write Latin compositions in support of propositions which on the one hand were deemed true in the eyes of the learned and on the other were considered difficult to handle when the student was not allowed to discuss them in his native tongue. Indeed, the chief use of the topics had historically been to encourage fluency in Latin within a culture which regarded the acquisition of that language as a necessary part of learning and religion;

[68] *Ibid.*, p. 54.   [69] *Ibid.*, p. 127.

and within such a context the topics possessed a real but limited value. Even there, however, they encouraged the idea that the verbal copiousness which they sought to produce was a desirable end in itself, when as a matter of fact it is a desirable end only when it is coupled with the highest regard for accuracy and consistency of verbal statement. Since Locke's whole emphasis was upon the need to develop in students a true respect for these two latter qualities, it is understandable that he would not think highly of an educational machinery which would overlook them in order to give undue stress to some lesser goal.

The final characteristic of the new British logic of the eighteenth century was the belief that truth is achieved when verbal statements correspond to the factual states with which they are dealing. William Barron, professor of logic, rhetoric, and metaphysics at St. Andrews between 1778 and 1803, was one of the new logicians who defined this theme with great clarity and directness. Said he:

> Truth relates to the enunciation of knowledge, and is the agreement of ideas with words. If I assert that the British is a free government, and that the English are more industrious than any other nation in Europe, I maintain truth, because my words actually correspond to accurate ideas of the facts.[70]

There can be no doubt that Barron had Locke's *Essay* in mind when he defined truth in this way, inasmuch as his definition bears a striking resemblance to Locke's own as set forth in Chapter v of Book iv. That chapter, which is entitled "Of Truth in general," begins by remarking that, since truth is what all men search for or at least pretend to search for, its exact nature is something that requires careful examination, so that we may understand in what it consists, and how the mind may distinguish it from falsehood. At this point, Locke defined truth as follows:

> *Truth* then seems to me, in the proper import of the Word, to signify nothing but *the joining or separating of Signs, as the Things signified by them, do agree or disagree one with another.* The *joining* or *separating* of signs here meant is what by another name, we call Proposition. So that Truth properly belongs only to Propositions: whereof there are two sorts, *viz.*

[70] *Lectures on Belles Lettres and Logic*, ii, 412.

Mental and Verbal; as there are two sorts of Signs commonly made use of, *viz. Ideas* and Words.[71]

This definition led Locke to speak of two aspects of truth: truth of thought, in which our ideas of things correspond to the things themselves, and truth of words, in which our ideas of things and our words about those ideas also correspond. Having discussed various troublesome questions connected with the understanding of these aspects, Locke returned once more to his main subject and once more he spoke of the nature of the concept of truth.

Truth [he said] is the marking down in Words, the agreement or disagreement of *Ideas* as it is. *Falshood* is the marking down in Words, the agreement or disagreement of *Ideas* otherwise than it is. And so far as these *Ideas*, thus marked by Sounds, agree to their Archtypes, so far only is the *Truth real*. The knowledge of this Truth, consists in knowing what *Ideas* the Words stand for, and the perception of the agreement or disagreement of those *Ideas*, according as it is marked by those Words.[72]

In the old logic, truth was acknowledged also to be the accurate correspondence between verbal propositions and factual states, but the acknowledgment tended always to be obscured or supplanted by the tidier belief that truth was achieved when a particular statement could be shown to have issued from a pre-existing self-evident axiom. In other words, as I indicated earlier, the old logic was prevailingly interested in defining truth in terms of consistency whereas Locke and his school preferred to define it in terms of accuracy. Nowhere is the difference between the old and the new logic more significant and more interesting than it is on this particular issue.[73]

---

[71] *Essay concerning Humane Understanding*, p. 344.

[72] *Ibid.*, p. 346.

[73] For other studies of Locke's contribution to logic, see the following: Blakey, *Historical Sketch of Logic*, pp. 271-282; Eduard Martinak, *Zur Logik Lockes: John Lockes Lehre von den Vorstellungen aus dem Essay concerning Human Understanding* (Graz, 1887); Walther Küppers, *John Locke und die Scholastik* (Berlin, 1895); A. Tellkamp, *Das Verhältnis John Locke's zur Scholastik* (Münster in Westfalen, 1927), pp. 34-45; W. & M. Kneale, *The Development of Logic*, pp. 312-313.

The anonymous treatise, *Lectures on Locke: or, the Principles of Logic*:

5. THE NEW LOGIC

The time has now come to turn to a particular study of the development of the new logic in eighteenth-century Britain. I should like to stress again that the influence of Locke in that development was gradual and cumulative rather than immediate. But it was inexorable and triumphant. Before the century ended, Locke's followers succeeded in doing what Molyneux had wanted done—they gave the universities a logic couched in another sort of language than that which had previously prevailed to the great hindrance of science.

---

designed for the Use of Students in the University (London, 1840), I have not seen. Nor have I examined William Knighton, *The Utility of the Aristotelian Logic; or the Remarks of Bacon, Locke, Reid and Stewart on that Subject considered; being the Substance of Three Lectures delivered to the Senior Students of the Hindu College, Calcutta* (Calcutta, 1847).

III   Other Voices: Le Clerc, Crousaz, Watts, Duncan, Wolff

As Locke's friend Molyneux pointed out in 1692, Jean Le Clerc's *Logica*, which had just appeared in print, bore unmistakable evidence of having borrowed some of its doctrines from Locke's *Essay concerning Human Understanding*. What makes this remark of interest to the historian of British logic is that the first of the several editions of Le Clerc's *Logica* appeared simultaneously in Amsterdam and London, thus becoming an immediate influence upon the reading public in Great Britain, and an immediate witness there to the value of Locke's *Essay* in the field of logical doctrine.[74] And when we notice, as we should do, that no printed logic anywhere in the world was earlier than Le Clerc's in calling attention to the logical value of the *Essay*, we have some reason to give Le Clerc's treatise the initial place in this section of the present chapter.

Le Clerc, a Protestant theologian and classical scholar, was born in Geneva in 1657, and he died in 1736 in Amsterdam, where he had settled in 1683 after spending a half-year preaching with success at the Walloon Church and the Savoy Chapel in London.[75] His occupation in Amsterdam was that of professor of phi-

[74] The title page of the first London edition reads as follows: "Logica: sive, Ars Ratiocinandi. Avctore, Joanne Clerico. . . . Londini, Impensis *Awnsham & Johan. Churchill*, apud Insigne *Nigri Cygni* in *Pater-Noster-Row*. 1692." This work is the first item in a volume also containing Le Clerc's *Ontologia* and *Pneumatologia*. The Edinburgh University Library holds a copy of the first Amsterdam edition of the *Logica* (1692), and also a copy of the fourth edition in England (Cantabrigiae, Typis Academicis, 1704). Notice of an English translation was entered in the Stationers' Registers on June 30, 1692, and was phrased thus: "*Logick, or, the Art of reasoning* in two parts. Written in Latin by John Clerke and put into English." See [George E. B. Eyre and Charles R. Rivington], *A Transcript of the Registers of the Worshipful Company of Stationers; From 1640-1708 A.D.* (London, 1913-1914), III, 404. A pamphlet entitled *An Account of the Life and Writings of Mr. John Le Clerc, . . . To this present Year M DCCXI* (London, 1712), sig. *1r-*2r, does not list such a translation, nor have I been able to prove that it was actually made. A copy of the first London edition of the Latin work is held by the Clark Library in Los Angeles.

[75] For additional details, consult the articles on Le Clerc in *Biographie Universelle, Nouvelle Biographie Générale, La Grande Encyclopédie*, and the *Encyclopaedia Britannica* (11th edn.).

losophy, literature, and ecclesiastical history at the Remonstrant Seminary; but he was also active between 1686 and 1726 as editor of three successive journals devoted to reviews of or excerpts from books published recently or formerly in the various countries of the European community. The first of these journals, the *Bibliothèque Universelle et Historique*, was issued each month from January, 1686, to December, 1693. It was superseded by the *Bibliothèque Choisie*, which came forth twice each year between 1703 and 1713. That in turn was superseded between 1714 and 1726 by another biyearly journal, the *Bibliothèque Ancienne et Moderne*. These periodicals made Le Clerc well known in the intellectual circles of Europe and America, and they brought him into contact with various famous personages, one of whom was John Locke.

Indeed, the January issue of the *Bibliothèque Universelle et Historique* for 1688 contained as its longest single item a condensed French version of Locke's *Essay concerning Human Understanding*. Le Clerc, to whom Locke had been introduced by the Dutch theologian Philip van Limborch in the winter of 1686 in Amsterdam, was instrumental not only in persuading Locke to publish an epitome of the *Essay* at a time when it was known only by rumor in learned circles, but also in becoming with Locke's consent the translator who put into French the condensation prepared by Locke in English.[76] The epitome published in Le Clerc's journal bore the following descriptive head:

Extrait d'un Livre Anglois qui n'est pas encore publié, intitulé ESSAI PHILOSOPHIQUE *concernant* L'ENTENDEMENT, *où l'on montre quelle est l'étenduë de nos connoissances certaines, & la maniere dont nous y parvenons.* Communiqué par Monsieur Locke.[77]

What followed occupies 94 of the 173 small pages of that issue of the journal.[78] A single page of the epitome is devoted to what would become in standard eighteenth-century editions of the *Essay* some 43 large pages constituting its first book. The most important sentence on that page is one which says that "I have

[76] See Bourne, *Life of John Locke*, II, 42, 99-100. See also Christophersen, p. 12.
[77] *Bibliothèque Universelle et Historique*, VIII (January 1688), 49.
[78] The epitome begins on page 49 and ends on page 142.

first undertaken to prove that our mind is in the beginning what one would call a *tabula rasa*; that is to say, without ideas and without knowledge."[79] Book II, which in final form would occupy some 200 pages divided among 33 chapters, is epitomized in 38 pages. Here, and throughout the rest of his work, Le Clerc gave his paragraphs Roman numerals to indicate their relation to Locke's similarly numbered chapters. The epitome of Book III extends to 25 pages and 10 numbered sections, and these contain the doctrines set forth in 83 pages and 11 chapters of Locke's final text. Le Clerc devoted 30 pages and 20 numbered paragraphs to Book IV, which in Locke's full essay would contain 132 pages and 21 chapters.

But this description shows only the quantitative aspect of the curtailment which the doctrine of the *Essay* underwent in the French epitome. The qualitative aspect also needs a word of comment. In 1688 the *Essay* had not yet reached its completed form in Locke's mind, and thus the epitome which he submitted to Le Clerc was a reduced version of something not yet fully worked out. Such a version would inevitably be incomplete in emphasizing the basic points of the final work. Nowhere is this incompleteness more important for the historian of logic than it is in the treatment which the epitome gives to Locke's ultimate criticism of the syllogism. As we know, Chapter XVII of Book IV of the final text of the *Essay* is devoted to this subject, and it covers 14 large significant pages of some eighteenth-century texts. In Le Clerc's epitome this chapter appeared as a paragraph containing 30 lines of text occupying part of one page and part of the next. These lines begin by emphasizing that reasoning has four parts: that of discovering proofs, that of arranging them in the order in which they have to be put in finding truth, that of perceiving more or less clearly the connection between ideas in each part of the deduction, and that of making a right judgment and of drawing a just conclusion from what has gone before. Then the epitome concludes its discussion of reason with these words:

From this it appears that the syllogism is not the great instrument of the reasoning faculty, that it only serves in the third part and solely again to show to others that the connection of

[79] *Ibid.*, p. 49. Translation mine. Christophersen is in error in saying that the epitome ignores Book I of the *Essay*.

two ideas, or rather of two terms, is good or bad by reason of the intervention of a third term. But the syllogism does not serve the reason in any way when it searches out any new knowledge whatever, or when it wishes to discover any truth previously unknown and the proofs upon which that truth is founded, these being the principal uses which one ought to make of his reason, as opposed to that of winning in a dispute or of reducing to silence those who wish to indulge in sophistry.[80]

These sentiments are certainly in harmony with those later to be developed in the final version of the *Essay*, but they need elaboration before they can be said to present an effective case against the syllogism or a proper case for inference as the most basic form of reasoning. Thus the capacity of the epitome to influence syllogistic theory would not appear to be great.

Le Clerc's *Logica* perfectly illustrates this latter observation. In an address to the reader of the work, Le Clerc was careful to specify what authorities he had consulted in writing each of its four parts. I should mention here that the first part deals with individual ideas and their linguistic equivalents, logical terms; the second part, with judgments and propositions; the third part, with method, whether analytic or synthetic; and the fourth part, with argument and syllogisms. Here is what Le Clerc said of his sources for Part I:

> Those things taught in Part I in connection with the seven species of ideas are customarily omitted altogether in other logics or are touched only in a light and perfunctory way. But nevertheless my readers will not deny, I hope, that such matters are of moment when the subject of simple perception is under analysis. For the rest, that I may not fail in frankness and ungratefully become guilty of a sin of the spirit, I shall publicly confess that I owe a very great deal to a distinguished book, written in English, to which its most modest and most acute author has given the title, *Essay concerning the Understanding*. When I first wrote the present treatise, I had seen his Epitome, from which I have obviously drawn many teachings, nor have I drawn from its stated principles merely a few implications,

[80] *Ibid.*, p. 137. Translation mine.

and I have distributed them in this book and throughout my whole work.[81]

The two other authorities whom Le Clerc mentioned in his preface are *The Port-Royal Logic* and Nicolas Malebranche's *De la Recherche de la Verité*.[82] The former of these works, said Le Clerc, supplied most of what he had to say about the synthetic method; and the latter had helped him in his discussion of the analytic method and of the uses and capacities of the mind. Le Clerc did not specify an authority for his second topic, judgment, or for his fourth topic, argument or syllogism. But his treatment of the syllogism obviously owed much to *The Port-Royal Logic,* and that famous and influential work gave him, indeed, his very

[81] *Logica* (London, 1692), sig. *3v. Translation mine. In later editions Le Clerc identified the "most modest and most acute author" as "Joannes Lockius." See his *Opera Philosophica in Quatuor Volumina Digesta* (Amsterdam, 1710), Vol. 1, sig. *10v. Le Clerc's Latin acknowledgement of his debt to the epitome reads thus in his first edition: "Caeterùm ne in ingenuitatem peccemus, ingrative animi peccatum admittamus, eximio libro Anglicè scripto, cui *Tentamen de Intellectu* modestissimus idémque acutissimus Scriptor Titulum fecit, plurima nos debere profitebimur. Cùm haec primùm scripsimus, Ejus Epitomen videramus, ex qua multa diserrè tradita hausimus, nec paucas, ex admissis Principiis consequentias deduximus; quae cùm in hoc Libro, tum per totum Opus sparsae sunt."

Le Clerc dedicated the first edition of the *Logica* to Robert Boyle and the accompanying *Ontologia* and *Pneumatologia* to Locke. In a letter addressed to Locke under the date of January 20, 1692, he announced that he had done these two things, and he spoke thus concerning the second: "J'ai fait dessein, si vous ne le trouver pas mauvais, de vous dédier l'*Ontologie*, et la *Pneumatologie*, où j'ai infiniment profité de vos lumières comme vous le verrez, et comme je l'ai déjà dit dans la Préface de ma Logique, où j'ai marqué votre ouvrage, comme l'un de ceux qui m'ont le plus servi." See *Lettres Inédites de Le Clerc à Locke,* ed., with an Introduction and Notes, by Gabriel Bonno, University of California Publications in Modern Philology, LII (Berkeley and Los Angeles, 1959), p. 49. Le Clerc dedicated later editions of all three of these works to Locke. *Ibid.*, pp. 103, 107.

[82] Malebranche's *De la Recherche de la Verité* was first published at Paris in 1674. Le Clerc spoke thus of *The Port-Royal Logic* (translation mine): "In Part III, in connection with whatever method, be it the synthetic or the analytic, that is customarily used in doing however many things, I have taken steps to follow at greater length and more accurately the example of a work written in French called the *Logic of Port-Royal*. I have drawn by turns from that book and from many others which deal with the synthetic method, but for the most part I have illustrated the doctrines by my own examples."

conception of the four parts into which logicians should divide their subject, although he did not treat these parts in the exact order which the Port-Royalists had followed. The only originality which Le Clerc claimed for his *Logica*, indeed, was that of appending a chapter of Part IV on the Socratic method of disputing. His treatment of the syllogism is conventional, and to him induction is merely an irregular form of syllogistic reasoning.[83] It is not likely that he would have remained undisturbed in his discussion of these crucial matters if he had studied the full final text of Chapter XVII of Book IV of the *Essay*. But the version of that chapter in the epitome is not such as to make the syllogism appear to need drastic reconsideration.

Thus Molyneux, who saw Le Clerc's *Logica* after having become thoroughly familiar himself with the full text of Locke's *Essay* in its first edition, was of course justified in preferring Locke's own logical theories to Le Clerc's borrowings from them. But had he known that Le Clerc had borrowed from the epitome rather than the full *Essay*, he would have understood Le Clerc's limitations to be the primary result of a failure in scholarship, not in insight.

Jean-Pierre de Crousaz, a compatriot and admirer of Le Clerc, would not have had a place in the history of eighteenth-century British logic if he had not attracted the attention of the heterodox Englishman already mentioned in these pages. That Englishman was John Henley.[84] Two years before Henley renounced his career in the established church to found The Oratory in Newport Market, London, and to become the self-styled restorer of the ancient elocution to the English pulpit, he added to his growing list of publications a two-volume work entitled *A New Treatise of the Art of Thinking; Or, A Compleat System of Reflections, Concerning the Conduct and Improvement of the Mind*.[85] This

---

[83] *Logica*, p. 167. [84] See above, Ch. 4, pp. 193-203.

[85] "London: Printed for Tho. Woodward at the *Half-Moon* over-against St. *Dunstan's* Church in *Fleet-Street*. M.DCC.XXIV." Henley's name does not appear anywhere in this work. We know, however, that he was the translator through his having claimed that office for himself in 1724 in a pamphlet bibliography of his own writings. For the title of that pamphlet, and for the title of the periodical in which Henley repeated the claim, see above, Ch. 4, p. 194 and n. 122. Jacqueline E. de La Harpe, *Jean-Pierre de Crousaz (1663-1750)*, University of California Publications in Modern Philology, XLVII (Berkeley

work declared itself to be a translation from the French of Mr. Crousaz, professor of philosophy and mathematics in the academy of Lausanne. In actual fact, Crousaz was at that time leaving Lausanne to become a member of the faculty of the University of Groningen in the Netherlands; but he was of Swiss origin, and he did teach at Lausanne in the earlier and the later stages of a long academic career, which ended in 1749, the year before his death.[86] The work which Henley translated in 1724 had been published originally at Amsterdam twelve years earlier, and in 1720, now called *La Logique* in its main title, it had been given a corrected and expanded edition in that same city.[87] This latter text, by the way, is the basis of Henley's translation.[88] In the very era in which Henley was seeing his version appear under Thomas Woodward's auspices in London, a two-volume Latin version of the parent work came forth in Geneva,[89] and three later editions of its complete French text and two editions of a French and one of a Latin abridgment, were due to be printed by 1746. Thus it had a much larger vogue in Europe than in England, where Henley's translation never reached a second edition, substantial and meritorious as it was.

Even in 1724, Henley could not claim to be the only Briton to

---

and Los Angeles, 1955), pp. 29, 270, attributes this translation to Benjamin Hoadly, I know not on what grounds. Her useful book I cite below as La Harpe.

[86] La Harpe, pp. 67-89, 113.

[87] The title of the first edition is as follows: *Système de Réflexions qui peuvent contribuer à la netteté et à l'étendue de nos connaissances, ou Nouvel Essai de Logique* (Amsterdam: F. L'Honoré, 1712). In the second edition the title page reads thus: "La Logique ou Systeme de Reflexions, Qui peuvent contribuer à la netteté & à l'étendue de nos Connoissances. . . . Seconde Edition revue, corrigée & augmentée considerablement. A Amsterdam. Chez L'Honoré & Chatelain. M. DCC XX."

[88] Crousaz dedicated the second edition of *La Logique* to Prince Louis of Hesse-Darmstadt. Henley's translation does not contain the dedicatory epistle, but otherwise it follows the text of the second edition, as a comparison of the two works shows.

[89] Its title page reads: "Ioh. Petri De Crosa, In Academia Lavsannensi, Philos. et Matheseos Professoris, Logicae Systema, Juxta Principia ab ipso in Gallico Opere posita; Nunc Latine conscriptum, emendatum, novis Observationibus ornatum, atque etiam, ubi conducibile visum est, ad usum Scholae paulò planiùs accommodatum. Genevae Apud Gabrielem De Tournes & Filios. M.DCC.XXIV." Cited below as *Logicae Systema*.

have reason to know who Crousaz was. It had happened in the year 1720 that the brilliant young Irish philosopher George Berkeley was returning homeward from the Continent and, while pausing at Lyons, engaged himself in writing a tract entitled *De Motu*, which he is thought to have submitted that year to the Royal Academy of Sciences in Paris in competition for a prize announced by the Academy for essays in the field of physics.[90] Berkeley did not win that particular prize. It was awarded instead to Professor Crousaz of Lausanne, who at the time was fifty-seven years old, while Berkeley was thirty-five. The works on which Berkeley's fame as a philosopher was to rest had already been published, but they had not yet gained wide acceptance at home or abroad. Anyway, they were not in competition for the prize which Crousaz received in 1721.

Many years later Crousaz was to become known in England in still another connection. In 1737 he published in French an essay criticizing the philosophical system espoused by Alexander Pope in the famous "Essay on Man." That criticism was soon issued at London in an English translation. Pope was dismayed when it appeared, and he was grateful when William Warburton answered it.[91] One is tempted to think that Pope's reputation would not have suffered serious damage if the criticisms by the Swiss logician had gone unanswered, but there can be no doubt that the debate between Warburton and Crousaz made the latter a more familiar person in England than he would otherwise have been, despite his having already had an English public for his *Art of Thinking* during fourteen years.

[90] See Alexander C. Fraser, *Life and Letters of George Berkeley*, D.D. (Oxford, 1871), pp. 85-86; also *The Works of George Berkeley*, ed. Luce and Jessop, IV, 3. See also La Harpe, pp. 43-45.

[91] See *An Examination of Mr. Pope's Essay on Man. Translated from the French of M. Crousaz* [by Elizabeth Carter] (London, 1739); see also *A Vindication of Mr. Pope's Essay on Man, from the Misrepresentations of Mr. De Crousaz* [by William Warburton] (London, 1740). Another examination of Crousaz's attack on Pope, entitled *A Commentary on Mr. Pope's Principles of Morality, or Essay on Man, By Monsr. Crousaz* (London, 1742) is attributed to Dr. Johnson; see *Boswell's Life of Johnson* (Oxford, 1934-1950), IV, 495. For another contribution by Johnson to the Pope-Crousaz controversy, see *The Works of Samuel Johnson* (Troy, N. Y., 1903), XII, 116-120. This first appeared as a Letter to the Editor, Mr. Urban, in *The Gentleman's Magazine*, XIII (1743), 152, 587-588.

This particular public was probably increased to some extent by a remark which Dr. Samuel Johnson made in 1748. That was the year when Robert Dodsley's *The Preceptor* came out in its first edition. A two-volume work designed to introduce young men and women to polite learning, *The Preceptor* contained twelve treatises of uneven quality, the best one of them being William Duncan's *The Elements of Logick*, which I shall discuss later. To this volume, as I have already indicated, Dr. Johnson contributed the preface, in which among other things he recommended that, if readers needed further help in logic beyond Duncan's treatise, they ought properly to take up the study of Crousaz, Watts, Le Clerc, Wolfius, and Locke's *Essay concerning Human Understanding*; "and if there be imagined any Necessity," he continued, "of adding the Peripatetic Logic, which has been perhaps condemned without a candid Trial, it will be convenient to proceed to *Sanderson, Wallis, Crackanthorp*, and *Aristotle*."[92] Why Dr. Johnson's list of Peripatetic logics available in England in the seventeenth and eighteenth centuries should have omitted Aldrich's popular *Artis Logicae Compendium* is something of a mystery, but otherwise he named the leading traditional and progressive logics of the age. Certainly he went beyond mere routine orthodoxy in including Locke's *Essay*, but he is safely within the accepted canon when he mentions Crousaz's *Art of Thinking*.

One more English comment upon Crousaz as a logician deserves to be remembered here before we turn to a discussion of the *Art of Thinking* itself. This time the comment comes from Edward Gibbon, author of the great eighteenth-century classic, *The History of the Decline and Fall of the Roman Empire*. Between 1753 and 1758, the young Gibbon was in residence in Lausanne, where he studied under Daniel Pavillard, a Calvinist minister, himself a disciple of Crousaz. Gibbon spoke of the earlier days of these studies in the following words:

> The first text of my philosophical studies, the book which taught me the use and conduct of my understanding, was the Logic of Mr. de Crousaz, a native and Professor of Lausanne, who died about five years before my arrival. His reputation is

---

[92] *The Preceptor*, I, xxv-xxvi. This work is also cited above, Ch. 2, p. 22, and Ch. 3, p. 139. Johnson's Preface is republished in his *Works*. See the edition just cited, XII, 154-175.

already faded; but his moderate and methodical writings were useful in their day to form the reason, the taste, and even the style of his countrymen; and he rescued the clergy of the Pays de Vaud from the heavy and intolerant yoke of the theology of Calvin. After I had transfused into my own mind the principles of Crousaz, as soon as I possessed some dexterity in the use of the weapons of arguments, I ventured to engage with his adversary Bayle, and his master Locke, the former of whom may be applied as a spur, and the latter as a bridle to the curiosity of a young philosopher. I carefully meditated the Essay on the Human Understanding, and I freely revolved the most interesting articles of the Critical dictionary.[93]

In still another attempt in his *Memoirs* to assess his debt to Crousaz, Gibbon said:

His System of Logic, which in the last editions has swelled to six tedious and prolix volumes, may be praised as a clear and methodical abridgement of the art of reasoning, from our simple ideas to the most complex operations of the human understanding. This system I studied, and meditated, and abstracted, till I have obtained the free command of an universal instrument, which I soon presumed to exercise on my catholic opinions.[94]

Gibbon had been converted to Catholicism at Oxford in 1753, and his outraged father had sent him at once to Lausanne to induce him to reacknowledge Protestantism. It is noteworthy that he returned to his father's faith in December, 1754, and that Crousaz had a part in that historic change of mind. Gibbon's reference in the passage just quoted is to the *Logique* in its last two editions, published respectively in 1741 and 1746 in six volumes.[95] There had been four volumes in the third edition, three in the second,

[93] *The Autobiographies of Edward Gibbon*, ed. John Murray, 2nd edn. (London, 1897), p. 234. Cited below as *Autobiographies*. See also *The Autobiography of Edward Gibbon*, ed. Oliphant Smeaton, Everyman's Library, pp. 64-65, 67, 72; also D. M. Low, *Edward Gibbon 1737-1794* (New York, 1937), pp. 46, 58, 67.

[94] *Autobiographies*, p. 136; also p. 397.

[95] The fourth edition was published in 1741 at Lausanne and Geneva. I have not seen a copy of the edition of 1746. Its existence is attested by the articles on Crousaz in the *Biographie Universelle*, the *Nouvelle Biographie Générale*, and *La Grande Encyclopédie*.

and two in the first. Thus Gibbon saw considerably more of Crousaz's complete work than the English readers of Henley's translation would have seen. But Gibbon was interested at Lausanne not only in subjecting his religious opinions to the test of a well-regarded system of logic but also in giving himself an easy mastery of French; and his labors with six volumes of a French text would accordingly have seemed doubly productive to his studious ambitions.

The *Art of Thinking*, so far as the two volumes of Henley's translation are concerned, runs to 919 pages, exclusive of the preface, the tables of contents, the index, and two lists of the publisher's other current productions, one list being at the end of the first volume, and the other at the beginning of the second.[96] The 491 actual pages of logical doctrine in the first volume are concerned not only with a definition of logic and with the dividing of the subject into four parts but also with a treatise upon the first part in two of its three major aspects. The 428 pages of the second volume are distributed so as to devote 98 pages to the rest of the discussion of the first part of logic and to handle each of the other three parts. Thus it becomes immediately obvious that Crousaz lavished almost two-thirds of his total space upon the first quarter of his subject, as if in his opinion it represented the logician's paramount concern, while the other three-quarters even in alliance with each other are made to seem insignificant by comparison.

Logic, or the art of thinking, declared Crousaz by way of defining his subject, "is a *System* of such Principles, Observations, and Maxims, as are able to furnish the human Understanding with a greater Degree of Penetration, Force, Extent, Exactness, and Readiness either to discover Truth of it self, or to comprehend it when proposed to it by others, or, lastly, to communicate it to them in its Turn upon its own Discovery."[97] The human understanding, in other words, is endowed by nature with the power to discover, comprehend, and communicate truth. As a formal discipline, logic proposes to collect and systematize the principles which govern the understanding in its natural exercise of these

[96] The copy in the Princeton University Library is exactly like that in the British Museum, except that it lacks the two-page list of Woodward's publications in Volume II.

[97] *Art of Thinking*, I, 2.

three capacities. The discovery of truth and the communication of truth to others are, however, the important operational concepts within this definition, comprehension being involved in both of them; and the second of these concepts brings logic and rhetoric into close relations with each other.

As for the systematizing of these governing principles, Crousaz proposed that they would be found to belong to one of four basic operations of the human mind. His own words upon this matter deserve our attention:

> In the first Place are form'd our *Perceptions*, that are called *Simple*, because they are only the Representation of Objects, without determining any thing about them, either affirmatively or negatively. . . . Afterwards we compare our Perceptions together, and observe their Connexion, or Opposition, which is call'd *Judging*. . . . In the same manner, as we compare our Perceptions in order to form our Judgments, we also compare our Judgments together, and from thence draw a Conclusion, which is call'd *Reasoning*. . . . *Lastly*, By rightly disposing a great Number of Thoughts, Reflections, Reasonings, Principles, and Conclusions, we form what is call'd a *Discourse*; and to succeed the better in the right ordering of so many different Parts, a certain *Method* is necessary: And this is the fourth Operation of the Understanding, to which Rules must be prescribed. And with respect to these four general Differences in our way of Thinking, we should divide *Logic* (according to some celebrated Authors) into four principal Parts.[98]

The celebrated authors referred to here could well have been Le Clerc, the Port-Royalists, and Gassendi. Their logics were divided into these same four parts. But the Port-Royalists, in particular, were so influential during the lifetime of Crousaz that most progressive logics followed their lead in this matter, as indeed Le Clerc himself had done. In regard to Crousaz, the Preface to the Latin edition of his *Logique* failed to mention Gassendi, but he did mention the Port-Royalists and Le Clerc, and it is obvious from what he said on that occasion that he considered them worthy of emulation in general.[99] Thus it is not surprising that he

[98] *Ibid.*, I, 2-3.
[99] *Logicae Systema*, I, sig. t7r. See below, pp. 326f., for his tribute to Le Clerc and the Port-Royalists. He spoke thus in Latin about the latter: "Feliciore

followed them in establishing perception, judgment, reasoning, and discourse as the focal points of logical doctrine.

Perceptions, as Crousaz understood the term, consist of sensations, on the one hand, or of ideas, on the other.[100] A sensation is a perception which has nothing but itself as its object. Thus if one feels thirst, or pain, or desire, one has a perception, but the perception does not have an object apart from itself. An idea, however, is a perception which has itself as one of its objects, and something different from itself as its other object. One sees a tree, for example, and one is aware not only of the act of perceiving but of the tree which is perceived. "In order therefore to understand the Things which exist without us," said Crousaz, "we must consult our Ideas, rather than our Sensations. By our Sensations we become acquainted with *our selves*, and our own Condition; but our Ideas lead us to the Discovery of *Nature*, and of the Condition of *Things*, quite different from our selves."[101] "The Course of this Work," added Crousaz, "will furnish us with divers Occasions to distinguish these two Methods of Thinking, and sufficiently evince the Necessity of this Distinction."[102]

The actual plan which Crousaz followed in discussing perceptions led to his analyzing them in relation to the mental faculties which produce them, in relation to the objects which they have, and in relation to the manner in which they take place. "These three Things, *Faculty*, *Object*, and *Manner of perceiving*, are the Sources of the Varieties of our Ideas," he declared; "and we shall lay down just so many general Heads, to which we shall in course refer our Remarks and Rules."[103] The first of these heads brings together his remarks upon the faculty of the understanding, of the senses, of the imagination, of the will, of the inclinations and passions, and of the memory. The treatment of these aspects of mental power occupies 278 pages of the first volume of Henley's translation. The second head occupies the remaining 199 pages of that volume, and it is devoted to an analysis of the two sorts of objects which perceptions have. "Those that have their *own Existence*, a *separate Existence*, are call'd *Substances*," ex-

---

successu *Ars cogitandi* prodiit, cujus iteratae Editiones in aetatis nostrae laudem meritò citabuntur."

[100] *Art of Thinking*, I, 10.

[101] *Ibid.*, I, 11-12.   [102] *Ibid.*, I, 12.   [103] *Ibid.*, I, 14.

plained Crousaz; "and we call *Modes* those Realities, which have not a separate Existence, and the Existence whereof is the same with the Existence of the Reality, of which they are Modes."[104] A piece of wax, for example, is a substance so far as its waxenness is concerned, Crousaz said; but it is a mode so far as it has a shape or figure of roundness or squareness, or the like. The third head under which perceptions are discussed takes up the first 98 pages of the second volume, and here Crousaz treated perceptions in relation to the manner in which men think of realities. After reminding his readers that his previous concern had been to account for the diversity in perceptions by tracing it to diversity in mental faculties or in objects perceived, he spoke as follows about his third heading:

> If we reflect never so little upon our own Experience, we shall be likewise convinced, that according to the different Degrees of Attention, and according as we treat a Subject with more or less Order, the Ideas we form of it, are more or less accomplished, or more or less perplexed. We must reduce to different Classes the Differences arising from that third Cause, and go on with our Endeavours to make each of our Ways of Thinking as just as possible.[105]

In covering this phase of the theory of perception, Crousaz treated clear and obscure ideas, distinct and confused ideas, simple and compound ideas, abstract ideas, general and determinate ideas, the five predicables of scholastic logic, and such other matters as total, partial, full, exact, imperfect, complete, and incomplete ideas. Special stress upon the logical term as the verbal equivalent of the logical idea and the logical perception occurs in the analysis given by Crousaz to the topics just enumerated.[106] Only when each of these topics had been handled did he feel that perception as the first part of logic had received its full measure of attention.

The second part of logic is considered by Crousaz to be an operation which produces not only an inward judgment upon the relation of two perceptions to each other but also an external record of that judgment in the form of a verbal statement. "The Act I now explain, when considered as within the Mind," said

---

104 *Ibid.*, I, 294.   105 *Ibid.*, II, 2.
106 *Ibid.*, II, 27-61, 81-86, 87-94.

Crousaz, "is called a Judgment; but when expressed, it is a Proposition."[107] "Therefore, when we judge," he summarized, "we have, 1. At least two Ideas. 2. We compare them. 3. We perceive, that the first contains the second, or excludes it; and lastly, we acquiesce in that Perception."[108] He proceeded then to discuss propositions both affirmative and negative, both true and false, both certain and uncertain. He had something to say of probabilities, of Pyrrhonism, of principles, of prejudices, and of false judgments. And of course he spoke severally of singular, of universal, and of particular propositions, and of propositions in compound or complex forms. "The famous Chancellor *Bacon*, who lived in an Age, when Men loved to speak after an extraordinary Manner, and who had accustomed himself to it, from the Schools," said Crousaz in his discussion of biased opinions, "has imposed singular Names on Prejudices, which have something mysterious, but at the same time ingenious, solid, and grand."[109] This remark led Crousaz to speak of what Bacon had called Idols—Idola Tribus, Idola Fori, Idola Specus, and Idola Theatri.[110] A willingness to accept Bacon as having relevance to the theory of logic is one more indication that Crousaz belongs in part among the new logicians of the eighteenth century. A traditionalist like Aldrich, it will be remembered, had denied that Bacon's *Novum Organum* had any connection with Aristotle's *Organon* except the title.[111] Still another indication of the incipient modernity of Crousaz is seen in his willingness to dismiss some of the hallowed dogmas of the scholastic logicians. Said he of them as he concluded his discussion of judgment:

> I will pass by the Subtilties in which they have taken a pleasure to indulge themselves about the Reduction of Propositions. I own, I should be tempted to expose the Follies that amused the old Schools to my Reader, did I know that he would reap from this reading the important Advantage of suspecting what passed thro' their Hands, and taking nothing from them without Examination. . . . What they teach likewise about Oppositions, Contradictories, Contraries, Subcontraries, does not seem to me to be of any Service. When I know how to examine the Truth of a Proposition in itself, I have nothing to do to inform

[107] *Ibid.*, II, 102.   [108] *Ibid.*, II, 105.   [109] *Ibid.*, II, 149.
[110] *Ibid.*, II, 149-150.   [111] See above, Ch. 2, p. 12.

myself, whether it be contradictory, contrary, or subcontrary to others that are true or false. To what purpose is it to know that this, *Every man is mortal*, being true, its Contradictory, *Some Man is not mortal*, is false. . . ? How, say I, do I assure myself of all this? I form to myself exact Ideas of every Subject, and Attribute, and I compare them together. The general Rule being therefore of clear, easy, and immediate Use, why should I load myself with pretended Helps, that are still more puzzling, and themselves draw their Force from the general Rule.[112]

Reasoning, Crousaz indicated as he took up the discussion of the third part of logic, is an extension of the act of judgment. Sometimes we are aware at once that one term in a judgment is included in or excluded from the other, and when this happens, the judgment is perfect without further effort. But sometimes we see the one term and the other without being sure that the second really includes or excludes the first. In this case, we have to enlarge the first term by connecting it to a third term which permits of a connection also with the second. "Thus to clear the Relation of two Ideas by means of a third, that inserts the second into the former," declared Crousaz, "is what we call *Reasoning*."[113] Everything necessary in this operation, he went on, can be reduced to three heads, and he promised to treat them one by one. The first would involve a discussion of the way in which the meaning of the two terms in a given judgment could be defined so that the judgment could be tested for validity; the second, of the way in which an outside third term could be located so as to permit the test for validity to proceed; and the third, of the way in which the third term would have to be connected with the other two terms in order that the test for validity could be properly concluded. Crousaz exactly lived up to his promise in regard to the development of these heads.

Thus he propounded two rules to be followed in clarifying the meaning of a judgment. The first rule consists in resolving any compound terms in the judgment into simple ones, so as to determine whether the judgment involves one question or several.[114] The second rule advises that the terms of each of the questions

---

[112] *Art of Thinking*, II, 190.   [113] *Ibid.*, II, 192.
[114] *Ibid.*, II, 193.

thus located be defined and compared, the definition being put in place of the thing defined, so as to avoid senseless, childish, ill-stated, and unimportant questions.[115] In explaining these two rules, Crousaz offered a number of examples of the ill effects attending controversies in which the terms at issue were not properly simplified and defined.

But even such simplifications and definitions cannot always result in our being sure that one term in the original judgment permits of its alleged connection with the other, and when this happens, we must look for some other term to use in testing that connection. "This third Idea, which must be discovered to form our Reasonings, is called a *Medium*," said Crousaz, "because it is placed, as a Tie, between the two others." "It is likewise called an *Argument*," he added; "a Term used to signify what illustrates, declares, and proves."[116] Since the discovery of this third idea was the heart of the process of research in the old science, it had naturally become also the heart of the old logic and of the old rhetoric. In elaborating it, dialecticians and rhetoricians had called it invention and had accommodated to it a system of topics or commonplaces to which I have already referred.[117] It is characteristic of Crousaz that he rejected the old system of commonplaces as an aid to invention and research and replaced it with two recommendations of his own.

Both of these recommendations concern the intellectual attitude which the investigator should require himself to have. "My first Direction towards the finding out of an Argument," Crousaz observed, "shall be therefore to compare with Attention the Idea of the Subject with that of the Attribute, and make them both present to me: For from this fixed Attention, which I give to the one and the other of these Ideas at the same Time, a third will arise, that will have a Relation to both of them."[118] The other direction has to do with alerting the mind as the investigation proceeds. Crousaz stated it thus:

Experience tells us, that the Fruitfulness of the Mind is very much animated and raised by Questions. A Man therefore must ask himself, what he must know to assure himself of the Rela-

[115] *Ibid.*, II, 200.   [116] *Ibid.*, II, 205.
[117] See above, Ch. 2, pp. 16, 27-28, 37, 48-49; Ch. 3, pp. 95, 97-99, 101.
[118] *Art of Thinking*, II, 205.

tion there is between the Subject of his Question, and the Attribute? What new Light can instruct him in it? What new Idea can clear it? When a Man, filled with this Desire, views a Question, it is an effectual Means to produce within himself what will answer that Desire.[119]

In illustrating the use of these two recommendations, Crousaz outlined a dispute which turned upon the question whether or not any war should ever be thought desirable; and having identified as its third term a situation which on the one hand could be prevented by war and on the other could be seen in itself as a monstrous condition of injustice and usurpation, he concluded that war in this situation must be counted a good.[120]

"The ancient Rhetoricians," said Crousaz in due course, "give Instructions different from ours, to assist us in the finding out of Arguments; I will represent, what a Man may think the most reasonable in their Method."[121] First of all, Crousaz declared, a third term cannot be used to prove the validity or invalidity of an alleged relationship between two other terms unless it has a clear connection with them; and all the imaginable connections which terms may have with each other can be distributed into classes. Thus any given third term will belong to one class of connections or to another. "This," Crousaz emphasized, "is a very true Conclusion; for there is no Argument [that is, no third term] without some Relation to the Question; and no Relation, that is not reducible to some one Class of Places, in which you may search for Reasons; or, of *Common Places*: for indeed these Places were expressed by Titles common to several Arguments, and contained all the general Ideas, that are applicable to many determinate Subjects." Secondly, continued Crousaz, when a third term is being examined to see whether or not it is connected with the other two terms so as to afford assistance in determining their connection with each other, "it is good to call to mind the Rules of that Relation, to which this Argument belongs, and attend to the Force of the Relation (for all are not of equal Force) and the Con-

[119] *Ibid.*, II, 206.

[120] *Ibid.*, II, 206-208. I have simplified Crousaz's argument in order to sharpen its illustrative force.

[121] *Ibid.*, II, 215. My two following quotations are from this same page.

formity of the Argument to all the Rules of that Relation it belongs to. . . ." But in registering these two counts of agreement with the theory behind the actual machinery of commonplaces, Crousaz made it plain that in the first part of his present work he had said everything essential upon the subject of the relation of ideas, one to another, and that many objections could be raised against the painstaking scholastics when they proceeded to elaborate this subject so far as to create a complex apparatus for drawing proofs from similitudes, adjuncts, causes, effects, and the like.[122] His own objections to this traditional lore of the commonplaces Crousaz proceeded to set forth with insight and effectiveness. He filed six objections in all, and they are such as to reveal once more why the doctrine of invention by means of the commonplaces would not survive in modern theories of argumentation and rhetoric.

The first objection to this doctrine, said Crousaz, is that it "cannot afford any great Assistance; for, if the Subject we are upon be but little known, it will not be so easy to know the *Like* to it, the *Opposites*, the *Adjuncts*, and the *Causes*; and if it be well enough known to lead the Mind to reflect, both easily and justly on all these Relations, it will, doubtless, be sufficient to fix our Attention on this Subject, and from our Ideas, thus attentively considered, we shall have a clear Knowledge of it, without the Necessity of distracting ourselves with Common Places."[123]

In the second instance, Crousaz declared, distracting ourselves with the commonplaces will actually prove hurtful, inasmuch as it will divide our attention. We ought to have our whole attention fixed upon the terms which make up the judgment under examination, not upon other matters more or less remote.

Thirdly, the commonplaces yield only general ideas, he went on, whereas ideas precisely connected with the question in hand will come from the study of its actual terms; and also the general ideas have the fatal disadvantage of being contradictory and insufficient:

Let the Question be again about the Justice of War: By looking into the *Common Places, viz.* that of *Causes*, the Effect is un-

[122] *Ibid.*, II, 215, 216; see also I, 354-491, where Crousaz explains his own theory of the relation of ideas to each other.
[123] *Ibid.*, II, 216.

just, if the Cause be unjust; and Pride and Revenge are the Causes of War. The same Common Place will tell us, that Defence against Injustice and Usurpation is a good Plea for War; thus, instead of Uncertainty from Ignorance, we are in doubt, by the Opposition of Arguments; and all this is from an equal Application of the general Idea of a Cause to two opposite Cases. . . . Let a Man make the Trial, or remember those that were made when he was a young Student, and he will own, that after having vainly consulted his Common Places one after another, a little Attention to the Question gradually produced such Ideas in him, as he had looked for elsewhere to no Purpose. He that knows something of the Subject he would reason upon, needs not to consult these Common Places; and he that consults them, can only draw general and insufficient Proofs from them.[124]

The ancient rhetoricians, Crousaz scornfully added, were content with the general and insufficient proofs that the commonplaces gave forth. "Provided they could in a short Time, without imparting any solid Knowledge to their Disciples, (such indeed they wanted themselves) make them talk readily and largely on Subjects they gave them, they were content."[125]

A fourth argument against the commonplaces Crousaz located in their tendency to make students prefer the appearance above the reality of reasoning. "The Art of finding Arguments to dispute upon a Subject that is little known," he remarked, "is deceitful, and only tends to spoil the Reason of a Man." And once students are taught these superficial and false methods of using their reason, they do not abandon them; "they do gravely in their Old Age, what they were taught to do foolishly in their Youth," said Crousaz; "and one Doctor follows the Steps of another, as Geese in a Line." The effect of such teachings is to create in men an ambiguous attitude towards truth. Cicero and Quintilian treated the commonplaces as a part of the theory of rhetoric out of deference to custom, Crousaz remarked, not out of a sense of their value. The case of Cicero is particularly ambiguous. When he praised illustrious orators, he did not commend their use of the commonplaces.

---

[124] *Ibid.*, II, 216-217.
[125] *Ibid.*, II, 217. My two following quotations are from this same page.

Yet he himself [said Crousaz] was much accustomed to this Method; in a View of Honour, and serving his Clients, he was obliged to take upon him all the Causes that were recommended to him: One Refusal would have procured him too many irreconcileable Enemies, since it would have been a Prejudice to their Cause. He likewise shone the brightest in the most equivocal Matters: Therefore he turned his whole Genius to find out and offer those Reasons that were the most feeble in themselves, in Colours the most proper to affect the Audience, upon every Subject, both for and against it. By this means his Eloquence became the most formidable to some, and helpful to others. But his Habit of viewing all that could be said for or against a Point at the same Time, and presenting both in the clearest Light, misled himself, and did not only in Theory tie him down to meer Probability, but made him always floating, irresolute, uncertain about what Party he ought to take, always dissatisfied with that he had taken; and it was the Cause afterwards, that the last years of his Life, as well as his Death, were unworthy of his high Station, his noble Sentiments, and beautiful Maxims, that shine in his Works. They will always be read with Admiration, but we shall ever be displeased to see that he who teaches them so well, was so wanting in the Practice of them.[126]

The last two of Crousaz's objections to the commonplaces concern certain values that they were alleged to have beyond those connected with the discovery of arguments. Men of low genius, said Crousaz, have imagined that the proper way to penetrate to the bottom of the thoughts of any author is to reduce each of his terms to its commonplace. Others have pretended that the commonplaces are a help in remembering a discourse. The former claim is ridiculous, Crousaz sternly contended. There can be no doubt that his comments on this theme are meant to satirize the methods followed by the Ramists in analyzing learned texts and in preparing learned compositions. Crousaz pointed as follows to one unfortunate commentator who used the Ramistic method in explaining a science: "*Greydanus* composed a Book of Physics, that was *Cartesian* at the Bottom; but all disposed according to the Common Places of *Ramus's* Logic. In so blind a Method you

---

[126] *Ibid.*, II, 218.

must have a great Attention to find that the Author was in the main a Man of Sense."[127] As for the claim that the commonplaces help the memory, Crousaz was even more emphatically in opposition. "Reason tells us," he declared, "that in a Discourse we ought always to set that before, which will give a Light to what follows. Therefore we must begin with that Part of the Subject that is easiest to be known, whether Adjunct, Effect, or Cause, &c. so that to handle different Subjects, each in the clearest Order, you must vary the Order of the Topics, and as soon as you vary it, the Memory will receive but a slender Assistance from it; and since that will not always hold, must not you vary your Discourses, in order to please, and to win Attention?"[128]

These words might well have concluded the case against the commonplaces, as Crousaz seems to have planned it. But he could not resist a final barrage at those who defended the utility of the method of commonplaces in literary composition. He said:

It is certain, Men do not use it in the Composition of Pieces, that turn upon Subjects of Importance. Neither the Masters of antient nor modern Eloquence were corrupted by this Method. In Dramatic Writings it is not followed. Lawyers would lose their Practice, and finish no Affair, did they recur to it in explaining of Wills, Laws, Contracts, or Decrees. So that a dry useless Form, abandoned by all the World, has taken refuge in the Church. Whether it be for public Edification, I appeal to Experience; but I think, that some etymological Remarks upon each Word, some Distinctions, and synonymous Terms; then an Enlargement on two or more Common Places, after having fatigued the Hearer, leave him as ignorant of the Text, and the Truths that flow from it, and as little confirmed in the Practice of Virtue, as if he had been otherwise employed.[129]

Having provided in these words his own personal testimony that the commonplaces of ancient dialectic and rhetoric were no

[127] *Ibid.*, II, 219-220. The work mentioned here is Joannes Greydanus's *Institutiones Physicae Libris Undecim Absolutae* (Leeuwarden, 1664). There was another edition at Bremen in 1671.

[128] *Ibid.*, II, 220-221.

[129] *Ibid.*, II, 221. In saying that no master of ancient eloquence had been corrupted by this method, Crousaz appears to forget what he had said of Cicero in the passage that I recently quoted.

longer used by his generation except in pulpit oratory, and that
their effect upon the sermon had been to make it boring and
sterile, Crousaz turned to the last subject that he had promised
to consider in his discussion of reasoning as the third part of logic.
The last subject involved the way in which the third term, once
it had been discovered, could be applied to the other two terms
in the judgment under examination so as to determine whether
that judgment was true or false. Here, of course, our author was
obliged by tradition and by his own inclination to describe the
syllogistic process, the central doctrine of the old logic. "That
peculiar Turn of Expression, which is used in the Schools for
Argumentation, is called a *Syllogism*," said Crousaz; "So that a
Syllogism is a certain Way of Reasoning, according to the Usage
of the Schools."[130] His handling of this subject, however, was not
rigidly scholastic, although it was more conventional than a complete disciple of Locke would have tolerated.

In approaching this subject, Crousaz spoke first of the danger
of permitting equivocal terms to enter into a syllogism. Next he
dwelt upon sophisms arising from the use of evidence or the use
of authority, and in the latter connection he mentioned man's
deference to custom and his tendency to resist change not by discussing in a reasonable way the objections to it, but by seeking to
discredit the character of its advocates or by crying out against
the corrupting effect of novelty in any form. Such efforts do not
in the long run succeed. "Truth, at equal Arms, will easily vanquish Error," he observed, "and Menaces and Punishments are
not requisite to support her, but rather render her suspected to
great and discerning Spirits."[131] Nevertheless, the fear of punishment can inhibit the progress of truth in a given society, even as
a more open society can benefit by the spirit of toleration. Upon
this point Crousaz gave an illustration of particular interest to his
British readers. "*F. Paul* durst not declare his Opinion upon the
Circulation of the Blood, for fear of the Inquisition," said he, "and
his Friend *Aquapendente* communicated it to *Harvey*, who, in a
free Country, got Honour by that Discovery."[132] These and other

[130] *Ibid.*, II, 261.

[131] *Ibid.*, II, 254. My next quotation is from this same page.

[132] Crousaz wanted this illustration to express his own approval of British
freedom and his disapproval of the Inquisition. But the illustration itself had
originally been cited by other writers to prove that Harvey should not be

similar observations upon the value of accepting reasonable change and upon the desirability of avoiding prejudice and false arguments led Crousaz to his discussion of the syllogism as the center of the art of reasoning.

Syllogisms were usually said to be regular or irregular, the former being composed of three propositions and the latter of more or fewer. Regular syllogisms were usually described as simple or compounded, that is, as categorical, on one hand, or hypothetical or disjunctive, on the other. The categorical syllogism was always made to consist of two premises and a conclusion, and its rules required that it deal with only three terms, that its premises cannot both be negative, and that one negative premise necessitates a negative conclusion. Hypothetical syllogisms invariably obliged one to affirm the antecedent or deny the consequent, while disjunctive syllogisms required a major premise that would enumerate all the compatible possibilities in the given case, so that the minor premise, by affirming one, could decisively eliminate the others. As for irregular syllogisms, they usually included such deviant forms as the enthymeme, the prosyllogism, the epicheirema, the dilemma, the sorites, and the induction. All of these celebrated terms and rules entered dutifully into Crousaz's analysis of syllogistic doctrines. He saw no reason to yield to the great authority of the Port-Royalists by preferring as a guide to proper syllogistic reasoning their one general bipartite rule instead of the three that he had stated. He quoted their rule as follows: "1. *That the Conclusion be contained in one of the Premisses. 2. That the*

---

given credit for discovering the circulation of the blood. A curious document in the history of attempts to deny this honor to Harvey is John Redman Coxe's *An Inquiry into the Claims of Doctor William Harvey to the Discovery of the Circulation of the Blood* (Philadelphia, 1834). Written to discredit Harvey, the *Inquiry*, pp. 183-186, quarrels repeatedly and to little purpose with an author who had explained why Father Paul should not be credited with having told Fabricius of Aquapendente of the discovery which Harvey later announced. For an estimate of the extent to which Fabricius may have influenced Harvey, see R. Willis, *William Harvey A History of the Discovery of the Circulation of the Blood* (London, 1878), pp. 143-147. See also Arturo Castiglioni, *A History of Medicine*, trans. and ed. E. B. Krumbhaar (New York, 1941), pp. 431-440, 515-524. There seems no reason now to question the statement by Norman Moore in his article on Harvey in *The Dictionary of National Biography* that the discovery of the circulation of the blood "remains to this day the greatest of the discoveries of physiology, and its whole honour belongs to Harvey."

other of the Premisses do manifestly shew it."[133] "I own," he went on, "a Syllogism thus qualified is good: But a Reflection that is to pass for a Rule, ought not only to be true, but also easily applicable." And after a brief discussion, he concluded that "the Use of this Rule supposes that of the three we have established."[134] Nor did he see any reason to quarrel with the traditional view that induction is an irregular form of syllogism. "Induction takes a great Number of Examples and particular Facts in several Premisses," he said, "to draw a general Conclusion from them. . . . But to be assured, that an Induction is demonstrative, we must be certain, that no Case has been forgotten; and therefore this Way of Arguing seldom rises above Probability."[135] "We seem to begin our Knowledge of Things by Induction," he added at once. "As we are born in Ignorance, and are naturally surrounded with Darkness, we grope along, inform ourselves by Trials, and having succeeded well in many particular Cases, we are led to draw a general Maxim from them. Thus the Arts have advanced." At this moment, Crousaz was not far from Locke and the new logic, but he did not seem to be able to go beyond himself to recognize that induction as a way of arguing had an identity of its own, and that its true character and importance could not be revealed so long as it was treated as an irregular syllogism. Indeed, as he was about to conclude the chapter in which he made the observations just quoted, he declared the syllogism to be the universal pattern of verbal expression. "All the Discourses of Men," he remarked, "are a Collection of Syllogisms of all Kinds, regular, irregular, simple, and compounded, varied in a thousand Manners."[136] These words fail to harmonize with Locke's description of the inference,[137] and they distinctly show that Crousaz was here a traditionalist at heart, even though he had not only rejected the scholastic doctrine of reduction of propositions and the ancient system of commonplaces, but also had demonstrated the relevance of Bacon's *Novum Organum* to eighteenth-century logicians.

The fourth part of logic as Crousaz conceived of it discussed the way in which we should arrange "a great Number of particu-

---

[133] *Art of Thinking*, II, 271. See also *Oeuvres d'Arnauld*, XLI, 283. See also above, Ch. 2, p. 56.

[134] *Art of Thinking*, II, 272.

[135] *Ibid.*, II, 280-281.   [136] *Ibid.*, II, 285.   [137] See above, pp. 289-291.

lar Conclusions, in order to come, by their Help and Interposal, to a total Conclusion." "That Part of Logic, which prevents a Perplexity in this Matter," added Crousaz, "is called Method."[138] Method gives three advantages to discourse: certainty, brevity, and fulness. The explanation of these three qualities occupies some 38 pages of Crousaz's text. What he said about them amounts to sensible cautionary advice, some of which is addressed directly to speakers. Here, for example, is what you should seek if you would be concise without being obscure: "1. To be entirely Master of your Subject. 2. To forget *yourself*, in a View of being only useful to those you address your Discourse to, or for whom you speak."[139] The same kind of cautionary advice is distributed throughout Crousaz's discussion of the way in which methods vary according to the exigencies of subject matter, as the writer or speaker treats geometrical truths, or the principles of morality, or the axioms of physics. As for the actual doctrines of method, itself, Crousaz enunciated them in relation to the method to be observed in instructing ourselves by the logical analysis of questions or by reading the works of others, and in relation to the methods to be observed in instructing someone else. When he spoke of the method of reading, he mentioned beauty of style, and cautioned his readers against thinking that they could be taught eloquence before they had meditated long upon things. "It is the Thoughts themselves that are the Basis of Eloquence," he remarked. "It is the Manner of Thinking that creates Beauty of Style. It is a gross Error to make it depend either entirely or principally upon the Expressions and Turns. Whether you would instruct or move, these Effects are owing to the Things which the Words signify, not to the Words themselves."[140] And these sentiments are confirmed by a Latin footnote in which Crousaz gives a passage of similar doctrine from Cicero's *De Oratore*, 1.12.50-51. As he came to the methods to be observed in instructing someone else, he recommended the procedures of analysis and synthesis, even as Le Clerc, the Port-Royalists, and other respected logicians of the previous century had done.[141]

[138] *Art of Thinking*, II, 298.
[139] *Ibid.*, II, 315.
[140] *Ibid.*, II, 364-365.
[141] See *Oeuvres d'Arnauld*, XLI, 362-368; see also above, Ch. 2, pp. 20-21, 40-41, 49.

Said he:

> That Method has been call'd Analytic, which in teaching fol-
> lows the very Order of Invention; and the opposite Method has
> receiv'd the Name of Synthetic. That is also called Analytic,
> which, to clear a Question, draws its first Light from the Ques-
> tion it self, and rises by Degrees to the Discovery of the Princi-
> ples that solve it; but the Synthetic lays hold at first on certain
> Principles different from the Question it self, and which it did
> not give Birth to, but were however provided for that Purpose.
> As our Notions ascend from certain particular Objects to gen-
> eral Maxims and Propositions, the ascending from Particulars
> to Generals is likewise called Analytic, and the descending
> from the Generals to the Particulars, Synthetic. Not but that
> general Questions may also be resolv'd by the Analytic, as well
> as particular ones by the Synthetic Way: But the antient
> Schools obscur'd all that came into their Hands, and fill'd every
> Thing with equivocal Terms.[142]

The two methods described by these words occupy a short chapter in Crousaz's text, and then he turned to such other aspects of
orderly discourse as definition, division, arrangement of proofs,
the conduct of refutation, the uses and abuses of disputation, and
the value of distributing continuous compositions into numbered
chapters and sections, and of learning the difficult art of transmitting ideas in dialogue form. What he said upon these matters
gives the concluding pages of his treatise a strongly practical tone
and a content almost entirely associated with the function of logic
in the communication of ideas from writer or speaker to reader
or listener. Indeed, the fourth part of logic as Crousaz framed it
emphasizes the presentation of ideas as distinguished from the
problems of research and discovery. But this emphasis should not
thoughtlessly be called a confusion of rhetorical with logical interests. It is rather a reflection of the second of the two important
operational concepts within Crousaz's definition of logic, and that
second concept stems originally from ancient dialectical theory,
which interested itself in the communication of ideas between a
learned author and the learned community. Rhetoric, it should
always be remembered, was originally the theory of communication in the situation in which a speaker or writer seeks to make his

[142] *Art of Thinking*, II, 377.

ideas available to the less learned segments of the public. During the eighteenth century, logic tended to abandon its interest in learned communication and to become preoccupied with the problems of scientific discovery. It was then that rhetoric began to add a concern for didactic literature to its previous interest in the popularization of ideas, its purpose being to make itself a generalized theory of discourse. Crousaz did not contribute to this change in the relations between rhetoric and logic. Instead he kept logic to its ancient dialectical function as well as its ancient preoccupation with the method of discovering truth.

When Crousaz translated his French logic into Latin in order to make it available to European learning, he did what Le Clerc and most other authors usually did for their Latin editions—he added an explanatory comment upon the influences which had shaped his own logical doctrines.[143] He spoke harshly of Aristotle's *Logic* as having been composed and used to enable the smart disputant to rise in the world by contradicting everyone whom he wanted to outshine. The utterances which this sort of doctrine has encouraged, said Crousaz, reflect discredit and dishonor upon mankind. The long reign of Aristotelian logic was ended, Crousaz went on, when Ramus's *Dialectica* at first supplanted it in various schools amidst a torrent of controversy, and later absorbed it so as to create a new compound of traditional doctrine, and in this guise to become the ruling fashion in schools of theology, metaphysics, and law.[144] As for events closer to his own time, Crousaz spoke thus:

> In the last century, but quite gently and timidly, to be sure, the yoke of authority began to be shaken off. The hard fact is that no school adopted Verulam's *Novum Organum* or Descartes's *Method*. With happier consequences the *Ars Cogitandi* came upon the scene, and its repeated editions in our own century will justly arouse admiration. In that same era the most learned Clauberg was writing; a great many professors undertook publicly to explain his *Logic*. The most celebrated and most elegant author of the work entitled *De Veritate Scrutanda* expounded

---

[143] *Logicae Systema*, I, sig. †6v-†7v.

[144] For details concerning Ramus's reform of logic and concerning the subsequent amalgamation of his doctrines with those of Aristotle, see my *Logic and Rhetoric in England*, pp. 146-165, 173-246, 282-317.

the art of analysis more fruitfully than his predecessors had done, and brought to light the chief sources of the errors which stem from our affections. The most famous and most justly celebrated *De Intellectu Humano*, by Mr. Locke, is a distinguished work, the best thing that we have from him, and it will always be numbered among the most useful of logics. The truly outstanding Mr. Le Clerc, a man of immense industry and with a learning as solid as it was vast, not only published a logic crammed to the top with the choicest observations of friendly witnesses, and splendidly furnished with original things, but also added to it an *Ontologia & Ars Critica* as a special contribution of his own, not previously attempted by anybody, however needful such a work had been.[145]

These are the works which he had read to the end and assiduously contemplated, Crousaz went on. Then he proceeded to mention the conflict that had arisen in his mind as he re-examined on the one hand the established Ramistic logic upon which he himself had been nurtured as a schoolboy, and on the other the new logic as it was expounded in the other works which he had enumerated. Out of this conflict came his decision to revoke the irrevocable laws of the old logic where they no longer served the purpose for which they had been intended. In this frame of mind he wrote his own work, and he plainly implied that it was to be a mixture of the old and the new.

One of the works which Crousaz placed in the new school had a much greater effect upon his *Art of Thinking* than did any of the others. It would be tempting, of course, to identify that one as Locke's, in view of Crousaz's own assertion that the *Essay concerning Human Understanding* would forever be counted among the most useful of logics. Indeed, several important witnesses have said of Crousaz that Locke was his master. Gibbon stated that very thing, as we have seen; and Professor La Harpe's good recent study of Crousaz declares that the latter's *Art of Thinking* shows Locke's influence, and that the theory of the origin of ideas

---

[145] *Logicae Systema*, I, sig. †7r. Translation mine. *De Veritate Scrutanda* is the Latin title devised by Crousaz to designate Malebranche's French work, *De la Recherche de la Verité*. Crousaz's tribute to Locke reads thus: "Clarissimi, & meritò celebratissimi, Dni. *Lockii* de *Intellectu Humano* eximium Opus, & Auctore suô dignissimum, *Logicis* utilissimis semper annumerabitur."

as set forth by the Swiss logician is singularly close to Locke's teachings on that same subject.[146] Yet if Crousaz had been deeply affected by Locke, he would certainly have been impelled not only to respond to Locke's attack on syllogistic logic but also to claim a new role for induction. These crucial steps he did not take. Thus the verdict has to be that there is very little in the *Art of Thinking* to connect it with Locke's *Essay* in respect to vital logical precepts.[147] But it can be said that *The Port-Royal Logic,* which Crousaz listed by its Latin title, *Ars Cogitandi,* was in fact the chief source from which his own *Art of Thinking* stemmed. The Port-Royalists had given logic a new direction and an influential new subject matter in the year preceding that in which Crousaz was born. Locke, we should remember, was at that time a young man serving as lecturer in Greek at Oxford. Crousaz did not slavishly follow the Port-Royalists. For example, as I pointed out above, he preferred the conventional three rules for the syllogism to the good but unnecessary two-sided rule proposed by them. And he found fault with their way of discussing the conventional syllogistic rules, even though he deemed it ingenious.[148] But he followed them in defining logic in terms of its investigative and its presentational offices.[149] If I may repeat statements already made, he followed them as well not only in making the basic structure of logic consist of the theory of perception, of judgment, of reasoning, and of method, but also in treating the method of instruction by speaking of analysis and synthesis. He followed them too in refusing to exclude from logic any subject

[146] La Harpe, p. 207. According to this view, Crousaz borrowed from Locke's theory of ideas, even as Le Clerc had done. Perhaps Crousaz was influenced by Le Clerc in deciding which part of the *Essay* had value for logic. See above, p. 308, for Gibbon's statement of Crousaz's indebtedness to Locke. For other statements to the same effect, see the articles on Crousaz in *Nouvelle Biographie Générale* and *La Grande Encyclopédie.*

[147] In a later abridgment of Crousaz's *Logique* (Amsterdam, 1737), II, 167, Locke's celebrated attack on rhetoric is quoted with full approval. For the English text of that attack, see the *Essay concerning Human Understanding,* Bk. III, Ch. x, Sec. 34. See also below, Ch. 6, pp. 490-491. Henley's translation does not contain this quotation, nor did the French text which he used.

[148] *Art of Thinking,* II, 338. See also *Oeuvres d'Arnauld,* XLI, 259-263.

[149] The Port-Royalists defined logic as follows: "La Logique est l'Art de bien conduire sa raison dans la connoissance des choses, tant pour s'en instruire soi-même, que pour en instruire les autres." See *Oeuvres d'Arnauld,* XLI, 125.

whatever that could be used to illustrate and enrich its doctrine, even if that subject could likewise be claimed for a treatise on politics or morality or physics. Thus he condemned those who would restrict each discipline so severely to preconceived boundaries as to make it impossible for one science to draw upon the field of another. "I never cou'd imagine the Sciences to be distinguish'd by Bounds or Limits so exact and inviolable," he cried, "as those that divide Kingdoms."[150] And these fervent words echo the very ones used by the Port-Royalists to free logic from the arbitrary limitations imposed upon it by Ramus.[151]

We must therefore conclude that Crousaz cannot be called a leader in the movement which led to the creation of a new logic in the late eighteenth century, although he cannot in any sense be classed as an opponent of that movement. He stood midway between the new and the old, unwilling on the one hand to take as conservative a position as Dean Aldrich had assumed in 1691, and unable on the other to be as advanced in his own era as the Port-Royalists had been in theirs. He accepted the five predicables of the old scholastic logic; yet he treated with some scorn the laborious pedantries lavished upon these terms by the Schoolmen,[152] and, as we have seen, he refused to concern himself with the scholastic machinery for the reduction of propositions. He did not respond to the provocative challenge which Locke had flung at syllogistic reasoning; yet he accepted Locke and Bacon as legitimate authorities upon logical doctrine.[153] He took the time-honored view that logic should recognize its responsibilities towards the communication of truth as well as towards its discovery; but he did not appear to anticipate that this arrangement might cease to appeal to logicians as they became more and more

---

[150] *Art of Thinking*, I, iv. This statement occurs in the Preface of Henley's translation and of the second edition of the French text.

[151] *Oeuvres d'Arnauld*, XLI, 113. Said the Port-Royalists: "Tout ce qui sert à la Logique lui appartient; & c'est une chose entièrement ridicule que les gênes que se donnent certains Auteurs, comme Ramus & les Ramistes, quoique d'ailleurs fort habiles gens, qui prennent autant de peine pour borner les jurisdictions de chaque science, & faire qu'elles n'entreprennent pas les unes sur les autres, que l'on en prend pour marquer les limites des Royaumes, & régler les ressorts des Parlements."

[152] *Art of Thinking*, II, 87-94.

[153] *Ibid.*, I, 335, 433. These references to Bacon are in addition to those already cited.

absorbed in the methods of scientific investigation. He considered the investigative mission of the old logic to be identified with the deductive analysis of logical judgments; yet he condemned the Scholastics for believing "that all we know on determinate Subjects, is drawn from general Propositions, as we draw a Book from a Library, and a Discourse from our Memory."[154] He accepted the syllogism of the old logic as the sole instrument of philosophical enquiry, induction being in his view one of its irregular forms; yet, as we said above, he recognized that all our knowledge begins in induction. He regarded skill in disputing as formerly "the most beautiful Flower of Philosophy, and the most shining Fruit of our Studies," and he laid down rules for the conduct of syllogistic disputations[155]; yet he said, as we know, that the disputatious utterances encouraged by Peripatetic logic were not a glorious chapter in the history of humanity, and on other occasions he took the opportunity to speak of academic disputes as quarrelsome, pretentious, and ill-mannered.[156] He dwelt upon the importance of discovering truth by a resort to his own two rules for the verbal analysis of a given proposition; yet we have surveyed in detail his condemnation of the old logic for its reliance upon the verbal analysis involved in the use of the traditional commonplaces. He tested the validity of some propositions by seeking to ascertain whether they were consistent with other propositions known to be true; yet he defined truth at other times as an accuracy of correspondence between our thoughts and judgments, on the one hand, and things as they really are, on the other.[157] Finally, his respect for the Port-Royalist dictum that the conclusion established by the syllogism is already in being in one of the premises, and needs only to be identified in the other premise, amounts almost to an endorsement of the *dictum de omni et nullo*, in which a statement about a particular thing is deemed valid, if it is consistent with a similar statement about a pre-existent class of similar things; yet he had earlier observed that "The Itch of establishing a first Principle, on which all the other should depend, has introduced the Method of proving one Principle by another, that is pretended to be more evident," and he condemned this practice by pointing out that "it inures us to turn our Eyes from the Evidence we have, in design to look after another

---

[154] *Ibid.*, II, 142.
[156] *Ibid.*, I, 133; II, 17, 404-405.
[155] *Ibid.*, II, 141, 264-265.
[157] *Ibid.*, I, 13; II, 110-112.

that is greater."[158] In all these various ways, he looked forward towards the new without being able to understand where it was destined to lead; and in all these other ways he looked back towards the old without approving of several of its celebrated rituals. In this posture of moderation he must now bow out of our story.

Perhaps the chief reason why Henley's translation of Crousaz never had a second edition in Britain is that in the year following its publication an Englishman of some note in the world of letters produced a logic that was destined to become one of the most popular textbooks of the next hundred years. The author in question was Isaac Watts, fifty-one-year-old pastor of a church in London, who had already published two volumes of sermons, some dissertations on the Christian doctrine of the Trinity, and a guide to prayer, and who had enjoyed for almost twenty years a considerable renown as a sacred poet and hymnist. In 1725 Watts had John Clark, Richard Hett, Emanuel Matthews, and Richard Ford, London booksellers, bring forth his *Logick: Or, The Right Use of Reason in the Enquiry after Truth, With A Variety of Rules to guard against Error, in the Affairs of Religion and Human Life, as well as in the Sciences*; and this didactic treatise eventually made Watts as well known in educational circles of the eighteenth and early nineteenth centuries as his hymns were in the Christian churches of Great Britain and America. In our own day, a fair number of his hymns are still a beloved presence in Christian worship, but his *Logick* has faded so completely into oblivion as to awaken surprise and disbelief when it is now mentioned as one of his writings.

Born in Southampton July 17, 1674, Watts was brought up by parents who had strong religious convictions and a settled determination to remain affiliated with the dissenting sect known as Independents or Congregationalists.[159] His father, twice imprisoned for nonconformity, taught his son Latin when the latter was only four years old, and saw to it that he entered Latin School at six and began to study Greek at nine, French at ten, and Hebrew

---

[158] *Ibid.*, II, 145.

[159] My account of Watts's life follows that given accurately and in detail by Arthur Paul Davis, *Isaac Watts, His Life and Works* (published dissertation, Columbia University, 1943). Cited below as Davis.

at thirteen or fourteen. Watts's brilliance as a student led to his being offered financial support for a career at Oxford or Cambridge, but he would have had to conform to the Church of England if he enrolled at either university, and he preferred instead to attend Thomas Rowe's Academy, a dissenting school, which like many others of its kind sought to offer advanced education not inferior to that of the regular university course.[160] Watts left Rowe's Academy in 1694 and spent the next two years at home writing hymns and pursuing his studies. On October 15, 1696, he entered the household of Sir John Hartopp, bart., as tutor of the latter's son, also named John. After half a dozen years with Sir John's family, during which Watts preached his first sermon and became assistant pastor of a dissenting church in Mark Lane, London, he took up an eight-year residence in the home of Thomas Hollis, who was later to bequeath money to found the first professorship of mathematics and natural philosophy at Harvard College.[161] The church in Mark Lane named Watts pastor in 1702, and he held that office for the rest of his life, although recurring illnesses greatly curtailed his clerical activities and forced him to live in virtual retirement. Between 1710 and 1712 he was guest in the family of a Mr. Bowes. During the latter year, he was invited to pay a visit to the luxurious mansion of Sir Thomas Abney, and he stayed there until his death thirty-six years later. This visit has been indicated as the most lengthy in fact or legend[162]; but when Watts himself in 1742 remarked that he had come under the Abneys' friendly roof intending to stay a week and had extended his visit to thirty years, Lady Abney graciously replied, "Sir, what you term a long thirty years visit, I consider as the shortest visit my family ever received."[163] In this connection we should remind ourselves that Watts was esteemed for his gentleness, his learning, his excellent conversation, and his

[160] For details, see Davis, pp. 10-15.

[161] *Ibid.*, p. 29.

[162] When Mr. Edward L. Pierce told the Massachusetts Historical Society that he was offering them for publication a letter written by Isaac Watts to Rev. Elisha Williams, President of Yale College from 1725 to 1739, he said: "Dr. Watts became in 1712 an inmate of the house of Sir Thomas Abney, once Lord Mayor of London, and remained there till his death, making, as has been said, the longest visit on record." See *Proceedings of the Massachusetts Historical Society*, Second Series, IX (Boston, 1895), 334.

[163] Davis, p. 32.

devoutness, and that he had at the same time the special attractiveness of a man whose hymns, psalms, and devotional poems
seemed to have a touch of divine grace about them. As early as
1706, his *Horae Lyricae* had brought him reputation, and his
Hymns and Spiritual Songs and *The Psalms of David*, published
respectively in 1707 and 1719, had made him famous. At the time
of his death in 1748, at the age of 74, he was deeply revered in his
own country and in America. It may surprise us now, but it surprised no one in the eighteenth century, that, when Dr. Samuel
Johnson published in 1781 the second installment of the series
now called *The Lives of the Most Eminent English Poets*, he gave
Watts a place in the eighth volume, not at the request of the booksellers who sponsored the series, but on his own initiative.[164]

Watts's *Logick* is connected with his term as tutor of young
John Hartopp, who became Sir John himself when his father died
in 1722. Watts preached the sermon at the funeral of the father,
the third baronet, and three years later dedicated his *Logick* to
the fourth baronet, his erstwhile pupil. In the dedicatory epistle,
Watts indicated that the present work represented a considerable
enlargement of the original sketch which he had prepared for the
assistance of Sir John's younger studies and had presented to him
at that time. "'Twas by the repeated Importunities of our
Learned Friend Mr. *John Eams*," the epistle declared, "that I
was persuaded to revise these *Rudiments of Logic*; and when I
had once suffer'd myself to begin the Work, I was drawn still on-

---

[164] Johnson contributed fifty-two biographical and critical sketches to the
booksellers' edition of the works of the English poets. Twenty-two of these
sketches were published at London in 1779 in a set of four volumes. The
other thirty sketches were published also at London in 1781 in a set of six
volumes. The entire ten volumes bore the title, *Prefaces, Biographical and
Critical, to the Works of the English Poets*. By Samuel Johnson. Volume the
First [-Tenth] (London, 1779-1781). The sketch of Watts appeared as the last
item in Volume VIII. It covered twenty-four pages. See William Prideaux
Courtney, *A Bibliography of Samuel Johnson*, revised and seen through the
press by David Nichol Smith (Oxford, 1915), pp. 140-141. In addition to the
ten volumes devoted to Johnson's sketches, there were 56 volumes devoted to
the actual works of the poets whom Johnson had treated, and there were two
volumes devoted to the Index. Thus the entire booksellers' project involved
68 volumes.

Johnson's fifty-two sketches appeared together in four volumes at London
in 1781, under the title, *The Lives of the Most Eminent English Poets*. The
sketch of Watts is in Volume IV, pp. 275-292.

ward far beyond my first Design, even to the Neglect, or too long Delay of other pressing and important Demands that were upon me."[165] The original sketch of the *Logick*, it appears, had had the title mentioned in the foregoing quotation. The John Eams (or Eames) referred to there was a dissenter and tutor of science and classics at Fund Academy in Tenter Alley, Moorfields, the exact locality in which John Ward's Academy was situated in the days before his elevation to the professorship of rhetoric in Gresham College.[166] "I will not presume, *Sir*," the dedicatory epistle went on, "that this little Book is improv'd since its first Composure, in Proportion to the Improvements of your manly Age."[167] With these complimentary words and others designed to remind Sir John of his early study of logic and its connection with his present maturity of observation, the dedication ended. It was dated *"London, Aug. 24. 1724."* Thus it must have been written at the Abneys' town house in Lime Street, for it was not until 1734 that they and their distinguished guest moved to their elegant new home in Stoke Newington.[168]

Watts's *Logick* bears a close family resemblance to that of Crousaz and of Le Clerc, and thus repetition would be involved in discussing it here in detail. It is, however, a solid and adequate treatise, and we should take note of its leading characteristics in order to understand why it was popular in its time and what sort of influence it exerted upon eighteenth-century attitudes.

In a quantitative sense, it contained 534 pages in its first edition, ten of which set forth the definition and the four main divisions of logic, and the other 524 pages, the doctrine within those divisions. Thus 210 pages discussed perceptions, ideas, and terms, these being the constituents of the first division. Judgment and propositions, as the second division, occupied 200 pages. The third division, reasoning and syllogism, accounted for 84 pages, and the fourth division, method, for 30 pages. There is sometimes

---

[165] *Logick* (London, 1725), pp. i-ii. I refer to this edition throughout my discussion.

[166] Watts called Eames "the most learned man I ever knew." See *The Dictionary of National Biography*, s.v. Eames, John. Before Watts published his treatise called *The Knowledge of the Heavens and the Earth made Easy* (London, 1726), he sent it to Eames for criticism and revision. See Davis, p. 87.

[167] *Logick*, p. v.   [168] Davis, p. 248, n. 38.

a value in quantitative analysis. In this case, it shows that Watts devoted three-quarters of his space to the first half of his subject, and less than one-quarter to the second half. To him perception and judgment were the points that young John Hartopp and his contemporaries should be taught at greatest length, while syllogism and method were to be given nothing beyond a conventional emphasis.

Throughout his discussion of these four divisions, and in his definition of his subject, Watts took the position that the doctrines of logic converge to form the theory of enquiry and also the theory of communication. "Logick," he remarked in the first sentence of his introduction, "is *the Art of using our Reason well in our Enquiries after Truth, and the Communication of it to others.*"[169] "Since 'tis the Design of *Logick*, not only to assist us in *Learning*, but in *Teaching* also, it is necessary," he observed as he spoke of terms in relation to conceptions of things, "that we should be furnished with some particular Directions relating to the *Definition of Names*, both in *Teaching*, and *Learning*."[170] Later, having ruled that a definition should contain nothing superfluous or tautological, he tested his own definition of logic in the light of this precept, and he spoke thus:

> So in the Definition which we have given of *Logick*, that it is the *Art of using our Reason well in our Search after Truth and the Communication of it to others*, it has indeed many Words in it, but it could not well be shorter. *Art* is the *Genus* wherein it agrees with *Rhetorick, Poesy, Arithmetick, Wrestling, Sailing, Building, &c.* for all these are *Arts* also: But the Difference or special Nature of it is drawn from its Object, *Reason*; from the Act, *using it well*, and from its two great Ends or Designs, *viz.* the *Search of Truth*, and the *Communication of it*: Nor can it be justly described and explained in fewer Ideas.[171]

Perhaps the best demonstration that Watts was concerned everywhere in his *Logick* with the functions of enquiry and communication is afforded, however, by his opening words as he entered the discussion of the fourth main division of his treatise. He said:

[169] *Logick*, p. 1. Italics are Watts's here and below.
[170] *Ibid.*, p. 132.
[171] *Ibid.*, p. 168. On p. 182, Watts defined rhetoric as follows: "*Rhetorick* is the Art of speaking in a manner fit to persuade."

'Tis not merely a *clear and distinct Idea*, a *well-formed Proposition*, or a *just Argument*, that is sufficient to search out and communicate the Knowledge of a Subject. There must be a Variety and Series of them disposed in a due Manner in order to attain this End: And therefore 'tis the Design of the *last Part of Logic* to teach us the *Art of Method*.[172]

As for the theory of enquiry itself, Watts wavered between his admiration for the improvements produced by the new science and his acquired theological disposition to define discovery in traditional deductive terms. An example of the former attitude is afforded when he was analyzing with great insight the prejudices born of an excessive veneration of the past. He spoke there as follows:

Again, To believe in all Things as our Predecessors did, is the ready way to keep Mankind in an everlasting State of Infancy, and to lay an eternal Bar against all the Improvements of our Reason and our Happiness. Had the present Age of Philosophers satisfy'd themselves with the *substantial Forms*, and *occult Qualities* of *Aristotle*, with the *solid Spheres, Excentricks* and *Epicycles* of *Ptolemy*, and the antient Astronomers; then, the great Lord *Bacon, Copernicus*, and *Descartes*, with the greater Sir *Isaac Newton*, Mr. *Locke*, and Mr. *Boyle*, had risen in our World in vain. We must have blunder'd on still in successive Generations amongst Absurdities and thick Darkness, and a hundred useful Inventions, for the Happiness of Human Life had never been known.[173]

But this resounding endorsement of the results achieved by the new science did not lead Watts to eulogize its investigative procedures or to question the investigative procedures of the old learning. He was content instead with things as they were when he came to speak of the logic of discovery. Thus, for instance, he envisaged new truth, not as something which emerges from the close observation of particular phenomena, but as something to be wrung from established truth by deductive processes. This view of scientific enquiry emerges at the outset of his discussion of the third part of logic:

[172] *Ibid.*, pp. 505-506.
[173] *Ibid.*, pp. 355-356. The entire chapter in which this quotation occurs is worth the special attention of the modern reader.

As the first Work of the Mind is *Perception*, whereby our *Ideas* are framed, and the second is *Judgment*, which joins or disjoins our Ideas, and forms a *Proposition*, so the third Operation of the Mind is *Reasoning*, which joins several Propositions together, and makes a *Syllogism*, that is, an *Argument whereby we are wont to infer something that is less known, from Truths which are more evident*.[174]

The notion that new truths emerge from truths already accepted is of course the basic implication of the *dictum de omni et nullo*, which postulates that, if a class of things is known to have a certain characteristic without exception, then that characteristic also belongs without exception to any particular thing that can be shown to belong to the class. Watts did not identify the basic law of the syllogism by the Latin phrase just given or by its English equivalent. But the *dictum* of the old logic is plainly involved in his conception of the basic law of the syllogism. "The *general Principle* upon which these universal and particular Syllogisms are founded," he said, "is this; Whatsoever is affirmed or denied universally of any Idea, may be affirmed or denied of all the particular Kinds or Beings, which are contained in the Extension of that universal Idea."[175] It must be emphasized, of course, that the truth or falsity of this principle was not an issue between the new and the old logic. The principle is undeniably true, as both schools avowed. The issue, however, was whether such a principle really explained the process by which new truth is discovered. Watts did not say anything to suggest that he was prepared to take the modern side of this issue, despite his enthusiasm for the discoveries which the moderns had made by other means than deductive analysis.

As for induction, Watts sided again with the traditional view, and considered that this form of reasoning had no independent status. To him induction was an irregular syllogism. Having discussed the epicheirema, the dilemma, the prosyllogism, and the sorites, he said, "To these Syllogisms it may not be improper to add *Induction*, which is, when from several particular Propositions we infer one general."[176] This definition is not intrinsically

---

[174] *Ibid.*, pp. 421-422.   [175] *Ibid.*, p. 429.
[176] *Ibid.*, p. 455; see also p. 483, where Watts refers to his preceding chapter as having treated "that Sort of Syllogism which is called *Induction*."

wrong, but it is perfunctory, and it forces induction into a questionable relation with the syllogism. The illustration which accompanies it in Watts's text is, however, even less satisfactory. It runs as follows: "*The Doctrine of the* Socinians *cannot be proved from the Gospels, it cannot be proved from the Acts of the Apostles, it cannot be prov'd from the Epistles, nor the Book of Revelations*; therefore *it cannot be proved out of the New Testament.*"[177]

The all-important principle to be used in ascertaining the truth or falsity of the conclusions established by enquiry was a somewhat ambiguous element in Watts's *Logick*, as indeed we would expect from his willingness to recommend the investigative methods of the old learning while applauding the achievements of the new. At times he defined truth as accuracy, and accuracy as the exact correspondence between an idea in the mind or a proposition in language, on the one hand, and the parallel thing in nature, on the other. In his discussion of ideas, he spoke thus: "Our Ideas are either *true* or *false*; for an Idea being the Representation of a thing in the Mind, it must be either a *true* or a *false Representation* of it. If the Idea be conformable to the Object or Archetype of it, it is a *true* Idea; if not, it is a *false* one."[178] And he expected the same kind of correspondence before a logical proposition could meet the test of truth. "A *true Proposition*," he said, "represents Things as they are in themselves; but if Things are represented otherwise than they are in themselves, the Proposition is *false*."[179] These definitions are all in harmony with the commitments of the new science, but not with the postulates of the deductive method of enquiry, as Watts had formulated them. That method defined truth as consistency, and consistency as the agreement established between something less known and something already evident. Watts approved of consistency as the test of truth, even as he also approved of accuracy. In fact, he accepted both standards when he spoke as follows during his discussion of true and false propositions: "Now it will follow from hence, that a *clear and distinct Perception or full Evidence of the Agreement and Disagreement of our Ideas to one another, or to*

---

[177] For a variant of this illustration, see Le Clerc, *Logica*, pp. 167-168. Le Clerc used the argument to prove that the unlimited authority of the Bishop of Rome could not be supported by anything in the New Testament.

[178] *Logick*, p. 65.   [179] *Ibid.*, p. 268.

things, is a certain *Criterion* of Truth."[180] It is not to the discredit of Watts that he accepted both standards. In fact, both standards are valid, and the acceptance of both was to be finally visible when logic came to terms with induction and learned to treat induction and deduction as equals. Watts did not anticipate that final solution of the problem, nor did he recognize that the problem actually existed. But he would have understood the final solution when it came, for he had already grasped the two concepts that would enter into it.

If Watts tended in the main to represent the old school as he spoke of the communicative function of logic, and as he analyzed deductive enquiry, the syllogism, the *dictum de omni,* the induction, and the nature of truth, he must be recognized, nevertheless, as something of a modern in other respects. One of these respects has to do with his attitude towards disputation. *"True Logic,"* he said in his dedicatory epistle, "is not that noisy Thing that deals all in Dispute and Wrangling, to which former Ages had debased and confin'd it; yet its Disciples must acknowledge also, that they are taught to vindicate and defend the Truth, as well as to search it out."[181] Elsewhere he spoke in disapproval of those logicians who endeavored to transform the doctrine of syllogistic moods and figures "into a Sort of *Mechanism,* and to teach Boys to syllogize, or frame Arguments and refute them, without any real inward Knowledge of the Question."[182] If these disparagements of disputation lack severity, and if Watts did not add substantially to them anywhere else in his *Logick,* we should understand that his own course of training at Thomas Rowe's Academy would have required him to participate every other day in the Latin disputations which were common features of higher education in eighteenth-century Britain, and that his practice of this art would have led him to see its value in the education of youth, even if it were not of primary value in testing the truths of science and scholarship.

Another respect in which Watts is to be counted a modern concerns his attitude towards the topics or commonplaces as instruments of discovery of the middle term needed to test the validity of the relation of the other terms to each other in the logical proposition. In his discussion of the middle term as the

[180] *Ibid.,* p. 272.   [181] *Ibid.,* p. iv.   [182] *Ibid.,* p. 434.

339

center of the syllogistic process, Watts introduced the doctrine
of topics or commonplaces, and indicated that this doctrine was
designed to assist in the discovery of middle terms or arguments
in connection with any enquiry whatever. Having listed the commonplaces to be remembered if the enquiry concerned grammar,
or logic, or metaphysics, or ethics, or theology, Watts observed,
"Now it has been the Custom of those who teach *Logic* or *Rhetorick* to direct their Disciples, when they want an Argument, to
consult the several *Topics* which are suited to their Subject of
Discourse, and to rummage over the *Definitions, Divisions* and
Canons that belong to each *Topic*." "This is called the *Invention
of an Argument*," added Watts, "and 'tis taught with much Solemnity in some Schools."[183] As for himself, Watts did not propose to
teach this form of invention with or without solemnity. He remarked instead:

> I grant there may be good Use of this Practice for Persons of
> a lower Genius, when they are to compose any Discourse for
> the Publick; or for those of superior Parts to refresh their Mem-
> ory, and revive their Acquaintance with a Subject which has
> been long absent from their Thoughts; or when their natural
> Spirits labour under Indisposition and Languor: But when a
> Man of moderate Sagacity has made himself Master of his
> Theme by just Diligence and Enquiry, he has seldom need to
> run knocking at the Doors of all the *Topics* that he may furnish
> himself with Argument or Matter of speaking: And indeed 'tis
> only a Man of Sense and Judgment that can use *common Places*
> or *Topics* well; for amongst this Variety he only knows what is
> fit to be left out, as well as what is fit to be spoken.[184]

As a substitute for the machinery of topics, Watts urged the
young students of his time to observe the world around them and
to examine thoughtfully what they saw. He spoke directly to them
upon this matter. *"Enlarge your general Acquaintance with
Things daily,"* he advised, *"in order to attain a rich Furniture of
Topics or middle Terms whereby those Propositions which occur
may be either proved or disproved*; but especially *meditate and
enquire with great Diligence and Exactness into the Nature,
Properties, Circumstances and Relations of the particular Subject*

[183] *Ibid.*, pp. 458-459.   [184] *Ibid.*, p. 459.

about which you judge or argue."[185] Nowhere is Watts more modern than in these words. And what he said against the ancient topical machinery of invention applied not only to logic but to rhetoric as well. Both disciplines were going to have to face the modern world without any illusions concerning the effectiveness of arguments derived primarily from a stock of ready-made ideas. Both disciplines were going to have to recognize that effective arguments come only from the knowledge of things. The influence of the scientific outlook upon logic and rhetoric is nowhere more evident than in the tendency of both arts during the eighteenth century to speak as Watts did against the use of commonplaces in the discovery of proofs.

Few textbooks of its time distributed their doctrines to a wider public than Watts's *Logick* did. At Glasgow in 1779 it achieved its twentieth British edition, and in the next forty-three years it was reprinted at least once in Glasgow, Berwick, and Leeds, at least twice in Edinburgh, and at least seven times in London. Meanwhile it had crossed the Atlantic to the United States, where it progressed from its first American edition at Philadelphia in 1789 to a sixth in 1819 at Boston.[186] The first American edition was based upon the sixteenth edition in Britain.[187] A copy of the eighth British edition (London, 1745) found its way into Thomas Jefferson's library.[188] In 1739 and 1740 Watts himself sent copies to New England for young libraries springing up in what still were the British colonies of Massachusetts and Connecticut.[189] As early as 1728, three years after its first publication, it was being used in the universities. On May 8 of that year, in a letter sent from "the Lady Abney's in Lime Street" to the Rev. Dr. Benjamin Colman, first in the line of pastors of the Church in Brattle Square, Boston, Watts wrote in part as follows: "The world has heaped unmerited honors on almost all my writings. Even Oxford

---

[185] *Ibid.*, p. 492.

[186] This inventory of editions has been compiled from catalogues of the following libraries: Princeton University, Bodleian, British Museum, Library of Congress, University of Edinburgh, Henry E. Huntington Library, and Boston Athenaeum.

[187] See Charles Evans, *American Bibliography*, VII, 375 (No. 22246).

[188] See Sowerby, *Catalogue of the Library of Thomas Jefferson*, V, 14.

[189] See Watts's letters as published in *Proceedings of the Massachusetts Historical Society*, Second Series, IX (Boston, 1895), 368, 377.

& Cambridge break thro' their bigotry & hatred of yͤ Dissenters, & use my Logic, my Astronomy, & my Poems."[190] The colleges and academies of America honored Watts in the same way as time went on.[191] Indeed, throughout the years between 1728 and 1785 the vogue of his *Logick* in institutions of higher learning does not appear to have slackened. When Jeremy Bentham attended Queens College, Oxford, in the first three years of the 1760's, the *Logick* was still in use as the standard English treatise in its field; but Bentham regarded it as "Old woman's logic," and he himself preferred what his tutor taught him from Sanderson's Latin *Logicae Artis Compendium.*[192] In publishing in 1781 his sketch of Watts for *The Lives of the Most Eminent English Poets*, Dr. Johnson said of the *Logick* that it "has been received into the universities, and, therefore, wants no private recommendation."[193] Then, too, as I mentioned earlier, Dr. Johnson had commented in 1748 upon current treatises on logic when he wrote his Preface to Dodsley's *Preceptor*, and he had recommended Watts at that time to students seeking to educate themselves in polite learning. Dr. Johnson's own copy of the *Logick* is now in the British Museum, and an examination of it reveals that on each of its 365 pages at least one word, and on some pages as many as eleven words, have been marked for quotation.[194] These markings were destined in themselves to strengthen Watts's reputation as a logician, for when Dr. Johnson published his famous *Dictionary* in 1755, it contained "literally hundreds of examples and definitions" from the *Logick*.[195] And finally John Shute, first Viscount Barrington, who was a lawyer, a politician, a dissenter, and a friend of Watts, is reported to have promised to read Watts's *Logick* at least once a year, as others read Cicero.[196] In the light of this array of facts, it is probably fair to say that in the English-speaking world more eighteenth-century students and serious general readers learned their lessons about logic from Isaac Watts than from any other source. This conclusion would certainly be true for the period between 1725 and 1750, when the *Logick* had no competitor to

---

[190] *Ibid.*, p. 341. [191] Davis, pp. 87, 255 n. 37.
[192] John Bowring, *The Works of Jeremy Bentham* (Edinburgh, 1843), x, 37.
[193] *Works*, xi, 48. [194] Davis, pp. 254-255, n. 35.
[195] *Ibid.*, p. 87. [196] *Ibid.*, p. 55.

rival it on equal terms. Even after 1750, when a first-rate competitor which had recently appeared was rapidly gaining respect and popularity, Watts's *Logick* continued to attract its share of students and general readers, and its appeal was to last well into the coming century.

The sources used by Watts in preparing this work deserve a word of explanation to correct a current misapprehension and to state the situation as it is. In his sketch of Watts as one of the eminent English poets Dr. Johnson mentioned the *Logick*, as we already know; and of it and its creator he said that "if he owes part of it to Le Clerc, it must be considered that no man, who undertakes merely to methodize or illustrate a system, pretends to be its author."[197] These words are cautious and charitable. But they have led to the less cautious affirmation that Watts followed Le Clerc, and perhaps they have also invited the sweeping and vague statement that he added materials from Locke and Aristotle as well.[198] It would be more accurate to say, however, that the work which obviously influenced Watts most of all is *The Port-Royal Logic*. In his definition of logic, he specified its communicative and its investigative function, as the Port-Royalists but not Le Clerc had done.[199] In ordering his discussion of the four parts of logic, he treated perception first, then judgment, then reasoning, and then method, as the Port-Royalists did; but Le Clerc had ordered the parts differently by making method his third topic, and reasoning fourth. When Watts gave the precepts governing the division of an idea into its parts, his fourth rule said, "Let not Subdivisions be too numerous without Necessity; therefore I think *Quantity* is better distinguished at once into a *Line*, a *Surface* and a *Solid*, than to say, as *Ramus* does, that *Quantity is either a Line, or a Thing lined*; and *a Thing lined is either a Surface or a Solid*."[200] This illustration and the reference to Ramus are to be found in *The Port-Royal Logic*, where Arnauld and Nicole, having objected to the Ramists for their insistence upon dichotomous

---

[197] *Works*, xi, 48.   [198] Davis, p. 86.

[199] For the definition of logic by the Port-Royalists, see above, n. 149. Le Clerc's definition reads as follows (*Logica*, p. 1): *Logicam*, seu *Dialecticam*, summatim consideratam, nihil esse aliud praeter *Artem bene ratiocinandi*, ex quo ejus nomen auditum est, omnes norunt."

[200] *Logick*, p. 205.

divisions, and having proposed that the division of an idea into three parts was sometimes the only natural course to take, spoke then as follows: "For example, is it not shorter, simpler, and more natural to say, All quantity is either a line, or a surface, or a solid, than to say, as Ramus did, quantity is either a line or thing lined; and a thing lined is either a surface or a solid?"[201] Watts made no attempt here to acknowledge his debt to *The Port-Royal Logic,* and only readers versed in the latter work would spot this borrowing. But he was not a plagiarist. He freely acknowledged on a later occasion that the Port-Royalists had been most ingenious in deriving the rules of the syllogism from four general axioms, and it is worthy of notice that he stated these four axioms in the formulations of the Port-Royalists, whereas Le Clerc in using the same source elected to omit one of the axioms and to state only the first three.[202] In other words, Watts plainly notified his readers that he knew and admired Arnauld and Nicole. Indeed, their logic was so widely known as to be either a mandatory source for any progressive logic of that era or an object of condemnation by those who like Dean Aldrich wanted to write a traditional one. Even so, Watts did not follow them slavishly. For example, he refused to treat the controversial fourth figure of the syllogism, on the ground that it was a useless form, whereas the Port-Royalists had given it adequate but unenthusiastic analysis.[203] It should not be understood, however, that Watts failed to make use of Le Clerc's *Logica.* Watts was a student at Thomas Rowe's Academy when that treatise appeared in London in 1692, and it was inevitable that he would read it in connection with his own studies and his duties as tutor of John Hartopp. His own *Logick* failed to mention Le Clerc by name. But his illustration of inductive reasoning is closely parallel to that in Le Clerc's *Logica,* as I pointed out above in the note appended to it. Moreover, his discussion of

---

[201] Translation mine. See *Oeuvres d' Arnauld,* XLI, 243. The Port-Royalists spoke thus: "Par exemple, n'est-il pas plus court, plus simple, & plus naturel de dire: *Toute étendue est ou ligne, ou surface, ou solide,* que de dire, comme Ramus, *magnitudo est linea, vel lineatum: Lineatum est superficies, vel solidum.*" My translation of this passage deliberately borrows Watts's formulations in order to sharpen the comparison.

[202] Compare Watts's *Logick,* pp. 432-434, with *Oeuvres d'Arnauld,* XLI, 258-263, and with Le Clerc's *Logica,* pp. 150-154.

[203] Compare Watts's *Logick,* p. 438, with *Oeuvres d'Arnauld,* XLI, 273-275,

judgment as the second part of logic resembles in various ways what Le Clerc said on the same subject.[204] And in distinguishing wholes as metaphysical, mathematical, physical, and logical, he followed the identical distinctions proposed in Le Clerc's *Ontologia*.[205] It seems fair to conclude that Le Clerc was one of Watts's sources, but that he was not as important to Watts as were the Port-Royalists. The authority whom Watts quoted most openly and at greatest length was John Locke, but these references fall within Watts's analysis of perceptions and ideas as the first part of logic, except for one short passage cited as he was bringing his chapters on reasoning to an end.[206] Locke was plainly not an influence in anything which Watts said on the syllogism and induction. If he had been, Watts's whole approach to logic might have been quite different from what it actually turned out to be.

As I mentioned above in passing, Watts's *Logick* encountered a first-rate competitor in Britain in the middle of the eighteenth century, and that competitor must now be discussed in some detail, not only because of its originality in applying Locke's teachings to the problems of logic, but also because of its creative relation to Thomas Jefferson's great work, the Declaration of Independence. It was entitled *The Elements of Logick*. Its author was William Duncan, a Scotsman, who had taken the degree of master of arts at Marischal College, Aberdeen, in 1735, and had gone some years later to London to seek a career as a professional writer.[207] At first he had supported himself by translating French

[204] Le Clerc's treatment of judgment covers fifty pages of the first edition of his *Logica* (pp. 47-96). The parallel section of Watts's first edition covers two hundred pages (pp. 221-420). Watts's discussion reads as if it were a freshly illustrated and sensibly expanded version of the important points stated by Le Clerc in a condensed style.

[205] Compare Watts's *Logick*, pp. 183-185, with Le Clerc's *Ontologia*, 7.5.

[206] For allusions to or quotations from Locke, see Watts's *Logick*, pp. 20-21, 42, 47, 68, 117, 177-179, 489. The reference on page 117 is to Locke's *A New Method of a Common-Place-Book*, and that on page 489 is to *The Conduct of the Understanding*. Otherwise, Watts cited Locke's *Essay*. Locke's *Conduct of the Understanding* furnished principles and ideas for Watts's similar work, *The Improvement of the Mind: or, A Supplement to the Art of Logick*, which Dr. Johnson praised in his sketch of Watts (*Works*, XI, 48).

[207] My account of Duncan relies in large part upon that by Andrew Kippis in his *Biographia Britannica* (London, 1778-1793), V, 500-504. Cited below as

and Latin works at the behest of booksellers, and one of his translations, for which he never received adequate credit, was published at London in 1743 as *The Satires, Epistles, and Art of Poetry of Horace*.[208] Then he turned to work of his own composing, and in 1748 he brought out his treatise on logic. It first appeared anonymously in the second volume of Robert Dodsley's two-volume compilation, *The Preceptor*, which was designed to introduce young persons to the various branches of learning. Later that same year, it was published by Dodsley as a separate work with Duncan properly identified as the author.[209] From that time onward it had two distinct careers, one as part of Dodsley's general course of education, and the other as an important educational venture in its own right.

It had not proceeded far in either career when an event occurred which did not damage its prospects for a continuingly favorable reception by the learned community—its author was appointed on May 18, 1752, to be professor of philosophy in his

---

Kippis. I also heed the sketch of Duncan in *Officers of the Marischal College and University of Aberdeen 1593-1860* ([Aberdeen], 1897), p. 45, and that by John Westby-Gibson in *The Dictionary of National Biography*.

[208] Duncan's edition and translation of these writings of Horace were published anonymously as Volume II of a work which contained in Volume I David Watson's edition and translation of Horace's *The Odes, Epodes, and Carmen Seculare*. Watson was indeed responsible for Volume I. But Volume II, as printed at London for J. Oswald in 1743, identified its editor and translator only by saying that it was being "Continued on the same Plan as the former Volume publish'd by D. Watson"; and by having its dedicatory epistle signed "The Translator." For evidence that Duncan was responsible for Volume II, see Kippis, p. 500. Later in the eighteenth century, both volumes, with David Watson's name on the title page of each, appeared at London under the title, *The Works of Horace*. The article on Watson in *The Dictionary of National Biography* makes no mention of Duncan's share in this enterprise.

[209] Its title page reads: "The Elements of Logick. In Four Books. By W. Duncan. *Doctrina sed Vim promovet insitam: Rectique cultus Pectora roborant*. Hor. London: Printed for R. Dodsley in *Pall-Mall*. 1748." An "Advertisement" preceding the title page speaks thus: "This Treatise was originally designed, to have been published by itself the Beginning of last Winter; but some Accidents intervening, it was inserted in the Second Volume of the *Preceptor*, and is now printed separately, as was first intended." There is a copy of this very rare book in the Puritan Collection of the Library of the Princeton Theological Seminary.

own college at Aberdeen. There were three professors of philosophy in Marischal College at that time, and they were supposed to divide the branches of this subject among them. Since logic was a most important branch, and since Duncan had published a fine book in that field, his chances of becoming professor of logic would have seemed excellent. Moreover, his only competitor for the post, Dr. Alexander Gerard, was his senior on the faculty by not even one day and his junior in age by almost eleven years. But illness intervened to prevent Duncan from entering upon his professorship before August 21, 1753,[210] and by that time Dr. Gerard was established in the chair of logic. Duncan was left with his second choice, the professorship of natural and experimental philosophy, and he apparently accepted it with good grace. A slight contrast to the concerns of this particular professorship was inadvertently provided by Duncan's next two publications, a translation of *The Commentaries of Caesar* (London, 1753), and another of *Cicero's Select Orations* (London, 1756). But his translation of Caesar's *Commentaries* was accompanied by his own learned treatise on the Roman art of war, and this at least was a subject which had some connection with the application if not the theory of natural science. Then, too, his *Elements of Logick* had exhibited a strong interest in mathematics, and this subject was of course a central part of the scientific curriculum of the time. Thus we need not assume that Duncan was unprepared for or secretly reluctant to carry out the assignment which fell to him. On the positive side, there is evidence that he was a successful teacher. One of his colleagues, Dr. Gerard himself, testified that Duncan as professor of natural science "was diligent, and very accurate."[211] And his students gave convincing evidence that they were drawn to him when in the year 1755 the thirty-three young men in attendance at his classes took up a collection among themselves and succeeded in raising five pounds sterling for the purchase of experimental instruments to be used in the teaching of natural science at Marischal College.[212]

One of those young men was William Small, who took the degree of master of arts that very year.[213] Small was destined to

---

[210] Kippis, pp. 503-504. [211] *Ibid.*, p. 504.
[212] Peter John Anderson, ed., *Fasti Academiae Mariscallanae Aberdonensis* (Aberdeen: Printed for the New Spalding Club, 1889, 1898), II, 322-323.
[213] *Ibid.*, II, 323.

go in 1758 to the College of William and Mary in colonial Virginia under appointment as professor of natural philosophy. It happened there that on August 14, 1760, his colleague, the Rev. Jacob Rowe, was expelled from his professorship of moral philosophy and logic because he had gotten drunk with undergraduates and had led them in a riot against the townspeople of Williamsburg. Events of this sort are not unknown in academic circles. What made this one important and fateful was that for the following year William Small not only carried out his own duties but Jacob Rowe's as well, and that young Thomas Jefferson, who had just entered the College of William and Mary, became Small's pupil in moral philosophy and logic. Relations between master and pupil were characterized by mutual understanding, mutual respect, and mutual affection. Jefferson said later of Small that he "probably fixed the destinies of my life." We may be sure that Small directed his pupil to his own master's excellent work, the *Elements of Logick*, and that it constituted the chief assignment in Jefferson's course in that subject. At any rate, the Declaration of Independence contains unmistakable echoes of Duncan's thinking, and it is constructed upon the exact organizational plan that Duncan recommended for works designed to create certainty and conviction among enlightened and critical readers.[214] Nowhere is the germinative relation between academic study and political action more evident than it is in this remarkable coincidence. Nowhere is it more certain that the historical study of the logics and rhetorics used as textbooks in a given century will make rich contributions to an understanding of the literary works produced at that time.

In the fifteen months between Duncan's appointment to the professorship at Marischal College and his actual entrance into that office, *The Monthly Review*, which had been founded in London in 1749 by Ralph Griffiths as a journal devoted to the critical appraisal of new books and pamphlets published in Great Britain and Ireland, violated its customary practice and ran a review of Duncan's *Elements of Logick*, which was by then four years old. The reviewer was William Rose, himself a Scot, and the date of

---

[214] For a detailed discussion of the influence exerted by Duncan upon Jefferson through the good offices of Small, see "The Declaration of Independence and Eighteenth-Century Logic," *The William and Mary Quarterly*, 3rd ser., XVIII (October 1961), 463-484.

his review was December 1752.[215] Rose acknowledged that Duncan's work fell outside the scope of strictly current literature; "yet, as it deserves to be much better known than we apprehend it is," he said, "such of our readers as have not had occasion to hear of it, will, we flatter ourselves, excuse our deviating a little from our usual method, in order to give them a short account of it."[216] Rose took notice of the strong prejudice created against logic by "those numerous, and too often frivolous and unnecessary distinctions, divisions and subdivisions, with which most of the books that treat of it abound." But he added at once:

> Our ingenious and judicious author, sensible of this, has presented us with a short system of *logick*, in a dress more agreeable and inviting, than that wherein any former ones, that we know of, have made their appearance. He treats his subject like one who is a thorough master of it, and disdaining to copy servilely after those who have gone before him, has struck out a plan of his own, conducted it with so much perspicuity and judgment, given so clear and distinct a view of the furniture of our minds for the discovery of truth, and laid down such excellent rules for the attainment of it, as render his work the best introduction to the study of philosophy and the mathematicks in our own, or perhaps in any other language.[217]

It is not easy to find fault with these opinions, even if we might be normally inclined to believe that a Scot in the presence of the English would speak nothing of a fellow Scot except in praise. As Rose indicated, Duncan's *Elements of Logick* is short, well-written, original, and excellent. And if it cannot in our own era be regarded as the best introduction to the study of philosophy and mathematics in English, it is nevertheless hard to name a work more deserving of such an accolade in eighteenth-century Britain.

Like Watts, Crousaz, and Le Clerc, Duncan followed the Port-Royalists in dividing logic into four parts, each of which dealt in the first instance with a separate power of the mind, and in the

---

[215] Like all articles in *The Monthly Review*, this one was anonymous. For the identification of its author as William Rose, see Benjamin C. Nangle, *The Monthly Review First Series 1749-1789 Indexes of Contributors and Articles* (Oxford, 1934), pp. xiii, 37-38, 93.

[216] *The Monthly Review*, VII (December 1752), 467.

[217] *Ibid.*, pp. 467-468.

second instance with the linguistic equivalent of that power. Thus he spoke successively of the ability of the mind to form ideas from sensory or reflective contact with the objects of experience, with its ability to respond intuitively to those ideas as their similarities or differences became instantaneously self-evident, with its power to deal rationally with ideas when their similarities or differences could not be established by intuition, and with its ability to arrange ideas into a complex structure of thought and discourse as the final steps in demonstrating how they were alike or different; and as Duncan spoke of these things, he identified their respective logical equivalents as terms, propositions, syllogisms, and discourses. He did not openly declare that these four divisions of logic were authorized by the Port-Royalists, and that he was consciously following their lead in this matter. But the Port-Royalists figured importantly in his hierarchy of values. Thus in his analysis of the syllogism, after having stated the main characteristics of each of the four standard figures, and after having then remarked that on the present occasion he would not go into the various subdivisions of each figure, he significantly said: "I shall therefore content myself, with referring the Reader to the *Port-Royal Art of Thinking*, where he will find the *Moods* and *Figures* of *Syllogisms* distinctly explained, and the *Rules* proper to each very neatly demonstrated."[218] We may conclude from this observation that Duncan intended his work to be a shortened version of *The Port-Royal Logic*, so far as the canons of logical doctrine were concerned, and that he would want his readers to make full use of that longer treatise whenever they felt his own pages to lack needed detail on this or that traditional point.

But Duncan superimposed upon the influential doctrines of the Port-Royalists an original and progressive concept of his own. That concept appeared at the beginning of his discussion of judgment, the second part of logic. Judgments were to him the basic units of human knowledge, as ideas were the constituent elements, and things the objects. Any of these units, he believed, had one of three actual foundations—intuition, experience, or testimony. Each of these three things had in turn an instrument and

---

[218] My quotations are all from *The Elements of Logick* as it was printed in Volume II of Robert Dodsley's *The Preceptor* (London, 1748). The quotation just given is on page 124. Italics and punctuation here and below are from that edition.

a kind of knowledge peculiar to it. The three foundations, the three instruments, and the three kinds of knowledge, became the subject of the most significant chapters of Duncan's *Elements of Logick*.

A mind furnished with ideas tends naturally to compare them one with another and to try to judge whether they belong or do not belong together. When by bare inspection of two ideas the mind discovers immediately what relation they have each to each, "the Judgments thence obtained," said Duncan, "are called *intuitive*, from a Word that denotes *to look at*: for in this Case, a mere Attention to the Ideas compared, suffices to let us see, how far they are connected or disjoined." Duncan added:

> Thus, *that the Whole is greater than any of it's Parts*, is an intuitive Judgment, nothing more being required to convince us of it's Truth, than an Attention to the Ideas of *Whole* and *Part*. And this too is the Reason, why we call the Act of the Mind forming these Judgments, *Intuition*; as it is indeed no more, than an immediate Perception of the Agreement or Disagreement of any two Ideas.[219]

Now intuition, Duncan went on, has demonstration or syllogism for its instrument and science for its product. His explanation deserves our notice:

> For whatever is deduced from our intuitive Perceptions, by a clear and connected Series of Proofs, is said to be demonstrated, and produces absolute Certainty in the Mind. Hence the Knowledge obtained in this manner, is what we properly term *Science*; because in every Step of the Procedure, it carries it's own Evidence along with it, and leaves no room for Doubt or Hesitation.[220]

Truths of this class, said Duncan, express changeless and immutable relations between the two ideas concerned. And of this nature are all the truths belonging to natural religion, morality, and mathematics.

When the bare inspection of two ideas fails to reveal what relation they have to each other, the mind has another recourse, and this ultimately brings into being another kind of knowledge.

[219] *Ibid.*, pp. 79-80.   [220] *Ibid.*, p. 80.

Duncan turned next to this. "The second Ground of human Judgment," he declared, "is *Experience*; from which we infer the Existence of those Objects that surround us, and fall under the immediate Notice of our Senses."[221] Experience has to be the basis of our judgment of the relation of two ideas when a study of them will not tell us what the relation may be. Is the idea of elasticity incompatible with the idea of hardness? We settle this problem, said Duncan, by consulting our experience with a piece of ivory and a stone:

> For being altogether Strangers to the true Nature both of Elasticity and Hardness, we cannot by the bare Contemplation of our Ideas determine, how far the one necessarily implies the other, or whether there may not be a Repugnance between them. But when we observe them to exist both in the same Object, we are then assured from Experience, that they are not incompatible; and when we also find, that a Stone is hard and not elastic, and that Air tho' elastic is not hard, we also conclude upon the same Foundation, that the Ideas are not necessarily conjoined, but may exist separately in different Objects.

> I might easily shew from innumerable other Instances, [said Duncan later on] how much our Knowledge, of the mutual Action of Bodies, depends upon Observation. The Bite of a Viper will kill. Plants are some salutary, some noxious. Fire dissolves one Body and hardens another. These are Truths generally known, nor is it less evident, that we owe their Discovery wholly to Experience.[222]

Thus as intuition is the foundation of scientific knowledge, argued Duncan, so is experience of natural. And the improvement of natural knowledge must rely not upon the syllogism but upon the method of trial and experience. On this latter all-important point Duncan took occasion later to speak as follows:

> As nevertheless it is certain, that many general Conclusions in natural Philosophy, are embraced without Doubt or Hesitation, nay, that we form most of the Schemes and Pursuits of Life upon that Foundation; it will naturally be asked here, how come we by this Assurance? I answer, not scientifically, and in

[221] *Ibid.*, p. 81.   [222] *Ibid.*, p. 81, 82.

the Way of strict Demonstration, but by Analogy, and an Induction of Experiments. . . . 'Tis not till after we have tried the Thing in a Variety of Experiments, and found it always to hold, that we begin to presume there may be really some such Connection, tho' our Views are too short and imperfect to discover it. Hence we are led to frame a general Conclusion, arguing from what has already happened, to what will happen again in the like Cases. . . . This is called Reasoning by *Analogy*; and it is, as we see, founded entirely upon Induction, and Experiments made with particular Objects: the more precise and accurate our Ideas of these Objects are, and the greater the Variety of Experiments upon which we build our Reasoning, the more certain and undoubted will the Conclusions be.[223]

But the experience of each man is limited to the objects which he himself can bring within his own scrutiny, inasmuch as other objects are so numerous that he cannot examine them all, and many are so distant that they cannot even be reached. "Life too is short," Duncan declared, "and so crouded with Cares, that but little Time is left for any single Man, to employ himself in unfolding the Mysteries of Nature. Hence it is necessary, to admit many Things upon the Testimony of others, which by this means becomes the Foundation of a great Part of our Knowledge of Body."[224] The things which a man studies through what others have said of them include not only objects existing in the present but actions that happened in the past. These latter, indeed, cannot possibly have a present existence, and they can be recreated for study only by taking notice of the records which they have left behind and the witnesses who saw them happen. "*Testimony* therefore is justly accounted a third Ground of human Judgment," said Duncan; "and as from the other two we have deduced *scientifical* and *natural* Knowledge, so may we from this derive *historical*; by which I would be understood to mean, not merely a Knowledge of the civil Transactions of States and Kingdoms, but of all Facts whatsoever, where Testimony is the ultimate Foundation of our Belief."[225]

Historical knowledge is not only characterized by having testimony as the basis of its judgments; it also has an instrument of its

---

[223] *Ibid.*, pp. 176-177.   [224] *Ibid.*, p. 83.
[225] *Ibid.*, pp. 83-84.

own to match the demonstrative syllogism of science and the induction and analogy of natural philosophy. Duncan called that instrument *"Criticism* and *probable Conjecture."*[226] These terms mean that when historical judgments are made to rest upon what witnesses have said or written, the witnesses must be shown to have been men of veracity, to have been competent judges, to have had the opportunity to be informed upon the matter in question, and so on, while the happenings of which the witnesses speak must be shown to be probable in themselves and harmonious with other known events of the time. Duncan concluded this part of his discussion as follows:

> By these and such like Arguments, founded partly on Criticism, partly on probable Conjecture, we judge of past Transactions; and though they are not capable of *scientifical* Proof, yet in many Cases we arrive at an undoubted Assurance of them. For as it is absurd to demand Mathematical Demonstration in Matters of Fact, because they admit not of that Kind of Evidence; it is no less so to doubt of their Reality, when they are proved by the best Arguments their Nature and Quality will bear.[227]

The three foundations of knowledge, each the guardian of its own instrument, each the support of its own kind of formal learning, correspond, as the preceding discussion has continuously implied, to three degrees of certainty. Highest in degree of certainty are the truths of mathematics, morality, and natural religion, and these subjects Duncan identified as science properly so-called. A somewhat lower degree of certainty is achieved in natural philosophy, and a still lower degree in history. On these three orders of certitude Duncan spoke directly when his treatise on logic was coming to an end. He said:

> In Matters of Science we argue from the Ideas in our own Minds, and the Connections and Relations they have one to another. And as when these Relations are set clearly and plainly before us, we cannot avoid perceiving and owning them, hence all the Truths of this Class produce absolute Certainty in the Mind, and are attended with a necessary and unavoidable Assent. It is otherwise in the Case of natural Knowledge. Intuition and inward Perception have here no Place. We discern not

[226] *Ibid.*, p. 180.   [227] *Ibid.*, pp. 179-180.

the Powers and Properties of those Objects that surround us, by any View and Comparison of the Ideas of them one with another, but merely by Experience, and the Impressions they make on the Senses. But now the Reports of Sense happening in some Instances to deceive us, we have no infallible Assurance that they may not in others; which weakens not a little the Evidence attending this Kind of Knowledge, and leaves room for Suspicion and Distrust. . . . If then absolute and infallible Certainty is not to be obtained in Natural Knowledge, much less can we expect it in Historical. For here Testimony is the only Ground of Assent, and therefore the Possibility of our being deceived, is still greater than in the Case of Experience.[228]

The inability of history and natural philosophy to achieve what was regarded as the absolute certainty of mathematics, of revealed morality, and of religious truths had of course been a constant supposition in traditional logic and had been paralleled by the great emphasis upon the deductive or syllogistic method of enquiry. Duncan's tendency to modify this supposition by admitting the practical reliability of conclusions in natural philosophy and history, and by thinking of inductive and critical methods of enquiry as being independent of the syllogistic method, represents not only a renunciation of the rigidities of the old habit of mind but also a positive step forward in the development of eighteenth-century British logic.

Duncan's discussion of method as the fourth part of logic offers yet another proof of his originality in treating the accepted patterns of logical theory. He adopted the conventional idea that method had two aspects, the analytic and the synthetic, and that each of these aspects had its investigative and its presentational functions. But his actual treatment of these subjects was more than merely traditional. His chapter on the analytic method, which he also called the method of resolution or the method of invention, outlined in coherent detail the successive steps to be taken as the human understanding seeks to hold within its span of attention a multitude of particular ideas, each with the same puzzling characteristic about it, and seeks then to discover some outside idea which will explain the presence of the puzzling characteristic and trace it to the operation of an underlying princi-

---

[228] *Ibid.*, pp. 176-179.

ple.[229] In describing these steps and their corollaries, Duncan emphasized the value of mathematics in training the mind to extend its dimensions, "enlarge its Compass of Perception, and accustom it to wide and comprehensive Views of Things,"[230] and he dwelt particularly upon arithmetic and algebra as indispensable disciplines in teaching the enquirer how to unravel puzzles. These recommendations would not be unfamiliar to anyone who had read the logics that preceded Duncan's, and yet Duncan would be recognized as having given his version of them an engaging effectiveness of expression. The same observation applies to Duncan's later chapter on the synthetic method, which he also called the method of composition, or of doctrine, or of instruction, or of science.[231] What he meant by calling it the method of science deserves a special comment.

Since science was to Duncan a term applied to all propositions which have the highest degree of certainty about them, and since mathematical truths rank high among such propositions, Duncan gradually developed the concept that the method used by the mathematicians offers the best possible definition of the synthetic method in logic. His first step in expounding this concept was taken in his discussion of judgment as the second part of logic. There he made it plain that propositions or judgments which achieved the certainty of science were to be classed either as self-evident or demonstrable. His own formulation of this distinction is as follows:

> When any Proposition is offered to the View of the Mind, if the Terms in which it is expressed are understood; upon comparing the Ideas together, the Agreement or Disagreement asserted is either immediately perceived, or found to lie beyond the present Reach of the Understanding. In the first Case the Proposition is said to be *self-evident*, and admits not of any Proof, because a bare Attention to the Ideas themselves, produces full Conviction and Certainty; nor is it possible to call in any thing more evident, by way of Confirmation. But where the Connection or Repugnance comes not so readily under the Inspection of the Mind, there we must have Recourse to Reasoning; and if by a clear Series of Proofs we can make out the

[229] *Ibid.*, pp. 148, 150-168.
[230] *Ibid.*, p. 152.   [231] *Ibid.*, pp. 148-149, 168-192.

Truth proposed, insomuch that Self-evidence shall accompany every Step of the Procedure, we are then able to demonstrate what we assert, and the Proposition itself is said to be *demonstrable*.[232]

By dwelling upon the procedures of proof in mathematics, Duncan proceeded to illustrate how demonstrations occurred. The mathematicians, he observed, begin their demonstrations by fixing the exact meaning of their terms by the process of definition. Their next care is to lay down the self-evident truths which are to be the foundation of their future reasonings. These self-evident truths in mathematics, Duncan went on, are either axioms or postulates. Axioms are self-evident speculative propositions, as exemplified by that which declares a whole to be greater than any of its parts; and postulates are self-evident practical propositions, as when we say that a circle may be described about any center with any radius. As for demonstrable propositions in mathematics, they too are speculative or practical, the former being known as theorems, and the latter as problems. "Since I am upon this Subject," said Duncan, "it may not be amiss to add, that besides the four Kinds of Propositions already mentioned, Mathematicians have also a fifth, known by the Name of *Corollaries*."[233] The last element in mathematical method, added Duncan, consists in "what they call their *Scholia*." These are analogous to annotations made by a scholar in editing a classical text. They may be affixed to definitions, to axioms, to postulates, to theorems, to problems, and to corollaries, their purpose being to clarify obscurities, answer objections, point to applications, or identify the mathematician who first discovered the proposition concerned. Here is what Duncan said as he sought to summarize all of the steps in his description of the method of the mathematicians:

They begin with Definitions. From these they deduce their Axioms and Postulates, which serve as Principles of Reasoning; and having thus laid a firm Foundation, advance to Theorems and Problems, establishing all by the strictest Rules of Demonstration. The Corollaries flow naturally and of themselves. And if any Particulars are still wanting, to illustrate a Subject, or compleat the Reader's Information; these, that the Series of

---

[232] *Ibid.*, p. 96.   [233] *Ibid.*, p. 101.

Reasoning may not be interrupted or broken, are generally thrown into Scholia. In a System of Knowledge so uniform and well connected, no wonder if we meet with Certainty; and if those Clouds and Darknesses, that deface other Parts of human Science, and bring Discredit even upon Reason itself, are here scattered and disappear.[234]

Up to this time, Duncan was still engaged with the discussion of the second part of logic, and his description of the method of mathematics had been inserted to reinforce his distinction between self-evident and demonstrable propositions. Not until he came to the fourth part of logic, and undertook to analyze what logicians had traditionally called the synthetic method, did he make it clear that his earlier discussion of the procedures of mathematical proof had been an important step in his continuing endeavor to show the synthetic method to be the exact duplicate of the method of mathematics. The identification of the two did not become final until Duncan, having explained the synthetic method, was writing the very last words of his *Elements of Logick*. Those words went thus:

> It is true the Method here laid down, hath hitherto been observed strictly, only among Mathematicians; and is therefore by many thought, to be peculiar to Number and Magnitude. But it appears evidently from what we have said above, that it may be equally applied in all such other Parts of Knowledge, as regard the abstract Ideas of the Mind, and the Relations subsisting between them. And since wherever it is applied, it necessarily begets *Science* and *Certainty*, we have hence chosen to denominate it the *Method of Science*, the better to intimate its true Nature and Extent.[235]

Duncan's admiration of mathematical method as a model for logic stemmed from something which Locke had said in his *Conduct of the Understanding*, as Duncan himself took pains to let us know in Book III of his treatise. Speaking there of the syllogism, and of the problems involved in finding a proper middle term for use in establishing the connection between the two other terms under consideration, Duncan remarked that no science furnishes more instances of the happy choice of middle terms than mathematics does. And he quoted Locke thus:

[234] *Ibid.*, p. 102. [235] *Ibid.*, p. 192.

Not that we look upon it as necessary, (*to use the Words of the great Mr.* Locke) that all Men should be deep Mathematicians, but that, having got the Way of Reasoning which that Study necessarily brings the Mind to, they may be able to transfer it to other Parts of Knowledge, as they shall have Occasion. For in all sorts of Reasoning, every single Argument should be managed as a Mathematical Demonstration, the Connection and Dependence of Ideas should be followed, till the Mind is brought to the Source on which it bottoms, and can trace the Coherence through the whole Train of Proofs. . . . Nothing does this better than Mathematicks, which therefore I think should be taught all those, who have the Time and Opportunity, not so much to make them Mathematicians, as to make them reasonable Creatures; for though we all call ourselves so, because we are born to it, if we please; yet we may truly say, Nature gives us but the Seeds of it. . . .[236]

It is surprising indeed that Duncan, after having perceptively followed Locke in recommending mathematical demonstration as the archetype of all argument whatever, and in seeing induction, analogy, criticism, and conjecture as equal partners of the syllogism in the development of human learning, should have done what he did when he spoke of the syllogism itself. On this subject he reverted to the tradition that Locke had strongly condemned. He treated the syllogism as the sole instrument to be used in the creation of scientific knowledge, although he had shown great insight in recognizing that reliable learning which might one day achieve the status of science could exist in natural philosophy and history and could rest upon such legitimate alternatives to the syllogism as repeated experiments and the critical evaluation of documents and testimony. He treated induction as an irregular type of syllogism when he spoke of it as a form of reasoning, although it is obvious from what he said about it elsewhere that it deserved consideration as an independent form. He called the *dictum de omni* and *de nullo* "the great Principles of Syllogistick Reasoning; inasmuch as all Conclusions whatsoever,

---

[236] *Ibid.*, pp. 121-122. The entire quotation, only part of which is given here, occupies thirty-three lines of Duncan's text, and is credited to Locke's *The Conduct of the Understanding.* For the first eleven lines of the quotation, see *Posthumous Works of Mr. John Locke*, pp. 30-31; for the rest, *ibid.*, pp. 26-27. Duncan's quotation is not entirely faithful to Locke's original text, but he does not change Locke's meaning in any real sense.

either rest immediately upon them, or upon Propositions deduced from them";[237] and yet he had in effect recognized that these principles do not explain the reasoning which takes place when the mind moves from the inspection of a particular case to a general conclusion covering all analogous cases. Nowhere in his treatment of reasoning as the third part of logic did he mention Locke's belief that the syllogism had little value in the search for new knowledge, and that an act of thought actually corresponded not to the form of the syllogism but to the form of inference. In fact, Duncan's third book tends throughout to be at odds with his other three books, as something traditional and ritualistic is at odds with that which seeks to come to terms with crisis and change. Even so, the third book is well written, brief, and interesting. If it repeats familiar doctrine, we must remember that Duncan believed this doctrine changeless and true so far as pure science was concerned. His real originality consisted in his wanting to superimpose upon old truths some new doctrines to guide the mind in natural philosophy and history, even if these important endeavors could not produce the highest degree of certainty.

On balance, Duncan's *Elements of Logick* must be regarded as the most challenging and most up-to-date book of its time, place, and class. Its analysis of the foundations, the instruments, and the reliability of natural philosophy and history meets the challenges that had to be met in releasing scholarship from the awkward limitations still being imposed upon it in the name of Aristotle. Its deliberate failure to recommend the use of the ancient machinery of topics as a means of invention and enquiry in science and learning is wholly in the most progressive spirit of its century. Its complete lack of interest in disputation as a device for establishing and communicating truth is also progressive, as is its conscious recognition that in many fields experiments could profitably be used as the best means to authenticate and enlarge knowledge. And finally, its recommendation that the method of mathematics should be adopted as the model for argumentative presentation in matters of politics, morality, and religion was responsive to one of the most critical needs of the seventeen-hundreds. That need had developed as the old rhetoric was losing its capacity to influence literary practice, and the new rhetoric had not as yet fully matured. The old rhetoric believed in the use of topics in inventing the subject matter of discourse; it believed in the exploitation

[237] *Ibid.*, p. 137.

of probabilities in arguing a case; it modeled its utterances upon the elaborate form of the classical oration; and it was spellbound by the ornamental possibilities of the tropes and the figures of style. The new rhetoric was to repudiate these standards, and to seek new ones in the content, the methods, and the style of science and scholarship. Thomas Jefferson paid William Duncan the compliment of writing the Declaration of Independence according to the requirements of Duncan's method of science. Thus the greatest public address of the eighteenth century was framed to conform to the laws of logic. If this fact seems paradoxical and somehow at variance with our expectation that a public address should adhere to the laws of rhetoric, we ought to remember that the new rhetoric of the age of science was not to be like the old rhetoric of the age of ritual, and that Jefferson with a momentous political message for the new era had the superb insight to accommodate that message to the only style which the new era would respect.

Duncan's *Elements of Logick* enjoyed a conspicuous popularity in Great Britain and America for seventy-five years after its first publication. In Dodsley's *The Preceptor*, it had eight London editions between 1748 and 1793, and a copy of one of the later of these was in Thomas Jefferson's library.[238] As a separate publication it was an even greater success. In this form it reached its ninth edition at London by 1800, and after the beginning of the year 1776 it appeared at Edinburgh on four successive occasions, at New York on two, at Albany on two, and at Philadelphia on one. On May 12, 1760, Duncan was drowned while swimming, and at that time he was not quite forty-three years old. Thus he did not live to see his *Elements of Logick* reach its full audience. But he did know in 1760 that it had had its third edition in *The Preceptor* and its fourth edition in its other form. Three months after his death, the Reverend Jacob Rowe of the College of William and Mary in distant Virginia was expelled from his professorship of moral philosophy and logic, and Duncan's former pupil, William Small, took over Rowe's duties. Had Duncan known what consequences for his *Elements of Logick* would flow from those events, he would no doubt have been pleased, but he would certainly not have considered the consequences unforeseeable wherever his work was taken to mean what he intended.

[238] Sowerby, *Catalogue of the Library of Thomas Jefferson*, I, 507. See also *The William and Mary Quarterly*, 3rd ser., XVIII (October 1961), 470, n. 23.

When Dr. Johnson wrote the Preface for *The Preceptor* to introduce to the British public Duncan's *Elements of Logick* and eleven other parts of polite learning, he mentioned several logics that might supplement Duncan's, if readers wanted to further themselves in that discipline, and one of those logics, as we know, was by an author whom he identified as Wolfius. Dr. Johnson's contemporaries would have recognized this as a reference to Christian Wolff, a German mathematician and philosopher, whose considerable reputation throughout earlier eighteenth-century Europe was associated with his success in developing, systematizing, and teaching the philosophical doctrines of Leibniz. Wolff was born in Breslau in 1679 and educated between 1699 and 1703 at the universities of Jena and Leipzig. After lecturing at Leipzig until 1706, he was invited by Frederick I, king of Prussia, to accept the chair of philosophy at Halle, and he remained there until 1723, enjoying great popularity as a teacher, attracting many disciples, and becoming known in wider and wider circles of European learning. As early as November 8, 1710, he was made a Fellow of the Royal Society of London. But despite his fame, he was forced to leave his post at Halle in 1723, thanks to the success of his enemies in convincing Frederick I that he should be sent into exile because his opinions might be such as to encourage insubordination in the Prussian Army. For the next seventeen years, Wolff found a refuge, a welcome, and a post of honor, at the University of Marburg. In 1733 he was made an associate member of the Royal Academy of Sciences of Paris. When Frederick II, later to be called the Great, came to the throne of Prussia in 1740, one of his first acts was to invite Wolff to return to his post at Halle, and Wolff accepted. But he found the scene of his early academic triumphs no longer productive of discipleship and adulation, even though the court and the university did everything possible to pay him homage. The fact was that the times had moved ahead of him, and that his teachings had become obsolete and unheeded. He died at Halle in 1754.[239]

[239] My sketch of Wolff's life depends upon the following published accounts: that by Hans W. Arndt in the introduction to his excellent edition of Wolff's German logic, in Christian Wolff, *Gesammelte Werke*, I. Abt. Band 1 (Hildesheim, 1965), which I cite below as Arndt; that by W. Schrader in *Allgemeine Deutsche Biographie*, XLIV (Leipzig, 1898), pp. 12-28; that by De Gérando in *Biographie Universelle*; that by Eugène Asse in *Nouvelle Biographie Générale*; and that by Andrew S. Pringle-Pattison in *Encyclopaedia Britannica*, 11th edn.

Dr. Johnson's mention of Wolff by his Latinized name indicates clearly enough that he was thinking of Wolff's logic in its Latin version. That work had been originally published at Frankfurt and Leipzig in 1728, and it was given later editions in those same two places in 1732 and 1740. It was entitled *Philosophia Rationalis, sive Logica, Methodo Scientifica Pertractata,* and its title page identified the author as Christianus Wolfius. But it had had an earlier existence as a German work published first at Halle in 1713 under the title *Vernünfftige Gedancken von den Kräfften des menschlichen Verstandes und ihrem richtigen Gebrauche In Erkäntniss der Wahrheit.* It was this vernacular version which achieved great popularity in Wolff's own country, where it counted its fourteenth edition by 1754.[240] It has been said of Wolff that he was virtually the first person in history to teach philosophy how to speak German. Certainly his German logic is a good witness to the truth of this assertion. Before it came out in its fourteenth edition, Jean des Champs translated it into French and published it in that form at Berlin in 1736; and it was produced at Venice in 1737 in an Italian version. No English version was in existence at the time when Dr. Johnson was writing the preface for Dodsley's *The Preceptor.* In fact, Wolff's treatise would not have been linked to the history of British logic by any ties of publication in Britain if it had not happened that an English version came out in London in 1770, some twenty-two years after Dr. Johnson had recommended its Latin text. The English version was called *Logic, or Rational Thoughts on the Powers of the Human Understanding.* It declared itself to be based upon the twelfth German edition, which had appeared in 1744.

Jean des Champs in an introductory statement affixed to his French translation of Wolff's logic gave some interesting details of the migratory life of European students during the eighteenth century, and of the drawing power of Wolff as a famous professor; and by a happy chance Jean threw in some proof that Wolff was admired by a man who would one day be a powerful king.[241] Jean and his brother started their academic careers by taking the

[240] Arndt, pp. 99.

[241] See "Avertissement du Traducteur" in *Logique, ou Réflexions sur les Forces de L'Entendement Humain, et sur Leur Legitime Usage, dans La Connoissance de la Verite* (Berlin, 1736). I here present the "Avertissement" in paraphrase, with interpolations of my own.

usual course in philosophy at Geneva under Swiss masters, and then they migrated to Germany to study theology. Despite their already having satisfied the requirements in the subjects taught by the celebrated Professor Wolff, they decided to attend his classes anyway; and so in the years 1727 and 1728 they studied under Wolff at Marburg. In 1727 Wolff had not yet published the Latin version of his logic, and thus Jean and his brother in order to comprehend his teachings had to master German, which they had neglected during their four years at Geneva. Once they had come to understand Wolff's native tongue, the idea was suggested to them that they translate his German logic into French. They did so and submitted their translation to Wolff, who understood French rather well even if he only spoke it a little. Wolff thought their French translation was faithful to his German, and he urged them to publish it. Family problems prevented their doing so at once, and after two years Jean's brother went away to take up his profession as pastor of the French church at Buchholz near Berlin. Jean continued to work on the translation, polishing it and adding things which Wolff had added to his own successive German editions. Then the crown prince, who would rule as Frederick II after 1740, and whose interest in French civilization was already well known, heard of the translation, and urged its publication, after having read it himself in part. Jean dedicated the translation to the crown prince when it was published at Berlin in 1736.[242] And his dedicatory epistle spoke thus of Wolff: "Mr. Wolff is certainly the greatest philosopher that there is in Europe. . . . The time has thus come at last when Germany is able to show in her turn a philosopher worthy to be compared to Descartes of France and to Newton of Great Britain."[243]

If we lay the German text of Wolff's logic alongside the French and the English versions, we can satisfy ourselves that Jean des Champs and his anonymous English fellow-translator strove for

[242] The dedicatory epistle is addressed thus: "A Son Altesse Roïale Monseigneur Le Prince Roïal." It is dated "Berlin, le 1 Septembre 1736," and is signed Jean des Champs.

[243] Translation mine. Jean des Champs's French text reads as follows: "Mr. Wolff est certainement le plus grand Philosophe qu'il y ait en Europe. . . . Le tems est donc enfin venu, où l'Allemagne pourra montrer à son tour un Philosophe, digne d'être comparé au Descartes de la France, & au Nevton de la Grande Bretagne!"

accuracy and inclusiveness in placing Wolff's doctrine into their own tongues. Each of the three works contains the same number of chapters; each version of each chapter contains the same number of separate sections; each German chapter title, each German term, each German sentence, finds its way to its French or English equivalent. Thus, like the parallel texts in French or German, the English translation discusses the following subjects: notions or ideas; the use of words or terms; propositions; syllogisms; the investigating of propositions by experience; the investigating of propositions by definitions; science, faith, opinions, and errors; estimating a person's power for examining truth; how to judge man's discoveries; how to judge books; how to read with profit; how to read judicious books, especially the Holy Scriptures; how to proceed so as to convince others; how to conduct refutation; how to proceed in disputation; and how to acquire the habit of using logic. The list of these subjects suggests, as the texts concerned conclusively prove, that Wolff saw logical doctrine as in part a scholastic science and in part a humanistic art. Prefixed to the English translation of Wolff's text are fifty-two pages devoted to a life of the author and twenty-four pages containing "The Author's Short View of the Following Logical Treatise," and under the latter heading we find a precise statement of Wolff's conception of his subject as a whole. "Logic I divide into two principal parts," he said, "the theoretical, or that which contains the rules of logic, and the practical, or that which comprises the manifold uses of these rules. To the first part, belong the four first chapters: to the second, the remaining chapters."[244] It should be added that the first of these two parts deals with perceptions, judgments, and reasoning, whereas the second deals with method. Thus Wolff gave a new twist to the four-part logic made popular by the Port-Royalists, but in the last analysis he covered the headings that they had prescribed, and that Le Clerc, Crousaz, Watts, and Duncan had also covered.

[244] The English translation has the following title page: "Logic, or Rational Thoughts on the Powers of the Human Understanding; with their Use and Application in the Knowledge and Search of Truth. Translated from the German of Baron Wolfius. To which is prefixed A Life of the Author. London: Printed for L. Hawes, W. Clarke, and R. Collins, in Pater-noster-Row. M DCC LXX." Cited below as *Logic, or Rational Thoughts*. The present quotation is on page lxvi.

During Wolff's exile at Marburg, he undertook to translate all of his writings into Latin, and his treatise on logic was an important part of that enterprise. To be sure, the logic in its Latin text appeared too late to benefit Jean des Champs and his brother, but it must have benefited later generations of itinerant students who were drawn to Wolff's classroom and yet were unable to understand him in German. As I indicated above, his Latin logic was first published in 1728. Although it contained the same basic doctrine that Wolff had put into his German logic, it dealt with that doctrine in a far more elaborate way. In fact, the Latin text fills 866 pages and amounts to 257,000 words, whereas the English translation and the German text contain about 50,000 words spread upon some 230 pages.[245] De Gérando remarked that the entire body of Wolff's philosophy occupied twenty-four quarto volumes when it was published in Latin, and that these could all have been digested into one volume without loss to anybody.[246] But De Gérando's judgment contains more wit than wisdom in its application to Wolff's *Philosophia Rationalis sive Logica*. This particular work, indeed, acts as a magnifying glass through which the parallel doctrines of the vernacular text can be seen in the largest and most illuminating perspective, and thus can be the more easily identified as a mixture of the strongly traditional and the mildly progressive.

One of the most obvious features of Wolff's traditionalism is delineated in his belief that logic is the instrument of communication as well as enquiry. In the second of the two main parts into which he divided logic, he devoted an entire section consisting of three chapters of his Latin text to the use of logic in searching for truth, and a later section consisting of five chapters to the use of logic in communicating truth to others.[247] In discussing the communicative function of logic, Wolff spoke of the way to convince others, the way to answer an opponent, the way to defend oneself, the way to conduct a disputation, and the way to offer instruction. In still another section of the second division of his

---

[245] These figures and estimates are based upon the third edition of Wolff's Latin logic, the sixth edition of his German logic, and the sole edition of his logic as translated into English.

[246] See *Biographie Universelle*, s.v. Wolf ou Wolff (Jean-Chrétien, baron de).

[247] *Philosophia Rationalis sive Logica*, Editio Tertia Emendatior (Francofurti & Lipsiae, M DCC XXXX), pp. 480-537, 706-797. Cited below as *Logica*.

Latin text, he discussed the use of logic in writing, judging, and reading natural history, civil history, and doctrinal works, and in connection with the latter kind of composition he gave attention to the analytical and the synthetic methods.[248] What he said on these subjects need not concern us here, inasmuch as his teachings are not different from those which I have explained in other connections. But it deserves to be emphasized that he was not inclined to ally logic exclusively with the methods of scientific investigation or to see that such an alliance might be possible at some future date.

Wolff was also strongly traditional in his view that the search for truth was essentially a deductive enterprise, anchored in axioms and definitions, conducted by syllogism rather than by induction, and guaranteed by the *dictum de omni et nullo*. These attitudes are all made evident throughout his discussion of reasoning as the third operation of the mind. Recognizing explicitly that the syllogistic method was everywhere in great disrepute, he declared that he chose still to adhere to it, not out of blind love of antiquity, not out of ignorance of modern discoveries, but out of an abiding faith in its value; and he proceeded to justify that faith by remarking that geometrical demonstrations can all be resolved into formal syllogisms, that discoveries in mathematics are made exclusively by syllogistic means, that in all other disciplines syllogisms are the only means to genuine demonstrations, and that the syllogistic method protects man against every possibility of error.[249] In line with these precepts, he held that every induction is an enthymeme comprehended under the general categorical syllogism[250]; he declared that the categorical syllogism was authorized by the *dictum de omni et nullo*, and he defined this dictum by saying, "Whatever can be affirmed of any genus or species can likewise be affirmed of that which is included within either of them," and "Whatever can be denied of any genus or species, can of the contents of that genus or species likewise be denied"[251]; he subscribed to the notion that the fundamental principle behind the *dictum* is the principle of contradiction, "whereby

[248] *Ibid.*, p. 633.

[249] I paraphrase these four reasons as they are stated in *Logic, or Rational Thoughts*, p. 94.

[250] *Logica*, p. 369.

[251] *Ibid.*, p. 294. Translation mine here and below.

we pronounce it impossible for the same thing to be and not to be at the same time"[252]; he paid tribute to the identical proposition, which he found illustrated by a proper logical definition and which he defined by saying that "if subject and predicate are responsive to the same idea, the proposition is called identical"[253]; and in his vernacular logic as translated into English he spoke thus of the ultimate bases of a syllogistical line of proof:

> Let no one imagine, that a proof can be comprised in a single Syllogism: For as we admit the Conclusion, only on account of the Premisses, we cannot be assured of its Truth, till we are convinced of the Justness of the Premisses. And therefore the Premisses are so long to be proved by other Syllogisms, till we come to such a Syllogism, as has for its Premisses either Definitions, Axioms, clear Principles taken from experience, or Propositions previously demonstrated.[254]

But in two respects Wolff's logical theories are more progressive than those of the determined Aristotelians of his time. For one thing, he altogether ignored the machinery of topics as a guide to the development of authentic knowledge. And for another thing he recognized the existence of an inductive process lying outside the realm of the syllogism, although he did not call it induction in any formal way. His discussion of the use of logic in the search for truth contains a chapter on experience in general, and another chapter on the processes by which judgments or propositions or truths are established. "A Judgment formed in consequence of such Experience," said Wolff, "I call *Intuitive*, to distinguish it from that other, to which we come by means of Syllogism, and which I call *Discursive*."[255] Wolff's subsequent analysis of intuitive judgments is close to what later logicians would call induction. In this connection we should have in mind that, as if indeed to anticipate the necessity of devising some kind of principle that would give induction as much authenticity as the *dictum de omni et nullo* gave the syllogism, Wolff proposed when he called induction an enthymeme that it rested upon a principle of its own, and in his Latin text he called that principle "Fundamentum Inductionis," and he stated it as follows: "Whatever can be affirmed or denied concerning lower particulars can be af-

[252] *Logic, or Rational Thoughts*, p. 77.
[254] *Logic, or Rational Thoughts*, p. 91.
[253] *Logica*, p. 223.
[255] *Ibid.*, p. 108.

firmed or denied universally concerning the higher orders within which the lower particulars are contained."[256] Awkward and static as this principle may be, it makes induction a more basic form of reasoning than the syllogism is, and it indicates that induction is not an aspect of the deductive process. Thus it is a step in the new direction.

The sources of Wolff's logical theory can be identified in a general way from the pages of his vernacular and his Latin texts. His most frequent references were to Leibniz, as one would expect from a dedicated student of that philosopher; Descartes and Aristotle were cited by Wolff with some regularity, and also Copernicus, Kepler, Newton, Galileo, Boyle, and Locke; and on rarer occasions he mentioned Spinoza, Ramus, Robert Hooke, John Wallis, Gassendi, and the Port-Royalists.[257] This is not the place for an analysis of the purport of Wolff's references to these various scholars, philosophers, and scientists. Nor would it be in order here to comment upon the uses to which Wolff put their doctrines. But it should be noted that, as a disciple of Leibniz, Wolff shared his master's opposition to many of Locke's doctrines. In 1696 Leibniz composed the first draft of his objections to Locke's *Essay*, but his final statements of those objections were not published until 1765. They contained a criticism, however, of Locke's doctrine that there are no innate ideas in the mind. Leibniz proposed to modify Locke's doctrine so as to recognize that the principle of identity and the principle of contradiction are innate ideas.[258] We can see in this proposal the principal reason

[256] *Logica*, p. 368. The Latin text of Wolff's definition of this principle reads thus: "Quod de singulis inferioribus affirmari vel negari potest, idem etiam de superiori universaliter affirmari vel negari debet, sub quo inferiora ista continentur."

[257] In the *Logica*, there are 27 references to Leibniz, 21 to Descartes, 10 to Newton, 9 each to Aristotle, Copernicus, and Kepler, 5 to Galileo, 3 to Boyle, 2 each to Hooke, Ramus, Spinoza, and Wallis, and one each to Locke and Gassendi. For other references by Wolff to Locke, see Arndt, pp. 107-108, 207-208, 216. For his one reference to the Port-Royalists, see Arndt, p. 225.

[258] For a brief account of Leibniz's reply to Locke's *Essay*, see Christophersen, pp. 54-56, 111. An excellent analysis of the fundamental difference between Leibniz and Locke in respect to the nature of language is given in Hans Aarsleff, "Leibniz on Locke on Language," *American Philosophical Quarterly*, I. 3 (July 1964), 1-24. The differences between Wolff's logical system and the system proposed by Locke originated in the same fundamental

why Wolff's logic treated experience and induction more as after-thoughts than as subjects of central concern to logicians, and why it regarded the syllogism as the proper tool of research and demonstration.

The English version of Wolff's logic never had a second edition. In the years immediately following the date of its only appearance in Britain, the competing treatises of Watts and Duncan had the English market under their strong control, and this fact alone would be enough to explain the indifference of the British public towards Wolff. But it should also be understood that in 1770 the most influential British thinkers would have considered Wolff's logical doctrine rather old-fashioned and obsolete. After all, in its German version it had ceased to appeal to Wolff's own country-men after 1754, and its Latin text did not command a new European public after 1740. Even so, however, its English version is known to have had one distinguished reader. Samuel Taylor Coleridge wrote marginal annotations in his copy of it when he was studying philosophy and logic in the latter part of the year 1800 and in the early months of 1801, and that copy is now in the British Museum.[259] After Coleridge had finished the English version, he no doubt felt it necessary to verify its readings against their source. At any rate, he obtained a copy of Wolff's German logic at that same period of his life, and he proceeded to give some attention to it. The definition of philosophy as it is given in the first sentence of Wolff's *Vernünfftige Gedancken* is transcribed in Coleridge's Notebooks on the pages which contain jottings for the months between December, 1800, and June, 1801.[260] Coleridge himself contemplated writing a major work on logic, and many of his manuscripts are involved directly or indirectly with that subject.[261] Thus it is to be expected that he

---

disagreements which led Leibniz and Locke to take opposite sides on the matter discussed by Professor Aarsleff.

[259] Coleridge's annotations on the English version of Wolff's logic are to be found in Alice D. Snyder, *Coleridge on Logic and Learning* (New Haven: Yale University Press, 1929), pp. 158-162. Cited below as Snyder.

[260] See *The Notebooks of Samuel Taylor Coleridge*, ed. Kathleen Coburn (New York, 1957-1961), Vol. 1 (Text), entries 891, 902, Vol. 1 (Notes), entries 891, 902.

[261] Snyder, pp. vii, 50-138. See also E. K. Chambers, *Samuel Taylor Coleridge, A Biographical Study* (Oxford, 1938), pp. 171, 226, 312-313.

would have made Wolff's text in English and German the focus of special study. Although by the year 1800 Wolff's logical system had become more interesting in a historical than in a doctrinal sense, Coleridge's annotations in the English version reflect his own interest in doctrine. At times he questioned the accuracy of certain English renderings of Wolff's German text, and at other times he questioned the validity of Wolff's statements in respect to minor logical distinctions. His comments nowhere seem to have been influenced by late eighteenth-century controversies between the new and the old logic, lively as those controversies had become in his own youth. In fact, the logic that he expected to write would probably not have been distinguished for its newness of outlook, if we may judge him from his manuscripts on logical matters, and if we equate newness of outlook in logic with attempts to carry out the prescriptions of John Locke.

IV   The New Accent: Reid, Kames, Campbell, Stewart

In 1733, when William Duncan was beginning his third year as student at Marischal College, a young man in his middle twenties named Thomas Reid was appointed librarian at that institution. There can be no doubt, of course, that Duncan and Reid became acquainted with each other almost at once, and that both of them became acquainted with George Campbell, who entered Marischal College in 1734.[262] As librarian, Reid did not have any teaching duties at that particular moment, but his appointment made him an officer of the college, and in that capacity he was in close contact with all one hundred and twenty members of the average student body of the time, even as the students in turn were closely associated with the few college authorities and with each other, regardless of all differences in academic rank. As we already know, Duncan was to play a significant part in the development of the new logic in eighteenth-century Britain, and, as we shall now see, Reid and Campbell were to play an even more significant part in the same development. Thus the mutual acquaintanceship of these three men at a formative period of their lives is in itself a historical fact of more than casual interest. It is unfortunate that a detailed account of their relations with each other during those years cannot be given. As the oldest and most experienced member of the trio, Reid must be assumed to have exerted more influence upon Duncan and Campbell than they did upon him. His later contributions to the new outlook in science and philosophy argue that he must have been a vital force in the community life of Marischal College between 1733 and 1737, the dates of his term as librarian. He would have been in a position to know Duncan during the last two years of the latter's four-year

---

[262] In the following account of the careers of Reid and Campbell, I have relied on the following sources: the articles by Leslie Stephen on these two men in *The Dictionary of National Biography*; *Officers of the Marischal College and University of Aberdeen*, pp. 29-30, 40-45, 74; McCosh, *The Scottish Philosophy*, pp. 95-106, 192-227, 239-245; Anderson, *Studies in the History and Development of the University of Aberdeen*, pp. 75-84, 88-89; and Dugald Stewart, "Account of the Life and Writings of Thomas Reid, D.D., F.R.S.E.," in *The Works of Thomas Reid, D.D.*, ed. Sir William Hamilton, bart., 7th edn. (Edinburgh, 1872), I, 3-38 (cited below as *Works of Reid*).

term as undergraduate, and to know Campbell for the first three years of his similar term.

Reid's earlier and later careers need a word or two of comment in connection with my present subject. He had attended Marischal College himself between 1722 and 1726, and had been awarded the degree of master of arts in the latter of those years. That degree, we should understand, was given at the time to all first graduates of Marischal College. The teachers who influenced him most were George Turnbull and David Verner. Turnbull as professor of moral philosophy and logic occupied the post that Alexander Gerard would later fill, whereas Verner was the predecessor of William Duncan in the chair of natural and experimental philosophy.[263] There must have been much talk of John Locke and the new learning in those years at Aberdeen. As I mentioned earlier, Locke's thesis that all of our ideas originate either in sensation or reflection was argued as a commencement exercise at Marischal College in 1730, and David Verner was the presiding officer on that occasion.[264] After Reid's graduation he studied divinity for several years, and in 1731 he received his license as preacher. At that point he decided not to plunge at once into the profession for which he had prepared himself but to spend the next two years in studious pursuits in his father's house. He was appointed librarian of Marischal College in 1733, and he must certainly have found time still further to deepen his learning in the four years in which he held that post. In 1737 he was made minister of the country parish of New Machar, and for the next fourteen years he performed the duties of a clergyman, even as he found time to continue his philosophical studies and to publish his first writing, "An Essay on Quantity."[265] The reputation which

[263] In the political troubles of 1717, the four members of the faculty of Marischal College were dismissed, and the four replacements were David Verner, John Anderson, George Cruden, and Patrick Hardie. Verner served in his post at Marischal College until his death in 1752, and Duncan was then chosen his successor. Anderson was succeeded by George Turnbull, Turnbull by William Duff, Duff by Alexander Innes, Innes by David Fordyce, and Fordyce by Alexander Gerard, whose appointment coincided with Duncan's. The successors of Cruden and Hardie need not concern us here.

[264] See above, pp. 272-273 and n. 21.

[265] This essay was first published by the Royal Society of London in their series entitled *Philosophical Transactions, giving Some Account of the Present*

he acquired in these latter endeavors led to his appointment in 1751 to the faculty of philosophy at King's College, Aberdeen, and now at last he was able to take up a career that had apparently never ceased to attract him. For thirteen years he reflected and lectured in Aberdeen on logic, ethics, physics, and mathematics.[266] He was one of the leaders in founding in 1758 an organization known as the Aberdeen Philosophical Society, to which his old associate, George Campbell, also belonged as a founding and original member.[267] Campbell was serving at the time as minister of Aberdeen, and in 1759 he was appointed principal of Marischal College for a term that lasted until 1796. At meetings of the Aberdeen Philosophical Society members read papers to each other and talked about their latest investigations. On several such occasions Reid himself presented the work which was to make him famous when it was published at London and Edinburgh in 1764. It was called *An Inquiry into the Human Mind, on the Principles of Common Sense,* and it was written to answer the sceptical philosophy of David Hume. To the Aberdeen Philosophical Society George Campbell also presented certain chapters of the work which would be published in 1776 under the title *The Philosophy of Rhetoric.* In the very year in which his *Inquiry into the Human Mind* appeared, Reid was invited to accept the chair of moral philosophy at the University of Glasgow as the replacement for the distinguished Adam Smith, who had recently decided to step out of academic work after a creative and influential professorial career which had included the delivery of a course of brilliant lectures on rhetoric in Edinburgh and Glasgow.[268] Reid remained

---

Undertakings, Studies, and Labours, of the Ingenious, in Many Considerable Parts of the World, Vol. XLV, For the Year 1748 (London, 1750), pp. 505-520.

[266] A manuscript digest of the lectures delivered by Reid at Aberdeen on logic was made by John Campbell and is now in the Edinburgh University Library, MS DK. 3. 2. See *Lectures on Rhetoric and Belles Lettres Delivered in the University of Glasgow by Adam Smith,* ed. John M. Lothian (London, 1963), pp. xxix-xxx. I have not consulted this manuscript. Lothian gives a brief quotation from it on the impracticability of trying to reduce the art of composition to rules or of attempting to lay down general precepts for analysis and synthesis.

[267] For an account of this Society, see McCosh, *The Scottish Philosophy,* pp. 227-229.

[268] These lectures are discussed below, Ch. 6, pp. 536-576.

as professor of moral philosophy at Glasgow for the rest of his life. One of his pupils during the academic year 1771-1772 was a young man named Dugald Stewart, a recent graduate of the University of Edinburgh. Stewart himself was about to embark upon an academic career that proved to be memorable, and he considered his year with Reid a necessary step in his own development as philosopher and teacher. When Reid went to Glasgow in 1764, there were some 300 students in that university, and at the end of his life the number had grown to 600. He died on October 7, 1796, six months almost to the day after the death of George Campbell in Aberdeen.

Three years after Reid's death, his "Statistical Account of the University of Glasgow" was published in the twenty-first and final volume of Sir John Sinclair's series called *The Statistical Account of Scotland*. In this essay Reid discussed the history, the modern constitution, the endowments, and the present state of the university to which he had devoted the last thirty-two years of his life.[269] His comments on the course of study in his own time are particularly relevant to our present history. Philosophy, as it was taught at Glasgow and elsewhere during the eighteenth century, regularly included three major subjects, each of which had its appropriate subdivisions. Reid listed these three subjects as logic, moral philosophy, and natural philosophy, and he indicated that logic preceded the other two in the order in which they were studied and taught.[270] He himself, of course, was professor of moral philosophy, and although he did not mention any names, we know from other sources that his recent predecessors in this field at Glasgow were in reverse chronology Adam Smith, Thomas Craigie, Francis Hutcheson, and Gerschom Carmichael. We also know that natural philosophy was taught at Glasgow by John Anderson between 1757 and 1796, and that Anderson's immediate predecessors were Robert Dick and Robert Dick's father. As for the remaining branch of philosophy, we know that George Jardine was professor of logic when Reid prepared his account of the University of Glasgow, and that Jardine's recent predecessors were John Clow, Adam Smith, and John Loudon. Adam Smith occupied the chair of logic at Glasgow for only one year, and then

[269] *Works of Reid*, II, 721-739.   [270] *Ibid.*, II, 734-735.

he transferred to moral philosophy.[271] It is especially interesting to take notice of Reid's words concerning the teaching of logic during his own career. He emphasized that a change was occurring in the manner in which this subject was presented in the classroom; that the former deference to Aristotle was being replaced by a new attitude; and that the present professor was giving logic a much wider application than it formerly had. Let us look directly at Reid's own description of what logic had been and what it was as his colleague Jardine conceived of it in the seventeen-nineties:

> Before the student entered upon the subjects of moral and natural philosophy, it was thought proper to instruct him in the art of reasoning and disputation; and the syllogistic art, taken from the Analytics of Aristotle, was, for many ages, considered as the most effectual and infallible instrument for that purpose. It was supposed to afford a mechanical mode of reasoning, by which, in all cases, truth and falsehood might be accurately distinguished. But the change of opinions on the subjects of literature, and on the means of comprehending them, has occasioned a correspondent alteration in the manner of treating this part of the academical course. The present Professor, after a short analysis of the powers of the understanding, and an explanation of the terms necessary to comprehend the subjects of his course, gives a historical view of the rise and progress of the art of reasoning, and particularly of the syllogistic method, which is rendered a matter of curiosity by the universal influence which for a long time it obtained over the learned world; and then dedicates the greater part of his time to an illustration of the various mental operations, as they are expressed by the several modifications of speech and writing; which leads him to deliver a system of lectures on general grammar, rhetoric, and belles lettres. This course, accompanied with suitable exercises and specimens, on the part of the students, is properly placed at the entrance to philosophy: no subjects are likely to be more interesting to young minds, at a time when their taste and feel-

[271] These statements concerning the faculty of the University of Glasgow in Reid's time are based upon information published in W. Innes Addison, *A Roll of the Graduates of the University of Glasgow From 31st December, 1727 to 31st December, 1897* (Glasgow, 1898), pp. 682-690.

ings are beginning to open, and have naturally disposed them to the reading of such authors as are necessary to supply them with facts and materials for beginning and carrying on the important habits of reflection and investigation.[272]

In this account of Jardine's course in logic at Glasgow Reid did not mention any of the writers associated in his own century with the decline of respect for the syllogistic method of Aristotle, and had he done so, he would not have mentioned himself. But he deserves special credit for the part he played in making necessary a fresh evaluation of the syllogism. His most influential contribution in this regard was made in a little essay which he published in 1774 as a solicited contribution to a two-volume treatise by Lord Kames on the human species. Kames, also known as Henry Home, was a member of the legal profession in Scotland for the fifty-eight years between 1724 and 1782, his title having been conferred upon him as a result of his appointment to the Scottish bench as ordinary Lord of Session in 1752.[273] He wrote voluminously on various subjects, but his reputation in the British literary community was established by his three-volume work, *Elements of Criticism*, published in 1762 in Edinburgh. It was this work, indeed, which made him known as the inventor of the science of philosophical criticism and which called him to the attention of such literary celebrities of the time as Dr. Johnson and Oliver Goldsmith.[274] Kames's treatise on the human species must have occupied him for many years, but he gave particular attention to it after his *Elements of Criticism* had appeared. He planned it as a long work on the progress of humanity considered at first without regard to the society in which man lives and then in regard to that society. The latter topic became involved with such large matters as the origin of national societies, the theory and forms of government, the rise and progress of states, the na-

[272] *Works of Reid*, II, 735.

[273] For further information about Kames, see Alexander Fraser Tytler, *Memoirs of the Life and Writings of the Honourable Henry Home of Kames . . . Second Edition. In Three Volumes* (Edinburgh, 1814). Cited below as Tytler. The name "Home" is pronounced "Hume." See Tytler, I, 99.

[274] See G. F. R. Barker's article, "Home, Henry, Lord Kames," in *The Dictionary of National Biography*, for opinions by Johnson, Goldsmith, and Dugald Stewart on Kames's *Elements of Criticism*. For a discussion of Kames as the inventor of philosophical criticism, see Tytler, I, 377, 396.

ture of war and peace, the rise and fall of patriotism, the administration of finances, of military affairs, and of the police, and the
nature of man's progress in science, in the use of reason, in morality, and in theology. As he proceeded to write successively upon
these subjects, Kames felt that he needed "a fair analysis of Aristotle's logics" to complete his account of man's progress in science
and the use of reason, and his friend Dr. Reid of Glasgow seemed
to him the proper choice for that assignment. Reid "relished the
thought," performed the assignment, and published his results as
an Appendix to Kames's survey of the principles and progress of
reason. Reid's analysis was entitled "A Brief Account of Aristotle's
Logic. With Remarks." Kames decided to publish anonymously
the work in which the "Brief Account" appeared, and to call his
big treatise *Sketches of the History of Man*.[275]

We may safely state that Reid's "Brief Account" was prepared
over a six-year period between the autumn of 1767 and the corresponding season of 1773. The evidence for this assertion is found
in a letter written by Reid from Glasgow College on October 31,
1767, to David Skene, doctor of medicine, dean of the faculty of
Marischal College, and a founding member of the Aberdeen Philosophical Society.[276] The letter in question contained the information that the chemists in Glasgow were seeking to discover a substance which could be used in stamping cambric when it came
from the loom and which would not fade out when the fabric was
bleached. Bleached cambric that was not stamped could be declared contraband under an act of parliament. Thus an unmarked
bolt of British fabric of this kind would be in danger of seizure
by the government on the charge that it had been smuggled into
Britain from France, and Scottish looms would be the losers.
After his reference to these matters, Reid wrote thus to David
Skene:

> I passed eight days lately with Lord Kaims at Blair-Drum-
> mond. You were very honourably mentioned. My Lord has it

[275] For the quotations just given, and for Kames's whole story of the invitation to Reid to prepare the "Brief Account" for him, see *Sketches of the History of Man. In Two Volumes* (Edinburgh: Printed for W. Creech, Edinburgh; and for W. Strahan, and T. Cadell, London, 1774), II, 165-167. This is
the first edition of the *Sketches* and of Reid's "Brief Account."

[276] For a short account of David Skene, see Anderson, *Studies in the History
and Development of the University of Aberdeen*, pp. 153-155.

much at heart to have a professor of practical mechanicks established at Edinburgh, and wants only a proper person. He is preparing a fourth edition of his "Elements." I have been labouring at *Barbara Celarent* for three weeks bygone; and on Monday begin my own course. I do not expect such a crop of students as I had last year; but the College in general promises pretty well.[277]

Reid's casual statement that he had been working with the figures and modes of the syllogism for the three preceding weeks would indicate that, when he had lately spent eight days with Lord Kames, he had been asked to do an analysis of Aristotle's logic for the forthcoming *Sketches of the History of Man*, and that he was already at work on the assignment before his own college course opened. Reid did not lecture himself on logic at Glasgow, and thus his reference here would not be to his own preparation for the term soon to start. The learned community of the time contained many scholars who thought highly of Aristotelian logic, and an analysis of that topic would have to be well based and soundly argued if it were to get a fair hearing for any unfavorable criticism that it might level at the Stagirite.[278] Reid must have appreciated difficulties of this sort and must have wanted accordingly to spend upon his essay every minute of his available free time between his eight-day visit at Blair-Drummond and the season when the *Sketches* would be scheduled to go to press. Ultimately Kames's Preface to the *Sketches* would be dated at Edinburgh, February 23, 1774. Copy would have had to be in the hands of the printers not later than the preceding autumn. An

---

[277] *Works of Reid*, I, 49. I use Reid's spelling of his host's name.

[278] James Burnett, Lord Monboddo, a Scottish contemporary of Reid and Kames, is a case in point. A devoted classicist, Monboddo thought Aristotle a wonderful philosopher in every respect, whereas the language which Locke had made philosophy speak is, Monboddo said, "mere stammering, and is, in my opinion, as contemptible as the matter which he has made her utter." Monboddo was also an unfriendly critic of Reid. See McCosh, *The Scottish Philosophy*, pp. 248-249. Another unfriendly critic of Reid was Dr. John Gillies, historian and classical scholar, who severely objected to one of Reid's attempts in the "Brief Account" to shed light upon a statement in Aristotle's *Categories*. This particular objection is reprinted in Sir William Hamilton's edition of the *Works of Reid*, II, 684. Sir William himself was a later critic of Reid, his edition of the "Brief Account" being one of the most quarrelsome editorial performances on record.

allotment of six years for the preparation of his essay would not under the circumstances have seemed excessive to Reid, and it does in fact appear to be in accord with the evidence.

In conducting his analysis of Aristotle's logic, Reid devoted the first, third, and fifth of his six chapters to an exposition of successive parts of the *Organon*, and the second, fourth, and sixth chapters to successive evaluations of the doctrine that he had just expounded. Thus in his opening chapter he offered an interpretation of the *Categories* and the treatise *On Interpretation*, after having given a short characterization of Aristotle and a description of Porphyry's *Isagoge*, which of course had come by tradition to be accepted as part of Aristotelian logical theory. Reid's second chapter commented upon the doctrine of the five predicables, the ten categories, logical distinctions, logical definitions, the logical view of language, and the logical view of propositions. The two books of the *Prior Analytics* became the subject of his next chapter. Here he explained what the process of conversion of propositions means, what are the figures and modes of the pure syllogism, what the rules are for the invention of a middle term, and how syllogisms may be manipulated to perform various feats and to attain victory in disputations. The commentary upon these matters gave Reid his longest single chapter, the fourth, although his second chapter had been almost as long. In the course of the fourth chapter he spoke of Galen and Ramus as having made additions to Aristotle's theory of the syllogism; he spoke of the kind of examples used in textbooks to illustrate syllogistic modes and figures; he spoke of the *dictum de omni et nullo* as the axiom invoked by Aristotle to prove that, out of a possible 192 modes of the syllogism, or out of a possible 256 modes, if the fourth or Galenical figure be allowed, there are only fourteen modes capable of producing just conclusions; and he also spoke of the syllogism considered as an engine of science. The fifth chapter he devoted to the *Posterior Analytics*, the *Topics*, and the *Sophistical Elenchi*, and his final chapter, not so much to a judgment upon these last three treatises in the *Organon* as to a valuable and wide-ranging commentary upon the utility of logic and upon the ways in which it might be improved. Throughout his entire analysis of these logical writings, he attempted to make his readers understand the main points of the doctrine under discussion, even as a textbook on logic would do; but he also attempted to evaluate the doctrine in such a way as to make his readers aware of the historical context to which logic belongs and of the capacity of that context to influence logic or whatever else it contains. Thus his work gains a perspective not often emphasized in textbooks in its field.

It should be understood at this point that Reid was not posing as a classical scholar commenting upon the Greek text of Aristotle's *Organon* and seeking to convey in English exactly what that text might originally have meant. He explicitly disclaimed any such role. "In attempting to give some account of the Analytics and of the Topics of Aristotle," he said at the beginning of his third chapter, "ingenuity requires me to confess, that tho' I have often purposed to read the whole with care, and to understand what is intelligible, yet my courage and patience always failed before I had done. Why should I throw away so much time and painful attention upon a thing of so little real use?" After explaining that he would have given the *Organon* the closest study if he had lived in an age when a knowledge of it entitled a man to the highest standing in philosophy, he added: "All I can say is, that I have read some parts of the different books with care, some slightly, and some perhaps not at all."[279]

Upon what, then, did Reid depend in formulating his "Brief Account"? What texts were his primary sources, if he did not base his comments upon Aristotle's own text? The answer is that his "Brief Account" is a commentary upon Aristotelian logic as that logic was understood in the standard treatises upon it in the two centuries preceding that in which he was writing. He mentioned these standard treatises in various casual references, and from those references we can compile a list of the primary sources of his understanding of Aristotelian logical doctrine.

Four of these sources stand out. The most ancient was Ludovico Vives's *Dialectices Libri Quatuor*, first published at Paris in 1550. Reid twice referred to it, and he would of course have known that it represented the state of Aristotelian logic just before the time when Ramus's reforms became the rage in Europe.[280] Reid also referred twice to Ramus. On one occasion he

[279] My quotations are all taken from the text of the "Brief Account" as it appears in the second volume of the first edition of Kames's *Sketches*. The quotations just given are on p. 193.

[280] "Brief Account," pp. 169, 215.

called him a reformer in philosophy "who had a force of genius sufficient to shake the Aristotelian fabric in many parts, but insufficient to erect any thing more solid in its place," and it was at this point that Reid recalled Ramus's practice of dividing each whole and each part into two mutually contradictory subdivisions.[281] On the other occasion Reid said that Ramus had introduced new modes adapted to singular propositions, and that the friends of Aristotle had proved this improvement "more specious than useful."[282] Ramus's writings on logic are extensive and repetitious, but it is probable that Reid would have known them through Ramus's French treatise, the *Dialectique*, published at Paris in 1555, or its Latin counterpart, which came out at the same place one year later under the title *Dialecticae Libri Duo*. A third authority, mentioned by Reid with some emphasis, was Bartholomew Keckermann, whose *Systema Logicae*, when it appeared in 1600, gave the name of Systematic to the school which attempted to counteract the reforms of Ramus and to make Aristotle once more supreme in logic.[283] Reid's fourth source was Franco Burgersdijck, also a Systematic. His influential *Institutionum Logicarum Libri Duo* came out at Leiden in 1626, and to it Reid made two allusions.[284]

Other standard treatises belonging to the Aristotelian tradition were undoubtedly in Reid's mind when he wrote the "Brief Account," and his failure to identify them is not as surprising as an open reference to them would have been, since they were well known to everybody. A list of them would certainly have included the names of Sanderson, Wallis, and Aldrich, whom we have already discussed in these pages. When Reid referred on one occasion to certain unnamed logicians who have "divided that science into three parts," and when he explained at once that these parts were simple apprehension or terms, judgments or propositions, and reasoning or syllogism,[285] he was only putting into words what Aldrich, Wallis, and Sanderson had themselves authorized

---

[281] *Ibid.*, p. 182.   [282] *Ibid.*, pp. 202-203.

[283] *Ibid.*, p. 215. For a discussion of Keckermann's influence in the late sixteenth-century reaction against Ramus, see Howell, *Logic and Rhetoric in England*, pp. 283, 302-303, 310, 312, 320, 323.

[284] "Brief Account," pp. 177-178, 216. See Howell, pp. 309-311, 316.

[285] "Brief Account," p. 176.

in conformity with ancient practice. No doubt in Reid's mind also were treatises representing the development of logic during the early eighteenth century. Above all he would have known Duncan's *Elements of Logick*. And he probably knew Crousaz, too, for he said at one place that some recent writers on logic had quite properly introduced a discussion of Bacon's idols into their system, and Crousaz, as we know, did that very thing.[286]

In his evaluation of the five predicables, the ten categories, and the doctrine of logical definition, Reid was concerned to state not only what these terms meant in Aristotelian theory but also what value their counterparts in the emerging new logic might be thought to have. The five predicables, he said, were in fact the five relations which predicates of propositions bear to subjects, and were intended as a complete enumeration of all the possibilities involved. He thought the enumeration less than exhaustive either in the form in which it appeared in Porphyry's *Isagoge* or in the form which it was given in Aristotle's *Topics*. But he found the ancient enumeration at least as satisfactory as were the parallel modern enumerations set forth by Locke and Hume.[287] He took the same position towards the ten categories. As an attempt to muster every object of human concern under one of ten possible concepts, the Aristotelian doctrine of the categories probably did not exhaust all the possibilities dictated by such a magnanimous and admirable scheme, declared Reid; but it was as acceptable as the corresponding schemes formulated by such moderns as Locke, Hume, and James Gregory.[288] The case was different, however, when Reid discussed the Aristotelian theory of definition in relation to that which Locke had set forth with care, precision, and impressiveness. Of Locke's theory Reid spoke as follows:

> The principles laid down by Locke with regard to definition, and with regard to the abuse of words, carry conviction along with them; and I take them to be one of the most important improvements made in logic since the days of Aristotle; not so much because they enlarge our knowledge, as because they make us sensible of our ignorance, and shew that a great part

[286] *Ibid.*, p. 238. See above, p. 313.
[287] "Brief Account," pp. 177-179.　　[288] *Ibid.*, pp. 179-181.

of what speculative men have admired as profound philosophy, is only a darkening of knowledge by words without understanding.[289]

In this passage Reid had in mind two distinct chapters of Locke's *Essay*. The first chapter, entitled "Of the Names of Simple Ideas," declared that "*a Definition is* nothing else, but *the shewing the meaning of one Word by several other not synonymous Terms.*" This concept of definition Locke then explained thus:

> The meaning of Words, being only the *Ideas* they are made to stand for by him that uses them; the meaning of any Term is then shewed, or the Word is defined when by other Words, the *Idea* it is made the Sign of, and annexed to in the Mind of the Speaker, is as it were represented, or set before the view of another; and thus its Signification ascertained: This is the only use and end of Definitions.[290]

The other chapter, as Reid's own reference indicates, is entitled "Of the Abuse of Words." One of its most important sections declared that the first use of language was "*To make known* one Man's Thoughts or *Ideas* to another," and that this end was made impossible under any one of the following three conditions:

> *First,* When Men have names in their Mouths without any determined *Ideas* in their Minds, whereof they are the signs: or *Secondly,* When they apply the common received names of any Language to *Ideas,* to which the common use of that Language does not apply them: or *Thirdly,* When they apply them very unsteadily, making them stand now for one, and by and by for another *Idea.*[291]

These are the principles which Reid called "one of the most important improvements made in logic since the days of Aristotle." Reid did not actually state these principles as I have just done. No doubt he assumed that his readers would be already familiar with them. But he did state the Aristotelian conception of the perfect definition, and that conception required not only that a definition state the essence of the thing defined but also that the essence of anything consisted in the qualities which it shares

[289] *Ibid.,* p. 188.
[290] *Essay,* 4th edn., p. 246. Italics are Locke's.
[291] *Ibid.,* pp. 298-299.

with other things of the same kind and in the qualities which distinguish it from those other things.[292] The difference between the
Aristotelians and Locke upon this issue was that Locke confined
definitions to words and gave rules which applied only to the
process of clarifying verbal meanings, whereas the Aristotelians
gave rules which also applied only to the clarifying of verbal
meanings, and yet they postulated that the resulting definitions
clarified things and their essences. Reid explained this difference
by saying that, although Aristotelians distinguished between the
definition of a word and the definition of a thing, what they had
to say about the latter either had the same meaning as what they
had to say about the former or it had no possibility of meaning at
all. He added:

> All the rules of definition agree to the definition of a word: and
> if they mean by the definition of a thing, the giving an adequate
> conception of the nature and essence of any thing that exists;
> this is impossible, and is the vain boast of men unconscious of
> the weakness of human understanding.[293]

Reid's preference for Locke and his objection to the Aristotelians became apparent in fullest measure, however, when he
analyzed the syllogism. In the "Brief Account," indeed, Locke's
strictures against syllogistic method may be said to have received
their first important endorsement since the moment of their
origin. Locke had given them their earliest effective statement in
1690, and Reid was writing between 1767 and 1774. The interval
between these two happenings is filled, as we know, with logicians
who for the most part regarded Locke with admiration and who
sought in various ways to incorporate his teachings into their own
systems of logic. But the syllogism had remained unaltered in
their works, even when William Duncan, the devoted mid-cen-
tury disciple of Locke, was the author concerned. If it seems
strange that reform should have moved so slowly in those years,
we should remember that the direction of reform was not in this
case towards the abolition of the syllogism and the adoption of a
wholly new form of reasoning and enquiry but towards a redefi-
nition of the role of the syllogism in logic and life, and towards
the development of a method of enquiry already in being as a
subordinate part of the old system. It sometimes takes longer to

---

[292] "Brief Account," p. 186.   [293] *Ibid.*, p. 187.

modernize an ancient structure than to tear it down and build something new in its place. At any rate, the modernization of logic required a long time, and even after Reid had severely and effectively criticised the ancient Aristotelian structure, the process of modernization was to continue onward for some seventy years before it reached its ultimate fulfilment in John Stuart Mill's *System of Logic*.

Everything which Reid said against the syllogism emerged from his central conviction that the syllogistic procedure was not a proper instrument of scientific enquiry, and that the only proper instrument was induction. This theme is woven into the texture of several of the separate sections into which each of the main chapters of the "Brief Account" is divided. Nowhere is it stated better than in the epigraph at the head of the present chapter, and that epigraph is taken from the last section of Reid's last chapter, where he was speaking of the improvement of logic. The epigraph indicates that the syllogism in its long history was associated with disputatiousness and sectarianism as the methods of subjecting truth to scrutiny, with animosity and personal rivalry as the typical attitudes of the truth-seeker, and with practical irrelevance as the major characteristic of the conclusions that finally emerged from deductive enquiries. The epigraph also indicates that induction, as first described by Francis Bacon, was associated not only with the methods of scrutiny found in laboratories, observatories, and experimental procedures, but also with the zest involved in forcing nature to yield her secrets, and with the bounteous harvest of new truths which the past hundred years had produced. In passages which immediately precede and immediately follow the epigraph, Reid had other things to say of the great revolution wrought in human affairs by the change from deduction to induction. He spoke thus on those two occasions:

> After men had laboured in the search of truth near two thousand years, by the help of syllogisms, Lord Bacon proposed the method of induction, as a more effectual engine for that purpose. His *Novum Organum* gave a new turn to the thoughts and labours of the inquisitive, more remarkable, and more useful, than that which the *Organum* of Aristotle had given before; and may be considered as a second grand aera in the progress of human reason.[294]

[294] *Ibid.*, p. 236.

Lord Bacon has displayed no less force of genius in reducing to rules this method of reasoning, than Aristotle did in the method of syllogism. His *Novum Organum* ought therefore to be held as a most important addition to the ancient logic. Those who understand it, and enter into the spirit of it, will be able to distinguish the chaff from the wheat in philosophical disquisitions into the works of God. They will learn to hold in due contempt all hypotheses and theories, the creatures of human imagination, and to respect nothing but facts sufficiently vouched, or conclusions drawn from them by a fair and chaste interpretation of nature.[295]

These words of praise for induction, and these disparagements of the syllogism, echo what Reid had said in an earlier section of the "Brief Account," when, in speaking of the syllogism as an engine of science, he had declared:

The slow progress of useful knowledge, during the many ages in which the syllogistic art was most highly cultivated as the only guide to science, and its quick progress since that art was disused, suggest a presumption against it; and this presumption is strengthened by the puerility of the examples which have always been brought to illustrate its rules.

The ancients seem to have had too high notions, both of the force of the reasoning power in man, and of the art of syllogism as its guide. Mere reasoning can carry us but a very little way in most subjects. By observation, and experiments properly conducted, the stock of human knowledge may be enlarged without end; but the power of reasoning alone, applied with vigour through a long life, would only carry a man round, like a horse in a mill, who labours hard, but makes no progress.[296]

This image of the horse in the mill, I should like parenthetically to point out, bears a striking resemblance to that in Locke's *Conduct of the Understanding*, where Locke, in advocating a wide rather than a narrow field of observation for the man who would furnish himself with a rich store of ideas, said:

I do not say to be a good Geographer that a Man should visit every Mountain, River, Promontory and Creek upon the Face of the Earth, view the Buildings, and survey the Land every

---

[295] *Ibid.*, p. 237.   [296] *Ibid.*, pp. 210-211.

where, as if he were going to make a Purchase. But yet every one must allow that he shall know a Country better that makes often Sallies into it, and traverses it up and down, than he that like a Mill Horse goes still round in the same Tract, or keeps within the narrow Bounds of a Field or two that delight him.[297]

We must of course understand that Reid was not interested merely in pointing out the benefits which had come to mankind when the syllogism was abandoned as an instrument of scientific enquiry and induction introduced in its place. He was also interested in the reason why the syllogism had failed. Perhaps the most vivid way of stating that reason, as Reid conceived of it, is to say that the image of the mill horse is in fact the image of the weakness and futility of syllogistic logic. The image suggests a going round in circles, and in the last analysis Reid felt that syllogistic reasoning was circular by its very nature. His comments upon the *dictum de omni et nullo* is a case in point. "The general principle in which the whole terminates, and of which every categorical syllogism is only a particular application," said Reid, "is this, That what is affirmed or denied of the whole genus, may be affirmed or denied of every species and individual belonging to it."[298] Reid proceeded then to comment upon this principle in such a way as to indicate that he considered its point of arrival the same as its point of departure. It is, in short, a tautology. Here is the way Reid phrased his criticism of the *dictum*:

This is a principle of undoubted certainty, but of no great depth. Aristotle and all the logicians assume it as an axiom or first principle, from which the syllogistic system, as it were, takes its departure: and after a tedious voyage, and great expence of demonstration, it lands at last in this principle as its ultimate conclusion. *O Curas hominum! O quantum est in rebus inane!*[299]

The notion that the syllogism is a *petitio principii*, a begging of the question, the use of a proposition to prove itself, was to be

[297] *Posthumous Works of Mr. John Locke*, p. 15.
[298] "Brief Account," p. 213.
[299] The Latin verse is the first line of Satire I of Persius. As translated by G. G. Ramsay, *Juvenal and Persius*, The Loeb Classical Library (London, New York, 1918), p. 317, it reads: "O the vanity of mankind! How vast the void in human affairs!"

developed by George Campbell, Dugald Stewart, and John Stuart Mill. They were to hold that the conclusion of a syllogism is simply a restatement of its major premise, and that anyone who thought he was proving something by a syllogism was in fact proving a conclusion by using that conclusion as a witness to its own truth. If, for example, you wanted to prove Socrates mortal, and you proceeded to cite as evidence the propositions that all men are mortal, and that Socrates is a man, you would be using as evidence for your conclusion a major premise which is merely a broader form of the conclusion itself. So far as George Campbell and Dugald Stewart are concerned, it was Reid, I believe, who provided them with the first hint of this grave defect in syllogistic procedure. Not only did Reid suggest this defect when he used the image of the mill horse and when he analyzed the *dictum de omni et nullo,* but he even stated it quite openly in the closing pages of the "Brief Account." When he did so, he was engaged in comparing deduction and induction with reference to the differences that characterize their way of getting from evidence to conclusion, and with reference to the degree of certainty to be attached to inductive generalizations. His interest in acquitting induction of the charge that its conclusions were dubious probabilities kept him from emphasizing that the conclusions of syllogistic logic were tautologies. But he implied this latter thing, even so, and his words were to furnish George Campbell with an important idea, as we shall see later.

> In reasoning by syllogism, from general principles [declared Reid] we descend to a conclusion virtually contained in them. The process of induction is more arduous; being an ascent from particular premises to a general conclusion. The evidence of such general conclusions is not demonstrative, but probable: but when the induction is sufficiently copious, and carried on according to the rules of art, it forces conviction no less than demonstration itself does.[300]

After making these successful assaults upon the syllogism as the center of the old logic, Reid did not proceed with sustained attacks against such other Peripatetic fixtures as the disputation and the machinery of topics. But it is nevertheless quite evident that he did not share any of the enthusiasm which the old logic had

[300] "Brief Account," pp. 236-237.

389

lavished upon these things. My previous quotations from his text have shown that the laboratory, the observatory, and scientific experiments are to his mind the modern equivalents of the academic disputations of former days, and that as a means of deciding whether a truth is or is not valid, the modern methods are vastly superior to the ancient. But those who want a few further details concerning Reid's attitude towards the topics and towards disputation may find them in the second section of the fifth chapter of the "Brief Account," where Reid made some references to them both as features of Aristotelian logic. At that point he remarked quite truly that "Aristotle has furnished the materials from which all the logicians have borrowed their doctrine of topics: and even Cicero, Quintilian, and other rhetorical writers, have been much indebted to the topics of Aristotle."[301] Concerning Aristotle's contribution to the theory of disputation, Reid had this to say: "The last book of the Topics is a code of the laws, according to which a syllogistical disputation ought to be managed, both on the part of the assailant and defendant. From which it is evident, that this philosopher trained his disciples to contend, not for the truth merely, but for victory."[302] And in the "Brief Account" there is a later passage which speaks of disputation and the topics in connection with a general evaluation of the whole machinery of syllogistic logic. Not to quote it here would be to deprive ourselves of one of Reid's most effective paragraphs.

Although the art of categorical syllogism [Reid declared] is better fitted for scholastic litigation, than for real improvement in knowledge, it is a venerable piece of antiquity, and a great effort of human genius. We admire the pyramids of Egypt, and the wall of China, tho' useless burdens upon the earth. We can bear the most minute description of them, and travel hundreds of leagues to see them. If any person should, with sacrilegious hands, destroy or deface them, his memory would be had in abhorrence. The predicaments and predicables, the rules of syllogism, and the topics, have a like title to our veneration as antiquities: they are uncommon efforts, not of human power, but of human genius; and they make a remarkable period in the progress of human reason.[303]

[301] *Ibid.*, p. 223.   [302] *Ibid.*, p. 224.   [303] *Ibid.*, p. 234.

Reid's whole thesis that the old logic, impressive as it was, had outlived its usefulness, fell short of the later design of the new logic in one important respect. That respect had to do with the traditional emphasis upon logic as in part a theory of communication as well as of enquiry. Reid did not envisage the break one day to take place between logical theory and the theory of communication. He thought instead that logic, improved of course by its new concern for inductive procedures, would continue to have a voice in literary and rhetorical enterprises. Here is what he said upon these matters:

> In compositions of human thought expressed by speech or by writing, whatever is excellent and whatever is faulty, fall within the province, either of grammar, or of rhetoric, or of logic. Propriety of expression, is the province of grammar; grace, elegance, and force, in thought and in expression, are the province of rhetoric; justness and accuracy of thought are the province of logic.
>
> The faults in composition, therefore, which fall under the censure of logic, are obscure and indistinct conceptions, false judgment, inconclusive reasoning, and all improprieties in distinctions, definitions, division, or method. To aid our rational powers, in avoiding these faults and in attaining the opposite excellencies, is the end of logic; and whatever there is in it that has no tendency to promote this end, ought to be thrown out.[304]

These words indicate that Reid stood where Crousaz, Watts, and Duncan did in regard to the communicative offices of logical doctrine. That stand had traditionally been taken to mean that logic provided the theory of communication to the scholar when he spoke to the scholarly, whereas rhetoric provided the theory of communication to the scholar or to anyone else when the speaker or writer addressed the popular audience. Eventually, logic was to disclaim any responsibility for scholarly communication, and was to devote its energies to the methods of scholarly discovery. And at that point rhetoric, except when it was unwise or blind, was to endeavor to extend its ancient interests and to become the theory of scholarly as well as of popular communication. It is interesting to note that Adam Smith, Reid's predecessor in the chair of moral philosophy at Glasgow, had already seen the clear out-

[304] *Ibid.*, p. 235.

lines of this new rhetoric, and had devoted himself to an exposition of it in his lectures on rhetoric at Glasgow and at Edinburgh. More will be said on this subject in my next chapter. Meanwhile, we might observe that Reid's modernity did not extend as far as Adam Smith's in this one respect, although in other aspects of logical doctrine Reid was in the frontmost rank of advancing thought of his time.

It has been made very evident in this discussion of Reid's "Brief Account" that his logical doctrines owe a greater debt to John Locke than to any other modern writer. This point need not be further stressed. And yet on one of Reid's pages there is a passage which indicates his deep veneration for Locke's contribution to logical theory and his own identification of the works in which that contribution was expressed. That passage should be quoted here as we now take leave of Reid. It falls at the place where Reid was stressing that the chief means of improving our rational faculty is by exercising it in various ways and on different subjects rather than by studying formal treatises on logic. Then he spoke thus:

> I take this to be Locke's meaning, when, in his Thoughts on Education, he says, "If you would have your son to reason well, let him read Chillingworth." The state of things is much altered since Locke wrote. Logic has been much improved, chiefly by his writings; and yet much less stress is laid upon it, and less time consumed in it. His counsel, therefore, was judicious and seasonable; to wit, That the improvement of our reasoning power is to be expected much more from an intimate acquaintance with the authors who reason best, than from studying voluminous systems of logic. But if he had meant, that the study of logic was of no use, nor deserved any attention, he surely would not have taken the pains to have made so considerable an addition to it, by his *Essay on the Human Understanding*, and by his *Thoughts on the Conduct of the Understanding*. Nor would he have remitted his pupil to Chillingworth, the acutest logician, as well as the best reasoner, of his age; and one who, in innumerable places of his excellent book, without pedantry even in that pedantic age, makes the happiest application of the rules of logic, for unraveling the sophistical reasoning of his antagonist.[305]

[305] *Ibid.*, pp. 230-231.

Reid could well indicate in this revealing passage that Locke had been responsible for the great improvement in logic during the time between the date of his major writings on that subject and the date of Reid's contribution to Kames's *Sketches*. And we in turn can well say that Reid's "Brief Account" permits us to see with great clarity not only what Locke's improvements in logic had meant at their point of origin, but how far Reid himself had construed them towards still further improvements.

As I mentioned earlier, Reid's "Brief Account" appeared originally as an Appendix to Lord Kames's own sketch of the principles and progress of reason, and Kames's sketch was merely one part of his extensive treatise on the human species. What Kames actually said about the principles of reason amounts to a popular explanation of the nature of knowledge, whether intuitive or discursive, whether certain or probable, whether accepted as exact knowledge or as opinion and belief.[306] These matters have an obvious bearing upon logic, but Kames's discussion of them does not add anything new to the tradition that I have been describing in the present chapter. Thus I shall not give a systematic account of his views upon them. I should perhaps say, however, that his conception of the nature of truth is openly within the province of the new logic, inasmuch as he equated truth with accuracy rather than with consistency. After remarking that truth and error are qualities of propositions, he spoke thus: "A proposition that says a thing is what it is in reality, is termed a *true proposition*. A proposition that says a thing is what it is not in reality, is termed an *erroneous proposition*."[307] This definition of truth and falsehood is of course a part of the old logic as well as of the new, as I have said before; but the old logic honored it more in the breach than in the observance, whereas the new logic sought to devise a machinery that would make it workable and productive. In his discussion of the principles of reason, Kames made it repeatedly clear that his definition of truth was not something merely to be stated and forgotten. And when he took up the second of the two subjects in this particular sketch, and traced the progress of reason, he was even more bent upon giving the definition substance and body. The progress of reason in Europe, he declared, had

---

[306] For Kames's discussion of these matters, see *Sketches* (Edinburgh, 1774), II, 102-119.

[307] *Ibid.*, p. 102.

been slower than that of sculpture, painting, or architecture; and he found the particular cause of this slowness in the blind loyalty paid over the centuries to Aristotle. "Considering that reason for so many ages has been locked up in the enchanted castle of syllogism, where empty phantoms pass for realities," he remarked, "the slow progress of reason toward maturity is far from being surprising."[308] The remaining pages of Kames's account of the progress of reason were given to the enumeration of actual beliefs which on the one hand Kames considered to have been deeply cherished by mankind and on the other, to have postulated false conceptions of reality. He divided these beliefs under three heads, and explained the divisions thus: "First, Instances showing the imbecility of human reason during its nonage. Second, Erroneous reasoning occasioned by natural biasses. Third, Erroneous reasoning occasioned by acquired biasses."[309] One of the instances cited by Kames under the first of these heads was the Epicurean doctrine that each of the gods has a human figure, inasmuch as no being of any other figure has the use of reason.[310] As an example of an erroneous belief belonging to his second head, Kames cited the English legal requirement that an accused person had to state whether he was innocent or guilty when he was arraigned for felony or piracy, and that, if he stood mute, and refused to plead one way or the other, he was to be held guilty and sentenced as if he had been convicted by verdict or confession.[311] Under his third head, Kames gave as one of his examples the accusation filed by the church against Copernicus—that inasmuch as the Scriptures speak of the sun as moving, it is wrong for anyone to allege the contrary.[312] This illustration and many of the others in Kames's account of the progress of reason show his concern that propositions should be judged true or false according as they agree or disagree with the realities to which they refer. Thus this part of his sketch has value for the new logic, even if it deals with logical doctrine by implication rather than by overt statement.

It was in his later introduction to Reid's "Brief Account" that Kames made something more than a merely repetitious or implicit contribution to the new logic, and what he said in that introduction is properly to be emphasized as his chief title to mem-

---

308 *Ibid.*, p. 121.   309 *Ibid.*, p. 122.   310 *Ibid.*, pp. 122-123.
311 *Ibid.*, p. 141, n.   312 *Ibid.*, pp. 158-159.

bership in the select company of Scottish logicians of the new school.[313] The introduction, as we already know, explained why he had invited Reid to give an account of the ancient logic as a supplement to Kames's own sketch of the principles and progress of reason, and how Reid had relished the invitation and welcomed the laborious task which it imposed upon him. But after these explanations, Kames offered some comments upon the essay written by Reid in fulfilment of the invitation. These comments have a certain electrical quality about them, as if they were sparks thrown off by Kames's mind as he grasped the naked wires of Reid's argument and received the thrust of impulses from the current of Reid's alternating expositions and criticisms of Aristotelian logic. Kames's comments at that moment are all interesting. But for our purposes only one can now be mentioned. It has to do with Reid's implied but not openly stated thesis that the syllogism is in fact an argument in a circle.

Kames's distinctive contribution to the new logic is that he took Reid's implied thesis upon this subject and made it more explicit. Aristotle, said Kames, damaged man's reasoning faculty when he drew it away from the course which it would naturally have followed and imposed upon it an artificial and superficial mode of procedure. Kames continued:

> I say, superficial; for in none of his logical works, is a single truth attempted to be proved by syllogism that requires a proof: the propositions he undertakes to prove by syllogism, are all of them self-evident. Take for instance the following proposition, That man has a power of self-motion. To prove this, he assumes the following axiom, upon which indeed every one of his syllogisms are founded, viz. That whatever is true of a number of particulars joined together, holds true of every one separately. . . . Founding upon that axiom, he reasons thus: "All animals have a power of self-motion: man is an animal: *ergo*,

[313] Kames's *Introduction to the Art of Thinking* (Edinburgh, 1761) should not be taken as a work on logic, although its title might suggest as much. It is a collection of maxims, sententious sayings, moral precepts, reflections, apothegms, historical incidents, fables, and allegories. Kames intended it to provide thoughts for contemplation and encouragement, but not to provide instruction in logic. It went through six editions between 1761 and 1819. See T. E. Jessop, *A Bibliography of David Hume and of Scottish Philosophy* (London, 1938), p. 141. Cited below as Jessop.

man has a power of self-motion." Now if all animals have a power of self-motion, it requires no argument to prove, that man, an animal, has that power: and therefore, what he gives as a conclusion or consequence, is not really so; it is not *inferred* from the fundamental proposition, but is *included* in it. At the same time, the self-motive power of man, is a fact that cannot be known but from experience. I add, that the self-motive power of man, is more clearly ascertained by experience, than that of any other animal: and in attempting to prove man to be a self-motive animal, is it not absurd, to found the argument on a proposition less certain than that undertaken to be demonstrated? What is here observed, will be found applicable to the bulk, if not the whole, of his syllogisms.[314]

Kames went on to point out that Aristotle did not use the syllogistic mode of reasoning when he wrote on ethics, on rhetoric, and on poetry. If he failed in his own works to put in practice his own rules for reasoning, what then did he consider the function of the syllogism to be? Kames answered this question thus: "He certainly intended his system of logics, chiefly, if not solely, for disputation: and if such was his purpose, he has been wonderfully successful; for nothing can be better contrived than that system, for wrangling and disputing without end."[315] Nor did Kames ignore the opportunity to draw a parallel between dictatorship in science and dictatorship in matters of faith. "The despotism of Aristotle with respect to the faculty of reason," he remarked, "was no less complete, than that of the Bishop of Rome with respect to religion; and it has now become a proper subject of curiosity, to enquire into the nature and extent of that despotism, from which men are at last set happily free."[316] Kames then concluded his introduction with the following words:

> In my reveries, I have more than once compared Aristotle's logics to a bubble made of soap-water for amusing children; a beautiful figure with splendid colours; fair on the outside, empty within. It has for more than two thousand years been the hard fate of Aristotle's followers, Ixion like, to embrace a cloud for a goddess.—But this is more than sufficient for a preface:

[314] *Sketches*, ii, 166.   [315] *Ibid.*, ii, 167.   [316] *Ibid.*, ii, 167.

and I had almost forgot, that I am detaining my readers from better entertainment, in listening to Dr. Reid.[317]

Kames's *Sketches of the History of Man* enjoyed a considerable success in their first fifty years. As I indicated above, they came out originally as an anonymous publication in two volumes at Edinburgh in 1774, and in that same year and the next appeared as a four-volume work at Dublin with their author's name on the title page. A "considerably improved" second edition was published anonymously at Edinburgh in four volumes in 1778, and a third edition in two volumes at Dublin in 1779. Thereafter they appeared at Basle in 1796, at Glasgow in 1802 and 1819, and at Edinburgh in 1807 and 1813. They were published in a two-volume German translation at Leipzig in 1774-1775.[318] Reid's "Brief Account" not only enjoyed a large public as a result of these various printings of Kames's *Sketches,* but it also gained a public of its own in the opening years of the nineteenth century. Newly called the *Analysis of Aristotle's Logic, with Remarks,* it appeared in 1806 at Edinburgh in a small octavo; and it was reprinted under this same title in 1812, 1819, 1820, 1822, and 1837.[319] Thus its influence was repeatedly freshened well into the century in which the new logic was at last to find its most effective interpreter.

Two years after the date of the first edition of Kames's *Sketches,* George Campbell published his *Philosophy of Rhetoric,* and in it, as a necessary part of the discussion of his titular subject, he dealt with logic in such a way as to earn for himself a respected standing among the new logicians of his time. His contribution to the new logic has a positive and a negative side, and the latter was to be so spectacular as to overshadow the former and indeed to suggest that the former was of little account. But in seeking to give a fair impression of his total accomplishment, I shall speak of both sides, and I shall begin with what he created rather than with what he sought to destroy.

In the fourth and fifth chapters of the first book of the *Rhetoric,* Campbell made it very clear that the new rhetoric of his own dreams could not possibly do without logic, but that the kind of logic in which it would find its future support would be different

[317] *Ibid.,* II, 167.   [318] Jessop, pp. 141-142.   [319] *Ibid.,* pp. 164-165.

from the logic of the past. In his view, rhetoric, eloquence, and communication were interchangeable terms,[320] and they applied to the art "whose object it is, by the use of language, to operate on the soul of the hearer, in the way of informing, convincing, pleasing, moving, or persuading."[321] Whenever language is used, and discourse results, the student of rhetoric becomes interested in all aspects of the process, Campbell indicated; and the discourse itself, as the central part of the process, interests the student in relation to its sense and its expression. "Now it is by the sense," Campbell declared, "that rhetoric holds of logic, and by the expression that she holds of grammar."[322] "The sole and ultimate end of logic," he added at once, "is the eviction of truth, one important end of eloquence; though, as appears from the first chapter, neither the sole, nor always the ultimate, is the conviction of the hearers." From these observations it appears that rhetoric and logic have the goal of conviction in common, although to logic this goal is the final object, and to rhetoric, an important preliminary one. Thus the theory of logic, so far as the rhetorician is concerned, is the theory governing the establishment of the truth of propositions that enter into discourses, truth being a quality which propositions must have in order to impress the human understanding or to affect the human will. "Logical truth," Campbell explained, with the new logic in mind, "consisteth in the conformity of our conceptions to their archetypes in the nature of things."[323] Then he defined his meaning as follows: "This conformity is perceived by the mind, either immediately on a bare attention to the ideas under review, or mediately by a comparison of these with other related ideas. Evidence of the former kind is called intuitive; of the latter, deductive."

As this passage indicates, evidence is the key term in Campbell's analysis of the kind of logic to be envisaged by the new rhetoric, and to this term he devoted the whole of the fifth chapter of Book I. The theory of evidence represents what Campbell himself called natural logic.[324] Natural logic teaches that a state-

---

[320] See George Campbell, *The Philosophy of Rhetoric. In Two Volumes* (London: Printed for W. Strahan; and T. Cadell, in the Strand; and W. Creech at Edinburgh. MDCCLXXVI), I, ix, 14, 16, 25. I cite this edition, the first, throughout my present discussion.

[321] *Ibid.*, I, vii.   [322] *Ibid.*, I, 96.   [323] *Ibid.*, I, 103.   [324] *Ibid.*, I, 163.

ment is sometimes accepted intuitively as true, and that on all other occasions truth would have to be established by deductive means. An intuitive recognition of the truth of a statement would arise, said Campbell, from intellection, from consciousness, or from common sense.[325] Intellection is Campbell's term for perception, and perception is a man's instant awareness that a proposition corresponds or does not correspond to the facts which it embraces. Thus when one says that "one and four make five," it is obvious at once that the statement is true. Consciousness is Campbell's term for man's awareness that his sensations, his ideas, his passions, are realities of his experience. His concept of hot water and his concept of the pain which comes when hot water engulfs the hand would lead him, for example, to be intuitively sure of the truth of the statement that hot water is painful in contact with living flesh. Common sense was not used by Campbell to mean what we ordinarily understand by the term. He meant by it a human capacity to identify and accept the self-evidence of certain statements that depend upon the information supplied by sense and memory—the statement, for instance, that "The course of nature will be the same to-morrow, that it is to-day."[326] Campbell mentioned, by the way, that his use of this term was not different from that in Reid's famous *Inquiry into the Human Mind, on the Principles of Common Sense.*[327] In any event, common sense, consciousness, and intellection are the separate instruments of our ability to identify the truthfulness of many of the statements made in any discourse, according to Campbell's analysis. But when a statement comes to our attention, and we cannot decide upon its truth or falsity by these means, that is, by intuitive awareness, we have to resort to deductive evidence. There are two kinds of deductive evidence, said Campbell, the scientific and the moral.[328] Scientific evidence "is solely conversant about number and extension, and about those other qualities which are measurable by these."[329] Scientific evidence leads to mathematical truths, or to any truths which involve declarations capable of being ascertained and expressed in numbers. An example given by Campbell to illustrate truths of this sort is the famous proposition in Euclid, "The square of the hypotenuse is equal to the sum of the squares of the sides."[330] Moral

[325] *Ibid.*, I, 103-120. [326] *Ibid.*, I, 113. [327] *Ibid.*, I, 110, n.
[328] *Ibid.*, I, 120-162. [329] *Ibid.*, I, 121. [330] *Ibid.*, I, 123.

evidence, on the other hand, is made up of four components: of our experience conceived as the sum of what our senses teach us and our memory retains; of analogies to our experience; of testimony about the experience of others; and of calculations as to the likelihood that a given experience will come to pass in a situation in which a fixed number of other experiences have an equal chance of taking place.[331] Campbell's own terms for these four sorts of deductive evidence are respectively "experimental evidence," "analogical evidence," "testimony," and "calculations of chances."[332] He distinguished between experimental evidence and analogical evidence by saying that, if we could be experimentally sure of the circulation of the blood in human beings, we could also be sure analogically of the circulation of the blood in quadrupeds and even of the circulation of sap in vegetables. Testimony, of course, was to Campbell the written or oral record of something experienced in some way by someone else. The proper kind of testimony would enable us to be sure of the truth of the statement that "Caesar overcame Pompey." As for the calculation of chances, Campbell analyzed ways of determining the number of happenings or experiences to be expected from a set of known possibilities, as in the throw of a pair of dice, we could calculate what the chances were that any given marking on one of the six faces of one die would appear on its uppermost face, and what the chances were that this marking would correspond to markings on the upper face of the other die. Campbell's own summary of this chapter indicates how the various terms of his new logic will enter into the concerns of his new rhetoric. He said:

> So much for the various kinds of evidence, whether intuitive or deductive; intuitive evidence, as divided into that of pure intellection, of consciousness, and of common sense, under the last of which that of memory is included; deductive evidence, as divided into scientific and moral, with the subdivisions of the latter into experience, analogy, and testimony, to which hath been added, the consideration of a mixed species concerning chances. . . . This, though peculiarly the logician's province, is the foundation of all conviction, and consequently of persuasion too. To attain either of these ends, the speaker must always assume the character of the close and candid reasoner: for

[331] Ibid., I, 136-155.   [332] Ibid., I, 144, 146, 151.

though he may be an acute logician who is no orator, he will never be a consummate orator who is no logician.[333]

The negative side of Campbell's contribution to the new logic consisted in his devastating attack upon the syllogism, which, as we well know, was not only the center of the old logic but also the foundation of logical proof in the old rhetoric. His attack takes place in the sixth chapter of Book 1, and that chapter is entitled "Of the nature and use of the scholastic art of syllogizing." It is perhaps the most famous chapter on logic in any rhetorical treatise ever written. It was to be remembered for a long time, and it was to make contemporary logicians feel that they had to read it, even if it might seem a little odd to some of them that a rhetorician could have something important to say about their own discipline. The reason why they thought they had to read it was that it contained four upsetting arguments against the claims of the syllogism to the central place in the procedures of scientific enquiry and in the practices of real deductive proof. Let us now follow Campbell into this phase of his theory of logic.

The first of his upsetting arguments was that the scholastic art of syllogizing "has not the least affinity to moral reasoning, the procedure in the one being the very reverse of that employed in the other."[334] Campbell stated this argument after he had mentioned that the syllogism during many ages had enjoyed among the learned the highest reputation as the only legitimate means of acquiring knowledge, and that on this account he felt he must not pass it over in silence. Its lack of affinity to moral reasoning meant in Campbell's phraseology that the syllogism had no connection with what in his immediately preceding chapter he had called the moral as distinguished from the scientific branch of deductive evidence. Moral evidence came into play in establishing truth, we remember, when men argued from experience, whether by direct use of it, or by analogy, or by testimony, or by the calculations of chances. The argument from experience was always an ascent from particulars towards universals. It was what the old logic had discussed as the analytic method. On the other hand, the syllogism was always a descent from universals to particulars. It involved what the old logic had called the synthetic method. "The analytic is the only method which we can follow,"

---

[333] *Ibid.*, 1, 162-163. [334] *Ibid.*, 1, 165.

said Campbell, "in the acquisition of natural knowledge, or of whatever regards actual existences; the synthetic is more properly the method that ought to be pursued in the application of knowledge already acquired."[335] He added almost at once:

Now, the method of reasoning by syllogism, more resembles mathematical demonstration, wherein, from universal principles, called axioms, we deduce many truths, which, though general in their nature, may, when compared with those first principles, be justly styled particular. Whereas, in all kinds of knowledge, wherein experience is our only guide, we can proceed to general truths, solely by an induction of particulars.

Campbell's second upsetting argument was that, although the syllogism might seem to have an affinity to scientific as distinguished from moral evidence, and to belong therefore to the deductive branch of natural logic, it did not in fact deserve such a rating.[336] Campbell rested this argument upon two considerations: the mathematicians, he declared, do not demonstrate their theorems by the method of syllogism; and he himself had found the syllogism an indirect, tedious, and obscure implement in proving mathematical theorems, although on occasion he had had a measure of success in using it for this purpose. This whole argument, like the preceding, is conspicuous as an illustration of what Campbell had himself called the moral branch of deductive evidence. In other words, it is an appeal to experience. Go to the mathematicians, Campbell was saying in effect. See what they do. You will find that they do not follow the rules laid down in textbooks on the syllogism. And if you try to follow those rules yourself in proving mathematical theorems, you will find the syllogistic method tedious and artificial and unnecessary in comparison to its mathematical counterpart.

Campbell's third argument, the most upsetting one of all, was that the progress of all argument and investigation is "from things known to things unknown,"[337] or from things evident to things obscure, whereas the syllogism, in direct opposition to this natural movement, leads from the less known to the better known, from the more obscure to the more evident. He illustrated this point by analyzing a syllogism which stated as its major premise

[335] *Ibid.*, I, 166. [336] *Ibid.*, I, 167. [337] *Ibid.*, I, 168.

that all animals feel, and as its minor premise that all horses are animals, and as its conclusion, that therefore all horses feel. Said Campbell:

> It is impossible that any reasonable man who really doubts whether a horse has feeling or is a mere automaton, should be convinced by this argument. For, supposing he uses the names *horse* and *animal*, as standing in the same relation of species and genus, which they bear in the common acceptation of the words, the argument you employ is, in effect, but an affirmation of the point which he denies, couched in such terms as include a multitude of other similar affirmations, which, whether true or false, are nothing to the purpose. Thus *all animals feel,* is only a compendious expression, for *all horses feel, all dogs feel, all camels feel, all eagles feel,* and so through the whole animal creation.[338]

Implicit in this illustration is the notion that the syllogistic procedure proves a point by citing as evidence the same point stated in a more general way. But Campbell wanted to make this notion explicit. And so he did. In the most memorable passage of his attack on the syllogism, he spoke as follows:

> Logicians have been at pains to discriminate the regular and consequential combinations of the three terms, as they are called, from the irregular and inconsequent. A combination of the latter kind, if the defect be in the form, is called a paralogism; if in the sense, a sophism; though sometimes these two appellations are confounded. Of the latter, one kind is denominated *petitio principii*, which is commonly rendered in English *a begging of the question*, and is defined, the proving of a thing by itself, whether expressed in the same or in different words; or, which amounts to the same thing, assuming in the proof the very opinion or principle proposed to be proved. It is surprising that this should ever have been by those artists styled a sophism, since it is in fact so essential to the art, that there is always some radical defect in a syllogism, which is not chargeable with this. The truth of what I now affirm, will appear to any one, on the slightest review of what has been evinced in the preceding part of this chapter.[339]

[338] *Ibid.,* I, 170.   [339] *Ibid.,* I, 173-174.

With these words Campbell convicted the syllogism of being in effect a *petitio principii*, that is, a sophism, even when it was beyond reproach in respect to form and to sense. Its premises and its conclusion could be true; its terms could be cast in a lawful mood and figure; and yet it inevitably would embody the fallacy of proving a thing by itself. Campbell left the matter there without attempting to analyze further the problem that he had created when he exposed the basic defect in syllogistic procedure. The problem is this: if even a completely proper syllogism embodies a sophism, how can its defectiveness be accounted for? It can be shown to be consistent in form, and accurate in sense. In what other direction can we possibly look in explaining the fallacy that it contains? Can it be that the *petitio principii* of the syllogism falls outside of its sense and its form? An answer to these questions lies in a consideration not mentioned by Reid, Kames, and Campbell, and perhaps not even recognized by them. That consideration has to do with their conception of truth, as distinguished from the conception of truth inherent but not emphasized in the old logic. Reid and his school followed Locke in defining truth as the quality which a proposition has when it is in accord with the facts interpreted by it. These philosophers understood scientific enquiry to be a search for propositions that would accurately interpret factual states. The syllogism was in their view useless as an instrument of scientific enquiry because its conclusion always involved the same interpretation of a factual state as its premises had postulated. Thus it never could produce new truth, and an instrument incapable of producing new truth was a mockery in science or scholarship, and even more of a mockery in this case because the old logic had repeatedly emphasized that it guided the understanding in the quest for truth. Irrefutable as these statements are, they overlook the value of the syllogism as an instrument for establishing consistency between one affirmation and another. If a general proposition has been carefully established by induction, then it is true because it accords with the facts. But if a question arises whether some other proposition is or is not consistent with it, and if that question is settled by syllogistic means, and a consistency is established between the latter proposition and the former, then the second can be said to be true because it has been shown to be consistent with the first. The syllogism should never have been represented as an instrument of scientific enquiry, for in scientific enquiry one cannot establish a new truth by using that truth as a proof of itself. It should have been represented instead as an instrument of critical examination, in which the problem is not to find the correct interpretation of the facts but to find whether a given interpretation is consistent with the interpretation accepted as the established one. In this context, the syllogism would not be assailable for embodying a *petitio principii*, inasmuch as consistency can only be shown by proving that one statement is contained in another. Nor in this context can the syllogism be expected to do what observation and experiment do in science and scholarship. It was Campbell's shortcoming that he did not create a place for the syllogism in his new logic and rhetoric, even as it was his strength that he would not allow it to be there under the false pretenses in which it had in the past clothed itself. He needed to define truth as accuracy in the scientific phase of human endeavor, and to define truth as consistency when men needed to understand, interpret, and communicate their knowledge. He needed a logic for both of these activities, especially when he was engaged in creating a rhetoric that was to be responsible for the presentation of truth to the understanding, the imagination, the passions, and the will. He ended, however, by failing to satisfy fully the need which rhetoric has always had for the syllogism.

Campbell's final argument on his examination of the syllogism did make a start towards satisfying the need just mentioned, and thus it is not so much another attack on the syllogistic method as an attempt to show what legitimate functions that method performs. "The fourth and last observation I shall make on this topic," he said, "is, that the proper province of the syllogistical science, is rather the adjustment of our language, in expressing ourselves on subjects previously known, than the acquisition of knowledge in things themselves."[340] As Campbell explained this observation, he made it refer to the process of detecting such abuses of language as that in which an argument, having in reality only one term, or only two terms, and containing therefore only a single word or a single statement, is sometimes made to assume the character of a full standard syllogism composed of three terms and three statements. The following argument, as given by

[340] *Ibid.*, I, 174.

Campbell, illustrates how a pseudosyllogism of this sort would look in its fullest extent:

> Twelve, you allow, are equal to the fifth part of sixty;
> Now a dozen are equal to twelve;
> Therefore a dozen are equal to the fifth part of sixty.[341]

Campbell did not bother to explain the defect in this argument, but he plainly meant it to exemplify a syllogism having only one term, not the statutory three. That term is twelve. The major premise says that twelve are twelve; the minor premise repeats that twelve are twelve; and the conclusion, not to be outdone, concludes that twelve are twelve. Easy as it may be to detect this kind of nonsense when numbers are concerned, Campbell went on, the substitution of a term in metaphysics for the one used here might deceive even the acute and the wary into supposing that something was in fact being demonstrated, when the argument amounted to nothing.

Campbell's famous chapter on the syllogism came to an end shortly after his analysis of the pseudosyllogism just quoted. He knew full well that the cultural change from syllogistic to inductive procedures was momentous and climactic, and that logic and rhetoric would differ afterwards from what they had been before. His paragraph written to memorialize this change suggests that in his view the new rhetoric must come to terms, not with the old syllogizing, but with the new science.

> When all erudition [he said] consisted more in an acquaintance with words, and an address in using them, than in the knowledge of things, dexterity in this exercitation conferred as much lustre on the scholar, as agility in the tilts and tournaments added glory to the knight. In proportion as the attention of mankind has been drawn off to the study of Nature, the honours of this contentious art have faded, and it is now almost forgotten. There is no reason to wish its revival, as eloquence seems to have been very little benefited by it, and philosophy still less.[342]

The sources of Campbell's hostility to the syllogism need a word of comment. The chapter just analyzed begins by distinguishing two stages in that hostility, and one of these stages is

[341] *Ibid.*, I, 178.   [342] *Ibid.*, I, 182-183.

clearly connected by Campbell with its point of origin, whereas the other is not. The first stage was that in which, as a student of Locke's *Essay concerning Human Understanding,* he had read the articles of Locke's attack upon the syllogism and "was first convinced, by what Mr. Locke hath said on the subject, that the syllogistic art, with its figures and moods, serves more to display the ingenuity of the inventor, and to exercise the address and fluency of the learner, than to assist the diligent inquirer in his researches after truth."[343] We do not know the precise date when Campbell read the *Essay* and acquired these first views. The passage just quoted is prefaced by the indication that he had gotten them "long since" from Locke; and it is followed by the statement that they had been with him "a long time." We may properly assume that he first read Locke during his undergraduate course at Marischal College, and that his unfavorable opinion of the syllogism originated from that experience. No doubt he took the occasion then to discuss Locke's views with his fellow student William Duncan, and with Thomas Reid, then librarian of that institution. No doubt these early views, matured and consolidated but substantially unchanged, were the direct inspiration for Campbell's discussion of natural logic when he wrote his chapter on that subject for his *Rhetoric.* Locke had placed more value upon natural than upon scholastic logic, we remember, and the concept of natural logic was implicit in what he said of inference.[344] At any rate, we know that Campbell's chapter on natural logic was completed by 1760,[345] and it is entirely reasonable to assume that the first stage of Campbell's hostility to the syllogism was brought to fulfilment at that time, even as it is reasonable to assume that this stage had begun at Marischal College in the middle seventeen-thirties. But what of Campbell's sixth chapter—the one which charges that the syllogism is a *petitio principii*? This charge cannot be traced to Locke, and that particular chapter, as Campbell indicated in the Preface to the work containing it, was "but lately added."[346] Lately added? These words would certainly permit us to assume that the sixth chapter was written after Campbell had had the opportunity to read the first edition of Kames's *Sketches* and to absorb from it the implied charge by Reid and Kames that a syllogistic argument is inherently circular. Thus when Campbell re-

[343] *Ibid.,* 1, 164.
[345] *Rhetoric,* 1, iv.

[344] See above, pp. 277, 286, 289-291.
[346] *Ibid.,* 1, iv.

marked in his sixth chapter that his opposition to the syllogism was of long standing, and had originated in Locke, but that "on a nearer inspection" he had seen "a little further into the nature of this disputative science, and consequently into the grounds of its futility,"[347] we may confidently say that the second stage of his opposition began when he studied Kames and Reid, and that these names should be added to Locke's in any list of the sources of his views on logic.

William Duncan's name should also be added to the same list, although conclusive proof of this statement is lacking. It is very probable, however, that Campbell had read and been influenced by the successful logic of his erstwhile undergraduate associate at Marischal College, who was later to be member of the faculty at that center of learning when Campbell was its principal. The probability is increased, indeed, when we compare the general design of Campbell's chapter on natural logic with that of Duncan's chapters on self-evident and demonstrable propositions and on the method of science. Scottish literary ethics, particularly among writers who would be likely to read and respect each other's works, were not careless or lenient in the eighteenth century, and any writer would take pains to treat a given subject with as much originality as he could command, so as to avoid the charge of dependence upon someone else who had done a distinctively good job with the same subject. Thus we should not expect that Campbell would follow Duncan closely on matters of logic, unless such a dependence were not only discernible but openly acknowledged as well. Campbell did not openly acknowledge Duncan as one of the influences upon his own thinking, nor does he ever invite the charge that he borrowed from Duncan in such a way as to convict himself of plagiarism. Nevertheless, I believe that he read Duncan, and that Duncan influenced him in matters of spirit and outlook rather than in matters of literal doctrine. But Campbell, in advocating a logic that did not contain the syllogism, and that indeed denounced the syllogism as a *petitio principii*, went considerably beyond Duncan, despite Duncan's having also grasped certain large aspects of the new logic which Locke had taught the eighteenth century to envision.

[347] *Ibid.*, I, 165. For proof that Campbell had read Reid's "Brief Account," and thus would have also known Kames's introduction to it, see his *Rhetoric*, I, 209.

The originality of Campbell's criticism of the syllogism received public notice at once, and a striking feature of that notice is that it came from London rather than from Edinburgh. In the autumn of 1776, *The Monthly Review*, which I mentioned earlier as having given Duncan's *Elements of Logick* a favorable reception,[348] devoted ten pages of its October issue, and ten pages of its November issue, to a commentary upon *The Philosophy of Rhetoric*. Both of these installments were written by William Enfield, who was not only on the staff of *The Monthly Review*, but also had belonged since 1770 to the faculty of the Academy at Warrington, where as tutor in languages and belles lettres Joseph Priestley had first delivered in 1762 his *Course of Lectures on Oratory and Criticism*.[349] Enfield confined the first installment of his review to a critique of Book I of Campbell's work, and his second, to Books II and III. His ruling opinion was most favorable, and he expressed it early in his critique, when he spoke as follows:

> Among the writers who have distinguished themselves in this walk, we have met with few who have given us so much satisfaction as the Author of the present work. His plan is much more extensive than the title he has chosen seems to promise, and leads him to the philosophical investigation, not merely of the principles of rhetoric in the usual acceptation of the term, but of good writing in general. And, as far as he has executed his design, he has discovered a clearness of discernment and accuracy of observation, which justly entitle him to be ranked among the most judicious critics. That our Readers may form some idea of the extensive plan and masterly execution of this work, we shall take a brief survey of its several parts in the order in which the Author has disposed them.[350]

Enfield proceeded to survey the several parts of Campbell's treatise by making frugal comments of his own while quoting generously from his author's text. Of the 851 total printed lines in his two installments, 572 are given over to Campbell's own words. Our greatest present interest, however, is in noticing that, of the

---

[348] See above, pp. 348-349.

[349] See below, Ch. 6, p. 632. For the identification of Enfield as author of this review, see Nangle, *The Monthly Review*, pp. 15-16.

[350] *The Monthly Review*, LV (October 1776), 287.

406 total lines of the first installment, 283 are made up of direct quotations, and 242 of these latter are taken from the sixth chapter of Campbell's first book. In sum, Enfield considered Campbell's attitude towards the syllogism to be of overwhelming importance in any critical evaluation of this part of the treatise under review. Moreover, he specifically memorialized the sixth chapter for containing "curious and original observations on the syllogistic art."[351] Although he did not arrange the quotations so as to reveal the four arguments that Campbell wanted to level against the syllogism, he managed nevertheless to make Campbell's general point inescapable, and to dwell fully upon the particular claim that the syllogism is a *petitio principii*.

The efforts of Reid and Campbell on behalf of the new logic began to receive powerful support from another brilliant Scot before Campbell's *Rhetoric* had celebrated its tenth birthday as a printed book. That Scot was Dugald Stewart, whom I mentioned earlier as having attended Reid's lectures on moral philosophy in Glasgow in the academic year 1771-1772. Stewart was a son of Edinburgh. Born in that city on November 22, 1753, just three months after the beginning of William Duncan's tenure as professor of natural and experimental philosophy at Aberdeen, Stewart attended the University of Edinburgh between 1765 and 1769.[352] In that period and in that place, of course, he came under the influence of John Stevenson, who had taught logic and metaphysics there since 1730, and who had been one of the first Scots to introduce his students to Locke through Wynne's abridgment of the *Essay concerning Human Understanding*.[353] After Stewart's year at Glasgow with Reid, he returned to the University of Edinburgh to take charge of the course in mathematics as the substitute for his father, the professor of that subject, whose ill health

[351] *Ibid.*, p. 288.

[352] This account of Stewart relies mainly upon John Veitch's "Memoir of Dugald Stewart," in *The Collected Works of Dugald Stewart, Esq., F. R. SS.*, ed. Sir William Hamilton, bart. (Edinburgh, 1854-1860), x, vii-clxxvii. The "Memoir" is cited below as Veitch, the *Collected Works*, as Hamilton. I rely also upon Sir Leslie Stephen's sketch of Stewart in *The Dictionary of National Biography* and upon the account of Stewart in McCosh, *The Scottish Philosophy*, pp. 275-307.

[353] See above, p. 273. For Stewart's tribute to Stevenson, see his "Account of the Life and Writings of Thomas Reid, D.D.," in *Works of Reid*, I, 9-10.

was forcing him into retirement. Stewart and his father jointly occupied the latter's professorship after 1775, and in 1778 the son was not only awarded the degree of master of arts by his university but he was also asked to conduct the course in moral philosophy there in the temporary absence of his own highly respected former teacher in that field, Adam Ferguson. When Ferguson withdrew for a time from the faculty of Edinburgh in 1785, Stewart was appointed his successor in the chair of moral philosophy, and he held that post until 1820, although in 1810 he ceased his activity as teacher and turned his duties over to Dr. Thomas Brown. Stewart died in Edinburgh on June 11, 1828. The beautiful monument now standing on Calton Hill in that city as a memorial to him was designed by William Henry Playfair, the architect, whose classical buildings have encouraged people to call Edinburgh the Modern Athens. The memorial to Stewart is modeled upon a monument erected in the fourth century B.C. in that famous other Athens by a wealthy Athenian named Lysicrates to house the prize tripod awarded in a dramatic contest to the chorus which he himself had financed in large part from his own personal fortune. An open circular structure with its roof supported by columns in the Corinthian order, Playfair's monument testifies to the great esteem in which Stewart was held by his fellow citizens at the time of his death, and to the triumphant renown of his era in the intellectual history of Scotland.

Stewart's lectures on moral philosophy, delivered, repeated, and improved over the years between 1785 and 1810, have been preserved in an abridged form in a book which he published in 1793 as an aid to the students enrolled in his course, and which he called *Outlines of Moral Philosophy*.[354] In its opening pages Stewart said that "the great business of philosophy" is "to ascertain those established conjunctions of successful events, which constitute the order of the universe;—to record the phenomena which it exhibits to our observation, and to refer them to their general laws." "Lord Bacon," he remarked, "was the first person who was fully aware of the importance of this fundamental truth."[355] And he added, "The more knowledge of this kind we ac-

---

[354] For a convenient text of this work, see *The Works of Dugald Stewart in Seven Volumes* (Cambridge, England, 1829), III, 371-499. I cite this text below as *Outlines*.

[355] *Outlines*, p. 376.

quire, the better can we accommodate our plans to the established order of things, and avail ourselves of natural Powers and Agents for accomplishing our purposes." As for the method of philosophical investigation that he would use in his lectures, Stewart spoke as follows:

> The reformation in the plan of philosophical inquiry which has taken place during the last two centuries, although not entirely confined to physics, has not extended in the same degree to the other branches of science, as sufficiently appears from the prevailing scepticism with respect to the principles of metaphysics and of moral philosophy. This scepticism can only be corrected by applying to these subjects the method of induction.[356]

The general laws which moral philosophy would seek to discover by induction and recommend to the world would be ascertained, said Stewart, "by an examination of the principles of the human constitution and of the circumstances in which man is placed."[357] Such an examination would require, he added, that he speak first of man's intellectual powers as these were reflected in the human understanding, then of man's active and moral powers as these concerned the human will, and finally of man's political capacities as these are shown in man's membership in political communities. The vastness of the undertaking represented by Stewart's ensuing lectures can be shown by the topics which he covered under each of these three heads. In discussing the intellectual powers of man, he analyzed consciousness, perception, attention, conception, abstraction, association of ideas, memory, imagination, judgment, and reasoning. When he turned to man's active and moral powers, he spoke of our appetites (hunger, thirst, and sex), our desires (for knowledge, social organization, esteem, power, and superiority), our affections, both benevolent and malevolent, our self-love, our moral faculty, our perception of right and wrong, of merit and demerit, of free agency, of duties to God, of evidences of design in the universe, of the moral attributes of deity, of a future state, and of duties to our fellow creatures and to ourselves. Stewart's third major heading, which analyzed man as the member of a political body, led him to speak of the history of political society, the origin and progress of the arts, sciences, and commerce, the history of property, the origin and progress of

[356] *Ibid.*, pp. 377-378.   [357] *Ibid.*, p. 380.

government, the elements of political economy, and the nature of the different forms of political powers. In the universities of twentieth century America, the subjects taught by Stewart at Edinburgh would fall into the departments of psychology, philosophy, history, political science, economics, and sociology. A dozen modern professors, each specialized in a single one of the many subjects within these various general departments, would be required to do what Stewart or any other eighteenth-century professor of moral philosophy attempted by himself. If the eighteenth century seems presumptuous and naïve in having assumed that one man could accomplish what is now regarded as beyond one man's capacity, we should temper any criticisms of this kind by reflecting that that era gave higher education a great variety of new studies in fields never before explored, and that the importance to be attached to the mere existence of those studies at that time far outweighs the disadvantages which attended them in the form of occasional shallowness. It is also worth remembering that those new studies were not always shallow. Some of Stewart's ideas have a deep significance for our own day, as we may incidentally observe in the course of the following discussion. And all of them are expressed with clarity, grace, and good will—the very qualities which are now so often lacking in the writings of modern philosophers, social scientists, psychologists, and historians, all of whom are the academic descendants of Stewart and his era.

Whereas the *Outlines of Moral Philosophy* preserve a condensed version of Stewart's lectures of Edinburgh, certain other works of his contain many of the lectures in carefully revised, rewritten, and perfected texts, which read more like philosophical essays than like oral discourses. During the last thirty-six years of his life he published at wide intervals in three volumes a work which bears the general title, *Elements of the Philosophy of the Human Mind,* and the essays in that work represent refinements and extensions of his lectures on the first of his three heads, that of the intellectual powers of man. The initial volume of the *Elements* appeared at London in 1792, although it was not designated as Volume I until later. It contained a general introduction to the philosophy of the human mind and a specific analysis of perception, attention, conception, abstraction, the association of ideas, memory, and imagination.[358] Twenty-two years elapsed before

358 Hamilton, Vol. II.

Volume II came forth at Edinburgh, and by that time Stewart had ended his career as teacher, and had been concentrating for four years upon advanced philosophical endeavors. The essays in Volume II continued his analysis of man's intellectual powers by dealing in depth with what the *Outlines* had called judgment and reasoning.[359] The four chapters of this installment of the *Elements* are successively concerned with stating the fundamental laws of human belief, the principles of reasoning and deductive evidence, the nature and shortcomings of Aristotelian logic, and the design of a new logic of experiment and induction. Volume III of the *Elements*, published at London in 1827, the year before Stewart's death, discussed four other topics connected with man's intellectual powers—that of language, of imitation, of the varieties of intellectual character, and of the differences between human and animal faculties.[360] As for Stewart's other lectures on moral philosophy, those dealing with the second division of his subject are represented by essays making up a two-volume work published by him at Edinburgh in 1828 under the title, *The Philosophy of the Active and Moral Powers of Man*,[361] while those dealing with the third division are partly preserved in another two-volume work, *Lectures on Political Economy*, reconstructed from Stewart's manuscripts and his students' notebooks and published for the first time at Edinburgh in 1855 and 1856 in Sir William Hamilton's edition of Stewart's *Collected Works*.[362]

To the historian of eighteenth-century British logic, the second volume of Stewart's *Elements of the Philosophy of the Human Mind* is a work of great importance and originality, and it deserves to give its author a much higher standing among the thinkers of his era than he has heretofore been allowed to have. In his sketch of Stewart in *The Dictionary of National Biography*, Sir Leslie Stephen said, "He was a transmitter of Reid's influence far more than an originator," and this judgment no doubt explains why Stewart was given no attention whatever in Sir Leslie's *History of English Thought in the Eighteenth Century*. Even John Veitch's sympathetic "Memoir of Dugald Stewart" spoke everywhere of Stewart as disciple and of Reid as master, and James McCosh, who was proud of the Scottish philosophers, and who displayed an affectionate admiration for Stewart, claimed only

[359] Hamilton, Vol. III.
[360] Hamilton, Vol. IV.
[361] Hamilton, Vols. VI and VII.
[362] Hamilton, Vols. VIII and IX.

that "if Stewart owed much to Reid, Reid owed nearly as much to his grateful pupil, who finished and adorned the work of his master, and by his classical taste has recommended the common-sense philosophy to many who would have turned away with disdain from the simpler manner of Reid."[363] A comparative estimate of Reid and Stewart tends of course to be influenced by the critic's choice of the standard to be used in measuring their accomplishments. If we regard Reid as the great exponent of the principles of common sense, as indeed we must do in fairness to his most important work, and if we proceed then to trace the influence of those principles in Stewart's lectures and writings, we would have to conclude that Sir Leslie Stephen, John Veitch, and James McCosh had pronounced the only sensible verdict upon Stewart. But if we ask which one of these two philosophers was the greater exponent of the new logic, and had a profounder sense of its present force and its future character, we could not call Stewart Reid's disciple, unless our notion of discipleship allows the talented pupil to outdo his talented master. In his review of the substance of Stewart's lectures on moral philosophy, Veitch dwelt particularly upon the discourses contained in the first and third volumes of the *Elements,* and upon those in *The Philosophy of the Active and Moral Powers of Man* and those in *Lectures on Political Economy.* As to the essays on logic in the second volume of the *Elements,* Veitch brushed them aside merely by saying, "Space was also allotted to the theory of Induction and Syllogism."[364] Although he added later in reference to this theory that "Mr. Stewart has given greater attention to the character of Philosophical Method than Dr. Reid,"[365] he honored the brilliance and originality of Stewart's chapters on logic by an almost unbroken silence. McCosh did not commit the same error. He distinguished between the "perfected universal logic" of the school of Aristotle, and the "particular logic" of the school of Locke, Reid, and Stewart. "In regard to this latter logic," McCosh declared, "Stewart must ever be referred to as an authority."[366] And he added almost at once that "in regard to induction, I believe that Stewart's account of it is, upon the whole, the best which appeared from the time of Bacon down to his own age."[367] This latter judgment is true and just. My present chapter is

[363] McCosh, p. 300. [364] Veitch, p. xxxviii. [365] *Ibid.*, p. xcv, n.
[366] McCosh, p. 292. [367] *Ibid.*, p. 293.

written indeed in the conviction that the evidence provided by all the British logics of the seventeenth and eighteenth centuries justifies no other verdict upon Stewart than the one just now quoted from McCosh. But if this estimate is true, why then did McCosh hold the emergence of inductive logic in such low esteem as to say that Stewart, its first brilliant spokesman after Bacon, deserves only to be regarded as having finished and adorned the work of his master Reid? It is time, I think, to assert our independence of the opinion that emphasizes only the derivative character of Stewart's philosophy. It is time to say that his work on induction entitles him to be considered an impressive original thinker in his own right. A review of his treatment of logic can lead us to no other conclusion, as we shall now see.

Stewart unfolded his theory of logic in three distinct stages, and these are spread over the four numbered chapters and the unnumbered introductory and concluding sections of the second volume of the *Elements*.[368] The first stage, mainly confined to the introduction and the following two chapters, consisted in an outline of the principles of what Stewart called rational or practical or mental logic, these terms being intended to indicate the opposition between his system and that of artificial logic or the old scholasticism.[369] It is true, of course, that rational logic, as Stewart used the term, answered to what Campbell and Locke had understood the word natural logic to mean. The second stage, to which Stewart devoted all of his next chapter, was given over to an attack on the logic of Aristotle, and at that point he was obviously engaged in extending and intensifying the similar attacks already made by Campbell and by Reid. His fourth chapter, the longest in this particular volume, is devoted to the final stage of his theory, which he called the experimental or inductive logic, and here he was at work shaping a doctrine that must be credited with resourcefulness and genius. He could not have written that chapter, to be sure, if Bacon had not previously written the *Novum Organum* and *De Dignitate et Augmentis Scientiarum*, or Locke, the *Essay concerning Human Understanding*, or Reid, the "Brief Account," or Campbell, *The Philosophy of Rhetoric*. But

[368] The ensuing discussion is based upon Hamilton, Vol. iii, which I shall cite by page number, without repeating the volume number.

[369] Hamilton, pp. 6, 108. For a parallel distinction made by Stewart between the old and new logic, see *Outlines*, p. 398.

we on our part would not be reading Stewart's fourth chapter today if his contribution to inductive logic had contained nothing or very little beyond what these sources had furnished. Bacon and Locke and Reid and Campbell would all acknowledge, I believe, that Stewart gave their teachings a content not present in them before, and a style neither common nor mean. They would not have dismissed him as a mere stylish purveyor of borrowed doctrine.

Stewart's discussion of rational logic led him to speak of intuitive and deductive evidence somewhat in the manner of Campbell. As we know, intuitive evidence in Campbell's analysis depended upon the processes of intellection, consciousness, and common sense, and it was said to be in operation whenever we are able on the instant to identify the truth or falsity in an affirmation or denial presented to us by ourselves or others as an account of the relation between two ideas. Stewart did not in all respects follow Campbell's formulations in enumerating the mental faculties involved in an intuitive act, although the main difference between these two writers in treating this subject was that Stewart went into it more deeply and at greater length than Campbell did. For example, Stewart devoted some twenty pages to the doctrine of common sense as a factor in intuition, whereas Campbell dealt with it in half that space. The respect shown by Stewart for Campbell throughout his analysis of this part of rational logic is well illustrated in one of his observations as he spoke of the role of consciousness in intuitive evidence. "According to the common doctrine of our best philosophers," said he, "it is by the evidence of *consciousness* we are assured that we ourselves exist."[370] And his footnote upon this statement particularizes it by sending his readers to only one philosopher, Campbell, and to only one work, *The Philosophy of Rhetoric*. Deductive evidence in Campbell's natural logic is classified, we remember, as scientific (or demonstrative, as Campbell sometimes calls it) and moral, the latter type being subdivided into experience, analogy, testimony, and the calculation of chances. Stewart's longer account of deductive evidence proceeds upon the assumption that its two classes should be called demonstrative and probable,[371] and that probable deductive evidence, which is a very wide category indeed, comes from experience, analogy, and testi-

[370] Hamilton, p. 41.   [371] *Ibid.*, pp. 113-152, 153-182.

mony.[372] Stewart is judicious and thorough during his discussion of these subjects, but I shall not dwell here upon any of his separate points, or draw parallels between them and Campbell's. It is a matter of some interest to observe, however, that in his comments upon this second part of rational logic, he spoke briefly of the inherent circularity of syllogistic reasoning, and he added, "that it was not without good reason Dr. Campbell hazarded the epigrammatic, yet unanswerable remark, that 'there is always some radical defect in a syllogism, which is not chargeable with that species of sophism known among logicians by the name of *petitio principii*, or a *begging of the question*.' "[373]

The second stage in Stewart's progress through logical theory involved him in a direct and searching analysis of Aristotelian logic, which stood opposed in his mind to the rational logic of intuitive and deductive evidence, and to the method of experiment and induction. He began this analysis by revealing some contradictions in Aristotle's theory of proof. He continued it by giving a ringing endorsement to the charge made successively by Bacon, Locke, Reid, and Campbell that the syllogism had no value as an instrument of scientific enquiry. He carried it on by investigating the question whether syllogistic logic had any utility as an instrument in the legal process, in civil affairs, and in education. And he concluded it by commenting upon a recently initiated controversy concerning the legitimacy of the claim that Aristotle was the inventor of the syllogism. I shall confine my discussion to the first three of these four subjects, the last one being foreign to my present purpose.

In the year 1797 Dr. John Gillies, classical scholar and historian of Scottish birth and education, published his translations of Aristotle's *Ethics* and *Politics* in company with his introductory essay on Aristotle's life and his critical analysis of Aristotle's speculative works. He could not speak of the latter subject, of course, without dwelling upon the *Organon*, and he could not discuss the *Organon* without referring on the one hand to the attacks of Kames and Reid on the syllogism, and on the other to the *dictum de omni et nullo* as the immutable foundation of logic. "On the basis of this one simple truth, itself founded in the natural and universal

[372] *Ibid.*, pp. 171-180, 284-298.
[373] *Ibid.*, p. 74. Stewart's quotation represents the sense but not the exact language of the passage as it is found in Campbell's *Rhetoric*, I, 174.

texture of language," said Gillies of the *dictum*, "Aristotle has reared a lofty and various structure of abstract science, clearly expressed, and fully demonstrated."[374] Gillies proceeded to explain that, by using the *dictum*, Aristotle had made it possible to accept fourteen modes of the syllogism as legitimate modes, and to understand why the remaining 178 possible modes were illegitimate.[375]

This argument of Gillies became the first target of Stewart's criticism. As we have just seen, his own conception of the nature of evidence and of the human understanding was that, whenever one idea was affirmed or denied of another, the mind of the person to whom the affirmation or denial presented itself either accepted its truth or falsehood at once by intuition or attempted by the process of reasoning to establish whether it was true or false. In accordance with this distinction, which he accepted on the authority of Locke, Stewart traced all certainty to intuitive or deductive evidence, the latter being involved with the third idea to which the original two ideas could be referred for proof of the original affirmation or denial. Now it was Stewart's conviction "that the power of reasoning presupposes the power of intuition,"[376] and that, even when the third idea had been invoked to test the connection between the original two, the perception of its relation to them, and of their resulting relation to each other, was a matter of successive intuitive acts. Anyone who said that the deductive process was capable of being used to demonstrate the validity of itself not only denied that the perception of validity was a matter of the antecedent faculty of intuition but also asserted that a measuring stick could be proved accurate by holding it up against itself to show that it was of the correct length. In other words, Stewart regarded it as an illusion that the legitimacy or illegitimacy of any syllogism in any mode or figure could be demonstrated by syllogistic means. It would always turn out, he believed, that the syllogism used in the process of validating the syllogistic mechanism would be recognized as true or false only by an intricate series of intuitive acts, and that the question of legitimacy or illegitimacy was always settled by intuitive recogni-

[374] John Gillies, *Aristotle's Ethics and Politics, Comprising His Practical Philosophy, Translated from the Greek* (London, 1797), I, 71-72. Cited below as Gillies. For Gillies's references to Kames and Reid, see pp. 76-77.
[375] *Ibid.*, I, 73-77.   [376] *Outlines*, p. 397.

tion acting in itself or through its offspring, deductive evidence.
Here is what Stewart said to summarize his argument against the
propriety of using the *dictum* to prove that the syllogistic procedure was conclusive:

> A process of reasoning which pretends to demonstrate the legit-
> imacy of a conclusion which, of itself, by its own intrinsic evi-
> dence, irresistibly commands the assent, must, we may be per-
> fectly assured, be at bottom unsubstantial and illusory, how
> specious soever it may at first sight appear. Supposing all its
> inferences to be strictly just, it can only bring us round again
> to the point from whence we set out.[377]

His own theory of evidence also led Stewart to criticise Aristotle's distinction between the demonstrative and the dialectical
syllogism, and Aristotle's apparent willingness to imply that, inasmuch as the *dictum* was the groundwork of all demonstration,
then each other science must in turn rest upon its own basic
axioms, and that therefore axioms must be accepted as the
groundwork of all science whatever. Aristotle, it will be remembered, had divided syllogisms into two great classes, the demonstrative and the dialectical, and had said that the former were
certain, the latter, probable. But, argued Stewart, if the *dictum*
is made the final test of conclusiveness, then all syllogisms which
conform to the *dictum* are equally conclusive, and how is it therefore possible to classify some of them as less conclusive than
others? What Aristotle should have done, suggested Stewart, is
to recognize the difference between a conclusion founded upon
demonstrative evidence and a conclusion founded upon probable
evidence. The former might be called demonstrative, the latter
probable, but now the distinction would refer to propositions, not
syllogisms, and would rest upon their content, not upon their
form, content being the one thing that has to be considered whenever the certainty or probability of a proposition is in question.[378]
As for Aristotle's implied belief in axioms as the groundwork of
science, does not this also involve a contradiction in his system of
thought? At one point his admirers, and Dr. Gillies in particular,
claimed Aristotle as the discoverer of the idea that the first principles upon which any science depends are got by induction from
the information of sense; and at another point they claimed Aris-

[377] Hamilton, p. 189. [378] *Ibid.*, pp. 186-189.

totle as the creator of a proud science of demonstration founded upon a single axiom. "In what manner this apparent contradiction is to be reconciled," Stewart tartly declared, "I leave to the consideration of his future commentators."

> For my own part [he added at once], I cannot help being of opinion with Lord Monboddo, (who certainly was not wanting in a due respect for the authority of Aristotle), that the syllogistic theory would have accorded much better with the doctrine of Plato concerning *general ideas*, than with that held on the same subject by the founder of the Peripatetic school. To maintain that in all demonstration we argue from generals to particulars, and, at the same time, to assert that the necessary progress of our knowledge is from particulars to generals, by a gradual induction from the informations of sense, do not appear, to an ordinary understanding, to be very congruous parts of the same system; and yet the last of these tenets has been eagerly claimed as a discovery of Aristotle, by some of the most zealous admirers of his logical demonstrations.[379]

Having disposed of the contradictions involved in accepting the *dictum* as the groundwork of logic, Stewart proceeded next to endorse the conclusions of the new logicians towards the syllogism as an engine of science. What he said on this subject is contained in a statement about Bacon and Locke in his text, and a comment about Reid and Campbell in an attached footnote. It will do no violence to his meaning if text and footnote are combined so as to make a continuous observation, as follows:

> The remarks which were long ago made by Lord Bacon on the inutility of the *syllogism* as an organ of scientific discovery, together with the acute strictures in Mr. Locke's *Essay* on this form of reasoning, are so decisive in point of argument, and, at the same time, so familiarly known to all who turn their attention to philosophical inquiries, as to render it perfectly unnecessary for me, on the present occasion, to add anything in support of them. To some of my readers it may not be superfluous to recommend, as a valuable supplement to the discussions

[379] *Ibid.*, pp. 194-195. For Lord Monboddo's own statement of his views on this matter, see [James Burnett, Lord Monboddo], *Antient Metaphysics. Volume Fifth* (Edinburgh, 1797), pp. 183-188. For the claim that Aristotle discovered induction, see Gillies, pp. 40-53, 61.

of Locke and Bacon concerning the syllogistic art, what has been since written on the same subject, in farther prosecution of their views, by Dr. Reid in his *Analysis of Aristotle's Logic,* and by Dr. Campbell in his *Philosophy of Rhetoric.*[380]

As Stewart saw the matter when he was preparing the second volume of the *Elements* for the press, the four distinguished philosophers mentioned in the passage just quoted had left unanswered the question whether syllogistic logic had any value in education or practical affairs after its uselessness in scientific enquiry had been demonstrated. This unanswered question he himself set out to discuss. In outlining what his discussion involved, I shall begin where he ended and say that to him the syllogism would have only a slight value in the modern world. It might be of some use in the practice of law, he acknowledged, inasmuch as legal judgments "are formed in consequence of an application to particular cases of certain maxims which we are not at liberty to dispute."[381] "The case was similar in every branch of philosophy," he added perceptively, "as long as the authority of great names prevailed, and the old scholastic maxims were allowed, without examination, to pass as incontrovertible truths." The syllogistic art might also be of some use in civil affairs, Stewart continued; and in support of this statement he quoted Locke's translation of a passage from Bacon's *Novum Organum,* and he noted that, since Locke had cited this passage in the introduction to *The Conduct of the Understanding,* "the opinion which it expresses may be considered as also sanctioned by the authority of *his* name."[382] But what remains for the syllogistic art after its possible applications to law and civil affairs have been acknowledged? Almost nothing. Those who claim that it is valuable as a means of teaching students how to make a legitimate inference from premises should remember that this important skill is developed, not by learning the rules of the syllogism, but by learning how to use

---

[380] Hamilton, p. 202. Hamilton corrected Stewart's reference to Reid by inserting *Account* in brackets after *Analysis.* Apparently Hamilton did not remember that Reid's treatise appeared at Edinburgh in 1806 as a separate work under the title, *Analysis of Aristotle's Logic, with Remarks.* Stewart's reference thus needs no correction.

[381] Hamilton, p. 203.

[382] *Ibid.,* p. 204, n. For the passage translated by Locke from Bacon, see above, p. 276.

language with precision, how to ascertain the facts upon which our reasonings must proceed, how to avoid partial and narrow views of broad, complicated subjects, and how to correct the distortions which prejudices impose upon our opinions through the influence of authority and fashion. The mention of prejudices as a source of error in the process of inference led Stewart to recommend in *The Port-Royal Logic* a section entitled "Des Sophismes d'amour propre, d'intérêt & de passion,"[383] and of course he could have recommended in the same connection Locke's *Conduct of the Understanding*, since it is obviously in his mind throughout this part of his critique of Aristotelian logic. As for those who claim that the cultivation of the power of reasoning is a primary concern of education, and that the syllogistic art develops that power as nothing else can, they should remember, declared Stewart, that little benefit accrued to mankind in the ages when the lore of the syllogism was at the center of the educational process, and that the mastery of that lore created a whole series of bad intellectual habits. Stewart used the evidence of testimony to establish the proposition that scholastic logic was a futile business, and his witness was John of Salisbury, "himself a distinguished proficient in scholastic learning." Here is Stewart's quotation from John:

After a long absence from *Paris*, . . . I went to visit the companions of my early studies. I found them, in every respect, precisely as I had left them; not a single step advanced towards a solution of their old difficulties, nor enriched by the accession of one new idea:—a strong experimental proof, that, how much soever logic may contribute to the progress of other sciences, it must for ever remain barren and lifeless, while abandoned to itself.[384]

Stewart's quotation from John omitted one of John's observations about his old associates. "They had changed," he said, "in but one regard: they had unlearned moderation: they no longer knew

[383] Hamilton, p. 205, n. See *Oeuvres d'Arnauld*, XLI, 328-339.

[384] Hamilton, p. 207. See Daniel D. McGarry, *The Metalogicon of John of Salisbury* (Berkeley and Los Angeles, 1955), p. 100, for this passage in a more literal translation. Stewart's translation, however, is faithful to the spirit of John's original Latin.

restraint."[385] But if Stewart failed to mention the bad intellectual habits which John noticed among his former classmates, he did not fail to dwell at some length upon the bad intellectual habits which an addiction to debate and controversy had fostered in more recent times. He noted that lawyers were taught by debates over points of fact and law to be ingenious, subtle, and witty, but they were not taught to have truly enlightened minds.[386] He noted also that the controversial writer was taught to confine his attention only to one side of a question, and thus on occasion to become "the sceptical dupe of his own ingenuity."[387] And at one point he expressed such an unfavorable opinion of disputation and disputants as to deserve special quotation.

> For my own part [he said], so little value does my individual experience lead me to place on argumentative address, when compared with some other endowments subservient to our intellectual improvement, that I have long been accustomed to consider that promptness of reply, and dogmatism of decision, which mark the eager and practised disputant, as almost infallible symptoms of a limited capacity; a capacity deficient in what Locke has called (in very significant, though somewhat homely terms) *large, sound, roundabout sense.*[388]

And finally, to those whose professions would require skill in polemical warfare, and who might wonder whether the study of Aristotelian logic would be therefore of special benefit to them, Stewart spoke as follows:

> My own opinion is, that, in the present age, it would not give to the disputant, in the judgment of men whose suffrage is of any value, the slightest advantage over his antagonist. In earlier times, indeed, the case must have been different. While the scholastic forms continued to be kept up, and while schoolmen were the sole judges of the contest, an expert logician could not fail to obtain an easy victory over an inferior proficient. *Now,* however, when the supreme tribunal to which all parties must appeal, is to be found, not *within,* but *without* the walls of universities; and when the most learned dialectician must, for his

---

[385] McGarry, p. 100.   [386] Hamilton, pp. 207-208.
[387] *Ibid.,* p. 209.
[388] *Ibid.,* pp. 211-212. For the quotation from Locke, see above, p. 277.

own credit, avoid all allusion to the technical terms and technical forms of his art, can it be imagined that the mere possession of its rules furnishes him with invisible aid for annoying his adversary, or renders him invulnerable by some secret spell against the weapons of his assailant? Were this really the case, one might have expected that the advocates who have undertaken its defence (considering how much their pride was interested in the controversy) would have given us some better specimens of its practical utility, in defending it against the unscientific attacks of Bacon and Locke. It is, however, not a little remarkable, that in every argument which they have attempted in its favour, they have not only been worsted by these very antagonists whom they accuse of ignorance, but fairly driven from the field of battle.[389]

These remarks did not conclude Stewart's case against Aristotelian logic, but they must conclude my present analysis of what he said. Perhaps I should mention that Stewart's sense of fairness prompted him to recognize Leibniz as having views contrary to his own on the art of the syllogism,[390] and that his sense of cultural interconnections led him to suggest the need of a study of the terms of the old logic as a way of understanding the many vocabularies which it had directly influenced. In this latter connection he spoke as follows: "The technical language connected with it is now so incorporated with all the higher departments of learning, that, independently of any consideration of its practical applications, some knowledge of its peculiar phraseology may be regarded as an indispensable preparation both for scientific and for literary pursuits."[391] This concession, however, was not to be carried so far as to allow the old logic to return to the curriculum with its old authority or its old pretensions. Stewart's final verdict upon it would appear to be contained in the following statement: "That nothing useful is to be learned from Aristotle's logic, I am far from thinking, but I believe that all which is useful in it might be reduced into a very narrow compass; and I am decidedly of opinion, that wherever it becomes a serious and favourite object of study, it is infinitely more likely to do harm than good."[392]

[389] Hamilton, pp. 216-217.
[390] *Ibid.*, pp. 220-221.   [391] *Ibid.*, p. 222.   [392] *Ibid.*, p. 219.

The third and final stage in Stewart's exposition of his logical theory consisted of his careful and thorough construction of what he variously called the experimental or the inductive or the new logic.[393] Up to this point, he had endorsed and enriched the criticisms which Reid and Campbell had made against the logical doctrines of the Aristotelians, and he had adopted and strengthened Campbell's impressive design for a natural logic based upon the theory of intuitive and deductive evidence. He might well have chosen to be content with these two praiseworthy accomplishments. After all, Campbell was to stand in learned opinion of the future as one of the two most famous British rhetorical theorists of his century, his genius having led him to help not only in freeing rhetoric from its two-thousand-year bondage to the old logic of enthymeme, of example, and of merely probable proofs, but also in endowing it with a new sense of obligation to truth and a new grasp of the intuitive and deductive evidence which modern persuasion would demand of speakers and writers.[394] A corresponding endeavor in the field of logic would have been enough in itself to establish Stewart as a more distinguished logician than Reid, and to entitle him to an honorable place among the philosophers of his own country and time, even if it would have justified later critics in pointing out that he had carried the new logic no farther than Campbell did, and that he had attacked the old logic with no more effectiveness than might reasonably be expected of a man of middle genius who had only to make use of the cues provided him by such outstanding thinkers as Reid, Locke, and Bacon. But the fact is that Stewart was not content with those two accomplishments. He went beyond them to explore new ground and to give the new logic its writ of independence. His long fourth chapter in the second volume of the *Elements* is impressive in its scope. Here is a list of the subjects which it treated: the difference between Aristotle and Bacon in regard to the concept of causation; the inductive logic as the logic of physical causes; the inductive method as the method of observation, experiment, analysis, and synthesis; the difference between Aristotle and Bacon in regard to the concept of induction; the difference between the concept of analysis and synthesis in

---

[393] For these three terms in the context given them by Stewart, see Hamilton, pp. 230 and 322.

[394] See above, pp. 397-410; also below, Ch. 6, pp. 579-603.

Greek mathematics and that same concept in modern inductive science; the distinction between experience and analogy in the field of scientific evidence; the grounds afforded by analogy for scientific inference and conjecture; the use and abuse of hypotheses in philosophical enquiries; misapplications of the words experience and induction in the terminology of modern science, with illustrations from medicine and political economy; and the conflict in modern philosophical opinion about final causes as a legitimate object of research. These subjects were handled by Stewart with learning and discrimination. Comments upon his treatment of them all would be fully relevant in my present chapter, but it is obvious that I must impose severe limitations upon the extent of my discussion of them. Stewart's own words can always be consulted by those who wish information about anything that I may omit, and indeed about anything that I may say. His own words are well worth attention, and if these concluding pages of my account of the new logic help in part to demonstrate that fact, and to induce modern students to read him, I shall be content.

Late in his discussion of the new logic, Stewart referred to the inductive philosophy of the Newtonians and the hypothetical system of their predecessors, and he said then that at the beginning of his present endeavor he had pointed out "the characteristical peculiarities" which distinguished these two systems from each other.[395] Let us begin with his analysis of those peculiarities, and let us select for special comment what he said concerning the difference between the hypothetical and the inductive concepts of causation. The hypothetical system of ancient philosophy and the inductive system of Bacon and Newton were agreed that philosophy is the science of causes, but they did not agree upon the meaning of the concept of causation itself. The ancients believed that what the moderns would call physical causes were endowed with an inherent power or energy to produce their effects, as if causes had human attributes, whereas the moderns believed that physical causes were only the constant forerunners or antecedents of events transpiring after them, and that the business of ascribing human attributes to them was incapable of proof. Thus Aristotle had talked, not of physical, but of efficient, material, formal, and final causes, and the schoolmen had construed the fourth one

[395] Hamilton, p. 322.

427

of these terms to mean God, and had made it underlie and ultimately explain the other three, so as to impose an anthropomorphic interpretation upon the whole theory of causation. The attributing of human characteristics to God or to things not human seemed improper to the moderns. Was it not effrontery on the part of man to impose his human limitations upon God? In a sense, were not the latter-day Aristotelians the impious ones, even at the very moment when they called the moderns impious for seeming to deny the role of God in the happenings of nature and history? Stewart did not raise these precise questions in his own analysis of this matter, but he did insist that physical causation should not be confused with final causation. The latter, he felt, was a legitimate object of research, despite Bacon's celebrated apothegm in denunciation of it,[396] but it was essentially a metaphysical, not a physical question, and physics should proceed so as to eliminate from its theory of causation all unprovable anthropomorphic assumptions. A partial summary of Stewart's final position upon the necessity of preserving a careful distinction between these two kinds of causation is contained in his following words:

> According to the doctrine now stated, the highest, or rather the only proper object of Physics, is to ascertain those established conjunctions of successive events, which constitute the order of the universe; to record the phenomena which it exhibits to our observations, or which it discloses to our experiments, and to refer these phenomena to their general laws. While we are apt to fancy, therefore, (agreeably to popular conceptions and language,) that we are investigating efficient causes, we are, in reality, only generalizing effects; and when we advance from discovery to discovery, we do nothing more than resolve our former conclusions into others still more comprehensive.[397]

[396] *Ibid.*, pp. 335-336. Stewart quoted Bacon's apothegm in Latin, as follows: "*Causarum finalium inquisitio sterilis est, et tanquam Virgo Deo consecrata, nihil parit.*" The apothegm comes from *De Dignitate et Augmentis Scientiarum*, 3. 5. In English it would read: "The investigation of final causes is sterile and, like a virgin consecrated to God, bears no children." (Translation mine.) For Bacon's Latin text and James Spedding's translation of the apothegm, see *Works of Bacon*, II, 298; VIII, 512.

[397] Hamilton, p. 240.

In accordance with this fundamental distinction, Stewart proceeded to define inductive logic as the logic of physical causation. "When, by thus comparing a number of cases, agreeing in some circumstances, but differing in others, and all attended with the same result," he declared, "a philosopher connects, as a general law of nature, the event with its *physical cause*, he is said to proceed according to the method of induction." "This, at least," he added, "appears to me to be the idea which, in general, Bacon himself annexes to the phrase; although I will not venture to affirm, that he has always employed it with uniform precision."[398] Stewart's footnote upon this passage consisted in a Latin quotation of a fragment of aphorism 105 from Book I of Bacon's *Novum Organum*. As translated later into English by James Spedding, this fragment reads as follows: "But the induction which is to be available for the discovery and demonstration of sciences and arts, must analyse nature by proper rejections and exclusions."[399] Here, then, is Stewart's operational definition of the new logic, and his acknowledgment of its antecedents in Bacon's *Novum Organum*. We notice, of course, that the definition associates the new logic only with scientific enquiry. The old connection between logic and the enterprise of communication has been altogether abandoned. We notice, moreover, that the enquiry visualized by Stewart does not consist in the examination of general truths, but in the examination of natural phenomena with a view to bringing into being general truths in the form of laws of nature. If all of this seems commonplace to us today, we might remember that our truisms were once the advanced thought of revolutionaries, and that the history of logic in eighteenth-century Britain affords some support to this statement, so far as the connection between logical theory and the theory of scientific investigation is concerned.

The new logic envisaged by Stewart was to have at its base a principle no less commanding in its authority, but much less recalcitrant in its applications, than the Aristotelian *dictum de omni et nullo* had been. Stewart called this new dictum "the *inductive principle*." It consists, he said, in "our instinctive expecta-

---

[398] *Ibid.*, p. 246.

[399] *Works of Bacon*, VIII, 138 (for the translation) and I, 312 (for the Latin text).

tion of the continuance of the laws of nature; an expectation which, implying little, if any, exercise of the reasoning powers, operates alike on the philosopher and on the savage."[400] Stewart gave Thomas Reid credit for naming this principle, and he then quoted Reid as follows in further elaboration of its meaning:

> It is from the force of this principle [said Reid] that we immediately assent to that axiom upon which all our knowledge of nature is built, That effects of the same kind must have the same cause. For effects and causes, in the operations of nature, mean nothing but signs, and the things signified by them. We perceive no proper causality or efficiency in any natural cause; but only a connexion established by the course of nature between it and what are called its effects.[401]

Stewart went on to assert that this principle, this law of belief, had been systematically implied in all of Bacon's logical rules, although it did not receive his formal recognition.

> It is, indeed, only of late [Stewart added] that natural philosophers have been fully aware of its importance as the groundwork of the inductive logic; the earlier writers under whose review it fell, having been led to consider it chiefly by its supposed subserviency to their metaphysical, or to their theological speculations. Dr. Reid and M. Turgot were, so far as I know, the first who recognized its existence as an original and ultimate law of the understanding;—the source of all that experimental knowledge which we begin to acquire from the moment of our birth, as well as of those more recondite discoveries which are dignified by the name of science.[402]

[400] Hamilton, pp. 246-247.

[401] *Ibid.*, p. 247. For this passage in its source, see *Works of Reid*, I, 199. It occurs in *An Inquiry into the Human Mind, on the Principles of Common Sense*.

[402] Hamilton, pp. 247-248. In his "Account of the Life and Writings of Thomas Reid," Stewart clarified the present reference to Turgot by saying that Turgot had stated this law in an article in the French *Encyclopédie*. See *Works of Reid*, I, 24. The article in question was entitled "Existence," and it appeared in the *Encyclopédie*, VI (Paris, 1756), 260-267. It is reprinted in *Oeuvres de Mr. Turgot* (Paris, 1808-1811), III, 95-136.

When the inductive principle described by Reid and Stewart is compared with that proposed by Wolff, we can see that a drastic change in habits of thinking upon this subject had occurred in the middle years of the eighteenth century. As I mentioned earlier, the third edition of Wolff's Latin logic, published in 1740, had recognized as the "Fundamentum Inductionis" the principle that "Whatever can be affirmed or denied concerning lower particulars can be affirmed or denied universally concerning the higher orders within which the lower particulars are contained."[403] This conception of induction is anchored to the old belief that induction is an irregular syllogism, and that it accomplishes its purpose when by the process of a simple enumeration of particulars it records a common characteristic which all of them share. The inductive principle stated by Reid in 1764 records that, if two particulars behave towards each other today as cause to effect, they will behave in that same way tomorrow if the conditions are the same. The difference between this principle and Wolff's is the difference between predicting future results and taking stock of results already achieved. Wolff's system, and that of the Aristotelians in general, was centered upon the past, Reid's upon the future, even as the old system derived its truths from the experience of the past, and the new system, from the experience of yesterday, today, and tomorrow. The swing from one system to another seems almost to have had its effective moment between 1740 and 1764, although it had been in motion since the days of Bacon, and it gained momentum from Stewart after Reid had given it a name.

On July 6, 1803, Francis Balfour, a Scottish doctor of medicine attached to the East India Company's service, delivered in Bengal to a meeting of the Asiatic Society a learned paper containing extracts from his own translation of a Persian translation of an Arabic treatise entitled *Essence of Logic*.[404] This particular treatise, said Balfour in introducing his paper, coincided in every point with the logical system of Aristotle, and would confirm the

[403] See above, pp. 368-369.

[404] These facts and the ensuing quotations are taken from Balfour's paper as it was printed in *Asiatic Researches; or, Transactions of the Society Instituted in Bengal, For inquiring into the History and Antiquities, the Arts, Sciences, and Literature, of Asia*, VIII (London, 1808), 89-135.

supposition that Aristotle's works were translated into Arabic many centuries ago. It would also serve, he continued, to correct certain grave misunderstandings now current in the English-speaking world concerning Aristotle's logic. On this latter point he became very specific.

> To the logical system of this wonderful genius, [he remarked] modern philosophers of distinguished eminence, and amongst these, Lord Kaimes, have not hesitated to impute the blame of retarding the progress of science and improvement in *Europe* for two thousand years, by holding the reasoning faculty constrained and cramped by the fetters of syllogism.

> From some of the extracts contained in this paper, it will appear, 1st. That the mode of reasoning by *Induction*, illustrated and improved by the great Lord Verulam, in his *Organum Novum*; and generally considered as the cause of the rapid progress of science in later times, was perfectly known to Aristotle, and was distinctly delineated by him, as a method of investigation that leads to certainty or truth; and 2dly, that Aristotle was likewise perfectly acquainted, not merely with the form of Induction, but with the proper materials to be employed in carrying it on—Facts and Experiments.

When Balfour's learned paper was published in London five years after it was originally delivered, it fell into the hands of Dugald Stewart, who was then engaged in preparing for the press the second volume of his *Elements*. Stewart made the remarks that I have just quoted the subject of one of the most valuable and important sections of his chapter on inductive logic.[405] What he did was first to present Bacon's theory of induction, and then to present Aristotle's, taking notice in this latter connection that John Wallis in his *Institutio Logicae* had written as a sympathetic Aristotelian and had viewed Aristotle's theory of induction very much as Stewart himself was doing. Prefixed to Stewart's presentation of these two systems of induction was the announcement that, in his opinion, the attempt to identify Bacon with Aristotle on this subject was "like confounding the Christian graces with the Graces of Heathen Mythology."[406] I should like briefly to explain the evidence Stewart used to justify that announcement.

---

[405] Hamilton, pp. 253-263. [406] *Ibid.*, p. 256.

Stewart presented Bacon's theory of induction by quoting two Latin passages from Bacon's works.[407] The first passage consisted in a generous portion, but not all, of the text of aphorism 105 in Book 1 of the *Novum Organum*. Stewart had quoted a smaller part of this same aphorism, we remember, in his earlier definition of the inductive logic. The second passage was a four-line excerpt from a seven-line statement in the *Cogitata et Visa*, a small book containing Bacon's essential thoughts on the interpretation of nature. Stewart's two excerpts from Bacon's text read thus in translation:

> In establishing axioms, another form of induction must be devised than has hitherto been employed. . . . For the induction which proceeds by simple enumeration is childish; its conclusions are precarious. . . . But the induction which is to be available for the discovery and demonstration of sciences and arts, must analyse nature by proper rejections and exclusions; and then, after a sufficient number of negatives, come to a conclusion on the affirmative instances: which has not yet been done or even attempted, save only by Plato, who does indeed employ this form of induction to a certain extent for the purpose of discussing definitions and ideas. But in order to furnish this induction or demonstration well and duly for its work, very many things are to be provided which no mortal has yet thought of; insomuch that greater labour will have to be spent in it than has hitherto been spent on the syllogism. . . . And it is in this induction that our chief hope lies.[408]

> And he [Francis Bacon] also thought these thoughts: . . . that induction abides as the sole last support and refuge in all things . . . and in truth its name is scarcely known, and its strength and usefulness have thus far been hidden from mankind.[409]

As for induction in Aristotelian logic, Stewart noted that Aristotle had founded all human belief upon syllogism or induction, and had then defined induction as "an inference drawn from *all* the particulars which it comprehends."[410] In Stewart's judgment, this definition reduced the inductive process to a simple enumera-

---

[407] *Ibid.*, pp. 256-257.
[408] *Works of Bacon*, VIII, 138-139. Translation Spedding's.
[409] *Ibid.*, VII, 123, 124. Translation mine.   [410] Hamilton, p. 257.

tion of particulars. He remarked that Bacon had called that kind of induction childish. And in order to show that Aristotle's conception of the inductive process was not being treated unfairly by Bacon or by himself, Stewart proceeded to quote a passage from a respected recent Aristotelian, Dr. Wallis of Oxford. That particular passage, by the way, figured in my previous discussion of the analysis which Wallis's *Institutio Logicae* gave to induction as a type of syllogism.[411] Wallis, it will be remembered, believed that a complete enumeration of particulars made a perfect syllogism out of the inductive process. His illustration was that, inasmuch as Saturn, Jupiter, Mars, Venus, Mercury, and the moon derived their light from the sun, and inasmuch as they together with the sun constituted all the planets, it was therefore true that all the planets except for the sun borrowed from the sun their light. Wallis proudly called this induction a syllogism in Darapti. Having quoted it, Stewart remarked:

> If the object of Wallis had been to expose the *puerility* and the *precariousness* of such an argument, he could not possibly have selected a happier illustration. The *induction* of Aristotle, when considered in *this* light, is indeed a fit companion for his syllogism; inasmuch as neither can possibly advance us a single step in the acquisition of new knowledge. How different from both is the induction of Bacon, which, instead of carrying the mind round in the same circle of words, leads it from the *past* to the *future*, from the *known* to the *unknown*?[412]

My account of Stewart's theory of inductive logic will have to close after I have discussed the four terms used by him to indicate the four procedures of inductive enquiry. Stewart believed that every man, whether an ordinary human being or a philosopher, sought to obtain from his experience an accurate system of rules for the regulation of his conduct. The only difference between the average man and the philosopher in respect to this enterprise was one of degree. The philosopher carried his researches further than the average man would think necessary, and those researches consisted in a careful process of observation, experiment, analysis, and synthesis. Stewart considered that observation and experiment as steps in the process of converting the information of the average man into the scientific knowledge of the philoso-

---

[411] See above, Ch. 2, pp. 34-35.   [412] Hamilton, p. 258.

pher were in need of no special explanation. But the case was different with analysis and synthesis. These two terms had various meanings in ancient and modern philosophy, and Stewart proceeded to comment at some length upon them.[413] From his discussion emerged the view that analysis consisted in resolving "particular facts into other facts more simple and comprehensive," and that synthesis was the process of applying "these general facts (or, as they are usually called, these *laws of nature*) to a synthetical explanation of particular phenomena." "These two processes of the mind, together with that judicious employment of observation and experiment which they presuppose," declared Stewart, "exhaust the whole business of philosophical investigation; and the great object of the rules of philosophizing is to shew in what manner they ought to be conducted."[414] Analysis, said Stewart at a later point, necessarily sets out from known facts and conducts us to a general principle, whereas, if we apply that principle to phenomena different from those comprehended under the preceding analysis, we follow the process of synthesis.[415] These various explanations make it obvious, of course, that Stewart considered analysis and synthesis to be indispensable parts of the investigative procedures to which the inductive logic was wholly committed. Although he said nothing about their place in the old logic, we know for ourselves that they had served in it as methods of enquiry and as methods of communication as well. Stewart would not have wanted his silence upon this latter subject to suggest that analysis and synthesis were relevant only to the process of research. His position would almost certainly have been that the inductive logic numbered analysis and synthesis among its essential investigative procedures, and that, if those procedures, or close variants of them, were also to be considered essential in the communication of ideas, the new rhetoric would have to be the agent for adapting them to that use. The new rhetoric, not blind to this challenge, showed some tendency, as we shall see, to meet it.[416]

In the beginning of the present chapter, I mentioned that one important point of friction between the old logic and the new consisted in their holding dissimilar attitudes towards the definition of truth. Interested in the process by which an examination

[413] *Ibid.*, pp. 244-250, 263-283.   [414] *Ibid.*, p. 244.
[415] *Ibid.*, p. 275.   [416] See below, Ch. 6, pp. 563, 602, 639, 663.

of the facts of experience could lead to an accurate statement about those facts, the new logic defined truth as the condition which prevails when a verbal statement accurately corresponds to the facts that it has in view, and to the mental conception that has to serve as intermediary between the factual and verbal world. The inductive procedures of the new logic were calculated to guarantee that statements would correspond to the facts behind them, and those procedures were designed for no other purpose. The old logic, as we have repeatedly seen, was constrained to accept this same definition of truth; but at the same time, thanks to the historical situation in which it had to conduct its affairs, it was also inclined to think of truth as the quality which a statement has when it is exactly consistent with other statements known or believed to be true. The old logic got into difficulties after the Renaissance because its central instrument, the syllogism, was perfectly adapted to the task of testing the consistency between a conclusion and its premises, but it was by no means adapted to proving whether a conclusion accurately stated the facts which it presumed to interpret. Stewart had seen the inadequacy of the old logic in this latter connection, and his conclusion was that the old logic should be abandoned. But he had not seen the adequacy of the old logic as an instrument for testing the consistency of propositions. It is strange that he remained insensitive to this value of the syllogism. He was a mathematician as well as a moral philosopher, and he was particularly interested in geometry, as his father had been before him. He even discussed Euclidean geometry in the course of his chapter on the inductive logic, and he felt required to do so, he said, because analysis and synthesis in modern science were not like the same two procedures in ancient mathematics, and he thought he should try to clarify the differences between the two processes in those two fields of endeavor.[417] In the course of his comments on Greek geometry, he defined the Euclidean concept of truth, and it is that definition which could stand without alteration as the concept of truth in the old logic. It is that definition, indeed, to which John Sergeant subscribed, as I pointed out at the end of my second chapter. Stewart's definition of this concept came as he finished explaining what analysis and synthesis had meant to the ancient geometers.

[417] Hamilton, pp. 263-276.

According to these definitions of analysis and synthesis [he said], those demonstrations in Euclid which prove a proposition to be true, by shewing that the contrary supposition leads to some absurd inference, are, properly speaking, analytical processes of reasoning. In *every* case, the conclusiveness of an analytical proof rests on this general maxim, That *truth* is always consistent with itself; that a supposition which leads, by a concatenation of mathematical deductions, to a consequence which is true, must itself be true; and that which necessarily involves a supposition which is absurd or impossible, must itself be false.[418]

Had Stewart applied this geometrical thinking to logic as a whole, he would have seen not only that the new logic needed to be inductive in order to supply what the old logic had lacked, but also that the new logic needed to retain the syllogism in order to preserve what induction could not supply on its own. In other words, he would have seen that the true logic of the new era must be a logic of accuracy and of consistency, of induction and of syllogism, inasmuch as human knowledge could no more afford to sacrifice the value of coherence than to ignore the value of adhering strictly to the dictates of fact. Thus we must acknowledge that Stewart, in his enthusiasm for induction, overlooked some of the ancient virtues of the syllogism—the virtues which ancient logic had shared with geometry. But his enthusiasm for induction was nevertheless beneficial and creative, even if one-sided. He deserves full credit for having given the inductive logic of Bacon and Locke its fullest, its most perceptive, and its most brilliant eighteenth-century statement in Britain. I began this chapter with an account of Locke's contribution to the new logic of the new age, and in ending it with this account of Stewart, I feel that I have not fallen into an anticlimax, and that, if others think I have done so, the fault is not Stewart's, but mine.

[418] *Ibid.*, p. 265.

CHAPTER 6

We must not judge so unfavourably of Eloquence as to reckon it only a frivolous Art that a Declaimer uses to impose on the weak Imagination of the Multitude, and to serve his own Ends. 'Tis a very serious Art; design'd to instruct People; suppress their Passions; and reform their Manners; to support the Laws; direct publick Councils; and to make Men good and happy. The more Pains an Haranguer takes to dazzle me, by the Artifices of his Discourse, the more I shou'd despise his Vanity. His Eagerness to display his Wit wou'd in my Judgment render him unworthy of the least Admiration. I love a serious Preacher, who speaks for my sake; and not for his own; who seeks my Salvation, and not his own Vain-glory. He best deserves to be heard who uses Speech only to cloath his Thoughts; and his Thoughts only to promote Truth and Virtue. Nothing is more despicable than a profess't Declaimer, who retails his Discourses, as a Quack does his Medicines.

A Letter From the late Archbishop of Cambray To The French Academy; Concerning Rhetorick, Poetry, History: And A Comparison between the Antients and Moderns.
(Translated from the French by William Stevenson and published at London in 1722 with its author's *Dialogues Concerning Eloquence in General.*)

THE NEW RHETORIC
(1646–1800)

1 Rhetoric *versus* Rhetoric: A Litigation in Six Issues

In Chapter 3 we explored the Ciceronian rhetorical tradition as it was expounded by John Ward at Gresham College and by John Holmes at Holt School. Inasmuch as that tradition had been present in European education during the latter part of the seventeenth century and for much of the time throughout the preceding sixteen hundred years, it is not strange that in the eighteenth century it should have attracted disciples like Holmes and Ward, and that those disciples should have treated it as if it could be expected with some modifications to remain a law unto the distant future. But the hard fact is that British writers on rhetoric in the second half of the eighteenth century regarded Ciceronian rhetoric as an anachronism. They decided that it was not so much in need of repair as replacement. And so they formulated a new rhetoric to supersede the old. The present chapter is devoted to the task of understanding this development, even as in Chapter 5 we endeavored to understand a similar development in the field of logic. My primary concern will now be to identify the authors of the new rhetoric and to describe the actual content of their doctrine. But before I turn to them and their writings, I should like to sketch the nature of their opposition to the old rhetoric. As I see it, there were six issues involved in that opposition, and I wish to begin this chapter by analyzing each.

One important issue concerned the question whether rhetoric should continue to limit itself to persuasive popular discourse as exemplified by political, forensic, and ceremonial speeches, or should expand its interests to include learned and didactic discourses and perhaps even the forms of poetry. The old rhetoric under the authority of Aristotle and Cicero had of course chosen the former alternative—it had devoted itself to the principles governing the content, the form, the style, and the delivery of persuasive popular compositions, which primarily embraced the three kinds of speeches just enumerated, while it had given only incidental attention to the theory of popular exposition. The later addition of the epistle and the sermon to its interests had not required it to extend the range of its traditional doctrine. Meanwhile, the old logic or dialectic had claimed jurisdiction over the method of philosophical enquiry and over the theory of content and form in learned writing, didactic works, and philosophical disputation, while the old grammar had dealt with the problem of correctness of usage in all the various types of composition, whether spoken or written, whether in prose or verse. These arrangements were partially upset during the Renaissance. Then it was that logic, as we have seen, began to interest itself more and more exclusively in the principles of scientific enquiry and to separate itself more and more from its ancient connection with the theory of learned exposition and debate. As a consequence, rhetoric began to realize that in its own right it was equipped to be the custodian of the theory of exposition, now no longer the concern of logic, and that meanwhile it would also need to modernize its historic interest in the methods of popular communication. Eighteenth-century British rhetoric shouldered these obligations squarely and expanded its interests so as to become not only the theory of learned and popular oral and written discourses in their didactic and persuasive forms, but also the creative center of speculation about all the types of belles lettres.

A second issue concerned the question whether rhetoric should continue to limit itself to the field of artistic proofs prescribed by classical theory, or should expand its interests to embrace and to use the nonartistic proofs that classical rhetoric had mentioned only to ignore. It will be remembered in this connection that the nature of each of these two kinds of proof was explained and illustrated in Chapter 3, as I spoke of John Ward's adherence to the ancient doctrine of the supremacy of artistic over nonartistic means of persuasion. If rhetoric had followed Ward, it would in effect have chosen to believe that arguments drawn from set topics were preferable from its point of view to arguments drawn from the facts of the case under debate, and thus it would have separated itself from the new science that was coming to dominate modern culture, and would have made itself into the exponent of the cloudy and futile wordplay that De Quincey was actually to designate as its sole responsibility.[1] Eighteenth-century British rhetoric refused to limit itself to this kind of role, and if the eighteenth-century authors who best spoke for it had been properly heeded by De Quincey, he would never have deceived himself about it as absurdly as he did. In the view of the authors whom De Quincey ignored, rhetoric in a culture permeated by the standards of scientific and scholarly proof must become scientific and scholarly itself, and must argue from the facts of the case, not from suppositions that may represent mere popular misconceptions and prejudices. I am not saying that the eighteenth-century British authors of the new rhetoric won a permanent victory on this point. But they resolutely tried for victory, and it is a calamity for twentieth-century rhetoric that they did not completely prevail. The theory that valuable arguments emerge from commonplaces unfortunately continues still to have currency, even in circles presumably dedicated to high rhetorical standards.[2]

A third issue concerned the question whether the form of rhetorical proof should be described as fundamentally enthymematic, with induction considered a mere variant of the enthymeme,[3] or whether it should be described as fundamentally inductive, with the enthymeme an auxiliary or occasional form. This issue has been so thoroughly explored in my chapters on eighteenth-century logic as to make further exposition of it unnecessary at this moment. It was, of course, an issue concerning the structure rather than the content of modern rhetorical proof. To eighteenth-century British writers on rhetoric, the syllogistic structure was not the natural form of thought, and although some

[1] For an account of De Quincey's views on this matter, see my essay, "De Quincey on Science, Rhetoric, and Poetry," *Speech Monographs*, XIII (1946), 1-13.

[2] Edward P. J. Corbett's *Classical Rhetoric for the Modern Student* (New York, 1965), pp. 94-142, attempts to make the ancient theory of topics available to speakers and writers of the twentieth century. It is unfortunate, however, that Mr. Corbett should have presented this theory without having explained that rhetoricians of the seventeenth and eighteenth centuries gave it such a critical rejection as to make it obsolete, and that rhetoric should not accept it today without proclaiming it an aid only to the slow and the dull.

[3] For John Ward's identification of the induction with the enthymeme, see above. Ch. 3, p. 105.

arguments would appropriately fall into that form, and could be analyzed and discussed in terms of their major premise, their minor premise, and their conclusion, the basic pattern of rhetorical argument for the new age was that which would lead the audience to recognize intuitively the truth of the author's statement or would lead him to establish its truth from related facts or truths. This latter process was not syllogistic; it was more nearly in accord with the process of inference as described so memorably by John Locke. Eighteenth-century British rhetoric is to be congratulated for handling the forms of thought in this way, and for freeing the rhetorical critic from the sterility involved in attempting to force a reluctant modern speech into a strict conformity with the standards of the old logic. Even so, the modern rhetorical critic does not always choose to be emancipated; he occasionally prefers to reduce rhetorical reasonings to enthymemes against their natural inclination to yield to this sort of analysis, and when he does so, his critical judgments seem somehow to be the shadow of a shadow of reality. Only now and then is such a procedure in accord with the dynamics of discourse in the twentieth century, although for the discourse of earlier centuries it is still valid and useful as a tool of analysis and understanding.

Another issue concerned the question whether rhetoric should deal only in probabilities, or whether it is also its responsibility to achieve as full a measure of truth as the situation allows. The old rhetoric, as I explained in Chapter 3, was pre-eminently the rhetoric of probabilities, and in its heyday it invited the scorn and contempt of philosophers because it seemed content with statements that were at best only approximations of the truth, or at worst were outright falsifications. The new rhetoric was aware, of course, that the correspondence between a verbal statement and the facts to which it relates may vary from strict to approximate truth, on the one hand, or from strict to approximate untruth, on the other, and that approximations to truth are on many occasions the only available support for the verbal reasonings upon which human decisions must depend. Thus it would seem that the new rhetoric would have to confess itself to be a rhetoric of probabilities, too, if a situation allowed it no hope of certainty, and that, on this issue, there was not a sharp clash between it and the old rhetoric. But there was a difference, even so. It consisted

444

in the recognition on the part of the new rhetoric that its prob-abilities could no longer be as loose as they once had been in days when trained observers were few, and uncritical procedures abounded. Modern probabilities had to have the stamp of scien-tific methodology upon them. They had to have a much higher rating than that accorded to mere guesswork or armchair specu-lation. They had to be in their own realm as unassailable as scientific probabilities were among trained and careful scholars. Thus a reliance upon them would give a rhetorical argument bet-ter repute and stronger authority than the probable arguments of the old rhetoric enjoyed. And, of course, a rhetoric committed to such standards would be the normal outcome of a revolution in science and scholarship, whereas a rhetoric indifferent to such standards would earn a greater measure of contempt in a scien-tific culture than the old rhetoric at its worst had ever earned in less critical times. The eighteenth-century British writers on rhetoric tended to insist upon scientific standards for the prob-abilities that speakers and writers would have to use, and it was this insistence which makes their rhetoric different from that of the old Ciceronians. Twentieth-century rhetoric has not always held its arguments from probability to scientific standards, and it has greatly suffered as a result. But at least the standards are there to be recognized, and the eighteenth century is clearly on record as having been a crucial influence in giving modern rhetoric an interest in them.

A fifth important issue concerned the question whether a speech had to adhere to the six-part form so fully elaborated in Ciceronian rhetoric, or whether a simpler form was desirable. The old rhetoric was itself divided upon this matter. Aristotle had taught that a speech need only state its case and prove it, and that, if other parts were needed beyond statement and proof, they would ordinarily be limited to an introduction and an epilogue. But Cicero endorsed the elaborate scheme that Aristotle had con-sidered more as a system of options than as a rigid prescription, and thus it was that rhetorical discourse came to have a ritualis-tic arrangement consisting of an introduction, a narration, a parti-tion, a proof, a refutation, and a peroration. This ceremonial pat-tern was found by successive generations to be perfectly suited to their tastes in a culture dominated by splendid religious rituals and by elaborate political pageantries of imperial, royal, and aristocratic rule. But the Reformation and the Counter Reformation, on the one hand, and the rise of parliamentary government, on the other, tended to expose the uselessness of a merely ceremonial rhetoric and to create a thirst for the religious and political discourses that in content would be fully relevant to the facts of the given situation and in form would be simple and easy to grasp. The best example of a treatise designed to provide the pulpit with a functional modern rhetoric is Fénelon's *Dialogues sur L'Éloquence*, composed in 1679, first published in its French text in 1717, and first given a published English translation in 1722. Among other evidences of his determination to emphasize the inner realities rather than the external forms of ancient rhetoric, Fénelon advocated a simple and natural structure for the sermon,[4] and the same kind of structure for all other types of persuasive and expository discourse was recommended repeatedly by the late eighteenth-century British rhetoricians. The twentieth century has followed their example, and the six-part oration of Cicero is no longer considered a viable option in written or spoken argument and persuasion.

The sixth and final issue concerned the question whether rhetorical style should be ornate, intricate, and heavily committed to the use of the tropes and figures, or should be plain and unstudied. There were, of course, three oratorical styles described in ancient oratory, as John Ward quite appropriately pointed out, and an orator was not supposed to consider that the title to excellence in spoken or written discourse was conferred more often upon practitioners of one style than upon those of another. Yet the grand style with its emphasis upon the tropes and figures always tended to make the middle and the plain style seem unrhetorical, and the result was that oratory became associated in the public mind of the seventeenth and eighteenth centuries with stylistic intricacy, floweriness, and conscious ornament. The new rhetoric of eighteenth-century Britain summoned the middle and the plain style back to oratory and to discourse in general and tended to disparage the grand style in its showy and extravagant forms. Thus the new rhetoric took issue not so much with the old rhetoric as with the natural perversions that had been allowed to dominate the interpretation of ancient doctrine. These natural

---

[4] See my *Fénelon's Dialogues on Eloquence*, pp. 39-40, 111-114.

perversions are still in evidence today, but by and large twentieth-century rhetoric has followed the eighteenth century in regarding the plain style with special favor.

As we prepare now to turn to the actual authors of the new eighteenth-century British rhetoric, it should be emphasized that they did not all take the modern side of each of the six issues just identified. But they all tended to treat the Ciceronian tradition as something which needed to be measured against the requirement of a new time and to be rejected wherever it failed to meet the standard that the new time would impose. Thus they are all on the modern side in their sympathies, even if a certain shortsightedness tended on occasion to make this or that author adhere to the side of tradition on this or that specific issue. But two of these eighteenth-century Britons were wholly on the modern side. Both of them were Scots, and one of them, George Campbell, has already figured in the preceding chapter of this book as a prominent member of the new school of logicians of his generation. The other is Adam Smith, who in age was four years younger than Campbell, but who was two years ahead of Campbell in starting to give eighteenth-century rhetoric a new and revolutionary formulation in public. The work of these two authors will receive special attention in a later section of this chapter. Meanwhile, it is important that we examine the historical context to which they, and indeed all the other new rhetoricians, belonged, and that we identify the earlier authors to whom all of them were directly or indirectly indebted.

447

II Voices of the Royal Society: Wilkins, Boyle, Sprat, Glanvill, Locke

Well before it received its first charter in the year 1662, the Royal Society of London was an informal organization of scientists and scholars who had been drawn together in the common conviction that the inductive method as propounded by Francis Bacon was destined to create a new order of human knowledge and to bring about vast improvements in the conditions of human life. These scientists began to hold meetings in London about the year 1645.[5] One member of that fateful early group was John Wilkins, a clergyman interested in science, who had already written a work to prove that the moon might be habitable and that a man would make himself and his age famous if he were able to get to that planet either by applying wings to his own body or by training some huge bird to carry him or by constructing a flying chariot which would be capable of ascending into space "beyond the sphere of the earths magneticall vigor."[6] Another member of the group was John Wallis, a Cambridge graduate, a practicing cryptographer, a mathematician of some promise, and author of the Aristotelian logic that was analyzed earlier in these pages. Still another member was Robert Boyle, only eighteen years of age in 1645, son of an Irish nobleman, but different from most noblemen's sons of that era by reason of his having already dedicated himself to a career in the new experimental science. That original group also included Mr. Samuel Foster, the professor of astronomy at Gresham College, and such other scientists as Dr. Jonathan Goddard, Mr. Theodore Haak, and Dr. George Ent.[7] Sometimes their regular meetings were held at the Bull Head Tavern in Cheapside; sometimes at Dr. Goddard's lodgings in Wood Street; and sometimes at Gresham College in Mr. Foster's quar-

[5] The following account of the early history of the Royal Society is based mainly upon that in The Record of the Royal Society of London, 3rd edn. (London, 1912), pp. 1-47. Cited below as Record of the Royal Society.

[6] [John Wilkins], A Discourse concerning A New World & Another Planet In 2 Bookes (London, 1640), I, 237-239. The first edition of the first of these "2 Bookes" was entitled The Discovery of a World in the Moone (London, 1638), and it did not discuss these three ways of ascending from the earth to the lunar surface.

[7] Record of the Royal Society, pp. 3-4.

448

ters.[8] They gathered together at a fixed day and hour in every week, and they not only paid penalties for nonattendance but they also made weekly contributions towards defraying the cost of experiments resolved upon in their discussions. Their rules barred them from talking about divinity, politics, and general news.[9] The proper subject of their meetings was the new philosophy.

A few years after the inauguration of this London society, four of its most important members took up residence in Oxford, and it was of course inevitable that they would continue their scientific association in their new surroundings, and that they would attract new recruits to their ranks from the Oxford student body. Wilkins, first of the four to leave London, became warden of Wadham College in 1648, and it was in his quarters at Wadham that he and his friends held scientific colloquies after an earlier Oxford meeting place became unavailable.[10] Wallis joined them in 1649 upon his receiving from Cromwell the appointment to the Savilian professorship of Geometry, and Goddard did likewise in 1651 when he was named warden of Merton. Then in 1654 Boyle moved to lodgings in the High Street next door to University College, and soon the meetings of the scientists were taking place in alternation between his dwelling and that of Wilkins. Meanwhile —the precise year was 1651—a young man named Thomas Sprat enrolled at Wadham as an undergraduate, and the influence of the scientific environment upon him was so pronounced that he achieved later fame as the first historian of the Royal Society when it had at last established its official identity. In 1652 Joseph Glanvill and John Locke entered Oxford, the former at Exeter College and the latter at Christ Church. Wilkins, Wallis, Goddard, and Boyle were members of the first council of the Royal Society under its first charter of incorporation in 1662;[11] they and Sprat as well were designated original Fellows in the famous list announced on May 20, 1663, under the Society's second charter of incorporation; Glanvill was elected Fellow in 1664; and Locke, in 1668.[12]

---

[8] *Ibid.*, p. 5.

[9] Charles R. Weld, *A History of the Royal Society* (London, 1848), I, 36. Cited below as Weld.

[10] *Record of the Royal Society*, p. 6.

[11] *Ibid.*, p. 15.   [12] *Ibid.*, pp. 16-18, 312, 314.

It should be noted here that the motto on the armorial bearings of the Society is a Latin phrase, *Nullius in Verba*, and that on the surface the phrase seems only to commit unnamed somebodies to express unnamed things "in the words of no one else."[13] But there is more to the motto than that. Its words echo the fourteenth line of the first of Horace's *Epistles*, where Horace had proudly declared, "nullius addictus iurare in verba magistri," that is to say, "I am bound to swear in the words of no master." If we now construe the terse and obscure armorial motto in the full light of this Horatian context, we can see that it is being used by the Royal Society to renounce the authority of the past and to assert the right of the present to a fresh look at the facts and to the truths to be derived from them. Thus the motto in its full setting expands into a definition of the dominant vision of modern scholarship and science.

In carrying out its program, the Royal Society had inevitably to face the realization that the new knowledge which it was discovering had to be transmitted throughout the world of learning and had also to be distributed as widely as possible among the individuals who made up the general public. So far as John Wallis was concerned, these procedures of communication were taught by logic. It was with this conviction in mind that he dedicated his *Institutio Logicae* to the Lord President and Fellows of the Royal Society and conceived of it as a treatise not only upon scientific investigation but also upon the presentation of truth to others, whether under the auspices of history, or poetry, or oratory, or practical philosophy, or speculative philosophy, or mathematics, or formal pedagogy.[14] Other members of the Royal Society subscribed to the tenet that, while traditional logic offered the best guidance in the presentation of ideas between a learned man and his learned colleagues, it was the office of traditional rhetoric, as taught by Cicero, to guide writers and speakers in the presentation of ideas to the popular audience. John Ward, who became a Fellow of the Royal Society in 1723, is a conspicuous advocate of this belief, as we have already seen.[15] But Wallis and Ward represented the conservative wing of the Royal Society in respect to

[13] For a discussion of the choice of armorial bearings for the Royal Society, see Weld, I, 142-143.

[14] See above, Ch. 2, pp. 31-41.

[15] See above, Ch. 3, pp. 77-79, 95-96.

the theory of communication. There were others in that distinguished organization who wanted to develop a new rhetoric that would not contradict the procedures of the new science. Chief among these latter in the era when the Society was defining its earliest objectives were Wilkins, Boyle, Sprat, Glanvill, and Locke. An account of the contribution of each of these men to the new rhetoric is now in order.

Wilkins's *Ecclesiastes, or, A Discourse concerning the Gift of Preaching As it fals under the Rules of Art* has already been mentioned in these pages as one of the earliest British rhetorics to use the English word elocution as a term for rhetorical delivery rather than for rhetorical style.[16] But it has other distinctions of a larger kind, and these concern the new rhetoric. It was first published in 1646, and that date virtually coincides, of course, with Wilkins's earliest attendance at the London meetings of the group which grew into the Royal Society. *Ecclesiastes* became a popular work. By 1693 it had received a total of seven editions distributed among eleven different dates of issue, and its vogue continued with interruptions for the next hundred and fifty years.[17] Its attractiveness in the late seventeenth century was doubtless enhanced by the prestige enjoyed by its author in his later years as master of Trinity College, Cambridge, dean of the collegiate church of Ripon, and bishop of Chester. But even without such recommendations, it would have appealed to its own times by reason of its modernity of outlook.

Ecclesiastes is careful in its opening words to indicate that preaching, on the one hand, and science, on the other, must not be allowed to drift apart and become separate enterprises. Preaching, as one of the arts by which knowledge is disseminated, must be considered a reciprocal phase of the process by which new truths are brought into existence in the first place. "It is the

---

[16] See above, Ch. 4, p. 151.

[17] Its second edition was issued in 1646 and 1647; its third, in 1651; its fourth, in 1653 and 1655; its fifth, in 1656, 1659, and 1669; its sixth, in 1675 and 1679; and its seventh, in 1693. An eighth edition appeared in 1704, and a ninth in 1718. It was later given a place in Edward Williams's *The Christian Preacher; or, discourses on preaching, by several eminent divines*, the fifth edition of which appeared at London in 1843. My present discussion is based upon the third edition (London, 1651).

end of all *Sciences* and *Arts,*" Wilkins remarked in this connection, "to direct men by certain Rules unto the most compendious way in their *knowledge* and *practice*. . . . And there is nothing of greater consequence for the advancement of Learning, then to find out those particular advantages which there are for the shortest way of knowing and teaching things in every profession."[18] The connection between knowing and teaching, between understanding and presentation, between enquiry and communication, sets the theme for Wilkins's entire *Ecclesiastes*. Said he:

> There are two abilities requisite in every one that will teach and instruct another: Σύνεσις · Ἑρμηνεία. A right *understanding* of sound doctrine; and an ability to propound, confirm, and apply it unto the *edification* of *others*. And the first may be without the other. As a man may be a good *Lawyer*, and yet not a good *Pleader*; so he may be a good *Divine*, and yet not a good *Preacher*.[19]

These words plainly indicate that, although Wilkins considered the first of these accomplishments to be possible without the second, he did not visualize the second as something which could exist without the first or could be produced automatically by the first. Indeed, he specifically questioned the prevailing assumption that right understanding was in itself a sufficient guarantee of success in preaching.

> It hath been the usual course at the University [he said] to venture upon this calling in an abrupt overhasty manner. When Schollers have passed over their Philosophical studies, and made some little entrance upon Divinity, they presently think themselves fit for the Pulpit without any farther enquiry, as if the Gift of Preaching and sacred Oratory were not a distinct Art of it self. This would be counted a very preposterous course in other matters, if a man should presume of being an Oratour because he was a Logician, or to practise Physick because he had learnt Philosophy.[20]

To Wilkins, the art of sacred oratory depends in part upon a spiritual endowment, gained from above and improved only by prayer, humility, and holiness; but in part it may be acquired by man's own industry as he develops his general skill in the arts and languages, and as he seeks the particular and immediate helps

---

[18] *Ecclesiastes*, p. 1.　　[19] *Ibid.*, p. 2.　　[20] *Ibid.*, pp. 2-3.

available to him through the study of rhetorical principles. These helps provide the subject matter of the rest of Wilkins's treatise. As I indicated in my reference to his use of the word elocution, he discussed these helps under the headings of method, matter, and expression, these three terms being the organizing concepts of his theory of pulpit oratory. To method he devoted some twenty-three pages, to matter, one hundred and two, and to expression, six.

The five major components of Ciceronian rhetoric are the obvious framework of Wilkins's theory as a whole. Method to him was the process by which a sermon becomes well organized and thus gets the power to fasten itself into the memory of the preacher and his congregation. In other words, this part of Wilkins's theory embraced what the Ciceronians called *dispositio* and *memoria*.[21] Matter is of course Wilkins's term for *inventio* in the classical scheme.[22] The third part of Wilkins's theory covered rhetorical style, or *elocutio*, and rhetorical delivery, or *pronuntiatio*—two historic Latin terms which Wilkins in opposition to established custom respectively translated as "Phrase" and "Eloquution," and which he had previously classified also against common custom as ingredients of the concept of "Expression."[23] Despite these departures from standard procedure, Wilkins is orthodox in the way in which he distributed emphasis in treating the parts of rhetoric. That is, he regarded matter as more important than expression, even as the Ciceronians tended to do when they were dealing with rhetoric in its full extent.

The six movements of the classical oration furnish Wilkins with his theory of rhetorical form as he spoke of the parts of the sermon. Arguing that the preacher must prepare himself to "Teach clearly," "Convince strongly," and "Perswade powerfully,"[24] he concluded that the first of these functions produces the Explication, the second, the Confirmation, and the third, the Application,[25] these being the principal parts of an address from the pulpit. In addition, the sermon had three lesser parts, the Preface, the Transitions, and the Conclusion.[26] The seventeenth-century Ciceronians would have regarded Wilkins's use of these terms as sometimes the close and sometimes the more distant parallels of those used commonly to describe the parts of the standard secular oration, and Wilkins would of course have agreed with them.

[21] *Ibid.*, pp. 5-6. [22] *Ibid.*, pp. 27-28. [23] *Ibid.*, pp. 128-133.
[24] *Ibid.*, p. 6. [25] *Ibid.*, p. 7. [26] *Ibid.*, p. 10.

Wilkins would also have agreed with anyone who taxed him with being to some extent under the influence of the Ramists. One of the legacies which Ramus bequeathed to his disciples consisted in the practice of separating a whole into two or three major divisions, and of proceeding systematically to break those divisions up into parts, and those parts into subparts, until only indivisible units remained. Another legacy from Ramus involved the reduction of the places of invention to ten topics, one of which contained all nonartistic proofs, and the other nine, all varieties of artistic proofs. Wilkins shows evidence of having been a follower of these two sets of doctrines. In schematizing the process of developing a sermon that would "Convince strongly," Wilkins indicated that the resources to be used for this purpose fell under the heading of positive proofs or the heading of the solving of doubts; that positive proofs were to be drawn either from Scripture or from reason; and that those drawn from reason concerned doctrinal points or practical truths. The character of these dichotomies is Ramistic, of course. And also Ramistic is Wilkins's procedure when he analyzed the sources of positive proofs as a whole. Those drawn from reason, so far as they depend upon doctrinal points, he noted, are to be found in the nine topics of artistic proof in Ramus's scheme: cause, effect, subject, adjunct, opposites, comparatives, name, division, definition.[27] Those drawn from Scripture make up Ramus's single category of nonartistic proofs, where testimony, divine or human, becomes the foundation of argument.[28] Still another legacy that Ramus bequeathed to his followers and Wilkins inherited is found in the latter's use of the word Method to designate the theory of organization of discourse. Method is perhaps the most important word in the Ramistic lexicon, as Wilkins and his generation would have known full well, and its Ramistic bearing upon Wilkins's theory of disposition would not have been lost upon any of Wilkins's contemporaries.[29]

[27] *Ibid.*, p. 8. In Wilkins's list the fifth topic is indicated as "Dissentan," and the sixth as "Comparats." For a discussion of Ramus's analysis of the topics of dialectical invention, see my *Logic and Rhetoric in England*, pp. 155-157.

[28] *Ecclesiastes*, pp. 8, 17.

[29] Wilkins's knowledge of Ramism could have come to him from William Perkins's *Prophetica*, which under its English title is listed among the treatises which Wilkins recommended as supplements to his theory of preaching. For

In discussing matter as the second concept governing the theory of preaching, Wilkins emphasized three general procedures for the preacher who sought excellence of content in his sermons. The first procedure was prayer, the second, reading, and the third, meditation. Of the second of these procedures Wilkins said, "But now because amongst those helps of invention which fall under the rules of Art, this of *Reading* is one of the principall, therefore it will deserve a more large and particular consideration."[30] These words are meant to be serious—Wilkins devoted himself exclusively to a discussion of reading as it bears upon the substance of pulpit oratory, although what he said would have to be counted as a treatment of meditation as well. And what contribution to sermon-making is provided by the inventional scheme of traditional rhetoric, with its special system of topics? Wilkins did not neglect this question, but he did not answer it in the usual way. He remarked instead:

> There are some other helps of invention to which the Art of *Rhetorick* does direct, according to the subject we are to handle, whether Demonstrative (Praise, Dispraise), Deliberative (Perswade, Disswade), Judiciall (Accuse, Defend.) For each of which there are severall *Topicks*, but 'tis supposed that every Minister is acquainted with those things in his preparatory studies, and therefore I forbear any further mention of them.[31]

This passage, like that in which Wilkins had mentioned the topics of Ramus's dialectic, does not indicate any strong loyalty on his part towards the ancient machinery of rhetorical invention. It merely demonstrates that he was aware of the machinery and thought it potentially useful, even if he could not recommend it

---

that list, see *Ecclesiastes*, pp. 3-4. For a short analysis of *Prophetica*, see my *Logic and Rhetoric in England*, pp. 206-207. Wilkins's list also mentions John Henry Alsted's *Theologica Prophetica* and Bartholomew Keckermann's *De Rhetorica Ecclesiastica*, both of which were written in a full awareness of Ramus's theory of invention, although their aim was not so much to explain Ramism as to effect a compromise between it and the older Aristotelianism. See *Logic and Rhetoric in England*, p. 283.

[30] *Ecclesiastes*, p. 31.

[31] *Ibid.*, p. 127. This quotation as I give it alters the format and punctuation of Wilkins's text, but I have not altered the wording.

as a main source of the content of sermons. His attitude towards it, in short, is modern more by his lack of enthusiasm than by his open opposition.

In the third part of *Ecclesiastes*, however, Wilkins became a modern in a most overt, most positive way. His discussion of rhetorical style not only characterized that famous division of the old rhetoric by the new term, "Phrase"; it also proceeded then to endow that subject with a content as interesting for what it did not say as for what it said. In both respects Wilkins broke with a long-standing tradition.

"The *phrase*," he explained, "should be plain, full, wholesome, affectionate."[32] These four words indicate the kind of style to which the preacher should aspire, and the following quotations indicate what Wilkins intended that style to be:

It must be *plain* and naturall, not being darkened with the affectation of *Scholasticall* harshnesse, or *Rhetoricall* flourishes. Obscurity in the discourse is an argument of ignorance in the minde. The greatest learning is to be seen in the greatest plainnesse. The more clearly we understand any thing our selves, the more easily can we expound it to others. When the notion it self is good, the best way to set it off, is in the most obvious plain expression. . . . A Minister should speak *as the oracles of God*, I *Pet.* 4.11. And it will not become the Majesty of a Divine Embassage, to be garnished out with flaunting affected eloquence. How unsuitable is it to the expectation of a hungry soul, who comes unto this ordinance with a desire of spirituall comfort and instruction, and there to hear only a starched speech full of a puerile worded Rhetorick? . . . 'Tis a sign of low thoughts and designes, when a mans chief study is about the polishing of his phrase and words. . . . Such a one speaks only from his *mouth* and not from his *heart*.

It must be *full*, without empty and needlesse Tautologies, which are to be avoided in every *solid* businesse, much more in *sacred*. Our expressions should be so *close*, that they may not be *obscure*, and so *plain*, that they may not seem vain and *tedious*. To deliver things in a crude confused manner, without digesting of them by previous meditations, will nauseate

[32] *Ibid.*, p. 128.

the hearers, and is as improper for the edification of the minde, as raw meat is for the nourishment of the body.

It must be sound and *wholesome*, not tainted with any *errone-ous* corrupt doctrine, or the affectation of *novelty*. False opinions do many times insinuate themselves by the use of suspicious phrases. And 'tis a dangerous fault, when men cannot content themselves with *the wholesome forme of sound words*, but do altogether affect new light and new language, which may in time destroy practicall Godlinesse and the power of Religion.

It must be *affectionate* and cordiall, as proceeding from the heart, and an experimentall acquaintance with those truths which we deliver. *Quod procedit è corde redit in cor*: 'Tis a hard matter to affect others, with what we are not first affected our selves.[33]

In thus reducing oratorical style to a plainness that would be rich in clarity and learning, to a fulness that maintained severe restraints against tautology and tedium, to a soundness that prevented the corruptions of falsehood and novelty, and to a warmth that proceeded from a love of truth as revealed by human experience, Wilkins was formulating a chapter in the new rhetoric. Without apology or regret he was using his new terms to replace the elaborate Ciceronian tradition of the tropes and figures and the three kinds of style. And there can be no doubt that his terms befit a rhetoric which was seeking to become the literary arm of the new science, the verbal instrument of the new learning, and the persuasive medium of an awakening democratic culture. Nor can there be doubt that these terms harmonize with Wilkins's previous insistence that rhetoric is not simply to be devoted to exhortation but must also face its responsibilities in providing a doctrine for the exposition of truth.[34] In short, Wilkins's treatment of style, and his emphasis upon discourse as exposition, restore to rhetorical theory two of its important but long dormant themes.

After he had laid down his prescription for the new style, Wilkins brought his analysis of this part of rhetoric to a close with a few practical remarks. He acknowledged that the constant writing of sermons week after week would hamper the busy preacher, and that the memorizing of sermons would inhibit him not only

---

[33] *Ibid.*, pp. 128-130.   [34] *Ibid.*, pp. 7, 9, 11-17, 21, 25-26.

from understanding and feeling what his words were intended to mean but also from profiting by the advantages of immediate spontaneity in utterance. And he warned the young clergyman not to expect to acquire a good extemporaneous style except by study, experience, and frequent practice in writing.[35]

Ecclesiastes itself concludes with some remarks on delivery or elocution. All Wilkins said at this point was that the two extremes of boldness and fear were to be avoided in presenting a sermon from the pulpit, and that there were practical ways of overcoming either of these faults and of achieving the modesty and gravity which alone befit a minister's high calling. While it is true that Wilkins gave this part of rhetoric a new name, and that the new name was to be adopted by the elocutionists as the synonym for rhetoric itself, and as the manifestation of their own ignorance of what rhetoric had anciently meant, there is no reason to call Wilkins a forerunner of the elocutionary movement because he chanced to speak as he did. For him delivery was not to be separated from content and form. In fact, it was to be treated only as the fulfilment of a content and a form that he had considered at length in their respective doctrinal aspects. And in its own right delivery was to be handled with the greatest possible brevity, no doubt because this part of the preacher's problem rested less upon theory than upon practice. At any rate, Wilkins devoted to "Eloquution" only a page of text.[36] If the elocutionists had exercised that sort of restraint, the practices which they identified as the whole art of rhetoric would have subsided into an early and well-deserved oblivion, and the true art of rhetoric would perhaps have avoided the eclipse that the nineteenth-century elocutionists helped bring upon it.

Wilkins made one other contribution to rhetorical theory some five years after the publication of *Ecclesiastes*, and it deserves a word, not because it extended but because it reinforced what he had already said on the subject. It occurred in a work entitled *A Discourse Concerning the Gift of Prayer*.[37] Wilkins thought it

---

[35] *Ibid.*, pp. 131-132.   [36] *Ibid.*, pp. 132-133.

[37] The title page of the first edition, to which my present discussion refers, reads as follows: "A Discourse Concerning the Gift of Prayer. Shewing What it is, wherein it consists, and how far it is attainable by Industry, with divers useful and proper directions to that purpose, both in respect of Matter, Method, Expression. . . . *London,* Printed by *T. R.* and *E. M.* for Samuel Gellibrand, at the Ball in *Pauls* Churchyard. 1651."

strange that all kinds of activities had been reduced to rules and method, but that prayer, an activity of great consequence, had received almost no attention from those interested in the duties of the clergy.[38] He proposed to correct this error of omission. In his view, the gift of prayer, so far as it could be cultivated by human industry, depended upon the affections and the judgment. When a clergyman's affections were not stirred by a sense that prayer was a necessary and beneficial aspect of man's spiritual communion with God, he would be unable to pray with the effectiveness that his calling demanded, and Wilkins devoted some attention to the means that could be used in removing that kind of hindrance.[39] But the hindrances to which he mainly addressed himself concerned a clergyman's judgment or reason, and these he listed as want of Matter, want of Method, and want of Expression.[40] Thus his treatise on prayer turns out to have the same structural features that we noticed in his treatise on preaching. Nor does the resemblance between these two works end at this point. When he spoke of Method in prayers, he specified that these discourses, like sermons, have six parts, and he listed these parts as the Preface, the Confession, the Transitions, the Petition, the Thanksgiving, and the Conclusion.[41] Twenty-five of the thirty chapters into which the *Gift of Prayer* is divided are devoted to these aspects of Method. As for Matter, Wilkins advised that each clergyman keep a register of the remarkable passages of his life in respect to God's dealings with him and his with God, and that he arrange these items under commonplace heads for use when he needed to pray.[42] But to these and the other means of devising a suitable content for prayers Wilkins gave little space, although the parallel operation had been the chief subject of his theory of preaching. His treatment of Expression as the third division of his present subject was in the spirit of his discussion of rhetorical expression in his earlier treatise. Thus he counselled that, "because the language of *Canaan*, the stile of the Holy Ghost is undoubtedly the fittest for holy and spiritual services ... we should rather chuse, (where we may) to speak in Scripture expression."[43] Thus also he warned against the extreme of *"Negligence,* when men vent their thoughts in a rude, improper, unseemly phrase," and the extreme of *"Affectation,* either

[38] *Gift of Prayer*, sig. A2r.
[39] *Ibid.*, pp. 25-37.
[40] *Ibid.*, p. 38; also sig. A3r.
[41] *Ibid.*, p. 41.
[42] *Ibid.*, pp. 39-40.
[43] *Ibid.*, p. 47.

of too much neatnesse and elegance, or else of a mystical kind of phrase, not to be found either in Scripture, or any sober writer . . . which . . . being reduced into plain English, will appear to be wholly *empty*, and to signifie nothing, or else to be *full* of vain repetitions."[44] In recommending Scripture as the pre-eminent model for the style of prayers, Wilkins went so far later as to describe with approval four types of rhetorical ornaments which he found to be authorized, not only by their use in the Old and New Testaments, but also by their value in being "very proper, and powerful, both for the expressing and exciting our affections."[45] And he identified these figures as Exclamation, Expostulation, Option, and Ingemination, each of which he illustrated by relevant passages quoted not always accurately from the King James version of the Bible. By the way, it is obvious here and elsewhere in the *Gift of Prayer* that the King James version is the source of Wilkins's concept of the language of Canaan and the style of the Holy Ghost, even as that same work must be understood as having provided him in *Ecclesiastes* with a living and powerful illustration of the plain rhetorical style which the new science was to find inseparable from its needs.

The influences which led Wilkins to formulate his particular theory of style, and which in wider terms led English prose to change from the posture of ornateness during the Commonwealth to that of plainness during the Restoration, have been a subject of scholarly controversy in the twentieth century. The controversy has not concerned the question whether such a stylistic change actually occurred, or whether Wilkins had a part in it, but whether it originated in a reverence among seventeenth-century writers for the plain style of ancient Roman Stoicism, or in the hope of actualizing the scientific visions of Francis Bacon, or in an older humanistic antagonism to the stylistic mannerisms of certain sixteenth-century Ciceronians. In an important series of essays published between 1914 and 1924, Morris W. Croll called that older antagonism the Anti-Ciceronian movement and traced its origin to Marc-Antoine Muret and his disciple Justus Lipsius, both of whom were influential prose stylists of the sixteenth century, and both of whom recognized Tacitus and Seneca as ancient masters of the stylistic plainness that they themselves wanted

44 *Ibid.*, p. 48.   45 *Ibid.*, pp. 48-49.

Renaissance writers to adopt.[46] Croll's theory was supplemented in 1930 by Richard Foster Jones, who argued that, while the Anti-Ciceronian movement was a strong influence in producing a change in the standards of seventeenth-century prose, there was another force acting partly in the same and partly in a different direction, and that other force should be regarded as a separate entity and identified with the rise of the new scientific philosophy of Francis Bacon and with the active support which Bacon's philosophy received from the group later organized into the Royal Society.[47] In the course of his article, Jones pointed out that John Wilkins's *Ecclesiastes* was one of the first works after Bacon's *Instauratio Magna* to bring the ideological consequences of the new science into focus upon the development of a stylistic program which the scientists themselves could approve of, and he mentioned Boyle, Sprat, and Glanvill as associates of Wilkins in that development. Jones's thesis was called somewhat obliquely into question in 1951 in George Williamson's *The Senecan Amble: A Study in Prose Form from Bacon to Collier*. Williamson intimated that the epistles of Seneca were more influential than seventeenth-century science in changing the standards of prose style from ornateness to plainness, and in causing Wilkins to adopt the stylistic program set forth in his *Ecclesiastes*.[48] It is true, of course, as Williamson indicated, that Seneca had condemned dialectical subtlety, verbal intricacy, affectation, insincerity, and excessive polish as traits of philosophical discourse,[49] and that Wilkins himself had referred to Seneca for a supporting opinion when he made analogous points in respect to pulpit oratory.[50] But surely Wilkins cannot have been so artless as to have had nothing in mind but a desire to follow Seneca when he made Seneca's stylistic theories the support for his doctrines of expression. Per-

[46] See *Style, Rhetoric, and Rhythm, Essays by Morris W. Croll*, ed. J. Max Patrick and Robert O. Evans, with John M. Wallace and R. J. Schoeck (Princeton, New Jersey, 1966), pp. 7-44, 107-162.

[47] See "Science and English Prose Style in the Third Quarter of the Seventeenth Century," PMLA, XLV (1930), 977-1009. Cited below as Jones.

[48] See *The Senecan Amble* (Chicago, Illinois, 1951), pp. 250-255. Cited below as *Senecan Amble*.

[49] See *Seneca ad Lucilium Epistulae Morales with an English Translation by Richard M. Gummere . . . in Three Volumes*, The Loeb Classical Library (London and New York, 1917-1925), I, 313-331; II, 137-147; III, 319-331.

[50] *Senecan Amble*, pp. 251-253.

haps Williamson's attitude on this point represents the occupational bias of literary scholarship in favor of a literary explanation of any change in literary standards. At any rate, Williamson seems to give no scope whatever for the possible influence of Wilkins's scientific interests upon his theories of style, even though those interests were well established before he wrote *Ecclesiastes* or became a member of the group which ultimately founded the Royal Society. Indeed, the strongest of all suppositions upon this matter is that Wilkins sought the authority of Seneca when he was formulating his stylistic program, not because Seneca was more important to him than his scientific interests were, but because Seneca offered him from out a hallowed past a classical endorsement of the stylistic program that the new science was beginning to need and demand. This likely hypothesis makes it impossible for me to agree with Williamson that Wilkins's "doctrine of style derives more from Seneca than from science."[51] Nor can I agree with Jones that the stylistic program advocated by the early Royal Society was different in kind from that of the Anti-Ciceronians of the preceding century.[52] Differences there are, and Jones has pointed them out, but they seem incapable of giving the two movements two completely separate identities. At the bottom of each was the recognition that a new era had dawned, that new knowledge was available to scientist and scholar, and that the new knowledge would alter the methods pertaining to its discovery and its transmission. Thus the Anti-Ciceronian movement of the sixteenth and seventeenth centuries, and the stylistic program of the Royal Society in the latter of those two eras, stand as successive products of the same developing set of causes, and those causes would have brought into being a growing preference for plainness in English prose style even if Tacitus and Seneca had not been particularly admired at the same time.

Wilkins's interest in science was at work not only upon the stylistic theory that he propounded in *Ecclesiastes* and the *Gift of Prayer* but also in his immensely toilsome later endeavor to create what might be called a special vocabulary for the communication of scientific knowledge across the linguistic barriers between one nation and another. This special vocabulary was the

[51] *Ibid.*, p. 255.　　　　　　[52] Jones, pp. 1004-1009.

subject of a 626-page volume published by Wilkins at London in 1668 under the title, *An Essay Towards a Real Character, And a Philosophical Language*. The principal design of this treatise, Wilkins remarked, is to devise "a *Real universal Character*, that should not signifie *words*, but *things* and *notions*, and consequently might be legible by any Nation in their own Tongue."[53] "To this purpose," he added at once, "is that which *Piso* mentions to be somewhere the wish of *Galen*, That some way might be found out to represent things by such peculiar *signs* and *names* as should express their *natures; ut Sophistis eriperetur decertandi & columniandi occasio*." "There are several other passages to this purpose," he went on, "in the Learned *Verulam*, in *Vossius*, in *Hermannus Hugo*, &c. besides what is commonly reported of the men of *China*, who do now, and have for many Ages used such a general Character, by which the Inhabitants of that large Kingdom, many of them of different Tongues, do communicate with one another, every one understanding this common Character, and reading it in his own Language." As these words would imply, Wilkins gave his attention respectively to the signs and to the names that could be used in connection with his own accompanying tables and his own specially designed philosophical grammar to enumerate and describe all things and ideas known to human experience. His signs turned out to be a system of marks supposedly capable of identifying their own meaning; and his names, a set of terms constructed according to his own philosophical principles, and spelled out partly in letters of the Roman alphabet.[54] He appended to the four hundred and fifty-four pages in which these matters were discussed a work called *An Alphabetical Dictionary, Wherein all English Words According to their Various Significations, are either referred to their Places in the Philosophical Tables, Or explained by such Words as are in those Tables*.[55] This work and the one to which it is annexed were begun by Wilkins in the years between 1650 and 1659, when, as warden of Wadham, he had not only leisure for such a task but

---

[53] *An Essay Towards a Real Character, And a Philosophical Language* (London, 1668), p. 13. Cited below as *An Essay*.

[54] *Ibid.*, pp. 385-434.

[55] The work has its own title page. The imprint reads: "London, Printed by *J. M.* for *Samuel Gellibrand* and *John Martin*, 1668." It contains 157 pages. The John Martin mentioned in the imprint was printer to the Royal Society.

also the direct encouragement of Dr. Seth Ward,[56] then Savilian professor of astronomy at Oxford and himself a resident of Wadham and an active member of the Oxford branch of the emerging Royal Society. Despite Ward's support, and despite the official endorsement which the Royal Society gave to *An Essay Towards a Real Character*,[57] it did not succeed in accomplishing what Wilkins wanted it to do. But at least it demonstrated throughout its vast laborious extent that a basic problem connected with the transmission of the new science was deemed by Wilkins to be worthy of a tremendous investment of his own energy and toil. A passion for the revival of a merely Senecan plainness in style would scarcely seem able to account for the depth and scope of Wilkins's passion for a new scientific medium of communication.

In the very period which witnessed the beginnings of the work just discussed, and in Oxford lodgings not far from those of Wilkins and Seth Ward, Robert Boyle was giving final shape to a treatise that has great relevance for the new rhetoric and the new style of seventeenth-century Britain. When it was published at London in 1661, the treatise was entitled *Some Considerations Touching the Style of the H. Scriptures*.[58] It was dedicated to Boyle's brother Roger, earl of Orrery, who was well known not

[56] *An Essay*, sig. b2r.

[57] *Ibid.*, sig. a1r. On the page preceding the title page is a notice dated Monday, 13th of April, 1668, saying that "At a Meeting of the Council of the Royal Society: Ordered, *That the Discourse presented to the* Royall Society, *Entituled,* An Essay towards a Real Character, and Philosophical Language, *be Printed by the Printer to the* Royal Society, Brouncker *Presi*." Wilkins dedicated the work to Lord Brouncker.

[58] The title page continues: "*Extracted from several parts of a Discourse (concerning divers Particulars belonging to the Bible) Written divers Years since to a Friend.* By the Honorable Robert Boyle, Esq;. London, Printed for *Henry Herringman*, at the *Anchor* in the Lower Walk in the New-Exchange. M.DCLXI." I cite the second edition (London, 1663) under the short title, *Style of the H. Scriptures*.

The full Discourse to which the title refers was begun by Boyle during the period of his foreign residence between 1638 and 1644, but the major part of it was written in the early sixteen-fifties, and the task of selecting the extracts that were finally printed can be confidently assigned to the years between 1654 and 1661, when Boyle was residing in Oxford. Indeed, these dates clearly emerge from Boyle's own account of the composition of the book as set forth in his address "To the Reader," sig. B7v-B8v.

only as a statesman and soldier, but also as author of a popular romance, *Parthenissa*. Boyle wrote his work with three major objects in view: to prompt Roger to write a far better book on the same subject;[59] to furnish devout persons "with something to Allege on the Scriptures Behalf, who are better furnish'd with Affections than with Arguments for it";[60] and to offer testimony in his own person "that the Study of the Works of Nature has not made me either Disbelieve the Author of them, or Deny his Providence, or so much as Disesteem his Word, which Deserves our Respect upon several Accounts, and especially that of its being the Grand Instrument of Conveying to us the Truths and Mysteries of the Christian Religion: My Embracing of which I know not why I should be Asham'd to own, since I think I can to a Competent and Unprepossess'd Judge give a Rational Account of my so doing."[61] As if to emphasize particularly his lack of confidence in his own ability to write upon his present subject, Boyle took pains to admit that he had "yet too great a Concern for the Knowledge of Things to be a diligent or solicitous Considerer of Words; and so was more fit to write almost of any thing, than of a Style, or of Matters Rhetorical."[62] But on this latter subject he had no reason to underrate himself. His contribution to the new rhetoric cannot be accepted as an example of his own unfitness to discuss it.

The quality of his approach to these "Matters Rhetorical" is strikingly revealed in the discriminating way in which he first clarified the concept of style as it applied to current criticisms of the Bible. His words show a grasp of fundamental issues. He said:

> Now those allegations against the Scripture we are to examine being but too various, it will be requisite for us, to consider the Style of it not in the stricter acception, wherein an Authors style is wont to signifie the choice and disposition of his words, but in that larger sense, wherein the word Style comprehends not only the Phraseology, the Tropes and Figures made use of by a Writer, but his Method, his lofty or humbler Character (as Orators speak) his Pathetical or languid, his close or in-

[59] *Style of the H. Scriptures*, sig. A5r.
[60] *Ibid.*, sig. C2r. This part of Boyle's work is set in italic type.
[61] *Ibid.*, sig. C2v.
[62] *Ibid.*, sig. B7v. For "solicitous" the second edition prints "sollitous," and the first edition, "sollicitous."

coherent way of writing, and in a word, almost all the whole manner of an Authors expressing himself.[63]

Thus style in Boyle's sense of the term included the third part of traditional rhetoric and went on from there to embrace arrangement and to reach into the ethical, emotional, and logical ingredients of discourse. Only memory and delivery did not appear in his stylistic theory, but their presence on its periphery is indicated, of course, by his acknowledgment that not all, yet almost all, of the problems of authorship were his present concern as they applied to the Bible. What he rejected would of course have been of doubtful relevance anyway on the present occasion; but what he actually included must be taken to demonstrate the high quality of his critical perceptiveness.

The total argument of Boyle's treatise consists in the posing and the answering of eight objections raised by men of wit and learning against the style, not the authority, of the Scriptures. Objections made in such a spirit, Boyle said, have the effect of keeping other men from the proper study and veneration of the word of God.[64] As for the objections themselves, Boyle gave them separate articulation as follows: that the Bible is obscure; that it is unmethodical in arrangement; that it does not follow the rules of syllogistic logic; that it is often lacking in pertinence and utility; that it is sometimes trivial and irrelevant; that in places it contradicts what it has said elsewhere; that it compares unfavorably with other works on ethics and morality in the way in which its valuable teachings are widely separated by barren stretches of subject matter; and that it *"is so unadorn'd with Flowers of Rhetorick, and so destitute of Eloquence, that it is flat, and proves commonly Inefficacious upon Intelligent Readers."*[65] These objections were obviously not regarded by Boyle as having equal weight. To the refutation of the first seven, he devoted a total of 118 pages; and he gave 101 pages to the refutation of the final one.[66] What he said in answering each allegation casts a favorable

[63] *Ibid.*, p. 2. The main text of Boyle's work is chiefly set in Roman type, with quotations italicized.

[64] *Ibid.*, p. 1.

[65] *Ibid.*, p. 147. Italics are Boyle's.

[66] See *Ibid.*, pp. 30-147, for the first seven rebuttals, and pp. 147-247 for the eighth. I consider Boyle's "Digression against Prophanenesse" (pp. 177-220) as part of the eighth rebuttal.

light upon his learning, his critical standards, and his good judgment; and his arguments are continuously pertinent to the subject
of my present chapter. But I shall not do more on the present occasion than discuss his answer to the eighth objection. That was
the most important one, so far as he was concerned, and his refutation of it contains the most striking features of his contribution
to the new rhetoric. In answering it, he distributed his argument
under five distinct heads.

As a prelude to the first of these heads, he called attention to
the settled conviction among men of learning that the stylistic
standards of ancient rhetoric were not only superior but also hostile to those exemplified in the Bible. He mentioned the cardinal
of the preceding century who feared that a further reading of the
Scriptures would impair his Latinity. He mentioned orators of the
cardinal's own time and country who complained that the study
of the Bible corrupted their cherished Ciceronian style. He mentioned a dispute between himself and a famous but unnamed
prince on the style of the Scriptures, and he said that the prince's
contempt for that style complemented the cardinal's scorn.
Finally, he mentioned in sorrow an Englishman "who is recorded
to have solemnly preferr'd one of the Odes of *Pindarus*, before all
the Psalms of *David*."[67] These "Witty Disrespecters" of the Bible,
said Boyle, were only a few of the many he could enumerate, but
he thought it wise not to catalogue others. Even so, he had made
the issue clear. On one side were the Ciceronians dedicated to a
flowered and ornamental prose and to the traditional rhetoric
which institutionalized it. On the other side were the Biblical
scholars who admired the plainness of Scriptural prose and believed in the need to create a rhetoric which would teach its
methods and values. When Boyle, as an emerging luminary
among the new scientists of the seventeenth century, elected to
join forces with the Biblical scholars against the Ciceronians, he
took the side of Wilkins in bringing together the Anti-Ciceronian
movement that had originated a hundred years earlier and the
drive that the Royal Society would soon inaugurate towards the
development of a plain style for science. And the Bible set the
standard around which the two parties rallied.

Boyle's opening argument in answering the eighth objection
was that eloquence, if thought to consist in rhetorical embellish-

[67] *Ibid.*, p. 148.

ments, would have been improper in many parts of the Scriptures, even as it would be considered out of place and improper in works on law, medicine, and chemistry. If the harsh and uncourtly terms of these latter works, Boyle asked, are considered proper to their themes, must we not reasonably allow the same latitude to various Biblical passages? And at this point he drew a forceful parallel between plainness in Biblical style and the admired plainness of a celebrated secular work.

> I remember *Macchiavel*, in the Dedication of his famous Prince [he said], after he had (not *causelesly*) acknowledg'd to *Lorenzo de Medici*, (to whom his Book is address'd) that he had not stuff'd it with lofty Language, or big Words, nor Adorn'd it with any of those enveagling outward Ornaments, usual to other Authors in their Writings; gives this account of the Plainness of his style, . . . that *he thought fit either that nothing at all should recommend his Work, or that the only truth of the Discourse and the Dignity of the subject should make it acceptable,* and exact its welcome. If a meer Statesman, writing to a Prince, upon a meer civil Theme, could reasonably talk thus: with how much more Reason may God expect a welcoming Entertainment for the least Adorn'd parts of a Book, of which the Truth is a direct Emanation from the Essential and Supreme Truth, and of which the Contents concern no less than mans Eternal Happiness or Misery?[68]

If "our nice Italian Criticks," Boyle added, cannot be deterred from reading Machiavelli either by the plainness of his style or by the prohibition of his works by the Inquisition, how can they hope to cite the unaffected style of the Bible as their excuse for despising or at least neglecting that divine book? With this question, Boyle brought his first head of refutation to an end. He admitted that he had not detained his readers long upon the considerations involved in it. But he reminded them that he had dealt with this matter earlier, as indeed he had,[69] and that further elaboration was hence unnecessary.

His second head of refutation consisted in saying that rhetorical embellishments tend to disappear from the literal translations of any work, and that the Scriptures were especially vul-

[68] *Ibid.*, pp. 152-153.
[69] *Ibid.*, pp. 78-87, 101-147, esp. pp. 106, 124, 131.

nerable in this regard.[70] Most vernacular versions of the Old
Testament fail to recapture the niceties of the Hebrew speech or
of the Vulgate. "The Old French Riming Translation of *Virgil*,"
Boyle went on, "makes not the *Aeneids* much more Eloquent than
Hopkins and *Sternhold* have made the Psalms: which sure being
Written by a Person who (setting aside his Inspiration) was both
a Traveller, a Courtier, and a Poet, must at least be allow'd to
contain polish'd and fashionable Expressions in their own Language, how coursely soever they have been mis-rendred in Ours."
As for the Greek of the New Testament, it has a strongly Hebraic
style which does not lend itself to easy translation. These and similar observations make up Boyle's argument on this head. If he
seems here to imply the existence of ornaments as a native but
untranslatable ingredient of Biblical eloquence, whereas his previous head had tended to make eloquence rest on other considerations, the inconsistency is a defect in his phraseology rather
than in his basic argument, as I shall endeavor to show at a later
stage of the present discussion.

Boyle's third head of refutation contained the most important
of his ideas on the new rhetoric. Here he developed the argument
that the true standards of eloquence are to be found, not by
studying exclusively the persuasive powers at work in the great
eloquent works of one region of the world or of one epoch in
human history or of one great author of some one nation and era,
but by studying the persuasive powers at work in all eloquent
works of all regions, all times, and all authors. Here is a view that
denies final authority in rhetorical judgments to European works,
to authors of any given century, or to that master of masters,
Cicero himself. Here is a view that claims final authority for rhetorical judgments only when they can actually account for what
moves men in any region at any time or within the works of any
writer. Lest it be assumed that this summary of Boyle's third head

---

[70] *Ibid.*, pp. 153-158. In an earlier discussion of this same point, Boyle had
said (p. 9): "For whereas the Figures of Rhetorick are wont by Orators to be
reduced to two Comprehensive sorts, and one of those does so depend upon
the sound and placing of the words (whence the *Greek* Rhetoricians call such
Figures σχήματα λέξεως) that if they be alter'd, though the sense be retained,
the figure may vanish; this sort of figures I say, which comprises those that
Orators call *Epanados, Antanaclasis*, and a multitude of others, are wont
to be lost in such literal Translations as are ours of the Bible. . . ."

of refutation is extravagant and fanciful, he should be summoned to speak for himself upon these matters.

To European judges who claim certain passages in the Scriptures to be lacking in eloquence, Boyle declared with great emphasis "That the Eastern Eloquence differs widely from the Western."

> In those purer Climates [he went on], where Learning, that is here but a Denizon, was a Native; the most cherish'd and admir'd Coposures [*sic*] of their Wits, if judg'd by Western Rules of Oratory, will be judg'd Destitute of it. Their Dark and Involv'd Sentences, their Figurative and Parabolical Discourses; their Abrupt and Maim'd way of expressing themselves, which often leaves much place to Guesses at the Sense; and their neglect of connecting Transitions, which often leaves us at a loss for the Method and Coherency of what they Write; are Qualities, that our Rhetoricians do not more generally Dislike, than their's Practice.[71]

Boyle drew a parallel between these differences in the rhetorical procedure of East and West and those connected with the Jewish habit of writing from right to left, and the European habit of writing from left to right. Then he cited the Koran as a work extravagantly admired for its eloquence throughout Islam while "Persons that judge of Rhetorick by the Rules of it current in these Western Parts of the World, would instead of extolling it for the Superlative, not allow it the Positive Degree of Eloquence; would think the Style as destitute of Graces, as the Theology of Truth; and would possibly as much Admire the *Saracen's* Admiration, as they doe the Book."[72] With the Koran and the Bible in mind, Boyle brought his condemnation of regionalism in rhetorical standards to a close with the following words:

> Since *Mahomet*, whose Eloquence (almost as Prosperous as his Sword) was able to bring Credit and Proselytes even to such a Religion as His: since *Moses*, that so Celebrated Legislator, bred up in the Refining Court, and all the fam'd Wisdome of the Egyptians; . . . since these Applauded Writers, I say, whom the Eastern Nations so Much and so Justly Admir'd, by many of our Latinists are not thought Good Writers, because of our

[71] *Ibid.*, pp. 158-159.   [72] *Ibid.*, p. 161.

470

Differing Notions of Eloquence; nay, if amongst *Europeans* themselves, *Cicero* hath found Many Censurers, and a Book hath been published to prove that *Tully* was not Eloquent; may not we Rationally enough suppose, that the Grecian and Roman style amongst the Eastern Writers, may not be much better relish'd than their's is amongst us; and that consequently, in those parts of the Scripture whose Eloquence is not Obvious to us *Europeans*, the Pretended Want of Eloquence may be but a Differing and Eastern Kind of it?[73]

By a natural association of different regions with different epochs, as if customs separated by immense distances in space would be subject to the same variations as are customs separated by great intervals of time, Boyle spoke next of the unlikelihood that standards of eloquence would remain constant from age to age. Upon this point his words deserve special attention, for they recognize that change is inevitable in rhetoric as in logic or politics or taste, and that the rhetorical doctrine needed in seventeenth-century Britain would not necessarily be the same as that needed in the Middle Ages or in ancient Rome and Greece. At bottom, the post-Renaissance struggle in Britain between the old logic and rhetoric, on the one hand, and the new logic and rhetoric, on the other, involved a succession of disputes upon opposing concepts of subject matter and doctrine within the disciplines concerned; but the struggle also involved rival attitudes towards change itself. The advocates of the old doctrine seemed unable to accept the idea that change is to be expected in all fields of human endeavor. They behaved as if the procedures of enquiry and communication were stable and changeless—as if what Aristotle and Cicero had said and done upon these matters was not subject to amendment or alteration as time went on. The new outlook took careful note that changes had occurred and would continue to occur in all human arrangements. Boyle's identification of himself with this latter attitude places him in the ranks of the new rhetoricians as securely as anything does which he said in describing the doctrines that the new rhetoric should contain. Nevertheless, his observations upon those doctrines as they might be changed by history are interesting and important. And he made these observations in such a way as to establish a continuity

[73] *Ibid.*, pp. 162-163.

between them and his previous comments against regionalism in rhetorical standards. "Eloquence, the Dress of our Thoughts, like the Dress of our Bodies," he declared, in marking the transition between these two topics, "differs not only in several Regions, but in several Ages."[74]

> And oftentimes in That, as in Attire [he continued], what was Lately Fashionable, is Now Ridiculous, and what Now makes a Man look like a Courtier, may within these Few Lustres make him look like an Antick; though how purely 'tis the Mode that makes such things appear Handsome or Deform'd, may be readily collected from the Vicissitudes observable in Modes; Men by intervalls relapsing into Obsolete Fashions. That there are Great Changes in that Mode of Writing men commonly mistake for Eloquence, I shall produce no less Illustrious a Witness than *Seneca*, who in his hundred and fourteenth Epistle, (to omit other Passages in his Works) not only proves it at large, but shows that in some Ages, even the Faulty wayes of Expression, conspir'd in by the Wits of those Times, have pass'd for Eloquence. The Scripture Style then, though it were not Eloquent Now, may have excellently suited the Genius of Those Times its Several Books were written in; and have been very proper for those People it was Primarily design'd to Work upon.[75]

These latter words, with their explicit recognition that an author's design is to work upon his readers, and that a reader responds to this design, lead us to the center of Boyle's conception of eloquence in discourse. A work is eloquent when it moves men. With an eye steadily upon the end to be achieved, be it persuasion or pleasure, an eloquent writer chooses his means accordingly; and if he realizes that the means needed do not fall within the rules of a given school of rhetoricians, he does not hesitate to break away from the rules, even when Cicero wrote them. Boyle spoke thus upon these matters:

> And, if I would presume to be Paradoxical in a thing I so little pretend Skill in as Eloquence, I might further represent on this occasion, That Rhetorick being but an Organical or Instrumental Art, in order Chiefly to Perswasion, or Delight, its Rules

[74] *Ibid.*, pp. 163-164.   [75] *Ibid.*, pp. 164-165.

ought to be estimated by their Tendency, and Commensurateness to its End; and consequently, are to be conform'd to by a Wiseman, but so farr forth as he judgeth them Seasonable and Proper to Please or to Perswade: which when he sees he can do better by Declining them, than by Practising them, (as Orators, like Hunters, must oftentimes leave the most Beaten Paths, if they will not loss their Game) he should not scruple to preferr the End to the Means; the Scope of the Artist, to what the Schools are pleas'd to call the Scope of the Art; and to think it more Eligible to speak Powerfully, than to speak Regularly. And we may hence consider, that it may be somewhat Inconsiderate to judge of all Eloquence, by the Rules of it that *Cicero's* Admirers impose on us; and Confound their Systems of Precepts with the Art of Rhetorick, as if they were Equivalent, or of the same extent.[76]

The trouble of course was that the old rhetoric completely identified itself with Cicero's precepts, and regarded those precepts as the measure of eloquence, even if such a work as the Bible could not be made to conform to them. The new rhetoric defined its problem as that of asserting its right to exist outside of the strict Ciceronian boundaries. Boyle deserves great credit for his sagacity in bringing this latter problem into the open. He said:

For *Cicero* being reputed (and that Deservedly) an Eloquent man, and very Successfull in Perswading his thus and thus qualify'd Hearers; divers, whose Modesty or Despair kept them from aspiring to more than Imitation, observing that *Tully* often made use of such and such a Contrivance, and such and such Figurative forms of speaking, took the pains to reduce those Observations into Rules, which being highly applauded by their Successors, and by them recruited with some Resembling Rules drawn from the Practice of a few other Orators, were afterwards compil'd into an Art, which as I deny not to be a Great Help to the Imitation of *Tully* and *Demosthenes*, or those others from whose Structure and Fashions of speech such Institutions have been drawn, so I shall no more take it for a Compleat System of Rhetorick, than any Instructions deducible from the Journals of *Solomon's* Tarshish Fleets, and from the Grecian and Roman's Sea-Voyages, for the true and entire Art

[76] *Ibid.*, pp. 165-166.

of Navigation. For if other Persons, either by an Endowment or Improvement of Nature, can find other Equally, or more Happy and Powerfull or Moving (though never so differing) wayes of expressing themselves, they ought as little to be Confin'd by the Prescriptions acquiesc'd in before them, as *Columbus* thought himself Oblig'd to be by the Rules or Practice of Antient Navigators; whose Methods and Voyages, had he not boldly ventur'd to Vary from, and pass beyond, how Vast and Rich a Portion of the World had his Conformity left undiscover'd?[77]

Boyle elaborated these doctrines still further by remarking that China, despite its high civilization and its devotion to verbal learning, "has not car'd to receive Rhetorick into the Number of their Arts and Sciences, presuming, as one may guess, that the Confining men's Expressions to Establish'd Rules would not be so like to Enable those to express themselves Eloquently, that Nature has Indispos'd to do so, as to Hinder others from expressing themselves, as well, as, were they left to their full liberty, they would do."[78] And he made other trenchant observations upon wise and foolish methods of following the rules of rhetoric as established in the West, and of imitating applauded authors, faults and all. But his third head of argument against the eighth objection to the style of the Scriptures was now at an end, and he concluded by reminding the cardinal and the other critics who found the Bible inferior to Cicero "that 'tis no Marvel they should find *Cicero's* Writings to be so Conformable to their Laws of Art, whilst they frame those Laws of Art out of his Writings."[79] It is not unfitting that a scientist of the inductive school of Francis Bacon should allow his pioneering exploration of the territory of the new rhetoric to contain so witty a gibe at the old rhetoric for the *petitio principii* involved in its justification of itself.

The fourth head of Boyle's argument developed the point "That there are very Few, if any Books in the World, that are no more Voluminous, in which there is greater Plenty of Figurative Expressions, than in the Bible."[80] "Though this may seem Strange," Boyle continued, " 'tis no more than may be made Good by more than some Hundreds of Instances; there being few Tropes or

[77] *Ibid.*, pp. 166-167.
[78] *Ibid.*, p. 168. [79] *Ibid.*, p. 170. [80] *Ibid.*, pp. 170-171.

Figures in Rhetorick, of which Numerous Examples are not col-
lectible out of the Expressions of Holy Writ." These Biblical figures and tropes Boyle did not proceed to catalogue. He said that
a list of them would add too great a bulk to his present essay, and
that they were being identified and discussed anyway in a work
then reportedly in preparation by abler pens. With these remarks
and a few others he concluded the fourth head. If this argument,
like that under his second head, tended to associate Scriptural
eloquence with Ciceronian embellishments in apparent conflict
with the drift of his first and third heads, the inconsistency, as I
remarked above, is more in his language than in his thought.[81] His
first and third heads asserted in effect that when an author relies
upon his conviction that soberly uttered truth will carry sufficient
weight, and when that truth by its sheer power causes an audience to accept it forthwith, the author has achieved eloquence,
even if rhetorical embellishments have played no part in his presentation. Boyle's second and fourth heads implied that when an
author relies both upon the power of his sense of truth and the
attendant force which rhetorical embellishments can exert in
moving his hearers to accept what he says, he too has achieved
eloquence. The old rhetoric tended to emphasize too exclusively
the embellishments used in this latter case, and tended to think
of the former case as unrhetorical. What Boyle wanted was a
rhetoric capable of accounting for both cases, and the Bible, he
felt, represented both, and thus presented a broader base for
rhetorical speculations than did the works upon which the old
rhetoric rested.

Boyle's fifth and final head of refutation consisted in developing
the argument "that it is very farr from being consonant to Experience, that the Style of the Scripture does make it Unoperative
upon the Generality of its Readers, if they be not Faultily Indispos'd to receive Impressions from it."[82] Stated in affirmative
terms, this argument means that mankind's experience with the
Bible demonstrates how actual and how powerful the influence
of that work has been, despite the fashionable habit of disparag-
ing its style. Since Boyle's whole conception of eloquence rests
upon the demonstrable capacity of a work to exert influence upon
readers or hearers in its own way, it was of course necessary for

[81] See above, p. 469.   [82] *Style of the H. Scriptures*, pp. 151, 221.

him to comment upon the extent to which the Bible meets this crucial test. His previous comments upon it had been frequent but incidental. Now he made it a matter of primary concern.

More is at stake in this argument than the ordinary definition of response in its ordinary application to discourse. By everyday standards, the term response might refer to any kind of reaction of any listener or reader to a given verbal communication of whatever design or content. Thus it might refer to responses hostile to the author's intention, or to favorable responses which might be described in terms like understanding, or conviction, or persuasion, or delight. As we have seen, Boyle recognized that rhetoric would study all of these responses, but only a special kind of response would be evidence of eloquence in the Bible or in any other work. A limitation of this sort must be taken as the unstated culminating principle behind his critical theory. A response to a work becomes an evidence of eloquence, he would argue, if the response involved the reader's awareness that what he had just read was not only true but also of maximum spiritual benefit to mankind and to himself. This twofold response would not be produced by the generality of books, and thus the question of eloquence would not arise in evaluating them. They would require a critical vocabulary of lesser terms, evaluative or descriptive. But some books would produce this twofold response, and to them only would the term eloquence rightly apply. A clear indication of Boyle's own acceptance of the distinction between these two sorts of books is given in a passage which I have already cited. That passage outlined his comparison between the Bible and Machiavelli's *Prince*. Machiavelli, it will be recalled, acknowledged that he had intended his work to command a welcome solely because his readers would recognize its truth and the dignity of its subject, and to this end he had not stuffed it with lofty language and ornaments.[83] Boyle's comment deserves to be quoted again to show why Machiavelli's work falls below the level of eloquence, and why the Bible rises to that level:

If a meer Statesman, writing to a Prince, upon a meer civil Theme, could reasonably talk thus: with how much more Reason may God expect a welcoming Entertainment for the least Adorn'd parts of a Book, of which the Truth is a direct Emana-

[83] See above, p. 468.

tion from the Essential and Supreme Truth, and of which the Contents concern no less than mans Eternal Happiness or Misery?

In the light of this statement, Machiavelli's *Prince* would be seen as having the capacity to change men's minds upon the important civil themes which it discussed; but this effect, praiseworthy as it is, would not compare with what Boyle later called "the Transforming Power the Scripture has upon many of its Readers."[84] That is to say, when the response to a discourse means that the author's work has transformed the reader's attitude so as to make him accept the work as true and to apply that truth towards the salvation of man's soul and his own, the work is eloquent. And by this standard, Boyle would say, eloquence belongs solely to the Bible and to discourses of similar intent and effect.

One of the witnesses whom Boyle called to testify to the transforming power of the Bible upon its readers was Pico, the renowned Italian wit and scholar of the fifteenth century; and Boyle recorded Pico's testimony as an incidental aside under his fourth rather than his fifth head of refutation. He spoke of Pico as follows:

> Wherefore, I shall now only say, that the Eloquence of the Scripture hath been highly Celebrated by no small Number of Persons, highly celebrated for Eloquence; and that many, who thought themselves as Intelligent in Oratory, as those that Censure the Scripture, have suspected their own Eloquence of Insufficiency, worthily to Extol that of the Prophet *Esay*; and some of them, (amongst whom I cannot but name that Excellent Prince of *Mirandula*, whom even the greatest Rabbi of this Age, styles the Phoenix of His Age) who after having Unsatisfiedly Travell'd thorough all sorts of Human Volumes, have Rested and acquiesc'd only in these Divine Ones: which will not a little Recommend the Scripture, since we may apply to Books, what an Excellent Poet sayes of Mistresses,
>> *'Tis not that which First we love,*
>> *But what Dying we approve,*
> That we Express the highest value of.[85]

[84] *Style of the H. Scriptures*, p. 235.
[85] *Ibid.*, pp. 171-172. In marginal notes Boyle identified the Rabbi as Manasseh ben Israel, and the poet as Edmund Waller. For the verses, which Boyle

But Boyle did not seek to prove the transforming power of the Bible from the testimony of fine wits and immortal writers alone. The greatest part of mankind, he said, "have not that Quickness which is wont to make Men pass for Wits, though they may have other Abilities more Solid, and desirable."[86] "And yet that the Bible has a great Influence upon this Latter sort of Intelligent Readers," he continued, "I presume You will easily Believe, if You consider how many Great Scholars, not onely Profess'd Divines, but others, have by their Learned Comments and other Writings, endeavour'd either to Illustrate, or Recommend the Scripture; and how much a Greater number of Understanding and Sober Men, that never Publish'd Books, have Evinc'd the Scriptures Power over them, partly by their Sermons and other Discourses, Publick and Private, and partly by endeavouring to Conform their Lives to the Dictates of it: Which last Clause I add, because You can scarce make a better Estimate of what Power the Scripture has upon Men, than by looking at what it is able to make them Part with." In elaborating this latter point, Boyle mentioned the dangerous risks which men have run to buy and own the Bible when its purchase and ownership were punishable by death. Turning to further particulars, Boyle spoke of the Ethiopian Queen's treasurer, who read Isaiah even upon long journeys and who would ask any passer-by to explain its difficulties if he himself were in doubt about them;[87] of Edward VI, who imitated the early piety but not the later moral lapse of Joash;[88] of King Alphonso of Aragon, who spared "Time from Studies and his Distractions, to read the Bible Forty times with Comments and Glosses on it";[89] of Pope Urban VIII, who "could find Room in a Head Crowded with Affairs enough to have Distress'd *Macchiavel*, for Reflections upon the Scripture";[90] of Queen Elizabeth, "the Envy of the Princes of her Time," who was "how Eminent a Student and Happy a Proficient in the Study of the Bible";[91] and of the "Matchless *Lady Jane,* who had all the Qualities the Best Patriots could desire in a Queen, but an Unquestionable Title," and who "was a Conspicuous Studier of the Inspir'd Books."[92] To

---

alters somewhat, see Waller's "An Apology for having Lov'd before." The Prophet Esay is of course Isaiah.

[86] *Style of the H. Scriptures,* p. 222.

[87] *Ibid.,* p. 225.   [88] *Ibid.,* p. 226.   [89] *Ibid.,* p. 227.

[90] *Ibid.,* p. 228.   [91] *Ibid.,* p. 229.   [92] *Ibid.,* pp. 229-230.

these witnesses and to the various others omitted from my present account, Boyle did not hesitate to add himself. "And truly for my own Part," he declared, "the Reading of the Scripture hath Mov'd me more, and Sway'd me more Powerfully to all the Passions it would Infuse, than the Wittiest and Eloquentest Composures that are Extant in our Own and some other Languages."[93] Then, in concluding this final head of refutation, Boyle drew a striking parallel between the power which the plain style of the Bible has upon men and the magnetic force which the plain loadstone exerts upon metals within its range of attraction. Here he proved that the natural phenomena known intimately by the scientist can teach lessons to the scholar bent upon stating the rhetorical laws governing verbal phenomena. He said:

> Nor can I often Consider the Instances Experience affords us of the Efficacy of many Texts, (which some that Pretend to Eloquence accuse of having None) without sometimes calling to mind, how in the Book of Nature God has Veil'd in an Obscure and Homely Stone an Attractiveness (Unvouchsaf'd to Diamonds and Ruby's), which the Stubbornest of Metals do's Obsequiously acknowledge. And as the Load-stone not onely Draws what the sparkling'st Jewels can not move, but Draws stronglier, where Arm'd with Iron, than Crown'd with Silver: so the Scripture, not onely is Movinger than the Glitteringst Human Styles, but hath oftentimes a Potenter Influence on Men in those Passages that seem quite Destitute of Ornaments, than in those where Rhetorick is Conspicuous.[94]

The image of the loadstone and the diamond, the one homely yet compelling, the other beautiful yet unmagnetic, gives Boyle's readers an excellent epitome of his whole theory of eloquence in relation to the plain and the figured style. But the last three words of the passage just quoted contain an unfortunate ambiguity that deserves a word of comment as I conclude this account of Boyle's treatise on the Scriptures. Those three words say in effect that rhetoric becomes most conspicuously itself, most recognizable for what it is, when an author's effectiveness is accompanied by glittering ornaments, whereas, when words devoid of ornaments are exerting maximum power upon a reader, rhetoric is so incon-

[93] *Ibid.*, p. 243.   [94] *Ibid.*, pp. 246-247.

spicuous as not perhaps to exist at all. This terminology is at odds with Boyle's earlier statements. He himself had convincingly demonstrated that there was on the one hand a rhetoric of plainness and power, and on the other a rhetoric in which power existed in the company of ornament. His basic point had been that these two rhetorics, taken together, were to be regarded as the natural successor of that one which in the name of Cicero had equated power with embellishment and had dominated European criticism for centuries. In line with this basic point, Boyle would be obliged to say that a plain and moving style was as conspicuously rhetorical as its ornamental and effective counterpart could be. His failure at the very end of his treatise to be consistent with himself on this point suggests that the Ciceronian rhetoric which he was trying to upset lived on in his own mind even after he had effectively destroyed its right to be considered the whole of rhetoric in modern criticism, and that the effective plainness which he had all but recognized as a necessary part of the rhetoric of the future did not yet have for him a natural right to be called rhetoric. But if those three words fell short of registering his full thought upon this matter, the fault, like the two which I attributed to him earlier, is more a lapse in vocabulary than a defect in critical judgment.

Boyle's treatise on the Holy Scriptures reached a wide audience. In its original English text it was printed four times in the years between the beginning of 1661 and the end of 1675.[95] It was published twice in the early nineteenth century. The first of these latter editions was done by the Rev. P. Panter, chaplain of the Royal Navy, who felt that certain idiosyncrasies and irregularities in Boyle's usage needed correction and who therefore translated Boyle's text into what he called "Modern Language." The second nineteenth-century edition gave Boyle's treatise a place in a collection called *The Sacred Classics: or, Cabinet Library of Divinity*. A Latin translation of it appeared first at Oxford in 1665 and later at Geneva in two separate issues each dated 1680. Twentieth-century readers would probably find Boyle's antiquated style and looseness of organization a barrier to their easy enjoyment of this work. They might even agree with the modern critic

[95] For these and the following bibliographical facts, I rely on J. F. Fulton, "A Bibliography of the Honourable Robert Boyle," *Oxford Bibliographical Society Proceedings and Papers*, III (1931-1933), 38-41.

who suggests that it is unreadable by reason of its discursiveness.[96] Nevertheless, it has to be reckoned an influential treatise, and its value as a witness to the actual nature of the revolution taking place in British rhetorical standards and tastes among the earliest members of the Royal Society is indeed immense.

When the Royal Society received its second and definitive charter of incorporation—the year was 1663 and Boyle's treatise on the style of the Scriptures had been in print for about two years—one of its prominent original Fellows, Robert Hooke, who was to become its Curator and Experimenter and later its Secretary,[97] declared the Society to be the instrument for the improvement of man's knowledge of his physical environment, and in the same breath he took pains to deny its intention to reform other arts and disciplines. "The business and design of the Royal Society," he wrote at that time, "is—To improve the knowledge of naturall things, and all useful Arts, Manufactures, Mechanick practises, Engynes and Inventions by Experiments—(not meddling with Divinity, Metaphysics, Moralls, Politicks, Grammar, Rhetorick, or Logick)."[98] Now the curious fact about this statement is that its final clause turned out to be at odds with what happened, even as its beginning clause did not err in the least. For one thing, the original statutes of the Society, as adopted in the year of Hooke's forecast, meddled with rhetoric in a very real way. They did this by stipulating that, in all scientific reports made by members of the Society, "the matter of fact shall be barely stated, without any prefaces, apologies, or rhetorical flourishes; and entered so in the Register-book. . . ."[99] This particular kind of meddling, unportentous as it may appear, was so far-reaching as to rule out of scientific exposition all rhetorical styles except that of plainness, and the new rhetoric was to respond accordingly as time went on. Five years after the promulgation of the original statutes, the Society meddled with grammatical problems. In sponsoring the publication of Wilkins's *Essay Towards a Real Character, And a Philosophical Language*, it officially endorsed an attempt, as we have seen, to create not only a basic

---

[96] *Ibid.*, p. 39.
[97] *Record of the Royal Society*, p. 31; Weld, I, 137-138, 261.
[98] Weld, I, 146.
[99] *Record of the Royal Society*, p. 119.

vocabulary but also a philosophical grammar for the communication of scientific discoveries throughout the world.[100] As for logic, the extent to which the Society meddled with it through the writings of Locke and his followers has been traced in detail in my preceding chapter. Nor can there be any doubt that the Society also meddled with the other subjects which Hooke placed beyond its jurisdiction. To be sure, these interferences seem inevitable as we look back upon them. It is clear to us that a scientific change as revolutionary as that which the Society fostered was bound to meddle in some way or other with all of man's sciences and arts. But if we had stood by Hooke's side in 1663, we probably would not have seen much farther than he did into the nature of the impact which the scientific activities of the Society were to have upon such subjects as rhetoric, logic, and grammar.

The circumstances which surrounded the decision of the Royal Society to provide by original statute that science was to adopt the plain style are set forth in Thomas Sprat's famous work, *The History of the Royal-Society of London*. Published in 1667, as Wilkins was putting the finishing touches to the printing of his *Essay*, Sprat's *History* announced that it would do three things. First, it would "give a short view of the *Antient*, and *Modern* Philosophy"; secondly, it would relate from the Registers and Journals of the Society "the first Occasions of their Meetings, the Incouragement, and Patronage, which they have receiv'd; their *Patent*, their *Statutes*, the whole Order and Scheme of their *Design*, and the *Manner* of their Proceedings"; and finally, it would try "to assert the *Advantage* and *Innocence* of this work, in respect of all *Professions*, and especially of *Religion*; and how proper, above others, it is, for the present temper of the *Age* wherein we live."[101] Sprat assigned a main division of his *History* to each of these three endeavors. Thus he devoted the 51 pages of "The First Part" to a survey of ancient and modern learning, the 269 pages of the "Second Part" to the story of the Royal Society itself, and the 118 pages of "The Third Part" to a defense of

[100] See above, p. 463.

[101] I cite the 1667 edition in the facsimile text published with an introduction, notes, and appendices by Jackson I. Cope and Harold Whitmore Jones (St. Louis: Washington University Studies, 1959). For the quotations just given, see p. 4.

the Society against those who contended that its work would destroy the educational system, undermine Christianity, damage the Church of England, impair the manual trades and mechanic arts, inflict economic injury upon the nobility and gentry, and be hostile to the interests of the entire kingdom.

The story of the Royal Society as Sprat related it in Part 2 fell into three chronological periods. The first began at an unspecified date in the late sixteen-forties or early sixteen-fifties and ended with the Restoration.[102] The meetings held by scientists and scholars at Wilkins's lodgings in Wadham College were the earliest events in the history of the Society, according to Sprat, and as a graduate of Oxford by way of Wadham, Sprat indicated his pride in being able to trace the origin of the Society to his own alma mater.[103] The second chronological period, much shorter in time but richer in subject matter, covered the years between 1660 and 1662, the latter date being the year when the Society received its first charter of incorporation.[104] The third period reached from 1662 to an indeterminate date close to the time of publication of Sprat's *History*.[105]

In his treatment of the second of these periods, Sprat made some energetic observations about the attitude of the Society towards various rhetorical styles of the time, and it is these which hold particular interest for the historian of rhetoric.[106] But we should not assume that, because Sprat placed these observations within the second chronological period of the Society's development, they belong exclusively to that era. The Society would certainly have discussed the techniques, styles, and vocabularies of scientific exposition at intervals during their early years at Oxford, when Wilkins and Seth Ward were working together to devise a new language for science, and Boyle was preparing his *Style of the H. Scriptures* for the press. And they would certainly have discussed these same subjects in Sprat's hearing after they received their charter of incorporation. Indeed, these subjects must have been in the foreground of their interest on many later

---

[102] *Ibid.*, pp. 52-60.   [103] *Ibid.*, p. 53.   [104] *Ibid.*, pp. 60-115.

[105] *Ibid.*, pp. 115-320. Sprat included within these pages some 14 documents to illustrate what sort of enquiries the Royal Society was conducting, what sort of reports its members were writing, and what sort of experiments it was performing and discussing.

[106] *Ibid.*, pp. 61-62, 111-115.

occasions—when Locke's *Essay* was a new book, for example, or when John Ward lectured at Gresham College.

As we read Sprat's account of the attitude of the Society towards these rhetorical styles, we see in full perspective what the Society meant when they took statutory action against rhetorical flourishes, and at the same time we notice the similarity between their attitude and Boyle's insistence that a complete system of rhetoric in modern times must go beyond the rules of the Ciceronians to recognize such other rules as that of Biblical plainness.[107] That is to say, as Sprat analyzed the situation, the Society recognized two distinct rhetorics. One of these was the rhetoric of tradition. It was associated with the belief that the only true eloquence was produced by figures and ornaments, and that the only proper literary vocabulary consisted in what Sprat called "the devices of *Fancy*, or the delightful deceit of *Fables*."[108] The other was not yet defined so clearly as to force Sprat to acknowledge the rightfulness of its claim to an equal share of the title usurped by its rival, but it too has to be called rhetoric, and indeed it was destined to receive that name in the rhetorical treatises of Adam Smith, George Campbell, Joseph Priestley, and Hugh Blair during the eighteenth century.[109] It was the rhetoric involved in the basic endeavor of the Society "to make faithful *Records*, of all the Works of *Nature*, or *Art*, which can come within their reach."[110] And it is the rhetoric always involved in any serious attempt to set standards by which learned discourses can be composed so as to succeed in conveying knowledge to others. Sprat provided a memorable description of the clash between this rhetoric and that of the old tradition. Let us turn now to it.

The description occurs as Sprat was speaking of the fifth and last of the substantive activities to which the Society dedicated their meetings. The other four activities consisted in directing, judging, conjecturing upon, and improving experiments, and to each Sprat had devoted due attention. He spoke then as follows:

> But lastly, in these, and all other businesses, that have come under their care; there is one thing more, about which the

[107] See above, pp. 473-474.
[108] *History of the Royal-Society*, p. 62.
[109] See below, pp. 548-575, 580-606, 633-647, 650-671.
[110] *History of the Royal-Society*, p. 61.

Society has been most sollicitous; and that is, the manner of their *Discourse*: which, unless they had been very watchful to kccp in duc temper, the whole spirit and vigour of their *Design*, had been soon eaten out, by the luxury and redundance of *speech*. The ill effects of this superfluity of talking, have already overwhelm'd most other *Arts* and *Professions*; insomuch, that when I consider the means of *happy living*, and the causes of their corruption, I can hardly forbear recanting what I said before; and concluding, that *eloquence* ought to be banish'd out of all *civil Societies*, as a thing fatal to Peace and good Manners.[111]

In elaborating these sentiments, Sprat made it clear that by "eloquence" he meant ornaments. "They were at first, no doubt," he continued, "an admirable Instrument in the hands of *Wise Men:* when they were onely employ'd to describe *Goodness, Honesty, Obedience*; in larger, fairer, and more moving Images: to represent *Truth*, cloth'd with Bodies; and to bring *Knowledg* back again to our very senses, from whence it was at first deriv'd to our understandings."[112] At this point, Sprat began to speak with mounting emotion about the present use of the colors of rhetoric:

> But now they are generally chang'd to worse uses: they make the *Fancy* disgust the best things, if they come sound, and unadorn'd; they are in open defiance against *Reason*; professing, not to hold much correspondence with that; but with its Slaves, *the Passions*; they give the mind a motion too changeable, and bewitching, to consist with *right practice*. Who can behold, without indignation, how many mists and uncertainties, these specious *Tropes* and *Figures* have brought on our *Knowledg*? How many rewards, which are due to more profitable, and difficult *Arts*, have been still snatch'd away by the easie vanity of *fine speaking*. For now I am warm'd with this just Anger, I cannot with-hold my self, from betraying the shallowness of all these seeming Mysteries; upon which, *we Writers*, and *Speakers*, look so bigg. And, in few words, I dare say; that of all the

111 *Ibid.*, p. 111. Earlier, as a step towards making English literature excel that of any other modern nation, Sprat had proposed an "*Impartial Court of Eloquence*; according to whose Censure, all Books, or Authors should either stand or fall." (p. 43) That proposal he was now tempted to recant.

112 *Ibid.*, pp. 111-112.

Studies of men, nothing may be sooner obtain'd, than this vicious abundance of *Phrase*, this trick of *Metaphors*, this volubility of *Tongue*, which makes so great a noise in the World.[113]

If this is one of the two rhetorics that the Royal Society had in mind as they sought to perfect the manner of their scientific discourse, what of the other? Sprat described the Society's constructive action in respect to it. His words, oft-quoted but never weakened by repetition, are as follows:

> They have therefore been most rigorous in putting in execution, the only Remedy, that can be found for this *extravagance*: and that has been, a constant Resolution, to reject all the amplifications, digressions, and swellings of style; to return back to the primitive purity, and shortness, when men deliver'd so many *things*, almost in an equal number of *words*. They have exacted from all their members, a close, naked, natural way of speaking; positive expressions; clear senses; a native easiness: bringing all things as near the Mathematical plainness, as they can: and preferring the language of Artisans, Countrymen, and Merchants, before that, of Wits, or Scholars.[114]

The question whether the stylistic reform thus described by Sprat was the outcome of the scientific movement of the seventeenth century, or was instead produced by the Anti-Ciceronian movement of the sixteenth and seventeenth centuries, has been made in our time an important issue in the debate which I dwelt upon earlier in concluding my remarks on Wilkins's *Ecclesiastes* and *Gift of Prayer*. One participant in the debate, Richard Foster Jones, argued that the scientific program inaugurated by the followers of Francis Bacon "called for stylistic reform as loudly as for reformation in philosophy," and that Sprat's proposal for "a close, naked, natural way of speaking" was a striking response to the first part of that demand.[115] This conclusion was explicitly disputed two decades later by George Williamson. "As it was the Anti-Ciceronian style that Bacon advanced," said he, "so it is the Anti-Ciceronian style from which the Royal Society programme derived."[116] "The stylistic programme of the Royal Society, which

[113] *Ibid.*, p. 112.   [114] *Ibid.*, p. 113.

[115] Jones, p. 989; also pp. 986-988.

[116] *Senecan Amble*, p. 276. Williamson's entire chapter called "Reform and the Royal Society" is of great interest and value, even if his determination to

has been thought crucial to the reform of prose style in the Restoration," he also declared, "repeats in effect Bacon's revolt against Ciceronian *copia*, and associates itself with Senecan requirements."[117] But, as I intimated in my earlier discussion of this issue as it concerned Wilkins, the final truth does not seem to lie with Jones, who erred in making the stylistic program of the scientists into a direct revolt against Anti-Ciceronian prose style, or with Williamson, who mistakenly saw in the stylistic theories of the scientists a reflection of the ideals of Seneca and his Anti-Ciceronian followers rather than a direct response to the needs of the new science. The final truth as it concerns Sprat seems to be that his program for a scientific style is a consequence of the Anti-Ciceronian movement of the sixteenth century and of the scientific developments fostered by Bacon and his followers in the seventeenth century. In short, it is a continuation of the old revolt and an adaptation of its terms so as to fit the special demands of the new scientists. To this I would add that, if the scientific movement of the seventeenth century had not taken place, and if, even so, the Anti-Ciceronians had continued to flourish in that century without any of the support which science actually gave them, the rhetorics of the eighteenth century would have been limited to works like that of Ward or of Holmes, and the new rhetorics of Adam Smith and George Campbell would not have emerged at all.

Joseph Glanvill, an Oxford graduate, a member of the Royal Society after December 14, 1664, and a clergyman rather than a scientist, deserves mention in this chapter, but his contribution to the new rhetoric has been thoroughly analyzed elsewhere,[118] and I shall here treat it only in bare outline. But I hope that what I am about to say will be enough to suggest his importance to those unfamiliar with his work and to give his admirers the assurance that he is at least not being overlooked on the present occasion through any tendency to undervalue him. His career as a writer

---

deny the scientific movement any influence at all upon stylistic matters is curiously unconvincing and quixotic.

[117] *Ibid.*, p. 275.

[118] See my *Logic and Rhetoric in England*, pp. 392-397. But for a view at odds with mine, see Jackson I. Cope, *Joseph Glanvill, Anglican Apologist* (Saint Louis, Missouri, 1956), pp. 161-166. Cited below as Cope.

and preacher might be briefly characterized as having started out in an exuberant dedication to what Sprat contemptuously called "the easie vanity of *fine speaking*" and as having ended in a sober preference for the plain, unaffected, natural, and moderate style. Scholars are divided in their speculations upon the reasons for this change in Glanvill's literary practices. Richard Foster Jones attributed the change to Glanvill's growing admiration for the stylistic program of the Royal Society as he sought and received and continuingly experienced the benefits of belonging to that organization. Moreover, Jones used Glanvill as one of two conspicuous examples of the actual influence exerted by the stylistic ideals of the Society upon the nonscientific writings of the day.[119] In opposing Jones's view, Williamson took the position that Glanvill's conversion to the plain style was merely a change in his "humour," that is, in his personal preference and taste, as influenced by contemporary Anti-Ciceronian and Senecan attitudes, but not by the Royal Society.[120] The truth is that all of these influences working in complex association with one another made Glanvill move from the rhetoric of adornment to the rhetoric of plainness, even if in the end his plainness as a preacher cannot reasonably be expected to have matched or even approached the austere plainness of scientific exposition. It is against this background that his contribution to the new rhetoric should be understood and appreciated. That contribution was made in a work which he published at London in 1678 under the title, *An Essay concerning Preaching: Written for the Direction of A Young Divine; and Useful also for the People, in order to Profitable Hearing.*[121] "I shall handle the *Rules* of Preaching," declared

[119] Jones, pp. 989-998.

[120] *Senecan Amble*, pp. 281-282, 223-224.

[121] Cope, pp. 163-164, discusses Glanvill's *Essay concerning Preaching* as if Glanvill had written it to advocate adornment rather than plainness as the key to the rhetoric of the pulpit. I take this to be Cope's meaning when he says that in the *Essay* ". . . Glanvill is actually rehabilitating the rhetoricism he had earlier castigated. . . ." (p. 163 n.) What Cope has failed to grasp is the distinction between the rhetorical style taught by Glanvill in the *Essay* (1678) and the rhetorical style displayed by Glanvill in his first book, *The Vanity of Dogmatizing* (1661). Glanvill did not write his *Essay* to rehabilitate the literary manner that he himself had practiced in that earlier work. For a careful analysis not only of Glanvill's earlier stylistic practice but also of his repudiation of it in *Scepsis Scientifica* (1664) and of his final abandonment

Glanvill, "under these four Heads. It ought to be *plain, practical, methodical, affectionate.*"[122] To these heads, which respectively involve the problems of style, of content, of organization, and of persuasiveness, he silently added a fifth, and he made that one the occasion for remarks upon delivery, and its twin aspects of voice and gesture.[123] By what he said and did not say upon each of these matters, he earned his right to be considered a new rhetorician, and no one need be hesitant in acknowledging his importance in the seventeenth-century movement towards reform in rhetorical standards and styles. His importance for the new rhetoric, indeed, is not inferior to that of Wilkins and Sprat, although it must be counted somewhat beneath that of Boyle.

But the most important person in the movement towards a new rhetoric within the confines of the Royal Society during the first half-century of its existence was John Locke. In fact, as I said earlier, Locke was a primary influence not only behind the new logic of the eighteenth century but also behind its new rhetoric, despite his having written only a little upon the latter subject, and his not having been usually counted among the leading rhetorical theorists of the European tradition.[124] What Locke did in this field may be indicated in a comprehensive way by reminding ourselves that Wilkins, Sprat, Boyle, and Glanvill made their most distinctive contributions to rhetorical theory in their refreshing advocacy of the plain style for various kinds of modern discourse, whereas Locke not only added his strong voice to theirs upon this issue, but he went beyond them to take an influential stand upon subjects associated with all but one of the other issues that I outlined at the beginning of this chapter as the collision points be-

---

of it in his essay "Against Confidence in Philosophy, and Matters of Speculation" (1676), see Jones, pp. 989-998. If Glanvill's *Essay* can be said to advocate any kind of "rhetoricism" at all, it would have to be called the "rhetoricism" of the new rhetoric, not that of the old.

122 *An Essay concerning Preaching* (London, 1678), p. 11.

123 *Ibid.*, p. 78.

124 See above, Ch. 5, pp. 283-284. An attempt to tell the neglected story of Locke's influence upon modern rhetoric was made in my essay, "John Locke and the New Rhetoric." *The Quarterly Journal of Speech*, LIII (1967), 319-333. My present account of Locke as rhetorician draws at times upon the substance and the wording of that essay.

tween the old rhetoric and the new.[125] Since his attitude towards the ornamental and the plain styles is a natural development of that just described as belonging to his colleagues in the Royal Society, I shall begin with it in giving this account of his rhetorical speculations as a whole.

Locke felt that figurative language and the artifices of conventional eloquence must be excluded from discourses which have truth and knowledge as their subject matter, information or instruction or improvement as their aim, and the learned community as their audience. Such discourses must follow the rules of the plain style. These sentiments are the dominant theme of the famous concluding passage in Chapter x of Book III of *An Essay concerning Human Understanding*—the chapter entitled "*Of the Abuse of Words.*" The passage begins as follows:

> Since Wit and Fancy finds easier entertainment in the World, than dry Truth and real Knowledge, *figurative Speeches*, and allusion in Language, will hardly be admitted, as *an* imperfection or *abuse* of it. I confess, in Discourses, where we seek rather Pleasure and Delight, than Information and Improvement, such Ornaments as are borrowed from them, can scarce pass for Faults. But yet, if we would speak of Things as they are, we must allow, that all the Art of Rhetorick, besides Order and Clearness, all the artificial and figurative application of Words Eloquence hath invented, are for nothing else, but to insinuate wrong *Ideas*, move the Passions, and thereby mislead the Judgment; and so indeed are perfect cheat: And therefore however laudable or allowable Oratory may render them in Harangues and popular Addresses, they are certainly, in all Discourses that pretend to inform and instruct, wholly to be avoided; and where Truth and Knowledge are concerned, cannot but be thought a great fault, either of the Language or Person that makes use of them. What, and how various they are, I shall not trouble my self to take notice; the Books of Rhetorick

[125] Locke did not openly object to the Ciceronian doctrine that a rhetorical composition should normally be expressed in a six-part structure, nor for that matter did he openly advocate the simpler structure that the new rhetoric would endorse. Thus he cannot be said to have taken a clear stand on the fifth issue mentioned above in Sec. I of this chapter. But he would, I feel, almost certainly have recommended the simpler structure, if he had addressed himself to this question.

which abound in the World, will inform those who want to be informed.[126]

In the midst of this assertion that didactic and expository compositions must adhere to the plain style, there is of course a corresponding denunciation of ornament, and thus of the rhetoric which emphasized it. But this denunciation must be carefully examined if it is not to be misread. Locke's view is that rhetoric is highly censurable so far as it is a party to the use of misleading or distorted ideas, and so far as its artifices of style misdirect the judgment through their capacity to move the passions. But it is also his view that rhetoric is laudable so far as it teaches order and clearness, and so far as it acts either under the auspices of wit and fancy to provide literary pleasure in nonscientific writings or under the auspices of reason to make truth itself entertaining and delightful to people who are not trained as scholars. Thus to Locke there is a bad and a good rhetoric, and his castigation of the one must not be allowed to obliterate his acknowledgment of the other.

Against this background we may now properly evaluate what he went on to say in the few sentences which follow the passage just quoted. Those few sentences seem to make rhetoric a pariah among the arts, but actually they apply only to the extravagant, self-regarding rhetoric of the past. They read thus:

> Only I cannot but observe, how little the preservation and improvement of Truth and Knowledge, is the Care and Concern of Mankind; since the Arts of Fallacy are endow'd and preferred; and 'tis plain how much Men love to deceive, and be deceived, since the great Art of Deceit and Errour, Rhetorick I mean, has its established Professors, is publickly taught, and has always been had in great Reputation. And, I doubt not, but it will be thought great boldness, if not brutality in me, to have said thus much against it. *Eloquence*, like the fair Sex, has too prevailing Beauties in it, to suffer it self ever to be spoken against: And 'tis in vain to find fault with those Arts of Deceiving, wherein Men find pleasure to be Deceived.[127]

[126] *An Essay concerning Humane Understanding* (London, 1690), p. 251. I cite this edition throughout this part of my discussion of Locke. In later editions, the passage just quoted remains unaltered except for some minor changes in wording.

[127] *Ibid.*, p. 251.

As I mentioned in Chapter 5, Locke himself had served as Praelector Rhetoricus at Oxford in 1663.[128] That office would of course have made him an established professor publicly teaching rhetoric. If at that time rhetoric had been solely and exclusively the art of deceit and error, Locke would have had no alternative but to ignore his duties or to turn his back upon his concern for the preservation and improvement of truth and knowledge while choosing rather to give his students deliberate instruction in the arts of fallacy and deception. And if eloquence then had been impossible of achievement except as it came from the artificial and figurative application of words, Locke would have had no alternative but to endorse the ornamental style or to confess that he preferred to teach his students to be ineffective writers or speakers instead. But of course the alternatives confronting him as Praelector Rhetoricus were not thus narrowly restricted. He could, for example, have taken the view, already popularized by his friend Boyle, that there was an eloquence of adornment and an eloquence of plainness, and that, since the latter fell as truly within the scope of a teacher of rhetoric as the former, he for his part could emphasize them both, or recommend the latter alone as the best modern style. Or he could have taken the view which he himself was later to express in the passages just quoted—that there was on the one hand a rhetoric addressed to the passions and prone to involve distorted ideas, misdirected judgments, and highly colored expressions, while on the other was a rhetoric addressed to the reason and dedicated to the communication of truth and knowledge by means of coherent order and stylistic plainness. Thus he could easily have satisfied the demands of his appointment as Praelector Rhetoricus without destroying his commitment as scholar. But if he had chosen this course, as he undoubtedly did, he would have been a teacher of the rhetoric which belonged not to the receding past but to the emerging future.

Having thus far seen Locke as an eloquent advocate of the plain style, we may now proceed to observe that two of his further contributions to the new rhetoric concern matters which have a logical as well as a rhetorical dimension. I refer to his disparagement of the topics as a machinery for the invention of sub-

128 See above, Ch. 5, p. 265.

ject matter in argument, and to his obvious preference for a subject matter discovered by direct contact with the realities of the situation under discussion. I refer also to his disparagement of the syllogism, and its variant form, the enthymeme, and to his obvious preference for induction and the inference. In its rhetorical bearing, the first of these two pairs of attitudes means that Locke endorsed the procedures which require nonartistic arguments to be the essential content of discourse, and he rejected the procedures which lead discourse to consist of artistic arguments. In other words, he advocated arguments developed from factual materials, and he frowned upon arguments developed from the hallowed machinery of topics. The second of the two pairs of attitudes just mentioned means in its rhetorical implications that Locke endorsed induction as the generic form of proof, and he gave it priority over the enthymeme of tradition. Both pairs of attitudes represent reversals of ancient dogma. The classical rhetoricians had neglected nonartistic arguments, and artistic arguments they had exalted. And they had of course considered enthymematic reasoning the basic kind of proof, and had thought induction to be an errant enthymeme, as enthymeme was an imperfect syllogism. But these subjects have been thoroughly explored in earlier pages of this work, and I shall not need to deal with them further here.[129] It will suffice for the present to record them as parts of Locke's rhetorical theory, and to hope that their importance for the new rhetoric has already been adequately shown.

Another of Locke's contributions to the new rhetoric belongs also to logical theory, and has been discussed in its logical bearings in one of my previous chapters.[130] But I feel that its rhetorical aspects need some special attention. This contribution has to do with the kind of argument that is designed to lend a convincing degree of probability to a recommended proposition or course of action. And this kind of argument had historically been as much a part of rhetoric as of logic.

The old rhetoric had been committed to probable arguments by virtue of its commitment to artistic proofs and their corollaries, the rhetorical topics. Since artistic proofs had only a sub-

<hr />

[129] See above, Ch. 3, pp. 98 ff.; Ch. 5, pp. 259, 284 ff., 293 ff.; Ch. 6, pp. 442 f.
[130] See above, Ch. 5, pp. 288, 294-295.

sidiary probative value, it was inevitable that they and the topics which supported them would come under attack and would be abandoned as demands grew for proofs based upon the factual materials that nonartistic arguments represented. But even probable arguments derived from factual materials would present problems. They too could be loose or tight, superficial or profound, counterfeit or genuine, and it would be important for rhetoric to know the difference between one sort and the other, and to perfect an apparatus to control their uses. It was upon these latter considerations that Locke offered some influential remarks. And although he intended what he said to have reference more to the enterprise of enquiry than to that of communication, the thoughtful future students of rhetoric were certain to see that Locke spoke on this occasion with them also in mind.

Locke's discussion of probabilities occurred in his immensely popular work, *The Conduct of the Understanding*, which was originally written as a chapter of an enlarged version of the *Essay*.[131] As he was offering advice in that work to those who truly wished to follow reason but lacked the personal resources to command a full view of the question under investigation, he recommended as one antidote to their disability that they should exercise themselves "in observing the Connection of Ideas and following them in train."[132] In words later to be quoted and admired by William Duncan,[133] Locke added: "Nothing does this better than Mathematicks, which therefore I think should be taught all those who have the Time and Opportunity, not so much to make them Mathematicians, as to make them reasonable Creatures." And a few paragraphs later, returning to this theme, Locke connected a training in mathematics with the uses of probable arguments in enquiry. He said:

> I have mentioned *Mathematicks* as a way to settle in the Mind an habit of Reasoning closely and in train; not that I think it necessary that all Men should be deep Mathematicians, but that having got the way of Reasoning, which that study necessarily brings the Mind to, they might be able to transfer it to other parts of Knowledge as they shall have occasion. For in all

131 See above, Ch. 5, pp. 274-275.
132 *Posthumous Works of Mr. John Locke*, p. 26.
133 See above, Ch. 5, p. 359.

sorts of Reasoning, every single Argument should be managed as a Mathematical Demonstration, the Connection and dependence of Ideas should be followed 'till the Mind is brought to the source on which it bottoms, and observes the coherence all along, though in proof of probability, one such train is not enough to settle the judgment as in demonstrative Knowledge.[134]

This mention of "proofs of probability" led Locke to comment more at length upon them. Here is the crucial paragraph:

Where a truth is made out by one demonstration, there needs no farther Enquiry, but in probabilities where there wants demonstration to establish the truth beyond doubt, there 'tis not enough to trace one Argument to its source, and observe its Strength and Weakness, but all the Arguments, after having been so examined on both sides, must be laid in balance one against another, and upon the whole the Understanding determine its assent.[135]

Thus Locke saw argument from probability as an activity that must involve the examination of all alternatives and be disciplined by mathematics, if dependable results are to be achieved in the nondemonstrative parts of knowledge. A succession of generations bred to this standard would naturally come to expect that the standard applied not solely to the probable conclusions of natural philosophy and history, but to those advocated by lawyers, political speakers, pamphleteers, and other moulders of opinion. In other words, the standards of the learned community would impinge upon the theories of the rhetoricians, and a more disciplined kind of probable argument than had hitherto prevailed would become a new ingredient of eloquent discourse and of the theory which sought to explain it. We shall see later how the new rhetoricians of the eighteenth century made this ingredient a part of their program.

The final contribution which Locke made to the new rhetoric had to do with persuasion as the predominant aim of rhetorical discourse and with the three traditional oratorical types which

---

[134] *Posthumous Works of Mr. John Locke*, pp. 30-31. For Duncan's use of this idea from Locke, see above, Ch. 5, pp. 356-358.

[135] *Posthumous Works of Mr. John Locke*, p. 31.

had grown out of it. Locke's view was that, apart from its uses as an address to the wit and fancy on occasions when it sought to give pleasure and delight to its audience, discourse must be understood as being chiefly an address to the judgment for the purpose of transferring one man's knowledge of things to another. In other words, the ruling aim of discourse is communication or instruction, and its basic type, the exposition. This is not to deny that persuasiveness is an effect which discourse can and does produce. It is rather to deny that persuasiveness can be understood or accomplished except as exposition surrounds and controls it.

The old rhetoric had taken the position that persuasiveness was the dominant object of rhetorical discourse, and that exposition, if it entered at all, served only in a subordinate role. "Rhetoric may be defined," said Aristotle, "as the faculty of observing in any given case the available means of persuasion."[136] Before his time, to be sure, the sophists and indeed Plato himself had considered rhetoric to be the art of persuasive speaking,[137] but it was Aristotle's immense authority, not that of his predecessors, which made persuasiveness the paramount concern of oratory as it was institutionalized in the later schools of Rome and Europe. Cicero considered that it was the subordinate aim of the orator to teach as well as to persuade; yet by the time of Quintilian, teaching was rarely given even secondary attention as a function of rhetoric, while persuasiveness was given almost exclusive stress.[138] This meant that rhetoric was equated predominantly with the arts of popular appeal, and was made to consist of logical arguments, emotional pleas, and ethical inducements. This also meant that demonstrative, deliberative, and judicial oratory, as the three

[136] *Rhetoric*, 1355b 25-26. Translation by W. Rhys Roberts.

[137] For Plato's view, see his *Phaedrus*, 260-261.

[138] See *De Oratore*, 2.28.121; 2.29.128; 2.77.310; 3.6.23; 3.27.104. In these various passages instruction or exposition is given a place beside persuasion as a goal of oratory. But in *De Oratore*, 2.27.115, and in *Orator*, 21.69, persuasion alone is mentioned. Quintilian, *Institutio Oratoria*, 2.15.1-38, tends to associate persuasion with oratory, and to separate oratory and exposition. He quotes Socrates, indeed, as having allowed to Gorgias the power of persuading but not that of teaching: "Gorgias apud Platonem suadendi se artificem in iudiciis et aliis coetibus esse ait, de iustis quoque et iniustis tractare; cui Socrates persuadendi, non docendi concedit facultatem." *Institutio Oratoria*, 2.15.18.

kinds of rhetorical discourse described in Aristotle's *Rhetoric*,[139] became as it were the typical forms of nonpoetic popular composition. The neglect of exposition and didactic discourse within ancient rhetorical theory meant in part that those forms were considered learned communications and were supposed to be the property of dialectic. But they were given little attention even there. From the time of Aristotle to that of Ramus, dialectic was in large measure the art of learned disputation and only in a minor sense the art of expounding scientific matters to the educated community.

It was not Locke's object to assert the unimportance of persuasive discourse as a tool of social organization or a subject of study in school or university. But he did feel that the times required an art of impartial exposition to cope with the problem of delivering the new science of Boyle and Newton to the world of scholarship. And he saw that a man's knowledge of things was the true source of his right conduct, persuasions being in vain if ignorance opposed them, and unnecessary if knowledge preceded them. Thus he indicated that the theory of discourse must be so constructed as to recognize not only the necessity of an accurate correspondence between man's words, as verbal phenomena, and man's ideas or conceptions, as intellectual phenomena, but also the attendant necessity of an accurate correspondence between man's ideas and the things of the physical world.[140] Thus also he suggested that, whether words are intended as argument or exposition, they are ruled by the same law—a law which judges the effectiveness of discourse by its linguistic adequacy in transferring accurate ideas of things from one man to another without distortion, deceit, or undue difficulty. A law so formulated makes argument subordinate to exposition, in the sense that the persuasiveness of a discourse becomes a side effect of its expository fidelity to idea and fact, and its expository fidelity becomes the major standard to which it must adhere even when it turns into persuasion or argument.

Locke's closest approach to a definition of an acceptable rhetoric is made in Chapter x of Book iii of the *Essay concerning*

[139] 1358a 36-1358b 20.
[140] *An Essay concerning Humane Understanding*, pp. 185-186, 289-292.

Human Understanding. That chapter, as we know, is entitled, *"Of the Abuse of Words,"* and it ends with the passage which I quoted above to show Locke's contempt for a rhetoric of error and deceit, and his approval of a rhetoric of order and clearness. In an earlier paragraph of that same chapter, Locke paused to summarize what he had been saying about the abuses of language, and it happens that his summary stated the conditions to be met when words are put to their proper uses. Thus the conditions are in fact those which the new rhetoric must observe; they are the boundaries within which modern rhetorical theory must be written. Locke said:

> To conclude this Consideration of the Imperfection, and Abuse of Language; the *ends of Language in our Discourse with others,* being chiefly these three: *First, To make known* one Man's Thoughts or *Ideas* to another. *Secondly,* To do it *with* as much ease and *quickness,* as is possible; and *Thirdly,* Thereby *to convey* the *Knowledge* of Things. Language is either abused, or deficient, when it fails in any of these Three.[141]

If we paraphrased this passage with rhetorical persuasiveness in mind, we would be forced to concede that a persuasive use of language is deficient when it does not communicate the speaker's ideas to his hearers, or when it makes the process of transmission more difficult or slower than it need be, or when the speaker's argument through lack of factual soundness gives a distorted or false view of its subject. Scholars would agree, I believe, that these three standards ought to prevail in scholarly writing and speaking in the modern world, and that, if they did prevail, scholarly publication both oral and written would be rhetorically excellent. All Locke does in the passage just quoted is to recommend the scholarly standard as the standard for modern rhetoric, whether the speaker's aim be to expound a system of science, or to explain a series of historical events, or to argue a case in a court of law, or to preach a sermon from the pulpit, or to seek to influence public policy in parliament or the political arena. Emotional pleas and ethical inducements are no longer to be accepted in discourse merely because they were two of the three modes of

---

[141] *Ibid.,* pp. 248-249. Italics are Locke's.

persuasion outlined in Aristotle's *Rhetoric*.[142] They are now to be accepted only as they contribute to ease and quickness in conveying the knowledge of things and in making it accessible to humanity.

At this point it might be carelessly assumed that the passage just quoted was intended by Locke to refer only to philosophical discourse, and not to the kind of discourse traditionally associated with rhetoric. Such an assumption, however, is contrary to fact, as we can immediately see if we remember something which Locke once said in commenting directly upon the art of speaking. He happened one day to be in conversation with a company of friends upon the method to be followed by young men in conducting a program of reading; and his words on that occasion awakened so much interest that one of his hearers volunteered to copy the substance of what he had said if he would repeat it. Locke did so, and the ensuing discourse, entitled "Some Thoughts Concerning Reading and Study for a Gentleman," was ultimately published at London in 1720.[143] Among the thoughts expressed in that discourse was a passage on the standards to be met by the young man who speaks in public, and the passage in question is nothing but a restatement for the would-be orator of the doctrine which in the *Essay* served to define the new rhetoric.

Having begun his conversation that day by remarking that we read in order to improve our understanding, and that the improvement of the understanding had as its two objects the increase of our knowledge and the delivery of that knowledge to mankind, Locke said: "The latter of these, if it be not the chief end of Study in a Gentleman; yet it is at least equal to the other, since the greatest part of his business and usefulness in the world, is by the influence of what he says, or writes to others."[144] Locke proceeded then to comment upon the problem of increasing our knowledge, and he outlined three steps to this end. At that point he spoke as follows: "But that, as I have said, being not all that a Gentleman should aim at in reading, he should farther take care, to improve himself in the Art also of Speaking; that so he may be able to make the best use of what he knows."[145] What transpires

---

[142] 1356a 1-35.

[143] [P. Des Maizeaux], *A Collection of Several Pieces of Mr. John Locke* (London, 1720), sig. Aa3v, pp. 231-245.

[144] *Ibid.*, pp. 231-232.   [145] *Ibid.*, pp. 233-234.

for the next half dozen paragraphs is in fact the outline of an art of rhetoric for the delivery of any man's knowledge to others by means of the spoken word. Here are substantial excerpts:

> The Art of Speaking well, consists chiefly in two things, viz. Perspicuity, and right Reasoning.
>
> Perspicuity, consists in the using of proper terms for the ideas or thoughts, which he would have pass from his own mind into that of another man's. It is this, that gives them an easy entrance; and it is with delight, that men hearken to those whom they easily understand; whereas, what is obscurely said, dying as it is spoken, is usually not only lost, but creates a prejudice in the hearer, as if he that spoke, knew not what he said, or was afraid to have it understood.
>
> The way to obtain this, is to read such Books as are allow'd to be writ with the greatest clearness and propriety, in the language that a man uses. An author excellent in this faculty, as well as several other, is Dr. Tillotson, late Archbishop of Canterbury, in all that is publish'd of his. I have chose rather to propose this pattern, for the attainment of the Art of Speaking clearly, than those who give rules about it; since we are more apt to learn by example, than by direction. . . .
>
> Besides Perspicuity, there must be also right Reasoning; without which perspicuity serves but to expose the speaker. And for the attaining of this, I should propose the constant reading of Chillingworth, who by his example will teach both Perspicuity, and the way of right Reasoning, better than any book that I know. . . .[146]

Locke did not consider these two standards hostile to those of the old rhetoric. Indeed, in some observations that I omitted from the last quotation, he recommended that, if students wanted to learn rhetoric by direction rather than by example, they should turn to Cicero's *De Oratore* and *Orator*, to Quintilian's *Institutio Oratoria*, and to Boileau's translation of Longinus's "On the Sublime." Thus he mentioned the old rhetoric by its most respected classics, and he did not speak in disparagement of them. Nevertheless, he obviously felt that the study of actual examples of eloquence would best reveal to students the secrets of eloquent

---

[146] *Ibid.*, pp. 234-235.

speaking, and that the standards of perspicuity and right reasoning were the best guides to the analysis of those examples and to the discovery and control of the sources of their effectiveness. Beyond these limits he did not go in speaking on that particular occasion of the art of making ideas pass from the mind of one man to that of another by the medium of language.

In retrospect, it appears that Locke's contribution to the new rhetoric consists in his having given British learning a fresh and enduring set of expectations concerning discourse. His account of the three ends of language, and his emphasis upon communication as the basic purpose of verbal composition, led the intellectual community to see popular and learned exposition as the basic kind of speaking and writing when the human understanding was being addressed, and to see the old preoccupation of rhetoric with persuasion and the three kinds of speeches as a reflection of past rather than present necessities. His vision of a severely judicious, openly mathematical approach to the evaluation of probabilities, and his accompanying preference for factual as distinguished from topical materials in public addresses, gave critics and listeners a new set of measurements to apply to what they heard and read, and speakers a new set of obligations respecting the reliability of the content and sources of their evidence in discourses before popular or learned meetings. His disparagement of syllogistic procedures, and his memorable demonstration of the viability of the process of natural logic and inference, brought to the learned community the recognition that formal discourse did not have to conform to the deductive routines prescribed by the priests of the old learning, and was now free to become the flexible instrument of inductive scholarship and empirical wisdom. Finally, his denunciation of prearranged contrivances of style, and his advocacy of the plain and perspicuous utterance, helped to convince all sectors of the public that speeches and writings did not have to keep to the vocabulary of the initiated, but could use the idiom of everyday life. These attitudes all belong demonstrably to Locke, and they were grasped at least in part by Wilkins, Boyle, Sprat, and Glanvill. Locke's immense popularity in Great Britain throughout the entire eighteenth century made him nevertheless the most influential of the gifted group of reformers of rhetoric in the Royal Society of his day, and thus he deserves a special place in the esteem of historians of rhetorical theory. Locke's total achievement as a thinker, says his able recent biographer, "marked a new beginning, not only in philosophy, but in the way in which men thought about the world."[147] Only words of this sort can justly characterize what Locke's speculations on rhetoric really mean.

[147] Maurice Cranston, *Locke*, in Writers and their Work, No. 135, Published for The British Council and The National Book League by Longmans, Green & Co. (London, 1961), p. 8.

III   Influences from Abroad: Lamy, Fénelon,
Rapin, Bouhours, Rollin

At various times between 1672 and 1734, French treatises on
rhetoric were brought out in English translations and thus came
to have a place in the history of British attitudes towards the
theory of discourse. One of these treatises was Michel Le Faucheur's *Traitté de l'action de l'orateur*, which, as we have seen,
had a dominating influence in the early stages of the British elocutionary movement of the eighteenth century.[148] But so far as the
new rhetoric of that era is concerned, the most important French
authors to have had a British public were Bernard Lamy,
François de Salignac de la Mothe Fénelon, René Rapin, Dominique Bouhours, and Charles Rollin. Each of these rhetoricians
will now receive specific comment. I have already spoken of
Lamy and Fénelon in connection with their willingness to question certain features of the Ciceronian rhetorical doctrine that
prevailed in their times, but I feel that each should be mentioned
again in the setting of the present chapter, lest his contribution
to the new rhetoric appear smaller than the circumstances actually warrant. As for Rapin, Bouhours, and Rollin, they had
nothing new to say about rhetoric, but they helped to define its
new place among the academic arts and sciences, and thus they
deserve a brief notice here.

The chief contribution of Lamy to the new rhetoric consisted
in his unconventional attack on the topics of rhetorical invention
as he was producing his otherwise conventional rearrangement
of Ramistic and Ciceronian theories of speaking.[149] The treatise
in which his attack occurred was first published anonymously at
Paris in 1675, and at that time it was called *De l'Art de Parler*.
When it reached its third French edition in 1688, its title was
changed to *La Rhétorique, ou l'Art de Parler*, and Bernard Lamy
was identified as its author. Meanwhile, it had come out at London in 1676 in an English translation called *The Art of Speaking*.
The anonymity of the original French treatise, and the obvious
resemblance between its attack on the topics and the similar at-

[148] See above, Ch. 4, pp. 164-181.
[149] My present account of Lamy's work relies upon that in my *Logic and
Rhetoric in England*, pp. 378-382.

tack in *The Port-Royal Logic,* led the English publisher to attribute it to "Messieurs du Port Royal," and the Port Royalists continued to be given credit for it in reprints of the English Translation in 1696 and 1704. What Lamy had to say in denunciation of the topics has been quoted in Chapter 3, and there is no need to repeat his words here.[150] It will be recalled that his attack is vigorous and convincing, and at first glance we might be inclined to value it highly as an influence in the decline and fall of the topics as a method of rhetorical invention. But in fact its value in that direction is not easy to assess. Lamy himself is in part responsible for this situation, precisely because, like the Port Royalists before him, he did not allow the topics to disappear altogether from inventional theory, but instead he preceded his at-attack upon them with a serious if somewhat perfunctory exposition of their various types and uses, with the result that he seemed to affirm in one breath what he denied in the next. Then again there is difficulty in deciding whether Lamy's ambivalence towards the topics would be a particular factor in their decline when the similar ambivalence of the Port Royalists would have been much more widely influential because they were much more widely read. Then again there is difficulty in deciding whether the ambivalent attitude of Lamy and the Port Royalists, counted together as a force against the survival of the topics, could possibly match the tremendous influence of Locke, who made the topics utterly meaningless by his revolutionary exploration of the true sources of knowledge. As against the Port Royalists, Lamy's castigation of the topics sounds more like an echo than an original voice. As against Lamy and the Port Royalists, Locke's utterances upon this matter sound like powerful claps of thunder drowning out the cheerful patter of rainfall. Still, it was advantageous, no doubt, to have Lamy echo for rhetoric what the Port Royalists had said upon a parallel matter in logic, and thus to record something on the rhetorical side to counteract John Ward's bland later assumption that the topical system of rhetorical invention was almost as good as new.

Fénelon's *Dialogues Concerning Eloquence* must be counted a far more important rhetoric than that of Lamy, whether we are thinking of its French text as first published at Amsterdam in 1717

[150] See above, Ch. 3, p. 92.

or of its first English text as fashioned by William Stevenson and brought out in 1722 at London.[151] In fact, it is one of the most important rhetorics to appear anywhere in Europe during the eighteenth century. When I published in 1951 the fourth English translation that it had received in the preceding two hundred and twenty-nine years, I called it "the first modern rhetoric," and I explained its relation to what had gone before and come after it by saying that Fénelon "began rhetoric anew."[152] These judgments have been strengthened, so far as I am concerned, by my subsequent studies of the development of rhetoric in that period. Thus it seems altogether proper here to hail Stevenson's version of the *Dialogues Concerning Eloquence* as the best self-avowed rhetoric among the earliest writings on the new rhetoric in English. Scholars who deal with subjects connected with British rhetoric of the eighteenth century damage their own work beyond repair if they neglect this important treatise.

The new rhetoric, as Fénelon conceived of it, emerged from the rhetoric of the past, but it was not on the one hand a copy of the past as seen by the fashionable scholarship of his own times, nor on the other an attempt to revive the past in the spirit of a pedantic antiquarianism. He intended his rhetoric to preserve what was still valid and to reject what was stale and obsolete in the great classical tradition. So far as he was concerned, the masterpieces of that tradition consisted primarily of Aristotle's *Rhetoric*, Cicero's *De Oratore* and *Orator*, Quintilian's *Institutio Oratoria*, Plato's *Phaedrus, Gorgias,* and *Republic,* Longinus's *On the Sublime*, and St. Augustine's *De Doctrina Christiana*. Fénelon wanted above all to reduce these works to a rhetoric that would contain nothing but their most durable precepts. That he was thinking in these very terms as he constructed his *Dialogues Concerning Eloquence* is unmistakably indicated in that work itself. The dialogues consist of conversations among three participants, who are identified only as A, B, and C, in order, no doubt, to make it difficult for a reader to attribute their opinions to actual living

[151] For the full title of the first edition of Stevenson's translation, see above, Ch. 3, p. 94. That edition is cited throughout my present discussion whenever I quote Fénelon's actual text in an English version. Thus the word "Stevenson" followed by a page number will refer to the corresponding page number of the first edition of Stevenson's work.

[152] For information about the source of these quotations, see above, Ch. 3, n. 37.

persons. But it is plain that A represented Fénelon. On one occasion, when B asked how orators ought to speak, A answered in these significant words:

> Instead of giving you my own Opinion, I shall go on to lay before you the Rules that the Antients give us: but I shall only touch upon the chief Points: For, I suppose, you don't expect that I should enter into an endless Detail of the Precepts of Rhetorick. There are but too many useless ones; which you must have read in those Books where they are copiously explain'd. It will be enough if we consider the most important Rules. Plato in his *Phaedrus* shews us, that the greatest Fault of Rhetoricians is their studying the Art of Perswasion, before they have learn't, (from the Principles of true Philosophy), what those things are of which they ought to perswade Men.[153]

The passage then went on to explain Plato's view "that none but a Philosopher can be a true Orator," and to emphasize Cicero's endorsement of that same doctrine.[154] But so far as we are presently concerned, the most important thing about this passage as a whole is that Fénelon in the person of his dramatic spokesman indicated his awareness of two ancient rhetorics, one of which was largely useless, and the other, important; and that he proceeded to name Plato's *Phaedrus* as an authority upon the latter when he again took up the task of reconstructing it.

In their actual scope, the *Dialogues Concerning Eloquence* reach far beyond the conventional discourses so extensively emphasized in ancient rhetoric. The dialogues began when the three spokesmen happened one day to meet and to fall into a discussion of a sermon which B had just heard and had greatly admired. Thus pulpit oratory was brought at once into focus, and it remained a major subject of comment throughout the first meeting and the two others which finally proved necessary to satisfy the desire of each spokesman for his proper share in the discussion. But other kinds of discourse came into focus, too—secular oratory, epic poetry, tragedy, the Hebrew and Christian Bibles, and the writings of several distinguished Fathers of the Church. The opinions expressed during the dialogues were discordant at first, but they gradually moved towards agreement upon what the spokesmen considered to be acceptable aims, legitimate methods,

[153] Stevenson, pp. 53-54.   [154] *Ibid.*, pp. 54-59.

and preferable models of discourse in all its branches, whether rhetorical or poetic. As if to emphasize Fénelon's sense of kinship with Plato, A acted throughout as a kind of Socrates. Thus he exposed the weaknesses of fashionable assumptions about excellence in speaking and writing; and thus he sought to merge discordant opinions into consensus. At one point, as if to echo what he had said earlier about not entering into endless detail on the present occasion, he disclaimed any thought of giving his companions "a compleat System of Rhetorick,"[155] but nevertheless he stuck to his task of creating the essential philosophy which a complete rhetoric needs if it is to outlive the time taken to produce it.

That philosophy would have pleased Robert Boyle, for, like Boyle, Fénelon defined literary excellence in terms of eloquence, and he went on not only to equate eloquence with the success of a discourse in moving men, but also to identify that latter capacity with the effect which a discourse produces when it makes deeply human truth visible to those who read or hear. In other words, Fénelon said in effect that words move men by opening men's eyes to the hidden truths of their being, and that when a discourse strikes them in this way, it may only then be called eloquent and excellent. This argument is the burden of the three dialogues. One formulation of it occurred at the end of the first dialogue in the following speech by A:

> Plato says an Oration is so far eloquent as it affects the Hearer's Mind. By this Rule you may judge certainly of any Discourse you hear. If an Harangue leave you cold and languid; and only amuses your Mind, instead of enlightening it; if it does not move your Heart and Passions, . . . it is not truly eloquent. Tully approves of Plato's Sentiments on this Point; and tells us that the whole Drift and Force of a Discourse shou'd tend to move those secret Springs of Action that Nature has plac'd in the Hearts of Men. Wou'd you then consult your own Mind to know whether those you hear be truly eloquent? If they make a lively Impression upon you, and gain your Attention and Assent to what they say; if they move and animate your Passions, so as to raise you above yourself, you may be assur'd they are true Orators. But if instead of affecting you thus, they only please or divert you, and make you admire the Brightness of

[155] *Ibid.*, p. 86.

their Thoughts, or the Beauty and Propriety of their Language, you may freely pronounce them to be mere Declaimers.[156]

And there are other formulations of this basic argument at other points in the dialogues. Thus in comparing Isocrates and Demosthenes, A said that Isocrates stands as the orator who seeks to polish his thoughts, to give harmonious cadences to his periods, and to guarantee that his words are nicely disposed, whereas, in listening to Demosthenes, "One cannot but see that he has the Good of the Republick entirely at heart; and that Nature itself speaks in all his Transports."[157] Thus in comparing the young Cicero with the Cicero of the philippics, A remarked that the orations of the former were marred by the display of their author's ambition, his desire for fame, and his lack of concern for the justice of his cause, whereas in his later life, "When he endeavour'd to support and revive expiring Liberty, and to animate the Commonwealth against Antony his Enemy; you do not *see* him use Points of Wit and quaint Antitheses. He's *then* truly eloquent."[158] Thus finally in comparing the greatest secular classics with those in the Old Testament, A spoke as follows:

> Homer himself never reach't the Sublimity of Moses's Songs; especially the last, which all the *Israelitish* Children were to learn by-heart. Never did any Ode, either *Greek*, or *Latin*, come up to the Loftiness of the *Psalms*: particularly that which begins thus; *The mighty God even the Lord, hath spoken,* surpasses the utmost Stretch of human Invention. Neither Homer nor any other Poet ever equal'd Isaiah describing the Majesty of God, in whose Sight the *Nations of the Earth are as the small Dust;* yea *less than nothing, and Vanity;* seeing it is *He that*

---

[156] *Ibid.*, pp. 63-64. The clause omitted from this quotation is such an inept translation of Fénelon's French text as to deserve oblivion. The sentence in which the clause appears reads thus in *Oeuvres de Fénelon* (Versailles and Paris, 1820-1830), XXI, 41: "Tout discours qui vous laissera froid, qui ne fera qu'amuser votre esprit, et qui ne remuera point vos entrailles, votre coeur, quelque beau qu'il paroisse, ne sera point éloquent." Stevenson translated the omitted clause as "however florid and pompous it may be." Floridity and pomposity do not mean in English what "beau" means in Fénelon's French text. The French text just cited is referred to below as *Dialogues sur L'Éloquence.*

[157] Stevenson, p. 14.   [158] *Ibid.*, p. 72.

stretcheth out the Heavens like a Curtain, and spreadeth them out as a Tent to dwell in.[159]

It would be a disservice to these formulations to represent them in our own time as a mere attempt to make the prejudices, presuppositions, and provincialisms of early eighteenth-century Catholic France appear to have divine authority, universal application, and immutable validity. Instead, we should regard them as formulations based upon the experience that humanity has actually had with human discourse. Thus their validity is to be ascertained in terms of the accuracy with which they reflect what feelings readers and listeners have in the presence of the words of writers and speakers. Fénelon seems to be declaring that, no matter what specific classics a people may choose as their own cultural possessions, their choice will be based in the first instance upon the capacity of those classics to move them, and they will know that such a capacity as this will be linked to the intensity with which those works give readers a passionate and deep vision into what they can accept as the profoundest personal truths about themselves. Thus Fénelon is not merely recommending Demosthenes over Isocrates, or the old over the young Cicero, or Moses over Homer. He is saying rather that any set of classics compiled by any people at any time will be chosen by the principles which have led Western Europe of the eighteenth century to make its choices, and that those principles grow out of the affective power of discourses, and the readiness of that power to become operative upon human beings as they respond to the conditions of truth within discourses and to the conditions of intelligence and feeling within themselves. Stated in these terms, Fénelon's principles of rhetoric are descriptive rather than prescriptive, a posteriori rather than a priori. And it is in these terms that their actual propriety must finally be judged at any time.

We are now in a position to see that the rhetoric created by Fénelon in the *Dialogues Concerning Eloquence* serves not only as a brilliant summary of the enduring principles of classical doctrine, but also as a fine preliminary statement of the new rhetoric of eighteenth-century Britain. As a matter of fact, it belongs on the modern side of four of the six issues separating the old rhet-

[159] *Ibid.*, pp. 151-153.

oric from the new, and the only reason why it is silent on the other two issues is that they were not immediately involved in the subjects which A, B, and C were discussing.[160] A brief comment upon Fénelon's attitude towards these four issues is now in order.

As we have seen already, the *Dialogues Concerning Eloquence* are on the side of modern rhetoric in refusing to limit rhetorical theory to persuasion alone and to the three kinds of speeches anciently considered to be its true central province. It is Fénelon's view instead that persuasion is subordinate to instruction in any final decision upon the question whether a given discourse deserves the title of eloquence, and that instruction is also the dominant aim of truly eloquent discourses which seem bent only upon giving pleasure and delight. When A quoted the complaint of Plato in *Phaedrus* that the greatest fault of rhetoricians was their acceptance of the study of persuasion as something which could be separated from the study of what men should be asked to believe or do, he was in effect saying that the persuasive content of any profoundly moving discourse could be determined only in relation to its instructional substance, and that rhetoricians must pay attention to the latter as the means of providing the former, if they have any concern for literary quality as opposed to literary trash. The same note was sounded over and over again in the *Dialogues Concerning Eloquence*. It was sounded when C in the first dialogue momentarily took A's side against B by remarking, "As for my part, I don't care whether a Preacher's Thoughts be *fine* or not, till I am first satisfied of their being *true*."[161] It was sounded later in the first dialogue when A reminded B of his having already granted that "Instruction is the proper End of Speech,"[162] and when B admitted that in an ideal state orators should be forbidden to speak anything but the truth, and that they should always speak to instruct, to correct mankind, and to strengthen the laws.[163] And it was sounded in the second dialogue when A, confronted by the charge that his emphasis upon the power of discourse to move men seemed to make rhetoric into the art of emotional appeal, proceeded to identify the orator as a philosopher who knew how to demonstrate the truth about his subject in such a way as "to give his accurate Reasoning all the

[160] The two issues not treated by Fénelon concern the modern as distinguished from the ancient view of probability and of inductive reasoning.

[161] Stevenson, p. 8.   [162] *Ibid.*, p. 33.   [163] *Ibid.*, p. 38.

natural Beauty and Vehemence of an agreeable, moving Discourse, to render it intirely eloquent."[164] On that occasion, A went on to define persuasion. B had asked what a hearer could possibly need after he had been fully convinced of the truth of a statement.[165] A replied:

> There is still wanting what an Orator wou'd do more than a Metaphysician, in proving the Existence of God. The Metaphysician wou'd give you a plain Demonstration of it; and stop at the speculative View of that important Truth. But the Orator wou'd further add whatever is proper to excite the most affective Sentiments in your Mind; and make you love that glorious Being whose Existence he had proved. And this is what we call Perswasion.[166]

The examples could be multiplied. But surely the attitude of Fénelon towards the relation of persuasion to instruction needs no further elaboration. Nor does it need to be emphasized that Fénelon, in making rhetoric into the theory of eloquent discourse, and in defining eloquence as truth turned vehement and compelling, expanded rhetorical theory to the point where it embraced not only oratory but poetry. We are not concerned at the moment with the basic weakness of Fénelon's attempt in the *Dialogues Concerning Eloquence* to construct an adequate distinction between rhetorical literature, on the one hand, and the forms of poetry, on the other. That matter has been discussed elsewhere.[167] What needs emphasis here is that Fénelon thought of rhetoric as embracing many types of discourse, and in this respect he was thoroughly in harmony with the developing new rhetoric of the eighteenth century.

He was also in harmony with the new rhetoric in his insistence that the topical machinery of invention could not possibly have a place in discourse intended to have eloquence as its goal. This insistence is a memorable feature of the *Dialogues Concerning Eloquence*. As A finished his comment upon the Platonic and Ciceronian requirement that the orator be a man of great learn-

[164] *Ibid.*, p. 67.
[165] Stevenson's translation erroneously attributes this speech to C.
[166] Stevenson, p. 68.
[167] See my essay, "Oratory and Poetry in Fénelon's Literary Theory," *The Quarterly Journal of Speech*, XXXVII (1951), 1-10.

ing, C turned suddenly into a man of wit and remarked that he had noticed on plenty of occasions a distinct lack of preparation and knowledge on the part of talented speakers. "It even seems," he added, "that they are not speaking because they are overflowing with truths, but that they are seeking for truths because they are overflowing with a desire to speak."[168] This observation, which sharpened its point by taking the form of the figure known as antimetabole, led A to refer to the thin and undernourished speeches of those who had no extensive fund of knowledge behind the ideas which they hurriedly put together for the particular occasion. He went on thus:

> They ought to have imploy'd several Years in laying up a plentiful Store of solid Notions: and then after such a general Preparation, their particular Discourses wou'd cost them but little Pains. Whereas if a Man, without this preparatory Study, lay out all his Application upon particular Subjects, he is forc'd to put off his Hearers with florid Expressions, gaudy Metaphors, and jingling Antitheses. He delivers nothing but indeterminate common-place Notions; and patches together Shreds of Learning and Rhetorick which any one may see were not made one for another. He never goes to the Bottom of Things, but stops in superficial Remarks, and ofttimes in false ones. He is not able to shew Truths in their proper Light, and full Extent; because all general Truths are necessarily connected among themselves: so that one must understand almost all of them, before he can treat judiciously of any one.[169]

That Fénelon had the topics of rhetorical invention in mind when he wrote these words for A to utter is conclusively proved by his French text. Stevenson's sentence saying, "He delivers nothing but indeterminate common-place Notions," is a translation of one in which A said, "on ne traite que des lieux communs,"[170] and the last two words of this latter clause are the technical French terms for the commonplaces or topics of classical rhetoric. After A's use

[168] On this occasion I give my own translation as being more responsive to Fénelon's text than Stevenson's is. Fénelon's text reads (*Dialogues sur L'Éloquence*, p. 38), "il semble même qu'ils ne parlent pas parce qu'ils sont remplis de vérités, mais qu'ils cherchent les vérités à mesure qu'ils veulent parler."

[169] Sevenson, pp. 60-61.

[170] *Dialogues sur L'Éloquence*, p. 39.

of these terms, a brief exchange of remarks occurred between C and A, and then C spoke as follows:

> Your judicious Observation puts me in mind of a Preacher I am acquainted with; who lives, as you say, from hand to mouth; and never thinks of any Subject till he be obliged to treat of it: and then he shuts himself up in his Closet, turns over his Concordance, *Combefix* and *Polyanthea,* his Collections of Sermons; and Common-place Book of separate Sentences and Quotations that he has gather'd together.[171]

And soon after this remark, the first dialogue and the passages devoted to the rhetorical topics came to an end. There is no ambivalence here—no tendency to give the topics a favorable word after these sarcastic disparagements. There is only visible a determination by Fénelon to discard the topics as a sorry substitute for learning, and that determination was as unambiguous as it was modern.

Fénelon turned out to be modern on a third score—that of the theory of rhetorical arrangement. He rejected in explicit terms the six-part oratorical structure of the Ciceronian tradition, and he substituted for it a structure dictated by the requirements of the speaker's subject. His recommendations upon this matter were given a careful exposition in the second dialogue,[172] and an excellent summary as the first dialogue was getting under way. I shall quote only the summary here. It was spoken by A in answer to B's admiring description of the intricate and self-conscious arrangement of the sermon which had started their whole discussion of rhetoric and eloquence. A expressed his distaste for the sermon after B had reconstructed it in terms of its text, its introduction, its transition, its division into three antitheses, its amplification of each antithesis, and its moral and emotional portraiture. The text of the sermon, said A, represented a false application of the Scripture; the introduction told a secular epi-

---

[171] Stevenson, pp. 62-63. Combefix designates François Combéfis, whose *Bibliotheca patrum concionatoria* was a reference book for preachers. The *Polyanthea,* another reference book for preachers and indeed for all authors, was first published at Savona in 1503, its original compiler being Dominicus Nanus Mirabellius. Under his name and that of a succession of four other compilers it was often republished at Continental presses during the sixteenth and seventeenth centuries. See my *Fénelon's Dialogues on Eloquence,* p. 86.

[172] Stevenson, pp. 114-120.

sode in a cold and childish but vain and affected spirit; and the division was contrived and artificial. Upon this latter point, A spoke as follows:

> When one chuses to divide a Sermon, he shou'd do it plainly, and give such a Division as naturally arises from the Subject itself, and gives a Light and just Order to the several Parts; such a Division as may be easily remember'd, and at the same time help to connect and retain the whole; in fine, a Division that shews at once the extent of the Subject, and of all its parts. But, on the contrary, here's a Man who endeavours to dazzle his Hearers, and puts them off with three Points of Wit, or puzzling Riddles, which he turns and plies so dexterously, that they must fancy they saw some Tricks of Legerdemain. Did this Preacher use such a serious grave manner of Address as might make you hope for something useful and important from him?[173]

A remarked later that the organization of sermons by contrivance and artifice, and by elaborate rules prescribing that discourses fall into two or three parts, was not the practice of the Fathers of the Church, nor was it the practice of such classical orators as Isocrates and Cicero. It was instead "a modern Invention which we owe originally to the Scholastick Divines."[174] This attempt by A to place the blame for ritualistic and elaborate rhetorical organization upon the scholastics alone is not historically accurate, for the scholastics had developed their rituals from Cicero's *De Inventione* and the anonymous *Rhetorica ad Herennium*, and thus they had in fact relied not on themselves but on unimpeachable ancient authority. What A should in justice have done was to say that *dispositio* in classical rhetoric was represented by two theories, one of which prescribed simplicity and was authorized by Aristotle's *Rhetoric* and in the main by the mature Cicero, while the other prescribed elaborateness and was the favorite doctrine of the young Cicero and of the schoolmasters of the Greek and Latin tradition. But our present concern is for Fénelon and the new rhetoric, and in this connection it is obvious that A as Fénelon's spokesman was in the camp of the moderns in recommending naturalness and simplicity as the only acceptable basis for the structure of discourse, even as those two

[173] *Ibid.*, p. 9.   [174] *Ibid.*, p. 115.

qualities had also been highly regarded now and then in classical doctrine.

The fourth and final way in which Fénelon's *Dialogues Concerning Eloquence* belong to the new rhetoric is in the field of stylistic theory. Fashionable sermon-making in Fénelon's youth obliged the preacher to phrase his thoughts in the language of the tropes and figures so elaborately treated in Ramistic rhetoric and in the fourth part of the classical Ciceronian system.[175] This obligation meant that good literary style was considered to be a systematic repudiation of the style of ordinary conversation, a trope being by definition a word used outside of its customary orbit, while a figure by definition was a verbal arrangement that violated the patterns of everyday speech. Thus if a speaker sought to praise Hector's bravery in battle by saying that Hector was a lion in the fight, he would be transferring the word "lion" to an unaccustomed human context, so as in one sense to violate customary usage and in another to impress upon the new context a striking value from the old; and this sort of departure from normal speech made up the trope known as metaphor. Or if a speaker, wishing to defend Paris for having chosen the beautiful Helen rather than empire or victory, said of him, as Isocrates did,[176] that he was to be excused for wishing to live with her for whom so many of the demigods would have been content to die, he would be phrasing his thought in a contrived opposition to give Paris's human and mortal choice the qualities of godlike and eternal importance; and this sort of departure from normal patterns of speech made up the figure known as antithesis. It was Fénelon's conviction that the preachers of his time were exploiting the tropes and the figures at the expense of thought and doctrine, and perhaps his chief purpose in writing his *Dialogues Concerning Eloquence* was to reverse this tendency and to summon thought and doctrine back to their rightful place in discourse and in conduct. At the same time, Fénelon was aware that any attempt to exclude the tropes and figures from discourse would be unrealistic and unworkable. Thus his endeavor became that of creating a standard which could be used in differentiating between the right and the wrong kinds of ornament in style.

[175] For details, see my *Fénelon's Dialogues on Eloquence*, pp. 6-36.

[176] For Fénelon's discussion of this passage in Isocrates, see *Dialogues sur L'Éloquence*, p. 74; also Stevenson, pp. 123-124.

His standard, as one would expect, grew out of his conception of the nature of eloquence itself. As I explained above, discourse could be called eloquent in Fénelon's view only when it moved the hearer or reader by convincing him of its truth and by making that truth his passionate concern; and it was this line of thought which gave Fénelon his principle for distinguishing bad ornament from good. Shortly after the beginning of the second dialogue, he had A articulate this principle as follows:

> We have seen [said A] that Eloquence consists not only in giving clear convincing Proofs; but likewise in the Art of moving the Passions. Now in order to move them, we must be able to paint them well; with their various Objects, and Effects. So that I think the whole Art of Oratory may be reduc'd to *proving, painting*, and *raising* the *Passions*. Now all those pretty, sparkling, quaint Thoughts that do not tend to one of these Ends, are only *witty Conceits*.[177]

Later in the second dialogue, Fénelon discussed style as a major subject, and when he did so, he developed still further the thesis that good ornaments were those introduced to give discourse its capacity to persuade men through proof, portraiture, and movement, whereas bad ornaments—the "witty conceits" of the passage just quoted—were introduced with some lesser aim in view. This thesis was in A's mind when, in answer to B's question whether or not any antitheses should be allowed in discourse, he replied:

> Yes: when the Things we speak of are naturally opposite one to another, it may be proper enough to shew their Opposition. Such Antitheses are just, and have a solid Beauty, and a right Application of them is often the most easy and concise manner of explaining Things. But 'tis extremely childish to use artificial Turns and Windings to make Words clash and play one against another. At first, this may happen to dazle those who have no Taste: but they soon grow weary of such a silly Affectation.[178]

The same thesis concerning the basic difference between good and bad ornament was implied in A's praise of the style of Virgil, Homer, and the Bible. Of them he spoke thus:

[177] *Stevenson*, pp. 73-74.   [178] *Ibid.*, p. 126.

When Virgil represents the *Trojan* Fleet leaving the *African* Shore or arriving on the Coast of *Italy*, you see every proper Circumstance exactly describ'd. But we must own that the Greeks enter'd still further into the particular Detail of Things; and follow'd Nature more closely in representing the smallest Circumstances. For which reason, many People wou'd be apt (if they dar'd) to reckon Homer too plain and simple in his Narrations. In this antient beautiful Simplicity, (which few are able to relish,) this Poet very much resembles the Holy Scripture: But in many Places the Sacred Writings surpass his, as much as he excells all the other Antients, in a natural and lively Representation of Things.[179]

This same thesis is deeply involved in what A went on to declare shortly after the words just quoted. In fact, if any single speech in the *Dialogues Concerning Eloquence* can be said to represent Fénelon's entire theory of rhetorical style, the following speech does:

There ought to be a Variety of Stile in every Discourse. We shou'd rise in our Expression when we speak of *lofty* Subjects; and be familiar, on common ones, without being coarse or grovelling. In most Cases, an easy Simplicity and Exactness is sufficient: tho' some Things require Vehemence, and Sublimity. . . . Most of those who aim at making fine Harangues injudiciously labour to cloath all their Thoughts in a pompous gaudy Dress: and they fancy that they have succeeded happily, when they express some general Remarks in a florid lofty Stile. . . . But the Stile of a true Orator has nothing in it that is swelling or ostentatious: he always adapts it to the Subjects he treats of, and the Persons he instructs: and manages it so judiciously that he never aims at being sublime and lofty, but when he ought to be so.[180]

Fénelon's stylistic theory is of course closely parallel to that advocated by the Anti-Ciceronians of the seventeenth century, and it is not antagonistic to the views held by the early members of the Royal Society. I mentioned above that Fénelon's conception of eloquence is akin to Boyle's, and I would recommend, indeed, that Boyle's treatise on the Holy Scriptures and Fénelon's *Dia-*

---

[179] *Ibid.*, p. 129.   [180] *Ibid.*, pp. 130-132.

logues Concerning Eloquence may be read as complementary expositions of the same theory of style. A similar recommendation might be made in regard to the stylistic theories of Fénelon and Sprat. The reader of the first edition of Stevenson's translation notices on three occasions that the translator used quotations from Sprat's *History of the Royal-Society* as glosses upon his version of Fénelon's text, and that the longest of these glosses was that in which Sprat denounced "*these specious* Tropes *and* Figures," and "*this vicious Abundance of* Phrase, *this Trick of* Metaphors, *this Volubility* of Tongue, *which makes so great Noise in the World.*"[181] Thus did Stevenson, himself a clergyman, see the affinities between the stylistic plainness that Sprat wanted the critics to recognize as a literary necessity for the new science and the stylistic restraint that Fénelon wanted the critics to accept as one of the proper marks of literary excellence in general. But even without Stevenson's help, the modern reader would be quick to identify the analogies between Sprat and Fénelon in the domain of style, and he would also be likely to see that Fénelon's theory of rhetorical expression reinforces that of Wilkins, Boyle, Glanvill, and Locke.

During the past two hundred and fifty years the *Dialogues Concerning Eloquence* have been frequently reprinted and widely read throughout the European and American communities. Stevenson's version, which first appeared in 1722, had later editions at Glasgow in 1750 and 1760, at Leeds in 1806, at London in 1808 and 1810, at Boston in 1810, and at various places and times thereafter either by itself or in company with other treatises on preaching.[182] The second English version was published at London in 1847 and 1849; it was the work of Alfred Jenour, like Stevenson a clergyman, and it was called *Hints on Preaching.* Samuel J. Eales, also a clergyman, produced the third English

---

[181] *Ibid.*, p. 30. My quotation follows Stevenson's punctuation. On this occasion, Stevenson quoted 18 lines of Sprat's text; previously (p. 19) he quoted 11 lines, and later (pp. 50-51), 14 lines. In addition, in his translation of Fénelon's *Letter*, he quoted Sprat on three other occasions, for a total of 109 lines (see pp. 201-202, 208-209, 213).

[182] This entire bibliographical account of Fénelon's work depends upon that in Harry Caplan and Henry H. King, "Pulpit Eloquence, A List of Doctrinal and Historical Studies in English," *Speech Monographs*, Vol. XXII, No. 4 (Special Issue, 1955), 27-28. See also my *Fénelon's Dialogues on Eloquence*, pp. 46-52.

version towards the end of the nineteenth century, and it had editions at London in 1896 and 1897. As I mentioned above, I myself did the fourth English version, which came out at Princeton in 1951. A German and a Spanish version were published in the eighteenth century, each having been subsequently reprinted, and a Dutch version appeared at Amsterdam in 1817, as if to remind everyone that the French text had first been published in that city just one hundred years earlier. The French text, I should add, also received many editions in its own country, at least six of which came out in the eighteenth century, and at least thirteen in the century that followed. In Chapter 3 of this present study, we saw that John Ward and John Holmes greatly admired the work, even if it did not succeed in inducing them to omit from their own reconstructions of classical rhetoric what Fénelon felt compelled to omit from his.[183] The value placed upon it by eighteenth-century British readers is reflected not only by the testimony of Ward and Holmes, but also by that of various other Britons, one of whom I shall quote by way of concluding my present account. His name was David Fordyce, and he taught moral philosophy at Marischal College, Aberdeen, for the nine years that preceded his death in 1751. One of his works was structured as a dialogue on eloquence between a man named Theodorus and his two companions, Agoretes and Philonous. At one point in the dialogue, Theodorus, who represents the author himself, spoke as follows:

> But what need I enter farther into the Detail of Pulpit eloquence? If you want to see the whole Machinery and Apparatus of it, displayed in the compleatest Manner, I refer you to the great and good *Prelat* of Cambray's *Dialogues* on that Subject; who was himself the justest Critic, and one of the best Models of Eloquence that I know.[184]

Three of Fénelon's contemporaries and fellow-countrymen also belong to the history of the new rhetoric in eighteenth-century Britain. Unlike Fénelon, their actual writings on rhetoric are not of great intrinsic interest, but it is nevertheless true that their works as a whole must be credited with having given the new

[183] See above, Ch. 3, pp. 93-94, 133.
[184] David Fordyce, *Theodorus: A Dialogue concerning The Art of Preaching* (London, 1752), p. 223.

British rhetoric a novel way in which to characterize its expanding eighteenth-century interests. What these writers did was to create in France and export to Britain a new sort of terminology in which to describe the association between the doctrines of traditional rhetoric, on the one hand, and the production and criticism of literary works of all kinds, on the other; and this development took place at the very time when the new rhetoric was in need of a fresh formulation by which to show that its role in literary endeavors was now much broader than it had been when rhetoric was considered to be only the theory of deliberative, forensic, and epideictic speeches. In more explicit terms, these three French critics made rhetoric an associate of the literary concept called "belles lettres." As a result, when English translations of the works of these critics were published in England, the term "belles lettres" was converted at first into such English phrases as "polite learning," "fine letters," and "fine learning," and later it became a naturalized English term in its own right, so that, when the new rhetoric finally emerged, it could feel free to associate itself with this smart imported phrase and use it to designate its new interests. René Rapin, Dominique Bouhours, and Charles Rollin were the three critics mainly responsible for this outcome, although of course their original French terminology was to be given an English habitation and an English status by the English translators of their works. Let us now examine such of these works as are relevant to the history of the new rhetoric, and let us discuss them in the order in which they were first published in English translations.

Born at Tours in 1621, René Rapin entered the Society of Jesus in 1639 and became a writer of literary criticism and Latin verse after spending nine years as professor of what one of his biographers calls "les belles-lettres et la rhétorique."[185] This particular title may have been conferred upon Rapin's professorship by his biographer rather than by his actual contemporaries, but in either event it describes with great accuracy what the major subjects of his critical writings were to be. When those writings were collected and published together for the first time at Paris in 1684,

---

[185] See *Bibliothèque de la Compagnie de Jésus*, Pt. 1, s.v. Rapin, René. I rely largely upon this source for my bibliographical information about Rapin's French works. See also *Biographie Universelle*, s.v. Rapin, René.

they advertised to the world that Rapin had focused his attentions as critic not only upon eight ancient authors who, in his own words, "have particularly excelled in the belles lettres," but also upon the fields which constituted what he openly called the belles lettres in their four major parts.[186] These four parts were poetry, history, and philosophy, in addition to rhetoric, which Rapin treated first and called eloquence. The eight ancient authors who particularly excelled in these fields were Demosthenes and Cicero for eloquence, Homer and Virgil for poetry, Thucydides and Livy for history, and Plato and Aristotle for philosophy. It is safe to say that these writings of Rapin became greatly influential in establishing belles lettres as a critical concept in European learning, and in making that concept designate not only the chief branches of literature but also the disciplines by which the varieties of literature are brought into being.

In his treatise on Demosthenes and Cicero, which was first published at Paris in 1670 under the title, *Discours sur la Comparaison de l'Éloquence de Démosthène et de Cicéron*, Rapin conducted an investigation into the relative merits of those two great orators, and the interesting thing is that, while being very careful to refuse to pronounce either one the superior of the other, he left no doubt that Cicero was his own favorite. He started his investigation by stating Aristotle's doctrine that persuasion occurs through the credence which the speaker establishes with the listeners, and that the three means by which this credence is built up are derived from the worth of the speaker, the disposition of the hearers, and the manner of procedure in the speech.[187] With these criteria as his guide, Rapin proceeded to speak of his two orators with respect to the persuasive effect of

---

[186] These two volumes bear the following titles: 1) *Les Comparaisons des Grands Hommes de l'Antiquité, qui ont le plus excellé dans les belles Lettres*; 2) *Les Réflexions sur l'Éloquence, la Poétique, l'Histoire, et la Philosophie. Avec le Jugement qu'on doit faire des Auteurs qui se sont signalez, dans ces quatre Parties des belles Lettres*. Both volumes were published at the press of François Muguet. As if to anticipate the time when they would appear under the title, *Les Oeuvres de René Rapin*, the first volume of the 1684 edition was designated "Tome premier," the second, "Tome second." They first appeared as *Les Oeuvres de René Rapin* at Amsterdam in 1693.

[187] *Oeuvres du P. Rapin* (La Haye, 1725), I, 9.

their personalities, of their emotional appeals, and of their procedures in the use of logic, style, and delivery. In discussing them under this third head, Rapin observed that there were in reality two rhetorics, one of the mind and understanding, the other of the heart and will, and that, although the former produced the more lasting effects upon the hearers, it was in reality not true rhetoric but simple instruction, whereas the latter came the closer to being what the art of persuasion ought properly to be.[188] To Rapin, Demosthenes was master of the rhetoric of the mind and understanding, Cicero, of that of the heart and will. Rapin's tendency to believe that appeals to the emotions were somehow more purely rhetorical than were the appeals to logic, and that simple instruction was somehow not a valid rhetoric, constitutes what seems to be the foundation of his preference for Cicero over Demosthenes, and it is the chief reason, of course, for the verdict that he was somewhat at odds with the new rhetoric of his time. Nevertheless, his comparison of Demosthenes to Cicero displays real classical learning and a firm command of the Aristotelian approach to rhetorical criticism. Thus it has genuine merit in its own right, however lacking it may be in the articulation of new attitudes towards rhetorical effectiveness.

The same kind of verdict must be pronounced upon Rapin's treatise upon rhetoric. Published originally at Paris in 1671 under the title, *Réflexions sur l'Usage de l'Éloquence de ce Temps*, this work was later to establish rhetoric as the first of the four parts of the belles lettres in Rapin's final scheme, as I said above, and it was divided so as to contain comments upon rhetoric in general, upon rhetoric at the bar, and upon rhetoric in the pulpit. When it later appeared in the collected editions of Rapin's works, its author explained in a preface what his chief inspirations in this branch of belles lettres had been, and these turn out as safely traditional. Said he on that occasion:

> Of all the subjects which I have to treat in this second volume, there is not one concerning which I would be able to render a more exact account to the public than I can do in this treatise on eloquence: instructed as I am in this matter through such good recollections as those furnished by the Rhetorics of Aristotle, Cicero, and Quintilian, who have treated eloquence so as

[188] *Ibid.*, I, 77-81.

to leave nothing to be desired, so perfect are their works in this field, and so fully have they carried out the idea which they give of it.[189]

These words are not to be taken, however, as a promise that Rapin's treatise on rhetoric is a systematic exposition of the ancient authorities whom he mentions thus admiringly. What he did instead was to offer comment upon various rhetorical subjects connected with each of his three divisions. For example, he discussed eloquence and political freedom, natural endowment and study, true and false eloquence, the value of good delivery, the uses of logic, the varieties of oratorical style, the antinomies between eloquence and the law, the childishness of a reliance upon commonplaces in legal oratory, demonstrative oratory as the third ancient type of oratorical composition, the antinomies between scholasticism and sacred eloquence, the eloquence of the Scriptures, the preacher's own piety and virtue as elements in sermons, and so on. He treated these subjects from the point of view of classical rhetoric, and his observations are sound and useful. At the end of the third part of his treatise, he descended to particulars and praised two recently deceased members of his own religious order, Claude de Lingendes and André Castillon, who merited attention, said he, as "the two most perfect of all the preachers whom I have known in this century."[190] These critiques give his treatise on rhetoric an attractive contemporary dimension, and they invite comparison in this respect with Fénelon's *Dialogues Concerning Eloquence*, which had also evaluated certain preachers of the time.[191] But Fénelon's evaluations, and indeed the whole thrust of his theory of rhetoric, were different from Rapin's in tone and emphasis. To Rapin, perfect eloquence consisted in doing once again what great speakers had done in earning their claim to oratorical distinction. In the case of Claude de Lingendes, this meant that he was praiseworthy in Rapin's

---

[189] *Ibid.*, II, sig. †6r. Translation mine, here and below.

[190] *Ibid.*, II, 80. Lingendes died in 1660, Castillon in 1671, the latter year being that in which Rapin first published his *Réflexions sur l'Eloquence*. As he began his account of these two preachers, Rapin declared that he would not aspire to speak of anyone then living. For additional details concerning Lingendes and Castillon, see under their names in *Bibliothèque de la Compagnie de Jésus*, Pt. 1.

[191] See my *Fénelon's Dialogues on Eloquence*, pp. 98-99.

eyes for his having made full and proper use of all the ethical, emotional, and logical resources of the rhetorical art. In the case of André Castillon, this meant that he appeared to Rapin to command these same resources and to use them in such a way as to make them seem the product not of art but of nature.[192] *Ars oratoriae est celare artem.* To Fénelon, on the other hand, perfect eloquence consisted in moving men to take the side of good over evil, truth over falsehood, beauty over ugliness, altruism over selfishness. The difference between Fénelon and Rapin can be summed up in many ways, but so far as we are presently concerned, it can best be characterized by saying that Rapin held to a standard that reflects traditional conceptions of rhetoric, and Fénelon, to a standard that anticipates what rhetoric was trying to become.

When the collected edition of Rapin's writings was first published in an English translation at London in 1706, it established in learned circles in Britain the idea that the belles lettres had four principal branches and eight pre-eminent authors, so far as the literature of ancient Greece and Rome was concerned.[193] But at that stage in the development of the English language, "belles lettres" was not acceptable as an English term, and thus Rapin's translators, the chief of whom was Basil Kennett, of Corpus Christi College, Oxford, had to render it by equivalent English expressions. A similar problem had not presented itself in 1672 to the translators or rather the paraphrasers who had published at London and at Oxford the earliest English versions of Rapin's treatise on eloquence and his comparative study of Demosthenes and Cicero.[194] At that time these two treatises existed only as sep-

[192] *Oeuvres du P. Rapin,* II, 83.

[193] See *The Whole Critical Works of Monsieur Rapin, In Two Volumes. . . . Newly Translated into English by several Hands* (London, 1706). There was a second edition at London in 1716, and a third at the same place in 1731. On the title page of the latter Basil Kennett "and others" are designated as the translators. One of these others was Thomas Rymer, who translated Rapin's *Réflexions sur la Poetique;* another was T. Taylor, who translated the *Comparaison de Thucydide et de Tite Live.*

[194] For an account of the 1672 Oxford editions of these two translations, see Falconer Madan, *Oxford Books* (Oxford, 1931), III, 270-272. I have examined the 1672 London translation of Rapin's *Réflexions sur l'Usage de l'Éloquence de ce Temps,* a copy of which is in the Princeton University Library. It is entitled *Reflections upon the Eloquence of These Times; Particu-*

arate publications in their original tongue, and Rapin himself had not yet put them under a covering title or a covering preface in which their connection with the whole range of the belles lettres was stressed, as it came to be stressed in the first collected French edition of 1684. In other words, the paraphrasers of 1672 did not have to cope with the term "belles lettres" at all. But Kennett had to cope with it thirty-four years later, for there it was in the title and preface of the French edition that he was using. Kennett proceeded to handle the term by failing to keep it as part of the title of the collection and by making it equivalent elsewhere to such expressions as "fine Letters," "Politeness," "Polite Learning," "Learning," "Knowledge," and "fine Learning."[195] If Kennett's translation of Rapin's preface to the collected edition of his works had been the only means of introducing the English public to the concept of "belles lettres," it is obvious that Kennett would have made the concept familiar enough, but that he could not be credited with having helped to make "belles lettres" itself into an English term. In 1706 the latter development was still in the future.

So far as the adoption of "belles lettres" into the English vocabulary is concerned, the influence of Dominique Bouhours and his English translators is altogether similar to that of Rapin and Basil Kennett. Bouhours, a native Frenchman, was a member of the Society of Jesus from 1644 to the time of his death in 1702. In those fifty-eight years he published a considerable number of books, but only one of them is relevant to my present subject. It came out first at Paris in 1687 under the title, *La Manière de bien Penser dans les Ouvrages d'Esprit*, and its French text was reprinted twenty-four times in the next hundred years, and was translated into English, Latin, and German.[196]

---

larly of the Barr and Pulpit. Its text differs markedly from that done by Kennett in 1706. I have not seen the Oxford editions of 1672.

[195] For these six phrases, see *Works of Monsieur Rapin* (London, 1706), I, sig. b1r, b1v, b2v-3r. Each phrase is a translation of "belles lettres" in the corresponding places in Rapin's preface, which he entitled "Le Dessein de cet Ouvrage en general et en particulier."

[196] See *Bibliothèque de la Compagnie de Jésus*, Pt. 1, s.v. Bouhours, Dominique. The work of Bouhours as critic is discussed by George Saintsbury, *A History of Criticism and Literary Taste in Europe*, 2nd edn. (New York, 1902-

In the "Avertissement" which accompanied the French text of this work, Bouhours explained what he did not intend, and what he did intend, the work to be.[197] He did not intend it, he said, to have any formal or material connection with the work called *The Art of Thinking*, and of course he meant this title to designate what would later become known as *The Port-Royal Logic*. In expanding this theme, Bouhours stressed that his work did not seek to use the method of Aristotle or of Descartes in order to lay down rules governing the three operations of the understanding. In other words, it did not endeavor to teach readers how to conceive simple ideas, how to reason with exactness, or how to form correct judgments in the affairs of daily life or in familiar, ordinary discourses. What it did, rather, was to seek to show its readers how to form correct judgments in matters concerning eloquence and the belles lettres. Not only did Bouhours use at this point the French words "l'éloquence" and "belles Lettres"; he also went on to comment that by them he meant works of genius in the fields of history, poetry, and oratory.[198] And he said next that he proposed to use the form of a dialogue rather than that of a treatise in order to demonstrate how correct judgments in these fields could be made.

> For the rest [he added], although this work does not treat things in the method of the schools, and although it does not profess to teach the oratorical art, it still could be called, so far as its thoughts are concerned, a thornless logic, neither dry nor abstract, and even more, a short and easy rhetoric, which instructs rather by examples than by precepts, and which has scarcely any other rule than that of lively and sparkling good sense. . . .[199]

Needless to say, these promises were fully kept by Bouhours in the work which unfolded beyond this "Avertissement." The work consists of four dialogues between two participants named Eudoxe and Philanthe. Dialogue 1 deals with false and true

---

1904), II, 315-316; by George Williamson, *Senecan Amble*, pp. 197-198, 240, 265, 362-363; and by E. B. O. Borgerhoff, *The Freedom of French Classicism* (Princeton, 1950), pp. 192-193, et passim.

[197] See *La Manière de bien Penser dans les Ouvrages d'Esprit* (Paris, 1715), pp. iii-viii.

[198] *Ibid.*, p. iv.   [199] *Ibid.*, p. vi. Translation mine.

thoughts and with the nature of the difference between them. Dialogue II deals with sublimity, agreeableness, and delicacy as three traits which must accompany truthfulness if thoughts are to succeed in achieving literary distinction. Dialogue III identifies bombast, affectation, and subtlety as three traits which prevent truthfulness from reaching literary excellence, bombast being mistaken sublimity, affectation, mistaken agreeableness, and subtlety, mistaken delicacy. Dialogue IV postulates that, in addition to truthfulness, sublimity, and agreeableness, a great literary work must have plainness, clarity, and intelligibility in its style. And these various topics are everywhere discussed in relation to the historical writings, the oratory, and the poetry of ancient Greece and Rome, and of modern France, Italy, and Spain. Eudoxe is an ardent defender of the ancients, his particular heroes being Cicero, Virgil, Livy, and Horace, and his taste being centered in a love for the reasonable and the natural in works of genius. On the other hand, Philanthe does not value the Greeks and the Romans as much as he does Lope de Vega and Tasso, and the literary qualities which delight him most are those connected with flowery decoration and sparkle.[200] Eudoxe, the spokesman for Bouhours, gradually overcomes Philanthe in the course of their four-day argument, and the work ends as the latter, fully committed to the cause of "le bon sens," goes home resolved to proclaim himself henceforth the foe of false wit in literature.[201]

The four dialogues between Eudoxe and Philanthe were published in an English translation at London in 1705 under the title, *The Art of Criticism: or, The Method Of making a Right Judgment Upon Subjects of Wit and Learning*. It was entirely appropriate, of course, that the translation should be called *The Art of Criticism*, although no French text of the work ever authorized the addition of that phrase to Bouhours's title. In two other respects, however, the translation is a disappointment to the historian of English rhetoric. First of all, the translator is identified merely as "a Person of Quality," and thus his work does not help in establishing who he was or what other interests he had. And secondly, by failing to translate the "Avertissement" which prefaces Bouhours's French text, he made it impossible for English readers to be aware of Bouhours's conception of the relation of

---

[200] *Ibid.*, p. 2.   [201] *Ibid.*, p. 526.

the work to rhetoric, to logic, and to the belles lettres, and he made it impossible for us to know how he would have converted the term "belles lettres" into English. In the latter connection, it is most unlikely that in 1705 any English author would have used the French term as an English phrase. He would more probably have rendered it into "polite learning" or "fine letters," as Basil Kennett was doing at that very time. The first recorded use of "belles lettres" as an English term, according to *A New English Dictionary*, is that by Jonathan Swift in *Tatler*, No. 230, on September 28, 1710, when Swift, in protesting against fads in current writing, spoke thus: "I say nothing here of those who handle particular Sciences, Divinity, Law, Physick, and the like; I mean the Traders in History and Politicks, and the *Belles Lettres*."[202] The "Person of Quality" who translated Bouhours in 1705 cannot be expected to rival Swift in the matter of the enrichment of the English vocabulary, but it would have been interesting, even so, to know whether he would have anticipated the conservative usage of Kennett or the liberal usage of Swift in respect to the treatment which "belles lettres" might at that time have received at his hands.

The complaints just recorded against the first English translation of Bouhours's *Manière de bien Penser dans les Ouvrages d'Esprit* do not apply to the second translation, which appeared at London in 1728 under the title, *The Arts of Logick and Rhetorick, Illustrated By Examples taken out of the best Authors, Antient and Modern, In all the Polite Languages. Interpreted and Explain'd By that Learned and Judicious Critick, Father Bouhours. To which are added, Parallel Quotations Out of the Most Eminent English Authors in Verse and Prose*. This book, which the translator acknowledged to be less of a translation than a paraphrase,[203] was the work of John Oldmixon, his name being appended not to the title page but to the letter which dedicated the book to George Dodington, Esq., Lord Lieutenant of the County of Somerset. Oldmixon changed things so as to eliminate the fiction that the doctrines set forth by Bouhours had been uttered in the course of four dialogues between Eudoxe and Philanthe, but

---

[202] For the text of this quotation as I give it here, see *The Prose Works of Jonathan Swift*, ed. by Herbert Davis (Oxford, 1939-1959), II, 174. Swift's text is printed in italics, with "Belles Lettres" in roman.

[203] *The Arts of Logick and Rhetorick* (London, 1728), p. xix.

he preserved the four-part structure and the basic content of his source. What interests us particularly at present about his paraphrase of Bouhours, however, is that, in presenting Bouhours's "Avertissement," he not only translated "belles lettres" into "polite Learning," and specified that this phrase embraced works of history, poetry, and eloquence, but he also suggested that his own title was dictated by what Bouhours had said when he called his original work a discourse on "both the Arts of *Logick* and *Rhetorick*."[204] Moreover, by adding copious English illustrations to those given by Bouhours in French, Italian, Latin, and Spanish, and by speaking words of blame or praise for English writers, Oldmixon gave the arts of logic and rhetoric a central place in the study and criticism of the literature of his own land. He implied, in fact, that he could appropriately call a book *The Arts of Logick and Rhetorick*, while using it to introduce English readers to a favorable or unfavorable appraisal of such of their own poets and dramatists as Spenser, Shakespeare, Milton, Dryden, Pope, Cowley, Congreve, Addison, Prior, and Waller, to such of their own satirists as Swift, to such of their own preachers as Tillotson, to such of their own historians as Echard, and to such of their own philosophers as Bacon, Hobbes, and Locke. By putting rhetoric in this kind of framework, Oldmixon was helping to prepare the way for its later emergence in England as the acknowledged custodian of the belles lettres, and herein lies his only contribution to our present history.

Charles Rollin, classical scholar, historian, and one-time rector of the University of Paris, resembles Rapin and Bouhours in having writtten works on rhetoric and the belles lettres, and in having had those works translated into English. But Rollin's translator did something which had not been done either by Kennett in his work with Rapin or by Oldmixon in his work with Bouhours—he made "belles lettres" into an officially recognized English term. This development will now receive brief notice.

So far as we are presently concerned, Rollin's chief literary effort was a set of treatises on literary studies, published at Paris in four volumes between 1726 and 1728, and called *De la Manière d'Enseigner et d'Etudier les Belles Lettres, par rapport à*

---

[204] *Ibid.*, p. 3.

l'esprit et au coeur.[205] To Rollin, the belles lettres embraced the study of the Greek, the Latin, and the French languages, the study of poetry, the study of rhetoric, the study of sacred and secular history, and the study of philosophy as the regulator of morals, the perfectioner of reason, the custodian of curious knowledges, and the inspirer of respect for religion. The first of Rollin's four volumes upon these subjects was given over to his treatises on languages and on poetry; the second, to his treatise on rhetoric; the third and part of the fourth, to his treatise on history; and another part of the fourth, to his treatise on philosophy. The final three hundred pages of that fourth volume contained a dissertation by Rollin on the internal government of colleges and on the responsibilities of administrative officers, teachers, parents, and students to the educational enterprise itself. Rollin was later to publish in thirteen volumes between 1731 and 1738 a major work on ancient history, called *Histoire Ancienne*, and between 1738 and 1741, he was to contribute nine volumes to a sixteen-volume work called *Histoire Romaine*. Thus it is not strange that, in his treatise on the belles lettres, he gave more attention to history than to any other field of literature. As for the other four parts of the belles lettres, he bestowed the largest amount of attention upon rhetoric, and that, too, is not strange, since Rollin was professor of eloquence at the Royal College when his work on the belles lettres was published, and some years earlier he had published a Latin edition of Quintilian's *Institutio Oratoria.*[206] With these and his other credentials, he would be accepted, of course, as an authoritative spokesman for everything that concerned the academic side of literary studies.

In the volume which he devoted to what he himself called "La

[205] The Princeton University Library has John Witherspoon's copy of the "Seconde Edition" of the first two volumes of this work, and of the first edition of volumes three and four. My discussion of the French text is based on this copy, each volume of which bears the following imprint: "A Paris, Chez Jacques Estienne, rue saint Jacques, à la Vertu. M.DCC.XXVIII. Avec Approbation & Privilege du Roy." The title page of each volume identifies Rollin as "ancien Recteur de l'Université, Professeur d'Eloquence au college Roial, & associé à l'Academie Roiale des Inscriptions & Belles Lettres."

[206] See *M. Fabii Quintiliani Institutionum Oratoriarum Libri Duodecim ad usum scholarum accomodati* (Paris, 1715). In 1717, also at Paris, Rollin brought out a small work called *Praeceptiones Rhetoricae*, which I have not seen.

Rhétorique," Rollin divided his subject into three major chapters, one of which set forth precepts, another of which discussed
composition, and the third and longest of which treated in five
large sections the problems connected with the study and explication of authors. In the first of these large sections, Rollin analyzed
the plain, the sublime, and the intermediate oratorical styles.
Then, in a very long section, he spoke on seven separate subjects
connected with reading and explication, these being reasoning
and proofs, content, choice of words, arrangement of words,
figures of words and thoughts, oratorical precautions, and verbal
appeals to the passions. Finally, in the three concluding sections,
Rollin spoke successively of the eloquence of the bar, the eloquence of the pulpit, and the eloquence of the sacred Scriptures.
His chief authority for the theory of the sublime style was Longinus.[207] In his treatment of the eloquence of the pulpit, he referred
on numerous occasions to St. Augustine's *De Doctrina Christiana*
and on one occasion to Fénelon's *Dialogues Concerning Eloquence*, which he pronounced excellent in its rules for preaching.[208] His admiration for Cicero's oratory led him, as he discussed the rhetoric of the bar, to quote a long passage devoted by
René Rapin to the praise of that orator and to question whether
Fénelon was representative of French taste when he placed the
eloquence of Cicero below that of Demosthenes.[209] Once in his
discussion of the sublime, and often as he spoke of the content of
compositions, he quoted Bouhours by way of developing his own
views.[210] But it must be emphasized above all that Rollin's treatise
on rhetoric owes almost everything to Quintilian and Cicero. This
debt can be detected everywhere in Rollin's doctrine, and he of
course made no secret of it. He repeatedly adorned his pages
with footnotes containing Latin quotations from Cicero's *De Oratore, Orator*, and *Brutus*, and from Quintilian's *Institutio Oratoria*. And his quotations from Quintilian outnumber those from
Cicero in a ratio of sixteen to ten.

Rollin's entire work on literary studies was published in a four-
volume English translation at London in March, 1734, under the

---

[207] *De la Manière d'Enseigner et d'Etudier les Belles Lettres* (Paris, 1728),
II, 5, 11, 100-114, 179.

[208] *Ibid.*, pp. 459-463, 469, 472-479, 483, 495, 497-499, 504, 525-527, 534 (for
references to *De Doctrina Christiana*); pp. 531-532, for reference to Fénelon.

[209] *Ibid.*, pp. 389-395. [210] *Ibid.*, pp. 109, 173-212.

title, *The Method of Teaching and Studying the Belles Lettres, or An Introduction to Languages, Poetry, Rhetoric, History, Moral Philosophy, Physicks, &c.*[211] In 1737 at the same place the translation came out in a second edition, and in 1810 an eleventh edition appeared. The British Museum holds a copy of a third edition at London in 1742, and the Bibliothèque Nationale, a copy of a third edition at Edinburgh in 1759.

So far as the rhetorical doctrine in the second volume of this translation is concerned, British learning of the middle years of the eighteenth century would not have found it novel or ingenious. After all, John Ward's lectures at Gresham College were being repeated year after year in that era. Not only were they better than Rollin's second volume, if one wanted nothing beyond a patient, sound, and comprehensive understanding of the rhetorical system of Cicero and Quintilian, but also they were available to the reading public after 1759 and thus were in the reach of anybody interested in that subject. Nevertheless, Rollin's translator did something which Ward failed to do, and that, at least, proved to be helpful to the new rhetoric.

Here is a brief account of what he did. In 1736, two years after the date of the first edition of his translation of Rollin's treatise on the belles lettres, there appeared at London the second edition of a famous English lexicon, Nathan Bailey's *Dictionarium Britannicum*. In it, for the first time in the history of English lexicography, "belles lettres" was listed as an English term. Moreover, the new term was defined on that occasion as "Literature, the Knowledges of Languages and Sciences also." There had been no entry at all for "belles lettres" in the *Dictionarium Britannicum* when it appeared in its first edition in 1730. Nor had there been any entry for it in Bailey's lexicon when that work appeared in 1721, 1724, 1726, 1727, 1728, 1731, or 1733 under its alternate title, *An Universal Etymological English Dictionary*. In other words, Bailey's lexicon did not recognize the term "belles lettres" before 1734, and in 1736 it made it part of the English vocabulary. Moreover, Bailey and his fellow compilers did not define the term in 1736 as Basil Kennett had defined it in 1706, when he trans-

---

[211] See "Register of Books publish'd in March 1734," in *The Gentleman's Magazine*, IV (1734), 167. The translator has not been identified. There is a copy of the first edition of this translation at the British Museum.

lated it in six different ways, or as John Oldmixon had defined it in 1728, when he used one of Kennett's terms to show its meaning. Instead, Bailey's compilers defined the term as an expression for the kinds of literature and for the knowledge of languages and science. Who can doubt that the crucial factor in the listing of "belles lettres" in 1736 under this quite unexpected definition was the appearance of the translation of Rollin's treatise on the belles lettres in 1734? Consider what the translation did. It treated "belles lettres" as an English term. It gave this term high visibility as part of its title. It established this term as a generalized word for an entity made up of languages, poetry, rhetoric, history, moral philosophy, and physics. It coined this generalized word at a time when the English vocabulary had no single native word or phrase for that particular entity, as Kennett and Oldmixon had both shown. And it offered collateral evidence from its title page that this term issued from the highest circles of French learning. Under these circumstances, it appears highly unlikely that Bailey and the other compilers of the second edition of the *Dictionarium Britannicum* sought any authority but the translation of Rollin's treatise on the belles lettres when they decided in 1736 to make this term English and to define it as they did.

Once "belles lettres" was accepted by British learning as a word for the kinds of literature and for the disciplines that create literature, it rapidly gained popularity in academic circles, and its popularity was particularly in evidence in Scotland. Indeed, well before the publication of the English translation of Rollin, the term "belles lettres" was occasionally used by British writers as a foreign expression to give smartness and style to something they wanted to say. We have already seen one instance of this practice in Swift's *Tatler* in 1710. But there were other instances. When, at the end of the second decade of the eighteenth century, Charles Mackie became the first professor of history at the University of Edinburgh, his official title being "Professor of Universal Civil History," he decided to enlarge that already enormous academic field of effort by including in his lectures some account of the history of literature and science. One result of this innovation was that a student of his, Robert Duncan, in a letter sent from abroad in 1724, addressed him as "Professor of History and

Belles Lettres."[212] Another result was that a friend of Mackie named John Mitchell wrote to him in 1726 to say among other things that he was "exceeding glad that the *Belles Lettres* meet with so good entertainment with you."[213] But after Bailey's *Dictionarium Britannicum* in 1736 had recognized "belles lettres" as an English term, and successive editions of the English translation of Rollin had accustomed British readers to its use, there was a gradual increase in the frequency of its appearances in speech and print. In 1755, when Dr. Samuel Johnson's *A Dictionary of the English Language* appeared in its first edition, "Belles Lettres" was one of its entries. Not only did Dr. Johnson define it as "Polite literature," but he quoted a passage from *Tatler* to show how it was used.[214] Sometime around 1755 or 1756, one of the student societies at the University of Edinburgh was known as the Belles Lettres Society, and it was designed to afford its members an opportunity to improve themselves in knowledge and in public speaking.[215] In 1761 John Miller's translation of Charles Batteux's *Cours de Belles-Lettres* appeared at London under the title *A Course of the Belles Lettres: or the Principles of Literature*. Between 1761 and 1764, a club called The Belles-Lettres Society flourished in Edinburgh, with Hugh Blair one of its members.[216] A royal document dated April 27, 1762, conferred upon that same Hugh Blair the title of "Regius Professor of Rhetoric and Belles Lettres" at the University of Edinburgh. In this connection it is interesting to notice that, when Blair was originally appointed to his professorship by the Town Council of Edinburgh on June 27, 1760, his post was designated simply as that of "Professor of Rhet-

[212] See L. W. Sharp, "Charles Mackie, the First Professor of History at Edinburgh University," *The Scottish Historical Review*, XLI (1962), 29. Cited below as Sharp. For the actual date of Duncan's letter, see *Historical Manuscripts Commission. Report on the Laing Manuscripts Preserved in the University of Edinburgh*, II (London, 1925), 215-216.

[213] Sharp, p. 29.

[214] In Bailey's *An Universal Etymological English Dictionary* as published at London in 1751, "Belle-Lettres" [*sic*] is defined as "Polite Literature." It was this definition that Dr. Johnson used four years later. In Bailey's *Dictionary* as published at London in 1755, "Belles Lettres" is defined as "Polite literature, the knowledge of languages and sciences." This definition reverts in part to that given in the *Dictionarium Britannicum* for 1736.

[215] See *Transactions of the Royal Society of Edinburgh*, I (1788), 49.

[216] See R. M. Schmitz, *Hugh Blair* (New York, 1948), p. 25.

orick."[217] Jean Henri Samuel Formey's *Principes Élémentaires des Belles-Lettres*, first published at Berlin in 1758, was brought out in Sloper Foreman's English translation at London in 1766 and at Glasgow in 1767 under the title *Elementary Principles of the Belles Lettres*. Then, of course, in 1783 at London Hugh Blair published in two volumes his *Lectures on Rhetoric and Belles Lettres*, which will be discussed later in this chapter. The great popularity of Blair's work in England and America did more than anything else to fix the association between rhetoric and the belles lettres and to give both of these terms a reference to all the forms of discourse—orations, historical works, philosophical treatises and dialogues, epistles, fiction, pastoral poems, lyric poems, didactic poems, biblical writings, epic poems, tragedies, and comedies. Moreover, during the late seventeen-seventies, as Blair's lectures at Edinburgh were steadily gaining in celebrity, William Barron became professor of logic at another Scottish university, St. Andrews, and after his death in 1803, his academic lectures, published at London in 1806 in two volumes with the title *Lectures on Belles Lettres and Logic*, gave one more proof of the popularity of "belles lettres" as a collective term for the types of literature, and added the reminder that logic as well as rhetoric was by tradition a theory of literary composition and thus could still claim in its reminiscent moments to be the custodian of the actual literature created and explained by its ancient principles.

[217] *Ibid.*, pp. 62-63. See also *University of Edinburgh Charters, Statutes, and Acts of the Town Council and the Senatus 1583-1858*, ed. Alexander Morgan (Edinburgh, 1937), p. 177.

Adam Smith's Lectures at Edinburgh and Glasgow

Before the summer of 1958, historians of eighteenth-century British rhetoric were unable to connect Adam Smith with the drastic changes that took place in rhetorical theory in Britain during the 1700's. They knew that Smith delivered a course of lectures on rhetoric in Edinburgh during the fall and winter of 1748-49, and that, according to some authorities, he repeated those lectures at the same place and during the same seasons in 1749-50 and 1750-51.[218] They also knew that Smith continued to deliver those lectures, or revisions of them, as part of his duties as professor of logic and later as professor of moral philosophy at the University of Glasgow from October, 1751, to December, 1763. But Smith's biographers had made it clear to everyone that, as he saw death draw near, he gave orders to have all his papers destroyed, except for some which he judged ready for publication, and that two of his friends accordingly burned sixteen volumes of his manuscripts, the lectures on rhetoric among them.[219] That event has been a source of frustration for all students of Smith's influential career, but it was particularly damaging to the attempt of historians of British rhetoric to evaluate in any substantial way what Smith may have contributed to their subject. They were to have no choice, it appeared, but to confine themselves to what Smith's contemporaries had said about his rhetorical theory, and to leave unanswered the question of his connection with the changes which that theory was undergoing in his lifetime.

Unsatisfactory as that situation was, it seemed upon examination to fall short of being completely hopeless. Three unusually well-qualified witnesses among Smith's contemporaries had taken pains to make written comments upon his lectures on rhetoric,

---

[218] See Tytler, I, 266; also John Rae, *Life of Adam Smith* (London, 1895), pp. 30, 36. William Robert Scott, *Adam Smith as Student and Professor* (Glasgow, 1937), pp. 50-54, considered Smith's lectures in 1750-51 to be on jurisprudence instead of rhetoric, but, of course, Smith might have given both of these sets of lectures in that last year at Edinburgh.

The whole of my present discussion of Adam Smith's theory of rhetoric appeared originally as an article in *Speech Monographs*, XXXVI (1969), 393-418.

[219] Rae, pp. 32, 434. See also Francis W. Hirst, *Adam Smith* (New York, 1904), p. 19.

and their testimony was readily available to all scholars. Those three contemporaries were John Millar, James Wodrow, and Hugh Blair. What they had to say does not lack interest for any of the connections in which Smith's life could be viewed. But to all with my present interests, those three witnesses made a shadowy matter emerge in some semblance of outline.

John Millar heard Smith's original lectures on rhetoric in Edinburgh, and he heard them again during Smith's first year at Glasgow. After Smith's death in 1790, Millar gave Dugald Stewart his impressions of the Glasgow lectures, and Stewart incorporated them into his "Account of the Life and Writings of Adam Smith, LL.D.," which he read at meetings of the Royal Society of Edinburgh on January 21 and March 18, 1793. Here are some of Millar's observations:

> In the Professorship of Logic, to which Mr Smith was appointed on his first introduction into this University, he soon saw the necessity of departing widely from the plan that had been followed by his predecessors, and of directing the attention of his pupils to studies of a more interesting and useful nature than the logic and metaphysics of the schools. Accordingly, after exhibiting a general view of the powers of the mind, and explaining so much of the ancient logic as was requisite to gratify curiosity with respect to an artificial method of reasoning, which had once occupied the universal attention of the learned, he dedicated all the rest of his time to the delivery of a system of rhetoric and belles lettres. The best method of explaining and illustrating the various powers of the human mind, the most useful part of metaphysics, arises from an examination of the several ways of communicating our thoughts by speech, and from an attention to the principles of those literary compositions, which contribute to persuasion or entertainment. . . .
>
> It is much to be regretted, that the manuscript containing Mr Smith's lectures on this subject was destroyed before his death. The first part, in point of composition, was highly finished; and the whole discovered strong marks of taste and original genius. From the permission given to students of taking notes, many observations and opinions contained in these lectures, have either been detailed in separate dissertations, or ingrossed in

general collections, which have since been given to the public. But these, as might be expected, have lost the air of originality and the distinctive character which they received from their first author, and are often obscured by that multiplicity of common-place matter in which they are sunk and involved.[220]

Millar's judgment of Smith's lectures is not unlike James Wodrow's. Wodrow was serving as Library Keeper at the University of Glasgow when Smith went there to be professor of logic. In a letter written sometime after 1776 to the Earl of Buchan, Wodrow spoke thus with Smith's lectures on rhetoric at Glasgow in mind:

> Adam Smith delivered a set of admirable lectures on language (not as a grammarian but as a rhetorician) on the different kinds of characteristics of style suited to different subjects, simple, nervous, etc., the structure, the natural order, the proper arrangement of the different members of the sentence etc. He characterized the style and the genius of some of the best of the ancient writers and poets, but especially historians, Thucydides, Polybius etc. translating long passages of them, also the style of the best English classics, Lord Clarendon, Addison, Swift, Pope, etc.; and, though his own didactic style in his last famous book (however suited to the subject)—the style of the former book was much superior—was certainly not a model for good writing, yet his remarks and rules given in the lectures I speak of, were the result of a fine taste and sound judgment, well calculated to be exceedingly useful to young composers, so that I have often regretted that some part of them has never been published.[221]

As for Hugh Blair, he, like Millar, heard Smith's original lectures on rhetoric in Edinburgh, and, like Millar and Wodrow, he made a comment upon the content of the manuscript from which the lectures issued. His comment appeared first in 1783 in the ear-

[220] *Transactions of the Royal Society of Edinburgh*, Vol. III, Pt. I (Edinburgh, 1794), pp. 61-62. Tytler, I, 267, listed Millar among those who attended Smith's original lectures on rhetoric in Edinburgh.

[221] Scott, pp. 51-52. Wodrow's reference to Smith's "last famous book" dates his letter after the publication in 1776 of *The Wealth of Nations*. The "former book" mentioned by Wodrow is *The Theory of Moral Sentiments*, which brought earlier fame to Smith when it was published at London in 1759.

liest edition of his own *Lectures on Rhetoric and Belles Lettres* in a footnote connected with his discussion of the plain style.

> On this head, of the General Characters of Style, particularly, the Plain and the Simple [remarked Blair], and the characters of those English authors who are classed under them, in this, and the following Lecture, several ideas have been taken from a manuscript treatise on rhetoric, part of which was shewn to me, many years ago, by the learned and ingenious Author, Dr. Adam Smith; and which, it is hoped, will be given by him to the Public.[222]

These testimonials are useful as a sketch of the content and value of Smith's lectures on rhetoric, even if they are so generalized as to prevent us from judging whether Smith's approach was definitely antitraditional. But they certainly do not suggest that the lectures were unimportant. Nevertheless, Francis Hirst spoke disparagingly of them in his book on Smith in the series devoted to English men of letters. After noting that the manuscript of these lectures was destroyed shortly before Smith's death, Hirst loftily concluded that "the world is probably not much the poorer."[223] These words are particularly unimaginative in the light of Hirst's own lively account of the way in which a student notebook containing a transcript of Smith's other lectures at Glasgow in 1762-63 on the subject of justice, police, revenue, and arms had been recovered from an attic in 1876 by Charles Maconochie and published at Oxford in 1896 under the editorship of Edwin Cannan, after having been regarded for more than a century as casualties of Smith's request in 1790 that his manuscripts be burned.[224] If the recovery and publication of that notebook were instruments, as Hirst jubilantly declared them to have been, in disposing of the legend "that Adam Smith was little more than a borrower from the French school, a mere reflector of the Reflexions of Turgot,"[225] might not Hirst have deemed it possible that the discovery of a student notebook containing a transcript

---

[222] (London, 1783), I, 381. (Cited here and below in the facsimile reprint edited by Harold F. Harding and published in 1965 by Southern Illinois University Press.) Tytler, I, 267, listed Blair as a member of Smith's audience when the lectures on rhetoric were first delivered in Edinburgh. See also Schmitz, p. 20.

[223] Hirst, p. 19.   [224] *Ibid.*, pp. 68-71.   [225] *Ibid.*, p. 71.

of Smith's lectures on rhetoric could become instruments in disposing of the legend that Smith's opinions on this subject were almost worthless?

At any rate, that possibility existed, and it became a reality as the year 1958 was advancing from summer to autumn. The scholar responsible for bringing this reality about was John M. Lothian, Reader in English in the University of Aberdeen, and one-time Professor of English Literature in the University of Saskatchewan. In the newspaper, *The Scotsman*, for Wednesday, November 1, 1961, under the headline, "Long-Lost MSS. of Adam Smith / Literature lectures found in Aberdeen," Lothian announced his discovery of a notebook containing a student's transcript of Adam Smith's lectures on rhetoric. Here is part of what Lothian wrote on that occasion:

> It was with a kind of solemn jubilation that I realised, in the late summer of 1958, that certain volumes of manuscripts, which I had purchased at the sale of books from a manor house in Aberdeenshire, were indeed the long-lost lectures on Rhetoric and Belles-Lettres of the great Adam Smith, which his friends had frequently urged him to publish and which he had been so resolutely determined to destroy.

In that article in *The Scotsman*, Lothian also announced the discovery of another student notebook containing a more detailed transcript of the lectures which Cannan had edited in 1896 from the notebook recovered by Maconochie; and he indicated that his findings as a whole made a very considerable addition to the known corpus of Smith's writings. "Between 70 and 80 thousand words of Adam Smith's hitherto unknown lectures on literature," he declared, "and about 170,000 of a new version of his views on the philosophy of history, law, and economics, had suddenly become available for the student and the scholar, and would certainly be put to use by all those in any way interested in the man and his period." Jacob Viner has calculated that this new version of Smith's lectures on philosophy, law, and economics contains "substantially over 50 per cent more matter" than did the version edited by Cannan.[226] But its discovery, even so, is not likely to

[226] See his "Guide to John Rae's *Life of Adam Smith*," p. 11, published as the Introduction to the facsimile reprint (New York, 1965) of the 1895 edition of Rae's *Life*.

yield richer results than those which we can expect from Lothian's discovery of a really substantial version of Smith's lectures on rhetoric.

Lothian himself as the first scholar to put this latter discovery to use achieved mixed results. In 1963 he brought out an excellent edition of Smith's lectures on rhetoric as they were recorded in the transcript which a student in the University of Glasgow had presumably made when he heard Smith deliver them in the academic year 1762-63.[227] But Lothian's attempt in the introduction to that edition to evaluate Smith's contribution to rhetorical theory fell considerably short of success. So far as it supplies an account of the Scottish milieu in which Smith's lectures were delivered, it performs a necessary service for scholars interested in Smith's life and for historians concerned with British rhetoric. But it gives no adequate insight into the nature and quality of Smith's work with rhetorical theory. If Lothian had interpreted Smith's lectures as the outcome of immediately previous developments in British rhetoric and logic, he would have seen that a new view of rhetoric had been gaining headway in Britain in the century before 1748, thanks to such effective critics of the old rhetoric as Boyle, Sprat, and Locke; and he would have been forced to conclude that Adam Smith's lectures gave that new rhetoric its earliest and most independent expression. A judgment of this kind could not have been substantiated at any time before 1958, but it can be substantiated now, and Lothian, who edited the materials on which it rests, was not aware that it should be pronounced.[228]

My present purpose being to set forth the facts which support this judgment, I shall proceed first to clarify the relation of Smith's lectures to his own life and to the cultural life of Scotland.

[227] Lothian's work is entitled, *Lectures on Rhetoric and Belles Lettres Delivered in the University of Glasgow by Adam Smith Reported by a Student in 1762-63* (London, 1963). I cite the Introduction and Notes as Lothian, and the text of the work as Adam Smith.

[228] For three other appraisals of Smith's lectures on rhetoric, see Vincent M. Bevilacqua, "Adam Smith's Lectures on Rhetoric and Belles Lettres," *Studies in Scottish Literature*, III (1965-66), 41-60; also Frank Morgan, Jr., "Adam Smith and Belles Lettres," (unpubl. diss., The University of Mississippi, 1966), described in *Dissertation Abstracts*, Vol. XXVII, No. 11, 3846-A; also Vincent M. Bevilacqua, "Adam Smith and Some Philosophical Origins of Eighteenth-Century Rhetorical Theory," *The Modern Language Review*, LXIII (1968), 559-568.

Smith entered the University of Glasgow in 1737 at the age of fourteen and graduated with great distinction as master of arts in 1740.[229] For the next six years he held the Snell Fellowship at Oxford, where he was a member of Balliol College, his studies being mainly in the field of Greek, Latin, French, Italian, and English literature.[230] His future plans as of that time could have been deduced from the terms of the Snell Fellowship—it required its Scottish beneficiaries to prepare at Oxford to take orders in the Church of England under the solemn promise that they would later become practicing clergymen only in Scotland.[231] But something caused Smith to change those plans and to return to Scotland in 1746 with at least four years of his Fellowship still unexpended.

From 1746 to 1748 he lived quietly with his mother at Kirkcaldy, thinking no doubt that he would one day acquire a professorship in a Scottish university or gain employment as tutor and traveling companion of a nobleman's son.[232] In that period he made the acquaintance of Henry Home, who in 1752 would become Lord Kames. Kames had visions of creating in Scotland a growing community of speakers and writers of distinguished and correct English, and he was so far successful on the literary side of this aspiration as to have Adam Smith say later of the famous Scottish authors of the generation to which Smith himself belonged that "we must every one of us acknowledge Kames for our master."[233] It was Kames who, having been made aware of Smith's six-year residence at Oxford and of his accomplishments in ancient and modern literature, proposed that Smith deliver a course of public lectures in English on rhetoric and belles lettres for the benefit of any interested students at the University of Edinburgh and for the improvement of literary taste among any subscribing citizens of the surrounding city. Lectures on literary subjects were of course being delivered regularly at that time in the University, and John Stevenson, whom I mentioned above as an early Scottish disciple of Locke and as the teacher of Dugald Stewart, made literary subjects a part of his academic course in logic, as Smith was later to do at Glasgow, and William Barron

[229] Scott, pp. 36, 136-137, 392. [230] Rae, pp. 22-24; Scott, pp. 40, 42.
[231] Scott, pp. 42-43. [232] Rae, p. 30.
[233] Tytler, I, 218, 219-266.

at St. Andrews.[234] But Stevenson's lectures were not available to the townsmen of Edinburgh, and besides, like most academic discourses of that time and place, they were pronounced in Latin.[235] Thus to Kames they would probably not have been considered competitors of the English lectures which would be needed if Scotland were to become the center of correct English speech and style. At any rate, Kames, in association with James Oswald and Robert Craigie, two other friends of Smith, joined in urging Smith to deliver a course of public lectures on rhetoric and belles lettres, and he yielded to their solicitations.[236]

His lectures were accordingly delivered in the late fall and winter of 1748-49, as I said above; and they were probably not held at a location within the University, as Rae thought, but at the quarters of the Philosophical Society of Edinburgh.[237] This Society, which had been founded in 1731, and which numbered Kames among its members, did not hold regular meetings during the years in which Smith delivered his Edinburgh lectures, and thus its quarters would have been open to such events as the lectures represented.[238] Students of law like John Millar, lawyers and sponsors of an improved English speech like Kames and Alexander Wedderburn, students of theology and rising young preachers like Hugh Blair, present and future members of parliament like James Oswald and William Johnstone, and various other groups interested in matters of literary taste and fashion, made up the audience of some hundred or more persons to whom Smith lectured that first year.[239] His discourses were a financial and literary success, and he repeated them during the fall and winter of one and possibly both of the two following years.

They contributed to his own career by leading directly to his

[234] For an account of Stevenson's academic course at Edinburgh, see above, Ch. 5, p. 273.

[235] Bower, *The History of the University of Edinburgh*, II, 275. See also Thomas Somerville, *My Own Life and Times 1741-1814* (Edinburgh, 1861), pp. 12-14.

[236] Scott, p. 48.

[237] Scott, pp. 49-50. Also see Rae, p. 32.

[238] Tytler, I, 256-259. This Society grew into The Royal Society of Edinburgh.

[239] Tytler, I, 266-267; Rae, p. 32; Scott, p. 46. For an account of Wedderburn's efforts to improve his own English pronunciation, see above, Ch. 4, pp. 157-159.

appointment in 1751 to the professorship of logic and in 1752 to the professorship of moral philosophy at Glasgow, these two positions being flexible enough to allow him to continue his lectures on rhetoric and belles lettres in connection with the subjects which his academic titles would require him to teach. But they also contributed a new institution to the cultural life of Edinburgh. That is to say, they led to Robert Watson's being named to continue the public lectures on rhetoric after Smith departed for Glasgow, and to Hugh Blair's assignment to the same duties after Watson departed for St. Andrews.[240] And they led as well to Hugh Blair's later appointment as Professor of Rhetoric and then as Regius Professor of Rhetoric and Belles Lettres at the University of Edinburgh. In other words, after having been instituted as a course of extra-academic lectures in English on the subject of rhetoric, they so far proved their value as to lead the University to give a place in its curriculum within a few years to what had grown out of them. And when this new development was taking place, John Stevenson is said to have protested against it on the ground that Hugh Blair was usurping a function that had long been performed within his own course in logic.[241] His complaint had some foundation, of course. But in 1760 he himself was sixty-five years old, and the educational reforms which he had introduced as a youth were becoming obsolete. Thus his case against Blair would hardly have been strong enough to carry the day, and carry the day it did not.

Even though Lothian's edition of the student notebook brings us much closer to Smith's actual accomplishments as a rhetorician than we have ever been before, we must keep in mind that it does not enable us to speak with finality of this part of his career or even to be sure that a given opinion ascribed to him in the notebook is beyond question his. Here are the difficulties. First, there is a possibility that our student will have distorted Smith's opinions by condensation or will have made errors in hearing and recording what Smith said. Secondly, there is a possibility that our student would have turned his notes over to an unknown copyist, and that what Lothian edited is not what the student heard and recorded, but what the copyist found implied in the student's notes. Thirdly, there is a possibility that the notebook

---

[240] Tytler, I, 272-275; also Schmitz, pp. 62-63.
[241] *The Scots Magazine*, LXIV (1802), 22.

will be occasionally misinterpreted by a modern scholar seeking to make it suitable for publication. And lastly, there is a possibility that a course of lectures pronounced in any given year of a professor's academic career will be lower in quality than that course in earlier or later years, and that Smith's lectures in his penultimate year at Glasgow may not have represented him at his best.[242] But when we have acknowledged that each of these limitations may weaken our evaluations of his rhetorical theory to an unknown and incalculable degree, we still have to try to make them anyway, recognizing as we must that Smith was a man of real genius, that he actually lectured on rhetoric, that his contemporaries were impressed by his lectures, and that at last we do have access to a substantial and no doubt largely accurate version of what he said. Under these circumstances we shall proceed to pass judgment upon Smith's theory of rhetoric as best we can, and to see whether he made as large a contribution to the development of the new rhetoric as I just now said he did.

One important statement should be made once more about these particular lectures: Smith intended them, not as discourses on ancient and modern literature, but as discourses to expound a system of rhetoric. He himself made this point clear as he was lecturing on the tropes and figures. After taking the grammarians to task for arguing that these contrivances of language are the cause of any stylistic beauty that a literary work may have, Smith spoke as follows:

> It is, however, from the consideration of these figures, and divisions and sub-divisions of them, that so many systems of rhetoric, both ancient and modern, have been formed. They are generally a very silly set of books and not at all instructive. However, as it would be reckoned strange in a system of rhetoric entirely to pass by these figures that have so much exercised the wits of men, we shall offer a few observations on them, though not on the same plan as the ordinary writers proceed on.[243]

[242] For a most thoughtful analysis of the problems confronting Lothian in his edition of Smith's *Lectures on Rhetoric and Belles Lettres*, see Ernest C. Mossner's review of that work in *Studies in Scottish Literature*, II (1964-65), 199-208.

[243] Adam Smith, pp. 23-24.

The significance of these words is that they add Smith's own authority to that of Millar, Wodrow, and Blair in identifying rhetoric as the subject of his lectures.

In the twentieth century, rhetoric has so far lost its respectability as to be thought an unseemly study for a first-rate mind. Accordingly, Smith's modern admirers have often felt constrained to retitle the lectures under consideration here. Thus Rae and Hirst spoke of Smith's first discourses at Edinburgh as "lectures on English literature."[244] Thus Scott said that "the subjects of the Edinburgh lectures may be taken, at least provisionally, to have been two courses on Literature and Literary Criticism, followed by a final course on Jurisprudence."[245] Thus Lothian, who as a rule uses "rhetoric" to characterize the subject of these lectures, and who says that the two volumes of the notebook containing them "carried on the spine of each volume in neat hand-writing the inscription, 'Notes of Dr. Smith's Rhetorick Lectures,' " nevertheless refers in his article in *The Scotsman* to "Adam Smith's hitherto unknown lectures on literature," and on another occasion he quotes Smith's remark that elaborate treatises on the figures are silly and not at all instructive, but he omits that part of the passage in which Smith identifies his own subject as rhetoric.[246] Thus finally Ernest C. Mossner, in his review of Lothian's edition, says that " 'Dr. Smith's Rhetorick Lectures,' as they were called by the copyist, might with some justice be called Lectures *against* Rhetoric, taking rhetoric as the ancient logic of multiplicity of divisions and subdivisions."[247]

But despite modern opinions to the contrary, the historian of rhetoric is forced to insist that the tradition of a respectable and learned rhetoric flourished in the 1700's, and that Smith not only identified himself with it but also through his efforts sought to bring it into partnership with the needs of his own day. His "anti-rhetoric" is therefore not in truth the opposite of rhetoric, but the very essence of rhetoric as he conceived of it in its modern form.

One other important thing has now to be said about Smith's lectures: he brought rhetoric and belles lettres together, not in line with the plan of previous writers like Rapin, Bouhours, and Rollin, but on a plan quite his own.

[244] See Rae, p. 36; Hirst, p. 19.   [245] Scott, p. 51.
[246] See Lothian, pp. xii, xxxii.
[247] *Studies in Scottish Literature*, II (1964-65), 206.

As we have seen, Rapin conceived of rhetoric as that branch of the belles lettres which taught how to compose traditional orations or how to judge the classical orations of such masters as Cicero and Demosthenes; and in his view, rhetoric is what it had been in the systems of Aristotle and the major Latin rhetoricians.

Bouhours considered logic and rhetoric to be the disciplines associated with the composition and criticism of all literary works, with logic the guide to thought, and rhetoric, to style. This position, of course, is vaguely Ramistic, although Bouhours hardly did more than suggest to the initiated that Ramus's way of separating logic from rhetoric was an influence upon him.

As for Rollin, he regarded rhetoric as one of the five components of the belles lettres, its purpose being the preparation of students for careers at the bar or in the pulpit, and its means, the study of the precepts of classical rhetoric, the assiduous practice of composition, and the thorough mastery of literary works renowned for eloquence. In other words, he, like Rapin, was essentially an eighteenth-century Ciceronian, even if he especially admired Cicero's disciple, Quintilian.

And what of Adam Smith? Well, his system of rhetoric and belles lettres differs in at least two ways from those just mentioned. First, he made rhetoric the general theory of all branches of literature—the historical, the poetical, the didactic or scientific, and the oratorical. And secondly, he constructed that general theory, not by adopting in a reverential spirit the entire rhetorical doctrine of Aristotle, or Quintilian, or Ramus, but by selecting from previous rhetorics what he considered valid for his own generation, and by adding fresh insights of his own whenever he saw the need to do so. As a result of these two innovations, his system of rhetoric is on the one hand more comprehensive and on the other hand more independent than are those of his French predecessors.

Lothian is right in observing that Smith's lectures on rhetoric "were the first of their kind, as far as we know, to be given in Great Britain."[248] But he errs when he qualifies this observation by adding, "though something similar had been given by Rollin in the University of Paris." Rollin's lectures at Paris have their parallel in Great Britain, not in Adam Smith's lectures at Glas-

[248] Lothian, p. xxiii.

gow, but in John Ward's lectures at Gresham College. Like Rollin, Ward was dedicated to the rhetoric of Cicero and Quintilian. But Adam Smith, as I said earlier, was dedicated to the rhetoric of Boyle, Sprat, and Locke. Between his outlook and that of Rollin were the differences which divide the modern from the ancient rhetoric. And those differences become fully visible for the first time in the history of rhetorical theory when we study Adam Smith's rhetoric in detail and see how far he was justified in saying that he was not following "the same plan as the ordinary writers proceed on." Let us now inspect the extraordinary plan that he chose to follow instead.

In that course at Glasgow in 1762-63, Smith delivered thirty lectures on rhetoric and belles lettres. The first lecture is unhappily not recorded in our student's notebook, and therefore in undertaking to assign terms to the major subjects discussed in the series as a whole, we cannot take advantage of any hints that Smith's introductory discourse would have made in this direction. The other twenty-nine lectures, however, may reasonably be said to fall under one or the other of two heads of doctrine. We could give titles to these heads by using the terms proposed for them by Millar, but in the interests of brevity and precision I propose that we use the term "communication" and the term "forms of discourse" to identify them. To the subject of communication Smith devoted ten lectures, and to that of the forms of discourse, nineteen. As we proceed to discuss the lectures dealing with each of these subjects, what I said a moment ago will become increasingly clear. In other words, it will be seen that Smith was not attempting to look at rhetoric through the eyes of Aristotle, Cicero, and Quintilian, although he could have expounded their doctrine adequately if he had wanted to do so. What he did instead was to see rhetoric not only as the theoretical instrument for the communication of ideas in the world which Locke had done so much to render intelligible to itself, but also as the study of the structure and function of all the discourses which ideas produce as they seek passage from person to person and from age to age. If Adam Smith drew his rhetorical system from the past, he drew it from the past which is always seeking to prepare for the future rather than from the past which is always seeking to preserve itself against change.

The ten lectures devoted by Smith to the first of his major subjects make two significant points about rhetoric. One is that communication is the fundamental process that rhetoric studies. The ancients had made persuasion the goal of rhetorical discourse, and Smith did not set out to quarrel openly with that particular way of formulating the end sought by oratory and its companion forms of literary composition. But he proceeded instead to stress repeatedly that discourse takes place in order to transfer ideas and attitudes from speaker to audience. Thus his system of rhetoric takes the position that persuasive discourse is the species, and communicative discourse the genus, in the classification of the functions of literature, and that persuasion is to be understood more properly as a subordinate than as a generic function, if rhetoric is to achieve its true status among the learned disciplines. The other significant point made by Smith in the ten lectures is that the only acceptable modern style for a rhetoric committed to the goal of communication is the plain style. John Locke would have particularly approved of this point and of the one which defined rhetoric in terms of its communicative function. Indeed, Locke himself made analogous points about the art of speaking, as we know from the passage which I quoted above.[249] Let us now turn to Smith's ten lectures in order to see how far he develops these two points as continuing themes. We shall find, however, that he develops them, not as separate propositions, but as different aspects of the same proposition.

In the second, and again in the sixth, the seventh, the eighth, and the eleventh lectures, Smith took pains to state and repeat the doctrine that discourses have communication as their main function and plainness of style as their chief means. He introduced this doctrine in connection with his discussion of such other subjects as perspicuity, the tropes and figures of speech, and the practices of modern English authors.[250] Perhaps his best statement of the doctrine occurred in his sixth lecture, as he was preparing to treat the tropes and figures, those immensely popular ingredients of traditional rhetoric. As he approached them, he observed that they came into being whenever "an expression is used in a different way from the common."[251] By this he meant,

[249] See above, p. 500.

[250] See the following passages of Lothian's edition: pp. 4 (lines 25-29), 22 (lines 26 ff.), 29 (lines 10-15), 36 (lines 1-8), and 51 (lines 1-8).

[251] *Ibid.*, p. 24.

of course, that the tropes and figures are so many repudiations of the ordinary ways of saying things; they are examples of the plain style in reverse. Recalling that the traditional rhetoricians like Cicero and Quintilian had found in these figures "all the beauties of language, all that is noble, grand, and sublime, all that is passionate, tender, and moving," Smith offered the following comment:

> But the case is far otherwise. When the sentiment of the speaker is expressed in a neat, clear, plain, and clever manner, and the passion or affection he is poss[ess]ed of and intends, *by sympathy*, to communicate to his hearer, is plainly and cleverly hit off, then and then only the expression has all the force and beauty that language can give it. It matters not the least whether the figures of speech are introduced or not.[252]

At this point, our student's notebook has an insertion which contains an alternative statement of the passage just cited, as if Smith had said it in one way in one year, and in another way in another year, with the result that our student had access to two versions of it and chose to include both to emphasize the importance that Smith attached to the doctrine involved. The insertion reads as follows:

> When your language expresses perspicuously and neatly your meaning and what you would express, together with the sentiment or affection this matter inspires you with, and when the sentiment is nobler and more beautiful than such as are commonly met with, then your language has all the beauty it can have, and the figures of speech contribute or can contribute towards it only so far as they happen to be the just and natural forms of expressing that sentiment.[253]

Still another form of this doctrine concerning the communicative function of discourse and the consequent necessity of plainness in style occurs in the eighth lecture, and on this occasion both sides of the doctrine are stressed once more, as they were in the earlier of the two passages, just quoted.

> Having in the foregoing lecture made some observations on tropes and figures [said Smith], and endeavoured to show that

[252] *Ibid.*, pp. 22-23. (The bracketed syllable is Lothian's.)
[253] *Ibid.*, p. 23.

it was not in their use, as the ancient rhetoricians imagined, that the beauties of style consisted, I pointed out what it was that really gave beauty to style, that when the words neatly and properly expressed the thing to be described, and conveyed the sentiment the author entertained of it and desired to communicate to his hearers, then the expression had all the beauty language was capable of bestowing on it.[254]

And in the eleventh lecture, Smith once again laid stress upon the communicative function and the plain style of rhetoric, as he was about to enter upon his analysis of the second of the two major heads of his rhetorical system. He said:

In some of our former lectures we have given a character of some of the best English prose writers, and made comparisons betwixt their different manners. The result of all which, as well as the rules we have laid down, is that the perfection of style consists in express[ing] in the most concise, proper, and precise manner the thought of the author, and that in the manner which best conveys the sentiment, passion, or affection with which it affects—or he pretends it does affect—him, and which he designs to communicate to his reader. This, you'll say, is no more than common sense: and indeed it is no more. But if you will attend to it, all the rules of criticism and morality, when traced to their foundation, turn out to be some principles of common sense which every one assents to: all the business of those arts is to apply these rules to the different subjects, and shew what the conclusion is when they are so applied.[255]

As these words indicate, comparative comments upon English prose writers were a continuing feature of Smith's first eleven lectures. It is now time to observe that those comments enabled Smith to establish Swift as the still unappreciated but nevertheless fully qualified master of the best modern style, and to establish Lord Shaftesbury as a prime example of the writer who, though widely admired, was in fact a representative of outworn stylistic conventions. In his eighth lecture, Smith first dwelt in detail upon the differences between these two writers, although he made frequent mention of both on earlier and later occasions.

[254] *Ibid.,* p. 36.
[255] *Ibid.,* p. 51. (The bracketed syllable is Lothian's.)

The eighth lecture immediately followed those in which Smith had discussed the figures of speech and had vigorously asserted that these devices, founded as they were upon the notion that good literary style must involve a systematic repudiation of the ways of common speech, should not in fact be regarded as the indispensable conditions of stylistic beauty. With that denial fresh in his students' minds, Smith applied it to the literary fashions of their own day, and he made it obvious to his hearers that the current admiration for Shaftesbury and the current disrespect for Swift merely equated stylistic beauty with figurative language and with very little else. Here are a few of his observations on these subjects:

> We in this country are most of us very sensible that the perfection of language is very different from that we commonly speak in. The idea we form of a good style is almost contrary to that which we generally hear. Hence it is that we conceive the further one's style is removed from the common manner, it is so much nearer to purity and the perfection we have in view. Shaftesbury, who keeps at a vast distance from the language we commonly meet with, is for this reason universally admired. . . . Swift, on the other hand, who is the plainest as well as the most proper and precise of all the English writers, is despised as nothing out of the common road; each of us thinks he would have wrote as well. And our thoughts of the language give us the same idea of the substance of his writings.[256]

Smith went on to emphasize, however, that Swift was the exemplar of the modern and Shaftesbury of the outmoded style, not simply because the one avoided and the other adopted the tropes and figures, but because the one was profoundly and the other superficially learned. This point emerges only when we probe more deeply than we have done hitherto into the great contrast which Smith drew between these two writers. Shortly after he expressed the sentiments just quoted, Smith laid down the rule that a good writer must meet the following conditions: "first, that he have a complete knowledge of his subjects; secondly, that he should arrange all the parts of his subject in their proper order; thirdly, that he paint [or] describe the ideas he has of them several in the most proper and expressive manner—this is the art of

[256] *Ibid.*, p. 38.

painting or imitation (at least we may call it so)."[257] Then he stressed at once that Swift met these three criteria beyond question. He spoke thus in this connection:

> Now we will find that Swift has attained all these perfections. All his words shew a complete knowledge of his subject. He does not, indeed, introduce anything foreign to his subject, in order to display his knowledge . . . ; but then he never omits anything necessary. . . . One who has such a complete knowledge of what he treats will naturally arrange it in the most proper order. This we see Swift always does. . . . That he paints but each thought in the best and most proper manner, and with the greatest strength of colouring, must be visible to anyone at first sight.[258]

In direct contrast to his view of Swift, Smith emphasized later that Shaftesbury's greatest defect consisted in his failure to meet the first of these three criteria. In the eleventh lecture, Smith subjected Shaftesbury to a penetrating analysis, and therein the theme recurs several times that Shaftesbury's style stems from his feeling of insecurity about his own learning. Smith mentioned that Locke was Shaftesbury's tutor, but that Shaftesbury preferred rather to follow his own whims than to master the metaphysical profundities of his preceptor. Thus Shaftesbury cultivated the fine arts, spoke with some show but with no true distinction in both Houses of Parliament, indulged himself in the pleasures of the imagination, allowed the delicacy of his sentiments to alienate him from his bent towards Puritanism, found Hobbes and the scholastics almost equally disagreeable, and finally embraced Platonism as the main guide to what he hoped to establish as the best modern philosophy.[259] At the same time, however, Smith went on, Shaftesbury found "abstract reasoning and deep searches" too fatiguing for his delicate frame.[260] Natural philosophy he did not seem "to have been at all acquainted with" —indeed he showed "a great ignorance of the advances it had then made, and a contempt for its followers," no doubt because "it did not afford the amusement his disposition required, and the mathematical part particularly required more attention and abstract thought than men of his weakly habit are generally capa-

[257] *Ibid.*, p. 38. (The bracketed word is Lothian's.)
[258] *Ibid.*, pp. 38-39.   [259] *Ibid.*, pp. 52-54.   [260] *Ibid.*, p. 52.

ble of."[261] And, after having arranged this balance sheet of Shaftesbury's liabilities and assets, Smith drew a very revealing conclusion, which deserves to be identified as a reflection of the dislike of the new rhetoric for superficiality of subject matter and the ornate style as its necessary concomitant. He spoke thus of Shaftesbury as he was preparing to take leave of the themes of his first eleven lectures: "As he was of no great depth in reasoning, he would be glad to set off by the ornament of language what was deficient in matter. This, with the refinement of his temper, directed [him] to make choice of a pompous, grand, and ornate style."[262]

In his twelfth lecture, as he took up the discussion of the forms of discourse, Smith proposed that every written composition intends either to relate some fact or to prove some proposition, in connection with its basic communicative function; and that, as a result, discourses must have one of three forms. The first form, which emerges from the attempt to relate facts, he decided to call narrative discourse. The two other forms he decided to call didactic discourse and rhetorical discourse, although on another occasion he was to change his mind and call the latter form the oratorical.[263] Didactic discourse, he said, emerges from the attempt to prove a proposition when proof can be accomplished by putting both sides of a question before an audience, and by giving each side its true degree of influence. Rhetorical or oratorical discourse emerges from the attempt to prove a proposition when proof can be accomplished only by magnifying one side and by diminishing or concealing the other. Didactic discourse seeks conviction, rhetorical discourse, persuasion. Smith clarified this distinction thus:

> Persuasion, which is the primary design in the rhetorical, is but the secondary design in the didactic. It endeavours to persuade us only so far as the strength of the argument is convincing: instruction is the main end. For the other, persuasion is the main design, and instruction is considered only so far as it is subservient to persuasion, and no further.[264]

[261] *Ibid.*, p. 53.
[262] *Ibid.*, p. 54. (The bracketed word is Lothian's.)
[263] *Ibid.*, pp. 58, 124.   [264] *Ibid.*, p. 58.

At this point Smith paused to comment upon the analogy between his three forms of discourse and the three forms of ancient oratory. But he developed the analogy in such indefinite terms as to lead us to suppose that the student's notebook may not here be an accurate guide to what he actually had in mind.[265] It seems obvious, from his final nineteen lectures as a whole, that his classification of discourses, so far as he had thus far permitted it to emerge, is like the ancient classification of orations more by reason of its threefold structure than by reason of its actual contents and intentions. I mean that Smith intended narrative discourse to cover historical writings, and didactic discourse to cover philosophical argument and scientific exposition, while oratorical discourse was limited to deliberative, forensic, and demonstrative oratory in its ancient and modern forms. Thus rhetoric, as he was thinking of it in the twelfth lecture, was the theory of all kinds of nonpoetical discourse. In fact, if we were to attempt to develop an analogy between his theory and its parallels in the ancient world, we would have to say that his rhetoric embraced what ancient rhetoric and dialectic were designed together to embrace, and what they had indeed continued to embrace during the middle ages and the early Renaissance.

As his lectures proceeded, Smith widened his conception of the forms of discourse so that it included poetic compositions. Thus rhetoric became for him what the ancients had treated as the three disciplines of rhetoric, dialectic, and poetics. This development occurred in his twenty-first lecture. He had just finished his discussion of narrative discourse, and didactic discourse should by rights have been his next subject. But he was arrested by the thought that historical narratives and poetical narratives had much in common, and that the rules governing the historian and biographer often applied to the poet, too. For what is it that makes up the essential differences between history and historical poetry? "It is no more than this," he declared, "that the one is in prose, and the other in verse."[266] His momentary preoccupation with this difference led Smith to say that poetical compositions were designed not to relate facts and not of course to prove propositions but rather to afford pleasure and entertainment.[267] Thus it turned out that his nineteen final lectures dealt with three kinds of communication—instruction, persuasion, and entertain-

[265] *Ibid.*, pp. 59-60.   [266] *Ibid.*, p. 113.   [267] *Ibid.*, pp. 113-114.

ment, and with four resulting forms of discourse—history, poetry, didactic writing, and oratory. And it turned out, too, as these concepts were substituted for those of traditional rhetorical theory, that rhetoric for the first time measured itself against the needs of the modern world and became fully and triumphantly responsive to those needs. Nothing quite like this had ever happened to rhetoric before.

To historical discourse Smith devoted nine lectures, and he made this part of his discussion unfold under five heads.[268] Thus he spoke first of the kind of facts that entered historical narration, and he proceeded next to comment upon the historian's manner of narration, his methods of arranging his work, and his style of writing. Finally he spoke of ancient and modern historians. As a rhetorician seeking to make a distinctively rhetorical contribution to the work of any future historian among his hearers, Smith aimed his discussion of these five heads at the problems involved in the literary presentation of historical materials. For example, in respect to the methods of arranging an historical work, he said that, "In general, the narration is to be carried on in the same order as that in which the events themselves happened."[269] But this rule should not be followed if the historian is tracing a series of events in one locality and a simultaneous series in another locality. The best method here would be to narrate those events "that happened in the same place for some considerable succession of time, without interrupting the thread of the narration by introducing those that happened in a different place."[270] And in addition to considerations of time and space as determinants in the ordering of a work of history, Smith recommended also that the order of cause and effect is often highly successful. As for historical style, Smith discussed it also with reference to the problems of future historians. In fact, he succeeded in making this part of his discussion helpful alike to young historians and orators:

> An historian, as well as an orator, may excite our love or esteem for the persons he treats of: but then the methods they take are very different. The rhetorician will not barely set forth the character of a person as it really existed, but will magnify every particular that may tend to excite the strongest emotions in us. He will also seem to be deeply affected with that affection

[268] *Ibid.*, pp. 59-112.   [269] *Ibid.*, p. 93.   [270] *Ibid.*, p. 93.

which he would have us feel towards any object. . . . The historian, on the contrary, can only excite our affection by the narration of the facts and setting them in as interesting a view as he possibly can. But all exclamations in his own person would not suit with the impartiality he is to maintain and the design he is to have in view, of narrating facts as they are, without magnifying them or diminishing them.[271]

Under his fifth head, Smith discussed in some detail the ancient and modern historical classics, and this subject occupied him for two lectures. He had spoken earlier of the design of historical writing, and had said then that the historian's aim as an author consisted, not in seeking to entertain the reader, as an epic poet might desire to do, but rather in seeking to offer him instruction, so that mankind, by coming to know the more interesting and important events of human life, and by coming to understand what caused them, could learn the means by which good effects might be produced and evil effects avoided in human affairs.[272] This definition of the historian's design became one of Smith's themes when he discussed the historical classics. In fact, he said that Thucydides was the first historian to recognize this aim as the proper goal of historical authorship. Thucydides tells us, Smith remarked, of his having undertaken his history of the Peloponnesian War so that, "by recording in the truest manner the various incidents of that war, and the causes that produced [it], posterity may learn how to produce the like events or shun others, and know what is to be expected from such and such circumstances."[273] "In this design," Smith added, "he has succeeded better perhaps than any preceding or succeeding writer." Smith went on, however, to pay his respects to other distinguished historians of antiquity—Herodotus, Xenophon, Caesar, Polybius, Livy, and Tacitus. As for the moderns, he thought that Machiavelli surpassed Guicciardini among the Italians, and indeed that Machiavelli surpassed all the moderns in having dedicated himself in the true spirit of history "to relate events and connect them with their causes, without becoming a party on either side."[274] And Smith proceeded next to observe that Britain's two leading historians, Clarendon and Burnet, did not measure up to Machia-

271 *Ibid.*, p. 96.   272 *Ibid.*, p. 85.
273 *Ibid.*, p. 102. (The bracketed word is Lothian's.)
274 *Ibid.*, pp. 110-111.

velli's standard, inasmuch as both of them had written not to present the facts but to praise or denounce parties.[275]

In a brief concluding paragraph of his second lecture on the great historians, Smith remarked that Paul de Rapin-Thoyras' *L'Histoire d'Angleterre* was the most candid of all historical accounts of England, but that Rapin had been guilty of entering too much into the private lives of monarchs and too little into the affairs of the body of the people.[276] Lothian tells us in a footnote that our student's notebook contains in the margin against this reference to Rapin an annotation reading, "10 years ago. A better now," and he indicates without comment that the first volume of what came to be called David Hume's *History of England* had appeared in 1754, and the last volume in 1762.[277] It seems obvious, indeed, that the student's marginal annotation refers to Hume's *History*. But, if the annotation came from the student and not from something Smith said in the lecture that day in January, 1763, it suggests that Smith did not change his lectures from year to year, and that his reference to Rapin rather than to Hume helps to attach the date of composition of this lecture, and perhaps of many of the others, to the period in which he first delivered them in Edinburgh.[278] At that time, the earliest installment of Hume's *History* was six years in the future, and Rapin's *L'Histoire d'Angleterre*, which very probably figured in Smith's wide reading in history and literature at Oxford, had appeared almost a quarter of a century before.

Poetical composition, the second of the four forms of discourse involved in Smith's system of rhetoric, was treated in a single lecture, the twenty-first in the series, and it was placed immediately before didactic and oratorical and immediately after historical composition by virtue of the narrative element which it shared with history. As we have seen, Smith considered that history, didactic discourse, and oratory were designed to produce a composite effect upon mankind, and that the ingredients of this effect

---

[275] *Ibid.*, pp. 111-112. [276] *Ibid.*, p. 112.

[277] See Jessop, pp. 28-30.

[278] See Lothian, pp. xii, xvii, for evidence to show that Smith's lectures on rhetoric at Glasgow were repetitions of those presented in Edinburgh. But not all evidence points in that direction. For example, Smith's twenty-first lecture ends with a reference to Gray's "Elegy written in a Country Church-Yard," first published on February 15, 1751, when the Edinburgh lectures had probably just ended.

entitled it on some occasions to be called instruction, on other occasions, conviction, and on still other occasions, persuasion, according as the author's purpose required him to be a neutral expositor or an active advocate. Moreover, these forms of discourse were bound by their mission to a common set of resources. That is to say, they were to confine themselves to facts and actualities; they were to keep to prose as their natural medium of communication; they were to reconcile themselves to their own inherent inability ever to arouse the highest degree of attention or the deepest degree of feeling in an audience; they were always to seek to achieve a full measure of unity of thought; and they were to establish their separate identities by calling themselves histories, or philosophical dissertations, or scientific treatises, or orations, in proportion as they found themselves differing from each other in respect to natural gradations in their content and aim. But poetical compositions, in Smith's critical philosophy, were set apart from all other writings by virtue of their having a special function of their own—that of affording mankind pleasure or entertainment. As the means to this end, poetical compositions were to exercise license in inventing their stories; they were to choose to express themselves in verse that would delight the ear; they were to take special pride in their inherent ability to surpass the other forms of discourse in beauty, strength, and conciseness; they were always to seek to achieve propriety in character portrayal and unity of interest, time, and place; and they were to establish their separate identities by calling themselves tragedies, comedies, epics, odes, elegies, or pastorals, in recognition of the differences that inhere in changes from the mood of grief to that of laughter, from the technique of direct presentation to that of narrative, and from a subject involving many events to that involving only a single action. These distinctions and terms form the outline of the single lecture devoted by Smith to poetical compositions.[279] A further analysis of that lecture can hardly be undertaken here. But as we take leave of it, we should remember that it has presented us with the opportunity of seeing the new rhetoric undertake to present the theory of poetical literature as one of the natural responsiblities of rhetoric in its endeavor to make itself into a general theory of discourse for the modern world.

[279] Adam Smith, pp. 113-123.

As I said earlier, Smith intended to treat didactic composition immediately after he had finished the last of his nine lectures on the writing of history, but he suspended that plan in order to deliver a single lecture on poetry instead. When the latter discourse had been pronounced, and didactic composition had again emerged for consideration, he disappointingly remarked that, since its rules were very obvious, he would pass them over so as to allow himself to give his attention at once to the forms of oratory.[280] In line with this new plan, he devoted his next two lectures to demonstrative or epideictic eloquence, and he seemed now to be bent upon continuing in this vein until deliberative and judicial eloquence had also been covered. In fact, it appeared quite possible that he had decided to omit didactic composition altogether from his system of rhetoric in line with his earlier remark that its rules could be easily deduced from what had been said of historical composition.[281] Such a decision would have meant that the earliest British treatise on the new rhetoric was to fail to bring within its jurisdiction what had formerly been the property of dialectic. It would also have meant, of course, that didactic composition, which was already being rejected as an object of doctrinal concern by the new logic, had not yet been declared eligible for admission within the new rhetoric and so was drifting along by itself without any affiliation whatever with its traditional associates in the enterprise of communication. Fortunately, however, Smith's decision to forego the discussion of didactic composition did not prove final. In fact, he openly revoked it at the beginning of his twenty-fourth lecture, and what he then said upon didactic composition gave rhetorical theory a refreshing new dimension.

Didactic composition has two aims, said Smith in the course of that twenty-fourth lecture: it seeks to prove a proposition to an audience that needs only to be convinced; or it seeks to deliver a system of science to the community of learning.[282] Thus in its rhetorical aspect it must provide doctrine that looks towards the effective literary presentation of philosophical argument or scientific knowledge. In other words, rhetoric at this point interests itself in discourse addressed to the learned audience, and its mission is to provide a theory to guide the literary endeavors of

---

[280] *Ibid.*, p. 124.   [281] *Ibid.*, p. 113.
[282] *Ibid.*, pp. 136, 138; see also p. 58.

philosophers and scientists. Smith's discussion of this theory is obviously designed to offer concrete advice to future authors in these two fields, as his lectures on history and on poetry had been designed with future historians and poets in mind.

In proving a proposition, Smith remarked, the young philosopher or scholar should state what he wishes to have his audience accept. Then he should do one of two things: if his task is relatively uncomplicated, he should proceed immediately to advance the arguments which his proposition needs for its support; but if there are complications, he may have to proceed to advance several subsidiary propositions, and to offer argumentative support for each, on his way toward proof. The more complex method Smith found to be illustrated by Shaftesbury's *Inquiry into the Nature of Virtue*, but he took pains to point out that this illustration was meant to endorse the perfection of Shaftesbury's method rather than the soundness of his reasoning.[283] In words reminiscent of those used in a similar connection in the *Rhetorica ad Herennium*, Smith then advised the young philosopher that three was a very proper limit to set upon the number of subordinate propositions which might be advanced in support of a major one, for the reason that "Three is the number of all others the most easily comprehended: we immediately perceive a middle and one on each side."[284] Indeed, Smith added, "There are more sermons and other discourses divided into this number of heads than into any other." But he argued that there could safely be five heads, too, and he commented upon differences between the problem involved in comprehending at a glance the number of windows in one of the walls of a building and that involved in seeing in the mind's eye the number of propositions in a discourse. This part of his discussion he brought to a close with the remark that the divisions, subdivisions, and subsubdivisions employed by Aristotle in the *Ethics* "are carried so far that they produce the very effect he intended to have avoided by them, viz. confusion."[285]

When didactic composition undertook to fulfill its second aim, that of delivering a system of science to the learned public, it had a choice of either of two methods. Smith indicated that the first method had originated with Descartes, but that it was neverthe-

[283] *Ibid.*, p. 136.
[284] *Ibid.*, p. 137. Cf. *Rhetorica ad Herennium*, 1.10.17.
[285] *Ibid.*, p. 138.

less entitled to be named after Newton. It consisted in advancing one or a very few principles at the beginning of a discourse and in using them thereafter to explain the natural connection among the rules or phenomena under discussion. The second method, which Smith associated with Aristotle, began by enumerating the subjects one had to explain and proceeded to take up each subject in turn so as to reduce it to its essential principles but to make no attempt to reconcile one principle with another. Smith illustrated this second method by commenting thus upon what Virgil had done in composing the four books of his *Georgics*: "His design is to give us a system of husbandry. In the First he gives us directions for the cultivation of corn; in the Second, of trees; in the Third, of cattle; in the Fourth, of the insects called the bees."[286] And how would the *Georgics* have had to be changed in order to become an illustration of the first method? What would the method of Descartes and Newton have done to it? Smith addressed himself directly to these questions in the following words:

> If Virgil had begun with inquiring into the principle of vegetation, what was proper to augment it, and *ex contra*, in what proportion it was in different soils, and what nourishment the different plants required, and, putting all these together, had directed us what culture and what soil was proper for every different plant, this would have been following the first method, which is, without doubt, the most philosophical one.[287]

In seeking somewhat later to clarify in other terms the differences between the Newtonian and the Aristotelian methods, Smith remarked that "It gives us a pleasure to see the phenomena which we reckoned the most unaccountable, all deduced from some principle (commonly, a well-known one) and all united in one chain, far superior to what we feel from the unconnected method, where everything is accounted for by itself, without any reference to the others."[288] We need not be surprised, Smith went on, that Descartes, whose philosophy contains hardly a word of truth, could yet have gained an almost universal acceptance among the learned men of Europe. For here was a case where a philosophic method was so good as to be able to survive in spite of the weaknesses of the philosophy within which it was woven.

[286] *Ibid.*, p. 139. [287] *Ibid.*, p. 139. [288] *Ibid.*, p. 140.

"The great superiority of the method over that of Aristotle, the only one then known," said Smith with a touch of sportive mockery, "and the little inquiry which was then made into those matters made them [that is, European scholars] greedily receive a work which we justly esteem one of the most entertaining romances that have ever been wrote."[289]

The Newtonian and the Aristotelian methods thus recommended by Smith to students interested in didactic composition were borrowed from the old logic, as he himself made no effort to conceal. In fact, what the old logic tended prevailingly to call the method of analysis became in Smith's system the Aristotelian method; and the Newtonian (or Cartesian) method as set forth by him was what Ramus had called the method of science and what Ramus's immediate successors had tended to call the method of synthesis. Interestingly enough, Ramus had cited Virgil's own arrangement of the *Georgics* as an example of the method of science, whereas Smith, as we have seen, considered that the *Georgics* could be made to illustrate that method only if the work were completely rewritten and rearranged.[290] Since Ramus flourished almost a century before Descartes, it is obvious that Smith was historically inaccurate in making Descartes appear to be the originator of the Newtonian method. Indeed, Smith would only have been on safe ground in this instance if he had said that the Newtonian and the Aristotelian methods, as he described them, were derived from concepts quite familiar in Plato's time, and that those concepts had had an active history from that date to Smith's own epoch.[291] But I mention this inaccuracy without intending to suggest that it is important. What seems to me to be important is that rhetorical theory under Smith's inspired leadership borrowed from the old logic the doctrines and methods which guide the literary presentation of scientific knowledge, and made those doctrines and methods its own, thereby giving itself the opportunity to be to the modern world what dialectic and rhetoric had

---

[289] *Ibid.*, p. 140. (The bracketed phrase is mine.)

[290] For Ramus's views on Virgil's *Georgics* as an illustration of the method of science, see his *Dialectique* (Paris, 1555), pp. 124-125. See also my *Logic and Rhetoric in England*, p. 163.

[291] See Plato, *Phaedrus*, 265-266; also Neal W. Gilbert, *Renaissance Concepts of Method* (New York, 1960), pp. 3-4, 110, 171-172, 184; also my *Logic and Rhetoric in England*, pp. 21-22, 160-165, 289-291, 297, 306-308, et passim; also above, Ch. 2, pp. 20-21, 40-41, 49; Ch. 5, pp. 302-303, 324-325, 328, 355, 401.

together been to the ancients. Rhetoric had always had the capacity to meet a challenge of this kind, simply because the theory and practice of addressing the popular audience teach much that is necessary, and little that is irrelevant, to the task of addressing men of learning. But it was not in a position to meet the challenge while logic retained control of the theory of learned communication, and while rhetoric itself was blind to anything but its ancient rituals. It was Smith who taught rhetoric to see beyond those rituals and to assert jurisdiction over what logic no longer wanted to control.

Oratorical composition, the fourth form of discourse in Smith's system of rhetoric, brought him and his hearers to what had formerly been the sole concern of the rhetorician. It also brought him and his hearers into contact with the whole of the ancient rhetorical tradition. Here would have been the place for a display of conservatism on Smith's part, if he had been disposed to concentrate upon past glories and hallowed principles rather than upon present exigencies and new challenges. Here would have been the place where the spirit of the antiquarian might well have prevailed over that of the creative scholar. For was not traditional rhetoric an impressive structure? Had it not been given its great ancient authority by Aristotle himself, and had it not acquired from the eloquent Cicero the right to be regarded as the only avenue to eloquence? Had it not accommodated itself to Christianity and become the long-drawn aisle to greatness in the pulpit and to blessedness in the sight of God's vicars upon the earth? Was it not worthy of adaptation to modern times with only the few modifications that might be necessary to make it responsive to recent regrettable lapses in the standards of culture? These questions have caused twentieth-century rhetoricians to hesitate to raise too many objections to the old rhetoric of Aristotle and Cicero, and they caused eighteenth-century rhetoricians to hesitate even more. But they did not prevent Adam Smith from exercising his independent judgment or from offering severe criticisms of ancient doctrine.

As I have already indicated, Smith made the three kinds of oratory the subject of his last nine lectures, although he interrupted himself long enough to devote a large part of one lecture to didactic discourse. His own announced plan was to deal with each oratorical kind by speaking successively of its ends, its means, its structure, its style, and its distinguished practitioners;[292] and speak he did in these very terms when he treated demonstrative oratory. Thereafter he adhered to his plan with much less strictness. Thus he spoke of deliberative oratory largely with its practitioners in mind, doing little with the other four of his promised heads; and thus too he spoke of judicial oratory under all of his promised heads except style. His observations throughout these lectures are fresh, astute, and never commonplace, despite the losses which they must have suffered in the process of being transmitted to us through someone else's interpretations. But a complete discussion of those observations need not be undertaken here. What I shall do instead is to comment upon Smith's attitude towards the nature of oratorical composition in modern rhetoric and towards the traditional doctrines that lay behind the orator's work. Even so there will be several interesting things to notice.

First of all, Smith indicated that, so far as the later stages of civilization are concerned, demonstrative oratory must be considered less important than either of its companion forms. Audiences found pleasure in listening to it, but it never gave them sound argument. And speakers used it presumably to praise someone else but in reality to glorify themselves, without being able to connect it with the conduct of public business. Primitive man, Smith argued, sharply differentiated between the necessary labors of his daylight hours and the recreation which he sought in the evenings when his work was done.[293] For these latter times he devised dancing, music, song, and poetry. Panegyrics, or hymns to his gods and heroes, became a part of his recreation, and thus in its origin demonstrative oratory had no connection with workaday occupations. At a later stage of society, as commerce developed, and riches and opulence appeared, man began to cultivate prose, which "is naturally the language of business, as poetry is of pleasure and amusement."[294] Panegyrists turned away from poetry and accommodated themselves to prose, seeking meanwhile to perfect this new medium by embellishment; but panegyrics still endeavored not only to afford pleasure to their hearers, but also to commend men and institutions and to glorify the panegyrist himself.

[292] Adam Smith, pp. 124, 142, 164.
[293] *Ibid.*, pp. 131, 132.   [294] *Ibid.*, p. 132.

Men would much sooner consider what was to be done [said Smith], or consider the merit of those actions that have been done, than they would think either of commending men and actions, or of discommending them, and consequently would sooner apply themselves to the cultivation of the Deliberative and Judicial eloquence than of the Demonstrative. Their subjects are such as would be interesting both to speaker and hearers, whereas that of the latter could interest neither; for though the speaker gave out that his design was to commend some person or nation, yet the motive was the advancement of his own glory.[295]

In this context Smith discussed three of the leading panegyrists of antiquity, but he mentioned none of his own time. "There have been but very few," he said, "who have turned their thoughts this way."[296] And he cited Brutus's disapproval and Cicero's admiration of Isocrates, as expressed in Cicero's *Orator*, to suggest to his own Scottish audience that they would waste time if they read Isocrates "to discover the truth of the matter in question" or to be instructed "in order, method, argument, or strength of reasoning."[297] "But if we expect entertainment and pleasure from an agreeable writer," he added, "we will not be disappointed."

The second point to be mentioned in commenting upon Smith's attitude towards oratorical composition is that to his mind the authors of ancient textbooks in rhetoric made far too narrow an application of their highly schematized doctrine. Smith allowed this attitude to be expressed so much by implication, however, that it would probably not be noticed by anyone not closely familiar with Latin rhetoric in the form which it had in Cicero's *De Inventione*, in the anonymous *Rhetorica ad Herennium*, and in Quintilian's *Institutio Oratoria*. These elementary treatises taught that the exordium of the classical oration involved either of two procedures, the *insinuatio* or the *principium*, that is to say, the ingratiating approach or the direct opening.[298] The former of these was to be used in addressing an initially hostile, the latter in addressing an initially friendly audience. What Smith did was to give these two procedures new names and to treat them, not as

295 *Ibid.*, p. 130.   296 *Ibid.*, p. 130.
297 *Ibid.*, pp. 134-135. See *Orator*, 13.40.
298 See *De Inventione*, 1.15.20; *Rhetorica ad Herennium*, 1.4.6-11; *Institutio Oratoria*, 4.1.42.

strategies limited to a speaker's introductory remarks, but as methods applicable to the conduct of the entire deliberative oration. He spoke of these methods as he was finishing his account of didactic composition.

> The first may be called the Socratic method [he said], as it was that [of] which, if we may trust the dialogues of Xenophon and Plato, that philosopher generally made use. In this method we keep as far from the main point to be proved as possible, bringing on the audience by slow and imperceptible degrees to the thing to be proved, and by gaining their consent to some things whose tendency they cannot discover, we force them at last either to deny what they had before agreed to, or to grant the validity of the conclusion. This is the smoothest and most engaging manner.

> The other is a harsh and unmannerly one, where we affirm the things we are to prove boldly at the beginning, and when any point is controverted, begin by proving that very thing; and so on. This we may call the Aristotelian method, as we know it was that which he used.[299]

Smith's immediate explanation of the circumstances in which these two procedures were to be used broaden the textbook doctrine of the exordium so that it becomes applicable to the speech as a whole. He spoke thus:

> These two methods are adapted to the two contrary cases in which an orator may be circumstanced with regard to his audience. They may either have a favourable or an unfavourable opinion of that which he is to prove: that is, they may be prejudiced for, or they may be prejudiced against. In the second case we are to use the Socratic method; in the first, the Aristotelian.[300]

The third point to be mentioned as we assess Smith's attitude towards oratorical composition involves us in the problem of reconciling an inconsistency between one part of his system and another. In his discussion of deliberative oratory, that is to say, Smith would have us believe that "in general, in every sort of elo-

---

[299] Adam Smith, pp. 140-141. (The bracketed preposition is Lothian's.)
[300] *Ibid.*, p. 141.

quence, the choice of the arguments and the proper arrangement of them is the least difficult matter," and that Cicero and Quintilian had accordingly treated "the invention of arguments, or topics, and the composition or arrangement of them, as very slight matters and of no great difficulty";[301] but in his later treatment of judicial oratory, he indicated his awareness of the elaborate ancient machinery for the invention of arguments in legal and deliberative cases,[302] and he said at one point that "It is in the proper ordering and disposal of this sort of arguments that the great art of an orator often consists."[303] Here, then, we have on the one hand Smith's denial that the invention and arrangement of arguments are important matters in modern oratorical practice or in ancient rhetorical theory; and on the other hand we have his later affirmation that these two processes are important to the practicing speaker and that the ancients expended a great deal of effort in reducing them to rule and method. In his recent study of Smith's lectures on rhetoric, Vincent M. Bevilacqua, taking cognizance only of Smith's denial of the importance of invention and arrangement in ancient rhetorical theory, argues that the denial is based upon Smith's misunderstanding of the rhetorical works of Cicero and Quintilian, and that, "in accord with his misinterpretation, Smith proposed not a traditional theory of rhetoric, which included the classical arts of invention, arrangements, style and delivery, but a stylistic belletristic one."[304] "Indeed," adds Bevilacqua, "in Smith's lectures style alone is the pressing concern of rhetoric and the area of greatest artistic latitude." But the charge that Smith did not understand the ancient doctrines of invention and arrangement is destroyed by Smith's whole discussion of judicial oratory; and, as I have shown, the assertion that style alone is in his view the pressing concern of rhetoric would hardly serve to express what he conceived the pressing concerns of rhetoric to be.

What led Smith, then, to belittle in one place and to emphasize in another the importance of invention and arrangement in the theories of Cicero and Quintilian? This question cannot be given a final answer at this time. But a plausible hypothesis is that our

[301] *Ibid.*, p. 142.
[302] *Ibid.*, pp. 164-171, 175-176.   [303] *Ibid.*, p. 167.
[304] "Adam Smith's Lectures on Rhetoric and Belles Lettres," *Studies in Scottish Literature*, III (1965-66), 52.

student's notebook, in recording the earlier of these inconsistent statements, omitted some of Smith's oral elaborations or misstated some of his essential doctrine, and that therefore at this particular point the notebook does not bring us into contact with what Smith actually thought. At any rate, we should not allow a patently erroneous view of the position of invention and arrangement in Ciceronian rhetoric to stand as Smith's final opinion when it is obvious that he has given us later a more complete and a much more accurate opinion upon the same matter. I would not want to argue that Smith accepted the ancient doctrines of rhetorical invention or disposition in their totality. Indeed, it is obvious that he did not. What I am arguing is that those doctrines were heavily stressed in Cicero's *De Inventione*, in the *Rhetorica ad Herennium*, and in Quintilian's *Institutio Oratoria*, and that Smith knew from his reading of the *Institutio Oratoria* and possibly of the other two works, as his discussion of judicial oratory proves, that ancient rhetoric had not regarded those doctrines as "very slight matters."

Another point to be emphasized in this analysis of Smith's view of oratorical composition is that he regarded the oratory of one cultural establishment to be unsuited to a different establishment, and that, as a consequence, the rhetorical theory calculated to produce oratory under one set of conditions would not necessarily be the theory which ought to prevail when the conditions change. As we have seen, this idea is a characteristic of the new rhetoric, and Boyle had already stressed it effectively in his argument that the rhetorical theory meant to explain the orations of Cicero was not the sort needed to explain the Holy Scriptures. The idea also means, of course, that the rhetoric of pre-scientific times should not be made a law unto scientific times, and that, if Ciceronian rhetoric fitted the former of these epochs, it need not therefore bend the latter one to its inexorable will. Smith did not commit himself to these particular propositions in these exact terms. What he did rather was to show that deliberative oratory in ancient Athens was different from that of Rome, and would in all probability not have succeeded in Rome, and that judicial oratory in ancient Athens and Rome had proceeded on a set of assumptions no longer valid for judicial oratory in London.

In speaking upon the first of these matters, that is, upon the

deliberative oratory of Cicero and Demosthenes, Smith empha-
sized the contrast between patrician Rome and democratic
Athens. The Roman orators spoke as superiors to inferiors, the
Athenian orators, as equals to equals.

> In the one country [said Smith] the people, at least the nobles,
> would converse and harangue with dignity, pomp, and the air
> of those who speak with authority. The language of the other
> would be that of freedom, ease, and familiarity. The one is that
> where the speaker is supposed to be of superior dignity and
> authority to his hearers, and the other is that of one who talks
> to his equals. Pomp and splendour suit the former well enough,
> but would appear presumption in the other.[305]

"These considerations," continued Smith, "may serve to explain
many of the differences in the manners and style of Demosthenes
and Cicero. The latter talks with the dignity and authority of a
superior, and the former with the ease of an equal." And later he
spoke thus upon this matter: "Such, then, are the different manners of Demosthenes and Cicero, both adapted to the state of
their country; and, perhaps, had they been practised in the other
countries, they would have been less successful."[306]

The case is the same, Smith argued, when we compare the
forensic orators of Greece and Rome with those of modern
Britain. Here is part of what he said upon this matter:

> I shall now give ye some account of the state of the Judicial
> eloquence of England, which is very different from that either
> of Greece or of Rome. This difference is generally ascribed to
> the small progress which has been made in the cultivation of
> language and style in this country, compared with that which
> it had arrived to in the Old World. But [though] this may be
> true in some degree, yet I imagine there are other causes which
> must make them essentially different. The eloquence which is
> now in greatest esteem is a plain, distinct, and perspicuous
> style, without any of the floridity or other ornamental parts of
> the Old Eloquence. This and other differences must necessarily
> arise from the nature of the country and the particular turn of
> the people. The Courts were then much in the same manner as
> the Jury is now. They were men unskilled in the law, whose

---

[305] Adam Smith, p. 153. [306] *Ibid.*, p. 155.

office continued but for a very short time, and were often in a great part chosen for the trial of that particular cause, and not from any particular set of men, but only by ballot and rotation from the whole body of the people, and of them there was always no inconsiderable number. The Judges in England, on the other hand, are single men who have been bred to the law, and have generally, or at least are supposed to have, a thorough knowledge of the law, and are much versed in all the different circumstances of cases, of which they have attended many before, either as judges or pleaders, and are supposed to be acquainted with all the different arguments that may be advanced on it. This therefore cuts them out from a great part of the substance of the old orations.[307]

Smith's modernity of outlook towards rhetoric is nowhere seen to better advantage than in the words which followed these observations:

There can be no room for a narration, the only design of which is, by interweaving those facts for which proof can be brought with those for which no proof can be brought, that these latter may gain credit by their connection with the others. But as nothing is now of any weight for which direct proof is not brought, this sort of narration could serve no end. The pleader, therefore, can do no more than tell over what facts he is to prove. . . . And if he should assert anything for a fact, as the old orators frequently did, for which he can bring no proof, he would be severely reprimanded. The pleader has here no opportunity of smoothing over any argument which would make against him, as the judge will perceive it and pay no regard to what he advances in this manner. Nor can he conceal any weak side by placing it betwixt two on which he depends for the proof of it. . . . All these were particularly directed by the ancient rhetoricians. The inattention and ignorance of the judges was the sole foundation of it: as this is not now to be expected, they can be of no service.[308]

The next point to need attention concerns Smith's theory of oratorical structure. His modernity in this matter has two aspects:

[307] *Ibid.*, p. 190. (The bracketed word is Lothian's.)
[308] *Ibid.*, pp. 190-191.

his rejection of the classical doctrine that an oration has five or six parts, each elaborately conceived; and his assertion that, when everything has been taken into account, the orator must state his proposition and prove it, while giving heed to whatever his speech may require in the way of a simple introduction and conclusion. The first statement of this theory occurred in his seventeenth lecture, when he paused in his analysis of historical writing to emphasize the difference between the structure of an historical work and that of an exposition or an oration. "The didactic and the oratorical compositions," he declared on that occasion, "consist of two parts: the proposition which we lay down, and the proof which is brought to confirm this, whether this proof be a strict one, applied to our reason and sound judgement, or one adapted to affect our passions and by that means persuade us at any rate."[309] An extended form of this same idea appeared in his later discussion of forensic oratory, where he spoke thus of ancient rhetoricians:

> They tell us that every regular oration should consist of five parts. There are, it is true, two chief parts, the laying-down the proposition, and the proof. But in the connecting these two properly together and setting them out in the brightest light, the oration, they say, naturally divides into five parts. The *first* of these is the Exordium, in which the orator explains briefly the purpose of his discourse and what he intends to accuse the adversary of, or to acquit his client of. The *second* part is, according to them, the Narration. . . . In the practice of the modern Courts of Judicature the narration is never introduced. . . . The other three parts are the Confirmation, the Refutation, and the Peroration. . . . The Peroration contains a short summary of the whole arguments advanced in the preceding part of the discourse, placed in such a way as naturally to lead to the conclusion proposed. To this the Roman orators generally added some arguments which might move the judge to decide in one way rather than in another, by either showing the enormity of the crime, if the person accused be his opponent, and setting it out in the most shocking manner; or, if he is a defendant, by mitigating the action and showing the severity of the punishment.

[309] *Ibid.*, pp. 84-85.

This latter the Greeks never admitted of: the other is the natural conclusion of every discourse.[310]

Smith's mention of the Greek orators in the passage just quoted should remind us that Athenian oratorical practice was simpler than Rome's, and that Smith, in rejecting the elaborate Ciceronian theory of the oration, was in fact endorsing the simpler theory set forth in Aristotle's *Rhetoric*.[311] Thus the new rhetoric, so far as its theory of speech composition is concerned, turned away from the elaborate Ciceronian ideal and adopted the earlier and plainer formula of Aristotle. But it did so, not in a spirit of reverence for a greater as distinguished from a lesser figure of the past, but in a genuine search for an oratorical form that would best fit the needs of the modern world. Classical scholars who consider the ancients more perfect than the moderns, and who among the ancients prefer the Greek to the Roman orators and philosophers, should not be misled by Adam Smith's preference for Demosthenes and Aristotle over Cicero. For Smith was not an apostle of Demosthenes and Aristotle in a situation in which he thought them giants towering above the puny men of Rome. He was their apostle only when they spoke to his own time with more relevance than Cicero could command. And when their words ceased to be relevant on any issue, he was their apostle no further.

A matter upon which Smith was the apostle of neither Aristotle nor Cicero involved the utility of the topics in the invention of oratorical proofs, and this will be the final point that I shall stress in the present discussion of Smith's attitude towards oratorical composition. Aristotle and Cicero had considered the invention of artistic proofs to be the heart of their theories of rhetoric, as we know, and they had lavished their energies upon creating a system of topics to assist the orator in devising these proofs. Smith did not flatly reject this system. He discussed it in part, and it is plain that he did not find it altogether useless. But he spoke slightingly of it on occasion, and in general he expected the modern orator to rely upon direct proofs rather than upon those that issued from mere conjectures and suspicions.

One expression of this expectation occurs in a passage already

---

[310] *Ibid.*, pp. 172, 175, 176.
[311] 1414a 30. See also above, pp. 445-446.

quoted, where, after showing how the classical *narratio* was suited to the situation in which established facts could be mixed with mere unsubstantiated allegations so as to give the speaker's argument some degree of credibility, Smith said that in modern times, only direct proof being admissible, the classical *narratio* was no longer employed. But the best expression of this expectation occurs when Smith was discussing proof as one of the two indispensable parts of the modern oration. On that occasion he revealed his basic attitude towards the topical devices which classical rhetoric had recommended for the discovery of rhetorical arguments.

The Confirmation consists in the proving of all or certain of the facts alleged [he said], and this is done by going through the arguments drawn from the several topics I mentioned in the last lecture; and the Refutation, or the confuting of the adversaries' arguments, is to be gone through in the same manner. The later orators adhered most strictly to the rules laid down by the rhetoricians. We see that even Cicero himself was scrupulously exact in this point, so that in many, indeed most, of his orations, he goes through all of those topics. It would probably have been reckoned a defect to have omitted any one, and not to have led an argument from the topic *De Causa, Effectu, Tempore,* etc. This may serve to show us the low state of philosophy at that time. . . . In his oration in defence of Milo he has arguments drawn from all the three topics with regard to the cause; that is, that he had no motive to kill Clodius; that it was unsuitable to his character; and that he had no opportunity. These, one would have thought, could not take place in this case, and yet he goes through them all. He endeavours to show that he had no motive, though they had been squabbling and fighting every day—he had even declared his intention to kill him; that it was unsuitable to his character, although he had killed twenty men before; and that he had no opportunity, although we know he did kill him.[312]

Notice how Smith balanced the known facts of Milo's case against the glib conjectures which Cicero drew from the topic of cause. Notice how poorly the conjectures fare when the known facts confront them. Notice how Smith's analysis of this part of

[312] Adam Smith, pp. 175-176.

Cicero's famous speech is itself a witty exposure of the sterility of artistic arguments in a case where the nonartistic arguments directly controvert them. There can be little doubt that the students who heard Smith deliver this lecture would never have been able in their later lives to restrain their smiles when they thought of Smith's mocking comments upon Cicero's defense of Milo. Nor would they ever have been likely in their own practice as speakers or writers to prefer arguments drawn from the topics to arguments based upon the facts. As the expounder of the new rhetoric, Smith was never more effective than he was on this particular occasion.

In concluding this assessment of Smith's system of rhetoric and belles lettres, I should like to re-emphasize that Smith's rhetorical theory is remarkable for its originality, its validity, and its timeliness. It took the position that the new rhetoric must define its function as broadly communicative rather than narrowly persuasive and hence must assert jurisdiction over the forms of historical, poetical, and didactic composition no less than over the traditional kinds of oratory. It asserted that the new rhetoric must teach the eloquence of plainness, distinctness, and perspicuity. It decreed that the new rhetoric must abandon the ritualistic form of the Ciceronian oration and must adopt the simpler pattern of proposition and proof. And it required the new rhetoric to turn away from the artistic proofs and the topical machinery of the old rhetoric, and to adapt itself to nonartistic arguments and direct proofs instead. Only in two respects was Adam Smith silent upon the issues confronting the new rhetoric: he did not openly condemn the syllogistic orientation of ancient rhetorical theory or propose inductive procedures in its place; nor did he stress that probable arguments, as ancient and modern phenomena in popular discourse, must learn in the new era to conform to higher standards of validity than they had done before. These two issues were to be squarely faced and creatively resolved by George Campbell and were to produce Campbell's major contribution to the new rhetoric. But surely Adam Smith implied his endorsement of Campbell's later position on these issues, and thus he is not to be counted an opponent of the new rhetoric in respect to them.

In one sector of his rhetorical theory Smith showed himself seriously weak; and that was in his willingness to accept pleasure or entertainment as the sole distinguishing characteristic of poetical composition. Surely poetry gives its readers pleasure, but so on occasion does history or oratory or even didactic discourse. Thus Smith's theory of the distinction between poetical and non-poetical composition does not meet the most elementary standard of adequacy, and it could not survive comparison with a really effective standard like that, for example, which Aristotle developed in his *Poetics*. Aristotle's distinction insisted upon the existence of the principle of mimesis in all the forms of poetry, and upon the non-existence of that principle in historical writing, didactic writing, and oratory.[313] Smith was deeply interested in the principle of artistic imitation, and he wrote a short treatise upon that subject;[314] but his treatise did not apply the principle to poetical composition in any sense that would allow poetry to emerge as distinctively mimetic.

Aside from the inadequacy of his theory of poetry, however, Smith may confidently be called the earliest and most independent of the new British rhetoricians of the eighteenth century. It is a calamity indeed that the destruction of his manuscripts by his own request prevented his excellence as a rhetorician from being recognized and acclaimed until he had been dead for almost two hundred years. Rhetorical theory in the nineteenth century might have taken a better turn than it did, had Adam Smith's lectures been available to stand beside the works of Campbell and Blair when the latter authors became the leading exponents of the new rhetoric against Archbishop Richard Whately's successful revival of central parts of the rhetorical doctrine of Aristotle. Smith's steadily growing posthumous fame, and the distinction of his rhetorical teachings, might have helped the new rhetoric to prevail over Whately's Aristotelianism, even as the genius of John Stuart Mill decisively helped the new logic of Thomas Reid and Dugald Stewart to prevail over Whately's attempt to convert the nineteenth century to the Peripatetic logic of Dean Aldrich.

[313] For a discussion of this matter, see my essay, "Aristotle and Horace on Rhetoric and Poetics," *The Quarterly Journal of Speech*, LIV (1968), 325-339.

[314] For it, see "Of the Nature of that Imitation which takes place in what are called the Imitative Arts," in *Essays on Philosophical Subjects*, by the late Adam Smith, LL.D. (London, 1795), pp. 131-184.

v George Campbell and the Philosophical Rhetoric of the New Learning

According to his own testimony, George Campbell wrote the first two chapters of *The Philosophy of Rhetoric* in 1750.[315] At that time he was serving as pastor of the parish of Banchory-Ternan, where he had started his career in the church in 1748, after having been licensed as preacher in 1746, and after having pursued a still earlier career as apprentice lawyer in Edinburgh following upon his graduation in 1738 from Marischal College, Aberdeen. He showed those first two chapters to some of his friends, but he did nothing further with them until 1757, when he moved to Aberdeen as parish preacher and at once became a founding member of a literary club which was to call itself a year later the Aberdeen Philosophical Society.[316] "It was a difference in his situation at that time, and his connection with the gentlemen of that society, some of whom have since honourably distinguished themselves in the republic of letters, that induced him to resume a subject, which he had so long laid aside," said Campbell in commenting upon the influences which led him in 1757 to renew his concern for rhetoric.[317] The first thing he did in Aberdeen to further that concern was to present the two completed chapters as oral reports at meetings of his new club, which was then made up of John Gregory, David Skene, Robert Trail, John Stewart, and Thomas Reid, in addition to Campbell himself. Reid, it should be remembered, had been librarian of Marischal College when Campbell was there as an undergraduate,[318] and Reid was to distinguish himself in 1764 by publishing his *Inquiry into the Human Mind*. The next thing Campbell did, no doubt with the active encouragement of the club, was to devote himself between 1757 and 1760 to the composition of six more of the final eleven chapters of Book I, leaving Chapters 3, 6, and 10 still unwritten. Then

---

[315] As I mentioned earlier, the first edition of *The Philosophy of Rhetoric* (2 vols., London, 1776) is cited here. It is designated henceforth by the author's surname. For his account of the stages in which the work was composed, see that edition, I, iii-iv.

[316] This Society, as I said above, Ch. 5, n. 267, is described by McCosh, *The Scottish Philosophy*, pp. 227-229. See in the same work, pp. 239-245, for a sketch of Campbell's life.

[317] Campbell, I, iv.   [318] See above, Ch. 5, pp. 372-373.

he interrupted the work again, in part to provide time for the new duties which attended his appointment in 1759 as principal of Marischal College, and in part to allow himself to prepare for publication in 1762 a book devoted to an examination of David Hume's essay on miracles.³¹⁹ He returned once again to the *Rhetoric* in the middle 1760's, not only to make progress on the Introduction, the nine chapters of Book II, and the five chapters of Book III, but also to read portions of the developing work to his associates in the Philosophical Society.³²⁰ His appointment in 1771 as professor of divinity in Marischal College led him to begin in 1772-73 the delivery of a series of lectures on systematic theology and pulpit eloquence, the latter subject being an inducement not only for him to think of rhetoric in one of its most important practical applications but also to finish his long-delayed treatise on its philosophy. In the latter connection he read a paper before the Philosophical Society in 1772 on the advantages and disadvantages arising from the differences between patterns of verbal arrangement in the ancient languages and those in the modern languages³²¹—a matter which would also be discussed in the third book of *Rhetoric*. As for Chapter 6 of Book 1, it was almost certainly inspired, as I indicated above,³²² by the attacks which Reid and Kames published in 1774 against syllogistic reasoning; and thus it was written very close to the moment when the *Rhetoric* went to press in 1776, as doubtless were Chapters 9 and 10 of the first book as well.

Since no part of Campbell's *Rhetoric* was in existence before 1750, and since by that time Adam Smith had already fixed the characters of his rhetorical speculation and had presented them in his first and again in his second course of lectures, any possibility that Campbell could have influenced Smith is clearly out of the question. And Smith on his side did not directly influence Campbell. But Campbell's *Rhetoric* may have been instrumental in causing Smith to decide not to allow his own rhetorical system to be published. Was not Campbell's *Rhetoric* a seminal work? Did it not present a new and sensitive formulation of its subject? And

---

³¹⁹ Campbell's work, entitled *A Dissertation on Miracles* (Edinburgh, 1762), was described by William Rose in *The Monthly Review*, XXVI (London, 1762), 499, as "this candid, spirited, and sensible performance."

³²⁰ McCosh, pp. 228, 471.   ³²¹ *Ibid.*, p. 473.

³²² See Ch. 5, pp. 407-408.

did it not appear at the very moment when the publication of *The Wealth of Nations* had given Smith a fame that could scarcely have been augmented by the appearance of any unpublished work of his? From our vantage point in the twentieth century, affirmative answers to each of these questions would be a matter of course; and in the light of such a consideration, Smith's decision in 1790 to have his rhetorical manuscripts destroyed may well have presupposed the conviction on his part that Campbell's treatise as published in 1776 made unnecessary any further immediate effort to bring rhetoric up to date.

An author's use of a term is the best clue to the meaning which he assigns to it, and by this standard we can say that to Campbell rhetoric meant the art by which any sort of verbal discourse acquires the power to move mankind. In fact, rhetoric and eloquence are synonynous terms with him, the former being made prominent by its place in his title, and the latter, by its frequency in his text. His first announcement that he considered eloquence to be his subject came in his Preface,[323] and just prior to that announcement he said that the purpose of his treatise as a whole was not only to define his subject as the art of operating upon the soul of the hearer by means of language, but also to ascertain the principles which that art might have at its roots.[324] In his Introduction he spoke of "eloquence, or the art of speaking, in the extensive sense in which I employ the term."[325] His own title for Book I was "The Nature and Foundations of Eloquence." He began that book with the following definition: "The word *eloquence* in its greatest latitude denotes 'That art or talent by which the discourse is adapted to its end.' "[326] And he repeated that definition in Book II.[327] Small wonder, then, that in the index which his *Rhetoric* acquired when it was issued as a textbook in the nineteenth century, the term "rhetoric" is listed only to give it a cross-reference to "eloquence," while under the latter term important parts of the treatise as a whole are identified by descriptive phrases and located by suitable page numbers.[328]

The purpose to which discourse is adapted, or the function which it performs in operating upon the soul of the reader or

---

[323] Campbell, I, ix.   [324] *Ibid.*, I, vii.   [325] *Ibid.*, I, 13.

[326] *Ibid.*, I, 25.   [327] *Ibid.*, II, 130.

[328] See for example the Index in the edition published at London by William Tegg & Co. in 1850.

hearer, was described by Campbell in generic and in specific terms. All discourses aim generically, he thought, to transfer meaning from an author to his audience, whatever the specific purpose might be. Thus in his Introduction Campbell said of eloquence that "It is indeed the grand art of communication, not of ideas only, but of sentiments, passions, dispositions, and purposes."[329] Later he observed that "Language is the sole channel through which we communicate our knowledge and discoveries to others, and through which the knowledge and discoveries of others are communicated to us";[330] and at that time he listed the four operations of the communicative process as speaking, writing, hearing, and reading.[331] Nevertheless, his major emphasis was upon the specific functions of discourse, and these he identified at times under five and at times under four designations, the former number being merely the result of a bifurcation of one element in the latter. That is to say, he mentioned discourses which inform, or convince, or please, or move, or persuade;[332] and, by collapsing the first two of these purposes under a single head, he also mentioned discourses as being intended to enlighten, to please, to move, or to influence conduct.[333] Indeed, on one occasion he took exception to the Greek rhetoricians for their having defined rhetoric as the art of persuasion, and he said then that the defectiveness of their definition was exposed in the very writings which produced it, "since in a consistency with it their rhetorics could not have comprehended those orations called *demonstrative*, the design of which was not to persuade, but to please."[334]

Campbell's theory of eloquence rested upon one great principle: that the human soul is not indifferent to the intellectual and moral quality of its ideas—that it has within itself the disposition to be moved only by those ideas which it accepts as truthful and good. "Nor are those mental powers," he declared, "of which eloquence so much avails herself, like the art of war or other human arts, perfectly indifferent to good and evil, and only beneficial as they are rightly employed. On the contrary, they are by nature, as will perhaps appear afterwards, more friendly to truth than to falsehood, and more easily retained in the cause of virtue, than

[329] Campbell, I, 14. [330] *Ibid.*, II, 100. [331] *Ibid.*, II, 99.
[332] *Ibid.*, I, vii, 97; II, 5. [333] *Ibid.*, I, 26-35. [334] *Ibid.*, I, 33, n.

in that of vice."[335] The significance of this statement is emphasized by Campbell in a supporting footnote of twenty lines. But one of the passages contained in the footnote is in Greek, and the other in Latin, and the modern reader might be inclined to dismiss them both as extraneous ornament rather than essential doctrine. Such heedlessness would prevent him, however, from seeing what Campbell considered eloquent discourse to be.

The Greek passage was from the opening chapter of Aristotle's *Rhetoric*. Aristotle began that chapter by remarking upon the connection between the arts of rhetoric and dialectic, the latter art having already been thoroughly discussed in his *Topics*. These arts are alike, said Aristotle, in being applicable to questions that come under dispute—to questions which are answered affirmatively by some and negatively by others. Thus both arts develop the capacity to argue either side of an issue, "not that we should do both (for one ought not to persuade people to do what is wrong), but that the real state of the case may not escape us, and that we ourselves may be able to counteract false arguments, if another makes an unfair use of them."[336] At that point, Aristotle reiterated that "Rhetoric and Dialectic alone of all the arts prove opposites; for both are equally concerned with them." And he then made the observations which Campbell quoted:

> However, it is not the same with the subject matter, but, generally speaking, that which is true and better is naturally always easier to prove and more likely to persuade. . . . If it is argued that one who makes an unfair use of such faculty of speech may do a great deal of harm, this objection applies equally to all good things except virtue, and above all to those things which are most useful, such as strength, health, wealth, generalship; for as these, rightly used, may be of the greatest benefit, so, wrongly used, they may do an equal amount of harm.[337]

The belief that truth and virtue have a natural advantage over their opposites in any dispute which arises in human affairs had come to Aristotle from *Phaedrus*, Plato's matchless dialogue on

[335] *Ibid.*, I, 187-188.

[336] Aristotle, *The "Art" of Rhetoric*, trans. John Henry Freese, The Loeb Classical Library (London and New York, 1926), pp. 11-13.

[337] *Ibid.*, p. 13.

rhetoric. To Aristotle, however, this insight was not so much a principle of rhetoric as a guide to the use of such arguments and persuasions as rhetoric might provide. Indeed, had Aristotle given the insight major emphasis, he might not have slighted as he did the whole subject of nonartistic proofs in oratory, and he might not have said as much as he did about artistic proofs. For after all, these latter have only marginal value in establishing the truthfulness of propositions or the virtuousness of conduct. To Francis Bacon, however, this insight became the central principle of rhetoric. He gave it that status in the rhetorical doctrine which he first formulated in 1605 in his *Advancement of Learning*. And he gave it the same status when he restated and expanded the doctrine in 1623 for his Latin work, the *De Dignitate et Augmentis Scientiarum Libri IX*. The Latin passage which accompanied the Aristotelian quotation in Campbell's footnote was from the latter work, and to Campbell as to Bacon it stated the central principle in man's attempt to explain eloquent discourse.

The *De Augmentis Scientiarum* divides human learning into history, poesy, and philosophy; and in the third of these categories, after descending through a tight system of heads and subheads, it treats of rhetoric, which it discusses as one of the three great arts of transmitting knowledge, the other two being grammar and logic. The particular function of rhetoric in the communicative process, said Bacon, was to "illustrate," that is to say, to present under a great light the truths of reason, so that the imagination would be won to them, and would make them so powerful an influence upon the affections and appetites as to induce these latter faculties to join with reason in ruling the will.[338]

---

[338] Bacon's Latin phrase for the process of transmitting knowledge is "Ars Elocutionis seu Traditionis," and his English phrase, "Art of Elocution or Tradition." See *Works of Bacon*, II, 362; VI, 261. "Traditivam," he said later, "in tres partes dividemus; Doctrinam circa *Organum Sermonis*; Doctrinam circa *Methodum Sermonis*; et Doctrinam circa *Sermonis Illustrationem sive Ornatum*," that is, "The art of transmission I will divide into three parts; the doctrine concerning the Organ of Discourse [i.e. Grammar], the doctrine concerning the Method of Discourse [i.e. Logic], and the doctrine concerning the Illustration or adornment of Discourse [i.e. Rhetoric]." *Ibid.*, II, 410; IX, 108. Italics are Bacon's. Bacon probably used the term "Illustration" with the definition of the figure of Hypotiposis in mind. John Marbeck, *A Booke Of Notes and Common places* (London, 1581), p. 491, defined Hypotiposis as

If the affections, Bacon argued, were in the first place obedient to reason, there would be no great need of persuasions and insinuations to induce the will to follow truth. But the affections raised mutinies within the human soul, and would always vanquish reason, "if eloquence of persuasions did not win the imagination from the affections' part, and contract a confederacy between the reason and imagination against them." Bacon's next words, which I shall now quote in Spedding's translation, make up the Latin passage in Campbell's footnote:

> For it must be observed that the affections themselves carry ever an appetite to apparent good, and have this in common with reason; but the difference is that affection beholds principally the good which is present; reason looks beyond and beholds likewise the future and sum of all. And therefore the present filling the imagination more, reason is commonly vanquished and overcome. But after eloquence and force of persuasion have made things future and remote appear as present, then upon the revolt of imagination to reason, reason prevails.
>
> Let us conclude therefore that rhetoric can be no more blamed for knowing how to colour the worse side, than logic for teaching how to make fine sophisms. For who does not know that the principle of contraries is the same, though the use be opposite?[339]

As Campbell would have remembered himself, and as he would have expected his readers to remember, the passage just quoted was followed at once by Bacon's important observation, "that Logic differeth from Rhetoric, not only as the fist from the palm, the one close the other at large; but much more in this, that Logic handleth reason exact and in truth, and Rhetoric handleth it as it

---

follows: "It is a figure called Illustration, by the which the forme of things is so set foorth in words, that it seemeth rather to be séene with the eies, then heard with the eares." See also *A New English Dictionary*, s.v. Illustration. The Latin term for Hypotiposis is Descriptio. See Henry Peacham, *The Garden of Eloquence* (1593), ed. William G. Crane (Gainesville, Fla., 1954), p. 134, for an account of the way in which, by using Descriptio or Illustration, an orator could change ears into eyes.

[339] *Works of Bacon*, IX, 133-134.

is planted in popular opinions and manners."[340] For rhetoric, by presenting truth so as to make it visible to ordinary men, becomes to Bacon's mind the vital last step in the process of transmitting knowledge—the step which "illustrates" what grammar and logic know only how to state.

Campbell would also have expected his readers to remember that earlier in his *Rhetoric* he had called Bacon "perhaps the most comprehensive genius in philosophy that has appeared in modern times,"[341] and on that occasion had quoted another Latin passage from the *De Augmentis Scientiarum*. That passage, too, sheds great light upon the central principle of Campbell's *Rhetoric*. In Spedding's translation it reads thus:

> The doctrine concerning the Intellect . . . , and the doctrine concerning the Will of man, are as it were twins by birth. For purity of illumination and freedom of will began and fell together: and nowhere in the universal nature of things is there so intimate a sympathy as between truth and goodness. . . . I come now to the knowledge which respects the use and objects of the faculties of the human soul. It has two parts, and those well known and by general agreement admitted; namely, Logic and Ethic. . . . Logic discourses of the Understanding and Reason; Ethic of the Will, Appetite, and Affections: the one produces determinations, the other actions.[342]

This passage is followed immediately in the *De Augmentis Scientiarum* by a statement which Campbell did not quote but which he would certainly have wanted us to construe as a legitimate part of the process by which discourse achieves eloquence. It goes as follows:

> It is true indeed that the imagination performs the office of an agent or messenger or proctor in both provinces, both the judicial and the ministerial. For sense sends all kinds of images over to imagination for reason to judge of; and reason again when it has made its judgment and selection, sends them over

---

[340] I quote this passage as Bacon himself phrased it in the *Advancement of Learning*. See *Works of Bacon*, VI, 300. Spedding translates its final words as "in the opinions of the vulgar," and that particular phrase seems unfortunate —and Victorian. See above, Ch. 1, p. 4, for the earliest form of these words.

[341] Campbell, I, 12-13.   [342] *Works of Bacon*, IX, 60-61.

to imagination before the decree be put in execution. For voluntary motion is ever preceded and incited by imagination; so that imagination is as a common instrument to both—both reason and will; saving that this Janus of imagination has two different faces; for the face towards reason has the print of truth, and the face towards action has the print of goodness.

So far as rhetoric is concerned, said Campbell, as he embarked upon his perceptive elaboration of these ideas from the *De Augmentis Scientiarum*, truth and goodness stand in relation to each other as conviction to persuasion, or as an act of reason to an act of will. That is to say, the understanding decides whether an idea is truthful or not, and the passions establish its goodness, once it has met the test of truth. Campbell gave attention to the processes by which each of these faculties performs its particular function in the act of persuasion, and it will be helpful if I now discuss each process by itself.

"Logical truth," said Campbell, "consisteth in the conformity of our conceptions to their archetypes in the nature of things. This conformity is perceived by the mind, either immediately on a bare attention to the ideas under review, or mediately by a comparison of these with other related ideas."[343] The establishing of truth, remarked Campbell on another occasion, "though peculiarly the logician's province, is the foundation of all conviction, and consequently of persuasion too." "To attain either of these ends," he added, "the speaker must always assume the character of the close and candid reasoner: for though he may be an acute logician who is no orator, he will never be a consummate orator who is no logician."[344] "In order to evince the truth considered by itself," he observed still later, "conclusive arguments alone are requisite; but in order to convince me by these arguments, it is moreover requisite that they be understood, that they be attended to, that they be remembered by me; and in order to persuade me by them, to any particular action or conduct, it is further requisite, that by interesting me in the subject, they may, as it were, be felt."[345] "Would we not only touch the heart, but win it entirely to co-operate with our views," he observed on still an-

[343] Campbell, I, 103. Also quoted above, Ch. 5, p. 398.
[344] Campbell, I, 163. Also quoted above, Ch. 5, pp. 400-401.
[345] Campbell, I, 186-187.

other occasion, "those affecting lineaments must be so interwoven with our argument, as that, from the passion excited, our reasoning may derive importance, and so be fitted for commanding attention; and, by the justness of the reasoning, the passion may be more deeply rooted and enforced; and that thus, both may be made to conspire in effectuating that persuasion which is the end proposed."[346]

In deciding whether an idea conforms to the nature of things, the understanding could make a mistake, of course, and the resulting error or sophism might have an evil effect upon conduct. But, even so, the influence of the sophism would have to be explained, not as proof of the neutrality of the mind towards truth and falsehood, but as proof of its devotion to error only on those special occasions when error wears the garb of truth. Campbell spoke thus upon this matter in his objection to the use of obscure discourse as a device for weakening a convincing argument:

> A little sophistry here will, no doubt, be thought necessary, by one with whom victory hath more charms than truth; and sophistry, as was hinted above, always implies obscurity; for that a sophism should be mistaken for an argument, can be imputed only to this, that it is not rightly understood.[347]

"Good is the object of the will," said Campbell with Bacon's similar sentiments in mind, "truth is the object of the understanding."[348] And what is goodness? How are the virtues to be defined? Are truth and good one and the same thing? Can we say, as some have done, "that acting virtuously in any situation, is but one way or other of telling truth"?[349] No indeed, said Campbell in answer to these two latter questions. Such theses merely lead us in circles if we attempt to prove them. Can goodness, then, be defined by the reason? No, said Campbell, "no hypothesis hitherto invented hath shown that by means of the discursive faculty, without the aid of any other mental power, we could ever obtain a notion of either the beautiful or the good; and till this be shown, nothing is shown to the purpose."[350] Are we then to say that, when we represent something as good, and thus address ourselves to the heart rather than to the head, we are in fact addressing ourselves only

346 *Ibid.*, I, 36-37. 347 *Ibid.*, II, 137. 348 *Ibid.*, I, 203.
349 *Ibid.*, I, 205, n. 350 *Ibid.*, I, 204, n.

to the passions, and that therefore the virtues must be classed with them?

> By no means [remarked Campbell, with this very question in mind]. But without entering into a discussion of the difference, which would be foreign to our purpose, let it suffice to observe, that they [the virtues] have this in common with passion. They necessarily imply an habitual propensity to a certain species of conduct, an habitual aversion to the contrary; a veneration for such a character, an abhorrence of such another. They are therefore, though not passions, so closely related to them, that they are properly considered as motives to action, being equally capable of giving an impulse to the will.[351]

In the light of his distinction between truth and goodness, Campbell developed his famous theory of persuasion. Two things must be done, he said, by an author who would persuade others. "The first is, to excite some desire or passion in the hearers; the second is, to satisfy their judgment, that there is a connexion between the action to which he would persuade them, and the gratification of the desire or passion which he excites."[352]

> The former is effected [he went on] by communicating lively and glowing ideas of the object; the latter, unless so evident of itself as to supersede the necessity, by presenting the best and most forcible arguments which the nature of the subject admits. In the one lies the pathetic, in the other the argumentative. These incorporated together . . . constitute that vehemence of contention to which the greatest exploits of eloquence ought doubtless to be ascribed.[353]

Not only did Campbell take Bacon's *De Augmentis Scientiarum* as his authority for the theory that truth and goodness move the soul and thus are responsible for eloquence in discourse, but he also followed this same treatise in arranging literary forms in a system paralleling that by which the human faculties operate. As we have seen, Bacon assigned logical discourse to the reason and rhetorical discourse to the reason and imagination. Indeed, in dividing human learning into history, poesy, and philosophy, he stipulated that these forms of composition belonged respectively

---

[351] *Ibid.,* I, 206. [352] *Ibid.,* I, 200; II, 132. [353] *Ibid.,* I, 201.

to the memory, the imagination, and the reason. Thus it must be stressed that in Bacon's opinion the divisions to be acknowledged by the critic in dealing with literary types are dictated by the divisions identified by the philosopher in describing the mind. Campbell's theory of rhetoric is founded upon the same principle. He devoted a chapter to the faculties of understanding, imagination, memory, and passions, as they act independently, or join to affect will,[354] and he made it plain that divisions in the world of discourse responded to one or more of these powers of the mind. The understanding is the dominant faculty. "This prerogative the intellect has above all the other faculties, that whether it be or be not immediately addressed by the speaker, it must be regarded by him either ultimately or subordinately," he said; "ultimately, when the direct purpose of the discourse is information, or conviction; subordinately, when the end is pleasure, emotion, or persuasion."[355] As for the memory, it imposes its requirements upon all types of discourse, since an address to it is "more or less necessary on every occasion."[356] But the other faculties are somewhat more specialized in respect to their involvement in the forms of literature. "Knowledge, the object of the intellect," said Campbell in his opening chapter, "furnisheth materials for the fancy; the fancy culls, compounds, and, by her mimic art, disposes these materials so as to affect the passions; the passions are the natural spurs to volition or action, and so need only to be right directed."[357] These ideas he elaborated as follows:

When a speaker addresseth himself to the understanding, he proposes the *instruction* of his hearers, and that, either by explaining some doctrine unknown, or not distinctly comprehended by them, or by proving some position disbelieved or doubted by them. . . . In the one, his aim is their *information*; in the other, their *conviction*. . . .

The imagination is addressed by exhibiting to it a lively and beautiful representation of a suitable object. . . . Now the principal scope for this class being in narration and description, poetry, . . . especially epic poetry, must be ranked under it. . . . But that kind of address of which I am now treating, attains the summit of perfection in the *sublime*, or those great and noble

---

[354] Ch. VII of Bk. I.   [355] *Ibid.*, II, 5-6.   [356] *Ibid.*, I, 196-197.
[357] *Ibid.*, I, 28-29.

images, which, when in suitable colouring presented to the mind, do, as it were, distend the imagination with some vast conception, and quite ravish the soul.[358]

"But it is evident," Campbell continued, after giving a further account of the sublime, "that this creative faculty, the fancy, frequently lends her aid in promoting still nobler ends."

> From her exuberant stores [he explained] most of those tropes and figures are extracted, which, when properly employed, have such a marvellous efficacy in rousing the passions. . . . In this case, the address of the orator . . . assumes the denomination of *pathetic*. . . .

> Finally, that kind, the most complex of all, which is calculated to influence the will, and persuade to a certain conduct, as it is in reality an artful mixture of that which proposes to convince the judgment, and that which interests the passions, its distinguishing excellency results from these two, the argumentative and the pathetic incorporated together.[359]

One more instance of Campbell's concern for the relation between the faculties, on the one hand, and the orator's discourses, on the other, should be presented here, not because it advances what Campbell said on this point, but because it connects this point to his central concern for truth as the incentive of the soul:

> If the orator would prove successful, it is necessary that he engage in his service all these different powers of the mind, the imagination, the memory, and the passions. These are not the supplanters of reason, or even rivals in her sway; they are her handmaids, by whose ministry she is enabled to usher truth into the heart, and procure it there a favourable reception. As handmaids they are liable to be seduced by sophistry in the garb of reason, and sometimes are made ignorantly to lend their aid in the introduction of falsehood. But their service is not on this account to be dispensed with; there is even a necessity of employing it founded in our nature.[360]

Campbell's use of the word orator in the passage just quoted deserves a few words of comment. Here and throughout his entire *Rhetoric*, Campbell intended this word to refer not only to

---

[358] *Ibid.*, I, 29-30.   [359] *Ibid.*, I, 32-33.   [360] *Ibid.*, I, 187.

the maker of speeches but to the author of any kind of verbal composition whatever. In other words, oratory is Campbell's technical term for any discourses addressed to one or more of the mental faculties, and accordingly he classed as oratory what the modern literary critic would designate by such specific terms as scientific exposition, didactic and philosophical writing, argumentative discourse, history, oratory in the traditional sense, dramatic literature, epic poetry, narrative poetry, fiction, romance. "In the two preceding chapters," he remarked in a generalizing statement during the early stages of Book I, "I have considered the nature of oratory in general, its various forms, whether arising from difference in the object, understanding, imagination, passion, will; or in the subject, eminent and severe, light and frivolous, with their respective ends and characters." "Under these," he went on, "are included all the primary and characteristical qualities of whatever can pertinently find a place either in writing or in discourse, or can truly be termed fine in the one, or eloquent in the other."[361] As this statement would suggest, Campbell had previously declared that "The arts are frequently divided into the useful, and the polite, fine, or elegant."[362] But the point to be especially noticed is that he did not allow this distinction to become a dividing line between what rhetoric should properly cover and what it should not. "Eloquence and architecture, by which last term is always understood more than building merely for accommodation," he said, "are to be considered as of a mixed nature, wherein utility and beauty have almost equal influence."[363] Thus, with no thought that the poem is an example of fine and the oration of useful art, he could say later that "Poetry indeed is properly no other than a particular mode or form of certain branches of oratory," and he could repeat this idea still later in such a way as to make oratory the generic term for narration, description, epic poetry, and tragedy.[364] One of his most interesting chapters dealt with the little epic as an appeal to the imagination, comedy as an appeal to the passion of frolicsome contempt, and low satire, as an appeal to will and an incentive to the refinement of manners.[365] As for discourse in its nonpoetic branches, Campbell's *Rhetoric* also considered it oratory, of

[361] *Ibid.*, I, 82-83.　　[362] *Ibid.*, I, 7.　　[363] *Ibid.*, I, 8.
[364] *Ibid.*, I, 14, 30.　　[365] *Ibid.*, I, 41-83.

course; but here at least, the term as he used it was close to its traditional meaning.

He devoted a special chapter, for example, to oratory in its limited ancient sense, his emphasis being upon the judicial oration, the deliberative oration, and the sermon.[366] But his conception of the nonpoetical branch of oratory was not limited to these three forms. Indeed, in various scattered observations he made this branch consist also of conversational exchanges, familiar letters, philosophical dialogues, essays, political and philosophical writings, historical works, and didactic treatises, under which latter category he placed his own *Rhetoric*.[367]

There can be no doubt, however, that poetry, as Campbell conceived of it, stood somewhat apart from all nonpoetical compositions, and his thinking upon this matter obviously owed a debt to Bacon's *De Augmentis Scientiarum*. Bacon, we recall, had made poetry one of the three major divisions of human learning, its province being ruled by the imagination, while eloquence, as a subdivision of philosophy, was dependent upon reason, even though the imagination and will were instruments of its influence. To Bacon, indeed, philosophical discourse of all sorts, oratory included, differed from poetical compositions very much as the historian's concern for what is actual differs from the poet's concern for what is imagined. Bacon considered history to be the verbal record of the actual past, and in the composition of such a work the historian's memory is the dominant faculty, with reason and imagination in subordinate roles. Poesy, however, is the verbal record of an imagined past. The dominant faculty in its composition is imagination. Memory and reason are here subordinate. Thus Bacon called poesy "feigned history," that is, history as imitated by narrative, as made visible by drama, or as transformed by allegory.[368] And in the third of these categories he placed those poetic forms which present their truths "as it were through a veil; that is when the secrets and mysteries of religion, policy, and philosophy are involved in fables or parables."[369] Although Campbell did not match Bacon's great critical insight in respect to the definition of the differences between poetry and the other branches of composition, he followed Bacon's general plan, nevertheless, and his suggested formulation

[366] *Ibid.*, I, 248-277.
[367] *Ibid.*, I, ix, 26-29; II, 346.
[368] *Works of Bacon*, VIII, 440.
[369] *Ibid.*, VIII, 443.

of these differences constitutes an ingenious and distinctive aspect of his literary philosophy.

We have already observed that Campbell did not make poetry into the aesthetic branch of oratory and forthwith proceed to define its true nature in terms of the difference between fine and useful art. Nor did he identify poetry with verse and the other branches of oratory with prose. "In regard to versification," he remarked, "it is more to be considered as an appendage, than as a constituent of poetry."[370] What he did instead was to define the special character of poetry by associating it with the figurative or veiled as distinguished from the literal or open meaning of a literary text. This conception emerged on two distinct occasions in the *Rhetoric*.

It emerged first in connection with Campbell's discussion of the method by which a reader could detect nonsense in literary composition. When a literary text is intended as a literal statement, the method to be used in interpreting it consists in recognizing, said Campbell, that its words are merely the signs of things, and that their meaning is determined by having recourse to the things they signify.[371] If the meaning which a statement assigns to objects corresponds to the meaning which the objects independently have, then the statement may safely be said to make sense. Nonsense occurs when correspondencies of this sort cannot be established. Writings in the field of mystical theology or metaphysics, Campbell intimated, contain an abundance of general and abstract words, and seem eminently impressive to unsophisticated readers, but may turn out to have no meaning, once their words are made to define themselves in terms of the things signified.[372] Works which abound in metaphors, however, present a peculiar problem, he said, insofar as the words used therein are a sign of something that is itself a sign of something else, and when metaphor runs into allegory and enigma, the thought can be discovered only by seeing the literal sense of the words as an idea figuring forth a thought beyond. "Most readers," Campbell observed, "will account it much to bestow a transient glance on the literal sense, which lies nearest; but will never think of that meaning more remote, which the figures themselves are intended to signify." And he cast his own doctrine into a metaphor by remarking

[370] Campbell, I, 15.
[371] *Ibid.*, II, 115-116.
[372] *Ibid.*, II, 79-86, 123-129.

that a reader had to learn to detect the meaning of metaphorical composition by seeing it through "a double veil."[373]

The same theory of poetical interpretation emerged a second time when Campbell was explaining the uses of obscurity in literary composition.

The illustrations I have given on this topic [he said] will contribute in some measure to explain the obscurity that is requisite in allegories, apologues, parables, and enigmas. In all these sorts of composition, there are two senses plainly intended, the literal and the figurative: the language is solely the sign of the literal sense, and the literal sense is the sign of the figurative. Perspicuity in the style, which exhibits only the literal sense, is so far from being to be dispensed with here, that it is even more requisite in this kind of composition than in any other. Accordingly, you will perhaps nowhere find more perfect models both of simplicity and of perspicuity of style, than in the parables of the gospel.[374]

The figurative interpretation that is required in reading poetry necessitates the recognition that poetic truth is not the same as logical truth, although there is an analogy between the two. Thus Campbell observed that in pathetic or panegyrical compositions, "in order that the hearers may be moved or pleased, it is of great consequence to impress them with the belief of the reality of the subject." "Nay," he added, "even in those performances where truth, in regard to the individual facts related, is neither sought nor expected, as in some sorts of poetry, and in romance, truth still is an object to the mind, the general truths regarding character, manners, and incidents."

When these are preserved, [he went on] the piece may justly be denominated true, considered as a picture of life; though false, considered as a narrative of particular events. And even these untrue events must be counterfeits of truth, and bear its image; for in cases wherein the proposed end can be rendered consistent with unbelief, it cannot be rendered compatible with incredibility. Thus, in order to satisfy the mind, in most cases, truth, and in every case, what bears the semblance of truth, must be presented to it.[375]

[373] *Ibid.*, II, 117.   [374] *Ibid.*, II, 148-149.   [375] *Ibid.*, I, 98-99.

Campbell returned later to the perplexing problem of poetic truth, and once again he made it plain that the poet observed different standards from those prevailing in the other branches of oratory. He said:

> We know that fiction may be as plausible as truth. A narration may be possessed of this quality in the highest degree, which we not only regard as improbable, but know to be false. Probability is a light darted on the object, from the proofs, which for this reason are pertinently enough styled *evidence*. Plausibility is a native lustre issuing directly from the object. The former is the aim of the historian, the latter of the poet. That every one may be satisfied, that the second is generally not inferior to the first, in its influence on the mind, we need but appeal to the effects of tragedy, of epic, and even of romance, which in its principal characters, participates of the nature of poesy, though written in prose.[376]

Campbell did not proceed to elaborate more fully upon the differences between poetry and the other branches of oratory. Had he carried his researches further, he might have been led to go from Bacon to Aristotle, and to see that a connection existed between Bacon's distinction and that which Aristotle drew when he made poetry mimetic, and history and oratory, nonmimetic.[377] But Campbell at least came closer to suggesting the essential nature of poetry than did Adam Smith. To Smith, as we have seen, poetry differs from oratory as a pleasurable differs from a persuasive effect; and such a distinction does more to unite than to separate the two literary forms. By contrast, Campbell and Bacon unite them in respect to their capacity for significance, and divide them in respect to the way in which that significance is to be presented and understood. Their insight is worthy of praise, even if in the light of it Campbell seems to have erred in insisting that, despite the differences between oratory and poetry, the latter may be classed as a mode of the former.

Campbell like Bacon assigned the great process of communication (in Bacon's words, elocution or tradition) to the arts of gram-

[376] *Ibid.*, I, 211-212.

[377] See "Aristotle and Horace on Rhetoric and Poetics," *The Quarterly Journal of Speech*, LIV (1968), 325-339.

mar, logic, and rhetoric.[378] "As the soul is of heavenly extraction, and the body of earthly," said Campbell, "so the sense of the discourse ought to have its source in the invariable nature of truth and right; whereas the expression can derive its energy only from the arbitrary conventions of men, sources as unlike, or rather as widely different, as the breath of the Almighty and the dust of the earth."[379] This observation points to an important structural principle in Campbell's theory of discourse. It is by the sense, he said, that eloquence holds of logic, and it is by the expression that it holds of grammar and rhetoric.[380] True to this principle, Campbell dealt in his first book with eloquence as a concern of logic, while in the opening chapters of Book II, he dealt with it as a concern of grammar, and in the rest of the treatise, with it as a concern of rhetoric in the narrow sense which this term came finally to have in his critical lexicon. The logic of eloquence not only involved Campbell's two celebrated chapters upon matters related to logical theory, both of which have been analyzed elsewhere in my present work, but also his discussion of the forms of discourse, the nature of the audience, the reputation of the speaker, and the three special types of spoken address. The grammar of eloquence led Campbell to analyze literary usage and to expound the meritorious principle that grammatical truth in any language is achieved when speakers or writers conform to linguistic practices that are reputable, national, and current.[381] Students of the history of English usage would find this part of Campbell's *Rhetoric* refreshing and informative. As for that which Campbell came redundantly to call the rhetoric of eloquence, it involves a discussion of the traits of perspicuity and liveliness in English style, and at this point Campbell gave an attractive account of the stylistic practices of his own day. These matters and those embraced by his analysis of grammar and logic make up the whole of his distinguished contribution to the new rhetoric of eighteenth-century Britain.

Four evidences of Campbell's debt to Bacon's *De Augmentis Scientiarum* have not yet been mentioned in this account of the *Rhetoric*, and I should now like to dwell briefly upon the most

[378] See above, n. 338.   [379] Campbell, I, 99-100.
[380] *Ibid.*, I, 99; II, 1-3. See also above, Ch. 5, p. 398.
[381] Campbell, II, 2.

important one of them.[382] In fact, until that one is fully recognized, the modern reader cannot appreciate that a small connection openly established by Campbell between his work and the *De Augmentis Scientiarum* is intended as a large identification of his method with that advocated by Bacon for the development of new knowledge. Thus the *Rhetoric* is not simply influenced by Bacon; rather, it carries out a specific plan which to Bacon's mind would yield promising results towards the advancement of learning.

On the title page of each volume of the first edition of the *Rhetoric*, there is a quotation in Latin, and an indication that the quotation originates in the *De Augmentis Scientiarum*, Book v, Chapter 3. The quotation reads, "Certo sciant homines, *artes inveniendi solidas et veras adolescere et incrementa sumere cum ipsis inventis*," that is, "Let men be assured that the solid and true arts of invention grow and increase as inventions themselves increase."[383] This passage forms part of Bacon's discussion of the "Art of Inquiry or Invention," first of the four intellectual arts, the others being "Art of Examination or Judgment; Art of Custody or Memory; and Art of Elocution or Tradition."[384] In treating the art of invention, Bacon said that, so far as invention is a quest for new knowledge, it had to forget its past history and incorporate into its doctrine new precepts for conscious experimentation and new rules for the interpretation of nature, these latter being in Bacon's phrase the sphere of "the New Organon."[385] He later added to these two procedures a third, recognized already to a slight extent by some writers, he said, but not yet given the attention that its great utility deserved.[386] This third procedure was to consist in taking a particular subject and devising for it a set of directions which, if followed closely and systematically, could be expected to endow it with valuable new truth. This third procedure Bacon illustrated by drawing up a set of model directions for con-

[382] The three not discussed here concern Campbell's quotations from the *De Augmentis Scientiarum* in reference to fallacies of interpretation, to pretentious but empty writing, and to Raymond Lully's method of imposture. See Campbell, I, 182; II, 76, 128. See also *Works of Bacon*, II, 399, 431, 436; and (for Spedding's translation) IX, 97, 125, 129-30.

[383] See *Works of Bacon*, II, 289, for Bacon's Latin, and IX, 87, for Spedding's translation, which I quote here. The italics are Bacon's.

[384] *Works of Bacon*, IX, 63.

[385] *Ibid.*, IX, 64, 71. [386] *Ibid.*, IX, 86-92.

ducting an enquiry into the problem of the lightness and heaviness of bodies; and he proposed that each set of this kind be called a "topica particularis," that is, "a particular topic," to distinguish it from the general topics taught in the inventional systems of traditional rhetoric and logic. At one point in Bacon's discussion of the "topica particularis" he made the remark which Campbell put on his title page as the epigraph or theme-setting statement for his *Rhetoric*. Campbell would have expected his readers to understand this quotation in its context in the *De Augmentis Scientiarum*. He would have expected them to know, for example, that Bacon's very next words recommended the use of particular topics "so that when a man first enters into the pursuit of any knowledge, he may have some useful precepts of invention; but when he has made further advances in that knowledge, he may and ought to devise new precepts of invention, to lead him the better to that which lies beyond."[387] And then Bacon spoke thus, as Campbell would also have expected his readers to know:

> It is indeed like journeying in a champaign country; for when we have gone some part of our way, we are not only nearer to our journey's end, but we can likewise see better that part of the way which remains. In the same manner in sciences every step forward on the journey gives a nearer view of that which is to come.

Thus in the light of Campbell's epigraph as it occurs in its context in the *De Augmentis Scientiarum*, there can be no doubt that the *Rhetoric* represents the first attempt in history to construct a rhetorical theory under the acknowledged influence of Bacon's vision of the way in which new sciences would come into being as improvements upon past knowledge and as so many opportunities to get glimpses of truths still partially hidden from view. And it is indeed a curious circumstance that one of the foremost of the new rhetorics of eighteenth-century Britain should have issued directly from a prescription which the British founder of the new science had laid down for the advancement of learning. History appears at times to have a drift towards the appropriate.

Campbell did more than create the implication that his *Rhetoric* was intended both to represent an improvement upon the rhetorical doctrine of the past and to provide a foretaste of the

---

387 *Ibid.*, ix, 87.

doctrine that was to come. He actually stated his intention in these terms. His statement came at the end of his informal account of the history of rhetoric from the earliest times to his own day and beyond. There were four steps to be discerned in this history, he said. The first was that in which the natural capacities of human nature had led mankind to create verbal discourses well before the time when any principles governing such an activity existed. "As speakers existed before grammarians, and reasoners before logicians; so doubtless," he said, "there were orators before there were rhetoricians, and poets before critics."[388] In framing discourses that would operate upon the minds of others, these earliest authors were guided by their consciousness of what operated on their own minds, and by their practical experience with their fellows. As a second step, Campbell observed that, given a body of these verbal discourses as objects of study, the earliest rhetoricians had classified them according to the effects which they were intended to have, whether to explain, or to convince, or to please, or to move, or to persuade. The third step was taken when the precepts of rhetoric began to be formulated as a result of the study of these classes of discourse. What a discourse was intended to accomplish was compared with what it actually succeeded in accomplishing; the traits of successful and of unsuccessful discourses were noted; noted also were the circumstances that would enable a critic to discover what particular function a given discourse might perform and under what conditions it could be used; and out of this sort of study a set of principles had gradually evolved. This was the stage, said Campbell, in which rhetoric now found itself. The traditional rules for rhetorical and poetic compositions, as "transmitted to us from these distinguished names in the learned world, Aristotle, Cicero, and Quintilian," he remarked, "have been for the most part only translated by later critics, or put into a modish dress and new arrangement."[389] And now Campbell described what the final step should be: rhetoric must go beyond its concern for the study of specimens of discourse and enquire into the principles of human nature—the workings of the understanding, the imagination, the passions, the memory, and the will. Even as the success or failure of a given discourse had in the past been explained by considering only the

[388] Campbell, I, 16-17.   [389] Ibid., I, 19.

adjustment of its internal means to its external ends, so now its success or failure must be explained by studying its adjustment or lack of adjustment to the mental faculties which it is intended to address. By taking this final step, said Campbell, "we arrive at that knowledge of human nature, which, beside its other advantages, adds both weight and evidence to all precedent discoveries and rules."[390] "It is his purpose in this Work, on the one hand," Campbell had already said of his design in the *Rhetoric*, "to exhibit, he does not say, a correct map, but a tolerable sketch of the human mind; and aided by the lights which the poet and the orator so amply furnish, to disclose its secret movements, tracing its principal channels of perception and action, as near as possible, to their source: and, on the other hand, from the science of human nature, to ascertain, with greater precision, the radical principles of that art, whose object it is, by the use of language, to operate on the soul of the hearer. . . ."[391] And these endeavors, he later emphasized, "may be said to bring us into a new country, of which, though there have been some successful incursions occasionally made upon its frontiers, we are not yet in full possession."[392]

Within the terms just proposed, Campbell's *Rhetoric* is well fitted for a position of honor in this new country. That is to say, it is a rhetoric in which the principles of verbal composition are framed to stand in strict correspondence to Campbell's own way of explaining the operations of the human mind. First of all, under the authority of Francis Bacon, Campbell thought that the mind operated not only by delegating each of its separate powers to one of its separate faculties, but also by providing that each separate faculty would specialize in receiving its own kind of verbal communication, while being able to participate in the process by which certain ones of those communications could be made instruments of belief or action.[393] Thus rhetoric or eloquence, he declared, must teach that discourses are divided into

[390] *Ibid.*, I, 18.   [391] *Ibid.*, I, vii.   [392] *Ibid.*, I, 19.

[393] My present account of Campbell's *Rhetoric* has sought to show the full extent of Campbell's debt to Bacon's *De Augmentis Scientiarum*. For another approach to this same problem, see Vincent M. Bevilacqua, "Philosophical Origins of George Campbell's *Philosophy of Rhetoric*," *Speech Monographs*, XXXII (1965), 2-4.

classes as the mental faculties are divided into specialized functions. Secondly, under the authority of Aristotle and Bacon, Campbell thought that the human mind has a tendency to believe and act only in accordance with the promptings of its sense of truth and goodness. Thus rhetorical persuasion, he said, must recognize truth and goodness as its basic materials and must be forever responsive to them. Thirdly, under the authority of Locke and of Locke's disciples, Duncan, Reid, and Kames, Campbell thought that the human mind in its quest for truth reasoned naturally from the facts of experience to particular or general conclusions, and judged those conclusions by immediate intuition or by a mediate comparison with other related ideas.[394] Thus rhetorical proof, he said, must be aware of its foundation in natural logic and must abandon the sterile syllogizing taught in the schools. Fourthly, under the authority of Hume, Campbell thought that there was an association among the passions as well as the ideas of the mind, one passion or idea being likely to occur in company with another, whenever the two were connected by the mind's perception of their resemblance, their contiguity, or their causal, that is to say, their temporal and spatial relations, each to each.[395] Thus rhetoric, he said, must take cognizance of these principles of association in addressing discourse to the memory or (as in vehement oratory, tragedy, or comedy) to the passions. Fifthly, under the authority of Lowth, Vaugelas, and Priestley, Campbell thought that the human mind, through being accustomed to the linguistic usages of speakers or writers in a given community, accepted as correct a usage authorized by custom, and as incorrect a usage not so authorized, with attend-

[394] The contributions of Locke, Duncan, Reid, and Kames to Campbell's *Rhetoric* are discussed above, Ch. 5, pp. 406-408. See also Alta B. Hall, "George Campbell's *Philosophy of Rhetoric*, Book I, A Critical Edition" (unpubl. diss., Cornell University, 1934), for a sketch of Locke's influence upon Campbell; and for a mention of Reid's influence, see Douglas W. Ehninger, "Selected Theories of *Inventio* in English Rhetoric: 1759-1828" (unpubl. diss., The Ohio State University, 1949).

[395] Campbell, I, 197-199, 316-318. For a discussion of the extent to which Campbell was indebted to Hume, see Lloyd F. Bitzer, "The Lively Idea: A Study of Hume's Influence on George Campbell's *Philosophy of Rhetoric*" (unpubl. diss., State University of Iowa, 1962). See also, by the same author, "Hume's Philosophy in George Campbell's *Philosophy of Rhetoric*," *Philosophy & Rhetoric*, II (1969), 139-166.

ant consequences for the mind's reception of ideas.[396] Thus rhetorical usage, he said, must hold itself to grammatical practices that reputable, national, and current custom has established, if it would succeed in communicating ideas through language. Sixthly, under the authority of Locke, Berkeley, and Hume, Campbell thought that the human mind, accustomed to perceiving not only the connections among things, and the connections between things and words, but also the connection between one word and another in given contexts, betrayed a natural tendency, when puzzled by verbal meanings, to invoke its knowledge of the things presumably being signified, and by this means to make the words intelligible if they signified things, or to dismiss them as nonsense if they did not.[397] Thus rhetorical language, said Campbell, could assure itself of perspicuity, and avoid unintended ambiguity, only by observing between itself and things the connections which the mind has already been taught to observe. And seventhly, under the authority of Hume, Campbell thought that the imagination responded to "a lively and beautiful representation of a suitable object," the intensity of the response being determined by the vivacity and elegance of the expression.[398] Thus rhetoric, he said, must choose special rather than general terms, figurative rather than literal words, brief rather than verbose expressions, and orderly and neat rather than diffuse, rambling, and disorderly sentences. These seven principles of rhetoric and the seven psychological principles to which Campbell tied them may be said to furnish proof that his *Rhetoric* brought him indeed into a new country and put him into a fuller possession of it than any previous British rhetorician except Adam Smith had enjoyed. Smith's rhetoric is more original, more sociological, more conscious of its adjustment to sweeping historical change, than is that of Campbell. But Campbell is at all times a discriminating and resourceful interpreter of the ideas of an impressive cluster of creative modern philosophers and scholars, chief of whom is Bacon.

---

[396] For Campbell's references to Robert Lowth's *A Short Introduction to English Grammar*, see the following pages in the *Rhetoric*: I, 343-344, 360, 376, 401, 433, 488-490, 494, 496-497; for his reference to Claude Favre de Vaugelas's *Remarques sur La Langue Françoise*, see I, 349; and for his references to Joseph Priestley's *The Rudiments of English Grammar*, see I, 362, 375, 381, 401, 433, 437, 439, 470, 500, 506.

[397] Campbell, II, 92-129.   [398] *Ibid.*, I, 29, 190-194.

And, by virtue of Smith's refusal to publish his lectures during his lifetime, Campbell's *Rhetoric* must be called the leading British, and indeed the leading European, work on its subject to appear in the eighteenth century.

The preceding discussion has made it plain to any reflective reader that Campbell took the modern side upon each of the issues that in his time divided the old rhetoric from the new. Thus he refused to limit rhetoric to the three traditional types of oratory, but instead he made it into a general theory of discourse. Thus he refused to recognize artistic proofs and the ingenious topical system of Aristotle, and he stressed instead that rhetorical subject matter must come from intellection, consciousness, common sense, experience, analogy, and testimony.[399] Thus he subjected scholastic syllogizing to an even more destructive analysis than Locke had given it, and he prepared the way for the creation of a new inductive logic which rhetoricians of the future would have to accept.[400] Thus he did not endorse the practice of using loosely contrived probabilities as the only materials of rhetorical argument, and he proposed instead a careful method for the calculation of chances in cases where several outcomes were possible and predictions had to be made as to the likelihood that any one outcome would occur.[401] Thus he did not advocate the ceremonial six-part oration of the past, but instead he confined his structural recommendations to comments upon the methods of analysis and synthesis in dialectical procedures and upon the options available if a discourse were to be organized according to the principles governing the association of ideas and passions.[402] Thus finally he did not treat *elocutio* as if the tropes and the figures were its dominant ingredients, and the grand style somehow its truest and most desirable kind, but he emphasized instead that *elocutio* was founded in grammatical truth, that is, in the conformity of the speaker's ideas to those linguistic usages which are reputable, national, and current, and that, once grammatical truth was achieved, style had purity, and needed then to aim for perspicuity in addressing the understanding and for

---

[399] *Ibid.*, I, 103-151, 155-163; II, 123-129.

[400] *Ibid.*, I, 163-185.   [401] *Ibid.*, I, 151-155.

[402] *Ibid.*, I, 165-166, 195-199. Campbell's theory of oratorical structure is more fully developed in his *Lectures on Pulpit Eloquence* than in his *Rhetoric*. See below, p. 610.

vivacity in addressing the imagination, the passions, and the will.[403] In sum, it is not possible to convict Campbell of having ignored any of the disagreements which separated the traditional rhetoricians of his day from the moderns. And it is quite impossible to find that on any of these disagreements he sympathized with the past rather than the future.

Campbell's *Rhetoric* did not have a second edition until 1801, and by that time it had been in print for twenty-five years. Thereafter it grew steadily in popularity and influence by going through forty printings between 1801 and 1887. But then it suddenly lost its public. Thus it was an unread classic during the early twentieth century, when rhetoric began to shake itself loose from its preoccupation with voice and gesture and to seek to restore its broken lines of communication with its own great past. For example, the early twentieth-century American textbooks on public speaking did not recognize Campbell's *Rhetoric* as a major improvement upon Aristotelian theory and as the true standard which later rhetorics must be measured against in determining how far they had advanced their doctrines. Nor were early twentieth-century speculative writers on rhetoric free of the same sort of negligence. That is to say, Kenneth Burke's *Counter-Statement*, which sought to make rhetoric into a theory of literary form, was not visibly influenced by Campbell's *Rhetoric*, although Campbell had made his theory account in part for the form and in full for the content of eloquent discourse. As for I. A. Richards's *The Philosophy of Rhetoric*, it quoted Whately's *Elements of Rhetoric*, it mildly ridiculed Lord Kames's *Elements of Criticism*, and it mentioned Campbell's *Rhetoric* with respect, as it sought to define the role of rhetoric in modern criticism;[404] but although it did not wholly approve of Campbell's attitude towards the doctrine of usage, it neither disputed nor recognized the great value of Campbell's analysis of the method by which literary nonsense can be detected. If the problem of meanings is one of the most urgent of the tasks of the new rhetoric, Campbell must be said to have been taught by Locke, Berkeley, and Hume to be aware of it, and I. A. Richards, who contributed brilliantly to-

[403] *Ibid.*, I, 32, 339-511; II, 1-445.
[404] For Richards's references to Whately, see his *Philosophy of Rhetoric*, pp. 5-8; to Kames, see pp. 16-17, 38, 98-99, 101-108, 115, 124; to Campbell, see pp. 51-52, 103.

wards its solution, might have commended Campbell in that respect at least. Scholarship in rhetoric became interested in Campbell as recently as 1934, and thereafter various scholars have contributed to our understanding of his rhetorical theory.[405] In 1963 his *Rhetoric* received its first full-length twentieth-century printing, and the scholar responsible for that event was Lloyd F. Bitzer. Professor Bitzer's edition consists of a facsimile reprint of the text of the *Rhetoric* as published at London in 1850, and of an introductory essay by Bitzer himself on Campbell's achievements as rhetorician.[406] That essay lacks historical perspective, and it errs in arguing not only that Campbell believed feeling to be superior to reason in the governance of conduct, but also that "Vivacity, or the lively idea, is without doubt the key concept in Campbell's theory of rhetoric."[407] Campbell considered reason to be the dominant faculty, as we have seen. And in stressing repeatedly that an idea has power to move the soul only when the reason accepts it as truthful and the passions adopt it as good, he indicated unmistakably that vivacity of style in itself is unable to produce eloquence. But the point is, of course, that Bitzer's work, despite these deficiencies, will help to restore Campbell to a place of honor among British rhetorical theorists of modern times. Thus it should earn the gratitude of all concerned.

One episode in the history of Campbell's *Rhetoric* in the nineteenth century deserves special mention as I bring to an end my discussion of this particular part of his total achievement as a rhetorician. The episode concerns Herbert Spencer's well-known essay, "The Philosophy of Style," which Spencer published in *The*

[405] See above, nn. 393, 394, 395. See also John Crawford, "The Rhetoric of George Campbell" (unpubl. diss., Northwestern University, 1947); Clarence W. Edney, "George Campbell's Theory of Logical Truth," *Speech Monographs*, xv (1948), 19-32; Douglas W. Ehninger, "George Campbell and the Revolution in Inventional Theory," *Southern Speech Journal*, xv (1950), 270-276; Lloyd F. Bitzer, "A Re-evaluation of Campbell's Doctrine of Evidence," *The Quarterly Journal of Speech*, XLVI (1960), 135-140.

[406] *The Philosophy of Rhetoric*, by George Campbell, ed. Lloyd F. Bitzer, Foreword by David Potter (Carbondale, Illinois: Southern Illinois University Press, 1963). Cited below as Bitzer. My earlier comments upon the bibliographical history of the *Rhetoric* depend largely upon Bitzer's account, pp. xxix-xxxi.

[407] Bitzer, pp. xxiv-xxv.

Westminster and Foreign Quarterly Review on October 1, 1852. Like other articles in that periodical, Spencer's essay was headed by a list of books compiled to fix the attention of readers upon the subject to be covered. Spencer's list, which was never reprinted in the many later editions of his essay, consisted of four works: Richard Whately's *Elements of Rhetoric*; Hugh Blair's *Lectures on Rhetoric and Belles Lettres*; George Campbell's *The Philosophy of Rhetoric*; and Lord Kames's *Elements of Criticism*, mistitled *Elements of Rhetoric* on this occasion.[408] Complaining that "No general theory of expression seems yet to have been enunciated,"[409] Spencer devoted his essay to the task of correcting this shortcoming. His method of doing so was to announce that the economizing of the hearer's or reader's attention was the cardinal principle to which all the rules of rhetoric should be reduced. "Hence, carrying out the metaphor that language is the vehicle of thought," declared Spencer, "there seems reason to think that in all cases the friction and inertia of the vehicle deduct from its efficiency; and that in composition, the chief, if not the sole thing to be done, is, to reduce this friction and inertia to the smallest possible amount."[410] With this principle as guide, Spencer proceeded in the rest of the essay to argue that, when meanings are expressed in Saxon rather than in Latinized English, or in specific rather than in general terms, or in direct rather than in indirect sentences, or in figurative rather than in literal expressions, they have the power to the greatest possible extent to achieve an effortless reception on the part of the audience. In developing his thesis, Spencer quoted Campbell's *Rhetoric* with approval on one occasion, and on three other occasions he discussed points in such a way as to seem to have Campbell's similar discussions in mind.[411] But there are two other interesting things to observe

---

[408] See Herbert Spencer, *Essays: Moral, Political and Aesthetic* (New York, 1873), pp. 10, 20, for his quotations from Kames's mistitled work. The first quotation is from the *Elements of Criticism* (Edinburgh, 1762), II, 318, the second from II, 315.

[409] *Essays*, p. 10.

[410] *Ibid.*, p. 12.

[411] *Ibid.*, pp. 15, 16, 18-19, 26-27, where Spencer discusses successively the vividness of specific words, the proper arrangement of adjective and substantive, the proper arrangement of predicate and subject, and the superiority of the direct over the indirect sentence. For Campbell's treatment of these same topics, see the *Rhetoric*, II, 159, 312, 311, 316-317, 341.

about Spencer's relations to Campbell. One is that Spencer's complaint in regard to the lack of a general theory of expression seems to betray a surprising disregard for what Campbell's *Rhetoric* had succeeded in doing in that very direction some seventy-six years earlier. The other is that Spencer's theory of economy as devised to supply what he considered to be a deficiency in the record was in fact a constituent part of Campbell's theory of style and thus the record already contained it. Campbell expressed his own version of the theory of economy after he had presented several illustrations of sentences which were obscure through faulty arrangement.

> It may indeed be argued [he said], that, in these and the like examples, the least reflection in the reader will quickly remove the obscurity. But why is there any obscurity to be removed? Or why does the writer require more attention from the reader, or the speaker from the hearer, than is absolutely necessary? It ought to be remembered, that whatever application we must give to the words, is, in fact, so much deducted from what we owe to the sentiments. Besides, the effect that is exerted in a very close attention to the language, always weakens the effect which the thoughts were intended to produce in the mind. . . . A discourse, then, excells in perspicuity, when the subject engrosses the attention of the hearer, and the diction is so little minded by him, that he can scarce be said to be conscious, that it is through this medium he sees into the speaker's thoughts.[412]

If Spencer's essay can still be recommended to students of composition for the value of its principle of economy, then it seems obvious that Campbell's *Rhetoric*, which states that same principle and many others of similar worth, deserves also to be recommended to the same audience. And Campbell should take his place with Spencer in the wider company of theorists who in the last two hundred years have sought to create for our time as vital a rhetoric as that which Aristotle created for his.

Campbell's lectures on pulpit eloquence deserve a word as I bring to an end this appraisal of his work as rhetorician. Delivered initially in 1772-73, as I said earlier, these lectures were repeated in successive years until 1795, when Campbell's tenure as

---

[412] Campbell, II, 15-17.

professor of divinity and principal of Marischal College was ended by ill health and advancing age. As put into print in 1807, eleven years after his death, the lectures never had the benefit of the corrections which he would have wanted to make in preparing them for the public. But they had what it took to give them some vogue in the nineteenth century,[413] and to us on the present occasion they are of interest because they apply to the preacher the theoretical precepts that make Campbell's *Rhetoric* a major work in its field.[414]

In the course of the fifth of this series of twelve lectures, Campbell digressed to give his students a brief account of the stages in the growth of his professional interest in the practical applications of rhetorical theory. During his years as an apprentice lawyer in Edinburgh, he had given some attention, he said, to the forensic oratory of the ancients, and later, when he began to prepare for a career as preacher, he had carefully studied the similarities and differences between that kind of discourse and the eloquence of the Christian pulpit. Then, as a student of divinity, he and six or seven other students had formed a society to consider the doctrines of theology and the practical duties of a pastor, and they had added other students to the group as time went on. One thing they did, remarked Campbell, was to undertake "an inquiry into the nature of sermons and other discourses proper for the pulpit, the different kinds into which they might fitly be distributed, and the rules of composition that suited each."[415] After discussing this topic together, the group finally assigned Campbell to make an abstract of what had been said, and this abstract was then copied by each member who chose to do so, and was communicated at the pleasure of the copier to any interested party whatever. "I have a copy of this still in my possession," Campbell told his students, and he went on to observe, not

---

[413] See Harry Caplan and Henry H. King, "Pulpit Eloquence, A List of Doctrinal and Historical Studies in English," *Speech Monographs*, XXII, 4 (1955), p. 25. Caplan and King list twelve printings of the lectures between 1807 and 1849.

[414] My present discussion is based upon the following edition: *Lectures on Systematic Theology and Pulpit Eloquence*, By the late George Campbell (Philadelphia, 1810). The lectures on pulpit eloquence are printed on pp. 157-333. The "Advertisement," p. iii, indicates when they were first delivered.

[415] *Lectures on Pulpit Eloquence*, p. 213.

only that he was drawing upon it freely for his present lectures, and that such a society as he and his fellows had formed in those days illustrated how far all students could contribute to their own improvement, but also that he himself should not be considered the sole author of what he was presently saying about the composition of sermons. The abstract which Campbell had prepared at the request of his fellow students was to be regarded, he said, as "the outline of an institute of pulpit eloquence."[416]

Campbell's lectures upon the heads of that outline fell into three parts. First of all, he talked about the minister in his role as public speaker, and to this topic he devoted his first lecture. Secondly, he talked about the sermon as the product of three abilities, one of which had to do with the sentiments being expressed, another, with verbal expression, and still another, with pronunciation or delivery; and to each ability he devoted a single lecture. It should be remarked that, in speaking of verbal expression, he said that this activity was traditionally called elocution, and that the recent tendency to use the latter term to designate pronunciation was of dubious propriety.[417] Thirdly, he talked about the various kinds of discourses involved in the concept of Christian eloquence, and having discerned two classes in all, he devoted his last eight lectures to them.[418]

Thus he spoke first of discourses which he considered to be lectures rather than sermons. Lectures, he said, were of two kinds, each expository in nature, one kind being devoted to the explication of a text from Scripture, and the other, to the application of a text to practical issues concerning providence, grace, and the conduct of life. The importance which he attached to these two forms is indicated by what he said as he began to discuss them. "As the Bible," he remarked, "is with us protestants acknowledged to be the repository, and indeed the only original, full, and untainted repository of christian knowledge; and as the study of it is maintained to be a duty incumbent on every disciple of Christ, that kind of discourses with us commonly called *lectures,* have been devised as means of facilitating to the people the profitable reading of holy writ."[419] Thus it is no surprise that Campbell devoted the greater part of one of his own lectures to these two forms of discourse.

[416] *Ibid.,* p. 212.
[418] *Ibid.,* pp. 231-242, 243-333.
[417] *Ibid.,* p. 180.
[419] *Ibid.,* p. 231.

As for discourses properly called sermons, Campbell described them in the same sort of terminology that he had used in the *Rhetoric* to designate the five kinds of oratory and their relation to the four major mental faculties. Thus he said that there were explanatory sermons and controversial sermons, both of which were addressed to the understanding, and that there were commendatory sermons for the imagination, pathetic sermons for the passions, and persuasive sermons for the will.[420] The controversial sermon, he noted, resembled the forensic oration of ancient rhetoric, the commendatory sermon, the ancient panegyric, and the persuasive sermon, the ancient deliberative speech.[421] To these forms Campbell devoted only a small amount of attention. He gave one lecture on the first, one lecture on the second, and half a lecture on the third, as if indeed he expected his students to go to classical theory for whatever they might need in the way of additional information about each of them. "It is not my intention by these lectures," he said on a later occasion with this very expectation in mind, "to supersede the study of ancient critics and orators, but only to assist you in applying their rules and examples to cases so different from those with which alone they were concerned."[422] But what about the explanatory and pathetic sermons? Could the modern preacher hope to go to classical rhetoric for directions that might apply by analogy to them? No, said Campbell, there is in the ancient rhetorical institutes nothing that can be called analogous to these two forms.[423] So far as explanatory sermons and philosophical lessons are concerned, he added, "no person, as far as I know, has thought it necessary to lay down rules," whereas "The fourth kind, the pathetic, hath in point of aim more similarity to the eloquence of the theatre, tragedy in particular, than to that either of the bar or of the senate."[424] Here, then, are the precise areas in which Campbell might hope to make a distinctive contribution to rhetorical theory—the areas of exposition and irrational appeal. And he made his contribution, to be sure. But he did so in a way that belongs peculiarly to the new rhetoric—he slighted the pathetic sermon, which seeks to arouse passion, by devoting only half a lecture to it, and he emphasized the explanatory sermon, which aims to replace ignorance with knowledge, by discussing it in three full lectures.

[420] *Ibid.*, pp. 214-221, 243, 290, 305, 320, 325.   [421] *Ibid.*, pp. 221-223.
[422] *Ibid.*, pp. 310-311.   [423] *Ibid.*, pp. 223-224.   [424] *Ibid.*, p. 224.

Campbell's strong sympathy for the new rhetoric, and for the new logic as well, was in evidence in other parts of these discourses on pulpit eloquence, and I shall mention three additional instances of it in bringing this appraisal to an end.

One instance had to do with his attitude towards the structure of sermons. Woven throughout his last six lectures were comments and advice upon the divisions which sermons ought to have, and while the divisions of one kind were not exactly parallel to those of another, it is true that all kinds had a text, an introduction of subject, an explanation of the connection between subject and text, a partition, a discussion of parts, and a conclusion, with refutation and proof featured as the formula for the development of the controversial sermon.[425] These structural ingredients remind us, of course, of those of the classical oration. But Campbell treated them flexibly and never insisted that they should all be present in a given discourse. And he took occasion to condemn the Neo-Scholastic practice of dividing the body of the modern sermon into subject, predicate, and copula. Such a practice, he said, "is the genuine offspring of the dialectic of the schools, and fifty times more artificial, or if you will mechanical, than that which true rhetoric would inculcate."[426] "On the contrary, it is the business of the latter," he continued, "to bring men back from all scholastic pedantry and jargon, to nature, simplicity, and truth. And let me add, that discourses on this plan will be found much more conformable, in manner and composition, to the simple but excellent models to be found in sacred writ."

Another instance of Campbell's sympathy for the new rhetoric occurred in his discussion of the style of pulpit oratory. He urged his students as Scots to acquire an exact knowledge of English speech so that they would be understood "over all the British empire."[427]

Besides, from the greater intercourse we have now with England [he said later], it is manifest, that their idiom and pronunciation are daily gaining ground amongst us. In consequence of this, more will be expected than formerly from a public speaker, who in every improvement in regard to lan-

[425] *Ibid.*, pp. 245, 259, 263, 265, 277, 286, 291, 293, 307-308, 315, 322, 327, 330, 332.
[426] *Ibid.*, pp. 275-276.   [427] *Ibid.*, p. 182.

guage, which so nearly concerns his own department, ought to be among the first, rather than among the last.[428]

But over and above grammatical purity was rhetorical strength, and the style of sermons was rhetorically strong, said Campbell, when it was perspicuous and affecting.[429] The great enemies of perspicuity, he emphasized, were pedantry and ostentation of learning. "The pedant in literature is perfectly analogous," he declared, "to the hypocrite in religion."[430] "The nearer therefore your diction comes to the language of conversation, it will be the more familiar . . . , and so the more easily apprehended. In this too the style of scripture is an excellent model."[431] As for the affecting style, Campbell mentioned that it required not only what the French called *onction* but also what he himself would call grave and serious language.[432] And he promised to discuss this kind of style when he treated the pathetic sermon. But he did not do so. What he did instead was to devote some special attention to the style of the explanatory sermon, counselling that, in this kind of discourse, "the style should be remarkably simple and perspicuous," and the vocabulary free "of the cobweb distinctions of schoolmen and metaphysicians."[433]

A final instance of Campbell's sympathy for the new rhetoric is provided at the end of his first lecture. He was discussing there the contribution which the arts of grammar, dialectic, and rhetoric may make to pulpit eloquence. His remarks upon grammar at that point anticipate those which I have already quoted in connection with his emphasis upon the mastery of the idioms and usages of the English tongue.[434] By skill in dialectic, "I do not mean being well versed in the artificial dialectic of the schools," he said, "though this, I acknowledge, doth not want its use, but being conversant in the natural and genuine principles and grounds of reasoning, whether derived from sense or memory, from comparison of related ideas, from testimony, experience, or analogy."[435] "School logic, as was well observed by Mr. Locke," he added, "is much better calculated for the detection of sophistry than the discovery of truth. . . . But true logic . . . is best studied not in a scholastic system, but in the writings of the most

[428] *Ibid.*, pp. 183-184.   [429] *Ibid.*, p. 184.   [430] *Ibid.*, p. 187.
[431] *Ibid.*, p. 191.   [432] *Ibid.*, p. 192.   [433] *Ibid.*, pp. 280, 282.
[434] *Ibid.*, pp. 166, 182-184.   [435] *Ibid.*, p. 165.

judicious and best reasoners on the various subjects supplied by history, science, and philosophy." As to rhetoric, he went on, modern writers "appear to me to have made hardly any advance or improvement upon the ancients."[436] What is valuable in them, whether they are in French or English, "is servilely copied from Aristotle, Cicero, and Quintilian. . . ."[437] Campbell paused here to say that every public speaker ought to be directly conversant with Quintilian's *Institutio Oratoria*, with the *Rhetorica ad Herennium*, and with Cicero's *De Inventione* and *De Oratore*; but then he remarked that his students should also consult certain rhetorical treatises of more recent date. "Of modern authors considered in both views, as teachers of the art, and as performers," he said, "I would recommend what Rollin and Fenelon have written on the subject. . . ."[438] And to this short list of new rhetoricians, among whom the twentieth-century critic would want to rank Fénelon far higher than Rollin, Campbell added at once "the ingenious and truly eloquent Dr. Blair," noting as he did so that Blair's lectures on eloquence had lately been published. Campbell implied that his own name was eligible for inclusion in that list. For in the same lecture he recommended that his audience read what his *Rhetoric* had to say not only about the relations of eloquence to logic and grammar but also about pulpit oratory and its connection with the other modern kinds of public speaking.[439] Thus Campbell must be considered a good judge of the rhetoricians of his day as well as a good rhetorician himself. He saw his own time in its true light. And this verdict in his favor is easy indeed to pronounce today when we remember that, had his judgment been insecure, he might have recommended to his students that they read the rhetorical writings of Thomas Sheridan. During the era in which Campbell was composing his own theory of eloquence, Sheridan was clamoring for recognition as the true discoverer of the long-lost art of rhetoric, and his claims to that distinction had been filed before audiences in Scotland.[440] It is a mark in Campbell's favor that he was not impressed.

[436] *Ibid.*, p. 166.   [437] *Ibid.*, p. 167.   [438] *Ibid.*, p. 167.

[439] *Ibid.*, pp. 165, 167. Had his students read the *Rhetoric*, they would have noticed some close verbal similarities between it and the lectures. Compare the *Lectures on Pulpit Eloquence*, pp. 180, 214-216, with the *Rhetoric*, I, 96, 102, 26, 29-33.

[440] See above, Ch. 4, pp. 158, 234.

VI Discordant Consensus: Hume, Lawson, Priestley, Blair, Witherspoon

So far as the present history of eighteenth-century British rhetoric is concerned, only one aspect remains to be discussed, and I turn now to the five authors who give it content and interest. One of them was the eminent philosopher and historian David Hume; another was John Lawson, Irish Anglican, who served as professor of oratory and history at Trinity College, Dublin; another was Joseph Priestley, now remembered as the chemist who discovered oxygen, but in his own time chiefly known as a Nonconformist theologian and a sharp critic of British policy towards the American colonies; still another was Hugh Blair, whose professorship of rhetoric and belles lettres at the University of Edinburgh resulted, as we know, from the success of Adam Smith's lectures on those subjects in that city; and still another was the Reverend John Witherspoon, Edinburgh master of arts of the year 1739, who went to America in 1768 as sixth president of what is now Princeton University, and who engaged himself within a few weeks of his arrival there to give the students lectures on various subjects, one of which he designated as "Composition, and the Eloquence of the Pulpit and the Bar."[441] From each of these men came a work that deserves notice by anyone seeking to view eighteenth-century British rhetoric as a whole. My present task will be to comment upon these works in such a way as to show where each stands in relation either to the old rhetoric of John Ward and John Holmes or to the new rhetoric of Adam Smith and George Campbell.[442]

[441] See Varnum L. Collins, *President Witherspoon, A Biography* (Princeton, New Jersey, 1925), I, 112.

[442] Anselm Bayly's *The Alliance of Musick, Poetry, and Oratory* (London, 1789), dedicated to "The Right Honorable William Pitt, Chancellor of the Exchequer and first Lord of the Treasury," devotes 64 pages to oratorical and rhetorical matters, the principal points of emphasis being style, the parts of the oration, the accomplishments of the orator and preacher, preaching methods in England, and oratorical delivery. Bayly took the modern side in two ways: 1) by teaching that "The perfection of style then, and of general use, either in poetry, oratory or history, is the plain and middle" (p. 324); and 2) by admitting that the theory of oratorical structure, even when reduced to four parts, as the ancients of course allowed, was to be regarded less as a system of rigid guides and shackles than as something to be heeded only now

David Hume's short essay, "Of Eloquence," first published at Edinburgh in 1742 and subsequently republished on nine other occasions during its author's lifetime, argued that modern British eloquence was greatly inferior to that of ancient Greece and Rome and to that of advanced nations in modern Europe, even though the British people equalled or surpassed all others in respect to native genius, scientific learning, and the inducements which popular governments afford to orators.[443] Eloquence to Hume was associated with the art of speaking in public, and it came into being whenever a public discourse became the agent of the sublime faculties of the mind and took on qualities of vehemence in thought, style, and action. In other words, eloquent discourse had force and energy; it expressed itself in bold and striking figures; it inflamed the passions and elevated the imagination. And its greatest representative was Demosthenes, with Cicero not far behind. Indeed, the eloquence of Demosthenes set the standard for true taste, said Hume, and he went on to develop the idea that true taste in oratory was not associated with the refined verdict of science and erudition but with the verdict of the people.

Now to judge by this rule [said Hume], ancient eloquence, that is, the sublime and passionate, is of a much juster taste than the modern, or the argumentative and rational; and, if properly executed, will always have more command and authority over mankind. We are satisfied with our mediocrity, because we have had no experience of anything better: But

---

and then (pp. 337-338). Bayly's work, however, is hardly of major interest, and I shall not discuss it further here. I have not attempted in this history to do anything with unpublished lectures on rhetoric by such men as Thomas Reid, Robert Watson, James Beattie, and Alexander Gerard. Nor have I considered Lord Kames's *Elements of Criticism* as a contribution to rhetorical theory. Works like George Jardine's *Outlines of Philosophical Education* (Glasgow, 1825) and William Barron's *Lectures on Belles Lettres and Logic* (London, 1806) show how rhetoric and logic were handled together within the same course at Glasgow and St. Andrew's, but they are so completely in the school of Bacon, Locke, and Adam Smith as to make a discussion of them appear unnecessary at this time.

[443] See David Hume, *Essays Moral, Political, and Literary*, ed. T. H. Green and T. H. Grose (London, 1898), I, 163-174. For the bibliographical history of the works in which "Of Eloquence" was published before Hume's death in 1776, see Jessop, pp. 5-7, 16-17.

the ancients had experience of both, and, upon comparison, gave the preference to that kind, of which they have left us such applauded models. For, if I mistake not, our modern eloquence is of the same stile or species with that which ancient critics denominated ATTIC eloquence, that is, calm, elegant, and subtile, which instructed the reason more than affected the passions, and never raised its tone above argument or common discourse. Such was the eloquence of LYSIAS among the ATHENIANS, and of CALVUS among the ROMANS. These were esteemed in their time; but when compared with DEMOSTHENES and CICERO, were eclipsed like a taper when set in the rays of a meridian sun.[444]

At an earlier point in the essay, Hume specifically denied that historical changes in the conditions under which the orator practices his art could account for the decline of eloquence in modern Britain. Such things as the modern reliance of lawyers upon precise statutes and precedents, the culturally determined preference of modern judges for solid facts and arguments as the basis of decision, and the diminished presence of spectacular civil disorders and crimes of violence in modern life, were not in themselves reasons for declaring, he said, that the strains of ancient eloquence were unsuited to these later times. And he suggested that a few successful attempts in Britain to reach the heights of Demosthenes and Cicero would be all that are needed to excite emulation among British youth and to produce a succession of eloquent speakers. The French nation, which did not have the incentives of popular government to assist them, had achieved eloquence to a higher degree than Britain, said Hume, no doubt because, in the persons of great preachers like Fléchier and Bossuet, great pleaders like Patru, and great parliamentary orators like Talon, the French had fine modern specimens of ancient vehemence to emulate.

Hume's entire argument is of course an endorsement of the values of the old and a denial of the leading tenets of the new rhetoric. The new rhetoric, as interpreted by Francis Bacon and George Campbell, for example, affirmed that an audience is moved by discourse only when discourse makes truth visible, and that vehemence, passion, and force achieve a merely transitory

---

[444] Hume, *Essays*, I, 172-173.

influence in and by themselves. The new rhetoric, as interpreted by Adam Smith, affirmed that an audience bred to trust forthright argument and scientific standards of demonstration would not credit proofs derived from the ancient topics, however seductive those proofs might be made to appear under the ministrations of a brilliant stylist. The new rhetoric, as interpreted again by Adam Smith, would doubt whether Demosthenes or Cicero would ever succeed before popular audiences of other places and of later times, or whether the emulation of these great speakers by youths in different cultures could ever be expected to produce anything but disaster. And the new rhetoric, as interpreted this time by Robert Boyle, would argue that the Scriptures achieved the highest eloquence in their capacity to move mankind, even if their style seemed oddly plain and unadorned by the standards of Demosthenes and Cicero. In fact, despite his great acuteness of mind, and his disposition to regard events in the history of taste, wit, and philosophy as being subject to greater variations from one age to another than are events in civil history, Hume seems curiously static, curiously unhistorical, and curiously antiquarian, in his attitude towards eloquence. And yet he is so fully a member of the empirical tradition of Bacon and Locke, and so modern in his own literary idiom and style, that his essay "Of Eloquence" cannot be made to belong wholly to the school of the Neo-Ciceronians like Ward and Holmes.

John Lawson was appointed professor of oratory and history at the University of Dublin on the foundation of Erasmus Smith in 1753, and in 1758, the year before his death, he published as one of the results of that professorship a book entitled *Lectures concerning Oratory. Delivered in Trinity College*. The professorship in oratory and history had been founded in May, 1724, upon a grant from the governors of the estate of Erasmus Smith, a Londoner, who had died in 1691, after having arranged that his immense holdings in Irish lands under the Cromwellian settlement should become a source of income to endow educational programs at the University of Dublin and elsewhere.[445] Before he succeeded to that professorship, Lawson had graduated B.A. at

[445] See W. B. S. Taylor, *History of the University of Dublin* (London, 1845), pp. 65-67; Constantia Maxwell, *A History of Trinity College Dublin 1591-1892* (Dublin, 1946), p. 120.

Dublin in 1731, and had later become at the same institution a master of arts (1734), a Fellow (1735), a Senior Fellow (1743), a doctor of divinity (1745), Archbishop King's Lecturer in Divinity (1746), and first librarian.[446] The lectures that he later published were devoted, not to oratory and history together, but to oratory alone, as his title makes clear; and it is quite possible that earlier and later occupants of his chair were like him in emphasizing one of these subjects at the expense of the other. At any rate, this particular professorship was ruled in 1762 to belong exclusively to oratory.[447] Thereafter it seems, however, to have produced no publications during the rest of the century. In fact, Lawson's *Lectures* stand out as the only surviving printed documents connected with the teaching of rhetoric at Trinity College from 1724 to 1800 on the foundation of Erasmus Smith.[448]

Courses offered to students under that particular endowment extended throughout the college year.[449] Since Lawson tells us that he lectured at certain periods and at other periods held classes devoted to student exercises,[450] it is reasonable to assume that in a given college year he would deliver one lecture and hold one class period each week. At any rate, the twenty-three lectures in the work which he finally published would harmonize well with that kind of program. The following heads of doctrine indicate what his lectures were about: eloquence as a praiseworthy, difficult, and often disparaged accomplishment; ancient and modern eloquence; the rhetorical classics; imitation as a way of becoming eloquent; eloquence as an address to the understanding, to the passions, and to the outward senses; pulpit eloquence; elo-

[446] See Taylor, pp. 282, 442; also *Alumni Dublinenses*, s.v. Lawson, John; also *The Dictionary of National Biography*, s.v. Lawson, John (1712-1759). For an account of Archbishop King's Lectureship in Divinity, see Maxwell, *History of Trinity College*, pp. 92, 149.

[447] See Denis C. Heron, *The Constitutional History of the University of Dublin* (Dublin, 1847), p. 72.

[448] Lawson himself said of his plan to deliver lectures in connection with his professorship in oratory that it represented a new departure, "as Lectures on the present Argument have been long disused; or rather have never been carried on in a continued and regular Course." See *Lectures concerning Oratory* (Dublin, 1758), p. 4. He remarked earlier that the publication of his lectures was also a new departure. *Ibid.*, p. xiii. But apparently his successors in the professorship did not choose to follow these innovations.

[449] Taylor, p. 66.   [450] *Lectures concerning Oratory*, pp. x-xii.

quence as it may be represented in a fable or discussed in a fictitious dialogue; and eloquence as it concerns the practice of
composing poetry in Latin. What I should like to do now is to
comment upon certain ideas which Lawson developed in relation
to these heads of doctrine, my purpose being not to summarize
his lectures or to give a complete account of his teachings upon
any one subject but to show what kind of rhetorician he was.[451]

One of Lawson's basic ideas had to do with the relation of rhetoric to truth. Is rhetoric the art of misrepresenting things to people who are indifferent to falsehood? Or is it the art of getting
people to accept the truth in situations where they want only to
embrace it but are prevented from doing so by their own in-
dolence and prejudice? Lawson came to terms with these questions by answering the latter in the affirmative, and by citing
Bacon as a witness on his side.

> Some wise and thinking Men, among whom I find Mr. *Lock,*
> have been of Opinion [he said], that the Study of Eloquence
> ought to be discouraged, as being the Art of deceiving agree-
> ably. In which Censure, they have manifestly mistaken for the
> Art, the Abuse of the Art. She furnisheth Arms for the Defence
> of Truth only; if any bred up in her Schools have employed
> these in the Service of Falshood, their's, not her's, is the Re-
> proach; they are not her Sons, but Deserters from her. Elo-
> quence, saith Lord *Bacon,* is inferior to Wisdom in Excellence,
> yet superior in common Use. Thus the wise Man saith, *The wise
> in Heart shall be called prudent; and the Sweetness of the Lips
> increaseth Learning*; signifying, that Profoundness of Wisdom
> will help a Man to a Name or Admiration; but that it is Elo-
> quence, which prevaileth in active Life.
>
> Let us then consider Eloquence in this Light, in her genuine
> State, as the Handmaid of Truth.[452]

[451] For another study with this same object, see Ray E. Keesey, "John
Lawson's *Lectures concerning Oratory," Speech Monographs,* xx (1953), 49-57.
Keesey treats the lectures as if Lawson intended them mainly as a paraphrase
of the ancient doctrines of invention, disposition, style, and delivery—a verdict which leaves unrecognized the clear traces of modernity in his theory.

[452] *Lectures concerning Oratory,* pp. 126-127. The last part of the first
paragraph of this passage is a somewhat imperfect quotation from Bacon's
Advancement of Learning, its source being indicated by Lawson himself in
an accompanying footnote. See *Works of Bacon,* vi, 296-297. In Bacon's text,

This explanation occurred in the eighth lecture, when Lawson was preparing to discuss eloquence as it addresses itself to the understanding. But he expressed similar sentiments during the first lecture, when definitions were particularly in order. It may be that it is more estimable to find truth than to impart it, he said on that occasion, but truth must be imparted, nevertheless. He continued thus:

> For Mankind, however Curious and Lovers of Truth, will seldom give Admission to her, if presented in her own native unadorned Shape. She must soften the Severity of her Aspect, must borrow the Embellishments of Rhetorick, must employ all the Charms and Address of that, to fix, conquer, and win over the Distractions, Prejudices, and Indolence of Mankind. If because Reason is natural to Men, they were to be left to the Power of simple, unassisted Reason, the Minds of the Multitude would be in a State as destitute as their Bodies, if abandoned equally to Nature alone, without Raiment, without Houses. Eloquence we may therefore stile the Cloathing of Reason, which at first coarse and plain, a Defence meerly against the Rigour of the Seasons, became at Length a Source of Beauty. . . .[453]

Another of Lawson's basic ideas concerned the problem of organizing a system of rhetoric into its major parts. Should these parts be defined in Aristotelian terms as a set of authorial procedures enumerated as invention, disposition, elocution, and pronunciation? Or should these parts be defined in Baconian terms by considering that the precepts connected with a given discourse are determined by the characteristics of the mental faculty to which it is addressed? Lawson solved this problem by following Bacon's example in respect to the mainheads, and Aristotle's example in respect to the subheads, of rhetorical doctrine. Thus he devoted two lectures to eloquence as it concerns man's reason, two lectures to eloquence as it concerns man's passions, and seven lectures to eloquence as it concerns man's outward senses.[454] In

---

the word "Salomon" [sic] appears in place of Lawson's "the wise Man," and Bacon cited Solomon's aphorism in Latin, not in English. For the aphorism itself, see Proverbs 16.21.

[453] *Lectures concerning Oratory*, pp. 5-6; see also pp. 257-258, 278-280.

[454] Lawson's theory of the mental faculties must be regarded, however, as an attempt not so much to imitate as to revise the theory espoused by Bacon.

discussing the address to reason, he found it necessary to say something about invention and disposition, the first of which he described as *"Sagacity* in discovering Arguments," and the other, as *"Skill* in ranging them to the best Advantage."[455] Later, when he treated eloquence as an address to the outward senses, he introduced the subjects of elocution and pronunciation.[456] It should be admitted, of course, that the four authorial procedures of rhetoric also figure in Lawson's account of pulpit eloquence, and that he gave pronunciation full treatment only when he spoke of it under this latter heading.[457] Hence he can be criticized for repetitiousness in his handling of the four procedures, but he cannot be said to have bound himself to the idea that they alone were the proper heads for rhetorical theory.

Still another of Lawson's basic ideas concerned the question of the speaker's attitude towards what he is saying. Should the speaker feel in himself the emotion which he would invoke in his hearers? Or should he only appear to feel that emotion, and having achieved its external manifestations, exclude it from his own inner awareness, on the ground that to experience it is to become incapable of carrying out a rhetorical purpose? When Lawson faced these questions for the first time, he gave what appeared to be an unqualified affirmative answer to the former, but, on facing them later, he reversed himself completely, and allowed an affirmative answer to the latter to become his final position. Here is the full story. As he was treating discourses addressed to the passions, he laid down two rules for his students to follow in this

---

To Bacon, the precepts of rhetoric emerged from the study of the faculties of understanding, imagination, passions, memory, and will. To Lawson, "every Mode of Apprehension from simple Sensation up to the most abstract Reasoning, many of which we distinguish by the Names of the several Faculties, are only Actions of the same Faculty of the Understanding. . . ." (*Lectures concerning Oratory*, p. 154.) To be sure, Lawson did not adhere to this doctrine with any great consistency, for he later allowed the will to become a major faculty, and still later he named four faculties—reason, passion, imagination, and the outward senses—as having a place in the theory of discourse. (*Ibid.*, pp. 168, 219-222.) But the point is not so much that he altered the doctrine in respect to details as that he adhered to its main outlines in deciding what the true heads of rhetoric were. For his own enumeration of these heads, see *Ibid.*, pp. 25, 126, 153, 187.

[455] *Ibid.*, p. 127. [456] *Ibid.*, p. 187.
[457] *Ibid.*, pp. 359-376, 376-408, 409-411, 411-431.

kind of oratory, the first being to "Observe, which, of what Kind and Turn are the Passages, that most affect your selves and others; from thence take your Direction,"[458] and the second, to "Be yourself possessed with the Passion, you would excite." As Lawson himself took pains to indicate, the second rule as he phrased it was in fact a translation of Horace's famous lines, "Si vis me flere, dolendum [est] Primum ipsi tibi," and he might well have added, of course, that Cicero had anticipated Horace in subscribing to these same sentiments.[459] Between his eleventh lecture, in which he committed himself to Horace's doctrine, and his fifteenth lecture, wherein he announced his change of mind, Lawson read or heard that actors would be unable to express an emotion if they allowed themselves simultaneously to feel it; and he decided forthwith that speakers would be subject to the same inability. As he was discussing the tropes and schemes under the familiar thesis that "Figures are the Language of Passion,"[460] the moment came for him to announce this new position. He said:

> I have read, or met with in Discourse, an Observation which I think judicious and new: An Actor, who would excel, should appear to be possessed with the strong Passion his Part expresseth, and seem the Man he represents; but he should not feel that Passion, should not be that Man. Why? Because the Strength of the Passion would disable him from expressing it. . . .

> This Remark may help to explain some Things before said and unavoidably repeated concerning Points in which we often mistake. A good Speaker must seem to feel the Passion he would excite, he must have it's Air, it's Language, the Figures most expressive of it's actual Influence; but I now add, that he must not be under that actual Influence: However outwardly in Transport, he must retain a Fund of Coolness within, Reason must rule there, "Calm and serene ride in the Whirlwind,

---

[458] *Ibid.*, p. 169.

[459] *Ibid.*, p. 170. Lawson's quotation from Horace's Latin text omits the bracketed word. See *Ars Poetica*, 102-103. Moreover, Lawson's translation omits Horace's poetic concreteness. Horace actually said, "If you wish me to shed tears, you must first grieve yourself." For a similar sentiment in Cicero, see *De Oratore*, 2.45.189-190.

[460] *Lectures concerning Oratory*, p. 252.

and direct the Storm:" Otherwise losing Command of himself, he must stray from all the Rules of Eloquence.[461]

This new position as it applies to speakers would also have some support from Cicero,[462] and thus it is not in fact a reversal of the tenets of classical rhetoric. But it is not as common a classical view as that which Lawson had earlier expressed. It consequently stands in his system as something of a departure from the conventional form of classical doctrine, even as it is a departure from what he himself had previously said.

Another of Lawson's basic ideas concerned oratorical delivery, which Lawson prevailingly called pronunciation, in deference to ancient British custom, although on two occasions he spoke of this part of rhetoric as elocution, as if his fellow Dubliner Thomas Sheridan, who was campaigning at that moment for the adoption of the latter terminology, could not be altogether ignored.[463] Was the speaker to proceed on the assumption that delivery on the platform as in private conversation is a natural external manifestation of an inward state of knowledge and feeling, and that therefore his best procedure in speaking is to learn to concentrate in public upon the meaning of his words and to allow his mind to dictate such external things as emphasis and pause? Or was he to proceed on the assumption that delivery is a mechanical art to be cultivated as a singer would follow musical annotations contrived by somebody else? Lawson chose to endorse the former and to repudiate the latter method. In justification of his view, he asked his students to contemplate a situation which any of them might encounter in everyday life:

> You have, it is likely, heard one Person relate to several, to a Dozen, or more, assembled, an Event, containing many Circumstances; of some Length therefore and Variety; and farther of a Nature interesting greatly the Hearers. Here you observe all the Diversity before-mentioned, but more conspicuous from the Circumstances and Occasion, from the greater Diversity of Matter, and the stronger Effects upon the Audience, which, like Light reflected, act in their Turn by warming the Speaker. Nature herself dictates these unstudied Tones, familiar, low,

---

[461] *Ibid.*, pp. 255-256.   [462] See *Orator*, 17.55.

[463] For Lawson's use of "elocution" to signify delivery, see *Lectures concerning Oratory*, pp. 419 (line 20), 425 (line 12).

soft, quick, acute, loud, and vehement, as the Accidents related demand: To all which the Appearance of the Hearers, as by Sympathy, exactly corresponds.

Advance but a few Steps farther, and you arrive at the Point now under Consideration.

Transport in your Imagination, this Man into a Church. Employ him there, in laying before a large Assembly, Truths of the greatest Moment; wherein he is to explain, prove, encourage, exhort, deter, holding forth Rewards and Punishments without End. Manifest it is, that here also, the Manner of Speaking will remain the same.[464]

Lawson went on to show that the speaker in this latter situation would of course be speaking more loudly, more vehemently, than he did before, but that his whole pattern of delivery—his tones, his variations, his emphasis—would not have altered in any basic way. "It is still the same Nature," said Lawson, "that operates thro' all these Gradations; that reigns equally from the placid Sounds of familiar Dialogue, to the highest Strains of adorned Declamation."[465]

In contrast to this natural method of delivery, Lawson outlined a mechanical method which, as he had learned from Jean Baptiste Du Bos's *Réflexions Critiques sur la Poësie et sur la Peinture*, was seemingly in use in ancient times to teach actors how to pronounce their speeches, and could presumably be revived and used in the modern theatre or in oratorical instruction. After remarking upon the human propensity to want to substitute mechanical for natural procedures, as in the case of the ingenious artist who devised tables for making poetry by pure mechanism, Lawson obliquely introduced and explained Du Bos's system thus:

[464] *Ibid.*, pp. 413-414. The "Diversity before-mentioned" refers to the details of a preceding illustration that Lawson had used to make the point now again under discussion.

The relationship between Lawson's concept of oratorical delivery as expanded conversation and James A. Winans's more creative similar concept has been pointed out already, and need not concern us here. For details, see Ray E. Keesey's previously mentioned article in *Speech Monographs*, xx (1953), p. 54.

[465] *Lectures concerning Oratory*, pp. 414-415.

In like Manner, some learned Persons have imagined a Method of rendering just Pronunciation easy to all, in a Way which we may name mechanical; by marking the Tones, with which every Word in a Speech or Sermon, nay, every Syllable, is to be spoken, in the same Way, as Pieces of Musick are written: By which Means, any Person, even without Knowledge of the Sense, may learn to pronounce justly, in the same Manner as one may, by the Help of musical Notes, sing truly, a Song which he doth not at all understand. And it is farther affirmed, that this valuable Art was known to, and commonly practised by the Antients: Which, if it were true, would strongly concur with these Persons, and might recommend this Invention to present Study and Enquiry.[466]

Lawson proceeded to deny in vigorous terms that an art of this kind was actually practiced in ancient Greece and Rome, his major argument being that Cicero and Quintilian, who had speculated upon all aspects of rhetoric in the greatest detail, did not even hint of its existence.[467] Then he declared that, for a preacher preparing a sermon for delivery in the pulpit, a mechanical method of this kind "is altogether chimerical."[468] Lawson's refusal to accept this method as a legitimate part of the ancient rhetorical tradition is interesting, in view of the tendency of many elocutionists to justify mechanical methods of delivery by alleging them to have been a once-vital part of ancient education. And it is interesting, too, that, at a moment when pronunciation alone was be-

[466] *Ibid.*, pp. 423-424. Lawson himself identifies "some learned Persons" by a footnote which says, "Reflexions sur la Poesie, la Peinture, & la Musique. To. iii." These words are Lawson's French version of the English title under which a translation of Du Bos's *Réflexions* was published in Lawson's own time. Du Bos's French title did not contain the phrase, "& la Musique." For the translation, see *Critical Reflections on Poetry, Painting and Music. With An Inquiry into the Rise and Progress of the Theatrical Entertainments of the Ancients*. Written in French By the Abbé Du Bos . . . Translated into English by Thomas Nugent, Gent. (London, 1748). (The second volume gives the title as *Critical Reflections on Poetry and Painting*.) In Vol. iii, pp. 102-115, of this work occurs the discussion to which Lawson's view of the mechanical method refers. It is astonishing that Ray E. Keesey's previously mentioned article in *Speech Monographs*, xx (1953), p. 55, should say that the identity of the "learned Persons" in Lawson's passage is not clear. Lawson himself identified those persons by his inexact reference to the title of Du Bos's treatise.

[467] *Lectures concerning Oratory*, p. 424.   [468] *Ibid.*, p. 425.

ing declared by Thomas Sheridan to be the whole of a long-lost art of rhetoric, Lawson refused to be stampeded into believing that oratorical pronunciation was anything more than one of the important procedures which rhetoric undertakes to supervise. In fact, in his opening discourse, Lawson called it a matter of common knowledge, "that the chief Design proposed in the Establishment of the present Lecture, was to teach the Art of Speaking, the Rules of distinct, proper, graceful Pronunciation."[469] And he commented upon that design by saying that he himself would devote only a small share of his time to this part of rhetoric, and that anyway Aristotle had believed this part incapable of being taught through lectures.

Another of Lawson's basic ideas concerned the value of the topics as aids to rhetorical invention. Were these ancient devices still useful? Or were they unsuited to the modern world? Lawson's answer was that, while "the Moderns have not only neglected, but despised this whole Matter," he himself would want to say that the topics had tradition and utility to recommend them.[470] He noted that Bacon's *Advancement of Learning* had considered the *"Topical Part"* of rhetoric to be in need of enrichment, in the sense that it lacked "a Number of Observations on all common Heads, digested into convenient Order."[471] And he also noted that Cicero and Quintilian had endorsed the topics in principle and had framed many precepts to indicate how the principle would apply to oratory. As for himself, he felt that the use of a system of topics would prevent rambling and confusion in unpremeditated discourses, and would assist weak and dim minds to a greater inventiveness than that with which nature had endowed them. There is even an unelaborated hint in his account of pulpit oratory that a young preacher, having chosen a discourse to unfold his text, and a text to be the abstract of his discourse, might then secure some supporting ideas by a resort to the topics, particularly those anciently called comparatives and opposites. At least, the topical system of traditional dialectic and rhetoric comes to the mind of the modern scholar when he hears

[469] *Ibid.*, pp. 22-23.

[470] Except as I have noted below, this summary of Lawson's view of the topics is based upon the second and third pages of his eighth lecture (pp. 127-128).

[471] See *Works of Bacon*, VI, 297, 300-303.

Lawson give the following advice to his eighteenth-century students:

> When you have in this Manner determined on your Point, you should above all Things carefully consider it; revolve it often in your Mind, turn and return it, view it on every Side, in all Lights, in every Aspect and Position, in its several Connexions, Resemblances, Oppositions, Differences: Consult also those who have written well upon it, that you may have the fullest, most accurate Survey of it which is possible.[472]

But beyond these endorsements of the ancient topical system Lawson did not go. Indeed, in emphasizing the need for orators to speak from a rich fund of actual knowledge of the subjects involved,[473] he did much to indicate his unconscious sympathy towards the very moderns who for neglecting and despising the topics had earlier incurred his quiet censure.

Still another of Lawson's basic ideas, and the last with which we shall here be concerned, bore upon the question of the types of discourse within the jurisdiction of rhetoric. Were rhetorical discourses properly so-called to be limited to something like the three oratorical forms of antiquity? Or were rhetorical discourses to be considered to include all the didactic, oratorical, and poetic forms of literature? Lawson's answer to these questions is determined pretty largely by what he considered Aristotle's answer to have been. And he stated Aristotle's answer in his third lecture as he was in the act of bringing to an end his excellent summary of the latter's *Rhetoric*. Having noted in the course of the summary that Aristotle had construed rhetoric to be the art of the deliberative, the judicial, and the demonstrative speech,[474] Lawson cautioned his students not to expect more from the work than Aristotle had intended. Then he added:

> The Ground of which Precaution is this. He wrote it solely for the Instruction of those, who were to speak in Publick, in the great Council, or before the Assembly of the People, concerning Matters relating to the State, or judicial Causes. Hence the Poet, the Historian, the Philosopher, are not to search here for Rules useful in their particular Studies and Kinds of Writing;

[472] *Lectures concerning Oratory*, p. 375.
[473] *Ibid.*, pp. 134-139, 356-364.   [474] *Ibid.*, p. 45.

which although contained in the general Extent of Eloquence, belong not to the Scheme of our Author.[475]

At this point Lawson's students would certainly have remembered that in his first lecture he had defined the purpose of his own discourses in the terms that he was now applying to Aristotle's *Rhetoric*. Why am I delivering these lectures in English, he asked on that occasion, when it is generally expected that academic discourses should be in Latin? And he answered his own question as follows:

> Because, the End now proposed is Improvement in Eloquence; And how is this Eloquence to be exerted? In our own Tongue. Thus it is, we are to speak at the Bar, in the Senate, in the Pulpit. To it therefore must our Rules principally relate, and from those who have written in it, we must draw Citations and Examples: Which we cannot perform properly in a learned Language; for although Custom hath rendered familiar the Introduction of *Latin* Passages in *English* Discourse; yet *English* interwoven in a *Latin* Composition would, I suppose, appear absurd and monstrous.[476]

Although Lawson decided later to limit himself only to pulpit eloquence, and to omit lecturing on the oratory of the bar and senate,[477] he did not of course abandon on that account his conviction that these three forms of discourse were coextensive with the concerns of rhetorical theory. But when he said that oratory must be able not only to convince and persuade but also to instruct mankind,[478] he extended those concerns so as to include didactic discourse, at least by implication. And when he classified discourses by relating some to the understanding, others to the passions, and others to other faculties, he suggested that, since the speechmaker addresses all parts of the mind, while other authors address only one or two parts, the art of the speechmaker is therefore to be regarded as the theory which includes within itself all the basic rules governing any form of verbal composition.

Having now examined the six basic ideas which Lawson developed in his lectures on oratory at Trinity College, we are in a position to see what his standing should be among the rhetoricians of his time. Before we pass judgment upon him, however, we

[475] *Ibid.*, pp. 50-51.   [476] *Ibid.*, pp. 21-22.   [477] *Ibid.*, pp. 352-353.
[478] *Ibid.*, pp. 193-194, 215.

should mention one other aspect of his lectures—an aspect which consists not in his statement of a new article in his rhetorical doctrine but in his revelation of an influence that helps to explain his doctrine as a whole. That aspect became visible in his eighteenth lecture, and it amounted to an unexpected demonstration on his part that Plato's *Phaedrus* must be accepted as one of the great classics of the rhetorical tradition. At the end of his seventeenth lecture, his students would no doubt have sworn that, so far as he was concerned, Aristotle's *Rhetoric* and Cicero's *De Oratore* were the two chief rhetorical classics, for he had given a digest of each in his second lecture, and had not thereafter given attention in depth to any other treatise of that kind. But in the eighteenth lecture, as he concluded his discussion of elocution, and was about to proceed with the two remaining subjects of pronunciation and pulpit oratory, he reminded his students of his earlier promise to discuss Plato as a rhetorical theorist, and having apologized for his failure thus far to do so, he took him up at once.[479] He then gave a digest of *Phaedrus* not less careful or systematic than his previous digests of the *Rhetoric* and the *De Oratore* had been.

He recalled that Phaedrus had set the theme of the dialogue by reading aloud to Socrates a speech composed either by Lysias, the Athenian orator, or by Plato in imitation of Lysias; that Socrates responded by giving what he called a better speech on the same subject; that Socrates then made another speech in order to put the subject into its eternal, as distinguished from its temporal, perspective; and that, with these three specimens of rhetoric before them, Socrates and Phaedrus speculated upon the definition of rhetoric as an art, upon its basic rules, and upon the obligations which a philosophical rhetoric would require a speaker to assume towards the souls of the listeners and towards the discovery, organization, and presentation of truth. At one point in his digest of the dialogue, Lawson represented Socrates as having argued that, "If the Appearance of Truth perswades, must not Truth itself more effectually perswade?"[480] And he concluded his digest by declaring that *Phaedrus* "containeth the fundamental Precepts of Rhetorick; enlarged afterwards, and reduced into a regular System by *Aristotle*; to which succeeding Writers have added little new; even the Eloquence and Experience of *Tully* did not much more than adorn these."[481]

[479] *Ibid.*, pp. 31, 329.   [480] *Ibid.*, p. 333.   [481] *Ibid.*, p. 335.

To these comments upon Plato as rhetorician, Lawson appended a eulogy of him as an eloquent writer, mentioning among other things that his poetic style was not so much an impropriety as a natural consequence of his youthful ambition to become a poet. In fact, the question whether Plato should adopt philosophy or poetry as his calling, whether he should "Think with the Sage, or warble with the Muse," became the theme of a poem which Lawson composed and read to his students at the end of the eighteenth lecture.[482] Dedicated to Lord Chesterfield by eight heroic couplets, the poem, entitled "The Judgment of Plato," consisted of 327 lines in that same verse form, and while it did not show Lawson to be a poetic genius whom the world ought at last to recognize, it nevertheless was graceful and competent throughout. It imagined Plato wandering in a grove and pondering what to make of his life. Two females appeared. The one who spoke for poetry urged him not to prefer the want and meanness of the philosophic life to the immortal company of Orpheus and Amphion. At one point she said:

> In untun'd Prose let the harsh Sophist creep,
> And argue ev'ry Reader into Sleep,
> Obscurely useful, like the rugged Stone
> Doom'd in the massy Pile to lye unknown;
> While the fine Genius like the Di'mond bright,
> Polish'd and set by Art attracts the Sight,
> Destin'd on Crowns and royal Hands to glare,
> Or flame on snowy Bosoms of the Fair.[483]

But the female who spoke for philosophy won the contest. She scornfully asked:

> What Credit can the Muse's Words obtain,
> Whose Study's to deceive, whose Praise to feign?[484]

Then she told Plato what her program is:

> Then hear my Voice, e'er yet in Error's Way
> Thy Youth but half misled, for ever stray.
> By me instructed Good from Ill discern,
> To know thyself, Man's highest Knowledge, learn.

[482] *Ibid.*, pp. 337-351. The quotation just given is on p. 341.
[483] *Ibid.*, p. 344.   [484] *Ibid.*, p. 348.

I fix your Notions, Actions regulate,
Unfold the Duties of each Age and State,
With Precepts strengthen Reason's tott'ring Sway,
Quell Appetite, teach Passion to obey,
Explain from whence is Man, for what design'd,
His End, his Nature, his immortal Mind. . .

Be thou the first to light the moral Ray,
And pour on *Greece* the philosophick Day,
With mine for ever blended shall thy Name
Descend, and Truth and *Plato* be the same.[485]

And when Plato declared that he chose to follow her vision, she rewarded him by pronouncing that his utterances would henceforth be guided no more by herself than by the Muse of poetry:

The Store by me supply'd, with pleasing Art
Shall to Mankind a publick Good impart;
And whilst I deck the Soul, her Voice shall win the Heart.[486]

In a less fanciful spirit our judgment upon Lawson is that as a rhetorician he has as much of an affinity for the new rhetoric as for the old. Certain considerations which have already been mentioned, and others which we should now enter into the record, support no other verdict. Thus he confined rhetoric to three kinds of speeches, with Aristotle's similar limitation in mind; but he recognized the didactic function of oratory and the need for exposition as a distinct modern form. Thus he was respectful towards oratorical subject matter that issued from the topics of invention, but he devoted little space to the topics, while dwelling with some emphasis upon subject matter derived from direct knowledge of the case under discussion. Thus he admitted that rhetorical proof was predominantly enthymematic, but he thought the pattern of geometrical proof offered the orator the best instruction in the art of reasoning.[487] Thus he would have conceded that probable reasonings were sometimes the only possible basis for an address to the understanding, but he recommended truth as the best basis for argument, and he implied that the only probabilities which would be convincing are those bearing the clearest stamp of truth upon them. Thus he knew of the

[485] *Ibid.*, pp. 348-349.   [486] *Ibid.*, p. 351.   [487] *Ibid.*, pp. 129-133.

six-part oration prescribed in classical rhetoric, and of the four-part oration approved by Aristotle, but he was obviously more sympathetic towards the flexibility of the latter than the ritualism of the former.[488] Thus he criticized the Irish for disliking stylistic ornament and for preferring the plain style of science;[489] he declared that the supreme splendor of eloquence was found in the ornamental style;[490] but yet he noted that eloquence declined in ancient Greece after the conquests of Alexander, and that the story of the decline was in part the story of Demetrius of Phalerum, who stripped eloquence of the plain manly dress which it had worn in the speeches of Demosthenes, and clothed it instead not only with "Ornaments, pointed Turns, glittering Expressions, affected Appositions," but also "with all the little Prettinesses and Elegancies, which may adorn an Epigram, but are unbecoming of Truth and good Sense."[491] Moreover, in his lecture on the tropes and figures, Lawson declined to enumerate these devices of style with the tiresome exactness which preceding rhetoricians including Vossius had achieved, and he disparagingly characterized such implements as "these Minutenesses," while admitting himself unable to recommend that they be completely ignored.[492] Upon this issue and upon all others of those just specified, Lawson showed sympathy for the new and respect for the old rhetoric, and he cannot be finally classed as a dedicated advocate of either one. But apart from these issues, he took a stand which is peculiar in being both on the ancient and the modern side. That is to say, when he refused to endorse Du Bos's suggestion that the delivery of a speech could be reduced to the mechanical reproduction of sounds in accordance with a predetermined system of marks and musical notations, he had behind him the combined authority of the old and the new rhetoricians. Only the elocutionists espoused the mechanical method, and they apparently did so because they mistakenly thought it classical. How they managed against history and good sense to make it seem the whole art of rhetoric in many nineteenth-century schools and colleges is a problem that cannot be dealt with here. But Lawson most certainly gave them no support.

[488] *Ibid.*, pp. 46-47, 54, 140-151, 331, 376-408.
[489] *Ibid.*, pp. 3-6.
[490] *Ibid.*, p. 210.   [491] *Ibid.*, pp. 37-38.   [492] *Ibid.*, pp. 254-255.

Three years after the date of publication of Lawson's *Lectures*, a well-read young dissenting theologian named Joseph Priestley was appointed tutor in languages and belles lettres at Warrington Academy in northwest England, and he held that post until 1767, when he became minister of Mill Hill Chapel in Leeds.[493] His tutorship was marked by his being awarded the honorary degree of doctor of laws by the University of Edinburgh on December 4, 1764, in recognition of his status as teacher at Warrington, and by his being elected a Fellow of the Royal Society of London on June 12, 1766, under the terms of a Certificate which read that he was "Author of a Chart of Biography, and several other valuable works, a gentleman of great merit and learning, and very well versed in Mathematical and Philosophical enquiries."[494] As part of his program of instruction at Warrington, he delivered formal academic discourses on various subjects,[495] and those on rhetorical theory, first presented in 1762, and presumably repeated and improved during the next five years, were finally published in 1777 under the title, *A Course of Lectures on Oratory and Criticism*. It is of these that I shall now speak. There are thirty-five of them, and they are of special interest to the historian of rhetoric because they show what rhetorical instruction was like in English education during the late eighteenth century, and what

[493] See *The Dictionary of National Biography*, s.v. Priestley, Joseph, LL.D. (1733-1804).

[494] In *A Catalogue of the Graduates in the Faculties of Arts, Divinity, and Law, of the University of Edinburgh*, p. 257, Priestley is listed for the degree of doctor of laws as "Teacher of Languages and Belles Lettres in the Academy of Warrington." These words may be taken to indicate that his position at Warrington was considered an explanation of the degree which he was being awarded. For the wording of the Certificate attending his admission to the Royal Society, see W. Cameron Walker, "The Beginnings of the Scientific Career of Joseph Priestley," *Isis*, XXI (April 1934), 92. Walker errs, however, in saying (p. 83) that Priestley was awarded his degree at Edinburgh for his *Chart of Biography*. The *Chart of Biography* was first published on February 2, 1765—two months after the date of the degree. See Ronald E. Crook, *A Bibliography of Joseph Priestley 1733-1804* (London, 1966), p. 122.

[495] See his *A Course of Lectures; on the Theory of Language, and Universal Grammar* (Warrington, 1762), and his *An Essay on a Course of Liberal Education for Civil and Active Life. With Plans of Lectures on i. The Study of History and General Policy. ii. The History of England. iii. The Constitution and Laws of England* (London, 1765). For a bibliographical account of these works, see Crook, pp. 108, 127, 131.

could be made of it when it became the subject of a treatise by someone whose fame, like that of Robert Boyle, was ultimately to be linked with the development of modern chemistry.

Warrington Academy in that era must be understood as an institution of higher learning in the liberal arts and theology, not as a mere secondary school. Its primary purpose was to provide advanced education to dissenters, for this was a period in English history when the famous old universities were restricted by law to members of the established church, and the Nonconformists had to seek their education wherever they could. It should be understood, moreover, that Warrington and many other academies of the same kind attracted a considerable number of students who would have been eligible to go to the old universities, if they had wished, but who nevertheless chose not to do so because they opposed the prospect of studying under conditions of religious and intellectual censorship. Herbert MacLachlan, one of the foremost authorities on the dissenting academies, says of the one at Warrington that it made the town known between 1757 and 1786 as "The Athens of the North," and that its impact upon English intellectual life in those years was "comparable only to that of a great university like Oxford or Cambridge at a later period."[496] From that kind of environment emerged the lectures which now stand as Priestley's contribution to rhetorical theory.

The art of oratory, said Priestley in his first lecture, consisted of a set of precepts to direct each of the four important steps in the composition of discourse, and these steps were recollection, method, style, and elocution.[497] The precepts of recollection were designed to show the speaker or writer "which way to turn his thoughts, in order to find the arguments and illustrations with which his mind is already furnished." Method taught him "what disposition of the materials of a discourse will give them the greatest force, and contribute the most to produce the effect intended by it." Style demonstrated how his thoughts could be expressed in the most telling manner. And as for elocution, its purpose was to indicate, in those cases where the discourse was

---

[496] See his *English Education under the Test Acts Being the History of the Nonconformist Academies 1662-1820* (Manchester, England, 1931), p. 209.

[497] See *A Course of Lectures on Oratory and Criticism*. By Joseph Priestley, LL.D. F.R.S. (London, 1777), p. 5. My quotations from Priestley's definitions of these steps are all from that same page.

to be pronounced, "what tone of voice, or what gestures of the body, will best become, and add grace to the delivery of it." It is obvious at once, of course, that, in choosing to call this fourth step elocution rather than pronunciation, Priestley was adhering to the special terminology of the elocutionists, and particularly to that being advertised throughout Great Britain in the 1760's by Thomas Sheridan. Indeed, Priestley's own personal knowledge of Sheridan's teachings is a matter of open record: on two occasions in the lectures now under consideration Priestley quoted excerpts from the volume which Sheridan had published in 1762 under the title, *A Course of Lectures on Elocution.*[498] But the interesting thing is that, despite his endorsement of Sheridan's teachings so far as this matter of terminology is concerned, Priestley took a firmly classical position in setting up the mainheads of his theory of rhetoric. He mentioned in his Preface that John Ward's *System of Oratory* had supplied him with material for his own discussion of recollection, that is, invention,[499] and he could well have added that Ward, Aristotle, and Cicero, rather than Sheridan, were responsible for his partitioning of the art of oratory into the four steps which his first lecture prescribed.

But Priestley departed from classical orthodoxy almost at once, and he did so in such a way as to indicate that oratory would eventually become in his system a much more comprehensive concept than it had been with the classical rhetoricians. "All the kinds of composition," he said in the opening sentence of his second lecture, "may be reduced to two, viz. NARRATION and ARGUMENTATION. For either we propose simply to relate *facts,* with a view to communicate information, as in *History,* natural or civil, *Travels,* &c. or we lay down some *proposition,* and endeavour to prove or explain it."[500] Let us now see what these two types of discourse are made to mean in Priestley's lectures as a whole.

[498] *Ibid.,* pp. 288, 312. For the source of the first of these quotations, see Sheridan's "A Dissertation on the Causes of the Difficulties . . . in learning the English Tongue"; for the source of the second, see Sheridan's "Dissertation I," which he intended as the eighth lecture in his series on elocution. Both quotations may be found in his *A Course of Lectures on Elocution* (London, 1762), pp. 239, 153.

[499] *Course of Lectures on Oratory,* p. iii.

[500] *Ibid.,* p. 6. All my quotations from Priestley follow his style in respect to italics and capitalization.

Narrative composition, as Priestley explained it in the words just quoted, contained civil history and natural history or science, and thus it served to draw into oratorical theory the chief forms of expository discourse. But Priestley was to give it a still wider application, for in a later lecture, when he was speaking of the passions as a concern of the writer, he made it plain that narratives of all sorts were part of his present theory, and that this type of composition included feigned history and feigned biography as well as civil and natural history. He spoke thus on that occasion:

> The faithful historian, and the writer of romances, having the same access to the springs of the human passions, it is no wonder that the latter generally moves them more forcibly, since he hath the choice of every circumstance that contributes to raise them; whereas the former hath nothing in his power but the *disposition* of them, and is restricted even in that. I fancy, however, that no person of reading and observation can doubt of the fact, that more tears have been shed, and more intense joy hath been expressed in the perusal of novels, romances, and feigned tragedies, than in reading all the true histories in the world. Who ever, upon any occurrence in real history, ever felt what he must feel in reading Clarissa, George Barnwell, Eloisa, and many other well-contrived fictions.[501]

As for Priestley's second major category of composition, it included far more than the three kinds of speeches of classical rhetoric. In fact, Priestley made it embrace what the ancients treated separately as dialectical composition, on one side, and rhetorical composition, on the other. His intention in this regard became obvious when he was preparing to speak of the topics in connection with his discussion of the procedures of recollection or invention in argumentation. On that occasion he drew a distinction between universal and particular propositions, the essence of the distinction being that the former were true or false for all persons, or for all times, or for all places, and the latter were true or false only for the persons, the times, or the places to which they had reference. Thus *"man is mortal"* is Priestley's example of a universal, and *"France is larger than England,"* of

[501] *Ibid.*, pp. 80-81.

a particular proposition.[502] Priestley then said that he ranged all arguments under one or the other of these two kinds of propositions, "because the topics of argument suited to each are very considerably distinct." And the line which he drew between these two kinds of topics ended not only by making universal topics consist of definition, adjuncts, antecedents, consequents, means, analogy, contrariety, example, and authority, but also by enumerating particular topics as those relating to the person, the time, the place, the motive, the manner, the instrument, the evidence, and the applicable law.[503] The interesting thing to be observed about these distinctions is that they parallel two lines of cleavage in ancient thought: that which separated dialectic from rhetoric in respect to subject matter; and that which separated these two disciplines from each other in respect to the machinery of invention. That is to say, there were two sorts of proposition, the infinite and the definite, said the ancient theorists, and the former belonged to dialectic as the latter to rhetoric; and correspondingly there were two sorts of topical systems for the invention of arguments, the system for dialectic involving such general considerations as definitions, properties, and antecedents, and that for rhetoric, such specific matters as a person's age, sex, fortune, and character.[504] Thus at a time when logic was seeking to rid itself of the dialectical topics and of a concern for learned argument, Priestley drew those two matters into his rhetorical system, and thereby helped to expand the concerns of rhetoric beyond what they had been before.

With narration and argumentation given these definitions, Priestley conducted his discussion of recollection or invention in a somewhat defensive way. First of all, he specified that the topics were applicable to the composition of argument but not to the composition of narration. Here is what he said on this important matter:

[502] *Ibid.*, p. 9.   [503] *Ibid.*, pp. 10, 19.
[504] For the classical distinction between infinite and definite questions, see the following works by Cicero: *De Oratore*, 1.31.138; *Partitiones Oratoriae*, 1.4; *Topica*, 21.79. For the view that definite questions are in general the property of rhetoric, see Cicero, *De Inventione*, 1.6.8. For the classical antecedents of Priestley's discussion of the dialectical topics, see Cicero, *Topica*, 2-4. For the classical antecedents of Priestley's discussion of the rhetorical topics, see Cicero, *De Inventione*, 1.13.17; 1.24-26; 2.9-11; also Quintilian, *Institutio Oratoria*, 3.6.25-28; 5.10.23-32.

With respect to *Narration* of any kind, it is superfluous to say much about it under the first head of *Recollection,* or *Invention,* except so far as facts are wanted for the purpose of *argumentative discourses.* The chief assistance that those who compose only in the narrative style can expect from the art of oratory, is in *digesting* and *adorning* their compositions; and these articles will be considered in the second and third parts of these lectures.

The whole business, therefore, of artificial recollection must, in a manner, be confined to the use of those who compose *argumentative discourses,* whose minds are previously furnished with every argument and observation proper to be introduced into them; but who may not be able to find them so readily as they could wish.[505]

Secondly, he stressed repeatedly that the topical system of ancient dialectic and rhetoric was applicable to the resummoning of knowledge already in the author's possession but was not applicable to the problem of achieving originality in the subject matter of discourse. The passage just quoted provides one example of this unenthusiastic view of the function of the topics. Another example occurs as Priestley was about to bring his account of topical invention to an end. "I cannot help being of opinion," he said there, "that those persons, in particular, whose profession obliges them frequently to compose *moral essays* and *sermons,* in which the thoughts are not expected to be *original* (in which, therefore, their chief business is merely to *recollect,* and *digest* the most valuable materials upon each subject) would spend a few minutes to good purpose in pursuing a well-digested table of topics, before they sat down to write."[506] As he spoke these words, Priestley no doubt remembered what Bacon had said in a similar connection—that the "invention of speech or argument is not properly an invention: for to *invent* is to discover that we know not, and not to recover or resummon that which we already know."[507] But whether or not he was influenced at this point by Bacon, his tendency was surely to allow the topics a minor role in argumentation, inasmuch as originality of subject matter was beyond their power to provide. In the third place, Priestley

[505] *Lectures on Oratory,* p. 6.   [506] *Ibid.,* p. 23.
[507] *Works of Bacon,* VI, 268.

openly acknowledged that even in the minor role to which he had assigned them, the topics were only of marginal value. This admission came at the end of the three lectures which he conscientiously devoted to them. As he surveyed what he had been saying, he remarked that the topics had been lavishly used by the famous orators of antiquity and thus had a claim to our regard. But he then took back part of the endorsement which his own lectures had given them.

> I am very ready, however, to acknowledge [he said], that rhetorical topics are more useful in the composition of *set declamations on trite subjects*, and to *young persons*, than in the communication of original matter, and to persons much used to composition. Original thoughts cannot but suggest themselves, so that all the assistance any person can want in this case, is a proper manner of *arranging* them. And a person much used to composition will have acquired a habit of recollection, without any express attention to topics.[508]

These criticisms suggest, of course, that the new rhetoric, having judged the topics to be inapplicable to narration and exposition, and to the composition of original and mature argument, would begin to speculate upon what should be put in their place, so far as rhetorical theory is concerned. But Priestley did not move in that direction, and thus he missed an opportunity to become something more than a reluctant modern advocate of the ancient machinery of topical invention.

Priestley's account of method as the second step in literary composition was more comprehensive than his treatment of recollection can claim to be. That is to say, he considered method in relation to narration and to argumentation, and thus he did not slight either part of his system of rhetoric. Moreover, what he said about each kind of method is of more than passing interest.

To Priestley's mind, narrative method on a given occasion took one or more of six available forms. Civil historians, biographers, writers of books of travel, and authors of fiction and drama and romance, would normally choose, he thought, to unfold events in chronological order, "but by no means suffering a regard to it to interrupt the account of any *intire transaction*, or prevent their

---

[508] *Lectures on Oratory*, p. 24.

looking either backward or forward for an incident that would throw light upon any character or event."[509] Writers of natural history, as for example geographers, biologists, botanists, and geologists, would normally follow the order of place.[510] Didactic treatises, which Priestley classified as specimens of narration, would lend themselves to an arrangement in which the distinct parts of a subject were set forth and discussed, essential parts being put first, and ornamental parts, later; and this kind of arrangement, Priestley suggested, was the one that he was following for his present lectures on oratory.[511] And all writers of narrative of whatever kind, he said, would on occasion want to arrange events or phenomena in a causal order, or to discuss one event because of its similarity to another, or because of its connection with another through the principle of the association of ideas.[512]

As for the arrangement of argumentative discourse, Priestley set it forth, not in terms of the parts of the classical oration, as orthodoxy, at least so far as popular argument is concerned, would have prescribed, but in terms of the method dominantly associated in his time with the organization of philosophical argument. That is to say, Priestley advised the author of an argument to arrange his discourse either by the method of analysis or that of synthesis. Here are his own words upon this matter:

> Logicians speak of two kinds of method in argumentative discourses, the *analytic* and the *synthetic*; and the distribution is complete and accurate. For, in all science, we either proceed from particular observations to more general conclusions, which is *analysis*; or, beginning with more general and comprehensive propositions, we descend to the particular propositions which are contained in them, which is *synthesis*.[513]

In discussing the synthetic method of argumentation, Priestley emphasized that it was well illustrated by the geometrical method of mathematics. And he developed an analogy between these two methods by showing that the arguer should do what the geometer does: he should lay down a proposition, define its terms, demonstrate it by a resort to relevant axioms, that is, to self-evident

[509] *Ibid.*, p. 37. [510] *Ibid.*, p. 34. [511] *Ibid.*, pp. 40-41.
[512] *Ibid.*, p. 35. [513] *Ibid.*, p. 42.

truths, add any miscellaneous remarks or scholia in explanation of the more obscure of his procedures, and deduce further truths or corollaries from the conclusion that he proves.[514] As for the analytic method of argumentation, it consisted, not in "laying down propositions, and then entering upon the proof of them," but in beginning "with observations or experiments," and in showing how they led to the establishment of some principle or other.[515] The analytic method, Priestley observed, was illustrated by Locke's *Essay concerning Human Understanding*, by Hutcheson's *System of Moral Philosophy*, and by Hume's *Enquiry concerning the Principles of Morals*; and the synthetic method, by Hartley's *Observations on Man*. To the organizing principle of each of these treatises Priestley devoted two or more paragraphs of careful exposition.[516]

Anybody who has read the account of the synthetic method as William Duncan worded it in his *Elements of Logick* would be convinced, I believe, that Priestley had Duncan in mind when he drew his analogy for the students at Warrington between geometry and argumentation. Throughout his analysis of this method, Duncan spoke of the mathematician rather than the geometrician, and in this particular detail of terminology, at least, Priestley did not consistently follow Duncan's way of speaking. But in all other essential respects, Duncan said what Priestley was later to say: that in argument, as in mathematics, a proposition is first laid down; that its terms are then defined; that axioms or self-evident truths are then invoked to prove it; that scholia, or parenthetical comments, are added throughout, as they may be needed; and that corollaries flow naturally and of themselves to extend what has been finally proved.[517] In regard to his sources, Priestley said in his Preface that he would have been more particular in acknowledging them if he had been better able to recollect them and had thought it necessary to do so. "Let my reader consider this work," he added, "as a succinct and systematical view of the observations of others, interspersed with original ones of my own; and he will not, I hope, think that the perusal of it has been ill-bestowed."[518] These words invite us to conclude that Priestley's failure to mention Duncan's *Logick* as one of his sources may

[514] *Ibid.*, pp. 45-47, 48-52.　　[515] *Ibid.*, p. 55.
[516] *Ibid.*, pp. 58-59, 60-62.　　[517] See above, Ch. 5, pp. 357-358.
[518] *Lectures on Oratory*, pp. iii-iv.

have been caused by his forgetfulness or by his conviction that so popular a work would hardly need to be openly identified. But in any event, Priestley did something original with the tradition which Duncan and many other logicians had invoked in associating logical method with the procedures of analysis and synthesis; and his originality in this respect deserves a word of explanation.

What Priestley did was to create a theory of oratorical form by turning his back upon the classical doctrine concerning the six-part or the four-part oration and by substituting for it the doctrine concerning the form of philosophical argument. George Campbell had done the same thing, so far as his *Philosophy of Rhetoric* is concerned, but Campbell had not developed the idea at all, and had moreover tended to diminish it when he recommended an offshoot of the pattern of the six-part classical oration in speaking of the structure of sermons to his theology students at Aberdeen.[519] Now, Priestley developed the idea in considerable detail in the course of his four careful lectures on method in argumentative discourses. Thus he became the first rhetorician of his time to establish a new theory of rhetorical structure. And his *Lectures on Oratory* are the only eighteenth-century rhetorical work to which one could turn if one wanted to argue that the structure of that famous eighteenth-century political address, the Declaration of Independence, is authentically oratorical by standards openly enunciated in Jefferson's own time. In other words, the Declaration of Independence does not have proper oratorical form if one considers oratorical form to be defined by the classical oration; but the Declaration is a proper oration in Priestley's terms, and it could profitably be studied as an example of the argumentative procedures which Priestley had associated with the geometers. Jefferson could not have been influenced, of course, by anything which Priestley said in his *Lectures on Oratory*, for the latter work was not available to readers at the time when the Declaration was composed. Indeed, it was Duncan's *Elements of Logick* which had suggested to Jefferson the structural principle upon which he framed his immortal argument.[520] But that same principle became the official property of rhetoric when Priestley borrowed it from logic and made it stand where the doctrine of the six-part oration had stood without serious

---

[519] See above, pp. 602, 610.   [520] See above, Ch. 5, p. 348.

challenge since the days of Cicero. And since Duncan had called that principle the method of science, it can be said to represent scientific practices of organization when it became a part of rhetorical theory. It is appropriate indeed that a scientist like Priestley should have had a hand in producing a momentous change of this sort.

Priestley's discussion of style as the third part of the art of oratory introduced his students to a concept that had been carefully withheld from view during his preceding lectures. That concept involved pleasure as one of the effects which the author of any narration or any argument should on occasion aim to produce. Up to the moment when that concept emerged, his students had been told that the author aimed to produce either or both of two effects, that of relating facts and that of establishing propositions. But at the end of his discussion of method, Priestley said that these two effects must now be extended to include a third. Here are his words:

> I would observe, at the conclusion of this part of the course, that the whole use of topics and of the disposition of them, . . . hath for its object and end the *informing of the judgment*, and *influencing the practice*, and that this is the only direct and proper, at least the ultimate end of oratory. The pleasure that a discourse may give to the *imagination*, or the emotion it may raise in the *passions*, are things that are brought about more indirectly, being effected by the *manner* in which things that tend ultimately to *convince* and *persuade* are expressed. The orator may, indeed, intend to please or affect his hearers; but, if he understands himself, he only means to influence their *judgments*, or *resolutions*, by the medium of the imagination or the passions.[521]

This line of reasoning had several consequences in the lectures that followed. First of all, it led Priestley to associate the third part of rhetoric with pleasure as an end of discourse, whereas the first two parts had had to do with the more fundamental ends of conviction and persuasion. Secondly, it led Priestley to indicate that his ensuing lectures on style concerned the subject of criticism rather than that of composition, although, except for a lec-

[521] *Lectures on Oratory*, p. 68.

ture on taste, Priestley continued to keep the problems of composition uppermost in his hearer's minds. Indeed, Priestley's shift
from composition to criticism would probably have remained unnoticed by those who heard the lectures, so faint was his emphasis upon it. And even the reader of the lectures is likely to notice
it only if he happens to become aware that the headline at the top
of the pages from 72 to 313 of the first edition has changed from
"Lectures on Oratory" to "Lectures on Criticism." Thirdly, the
line of reasoning now under discussion led Priestley to divide the
subject of style into three forms of address, each of which could
be carried out either by narration or argument, the three forms
being that calculated to arouse the passions, that calculated to
engage the judgment, and that calculated to appeal to the imagination. These forms of address, which Priestley delineated at the
beginning of his twelfth lecture,[522] are the subject of the twenty-
four lectures which brought to an end his discussion of the third
part of rhetoric.

In the course of those twenty-four lectures, Priestley developed
the idea that, once assured of a subject matter and an organization capable of informing the judgment and directing the practice
of his audience, the author might seek to give that audience the
pleasure which comes from ornamental expression, provided that
his own genius and the occasion of his discourse permitted him
to achieve this important but subservient goal.[523] In a discourse
addressed to the passions, ornament would be achieved by the
vivid representation of scenes and ideas through such stylistic
devices as that of using the present tense in describing past action, or that of seeking the concrete word or the description of an
actual feature in portraying a real or a fictional event.[524] Ornament in a discourse addressed to the judgment would be achieved
by displaying qualities beyond those of good logic—for example,
the quality that words have when an author conveys his ideas
with earnestness, with a sense of conviction, and with a regard for
honesty, impartiality, and candor.[525] Ornament in a discourse addressed to the imagination would be achieved by the various
means that cluster around two general endeavors, and we cannot
do better than to quote Priestley's own statement of what those
endeavors are. "Every thing that hath a striking or pleasing effect

[522] *Ibid.*, p. 79.   [523] *Ibid.*, p. 69.   [524] *Ibid.*, pp. 79-107.
[525] *Ibid.*, pp. 108-124.

in composition," he said with the address to the imagination in mind, "must either *draw out and exercise our faculties,* or else, by the principle of association, must *transfer from foreign objects ideas that tend to improve the sense;* the principal of which are *views of human sentiments,* of the *effects of the human genius,* and of a *rise and improvement* in things."⁵²⁶ The first of these endeavors is particularized in Priestley's comments upon novelty, sublimity, uniformity, variety, comparisons, metaphors, and allegories; and the second, in what he said about such devices as contrast, burlesque, riddles, puns, antitheses, metonymy, synecdoche, personification, and climax. To Kames's *Elements of Criticism* and to Hartley's *Observations on Man* Priestley confessed himself greatly indebted at this point, although his debt to Hartley is visible in all major parts of his theory of oratory.⁵²⁷ In fact, one of the most original features of his theory is that he did what he set out to do—he used the principles of oratory to illustrate Hartley's doctrine of the association of ideas.

Of the many things which interest the historian of rhetoric as he reads Priestley's lectures on style, one only will be selected here for special notice. It occurs in Priestley's comments upon discourses addressed to the judgment, and it concerns the question whether the modern speaker will or will not gain credence with his hearers if he deliberately models his eloquence upon that of Greece and Rome. As we know, Adam Smith stressed that ancient eloquence would not succeed in modern Britain, and David Hume, that it would.⁵²⁸ Hume argued, indeed, that British eloquence could hope to rise above its present mediocrity only if British orators would learn to do what Demosthenes and Cicero had done with such great perfection. Without being aware of this particular difference of opinion, Priestley cast what amounted to a vote for Adam Smith's side of the case.

It is, likewise, proper that all Englishmen in particular should be informed [he said], that a person of a liberal education in this country can hardly ever be in such a situation, as

⁵²⁶ *Ibid.,* p. 279. For an earlier statement of these two endeavors, see *ibid.,* p. 136.

⁵²⁷ *Ibid.,* pp. iii, 95, 125 (for references to Kames); pp. i-ii, 25, 35, 57, 61-62, 72-73, 130, 200, 279 (for references to Hartley or to the principle of the association of ideas).

⁵²⁸ See above, pp. 569-571, 614-616.

will not render the imitation of some of the boldest, the most successful, and admired strokes of Roman, not to say Grecian eloquence, extremely improper and ridiculous. The English pulpit, the English bar, and the English senate, require an eloquence more addressed to the reason, and less directly to the passions, than the harangues of a Roman pleader, or the speech of a Roman senator. Our hearers have generally more good sense and just discernment, at least they are naturally more *cool* and phlegmatic; both which qualities check a propensity to strong emotions: and marks of great vehemence must appear absurd in a speaker, when the audience is unmoved, and sees nothing to occasion such emotion.[529]

Priestley's attitude upon this issue was not particularly consistent, to be sure, with his endorsement of the topics as a component of modern rhetoric. But it was consistent with all other aspects of his rhetorical theory. In those other aspects, indeed, he belonged with the new rhetoricians as completely as did Adam Smith and George Campbell.

Priestley never composed for publication his lectures on elocution or delivery as the fourth part of the art of oratory, and to that extent his rhetorical theory as it has come down to us is incomplete. But he indicated that he lectured on elocution once each week during his course, and that his lectures consisted of instructions to students while they were presumably engaged in speaking exercises of some kind or other.[530] His last two lectures on style were devoted to harmony in verse and in prose, and what he said in them relates to delivery, because harmony, of course, is manifest only as verse and prose are spoken aloud. In fact, he quoted John Mason in each of those two lectures, once to approve of the syllables which Mason used in indicating the standard of English iambic verses, and again to point out an offensive combination of sounds in Mason's style.[531] These two quotations were from Mason's *Essay on the Power and Harmony of Prosaic Numbers.*[532] It is highly probable that, in Priestley's lectures on delivery, there would be found some reference to Mason's *Essay on Elocution or Pronunciation,* for that little work was easily available in the era

[529] *Lectures on Oratory,* pp. 113-114.
[530] *Ibid.,* p. iv.
[531] *Ibid.,* pp. 299, 312.   [532] (London, 1749), pp. 15-16, 13.

when Priestley taught at Warrington, and, as we know, it had made a modest contribution towards popularizing "elocution" as a term for the oral presentation of discourse.[533] The actual doctrine which made up Priestley's view of delivery in oratory must, however, remain conjectural, and it could scarcely be expected anyway to have the philosophical and historical interest that attends his work with the other three parts of rhetorical theory.

As my preceding comments have indicated, Priestley's rhetoric is openly intended as an all-encompassing view of composition and criticism, with history, didactic writing, philosophical exposition, learned argument, popular address, fiction, romance, and poetry, included within its scope. I must now emphasize, however, that it fails in one important respect to achieve full stature as a general theory of discourse. That is to say, it appears to take for granted that the differences between the fictitious narratives of epic poetry, tragedy, comedy, and the novel, on the one hand, and the nonfictitious narratives of biography, memoirs, histories, and various didactic treatises, on the other, require no special treatment, so far as the writer and the critic are concerned. Thus the insight which led Aristotle to indicate that poetry is mimetic, while history and oratory and dialectical compositions are non-mimetic, has no parallel in Priestley's rhetorical system, nor does Francis Bacon's careful demonstration that history is the record of what has happened, and poesy, the record of what the imagination feigns to have happened.[534] To Priestley, a narrative or an argument may succeed in arousing passion or engaging the imagination, even as it informs the judgment and directs the practice of mankind, and thus it may appeal to the faculty of taste and stir the imagination to finer feelings of pleasure, while performing its more important business with the understanding and the will. If this means that poetry is being defined as the pleasure-giving aspect of any composition whatever, and that that aspect, when it happens to exist at all, is to be considered something extraneous to the essence of the work to which it belongs, then the poetic principle has hardly been recognized for what it truly is, and its significance has been discounted so far as to belie what it actually has meant to human life and culture. Priestley's system of rhetoric would therefore seem to begin by drawing poetry within its jurisdiction, and to end by leaving the poetic principle unrecognized.

[533] See above, Ch. 4, pp. 204-208.   [534] See above, pp. 591, 594.

And in that particular segment of its total accomplishment it can hardly be pronounced satisfactory.

The *Lectures on Oratory* have appeared six times in print.[535] The first edition, as I mentioned above, came out at London in 1777. One of the other five printings occurred at Dublin in 1781; three more, at London, in connection with successive issues in 1824, 1826, and 1833, of Volume XXIII of *The Theological and Miscellaneous Works of Joseph Priestley*, edited with notes by John Towill Rutt; and the final one, the only American edition, at Carbondale, Illinois, in 1965, under the editorship of Vincent M. Bevilacqua and Richard Murphy. This last printing contains not only a facsimile of the first edition but also an introductory essay by the two editors outlining the events in Priestley's life and commenting upon the bibliographical history and the rhetorical quality of the *Lectures on Oratory*. One useful feature of that introductory essay is its speculative reconstruction of Priestley's doctrine of oratorical delivery; but its analysis of the other aspects of Priestley's rhetorical theory lacks depth and precision. As an effort to provide modern scholars with a readable and attractive text of the *Lectures on Oratory*, the work of Bevilacqua and Murphy deserves of course to be commended. And if it serves to call attention to Priestley's rhetoric as a neglected but significant side of eighteenth-century critical theory, it will indeed be of real use to scholarship.[536]

Priestley's *Lectures on Oratory* had been in print for a little more than six years when another work of the same sort appeared, and

[535] For this bibliographical information, see Crook, *Bibliography of Joseph Priestley*, pp. 79, 107; also *A Course of Lectures on Oratory and Criticism* By Joseph Priestley, ed. Vincent M. Bevilacqua and Richard Murphy (Carbondale, Illinois, 1965), pp. xx-xxi, liv-lv.

[536] In his *The Language of Politics in the Age of Wilkes and Burke* (London and Toronto, 1963), James T. Boulton discusses Priestley's contribution to the debate in Britain between 1790 and 1793 over the French Revolution, and he also discusses contributions on that same occasion by Edmund Burke, Thomas Paine, Mary Wollstonecraft, James Mackintosh, and William Godwin. But Mr. Boulton does not recognize that the rhetorical theories of that era, and particularly Priestley's *Lectures on Oratory*, are important to the modern critic in defining the standards which the participants in that debate themselves observed. Why, in short, should Priestley the rhetorician be ignored by a student of Priestley the controversialist?

it was to become the most popular and most influential, but not the most meritorious, of all the new rhetorics of its age. It was written by Hugh Blair, and it contained the text of the forty-seven lectures which Blair had been delivering year after year in his capacity as first Regius Professor of Rhetoric and Belles Lettres at the University of Edinburgh. As we already know, Blair entitled the work, *Lectures on Rhetoric and Belles Lettres*, and he published it in two volumes at London and at Edinburgh in 1783.[537]

It is not hard to explain why Blair should have been willing at that particular time to give the public a printed version of his already celebrated lectures. First of all, he was aware that they represented a completely new development at his own university, and that King George III himself had conferred upon that development a special distinction in the academic world. These sentiments are expressed or implied in the first footnote which Blair appended to the published version of the work now under discussion.

> The Author [he remarked] was the first who read Lectures on this subject in the University of Edinburgh. He began with reading them in a private character in the year 1759. In the following year he was chosen Professor of Rhetoric by the Magistrates and Town-council of Edinburgh: and, in 1762, his Majesty was pleased to erect and endow a Profession of Rhetoric and Belles Lettres in that University; and the Author was appointed the first Regius Professor.[538]

In the second place, Blair said of his lectures that "The publication of them, at present, was not altogether a matter of choice," and he explained himself as follows:

> Imperfect Copies of them, in Manuscript, from notes taken by Students who heard them read, were first privately handed

[537] According to Schmitz, p. 94, the first edition appeared at London on June 7 and at Edinburgh on July 5, 1783. Bevilacqua and Murphy say that the first edition of Priestley's *Lectures on Oratory* appeared before April 13, 1777; see their edition, p. xviii.

My discussion of Blair's *Lectures on Rhetoric*, as I indicated above, is based upon the text of the first edition as printed in facsimile at Carbondale, Illinois, in 1965, under the editorship of Harold F. Harding. Harding's critical introduction is cited here as Harding.

[538] *Lectures on Rhetoric*, I, 3.

about; and afterwards frequently exposed to public sale. When the Author saw them circulate so currently, as even to be quoted in print, and found himself often threatened with surreptitious publications of them, he judged it to be high time that they should proceed from his own hand, rather than come into public view under some very defective and erroneous form.[539]

Thirdly, Blair ceased after 1783 to have use for a set of prepared academic lectures in connection with his own teaching, inasmuch as that year marked his retirement from the active duties of his professorship.[540] And, finally, the publishing firms of Strahan and Cadell in London, and Creech in Edinburgh, offered him £1500 in May, 1782, for the copyright of the lectures, and that sum was handsome enough to induce any author to agree to have his thoughts conveyed in print to the public.[541] In connection with the commercial aspects of the publication of the lectures, it must be observed, indeed, that Blair was unusual among rhetoricians of his time so far as to get a wide audience of general readers for his rhetorical writings.[542] Priestley, Lawson, Adam Smith, Sheridan, Ward, and even Campbell, were hardly his equals in this beguiling respect, at least.

As he indicated in his first lecture, Blair sought to give his hearers or readers the sort of advice that would help them to become either good writers and able speakers, if their profession required such abilities, or wide readers and judicious critics, if they had no practical motives in studying composition and literature.[543] To those in the former group, Blair emphasized that the

[539] *Ibid.*, I, iii. Blair indicated in a footnote to this passage that he had been quoted in the account of Addison in *Biographia Britannica*. And so he had. The second edition of that work (London, 1778, Vol. I, p. 62, col. 2) contains the following statement: "The ingenious Dr. Blair of Edinburgh, in his Lectures on Oratory (a manuscript copy of which we have seen), hath analyzed some of Mr. Addison's prose compositions; and, while he gives due applause to their excellencies, mentions, with judgment and candour, the places wherein the arrangement might be altered for the better."

[540] Schmitz, pp. 66, 93, 118.

[541] *Ibid.*, p. 94.

[542] Jessop, pp. 101-102, lists 28 editions of the *Lectures on Rhetoric*; Schmitz, p. 144, lists 62 editions. There were also numerous abridgments of the work. It was translated into German, French, Italian, Spanish, and Russian.

[543] *Lectures on Rhetoric*, I, 4-5.

study of composition was in fact the study of reason itself. "True rhetoric and sound logic," he said, "are very nearly allied. The study of arranging and expressing our thoughts with propriety, teaches to think, as well as to speak, accurately."[544] To those in the latter group, "rhetoric is not so much a practical art," he declared, "as a speculative science; and the same instructions which assist others in composing, will assist them in judging of, and relishing, the beauties of composition."[545] And he then offered the following definition of what true criticism should be:

> As rhetoric has been sometimes thought to signify nothing more than the scholastic study of words, and phrases, and tropes, so criticism has been considered as merely the art of finding faults; as the frigid application of certain technical terms, by means of which persons are taught to cavil and censure in a learned manner. But this is the criticism of pedants only. True criticism is a liberal and humane art. It is the offspring of good sense and refined taste. It aims at acquiring a just discernment of the real merit of authors.[546]

Having thus identified his audience as the community of aspiring critics and authors, Blair listed the subjects which he proposed to deal with in the ensuing course.

> They divide themselves [he said] into five parts. First, some Introductory dissertations on the nature of taste, and upon the sources of its pleasures. Secondly, the consideration of language: Thirdly, of style: Fourthly, of eloquence properly so called, or publick speaking in its different kinds. Lastly, a critical examination of the most distinguished species of composition, both in prose and verse.[547]

Blair carried out this program by delivering four lectures on taste, four on language, fifteen on style, ten on eloquence, and thirteen on the forms of composition. His treatment of each of these subjects will now receive brief comment.

The four lectures on the first subject dealt with the nature of taste, the nature and foundation of criticism, the true meaning of sublimity in composition, and the true meaning of beauty. Blair defined taste as " 'The power of receiving pleasure from the

[544] *Ibid.*, I, 6-7.   [545] *Ibid.*, I, 8.   [546] *Ibid.*, I, 8-9.
[547] *Ibid.*, I, 14.

beauties of nature and of art.' "[548] He declared it to be "a faculty common in some degree to all men."[549] And he summarized his discussion of it as follows:

> The conclusion, which it is sufficient for us to rest upon, is, that Taste is far from being an arbitrary principle, which is subject to the fancy of every individual, and which admits of no criterion for determining whether it be false or true. Its foundation is the same in all human minds. It is built upon sentiments and perceptions which belong to our nature; and which, in general, operate with the same uniformity as our other intellectual principles. When these sentiments are perverted by ignorance and prejudice, they are capable of being rectified by reason. Their sound and natural state is ultimately determined, by comparing them with the general Taste of mankind.[550]

These sentiments were not offered by Blair as original theories but as the synthesis of the views of such distinguished authorities as Gerard, D'Alembert, Du Bos, Kames, Hume, and Burke.[551] And the same authorities are at the basis of Blair's discussion of criticism, sublimity, and beauty. "True Criticism," he said, "is the application of Taste and of good sense to the several fine arts,"[552] taste being the power which forms the good critic as genius is the power which forms the orator and poet.[553] As for sublimity and beauty, they are terms associated in the first instance with the pleasures which we experience when we behold a natural object that impresses us as either awe-inspiring or serene; and in the second instance they are terms associated with the feelings that we have when a verbal description of that same kind of natural object impresses us in the same way as the object itself did.[554] Here is one passage in which Blair distinguished these two terms from each other:

> Beauty, next to Sublimity, affords, beyond doubt, the highest pleasure to the imagination. The emotion which it raises, is very distinguishable from that of Sublimity. It is of a calmer kind; more gentle and soothing; does not elevate the mind so much,

[548] *Ibid.*, I, 16. [549] *Ibid.*, I, 17. [550] *Ibid.*, I, 34.
[551] *Ibid.*, I, 17. [552] *Ibid.*, I, 36. [553] *Ibid.*, I, 41.
[554] *Ibid.*, I, 46.

but produces an agreeable serenity. Sublimity raises a feeling, too violent, as I showed, to be lasting; the pleasure arising from Beauty admits of longer continuance.[555]

Blair's four lectures on language began with the observation that language "is the foundation of the whole power of eloquence,"[556] and they proceeded to set forth the ideas which Blair by his own acknowledgment drew from Adam Smith, from Lord Monboddo, from James Harris, from Condillac, from Arnauld and Lancelot, from Rousseau, and from several other authorities.[557] Thus Blair traced the rise and progress of language before and after the invention of writing, and he spoke of the structure of language in general and of the English tongue in particular. In his discussion of the general structure of language, he quoted Campbell's *Philosophy of Rhetoric* on one occasion,[558] and when he turned to the structure of English, he referred again to Campbell, and to Greenwood, Lowth, and Joseph Priestley as well.[559] These lectures as a whole may be said to grow out of the need to emphasize what Blair felt to be the connection between grammar and rhetoric.

Blair's fifteen lectures on style dealt successively with perspicuity, ornament, the general characters of style, the methods by which a good style might be attained, and the accomplishments of Addison and Swift as stylists. Blair defined style as "the peculiar manner in which a man expresses his conceptions, by means of Language."[560] He treated perspicuity by accepting it as one of the two leading qualities of style, the other being ornament, and by discussing thereafter the problem of choosing words and the problem of arranging words into sentences. His analysis of this latter problem led him not only to speak of clearness and precision, unity, strength, and harmony, but also to refer his readers to such authorities as Demetrius Phalereus and Dionysius of Halicarnassus, among the ancients, and to Kames's *Elements of Criticism* and Campbell's *Philosophy of Rhetoric*, among the moderns.[561] Ornament, the other leading quality of style, he treated by devoting one lecture to the nature of figurative language, and three lectures to the common figures—metaphor, al-

555 *Ibid.*, I, 80-81. 556 *Ibid.*, I, 97. 557 *Ibid.*, I, 97-98.
558 *Ibid.*, I, 154-155. 559 *Ibid.*, I, 173, 179, 182. 560 *Ibid.*, I, 183.
561 *Ibid.*, I, 208-209.

legory, hyperbole, personification, apostrophe, comparison, antithesis, climax, and the like. All writers who treat of rhetoric, he observed, have insisted at large upon the figures of speech, and it would be an endless task to make references to their work. But he added that Marsais's *Traité des Tropes pour servir d'Introduction à la Rhetorique, & à la Logique* was sensible and instructive, and that Kames's *Elements of Criticism* might be consulted for definitions and illustrations of particular figures.[562] When Blair finished his treatment of these matters, he turned to the subject of the general characters of style, and at this point he made a decision of some consequence. That is to say, he recognized and rejected the ancient doctrine of three major styles, and he indicated that he was going instead to follow Adam Smith's teachings upon this matter, as those teachings had come to him from Smith's manuscript treatise on rhetoric.[563] Thus Blair proposed that writers differed from each other in style as they differed in respect to their ways of thinking, in respect to their rejection or acceptance of ornament, and in respect to their disposition to use ornament with simplicity or with studied affectation. In other words, styles were diffuse or concise, nervous or feeble, as their author's habits of thought varied; styles were dry, or plain, or neat, or elegant, or florid, as their authors ranged in attitude from dislike to love of ornament; and styles were natural or artificial as their authors felt ornament to be a natural thing or a seductive invitation to display their own virtuosity.[564] As for Blair's advice about the method of acquiring a good style, it is prudent and practical, and it consists of such pieces of ancient wisdom as that of seeking to have clear ideas before one begins to write or that of giving oneself frequent practice in composition.[565] We need not enumerate Blair's other recommendations on this head, nor would it be feasible to try to describe briefly what he said about the accomplishments of Addison and Swift as writers. But it is relevant to our present purpose to observe that his own taste in regard to these two authors coincides with that of the new rather than with that of the old rhetoric.

Blair's ten lectures on eloquence dealt successively with the nature of eloquent discourse, its history, its ancient and modern kinds, the six parts of the oration, the invention and disposition

[562] *Ibid.*, I, 272-273.

[563] *Ibid.*, I, 370-371, 381.

[564] *Ibid.*, I, 371-378, 379-385, 387-399.

[565] *Ibid.*, I, 402, 403.

of proofs, the pronunciation or delivery of the speech, and the means to self-improvement in public address. What Blair said upon each of these subjects must now receive brief consideration.

Eloquence is best defined, said Blair, as "the Art of Speaking in such a manner as to attain the end for which we speak."[566] And he explained at once what the terms of this definition meant to him:

> Whenever a man speaks or writes, he is supposed, as a rational being, to have some end in view; either to inform, or to amuse, or to persuade, or, in some way or other, to act upon his fellow-creatures. He who speaks, or writes, in such a manner as to adapt all his words most effectually to that end, is the most eloquent man. Whatever then the subject be, there is room for Eloquence; in history, or even in philosophy, as well as in orations. The definition which I have given of Eloquence, comprehends all the different kinds of it; whether calculated to instruct, to persuade, or to please. But, as the most important subject of discourse is Action, or Conduct, the power of Eloquence chiefly appears when it is employed to influence Conduct, and persuade to Action. As it is principally, with reference to this end, that it becomes the object of Art, Eloquence may, under this view of it, be defined, The Art of Persuasion.[567]

This definition of the nature and ends of eloquence makes it clear that Blair did not confine eloquence to spoken discourse alone, or to oratory alone, or to persuasion alone. He emphasized persuasion above the author's other goals, to be sure, but he obviously did so in the belief that persuasion, by virtue of its being a compound of instruction and conviction and pleasure and passion, is the goal which includes all the other goals. This conception of the ends of eloquence was obviously suggested to Blair by Campbell's *Philosophy of Rhetoric*, and there can be no doubt that Blair's definition of eloquence came from the same source. For, as we remember, Campbell had declared eloquence to be " 'That art or talent by which the discourse is adapted to its end.' "[568] Indeed, when Blair in a later passage defended eloquence against its detractors by remarking, "Give truth and virtue the same arms which you give vice and falsehood, and the former are likely to

[566] *Ibid.*, II, 2.   [567] *Ibid.*, II, 2-3.   [568] See above, p. 579.

prevail,"[569] he was echoing the argument that Campbell had borrowed from Aristotle and Bacon and had expounded throughout his treatise on rhetorical theory.

But it is not enough merely to note that two of Blair's conceptions—that regarding the ends of eloquence, and that regarding the connection of eloquence with truth and falsehood—are borrowed from Campbell. It has to be recognized at the same time that Blair differs from Campbell in respect to the attitude which he takes towards the latter of these conceptions. To Campbell, the latter conception was central; it was peripheral to Blair. To Campbell, the latter conception deserved great emphasis; Blair gave it only a passing mention. To Campbell, the latter conception was valid in rhetoric because it was valid in terms of the way in which the human faculties work together and apart; to Blair, the conception was valid without being deeply involved in the moral and intellectual nature of man. Thus Blair's rhetorical theory must be said to lack penetration and insight at a crucial moment in its development. It enables the critic to define an author's goal and to study the way in which that goal is reached through the author's skill in adapting his words to it. But it does not enable the critic to decide whether one example of the successful adaptation of words to the author's purpose is ever to be considered better or worse than another example. This problem can be decided, of course, only by considering what the words in each case mean, and once this consideration is introduced into criticism, the truth and goodness inherent in the substance of the words become central issues. Walter Pater's essay called "Style," first published in 1888, clarified these issues more fully than anyone had done since the time when Plato wrote *Phaedrus*. But Campbell clarified them, too, although he did not thereby achieve Pater's precision and comprehensiveness. As for Blair, he recognized what the issues were, but he did not venture to explore them. Perhaps he felt that it was unnecessary, or that it was risky and hazardous, to do so. In either case, however, his rhetorical theory at this point at least falls short of Campbell's in interest and quality.

Having defined the nature and goals of eloquent discourse, Blair turned next to its history, and he devoted the better part of two lectures to a survey of the oratorical achievements of Greece,

[569] *Lectures on Rhetoric*, II, 4.

Rome, and modern Europe. These achievements were a favorite subject of controversy in his time, and his own position in that controversy is a matter of some interest to the historian of rhetoric.

One thesis to emerge from this survey was that Demosthenes outranks Cicero on the scale of oratorical greatness. Blair remarked that his own high opinion of Demosthenes was supported by David Hume, the latter having expressed the opinion in his essay "Of Eloquence" that, "of all human productions, the Orations of Demosthenes present to us the models which approach the nearest to perfection."[570] Blair also remarked that most French critics gave a distinct preference to Cicero whenever they compared him with Demosthenes, and that Rapin indeed had supported this preference by attributing the superiority of Cicero to his familiarity with Aristotle's *Rhetoric* and the inferiority of Demosthenes to his having had the misfortune to deliver his famous speeches before the *Rhetoric* was published.[571] Blair dismissed this argument as childish. "Such Orators as Cicero and Demosthenes," he said, "derived their knowledge of the human passions, and their power of moving them, from higher sources than any Treatise of Rhetoric."[572] There was, however, one French critic, Blair noted, who preferred Demosthenes to Cicero, and that critic was Fénelon, "the famous Archbishop of Cambray, . . . himself surely no enemy to all the graces and flowers of composition." "It is in his Reflections on Rhetoric and Poetry," Blair continued, "that he gives this judgment." And Blair added not only that that treatise was usually published in company with Fénelon's *Dialogues on Eloquence*, but also that "These dialogues and reflections are particularly worthy of perusal, as containing, I think, the justest ideas on the subject, that are to be met with in any modern critical writer."[573]

Another thesis to emerge from Blair's survey was that, if we consider Demosthenes and Cicero together, they represent a standard of oratorical perfection not to be found anywhere in the modern world. Speaking of France and Britain as the best fitted of all modern nations to rise above that ancient standard, Blair passed the following judgment upon them:

[570] *Ibid.*, II, 32. Blair's statement of Hume's opinion is not enclosed in quotation marks, but it is nevertheless an exact quotation from Hume's essay.
[571] *Ibid.*, II, 32-33.   [572] *Ibid.*, II, 33.   [573] *Ibid.*, II, 33-34.

While, in other productions of genius, both in prose and in poetry, they have contended for the prize with Greece and Rome; nay, in some compositions, may be thought to have surpassed them: the names of Demosthenes and Cicero, stand, at this day, unrivalled in fame; and it would be held presumptuous and absurd, to pretend to place any modern whatever on the same, or even on a nearly equal, rank.[574]

At this point in his survey, Blair noted that Hume had asserted the inferiority of modern to ancient eloquence and had then supposed the reasons for this inferiority to lie beyond satisfactory explanation. On the latter point, said Blair, "I differ from him, and shall endeavour, before the conclusion of this Lecture, to point out some causes to which, I think, it may, in great measure, be ascribed. . . ."[575] When Blair's explanation of these causes came, it amounted to an interesting display of historical analysis. He said first of all that modern man had come to expect accuracy and closeness of reasoning upon public occasions, and had come to be suspicious of anything but reason and moderation in any particular speaker's attempt to elevate the imagination and to warm the passions.[576] He observed secondly that, in the British parliament, the high hand of arbitrary power in former reigns, and the subtle uses of ministerial influences at the present time, had tended to keep oratory from cultivating the vehemence which gave it an irresistible and certain effect in ancient assemblies.[577] Thirdly, he emphasized that arguments at the British bar had now to reflect a detailed knowledge of the law, and a continuing concern for precedent, and that the vehement old appeals to equity and to human feelings were no longer workable.[578] Fourthly, he remarked that the pulpit of the established church, with its distaste for anything approaching the evangelical zeal of the Puritan preachers, and with its practice of reading sermons from manuscript, was defining its modern role in terms of instruction and reasoning, not in terms of warmth and passion.[579] In connection with what Blair said under this fourth head, and under the other three heads as well, we can see with great clarity that he recognized the connection between oratorical practices and historical conditions, and that he saw the utter futility of using

[574] *Ibid.*, II, 38.　　　[575] *Ibid.*, II, 38 n.　　　[576] *Ibid.*, II, 41-42.
[577] *Ibid.*, II, 42-43.　　[578] *Ibid.*, II, 43.　　　[579] *Ibid.*, II, 43-44.

under modern circumstances a set of practices which once had worked to perfection, and which he himself happened to prefer.

Blair even carried his historical attitude into the advice which he later gave about imitating the ancient orators. Thus he warned prospective parliamentary speakers to have a proper regard for what the public ear would bear. "This direction I give," he said, "in order to guard against an injudicious imitation of ancient Orators, who, both in their pronunciation and gesture, and in their figures of expression, used a bolder manner than what the greater coolness of modern taste will readily suffer."[580]

> This may perhaps, as I formerly observed [he added], be a disadvantage to Modern Eloquence. It is no reason why we should be too severe in checking the impulse of genius, and continue always creeping on the ground; but it is a reason, however, why we should avoid carrying the tone of declamation to a height that would now be reckoned extravagant.

Thus also Blair warned the modern apprentice in legal oratory to "beware of considering even the judicial Orations of Cicero or Demosthenes, as exact models of the manner of speaking which is adapted to the present state of the Bar."[581] In words reminiscent of those used in a similar connection by Adam Smith, Blair spoke as follows of the dangers of imitating Roman oratory in Britain:

> In the famous cause of Milo, Cicero spoke to fifty-one *Judices Selecti*, and so had the advantage of addressing his whole pleading, not to one or a few learned Judges of the point of law, as is the case with us, but to an Assembly of Roman citizens. . . . To great advantage he may still be studied by every Speaker at the Bar. In the Address with which he opens his subject, and the insinuation he employs for gaining the favour of the Judges; in the distinct arrangement of his facts; in the gracefulness of his narration; in the conduct and exposition of his arguments, he may and he ought to be imitated. A higher pattern cannot be set before us; but one who should imitate him also in his exaggeration and amplifications, in his diffuse and pompous declamation, and in his attempts to raise passion, would now make

---

[580] *Ibid.*, II, 56-57.   [581] *Ibid.*, II, 76.

himself almost as ridiculous at the Bar, as if he should appear there in the *Toga* of a Roman Lawyer.[582]

But if Blair the historian is at pains to stress that ancient eloquence will not suit modern conditions, and should in many ways not be imitated by modern speakers, what becomes of the argument of Blair the critic that Demosthenes and Cicero set the standard for oratorical perfection, and that those who do not follow that standard represent oratory in a state of decline? The answer is, of course, that Blair should not have taken these latter positions if he had believed in the solidity of his historical analysis. His argument should instead have been, not that oratory fell into a decline when speakers abandoned the ancient vehemence, but that oratory changed. He should have seen that, when ancient vehemence moved men, and temperate discourse seemed to exercise no great influence, then in truth the ancient vehemence was the standard of perfection. But he should have gone on to stress that, when historical conditions made that ancient vehemence no longer effective, it could no longer be thought the standard, and that a new standard had to be formulated by seeking to discover what moved men in the new time. Robert Boyle, Adam Smith, and Joseph Priestley saw this issue much more clearly than did Blair. If we take Blair's argument seriously, we can find fault with him for saying in one breath that oratorical perfection is the perfection of Cicero and Demosthenes, and in the next breath, that oratorical perfection was not suited to the modern world and should not be sought by the modern student, as if the modern student should under no conditions seek to move his fellow creatures by the spoken or written word. The old humanists had argued that Cicero was eloquent, and that any discourse had to embody his rhetorical practices if the title of eloquence was to be conferred upon it. And their critics had replied that the Scriptures had not embodied Ciceronian practices, and yet had in fact moved men more deeply than Cicero had ever done. It was Boyle who pointed out that there were two standards of eloquence involved in this clash of opinion—one standard which equated eloquent discourse with ornament, and another which equated it with plainness. And Boyle was right, as were Adam Smith and Joseph

---

[582] *Ibid.*, II, 77-78.

Priestley in circumstances which differed in many respects, but not in basic issues, from those faced by Boyle. Compared to these critics, Blair seems feeble and equivocal upon this particular matter.

Next after Blair's historical survey of eloquence came his four lectures on the kinds of modern oratory, and at this point he dealt successively with speaking as it occurs in the modern court of law, the modern popular assembly, and the modern pulpit. "This division," he said, "coincides in part with the ancient one."[583] And he then explained that the modern legal speech was precisely like the ancient judicial oration, and the modern parliamentary address had elements in common with the deliberative speech and the panegyric of antiquity. Only the modern sermon, said Blair, had no counterpart in ancient rhetorical practice. During these four lectures Blair issued the cautions which I quoted a moment ago in commenting upon his attitude towards the imitation of Demosthenes and Cicero. The rest of what he said about the three kinds of oratory does not increase or diminish his stature as a new rhetorician and thus need not enter into my present discussion. I should say, however, that his method in these particular lectures was to set forth doctrine concerning each kind of oratory and to analyze an example of that kind. The doctrine involved problems of subject matter or invention, disposition or method, style, and delivery, but he did not force his treatment of these matters to parrot the distinctions which accompanied these familiar terms as they were used in the old rhetoric. Nor did he undertake to give each of these terms the same degree of emphasis for each kind of oratory. For example, he dealt at greater length with the style of parliamentary speaking than with that of the legal address or the sermon, and he tended to say of each kind of oration that he would treat its delivery when he came later to speak of the whole problem of pronunciation. As for his examples, they consisted of several passages from various speeches of Demosthenes to illustrate the parliamentary speech, of a sustained analysis of Cicero's oration for Cluentius to illustrate legal oratory, and of a similar analysis of a sermon by Bishop Atterbury to illustrate the eloquence of the pulpit.[584]

After he had disposed of these kinds of oratory, Blair turned

---

[583] *Ibid.*, II, 47.   [584] *Ibid.*, II, 61-73, 86-100, 127-155.

next to the doctrine of oratorical structure in its large aspects, and upon this subject he delivered two lectures, his successive points of emphasis being, "first, the Exordium or Introduction; secondly, the State, and the Division of the Subject; thirdly, Narration, or Explication; fourthly, the Reasoning or Arguments; fifthly, the Pathetic Part; and lastly, the Conclusion."[585] The bare announcement of these subjects would seem to promise that Blair's approach to the doctrine of oratorical arrangement would be largely traditional, and indeed it turned out that way. Thus, although he did not follow the ancients so as to make refutation a separate part of the oration, he nevertheless worked it into his scheme by subsuming it under the discussion of reasoning or arguments;[586] and although he appeared to veer from ancient theory when he made a separate part out of pathetic appeals, he still indicated that the proper place for this kind of discourse was the conclusion or peroration, as the ancients had taught.[587] Thus, too, although he respectfully cited Fénelon's opinion that it was stiff and unnatural to go through the motions of laying out a sermon into a system of formal parts, he chose even so to declare it to be his own opinion "that the present method of dividing a Sermon into heads, ought not to be laid aside."[588] Blair's traditionalism in these doctrines has to be understood, however, as unpedantic and flexible. That is to say, his style and vocabulary were always urbane and modern, and he did not insist that every discourse had to have each one of the six parts which his theory assigned to it. "There may be many excellent Discourses in public," he declared with reference to this latter point, "where several of these parts are altogether wanting; where the Speaker, for instance, uses no Introduction, but enters directly on his subject; where he has no occasion either to divide or explain; but simply reasons on one side of the question, and then finishes."[589]

In his discussion of arguments or reasonings as the fourth part of the standard oration, Blair made some observations which are completely untraditional, and these constitute, indeed, his best claim to the title of new rhetorician. "Now, with respect to Argu-

---

[585] *Ibid.*, II, 157.

[586] *Ibid.*, II, 157. In the fourth part of the speech, the speaker, said Blair, "will employ arguments for establishing his own opinion, and overthrowing that of his antagonist."

[587] *Ibid.*, II, 191.　　　　[588] *Ibid.*, II, 170.　　　　[589] *Ibid.*, II, 157.

ments," he said, "three things are requisite. First, the invention of them; secondly, the proper disposition and arrangement of them; and thirdly, the expressing of them in such a style and manner, as to give them their full force."[590] It was in his discussion of the first of these heads that he made one set of untraditional observations, and he made another set when he handled the second head. Let us look separately at each.

The invention of arguments, said Blair, is the most important aspect of the fourth part of the oration, but it is an aspect which lies beyond the scope of the art of rhetoric. He then spoke thus:

> The ancient Rhetoricians did indeed attempt to go much farther than this. They attempted to form Rhetoric into a more complete system; and professed not only to assist Public Speakers in setting off their arguments to most advantage; but to supply the defect of their invention, and to teach them where to find arguments on every subject and cause. Hence their Doctrine of Topics, or "Loci Communes," and "Sedes Argumentorum," which makes so great a figure in the writings of Aristotle, Cicero, and Quinctilian.[591]

After some comment upon the nature of the topical system of classical rhetoric, Blair pronounced that system incapable of producing anything but trivial discourse. "What is truly solid and persuasive," he declared, "must be drawn 'ex visceribus causae,' from a thorough knowledge of the subject, and profound meditation on it."[592]

> On this doctrine, therefore, of the Rhetorical Loci or Topics [he added], I think it superfluous to insist. If any think that the knowledge of them may contribute to improve their invention, and extend their views, they may consult Aristotle and Quinctilian, or what Cicero has written on this head, in his Treatise De Inventione, his Topica, and Second Book De Oratore. But when they are to prepare a Discourse, by which they purpose to convince a Judge, or to produce any considerable effect upon an Assembly, I would advise them to lay aside their common places, and to think closely of their subject. Demosthenes, I dare say, consulted none of the Loci, when he was inciting the Athenians to take arms against Philip; and where Cicero has

[590] *Ibid.*, II, 179-180.   [591] *Ibid.*, II, 180.   [592] *Ibid.*, II, 181-182.

had recourse to them, his Orations are so much the worse on that account.[593]

Somewhat less untraditional than this urbane assault upon the topics of invention was Blair's use of terms from eighteenth-century logic to describe the ways in which arguments should be conducted in the fourth part of the oration. Classical rhetoric had said that these arguments should be conducted by induction or deduction, induction being an irregular syllogistic process in which indisputable facts were adduced one after another so as to lead to the establishment of a related but disputable conclusion, and deduction, the process in which a major premise and a minor premise were laid down, and a conclusion drawn therefrom, under the rules governing regular syllogisms.[594] What Blair did was to identify these processes by calling the first the method of analysis, and the second, the method of synthesis, and thus, without making any substantive change in the doctrine involved, he took two traditional terms out of rhetoric, and replaced them by logical terms. Here is part of what he said on this matter:

> Two different methods may be used by Orators in the conduct of their reasoning; the terms of art for which are, the Analytic, and the Synthetic method. The Analytic is, when the Orator conceals his intention concerning the point he is to prove, till he has gradually brought his hearers to the designed conclusion. They are led on step by step, from one known truth to another, till the conclusion be stolen upon them, as the natural consequence of a chain of propositions. . . . This is much the same with the Socratic method, by which that Philosopher silenced the Sophists of his age. . . .

> But there are few subjects that will admit this method, and not many occasions on which it is proper to be employed. The mode of reasoning most generally used, and most suited to the train of Popular Speaking, is what is called the Synthetic; when the point to be proved is fairly laid down, and one Argument after another is made to bear upon it, till the hearers be fully convinced.[595]

[593] *Ibid.*, II, 182.
[594] For this doctrine in classical rhetoric, see *De Inventione*, 1.31-41.
[595] *Lectures on Rhetoric*, II, 182-183.

Blair is the fourth British rhetorician of his time to blend into rhetorical theory the logical methods of analysis and synthesis, the three others having been Adam Smith, George Campbell, and Joseph Priestley. In explaining the two procedures to be used by didactic composition when its mission was to deliver a system of science to the public, Smith dwelt upon the methods of analysis and synthesis; and Campbell mentioned the same two methods in connection with some remarks that he made about the difference between acquiring knowledge and communicating it.[596] As for Priestley, he went beyond Smith and Campbell to make the two methods stand for the entire theory of *dispositio* in oratory.[597] But Blair took a more conservative view. He assigned them, not to composition as a whole, and not to didactic discourse as an important modern form of composition, but to the composition of arguments in the fourth part of an oration. Thus at this point he represented the tendency to change minor details of terminology rather than major concerns of substance in rhetorical theory. And indeed throughout his lectures he showed this same tendency in one other interesting respect—what the old rhetoric had uniformly called *dispositio* or arrangement, Blair prevailingly called method.[598]

In the final stages of his discussion of eloquence, Blair addressed himself to the problem of oratorical pronunciation or delivery, and he made his single lecture on this subject consist of an outline of four basic and four higher requirements for speakers to observe. The basic requirements concerned loudness, distinctness, slowness, and propriety; and the higher requirements, emphasis, pauses, tones, and gestures.[599] Blair's own profound conviction was that speakers would attain a forcible and persuasive delivery "if they will only unlearn false and corrupt habits; if they will allow themselves to follow nature, and will speak in public, as they do in private, when they speak in earnest, and from the heart."[600] In other words, speaking effectively in public did not come from a conscious attention to rules regarding the use of voice and gesture.

[596] See above, pp. 561-564, 602.
[597] See above, pp. 639-642.
[598] *Lectures on Rhetoric*, II, 3, 27, 53-54, 83, 87, 169, 172, 173, 182-183.
[599] *Ibid.*, II, 206, 210. [600] *Ibid.*, II, 224.

For when a Speaker is engaged in a Public Discourse [said Blair in concluding this lecture], he should not be then employing his attention about his manner, or thinking of his tones and his gestures. If he be so employed, study and affectation will appear. He ought to be then quite in earnest; wholly occupied with his subject and his sentiments; leaving Nature, and previously formed habits, to prompt and suggest his manner of Delivery.[601]

Blair uttered these words when the elocutionary movement had gained great momentum in Britain, and Thomas Sheridan had succeeded in convincing a great many people that the true art of rhetoric as taught in ancient Rome was not only to be regarded as something confined exclusively to voice and gesture but was also to be cultivated in modern times as a sure corrective for bad taste, low morals, loose behavior, and general public corruption. Blair's teachings on delivery included a respectful acknowledgment of his indebtedness to Sheridan's *A Course of Lectures on Elocution*, and a quotation from that same author's *Lectures on the Art of Reading*.[602] But the truly remarkable thing about Blair's rhetoric is that it did not use the word elocution as a term for oratorical delivery, despite Sheridan's insistence in that direction. To Blair, elocution was properly a word for style, and pronunciation, the right word for delivery.[603] And by being traditional in this instance, Blair was also in fact a modern, for the new rhetoric did not subscribe to the terminology or to the rhetorical theory of the elocutionists.

Blair's final lecture on eloquence was practical in content and tone as it sought to indicate how any aspiring young speaker could improve himself in oratorical composition. Blair stressed that improvement in speaking would come from the development of high moral qualifications, the acquisition of deep and wide knowledge, the cultivation of habits of industry, the imitation of the best models, the actual composition and delivery of speeches and practice in writing, and the study of great critics and rhetoricians.[604] These pieces of advice show Blair to be a humanistic scholar, not a narrow technician, in his approach to the education

[601] *Ibid.*, II, 224-225.   [602] *Ibid.*, II, 205, 218.
[603] *Ibid.*, II, 1, 42, 60, 118, 203-225.
[604] *Ibid.*, II, 228, 233, 234, 235, 239, 242.

of an eloquent writer or speaker. Indeed, his whole conception of rhetoric is that, if it is to succeed in producing eloquence, it must never be content alone with delivery or style, but must recognize that its total obligation is to make sound ideas become verbal incentives to virtuous conduct. This particular lecture is especially interesting to the historian of rhetoric, however, in the view which it gives of the quality of Blair's own rhetorical learning. "It is to the original Antient Writers," he said, "that we must chiefly have recourse; and it is a reproach to any one, whose profession calls him to speak in public, to be unacquainted with them."[605] This observation led him to speak of the value of Aristotle's *Rhetoric*, Cicero's *De Oratore* and *Orator*, and Quintilian's *Institutio Oratoria*, to all aspiring speakers. And it is these works, we may be sure, which Blair himself had drawn upon most heavily in fashioning his own lectures on eloquence. But he also took pains again to praise Fénelon's *Dialogues on Eloquence*, and, as we know from his earlier lectures, he had a warm admiration for Adam Smith's Lectures on Rhetoric, which he had heard in 1748 and had used in manuscript some years later. As for George Campbell's *Philosophy of Rhetoric*, it too had earned his great respect. But he was not enthusiastic towards all the rhetoricians of his day. "Rollin, Batteux, Crevier, Gibert, and several other French Critics," he observed, "have also written on Oratory; but though some of them may be useful, none of them are so considerable as to deserve particular recommendation."[606] We might say, indeed, that Blair's strongly implied preference for Fénelon above Rollin is as sure a proof of his right to be called a new rhetorician as is his esteem for the rhetorical works of Adam Smith and George Campbell.

After Blair had concluded his lectures on eloquence, he turned next to the various forms of composition, and this subject occupied him for the thirteen lectures that now remained in his course. He had already discussed orations as one form of composition, and they did not become his subject a second time. What he did, however, was to talk about historical writings, philosophical writings, epistolary writings, fictitious histories, pastoral and lyric poems, didactic and descriptive poems, epic poems, tragedies, and comedies. Great works and great authors, ancient and modern, in each of these fields, were in effect his culminating

---

[605] *Ibid.*, II, 243.   [606] *Ibid.*, II, 242-243.

concern as these final lectures unfolded. Here was Blair the critic speaking of the literary compositions which his theory of rhetoric was designed to explain. "The Historian, the Orator, the Philosopher," he declared, "address themselves, for the most part, primarily to the understanding: their direct aim is to inform, to persuade, or to instruct. But the primary aim of a Poet is to please, and to move; and, therefore, it is to the Imagination, and the Passions, that he speaks."[607] It would be interesting indeed to show in detail how Blair discussed all the forms of composition in terms of this theme. But I must refrain from doing so here. I shall content myself instead with a few observations upon Blair's distinction between the poetic and the nonpoetic forms of composition, inasmuch as the quality of that distinction has much to do with his final standing among the new rhetoricians of his time.

"The most general division of the different kinds of Composition is, into those written in Prose," said Blair, "and those written in Verse; which certainly require to be separately considered, because subject to separate laws."[608] In accordance with this rhetorical partition, Blair proceeded to discuss historical writing, philosophical writing, epistolary writing, and fictitious history as forms of prose, his express stipulation being, as I noted above, that oratory also belonged under this head but would not receive further discussion; and later he discussed pastoral and lyric poetry, didactic and descriptive poetry, epic poetry, tragedy, and comedy, as forms of verse. The odd thing about this program as Blair outlined it is that it makes the laws of versification the principle by which poetry is separated from oratory, history, and philosophy, and thus it declares in effect that versified history or philosophy or oratory could in that form be called poetry. And at the same time it declares in effect that an epic poem translated into prose, or a tragedy written in prose, could in that form be denied its poetic standing. Moreover, it requires the critic to accept fictitious history and actual history as subject to the same set of laws, when as a matter of fact a prose fiction seems to obey the same basic laws that epic poetry adheres to. In other words, when Blair implied that the prose forms of composition in his scheme were subject to different laws from those governing the poetic forms of composition, he was in one of his most superficial mo-

---

[607] *Ibid.*, II, 312.

[608] *Ibid.*, II, 259.

ments, and any influence that his implication would have with later critics must certainly be judged unfortunate.

Blair realized his predicament himself when he came to discuss fictitious history, for it was obvious to him then that this form of prose did not adhere to the laws that governed historical writing. In treating modern British historians, he mentioned with obvious admiration the names of Hume, Robertson, and Gibbon,[609] and in his account of modern British fictitious histories, he found occasion to praise Defoe's *Robinson Crusoe*, Fielding's *Tom Jones*, and Richardson's *Clarissa Harlowe*, although he noted that British fiction was in general inferior to that of the French.[610] Throughout his treatment of fictitious history, however, he remained conspicuously silent about the possible kinship between this form of literature and regular historical writing; and he took pains instead to stress that fictitious history, on the one hand, and epic poetry and drama, on the other, were of the same kind. Here is what he said in this connection:

> In fact, fictitious histories might be employed for very useful purposes. They furnish one of the best channels for conveying instruction, for painting human life and manners, for showing the errors into which we are betrayed by our passions, for rendering virtue amiable and vice odious. The effect of well contrived stories, towards accomplishing these purposes, is stronger than any effect that can be produced by simple and naked instruction; and hence we find, that the wisest men in all ages, have more or less employed fables and fictions, as the vehicles of knowledge. These have ever been the basis of both Epic and Dramatic Poetry.[611]

It was at this point that Blair quoted a Latin passage from Bacon's *De Dignitate et Augmentis Scientiarum*, and that passage not only belongs to Bacon's analysis of poesy or feigned history but it also indicates why poetry and history march to different sets of laws. The passage reads thus in Spedding's translation:

So that this Poesy conduces not only to delight but also to magnanimity and morality. Whence it may be fairly thought to partake somewhat of a divine nature; because it raises the mind and carries it aloft, *accommodating the shows of things to the*

---

[609] *Ibid.*, II, 285. [610] *Ibid.*, II, 309-310. [611] *Ibid.*, II, 304.

desires of the mind, not (like reason and history) buckling and bowing down the mind to the nature of things.[612]

As this passage indicates, poetry deals with historical reality by accommodating that reality to the aspirations of the human imagination and by making it thereby speak, not of its specific but of its universal meaning, whereas history deals with historical reality by buckling the mind down to the actual record, and by making that record speak of its literal and specific self. And in line with this distinction, Bacon earlier ruled that verse had nothing to do with the essence of poetry, and that "true history may be written in verse and feigned history in prose."[613] Had Blair heeded Bacon, he would have drawn the line between history and poetry, not in terms of prose and verse, but in terms of actuality and fable, and under this principle he would have begun his discussion of poetical literature at the point where he took up the subject of feigned history and put himself in a position to express his own admiration for the novels of Defoe and Fielding.

Blair did not feel it necessary, however, to correct himself. He continued instead to take for granted that the very essence of poetry was somehow bound up with its tendency to use versification. Thus, when he had finished discussing feigned history as if its laws were those of actual history, he turned to what he regarded as true poetry, and he defined it as "the language of passion, or of enlivened imagination, formed, most commonly, into regular numbers."[614] Moreover, in justifying this definition, he specifically denied that the essence of poetry consisted in its being fictional or imitative.[615] His definition seems to allow a critic no choice but to class as poetry a passionate and imaginative discourse like Burke's *Reflections on the Revolution in France*, and to say that the absence of regular numbers in Burke's treatise can be explained as an allowable exception. In other words, Blair's definition does not provide an adequate explanation of the differences between oratory and poetry, and if a theory of rhetoric pretends to be a general theory of discourse, as Blair's did, it can

---

[612] *Works of Bacon*, VIII, 441. The passage which Blair quoted in Latin (*Lectures on Rhetoric*, II, 305) is indicated in my quotation by italics. In a footnote Blair provided his readers with his own translation of the quotation.

[613] *Works of Bacon*, VIII, 439.   [614] *Lectures on Rhetoric*, II, 312.

[615] *Ibid.*, II, 311-312.

hardly permit such differences as these to remain blurred and confused.

A modern student of Blair's rhetoric has declared that only twenty of Blair's lectures—the first ten of those on style and all of those on eloquence—make a direct contribution to rhetorical theory; and he intimates that the remaining twenty-seven lectures are intended to refer to such other disciplines as linguistics, the art of written composition, poetics, literary criticism, and literary history.[616] This opinion means that Blair's introductory lecture, his four lectures on taste, his four lectures on language, his five lectures on the literary works of Addison and Swift, and his thirteen lectures on the forms of literature, do not participate in his theory of rhetoric in any strict scholarly sense. If rhetoric is defined only as Aristotle, Cicero, and Quintilian conceived of it, then this opinion can of course be defended. But Blair had a larger idea. Like Adam Smith, George Campbell, and Joseph Priestley, Blair considered that modern rhetoric is rightfully the theory not only of the three spoken kinds of oratory, but also of the kinds of writing as well. He intended his lectures on taste to represent a theoretical approach to compositions primarily designed to please and to move. He intended his lectures on language and style to represent a theoretical approach to the medium in which the effects of pleasure and persuasion and instruction are produced. He intended his lectures on eloquence to represent a theoretical approach to persuasion as it can be accomplished in oratory. And he intended his lectures on the forms of composition to represent an illustrative critical approach to works embodying all the principles by which discourses achieve the capacity to instruct, or persuade, or move, or please mankind. When we see Blair's lectures in this light, we have to admit that all forty-seven of them are of concern to students of rhetorical theory so far as those students have to make themselves sensitive on the one hand to modern versions of the rhetoric of the past, or on the other hand to the emerging forms of the new rhetoric. Too often, alas, the rhetorical works of Blair and his contemporaries have been studied as if their sole rhetorical content abides at those points where they are obviously close to the old rhetoric of Aristotle and Cicero. If a wider view than that emerges from my present ac-

[616] Harding, I, xi-xii, xvii-xviii.

count, and if that view becomes an influence with future students of Blair, our understanding of him as a rhetorician will, I think, be greatly improved.[617]

John Witherspoon, the last of the great Scottish rhetoricians to figure in this history, was five years younger than Blair, and Blair survived him by six years, but there is more to be said about the relations of these two men than mere vital statistics suggest. They were in fact college friends who became antagonistic to each other in later life. Both were awarded the degree of master of arts at the University of Edinburgh on February 26, 1739, in company with three other young men, Blair being just under twenty-one years of age at the time, and Witherspoon, just over sixteen.[618] In that era, the Church of Scotland did not require an academic degree of those who were preparing for the ministry, and any student who took a degree had to print a thesis and defend it publicly. As a result of these academic obstacles, it would have been normal for Blair and Witherspoon, both of whom had decided to become clergymen, to avoid the graduation rituals, even if they incurred thereby the disapproval of at least some of their professors. But these two young men, and three colleagues, decided in November of 1738 that they would apply for permission to meet the requirements of the university rather than seek to become ordained without visible academic titles, and the university senate unanimously voted not only to approve of their self-denying application, but also to erase certain fees which the students concerned would otherwise have had to pay.[619] At that

[617] For a useful list of studies of Blair's rhetoric, see Harding, I, xxvii-xxxv. Blair's prospective new friends will want to consult Harding's introduction to the lectures (Harding, I, vii-xl), and not only Schmitz's analysis of them but also his contributions towards a complete inventory of Blair's writings and of works about him (Schmitz, 96-118, 139-158).

[618] For the names of these five graduates, see *A Catalogue of the Graduates in the Faculties of Arts, Divinity, and Law, of the University of Edinburgh*, p. 207. Witherspoon's name appears in the list as "Wederspun, Joannes." For the record of other spellings of his name, see Collins, *President Witherspoon*, I, 3-4, 13.

A condensed version of my present account of Witherspoon's rhetorical theory appeared in *University, A Princeton Quarterly*, No. 45 (Summer 1970), 26-30.

[619] See Schmitz, pp. 14-15.

hour, at least, Blair and Witherspoon must have felt that they had made common cause against worldly compromises and had shown a common dedication to high intellectual and spiritual standards. In the course of the next fifteen years, however, these two clergymen drifted apart on the very issue which had bound them together as undergraduates. Blair as a pastor in the Canongate Church in Edinburgh identified himself with a party of lenient Presbyterian theologians, the so-called moderates, who took a somewhat relaxed and worldly view of the application of religious dogma to social conduct, and Witherspoon, who was then in charge of the parish at Beith, adhered to the tenets of an austere Presbyterian orthodoxy. There is no occasion here to enter into an explanation of the issues which divided these two points of view. We need only notice that in 1753 Witherspoon published an anonymous pamphlet entitled *Ecclesiastical Characteristics*, and that this little work was not only highly successful in its use of the weapons of satire and ridicule against the moderates, but also it was very instrumental in making Witherspoon the object of admiration in his own party and the object of dislike on the other side.[620] Relations between Witherspoon and Blair would appear to have been distant after 1753.

Because Witherspoon's lectures on eloquence at Princeton between 1768 and 1794 consisted in a sustained discussion of composition, taste, and criticism, they have been repeatedly assumed to bear a striking resemblance to Blair's lectures on rhetoric at Edinburgh, at least so far as these three topics are concerned.[621] The first writer to mention this alleged resemblance was Ashbel Green, eighth president of Princeton, who was a student under Witherspoon and heard the latter deliver the lectures in question. In an address to the alumni of Princeton College in 1840, Green made the following observations:

Blair's Lectures on Belles Lettres are much more extended than those of Witherspoon, but the leading ideas of the two writers are wonderfully similar. I once asked my old master, whether there had not been some correspondence between him and Dr.

---

[620] For further details concerning this work and its popularity in Scotland, see Collins, *President Witherspoon*, I, 26-41; II, 238-239.

[621] The lectures were first published in *The Works of the Rev. John Witherspoon*, D.D. L.L.D. (Philadelphia, 1800), III, 375-495. My present analysis of them is based upon the text as given in this first edition.

Blair, on the subject of these lectures; and the answer was, that there never had been the interchange of a single thought between them, on any topic which they had severally discussed. The similarity remarked, therefore, is doubtless to be attributed, to these authors having studied under the same teachers, and thus derived their original train of thinking on the subjects in question, from a common source. They were either classmates or cotemporaneous members of the University of Edinburgh.[622]

It should be carefully noticed that, so far as this statement is concerned, Witherspoon was not asked to comment upon the alleged resemblances between his lectures and those of Blair. He was asked instead whether he and Blair had ever exchanged letters on the subjects which they had both treated, and his reply was an emphatic no. But what would he have said if he had been asked to comment upon the alleged resemblance, itself? We do not know, of course, but he could with justice have denied that there was a wonderful similarity between the two sets of lectures, and he could have asked all who doubted him to compare his text with that of Blair, and to see for themselves what the true state of affairs was. He could also have gone on to observe that he began to deliver his lectures upon his first arrival in Princeton in 1768; that Blair's lectures were not available to the general public until they were printed in 1783; that by 1783 he himself had fully established the subject matter of his own lectures, and had had the opportunity to refine and rehearse his rhetorical doctrine over a period of fifteen years; and that, after 1783, any knowledge which he might have acquired about Blair's lectures would hardly have caused him to amend or change his own text. He might have added, of course, that Green was right in attributing mere resemblances between himself and Blair to their having had at Edinburgh in the late 1730's certain teachers in common, one of whom, indeed, was John Stevenson, the early Scottish disciple of Locke.[623] For the rest, Witherspoon would doubtless have

---

[622] Ashbel Green, "Dr. Witherspoon's Administration at Princeton College," *The Presbyterian Magazine*, IV (October 1854), 468. Cited below as Ashbel Green.

[623] Blair's lectures have been loosely identified as a main source of Witherspoon's by Wilson B. Paul, "John Witherspoon's Theory and Practice of Public Speaking," *Speech Monographs*, XVI (1949), 274, and by Leland T. Chapin,

taken it for granted that anyone conversant with his lectures on eloquence would remember his having acknowledged in them his familiarity with such classical rhetoricians as Aristotle, Cicero, and Longinus, with such commentators upon classical rhetoric as John Ward and John Lawson, with such French authors as Lamy, Fénelon, Rollin, and Lévesque de Pouilly, and with such immediate British contemporaries as Alexander Gerard, Lord Kames, David Hume, Edmund Burke, and William Hogarth.[624] These were his chief points of reference as he discussed composition, taste, and criticism, and inasmuch as Blair drew ideas from many of the same sources, there would naturally be resemblances between his lectures and those of Witherspoon. But resemblances of this nature do not make Witherspoon dependent in any way upon Blair.

Witherspoon's lectures on eloquence were not published until six years after his death. It was Ashbel Green who found them in manuscript among Witherspoon's papers and advised the Philadelphia printer Woodward to insert them into the forthcoming edition of Witherspoon's works, "stating in a note, prefatory to those on Moral Philosophy, that the publication was posthumous, and that it had not had the advantage of the author's revision."[625] Thus the lectures as they were printed by Woodward may on

"American Interest in the Chair of Rhetoric and English Literature in the University of Edinburgh," *University of Edinburgh Journal*, xx (1961-1962), 119. Neither Paul nor Chapin, however, does more than assert a resemblance between Witherspoon and Blair, and a resemblance, as Ashbel Green pointed out, could be explained as evidence, not that Witherspoon followed Blair, but that both writers had studied under the same masters. For an account of Stevenson's influence at the University of Edinburgh, see above, Ch. 5, pp. 273, 410; Ch. 6, pp. 542-543.

[624] For Witherspoon's references in the lectures on eloquence to these authors, see his *Works*, Vol. III, as follows: to Aristotle, p. 412; to Cicero, pp. 389, 411-412; to Longinus, pp. 416, 488; to John Ward, p. 413; to Lawson, "One of our modern authors on eloquence," p. 484; to Lamy, p. 407; to Fénelon, p. 473; to Rollin, pp. 427, 431; to Lévesque de Pouilly, "A French author," p. 494; to Gerard, "Gerrad," p. 492; to Lord Kames, "Kaime," "the other Hume," pp. 437, 441; to David Hume, p. 476; to Edmund Burke, "Bourke," pp. 416, 491; to William Hogarth, pp. 489-491. Witherspoon mentioned several other authors; this list represents only his more conspicuous references. And it should be understood that he did not hesitate to disagree with any of the works which he cited.

[625] Ashbel Green, p. 267.

occasion misrepresent what Witherspoon intended to say. And they come to us under one other handicap—they do not represent everything which Witherspoon said as he delivered them. They represent instead a condensed system of notes which he wrote out and read to his classes, the arrangement being that the students would copy the notes as they were presented, and that Witherspoon would add illustrative comment and elaboration as he went along, so that at the end of each lecture hour the students would have a complete version of one particular lecture and would have to recite upon it later that same week.[626]

Witherspoon did not introduce the study of rhetoric into the Princeton curriculum. What we may confidently assume to have been the old rhetoric was part of the course of study when Witherspoon arrived,[627] and it would have consisted of part or all of the traditional Ciceronian system as taught by John Ward and John Holmes. Witherspoon's special claim to recognition in my present history is that he was the first to introduce the study of the new rhetoric into American higher education. He did so at Princeton by changing the course of study in such a way as to require all sophomores to take English grammar and English composition, while all juniors and seniors had to continue to take the latter of these subjects and to attend and recite upon Witherspoon's lectures on eloquence. Thus each graduating class heard these lectures twice over, and twice recited upon each. And in addition, of course, they practiced themselves in the various kinds of writing, and in the composition and delivery of speeches. This kind of instruction was intended to produce an acceptable degree of literary and oratorical competence in each graduate; and the rest of the curriculum would meanwhile have made him competent in classical literature, in mathematics, in geography, in history, in logic, in natural philosophy, in ethics, and in politics.[628] If the writings of several of the young men who graduated from Princeton under Witherspoon came later to constitute a distinguished part of American political literature of the late eighteenth and earlier nineteenth centuries, and after all, James Madison was one of those graduates, and his contributions to *The Federalist* have great literary merit, then perhaps some of the credit for this outcome belongs to Witherspoon's

[626] Varnum Lansing Collins, *Princeton* (New York, 1914), p. 88.
[627] *Ibid.*, p. 298.   [628] *Ibid.*, pp. 299-300.

lectures on eloquence and to his insistence that the new rhetoric be made into a serious and continuous ingredient of each student's undergraduate experience.

The first three of the lectures on eloquence were considered by Witherspoon to be preliminary discourses, and in them he laid down some general rules of good writing, after having developed various aspects of the theme that "To make what is called a complete orator, very great natural powers are necessary, and great cultivation too."[629] By orator he meant speaker and writer, as the other new rhetoricians customarily did; and he intended these two categories of authorship to include not only the parliamentary speaker, the legal speaker, and the preacher, but also the scientific writer, the historian, the controversialist, the writer of epistles and essays and dialogues, and the poet in his minor capacities, and in his epic and dramatic might.[630] As for the general rules of good writing, Witherspoon stressed the need to study and imitate the best examples, Addison being an excellent and Dr. Johnson a bad model;[631] and he urged his hearers not only to make practice in composition a regular part of their daily lives, but also to study grammar, orthography, and punctuation, to guard themselves against common faults of usage, and to learn to follow nature. Something of his own attitude towards good writing emerged when he warned his students against a swelling and bombastic style.

> The want of a fund of good sense and genuine taste [he said], makes ignorant persons fools, and scholars pedants. A plain man will tell you of taking a purge or a dose of physic, and you neither mistake him nor laugh at him. A quack of a physician will tell you of a mucilagenous decoction, to smooth the acid particles, and carry off the acrimonious matter that corrodes and irritates the internal coats of the stomach.[632]

And this same attitude was in his mind when he warned his students against expecting his own lectures to be distinguished ex-

[629] *Works*, III, 381.

[630] For evidence of Witherspoon's continuing concern in his lectures on eloquence for historical, scientific, argumentative, oratorical, and poetic forms of composition, see *Works*, III, 415, 431, 435-437, 440-443, 446-448, 457-463, et passim.

[631] *Ibid.*, III, 387; also pp. 428, 431, 433.

[632] *Ibid.*, III, 383-384.

amples of eloquence. Those with such expectations, he declared, "may just be pleased to observe, that a cool, plain, and simple manner of speaking, is necessary in teaching this, as well as every other art."[633]

At the beginning of his fourth lecture, Witherspoon outlined the program of his entire course. He had already said that he meant to discuss composition, taste, and criticism.[634] Now he made it possible for his students to detect that six of the seven subjects which his lectures would develop belonged to composition, and that taste and criticism were to be regarded as the seventh subject. Here is his own enumeration of the things which he proposed to do:

I. To treat of language in general, its qualities, and powers— eloquent speech—and its history and practice as an art.

II. To consider oratory as divided into its three great kinds, the sublime—simple—and mixed,—their characters—their distinctions—their beauties—and their uses.

III. To consider it as divided into its constituent parts, invention, disposition, stile, pronunciation and gesture.

IV. To consider it as its object is different, information, demonstration, persuasion, entertainment.

V. As its subject is different. The pulpit, the bar, and the senate, or any deliberative assembly.

VI. To consider the structure and parts of a particular discourse, their order, connexion, proportion and ends.

VII. Recapitulation and inquiry into the principles of taste, or of beauty and gracefulness, as applicable not only to oratory, but to all the other (commonly called) the fine arts.[635]

In accommodating this seven-part program to his actual discourses, Witherspoon devoted twelve lectures to composition and its attendant six major headings, and one lecture to both of his other announced concerns. Thus he treated language and eloquence in Lectures IV and V, the three great kinds of writing in

[633] *Ibid.*, III, 379. [634] *Ibid.*, III, 377.
[635] *Ibid.*, III, 399-400. The comma after "different" in item IV is inserted here on the authority of the text in John Witherspoon, *Lectures on Moral Philosophy and Eloquence*, Woodward's Third Edition (Philadelphia, 1810), p. 175.

Lectures VI through X, the four processes of creative effort in Lectures XI and XII, the four different goals of discourse in Lecture XIII, the three major kinds of speeches in Lectures XIV and XV, the oration and its parts also in Chapter XV, and the two remaining major subjects, taste and criticism, in Lecture XVI.

In his discussion of language and eloquence, Witherspoon lost no time in bringing these two topics into a close relation with the whole process of composition. Here is how he joined these elements together.

> Articulate language [he said] is intended to communicate our sentiments one to another. This may be considered as fully explained, by saying it includes information and persuasion. A conception in my mind, when spoken, its excellence consists in making another perceive what I perceive, and feel towards it as I feel. They may be afterwards amplified and extended; but these two particulars shew the true original purpose of speech. Eloquence is commonly called the art of persuasion, but the other must be taken in. We must inform before we can persuade, or if there be any such thing as persuasion without information, it is only a blind impulse.[636]

From this point on, Witherspoon traced the rise and progress of language as the chief means of communication, and the rise and progress of discourse calculated to communicate by means of its capacity to inform and persuade. Among his observations upon the progress of language from narrow, short, and simple forms to those of considerable complexity, he mentioned that in all uncultivated tongues figures were "frequent and very strong," and he drew upon his American experience to illustrate this fact. "The Indians in America," he observed, "have a language full of metaphors. They take up the hatchet, for going to war, and they brighten the chain, when they confirm a peace."[637] In commenting later upon the rise and progress of oratory and poetry, he noted that the latter form of composition, being committed to pleasure and immediate entertainment as its aim, could expect to find an audience in any age, whereas oratory could find an audience for its persuasions only when those persuasions belonged to a specific context and a particular moment.

[636] *Works*, III, 400.   [637] *Ibid.*, III, 405.

Perhaps to this we may add [he went on], that the incitements to poetry are more general. A poet pleases and obtains fame from every single person who reads or hears his productions; but an assembly, business, and an occasion are necessary to the orator. This last is likewise limited in point of place and situation. Oratory could not thrive in a state where arbitrary power prevails, because then there is nothing left for large assemblies and a diffusive public to determine; whereas poetry is pleasing to persons under any form of government whatever.[638]

As for the alleged superiority of ancient to modern speakers, Witherspoon objected to those critics who endowed Greek and Roman orators with a superhuman genius and made even their ordinary listeners into sages and visionaries. He summed up his own attitude towards these sentiments by speaking thus:

In short I take it for granted that an assembly of the vulgar in Athens was just like an assembly of common people among us, and a senate at Athens in understanding and taste was not superior to the senate of Great-Britain, and that some of them were but mere mobs; and that they were very disorderly is plain from what we read of Plato being pulled down from the desk when he went up to defend Socrates.[639]

Six points seem to me to deserve emphasis in Witherspoon's discussion of his second major heading, the kinds of writing. First of all, he made these kinds consist not only of the sublime mode, the simple mode, and the mixed mode, as the three great forms, but also of such lesser modes as that of plainness, of smoothness, of sweetness, of conciseness, of elegance, and so on. Secondly, he gave each of the great modes its own particular province, the sublime kind being found in epic poetry, tragedy, and oratory, the simple kind in scientific writing, in epistles, essays, and dialogues, and the mixed kind in history and in controversy. Thirdly, in discussing the sublime mode, Witherspoon relied in part upon Longinus, and indeed he defined the sublime mode in terms of three of the five characteristics which Longinus had attributed to it, these characteristics being greatness in an author's conceptions, strength in an author's feelings, and aptness in an author's

[638] *Ibid.*, III, 408-409. [639] *Ibid.*, III, 413.

figurative language. Fourthly, when he commented upon the greatness of an author's conceptions, Witherspoon admitted the difficulty of having in modern times an orator or writer who, by combining in his own person the gifts of the statesman, the general, and the scholar, could thereby be in a position to have wideness of view and largeness of mind; yet his own conviction, he said, was "that when statesmen are also scholars, they make upon the whole, greater orators and nobler writers, than those who are scholars merely, though of the greatest capacity."[640] Fifthly, at the outset of his remarks upon the simple mode of composition, he indicated the high value to be attached to it by telling his students that, "If I could explain this fully so as to make every one clearly to understand it, and at the same time incline you to admire and study it, I should think a very difficult and important point was gained." "I would observe therefore, in the very beginning," he went on, "it is a mistake to consider simplicity and sublimity as universally opposite, for on the contrary there is not only a great excellence in some performances which we may call wholly of the simple kind; such as a story told or an epistle written with all the beauty of simplicity, but in the most sublime and animated compositions, some of the greatest sentiments derive their beauty from being clothed in simple language."[641] Finally, as he was preparing to discuss the lesser modes of composition, he rejected the supposition that climate determines style, preferring to declare that style "rather takes its colour from the state of society, and the sentiments and manners of men . . ."; and he then added the following observations, almost as if he were warning his students against perpetuating in their own emerging republic the styles suited to royalty and aristocracy:

> When the manners of a people are little polished [he said], there is a plainness or a roughness in the style. Absolute monarchies, and the obsequious subjection introduced at the courts of princes, occasions [sic] a pompous swelling and compliment to be in request different from the boldness and sometimes ferocity of republican states.[642]

Invention was the first subject introduced by Witherspoon when he began to consider his third heading, the constituent parts of creative effort; and he disposed of it by affirming what

[640] *Ibid.*, III, 417. [641] *Ibid.*, III, 430. [642] *Ibid.*, III, 438.

the new rhetoric had come to accept as its most cherished doctrine. That is to say, he defined invention by saying that it "is nothing else but finding out the sentiments by which a speaker or writer would explain what he has to propose, and the arguments by which he would enforce it"[643]; and with these words he made it clear that invention had obligations to informative as well as to persuasive discourse. Moreover, he said that attempts to teach invention were futile, and that he himself preferred to leave it "to the spontaneous production of capacity and experience."[644] And at last, after some comments upon the teaching of invention by the old rhetoric, he dismissed the ancient machinery of topics from the Princeton curriculum without extenuation or sympathy. Here is what he said on that occasion:

> There have been books of common places, published, containing arguments and topics for illustration and even similitudes —sayings of the ancients, &c. but they are of very little use, unless to a person that has no fund of his own, and then one that makes use of them is like a man walking on stilts; they make him look very big, but he walks very feebly.[645]

At this point in his course of lectures, Witherspoon introduced the subject of disposition. "This is a matter of the utmost moment," he said, "and upon which instruction is both necessary and useful."[646] As if to lay special emphasis upon the importance to be attached to disposition as a field of concern in the new rhetoric, Witherspoon declared that he would discuss it at once as it concerned any kind of composition whatever, and that, in a later lecture, he would discuss it again as it applied in particular to a sermon or to a speech delivered at the bar or in the popular assembly.[647] Thus it happens that a large part of Lecture xi and almost half of Lecture xv are devoted to the problem of arranging discourse.

In Lecture xi Witherspoon stated what the values of order in composition are, and how order may be guaranteed. Good order, he said, makes a discourse clear, strong, easy to remember, beautiful, and brief.[648] Having given each of these qualities a terse and cogent treatment, he turned to the methods of bringing order to discourse, and these he discussed as they applied

[643] *Ibid.*, iii, 443.   [644] *Ibid.*, iii, 444.   [645] *Ibid.*, iii, 444.
[646] *Ibid.*, iii, 444.   [647] *Ibid.*, iii, 444-445.   [648] *Ibid.*, iii, 445-446.

to the whole composition, or to its subdivisions, or to its amplifications. "Every work, be it what it will, history, epic poem,
dramatic poem, oration, epistle, or essay," he said, "is to be considered as a whole, and a clearness of judgment in point of method, will decide the place and proportion of the several parts of
which they are composed."[649] "The necessity of order in the whole
structure of a piece," he said again, "shows that the rule is good
which is given by some, that an orator before he begin his
discourse, should concentrate the subject as it were, and
reduce it to one single proposition, either expressed or at
least conceived in his mind."[650] "Agreeably to this principle," he said yet again, "I think that not only the subject of a
single discourse should be reduceable to one proposition, but
the general divisions or principal heads should not be many in
number."[651] As for order in subdivisions, it should be clear and
plain, he declared, and it should make the subdivisions distinct,
proportionate to the size of the whole, coordinate in kind, exhaustive in extent, and connected with each other as naturally as is
possible.[652] These various requirements he was careful to illustrate, and the example which he chose to clarify "coordination in
kind" was close indeed to the lives of his students.

> This rule is transgressed [he observed] when either the things
> mentioned are wholly different in kind, or when they include
> one another. This will be well perceived if we consider how a
> man would describe a sensible subject, a country for example;
> New-Jersey contains (1) Middlesex. (2) Somerset county. (3)
> The townships of Princeton (4) Morris county.[653]

But what kind of order is required in the amplifications which
are needed to put flesh on the bony structure of discourse? This
question became Witherspoon's final topic in Lecture XI, and his
discussion of it deserves a word. "I once have said," he remarked
at this point, "that all reasoning is of the nature of a syllogism,
which lays down principles, makes comparisons, and draws the
conclusion. But we must particularly guard against letting the
uniformity and formality of a syllogism appear."[654] In other
words, the order required in amplifications must not be visibly
syllogistic; it must be relaxed and natural; and it must not call

[649] *Ibid.*, III, 447.　　　[650] *Ibid.*, III, 447.　　　[651] *Ibid.*, III, 447.
[652] *Ibid.*, III, 448-450.　　[653] *Ibid.*, III, 449.　　[654] *Ibid.*, III, 450-451.

attention to itself. "Sometimes the sensible ideas of time and place suggest an order," Witherspoon said, "not only in historical narrations and in law pleadings, which relate to facts, but in drawing of characters, describing the progress and effects of virtue and vice, and even in other subjects, where the connection between those ideas and the thing spoken of, is not very strong." "Sometimes," he added, "and indeed generally, there is an order which proceeds from things plain to things obscure." And his next words, which are a happy mixture of good sense and good style, mention another kind of order:

> The beginning of a paragraph should be like the sharp point of a wedge, which gains admittance to the bulky part behind. It first affirms what every body feels or must confess, and proceeds to what follows as a necessary consequence: In fine, there is an order in persuasions to a particular choice, which may be taken two ways with equal advantage, proceeding from the weaker to the stronger, or from the stronger to the weaker. . . . This is called sometimes the ascending or descending climax.[655]

When Witherspoon returned in Lecture xv to the subject of disposition, he handled a more conventional side of it than he did in Lecture xi, and he even seemed at that point to be on the verge of speaking of it in the terms used by the old rhetoric. But he mentioned the old terms only to discard them for his own new ones. Here are his words:

> Orators, or critics on oratory very early learned to analyze a discourse, and to enumerate the parts of which it is composed. They are a little differently stated by different authors; some reckon four, introduction, proposition, confirmation and conclusion; others, five, adding narration; others, six, adding refutation; and there are some discourses in which you may easily have each of these different things; but considering that we must take this matter so generally, as to include all kinds of composition, it would be I think as well to adopt the division in poetical criticism, and say that every regular discourse or composition of every kind, must have a beginning, a middle, and an end.[656]

[655] *Ibid.*, III, 451. [656] *Ibid.*, III, 478.

This passage is notable in indicating that a new rhetorician like Witherspoon, feeling obliged to construct a theory that would apply not only to the three kinds of speeches studied in traditional rhetoric but also to the other kinds of composition, found it sensible to reject the four-part, the five-part, and the six-part oratorical structures of antiquity, and to put in their place a new three-part structure drawn from poetics. As one reads the words just quoted, one understands what the new rhetoric was all about, and one sees that Witherspoon understood, too, although he would perhaps not openly have called himself a new rhetorician. I need not attempt to comment here upon what he said as he explained the details of his three-part doctrine of disposition. But if I did comment, the reader would agree, I believe, that Witherspoon's doctrine is firm and sensible.[657]

Next after disposition in Witherspoon's discussion of the third major heading of his total program came style and pronunciation, including gesture, and these subjects he handled in Lecture XII. He had already treated style, of course, in his lectures on the sublime, the simple, and the mixed kinds of writing, and what he added to the subject in Lecture XII is in the nature of practical advice, and need not concern us here. But his discussion of pronunciation has two characteristics that we should notice. First of all, he did not call this part of rhetoric elocution, as the school of Thomas Sheridan did, although he obviously knew of Sheridan's teachings in this field. On an earlier occasion, indeed, he had referred to Sheridan as an authority on the sounds of English vowels.[658] The new rhetoric never took kindly to Sheridan's use of the word elocution for pronunciation, and Witherspoon showed himself to be no exception to this general rule. Secondly, Witherspoon considered pronunciation "a famous subject, largely treated of by all critical writers,"[659] and he briefly gave five pieces of advice concerning it, one of which urged his hearers "to keep to the tone and key of dialogue, or common conversation as much as possible."[660] "In common discourse," he added, "where there is no affectation, men speak properly. At least, though even here there are differences from nature—some speaking with more sweetness and grace than others, yet there is none that falls into any of those unnatural rants or ridiculous

[657] *Ibid.*, III, 478-483.
[658] *Ibid.*, III, 404.   [659] *Ibid.*, III, 455.   [660] *Ibid.*, II, 456.

gestures, that are sometimes to be seen in public speakers." This doctrine, too, is characteristic of the new rhetoric, as indeed it was characteristic of the old. Only the elocutionists in their more extreme moments tended to contradict it and to imply that stage declamation rather than common conversation was the standard for oratorical delivery.

The fourth major heading in Witherspoon's treatment of eloquence concerned the ends or goals of discourse, and he devoted Lecture XIII to these subjects, developing the point that "The ends a writer or speaker may be said to aim at, are information, demonstration, persuasion and entertainment."[661]

> I need scarce tell you [Witherspoon added] that these are not so wholly distinct but that they are frequently intermixed, and that more than one of them may be in view at the same time. Persuasion is also used in a sense that includes them all. The intention of all speech, or writing which is but recorded speech, is to persuade, taking the word with latitude. Yet I think you will easily perceive that there are very different sorts of composition, in some of which one of the above mentioned purposes, and in others a different one, takes the lead and gives the colour to the whole performance. Great benefit will arise from keeping a clear view of what is the end proposed.

In the course of this lecture, Witherspoon kept his students reminded that he was talking to them about literary activity as it might affect them in any one of a dozen future ways. Thus his discussion of information as a goal of discourse was aimed at those who would write histories, or fables, or epistles, or communications intended for business or friendship.[662] Future scientific writers, whether of essays, or systems, or controversies, made up the audience of those for whom his remarks upon demonstration were intended.[663] Future lawyers, senators, or preachers became immediately aware that his comments upon persuasion applied above all to them.[664] And those who aimed to follow in the footsteps of Horace or Lucian or Fontenelle or Boileau or Cervantes or Shakespeare or Donne or Marvell or Swift or Pope would have seen their future literary aspirations recognized

---

[661] *Ibid.*, III, 457.
[662] *Ibid.*, III, 458.   [663] *Ibid.*, III, 459.   [664] *Ibid.*, III, 461-462.

in his comments upon entertainment.[665] The point here and elsewhere in Witherspoon's lectures is that his concept of oratory is coextensive with the forms of literary composition, and that oratorical theory, whether it is called rhetoric or not, is in fact the general theory of discourse. The point also is that Witherspoon, without condescension and without flattery, was talking about literary endeavors as if they rightly belonged among the normal ambitions and expectations of his students. In his capacity to speak to this kind of purpose, Witherspoon stands as a gifted and admirable teacher of the new rhetoric.

After having finished with the four goals of the writer or speaker, Witherspoon turned next to the pulpit, the bar, and the deliberative, or as he also called it, the promiscuous assembly, and he spoke in Lectures XIV and XV of the speaking that goes on in these arenas. His object at this point, as he himself phrased it, was to "delineate the character of an accomplished minister, lawyer and senator."[666] One of his comments to future clergymen was that "On the whole, a strict adherence to truth and nature, and taking the world just as it is, will be an excellent mean to direct us in every part of our public service."[667] His remarks to future lawyers included the following passage:

> This, indeed, may be said to be the country of law, not only on account of its being a free state, the character of which is, that not man, but the laws, have dominion, which is our glory, but because by the great multiplicity of our statutes it becomes an important and difficult science. For both these reasons there are great hopes proposed to persons of ability in this department. They have not only the reasonable prospect, if of tolerable abilities with diligence to provide an honorable subsistence to themselves, but it is the direct road to promotion, and the way of obtaining the highest offices in the state.[668]

And he began his advice to future speakers in deliberative assemblies with these words:

> I shall not be very long upon this subject, but as it is far from being improbable that some here present may in future life have occasion to act in that sphere, and to be members of the

[665] *Ibid.*, III, 462-463.
[666] *Ibid.*, III, 464.   [667] *Ibid.*, III, 470.   [668] *Ibid.*, III, 471.

provincial assemblies, I shall make a few remarks upon it to that purpose. In large deliberative assemblies of the political kind, there is nearly as much opportunity for fervor and passion, as there is to the divine, and more scope for wit and humor, than to the lawyer. For though no matters of a merely temporal kind, are of equal moment in themselves, with the things a minister has to treat of, yet men's passions are almost as much, and in many cases more excited and interested by them. The fate of nations, the welfare of our country, liberty or servitude, may often seem to want as violent an exertion of the passionate kind of eloquence, as any subject whatever.[669]

Remarking then that Hume, "though an infidel in opinion," was right in holding vehement emotional oratory to be capable even now of exerting great influence upon a large assembly, Witherspoon cited the following example:

Mr. Pitt, now Earl of Chatham, from being a colonel of dragoons, rose to the highest station in the British empire, merely by the power of a warm and passionate eloquence; there was never any thing in his discourses, that are remarkable either for strength of reasoning, or purity and elegance of style; but a very great impetuosity and fire, that carried his point in the British house of commons.[670]

These words and the others just quoted in this paragraph will have to suffice at the present time as an account of the general tenor of Witherspoon's messages to the future assembly speaker, the future lawyer, and the future minister. What seems most striking about these messages is that they brought the affairs of their time into Witherspoon's classroom and made his students see that eloquence was a part of the concern of mankind for liberty, national welfare, the rule of law, and moral truth. He appeared indeed to be saying that the teacher who does not stress these matters would teach eloquence to no purpose.

"I am now to conclude the discourses upon this subject," said Witherspoon in his final lecture on eloquence, "by an inquiry into the general principles of taste and criticism."[671] In many ways this lecture is the best of the series. Soon after he had started it with the words just quoted, Witherspoon drew a dis-

---

[669] *Ibid.*, III, 475-476.   [670] *Ibid.*, III, 476.   [671] *Ibid.*, III, 483.

tinction between the mechanic and the fine arts, and by his own enumeration he made the fine arts consist of poetry, oratory, music, painting, sculpture, and architecture. "It must be allowed," he said, "that, though these arts have some common principles of excellence, there are some persons who have a strong inclination after, and even a capacity of performing in some of them, and not in others."[672] "Yet commonly complete critics, and those who have a well formed taste," he added, "are able to perceive the beauty of the whole, and the relation of one to another." In other words, a skilled orator would probably make a poor showing in music or architecture, but a skilled critic of one art would not be at a complete loss in another. It was to his students in their capacity as critics that Witherspoon spoke in this lecture, and his thesis was "that there is a taste in the fine arts, and a real foundation for it in nature."[673]

The first thing which Witherspoon did as he prepared himself to state this thesis was to contradict an opinion expressed by John Lawson in his *Lectures concerning Oratory*. "One of our modern authors on eloquence," said Witherspoon, without identifying Lawson further, "has thought fit to take exception at the use of the word *taste*, as being of late invention, and as implying nothing but what is carried in judgment and genius."[674] Witherspoon's answer to this objection was that taste, though a modern term, was a perfectly good one, and that it had originated when French critics began at first to use the phrase *bon goût* to designate classic elegance and later came to extend the concept to all the other arts. "And as a sense of the beauty of the arts," he added, "is certainly a thing often distinct from judgment, as well as from erudition; the term seems not only to be allowable, but well chosen."[675] With one of the major terms of his final lecture thus established, Witherspoon turned to the exploration of his thesis and its corollaries.

This exploration consisted in Witherspoon's own critical and historical survey of celebrated treatises on the subject of beauty, imaginative pleasure, sublimity, taste, and pleasurable sensibilities. In the course of this survey, he dwelt in brief or at some

---

[672] *Ibid.*, III, 484.   [673] *Ibid.*, III, 486.

[674] *Ibid.*, III, 484. See Lawson's *Lectures concerning Oratory* (Dublin, 1758), pp. 15-21.

[675] *Works*, III, 484.

length upon the following works: Francis Hutcheson's *An Inquiry into the Original of our Ideas of Beauty and Virtue*; Joseph Addison's *Spectator*, Nos. 411-421; Jean-Pierre de Crousaz's *Traité du Beau*; William Hogarth's *The Analysis of Beauty*; Edmund Burke's *A Philosophical Enquiry into the Origin of our Ideas of the Sublime and Beautiful*; Alexander Gerard's *An Essay on Taste*; and Lévesque de Pouilly's *Théorie des Sentimens Agréables* in its English translation. By stating and evaluating the doctrines that these authors set forth, Witherspoon arrived at his own theory of taste, and that theory was that Gerard, in declaring taste to be made up of discrete internal sensations of novelty, sublimity, beauty, imitation, harmony, ridicule, and virtue, had come closest to describing the complete foundations of the subject, but that Gerard's list could be perfected by adding to it the sense of proportion and that of utility.[676] These, then, are the separate terms in which a critic's taste is to be explained. Not content, however, to leave those separate terms uncoordinated, Witherspoon, as a final step, turned to Lévesque de Pouilly for help in reducing them to a single law.

> After having thus attempted the analysis of the principles of taste and elegance [said Witherspoon], I would observe, that as nature seems to delight in producing many great and different effects from simple causes, perhaps we may find an ultimate principle that governs all these. A French author has written a treatise called the Theory of agreeable Sensations, in which he says that the great principle is, whatever exercises our faculties, without fatiguing them, gives pleasure; and that this principle may be applied to our bodily form, and to the constitution of our mind, to objects of external sensation, to objects of taste, and even to our moral conduct. It may no doubt be carried through the whole of criticism, and we may say this states the bounds between variety and uniformity, simplicity and intricacy, order, proportion and harmony.[677]

"You may see from the preceding remarks," concluded Witherspoon, "that the foundation is laid for taste in our natures; yet

[676] *Ibid.*, III, 492.

[677] *Ibid.*, III, 494. The English translation of Lévesque de Pouilly's anonymous treatise was published at London in 1749, at Edinburgh in 1766, and at London in 1774.

is there great room for improvement and cultivation; by investigating the grounds of approbation; by comparing one thing with another; by studying the best examples; and by reflection and judgment, men may correct and refine their taste upon the whole, or upon particular confined subjects."[678] And with a brief warning against "a finical nicety" in applying the principles of taste to a work of art, Witherspoon brought his lectures on eloquence to an end, so far as his delivery of them in a given academic term was concerned. Their final end would not come, perhaps, until the last graduate who heard Witherspoon deliver them had penned his last literary work, or had made his last speech, or had pronounced his last critical judgment upon another author's venture towards excellence in discourse.

More than two centuries have now elapsed since Witherspoon began to deliver these particular lectures, and it is interesting to notice that the subjects of composition, taste, and criticism, as they apply to activities performed in the language which the lectures represent, are still central features of the Princeton curriculum and find their fullest expression within the course offerings of the Department of English. But the relation of these three subjects to one another in respect to the emphasis given each has greatly changed since 1768. In Witherspoon's time, composition and the exercises which it entailed were made the chief features of literary study, while taste and criticism received only minor attention. Now the emphasis is reversed. Taste and criticism, as they involve the study of the best works of English and American literature, and as they require students to read, compare, reflect upon, and judge those works, are given major stress, and composition, as an openly acknowledged subject of concern, has lost its former dominance. In its theoretical and practical aspects this latter study is the present objective of a relatively small number of English courses, some of which emphasize public speaking, and others, such endeavors as the writing of exposition or drama or fiction or poetry. This is not the place for a debate upon the merits of either of these ways of distributing emphasis upon these academic disciplines. What I wish to do instead is to call attention to the difference between the present way and that established by Witherspoon in order to point out

[678] *Works*, III, 495.

that the new British rhetoric of the eighteenth century, as formulated by him and by his fellow Scots, Adam Smith, George Campbell, and Hugh Blair, led directly to the creation of the modern departments of English literature. Thus Witherspoon must be regarded as the founder of English literary studies at Princeton, and this achievement must be accepted as the natural outgrowth of his dedication to the new rhetoric of his time.

CHAPTER 7

The sole object of Logic is the guidance of one's own thoughts; the communication of those thoughts to others falls under the consideration of Rhetoric, in the large sense in which that art was conceived by the ancients; or of the still more extensive art of Education. Logic takes cognizance of all intellectual operations, only as they conduce to our own knowledge, and to our command over that knowledge for our own uses. If there were but one rational being in the universe, that being might be a perfect logician; and the science and art of logic would be the same for that one person, as for the whole human race.

John Stuart Mill, *A System of Logic, Ratiocinative and Inductive, Being a Connected View of the Principles of Evidence, and the Methods of Scientific Investigation* (London: John W. Parker, West Strand, M.DCCC.XLIII), I, 5-6.

CONCLUSION

As the preceding chapters have demonstrated in some detail, British logic had two and British rhetoric four distinct forms at the end of the eighteenth century. Let us now take a retrospective glance at the essential characteristic of those forms, so that we may see in outline what the separate strands of our argument have been, and how those strands are related to each other as parts of a single whole. A glance of this sort, it would appear, is one of the obligations which the conclusion of any lengthy discourse is supposed to fulfill; and when the discourse, as in the present case, has undertaken to be the history of the theory of discourse itself in an era of important change, that obligation becomes a matter rather to be honored in the observance than the breach. At any rate, I shall honor it in the observance on the present occasion.

One of the two forms of eighteenth-century British logic, we remember, stemmed from Aristotle's *Organon* and was available during the 1700's in Greek texts and Latin translations of its original source, and in various British digests, chief of which was Dean Aldrich's durable *Artis Logicae Compendium*.[1] This form of logic identified itself as a method of investigation and of learned presentation. It stressed the deductive examination of accepted truths as its main procedure of enquiry. It regarded the syllogism as its master implement, induction being considered an irregular syllogistic form. It considered the *dictum de omni* to be the principle from which the entire science of logic was derived. It thought of scholastic disputation as the outstanding philosophical activity in the field of enquiry and communication. It believed the ancient machinery of topics to be a useful means of subjecting questions to investigation or of helping to formulate

---

[1] Some other eighteenth-century textbooks in Aristotelian logic: J. Jennings, *Logica in usum Juventutis Academicae*; Gerschom Carmichael, *Breviuscula Introductio ad Logicam*; John Newbury, *Logic*; John Williams, *The Young Mathematician's Logic*; John Napleton, *Elementa Logicae*; Richard Murray, *Compendium of Logic*; N. Dralloc (i.e. John Collard), *An Epitome of Logic*.

them into connected discourse. And above all it implicitly assumed that the truth of a proposition was established by the process of showing it to be syllogistically consistent with accepted propositions.

The other form of eighteenth-century British logic was inductive. It had received its chief inspiration from Francis Bacon and John Locke, and its leading apostles in the 1700's were Thomas Reid, George Campbell, and Dugald Stewart. It became more and more interested in the methods of scientific investigation and less and less concerned with the methods of learned presentation. It stressed observation and experiment as the main procedures of enquiry; it regarded induction as the most basic instrument in logic; it considered that the syllogism by its very nature involved the use of a proposition to prove itself and that such a procedure could have no power to uncover truths not hitherto known; it thought the *dictum de omni* incapable of furnishing the entire substance of logical theory; it disparaged disputation as a means of investigation; it ignored or actively belittled the ancient machinery of topics; and it openly declared that a proposition was true, not when it could be shown to agree with accepted propositions, for they might be doubtful, but only when it could be shown accurately to interpret the facts within its purview.

As for eighteenth-century British rhetoric, its four forms, we recall, were derived either from Aristotle and Cicero or from attitudes associated with the rise of the new science.

First of all, there was the full-length rhetorical system of the ancient Greek and Roman theorists as interpreted in the 1700's by John Ward and John Holmes. It emphasized invention, arrangement, style, memory, and delivery. It limited itself to persuasive popular discourse, and it considered its chief literary products to be deliberative, forensic, and epideictic speeches. It stressed the use of artistic as distinguished from nonartistic proofs in oratory, and thus it continued to recommend the ancient machinery of rhetorical topics as aids to the invention of rhetorical subject matter. It took the position that rhetorical proof was characteristically syllogistic or enthymematic, and that induction was a variant of the enthymeme. It recommended the loose probable proofs of a bygone era as the chief guarantee of rationality in oratorical composition. It thought of a full-dress speech as having an introduction, a narration, a partition, a proof, a refutation, and a conclusion. And so far as the tropes and the figures and the three kinds of style were concerned, it treated them so as to suggest that lavish ornament used in connection with the grand style was somehow more truly rhetorical than was the plain unadorned speech of civil life.

Secondly, there was stylistic rhetoric. It consisted of materials identified with the third part of the traditional system, that is, with the kinds of style and the varieties of figurative language. It was as useful for the stylistic analysis of poems and novels and dramas as of orations. And its chief eighteenth-century British interpreters were Nicholas Burton, Anthony Blackwall, and John Stirling.

Thirdly, there were the elocutionists. These rhetoricians centered their energies upon oral delivery as that activity had been described under the fifth part of the traditional system. The practical applications of elocutionary dogma involved not only the pronunciation of speeches to audiences but also the reading of liturgy, the rendering of dialogue upon the stage, and the exchange of conversational elegancies in polite society. The elocutionists, it will be recalled, numbered among their leading eighteenth-century British spokesmen such men as Orator Henley, Thomas Sheridan, John Walker, and that unknown earlier figure who first translated Le Faucheur's *Traitté* into English.

Lastly, there was the new rhetoric. It thought of itself as the product of the teachings of Bacon and Locke. It maintained an interest in popular communication and in the three kinds of speeches traditionally associated with rhetorical doctrine, but it developed an interest in learned communication as logic withdrew from that field, and it became at length the general theory of literature, as it undertook to provide standards for the composition and criticism of persuasive, expository, didactic, historical, philosophical, and poetical forms of verbal expression. Its leading eighteenth-century British spokesmen were Adam Smith, George Campbell, Hugh Blair, and John Witherspoon, although it received various degrees of support from David Hume, John Lawson, and Joseph Priestley. It tended in its purest moments to ignore or condemn the artistic proofs and the topical machinery of ancient inventional theory and to recommend instead what the ancients called nonartistic proofs. It also tended to recommend inductive procedures in rhetorical argumentation, strict standards for probable arguments, simple formulas for the construction of speeches, and the concept of plainness in oratorical and literary style. And, as I hope to have adequately demonstrated, it received its best and most advanced British treatments in Adam Smith's lectures on rhetoric at Edinburgh and Glasgow between 1748 and 1763, and in George Campbell's *The Philosophy of Rhetoric.*

It was the fashion in the early nineteenth century for British logicians and rhetoricians to ignore what I have called the new logic and the new rhetoric of eighteenth-century Britain, and to say that the history of logic and the history of rhetoric were alike characterized by a curious tendency to exhibit nothing in the way of progress and improvement since Aristotle gave them both their definitive formulations. This fashion was brought to the attention of a large public by Richard Whately, whose *Elements of Logic* and *Elements of Rhetoric* were published at London in the middle 1820's. In both of these meritorious and widely circulated treatises, Whately considered it part of his task to provide a brief historical sketch of the subjects to which he was addressing himself, and in each sketch he took pains to deny that that particular discipline had had a history. Thus of logic he said that "The history of its discovery, as far as the main principles of the science are concerned, properly commences and ends with Aristotle; and this may perhaps in part account for the subsequent perversions of it."[2] And he opened his account of the history of rhetoric with a similar judgment.

It may be expected that, before I proceed to treat of the Art in question [he said], I should present the reader with a sketch of its history. Little however is required to be said on this head, because the present is not one of those branches of study in which we can trace with interest a progressive improvement from age to age. It is one, on the contrary, to which more attention appears to have been paid, and in which greater proficiency is supposed to have been made, in the earliest days of Science and Literature, than at any subsequent period. Among

[2] Richard Whately, *Elements of Logic*, 3rd edn. (London, 1829), p. 6. Cited below as *Logic*.

the ancients, Aristotle, the earliest whose works are extant, may safely be pronounced to be also the best, of the systematic writers on Rhetoric.[3]

We can perhaps excuse Whately for complying with the intellectual currents of his own times so far as to think that logic and rhetoric began and ended with Aristotle, and that what had happened to these two disciplines in ancient Rome, in the Italy, France, and England of the Middle Ages, in the European Renaissance, and in eighteenth-century Scotland, had not only failed to achieve the rank of improvements but at times had amounted to outright perversions. Even so, however, we are under no obligations to acknowledge that Whately's historical sketches of logic and rhetoric, and the words just quoted from both of them, have any value as history. They emphatically do not, even if a distinguished twentieth-century critic, Mr. I. A. Richards, endorsed them in their application to rhetoric when he himself was lecturing on the latter subject at Bryn Mawr in 1936.[4] Indeed, any scholar of the nineteenth or twentieth centuries who speaks as if the disciplines of logic and rhetoric have had no real history except as each has conformed to the dictates of Aristotelian theory is guilty of a naïve oversimplification of the actual state of affairs. In consenting to be ignorant of this aspect of the past, he is condemning himself in part at least to be forever a child. My present book, I hope, will serve to correct such mistakes, so far, at least, as it has succeeded in giving an accurate account of its two major subjects in the period to which it has limited itself.

What of the forms of logic and of rhetoric in the hundred years between the end of the eighteenth and the beginning of the twentieth centuries? And what of these forms in our own time? This is not the place for final answers to these questions, but they are good questions, nevertheless, and they deserve a full consideration on some occasion or other. My present subject cannot be defined to include them, and, besides, in doing it justice, I have had to take so much space that I can rightfully claim no more. What I should like to do here, however, is to outline in a general

[3] Richard Whately, *Elements of Rhetoric*, 3rd edn. (Oxford, 1830), pp. 9-10. Cited below as *Rhetoric*.
[4] I. A. Richards, *The Philosophy of Rhetoric*, p. 6.

way the answers that these questions would receive in the era between 1800 and 1850. After all, what's past is prologue, and therefore this concluding chapter may properly end by aspiring to give a preliminary view of the events which were to follow those traced in the preceding chapters.

The earliest important British contribution to nineteenth-century logical theory has just now been mentioned. It was Richard Whately's *Logic,* published as an article in the *Encyclopaedia Metropolitana* in 1825 and as a separate book in 1826.[5] That treatise, as I indicated on a much earlier occasion,[6] was founded upon Aldrich's *Artis Logicae Compendium,* which in its own right was enjoying great popularity at Oxford in the 1820's. But in reaffirming the standard teachings of the Aristotelian system, Whately took great pains to file repeated protests against the new logic of Locke, Campbell, and Stewart. He declared, for example, that Locke had no clear notion of the proper province of logic; that Campbell's attack on the syllogism was full of misapprehensions; and that Stewart's disparagement of the *dictum de omni* and his belief in the superiority of induction to deduction reflected little more than his general confusion of mind.[7] Thus Whately must be said to have been well acquainted with the new as well as the old logic and to have been fully aware of what he was doing when he chose to endorse the old. And indeed the intellectual process by which he arrived at this endorsement must be respected for its ingenuity, even if the endorsement itself seems out of keeping with its times and with the facts of the case.

The basic distinction in Whately's *Logic* is that discovery and reasoning are separate mental operations. Whately declared discovery to be the process by which a proposition previously unknown is brought into existence through observation, testimony,

---

[5] The *Encyclopaedia Metropolitana* was planned in the second decade of the nineteenth century, and it began to be published in serial parts in 1817 or 1818. By 1834, Parts 1 to 39 had been published, by 1839 Parts 40 to 48, and by 1845, Parts 49 to 59. I am unable to date the original Part which contained the *Logic* or that which contained the *Rhetoric.* Oskar Alfred Kubitz, *Development of John Stuart Mill's "System of Logic,"* Illinois Studies in the Social Sciences, Vol. XVIII, Nos. 1-2 (1932), pp. 20, 305, assigns the first appearance of Whately's *Logic* to 1825. Kubitz's work is cited below by his last name.

[6] See above, Ch. 2, pp. 59-60.

[7] See Whately, *Logic,* pp. 9, 19, 33, 215, 223-224.

and experiment.[8] He declared reasoning to be the process by which a proposition is brought into existence through argumentation, that is to say, through using two granted propositions to show that a third proposition is the necessary consequence of them.[9] It was Whately's contention that logic as a science limited itself to the latter process, and had nothing substantial to do with the former, important as the discovery of new truth obviously is. Suppose, he said, that the procedures of discovery could be reduced to scientific form, unlikely as such a supposition is.[10] Even so, that scientific form, however useful it turned out to be, would not "have the same object proposed with the Aristotelian Logic; or be in any respect a rival to that system." And to clinch his argument and to show exactly where he differed from the new school of logicians, he resorted to a metaphor. "A *plough*," he said, "may be a much more ingenious and valuable instrument than a *flail*; but it never can be substituted for it."[11] In other words, Whately's quarrel with the new logic was that it sought to identify itself with the process of preparing the ground, sowing the seed, and harvesting the new crop, whereas logic ought to restrict itself to the use of the flail upon the harvested crop as it lay spread over the floor of the barn and was beaten to make it yield the golden kernels of grain already contained in its ripened heads.

To Whately, the term induction had two distinct meanings, one of which related to the process of discovery, and was hence outside of the domain of logic altogether, while the other related to the process of reasoning, and was thus a part of logic. Here is Whately's own explanation of this distinction:

> In the process of Reasoning by which we deduce, from our observation of certain known cases, an inference with respect to unknown ones, we are employing a Syllogism in *Barbara* with the major Premiss suppressed; that being always substantially the same, as it asserts, that "what belongs to the individ-

---

[8] *Ibid.*, pp. 222-252. [9] *Ibid.*, pp. 215-221, 223.

[10] *Ibid.*, p. 243.

[11] *Ibid.*, p. 244. For a discussion of the application of this metaphor to the problem of interpreting the history of logic in the 1700's, see my essay, "The Plough and the Flail: The Ordeal of Eighteenth-Century Logic," *The Huntington Library Quarterly*, XXVIII (November 1964), 63-78.

ual or individuals we have examined, belongs to the whole class under which they come. . . ."

Induction, therefore, so far forth as it is an *argument*, may, of course, be stated Syllogistically: but so far forth as it is a *process of inquiry* with a view to obtain the Premises of that argument, it is, of course, out of the province of Logic.[12]

In line with these basic distinctions between discovery and reasoning, and between inductive enquiry and inductive argumentation, Whately proceeded on five major counts to affirm the values and points of view of the old logic. To him, logic stressed the syllogistic examination of accepted truths as its mode of enquiry, even if that mode could not produce new truths in the sense in which inductive methods produced them.[13] To him, the syllogism was the center of logical theory, and induction was an irregular syllogistic form.[14] The *dictum de omni* was in his view the great axiom from which all the principles of logic flowed.[15] To him argumentation was the outstanding activity for the logician, observation, testimony, and experiment being concerned with science, not logic.[16] And, finally, of course, Whately's actual conception was that truth and consistency are the same thing. Thus he emphasized that logic "furnishes rules to secure the mind from error in its deductions;"[17] that logic considers the syllogism to be "the form to which *all* correct reasoning may be ultimately reduced;"[18] and that the logician's object is "to lay down rules, not which *may* be followed with advantage, but which cannot possibly be *departed* from in sound reasoning."[19] The great contradiction in Whately's *Logic* as a whole is that he could make statements like these in one part of his work and yet could say in another part that truth, "in the strict logical sense, applies to Propositions, and to nothing else; and consists in the conformity of the declaration made to the actual state of the case."[20] And what is the contradiction here? It is this—that the conformity of a proposition to the actual state of the case can be established, not by Whately's deductive argumentation, but by the inductive

[12] *Logic*, pp. 216-217.
[14] *Ibid.*, pp. 216-217.
[16] *Ibid.*, pp. 1, 216, 223, 227, 248.
[18] *Ibid.*, p. 12.
[20] *Ibid.*, p. 318.

[13] *Ibid.*, pp. 226-229, 231-252.
[15] *Ibid.*, pp. 31-37.
[17] *Ibid.*, p. 1.
[19] *Ibid.*, p. 22.

methods of observation, testimony, and experiment, and that therefore Whately, in ruling these latter methods out of logic, was making it impossible for logic ever to establish truth in what Whately himself called the strict logical sense of the term. The new logic avoided this contradiction by making logic inductive while accepting the definition which Whately, the traditional logicians, and Locke himself had applied to truth. But Whately and his school were caught in the contradiction, and they refused to escape from it either by admitting induction into logical theory or by openly defining logical truth solely in terms of consistency instead of accuracy. Perhaps they did not see the contradiction, but it was there, nevertheless.

In one conspicuous respect, Whately's logical doctrines were uncharacteristic of the old logic. That is to say, the old logic had endorsed Aristotle's distinction between artistic and nonartistic proofs and had repeatedly advocated the use of the ancient machinery of topics for the invention of the former kind; but Whately in his role as logician ignored these matters altogether. The reason why he did so is perhaps best explained by citing a remark which he made in the later editions of his *Rhetoric*. "Aristotle's division of Persuasives into 'artificial' and 'inartificial,' . . . including under the latter head, 'Witnesses, Laws, Contracts,' &c.," he observed with rhetorical proofs of course in mind, "is strangely unphilosophical."[21] And he proceeded to argue that the materials upon which we construct an argument cannot be invented, inasmuch as they are in existence already, either in the form of "general maxims or particular testimony—Laws of Nature, or Laws of the Land." We may be sure that this line of reasoning would apply in Whately's view to logic no less than to rhetoric and would sufficiently explain why the theory of artistic proofs and of the topics did not appear in his work on the former as it did not in his work on the latter of these two subjects.

In 1843 an event of great importance took place—the new logic, which had been forming at Aberdeen and Edinburgh in the preceding century, became the subject of one of the greatest of all the masterpieces in the history of logical theory. That fine work

[21] *Elements of Rhetoric*, 7th edn., revised (London, 1846), pp. 39-40. This edition was reproduced in facsimile by Southern Illinois University Press at Carbondale in 1963, under the editorship of Douglas Ehninger, who supplied an "Editor's Introduction." That introduction is cited below as Ehninger.

was John Stuart Mill's *A System of Logic, Ratiocinative and Inductive; Being a Connected View of the Principles of Evidence and the Methods of Scientific Investigation.* If Whately's *Logic*, in Mill's own admiring words, "stated with philosophical precision, and explained with peculiar perspicuity, the whole of the common doctrine of the syllogism,"[22] it should be said of Mill that his treatment of deduction is also disciplined and luminous, while being singularly acute and profound, and that his treatment of induction makes this subject, for the first time in history, "the main question of the science of logic."[23] This is not the place for a survey of Mill's great work. All I can do is to call attention to the fact that on the one hand it brilliantly completed what Locke and Reid and Campbell and Stewart had envisioned for the new logic, and that, on the other, it did not destroy syllogistic logic in the process, but left it as a viable and important part, if no longer the whole, of the science of reasoning.

In other words, Mill's *System of Logic* took the modern side of the issues that separated the old logical doctrines from the new. It was concerned with scientific investigation, and, as the epigraph at the head of this chapter indicates, it dissociated itself completely from its former interest in the enterprise of communicating our thoughts to others. It drew observation and experiment

---

[22] John Stuart Mill, *A System of Logic* (New York, 1846), p. 114. In *The Westminster Review*, IX (January 1828), pp. 137-172, there appeared a long critique of Whately's *Logic*, which had been given a second edition the preceding year. As author of that critique, John Stuart Mill took the position that Whately's work was highly commendable, and indeed such an opinion is not open to serious question. What is remarkable, however, is that Mill said nothing to indicate any misgivings on his own part towards Whately's exclusion of inductive enquiry from the concerns of logical theory. Said Mill of Whately (p. 138): "His vindication of the utility of logic is conclusive: his explanation of its distinguishing character and peculiar objects, of the purposes to which it is and is not applicable, and the mode of its application, leave scarcely any thing to be desired." As set forth in that critique, Mill's own proposals for improvements in Whately's theories (pp. 156-172) did not embody any of the inductive principles that make his own *System of Logic* truly original and outstanding in its field. In fact, the whole tenor of Mill's critique makes it clear that, between 1828 and 1843, his logical theories underwent a revolutionary development. For an account of that development, see Kubitz, pp. 25-43, et passim.

[23] *System of Logic*, p. 171.

within the speculative concerns of logic, as if it were consciously seeking to prove Whately wrong in suggesting that the process of investigation could never adequately be brought into scientific form, and that only argumentation was capable of strict logical treatment.[24] It made reasoning consist of induction as well as deduction, and it made induction the very basis of all reasoning, not a mere irregular form of syllogism.[25] It endorsed Campbell's argument that the syllogism, so far as it claims to prove a conclusion, is a *petitio principii*, but it went beyond Campbell to show that we must not therefore dismiss syllogistic theory as useless.[26] It accepted the *dictum de omni*, not as the maxim upon which all reasoning is founded, but as a way of defining the meaning of the word "class."[27] And, of course, it ignored disputation as one of its constituent activities, and it also ignored artistic arguments and the machinery of topics. But what was its attitude towards truth? Well, the best answer to this question is found in a note which Mill began to append to later editions of the work now under discussion. That note refers to the Aristotelian logic devised by Sir William Hamilton in the middle years of the nineteenth century, but it could also refer, of course, to Whately's *Logic*. Because of its importance in helping us to differentiate the new logic from the old, I shall quote it almost in full:

> The view taken in the text, of the definition and purpose of Logic [said Mill of his own work], stands in marked opposition to that of the school of philosophy which, in this country, is represented by the writings of Sir William Hamilton and of his numerous pupils. Logic, as this school conceives it, is "the Science of the Formal Laws of Thought;" a definition framed for the express purpose of excluding, as irrelevant to Logic, whatever relates to Belief and Disbelief, or to the pursuit of truth as such, and restricting the science to that very limited portion of its total province, which has reference to the conditions, not of Truth, but of Consistency. What I have thought it useful to say in opposition to this limitation of the field of Logic, has been said at some length in a separate work, first published in 1865, and entitled *An Examination of Sir William Hamilton's*

[24] *Ibid.*, pp. 216-237.
[26] *Ibid.*, pp. 122-137.
[25] *Ibid.*, pp. 111-112, 131, 137, 171.
[27] *Ibid.*, pp. 116-118.

Philosophy. . . . For the purposes of the present Treatise, I am content that the justification of the larger extension which I gave to the domain of the science, should rest on the sequel of the Treatise itself. Some remarks on the relation which the Logic of Consistency bears to the Logic of Truth, and on the place which that particular part occupies in the whole to which it belongs, will be found in the present volume (Book II, Chap. iii. § 9).[28]

The confrontation between Whately's version of the old and Mill's version of the new logic put Whately's work into permanent eclipse, so far as the logical tradition that I have been examining here is concerned. The nineteenth century did not fully appreciate that this eclipse had occurred, for in 1862 Samuel Neil did a three-part article entitled "Modern Logicians" for his magazine, *The British Controversialist,* and that article featured only two logicians, Whately and Hegel.[29] Neil specifically excluded Mill from consideration, because, he said, Mill and other logicians of the same or opposite convictions had not yet been able to define the true connections between syllogistic and inductive theory.[30] But history did not agree with Neil, and by the end of the nineteenth century Mill's version of the new logic had effectively ended the long reign of Aldrich's *Artis Logicae Compendium* in its own form and in the form which it had under Whately's ingenious hand.

[28] *A System of Logic,* People's Edition (London, 1893), p. 8. The early editions of Mill's *System of Logic* did not contain the section to which the closing line of this quotation calls our attention. In fact, the first and second editions make Book II, Chapter III, end with Section No. 7, whereas in the People's Edition, this Chapter ends with Section No. 9. It thus seems clear that Mill's distinction between a logic of Consistency and a logic of Truth came to him as a result of his critical examination of Sir William Hamilton's logical theories. It is a tremendously useful distinction. Among its many functions, it serves to draw a clarifying line between Mill's role as a discursive logician and the role of those who, like Mill's contemporary George Boole, were creating a new mathematical and symbolic logic.

[29] See *The British Controversialist, and Literary Magazine* (London, 1862), pp. 1-12, 81-94, 321-333.

[30] *Ibid.,* p. 88. "Notwithstanding the labours of Mill, Whewell, Hamilton, De Morgan, Herschel, Lewes, Hampden, Morell, &c., &c.," said Neil, "we do not think that the true interpretation of the relationships of syllogism and induction has been reached."

Turning now to early nineteenth-century British rhetorical theory, we may say that its history is marked not only by a brisk resurgence of interest in a modified version of classical doctrine, but also by the continuation of the vogue of stylistic and of elocutionary rhetoric; and we may also say that its history is marked by the gradual transfer of the constituent parts of the new rhetoric of the eighteenth century to another field of knowledge. A brief account of these developments is now in order.

British interest in classical rhetoric was manifested in the early 1800's, not by a disposition to reinterpret the five-part Ciceronian program which Ward and Holmes had lovingly explained a hundred years before, but by an attempt to restate ancient doctrine as Aristotle rather than Cicero or Quintilian had conceived of it. As in the case of the revival of Aristotelian logic between 1800 and 1830, the chief writer responsible for bringing Aristotelian rhetoric into a new popularity in that same era was Richard Whately. Whately's *Elements of Rhetoric*, first published as an article in the *Encyclopaedia Metropolitana* in the middle 1820's, and as a separate book in 1828,[31] openly demonstrates that its author had carefully scrutinized the claims of the new rhetoric, as formulated by Campbell and Blair, and had then turned away from it, at least in basic ways, to express in his own terms some rival, and to him superior, claims of the ancient system in its most authoritative ancient form. Here are the details.

At the end of his historical sketch of rhetoric, to which I referred in the opening pages of this chapter, Whately remarked

[31] For an able study of the date of composition of Whately's *Rhetoric*, of its sources, and of its contributions to rhetorical theory, see Wayland Maxfield Parrish, "Whately and His Rhetoric," *The Quarterly Journal of Speech*, xv (February 1929), 58-79. Cited below as Parrish. Despite its general excellence, this article needs correction in respect to its conjecture that Volume I of the *Encyclopaedia Metropolitana* was published complete for the first time in 1829, and that, since Volume I now contains Whately's *Logic* and *Rhetoric*, those two works might therefore have first appeared in that year, so far as their printed career in the *Metropolitana* is concerned. The Volume I that appeared in 1829 contained in reality a collection of new or previously published articles making up the first volume of the *Metropolitana*'s Second Division, which limited itself to the Mixed Sciences. Whately's two articles belonged to the First Division, and that was given over to works on the so-called Pure Sciences. For a brief reference to the problem of ascertaining the date when Whately's *Rhetoric* appeared in the *Metropolitana*, see above, n. 5.

that few modern writers of ability had given serious thought to rhetorical theory, and that those few had added little or nothing of matter or method to the parallel system of the ancients. But even as he uttered these words, he apparently thought that they excluded things which might cry out against him if he did not mention them. At any rate, he proceeded to say that it would be most unjust for him at that point "to leave unnoticed Dr. Campbell's *Philosophy of Rhetoric*."[32] And he then characterized that treatise as "a work which does not enjoy indeed so high a degree of popular favour as Dr. Blair's, but is incomparably superior to it, not only in depth of thought and ingenious original research, but also in practical utility to the student." Whately did not want his readers to get the idea, however, that Campbell, for all his merits as a rhetorician, could ever be thought the equal of Aristotle, and thus he spoke of Campbell as follows:

> His great defect, which not only leads him into occasional errors, but leaves many of his best ideas but imperfectly developed, is his ignorance and utter misconception of the nature and object of Logic; on which some remarks were made in my treatise on that Science. Rhetoric being in truth an off-shoot of Logic, that Rhetorician must labour under great disadvantages who is not only ill-acquainted with that system, but also utterly unconscious of his deficiency.[33]

This intemperate accusation has no merit at all, if we examine it in relation to the facts that my present history has set forth. That is to say, it simply is not true that Campbell was utterly ignorant of the nature and object of logic. The three chapters on this subject in the first book of his *Rhetoric* are not the work of ignorance and misconception. All Whately's accusation really means is that Campbell's attack on the syllogism was squarely in the tradition of the new logic, and was a development of ideas sponsored by Bacon, Locke, and Reid, whereas Whately himself, as a spokesman of the old logic and a convinced Aristotelian, did not agree with Campbell on this matter. The proper issue between these two points of view was not whether Campbell was ignorant and Whately, truly informed, but whether Campbell had a better explanation than Whately of the problems that logic

[32] *Rhetoric*, p. 12.   [33] *Ibid*., pp. 12-13.

feels itself bound to study. If consistency between our premises and our conclusions is the only aspect of truth to concern us as logicians, then our logic may limit itself to the syllogism alone, but it should not thereupon resort to the tactics of disparagement to discredit those who insist that logic should also concern itself with the accuracy of correspondence between our premises and the facts behind them. Thus Whately's outburst against Campbell is merely an illustration of the way in which pejorative accusations take the place of factual statements and become a poor substitute for proof in controversy. It does, however, serve a useful purpose —it shows that one of the fundamental issues between the old rhetoric and the new was not whether the concerns of rhetoric and the concerns of logic belong together or apart, but whether the concerns of rhetoric are better served by syllogistic or by inductive theory. On this issue, Whately stood with Aristotle, of course, and Campbell, with the moderns.

To Whately, rhetoric was to be defined, not exclusively in relation to spoken discourse, but in relation to speaking and writing.[34] The term rhetoric in its primary signification, he observed, "had reference to public *Speaking* alone, as its etymology implies: but as most of the rules for speaking are of course applicable equally to Writing, an extension of the term naturally took place; and we find even Aristotle . . . including in his Treatise rules for compositions as were not intended to be publicly recited."[35] But Whately was unwilling to consent to a wider extension of the term—to such a wide extension, for example, as that proposed by the new rhetoricians. Therefore he refused to admit that rhetoric could be defined as "the Art of Composition, universally"; or that, by excluding poetry from it, one could legitimately make it embrace "all Prose-composition."[36] What he proposed to do himself, he said, was "to treat of *Argumentative Composition*, generally, and exclusively; considering Rhetoric (in conformity with the very just and philosophical view of Aristotle) as an off-shoot from Logic."[37] He went on to say that any speaker or writer entered the province of rhetoric when he sought to prove something by dis-

---

[34] The view expressed by Ehninger, pp. xii, xv, that Whately's *Rhetoric* is persistently focused upon the problems and methods of oral argumentation is misleading so far as it seems to neglect Whately's equally obvious emphasis upon writing.

[35] *Rhetoric*, p. 2.   [36] *Ibid.*, p. 4.   [37] *Ibid.*, p. 6.

course—when he became an advocate. Nor are philosophical works "to be excluded from the class to which Rhetorical rules are applicable; for the Philosopher who undertakes, by writing or speaking, to convey his notions to others, assumes, for the time being," remarked Whately, "the character of Advocate of the doctrines he maintains."[38] "And this view of the subject," he added somewhat later, "is the less open to objection, inasmuch as it is not likely to lead to discussions that can be deemed superfluous, even by those who may choose to consider Rhetoric in the most restricted sense, as relating only to 'Persuasive Speaking'; since it is evident that *Argument* must be, in most cases at least, the basis of Persuasion."[39]

With spoken and written argumentative composition established as the true subject of rhetoric, Whately outlined the plan that his own rhetorical treatise would follow:

> I propose then to treat, first and principally, of the Discovery of Arguments, and of their Arrangement; secondly, to lay down some Rules respecting the excitement and management of the Passions, with a view to the attainment of any object proposed, —principally, Persuasion, in the strict sense, i.e. the influencing of the Will; thirdly, to offer some remarks on Style; and fourthly, to treat of Elocution.[40]

This program is of course Aristotelian, if we consider that the first two books of Aristotle's *Rhetoric* deal with the problem of discovering logical, emotional, and ethical proofs, and that the third book discusses arrangement and style, while mentioning delivery only to dismiss it as unsuited to an elevated enquiry. Indeed, Parrish has pointed out that Aristotle's *Rhetoric* is Whately's principal source, and that Whately made at least thirty-nine specific references to it, not in such a way as to copy it but in such a way as to provide himself "with texts on which his own ruminative powers might work."[41] But it is also true, as Parrish has likewise noted, that Whately's other major source is Campbell's *Rhetoric*,

---

[38] *Ibid.*, p. 7.   [39] *Ibid.*, p. 9.

[40] *Ibid.*, p. 9. Parrish is in error in saying (p. 75) that "Whately was the first important writer to transfer the term 'elocution' from style to delivery." Joseph Priestley and Lawson had done the same thing, as had most of the elocutionists, of course.

[41] Parrish, pp. 73, 78.

despite Whately's adverse reaction to Campbell's attack on the syllogism.[42] In fact, Whately referred to Campbell or quoted him briefly or at length on at least nineteen occasions and for the most part with complete respect.[43] Thus it may be said of Whately that his ruminations upon Aristotle's ancient and Campbell's modern work produced a rhetorical theory which, as might be expected, was a mixture of the old and the new rhetoric. But it should be added that the weight of its few resemblances to the former is perhaps greater than that of its more numerous resemblances to the latter. At any rate, I would think it fair to put the matter in these terms, although I do not mean here to argue the point. All I shall attempt to do is to enumerate the resemblances which exist between Whately and traditional rhetoric, on the one side, and between him and the new rhetoric, on the other.

In round terms, Whately's *Rhetoric* is avowedly with the tradition in two and silently with the moderns in four major respects. That is to say, it is outspokenly traditional in its determination to restrict rhetoric to argumentative discourse and to deny it the right to speculate upon poetry and indeed upon prose composition as a whole. It is also outspoken, even brusque, in its traditional insistence that rhetoric must draw its logical theories from the old deductive rather than the new inductive logic. But it is quietly modern in its refusal to accept Aristotle's distinction between artistic and nonartistic proofs and in its complete neglect of the topical system of rhetorical invention.[44] It is also quietly modern (and openly Aristotelian as well) in its acceptance of proposition and proof as the basic necessities of oratorical structure, and in its recommendation that the introduction, the refutation, and the conclusion of speeches need be included only as special circumstances dictate.[45] It is quietly modern, too, in its concern for the creation of a means by which probable arguments in present-day discourse can be disciplined towards the greatest possible measure of credibility and exactitude.[46] And finally,

[42] *Ibid.*, pp. 73, 75, 76, 77.

[43] *Rhetoric*, pp. 58-59, 155-157, 175, 192-193, 195-196, 204, 234-235, 243-244, 246-247, 253, 276-277, 280, 282, 283, 297, 300, 303, 418-423, 431-437.

[44] See above, n. 21.

[45] *Rhetoric*, pp. 110-152. It is on p. 117 where Whately stated and commented upon Aristotle's division of a speech into two great parts, "The Proposition and the Proof."

[46] *Ibid.*, pp. 57-64, 65-69.

it is quietly modern in its conviction that perspicuity, energy, and elegance should be the great aims of the argumentative style, and that, if the demands of the two latter qualities conflict with each other on a given occasion, "the general rule to be observed by the orator is to prefer the energetic to the elegant."[47] In the whole matter of style, indeed, Whately took the modern side in his condemnation of the epideictic oratory of the ancients,[48] in his insistence that the business of an argument or persuasive discourse is to call attention to its subject, not to its verbal ingenuity,[49] and in his refusal to handle the tropes and figures at the length or in the variety that traditional rhetoric had made customary.[50]

As for British stylistic and elocutionary rhetorics of the early years of the nineteenth century, they offered themselves to the public, not only as integral parts of Whately's Neo-Aristotelian doctrine, but also as independent doctrines in their own right; and in the latter capacity each one of them tended to become identified, as indeed they had in the eighteenth century, with the whole of the art which they served. These independent rhetorics will receive only a very brief mention on the present occasion. In the period between 1800 and 1850, the rhetoric of style, that is to say, the rhetoric which limited itself only to the third part of the traditional system, and which treated that third part as if it were a complete entity in itself, was represented by such new publications as Alexander Jamieson's *Grammar of Rhetoric and Polite Literature* (London, 1818), Ralph Sharp's *The Flowers of Rhetoric, the Graces of Eloquence, and the Charms of Oratory* (London, 1819), and Larret Langley's *Manual of the Figures of Rhetoric* (Doncaster, 1835). In the same period, elocutionary rhetorics, which of course limited themselves exclusively to the fifth part of the traditional system, flourished in such abundance on all levels of education as to make the term rhetoric almost everywhere synonymous with the art of delivering speeches with the correct

[47] *Ibid.*, p. 320.

[48] *Ibid.*, pp. 238-239. Whately called epideictic discourse one of the kinds of "spurious Oratory."

[49] *Ibid.*, pp. 279, 323-324.

[50] For Whately's treatment of the figures, see *ibid.*, pp. 246-264, 311-318. Metaphor, simile, epithet, antithesis, and rhetorical question are the ones to which he devoted most of his attention.

accent, the appropriate emphasis, the proper pause, and the fitting gesture. The most influential early nineteenth-century British writers to give their support to the elocutionary movement were John Thelwall, James Wright, Benjamin Humphrey Smart, and Alexander Melville Bell. These men and their many associates wrote treatises to show how rhetorical pronunciation and gesture were to be practiced not only from the oratorical platform but also from the stage of the playhouse or from the lectern and the pulpit.[51] By separating themselves from any obligation to consider the theory of content and arrangement as parts of rhetorical doctrine, and by stressing instruction in voice and gesture as a mechanical rather than an intellectual or philosophic matter, the elocutionists made rhetoric appear to be the art of declaiming a speech by rote, without regard to whether the thought uttered were trivial or false or dangerous; and under auspices like these rhetoric became anathema to the scholarly community and sacred only to the anti-intellectuals within and outside the academic system. The chasm which yawned between the elocutionists, on the one hand, and the traditional or the new rhetoricians of the eighteenth century, on the other, was very wide, but it became still wider in the nineteenth century. Its width at its greatest extent cannot of course be measured by the techniques of the surveyor, but it can be suggested by a comparison of the intellectual level of the first sentence of Aristotle's *Rhetoric* with that of the first sentence of an American elocutionary textbook of the late nineteenth century. Both of these works, by the

[51] The following works may be cited to indicate the variety of situations to which elocutionary doctrine was applied in the early nineteenth century: Johann Jacob Engel, *Practical Illustrations of Rhetorical Gesture and Action, adapted to the English Drama*, trans. Henry Siddons (London, 1807); Thomas Ewing, *Principles of Elocution, containing . . . Rules, Observations, and Exercises on Pronunciation*, 2nd Ed. (Edinburgh, 1816); John Henry Howlett, *Instructions in Reading the Liturgy of the United Church of England and Ireland* (London, 1826); Henry Innes, *The Rhetorical Class Book: or, the Principles and Practice of Elocution Defined and Illustrated* (London, 1834); Richard Cull, *Garrick's Mode of Reading the Liturgy of the Church of England*, A new edition (London, 1840); A. M. Hartley, *The Academic Speaker, A System of Elocution designed for Schools and Self-Instruction* (Glasgow, 1846). A survey of the elocutionary movement in Great Britain in the nineteenth century is contained in Frederick W. Haberman's essay, "English Sources of American Elocution," to which I have already referred above, Ch. 4, n. 263.

way, were intended for mature students. Said Aristotle: "Rhetoric is the counterpart of dialectic." Said the elocutionary textbook: "Always inhale through the nostrils."[52]

During the nineteenth century the new rhetoric that I described in the preceding chapter changed its name and restricted its subject matter. These developments can best be made clear by saying that the subjects which were taught in eighteenth-century British institutions under the rubrics of oratory and criticism or rhetoric and belles lettres or belles lettres and logic were altered in the nineteenth century so as to retain their emphasis upon poetry, fiction, drama, and aesthetic criticism, while abandoning their concern for rhetoric as an active literary discipline, and while ceasing to give their further attention to the study of didactic works, histories, and philosophical treatises, considered as forms of discourse. In short, what might be called the department of rhetoric and belles lettres in an eighteenth-century Scottish university became the department of English literature in the universities of nineteenth-century Britain and America. And why was rhetoric made a ceremonial term or dropped altogether under this new dispensation? The answer at least in part is that rhetoric at the height of its popularity in eighteenth-century Scotland did not succeed in becoming a genuine theory of poetical literature, as it had aspired to be, and that its other concerns— oratory, didactic writing, history, and philosophical prose—could not be managed properly by later academic departments needing suddenly to devote all their efforts to the poetic and imaginative forms of literary effort. Then, too, as another part of the answer, there was the growing realization that rhetoric in the nineteenth century was being identified more and more closely with the elocutionists and was thus becoming less and less appropriate as a term for the truly operational parts of the theory of verbal composition.

At any rate, the facts themselves tell the story of what happened to the new rhetoric in nineteenth-century Britain and America. I shall cite only a few of them. In 1845 William Edmonstoune Aytoun was named professor of rhetoric and belles lettres at the University of Edinburgh, his title being that which had first been conferred upon Hugh Blair in 1762; but in 1858,

---

[52] See George L. Raymond, *The Orator's Manual*, 9th edn. (New York, Boston, Chicago, 1879), p. 15.

Aytoun was given a new title, that of professor of rhetoric and English literature, and the latter designation, with rhetoric no longer meaningful in relation to what Aytoun was expected to teach, became the rule where Blair lectured of old.[53] At Trinity College, Dublin, where, as we know, a professorship of oratory and history was created in 1724, the following events occurred: oratory and history were made separate chairs in 1762; in 1855, oratory and English literature were joined together in one chair; and in 1867 a separate chair of English literature was founded.[54] At Glasgow, the reforms of 1858 added the subject of English literature to the department of philosophy, in which Adam Smith had lectured in the 1750's on logic and moral philosophy as well as on rhetoric.[55] At St. Andrews, where William Barron, we remember, had lectured on belles lettres and logic in the closing years of the eighteenth century, the subject of English literature was introduced into the curriculum in 1861, in connection with the course in logic, and in 1896 a chair of English was established under the Berry bequest.[56] Alexander Bain became Professor of Logic and English at Aberdeen in 1860, and although he is chiefly remembered today for his work in psychology, he was the author of a treatise on rhetoric, and he taught English language and composition in a course that was to be continued later by William Minto and H. J. C. Grierson.[57] The Boylston Professorship of Rhetoric and Oratory at Harvard, first held between 1806 and 1809 by John Quincy Adams, who lectured on Ciceronian rhetoric, was transformed between 1851 and 1876 into a chair of English literature by Francis J. Child, the distinguished editor of a collection called *The English and Scottish Popular Ballads*; and since his day the Boylston Professorship has been held by teachers of English composition and by poets and literary scholars.[58]

[53] See Grant, *Story of the University of Edinburgh*, II, 360-361.

[54] See Maxwell, *History of Trinity College Dublin*, p. 195.

[55] See J. D. Mackie, *The University of Glasgow 1451-1951* (Glasgow, 1954), p. 273.

[56] See R. G. Cant, *The University of St. Andrews, A Short History* (Edinburgh and London, 1946), pp. 107-108, 126 n. 1.

[57] See Anderson, *Studies in the History and Development of the University of Aberdeen*, pp. 92-95. See also *A Calendar of the University of Aberdeen for the Sessions 1860-61 to 1863-64* (Aberdeen, 1900), pp. 3, 11.

[58] See Paul E. Ried, "Francis J. Child: The Fourth Boylston Professor of Rhetoric and Oratory," *The Quarterly Journal of Speech*, LV (October 1969), 268-275.

Finally, at Princeton, the subjects which John Witherspoon had introduced in 1768 in his lectures on composition, taste, and criticism, formed the nucleus around which Matthew Boyd Hope, called officially professor of belles lettres, and unofficially, professor of rhetoric, built Princeton's first course in English literature in 1846-47.[59] This latter event, and those which I have just mentioned as having occurred in the same era at Harvard, Aberdeen, St. Andrews, Glasgow, Dublin, and Edinburgh, are witnesses to the capacity of the new rhetoric of eighteenth-century Scotland to bring about the development of English literature as a field of study in nineteenth-century American and British universities. The new eighteenth-century British logic found an immensely gifted interpreter during the nineteenth century in John Stuart Mill, and he gave it definitive treatment. But the new rhetoric created by Adam Smith and George Campbell did not find its John Stuart Mill. It did not receive the kind of treatment that would have made it a general theory of discourse on the poetical and fictional as on the argumentative, persuasive, and expository side. Its glory was that it finally made English literature into an important academic subject. But that subject tended at once to reject rhetorical theory as one of its philosophical interests, and at the same time the elocutionists were making rhetoric synonymous with the sound, but not the substance and form, of discourse.

And that is where matters stood at the beginning of the twentieth century. When the term rhetoric was mentioned in that era, most persons thought of declamation. Quite a few thought of a figured and ornate style. Some remembered Whately's Aristotelian use of the term to designate the theory of argumentative and persuasive discourse in its oratorical and philosophical branches. An occasional scholar identified the term with George Campbell's use of it or with the older tradition associated with

[59] See Thomas Jefferson Wertenbaker, *Princeton 1746-1896* (Princeton, New Jersey, 1946), pp. 235-236. Hope served at Princeton under the official title of professor of belles lettres from 1845 to 1854, and of professor of belles lettres and political economy from 1854 to 1859. See *General Catalogue of Princeton University 1746-1906* (Princeton, New Jersey, 1908), p. 31. But, as Wertenbaker says, he was also responsible for a course in rhetoric. In fact, he is designated in handwriting as "Professor of Rhetoric" at the bottom of one of the pictures of him in a collection in Princeton University Archives.

the names of John Holmes, John Ward, Quintilian, and Cicero. But there was nobody then to see all of these meanings in their historical perspective or to tell others what he had seen. Attempts of the latter sort were later to be made, however, and my present book belongs among them.

INDEX

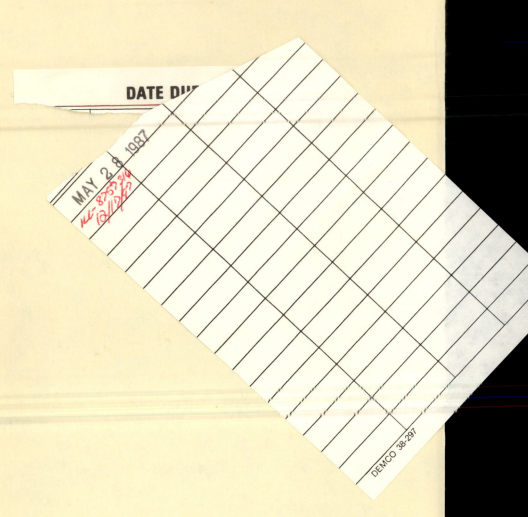